NATIONAL SECURITY MANAGEMENT

ELEMENTS OF DEFENSE ECONOMICS

Charles J. Hitch
and
Roland N. McKean

National Defense University
Washington, D.C.

NATIONAL DEFENSE UNIVERSITY
Washington, D.C.

ROBERT G. GARD, Jr., LIEUTENANT GENERAL, USA
President, National Defense University

THEODORE ANTONELLI, MAJOR GENERAL, USA
Commandant, Industrial College of the Armed Forces

HARRISON LOBDELL, JR., MAJOR GENERAL, USAF
Commandant, National War College

On 1 January 1977 the Department of Correspondence Studies, Industrial College of the Armed Forces, was transferred to the External Programs Directorate, National Defense University. This book was originally published by the Department of Correspondence Studies, Industrial College of the Armed Forces, in 1967.

Second printing, NDU, November 1977

FOREWORD

The purpose of this text is to introduce the student to some of the essential elements of economic analysis which have come to play a vital part in Defense management since 1961. Much of this volume reflects research conducted by The RAND Corporation for the U.S. Air Force; and one of the principal authors, Charles J. Hitch, was to have the opportunity to put some of his ideas to the test in his role as Assistant Secretary of Defense (Comptroller) from 1961 to the summer of 1965.

Their work, the authors state, is not designed to solve military-economic problems at the various levels.

> . . . We shall point out that certain policies stated in general terms, such as the protection of our deterrent forces, are extremely important, but we shall not, except in hypothetical examples, compare *specific* alternatives and indicate preferred strategies and weapon systems. This is the continuing task of responsible decision-makers and the analysts who advise and assist them. It can never be done once and for all because good solutions change with circumstances, and circumstances change constantly.

The authors' main purpose is "to help decision-makers, their advisers, and interested citizens in general, by showing how economic analysis—ranging from just straight thinking about alternative courses of action to systematic quantitative comparisons—can contribute to the selection of preferred (efficient, economical) policies and actions."

We introduce the student here only to portions of the authors' work. By way of essential background, we present in Part One the authors' view of economic factors that enter into the consideration of defense or national security problems (chapter I), and the kinds of threats that a nation's defenses are required to meet (chapter II).

Part Two is concerned with problems at a relatively high level—choices affecting the resources available for defense. Chapters III and IV are directly concerned with the determination of the defense budget—what the constraints are, and how we should choose the size of the budget.

Part Three is concerned with more specific problems—the problems of efficient choice within the departments responsible for defense—and with methods of analyzing various alternatives.

The authors' concern here is with "straight thinking" about military problems, especially the design of analyses and the use of appropriate economic criteria to aid in choosing preferred policies. In the four chapters comprising this part, the student is exposed to the complications associated with "incommensurables," uncertainty, the enemy, and time. Students with a strong interest in quantitative analysis and in some special problems and applications, looking at them as economic problems of choice, will want to consult the full work, *The Economics of Defense in the Nuclear Age*, from which this text is extracted, and the comprehensive bibliography acompanying that work. Students who need to reinforce and update their knowledge of general concepts of economics and of basic, college-level economics should consult one of the standard textbooks; some recognized writers on the subject are: Paul A. Samuelson, Melville J. Ulmer, George L. Bach, and Robert L. Heilbroner.

The College is indebted to The RAND Corporation for its permission to draw on the Hitch and McKean work for material to be used in orienting students in one of the basic disciplines of Defense management in today's environment.

CHARLES E. BARRETT
Professor of Economics

Industrial College of the Armed Forces
Washington, D.C.
5 May 1967

CONTENTS

ILLUSTRATIONS

PART ONE

ANALYTIC AND
FACTUAL BACKGROUND

I

DEFENSE AS AN ECONOMIC PROBLEM*

National security [1] depends upon many factors, which writers on the subject classify in different ways. Important among them are the morale of a country's soldiers, the number and ingenuity of its scientists, the character and skill of its political and military leaders, its geographic position relative to other countries, and even—in this nuclear age—the prevailing winds that blow across its expanses.

But national security also depends upon economic factors, which are variously interpreted and defined. Most speakers and writers who stress the importance of economic factors are referring to the economic strength of the nation, as contrasted with its military forces. They allege that the United States exerted a decisive influence in the later stages of World Wars I and II through its superior economic strength. Russia, it has been said, is more fearful of "Detroit" than of either the Strategic Air Command or the Divisions of NATO.

Other experts use the concept of economic factors more narrowly, to refer to the constraints on military forces imposed by the budget—the necessity to limit costs. Thus, Professor Kissinger [2] contrasts "doctrinal," "technological," and "fiscal" influences on our military strategy and concludes that the fiscal, as well as the technological, has been too influential at the expense of military

---

* The material which follows has been extracted from Charles J. Hitch and Roland N. McKean, *The Economics of Defense in the Nuclear Age* (Cambridge: Harvard University Press, 1960), with permission of the RAND Corporation.

[1] In most of this volume, the terms "defense" and "national security" will be used interchangeably. Wherever defense is used in a narrower sense, e.g., defense as opposed to offense, we believe the context will make this clear.

[2] Henry A. Kissinger, "Strategy and Organization," *Foreign Affairs*, April 1957, pp. 379–394.

doctrine. Similarly Mr. Hanson Baldwin complains that "In the Western World—though not in Russia—costs are a more decisive factor in shaping defense than is military logic." [3]

In this book we will be concerned with economics in its most general sense. Economics is not exclusively concerned, as the above interpretations imply, with certain types of activities (industrial) rather than others (military), or with the traditional points of view of budgeteers and comptrollers.[4] Being truly economical does not mean scrimping—reducing expenditures no matter how important the things to be bought. Nor does it mean implementing some stated doctrine regardless of cost. Rather economics is concerned with allocating resources—choosing doctrines and techniques—so as to get the most out of available resources. To economize in this sense may imply spending less on some things and more on others. But always economics or economizing means trying to make the most efficient use of the resources available in all activities in any circumstances.

In our view the problem of combining limited quantities of missiles, crews, bases, and maintenance facilities to "produce" a strategic air force that will maximize deterrence of enemy attack is just as much a problem in economics (although in some respects a harder one) as the problem of combining limited quantities of coke, iron ore, scrap, blast furnaces, and mill facilities to produce steel in such a way as to maximize profits. In both cases there is an objective, there are budgetary and other resource constraints, and there is a challenge to economize.

Economy and efficiency are two ways of looking at the same characteristic of an operation. If a manufacturer or a military commander has a fixed budget (or other fixed resources) and attempts to maximize his production or the attainment of his objective, we say that he has the problem of using his resources efficiently. But if his production goal or other objective is fixed, his problem is to economize on his use of resources, that is, to minimize his costs. These problems may sound like different problems; in fact they are logically equivalent. For any level of either budget or objective, the choices that maximize the attainment of an objective for a given budget are the same choices that minimize the cost of attaining that objective.[5] If the Bessemer process is the most economical method of producing steel from the one point of

---

[3] "Arms and the Atom—I," *New York Times*, May 14, 1957, p. 21.

[4] Problems of eliminating redundant overhead costs, preventing the padding of expense accounts, restricting the use of chauffeur-driven cars to top officials, etc., while important, are relatively narrow management problems, and not our concern in this book.

[5] This point is elaborated upon in Chapter V, below.

view, it is the most efficient from the other. If Missile X is the system that provides maximum deterrence with a $10 billion SAC budget, it is also the missile which most economically achieves that level of deterrence. In other words, there is no conflict of interest between the budgeteer who is supposed to be interested in economizing and the military commander who is supposed to be interested in efficiency—except in the determination of the *size* of the budget or the magnitude of the objective to be achieved. They should be able to agree on all the "subsequent" decisions.

For this reason it is misleading to imply, as do Kissinger and Baldwin in the articles just quoted, that economic or cost factors are necessarily in conflict with strategic, doctrinal, and technological considerations, and must somehow be reconciled with them, with not too much weight being assigned the economic. There *is* a conflict between defense and other goods in deciding on the size of the military budget.[6] Economizing involves deciding how much of other things to sacrifice in the interests of military strength. But in all decisions on how to spend the military budget —on what kinds of equipment and forces, to implement what kind of strategy—there is no such conflict. Strategy, technology, and economy are not three independent "considerations" to be assigned appropriate weights, but interdependent elements of the same problem. Strategies are *ways of using* budgets or resources to achieve military objectives. Technology defines the *possible* strategies. The economic problem is to choose that strategy, including equipment and everything else necessary to implement it, which is most efficient (maximizes the attainment of the objective with the given resources) or economical (minimizes the cost of achieving the given objective)—the strategy which is most efficient also being the most economical.

Strategy and cost are as interdependent as the front and rear sights of a rifle. One cannot assign relative weights to the importance of the positions of the front and rear sights. It does not make sense to ask the correct position of the rear sight except in relation to the front sight and the target. Similarly one cannot economize except in choosing strategies (or tactics or methods) to achieve objectives. The job of economizing, which some would delegate to budgeteers and comptrollers, cannot be distinguished from the whole task of making military decisions.

The problem of national security might in theory be regarded as one big economic problem. The nation has certain resources—now

---

[6] See Chapter IV, below.

and prospectively in the future—which are conventionally classified by economists as various sorts of land, labor, and capital. These resources can be used to satisfy many objectives of the nation and its individual citizens—national security, a high standard of living, social security, a rapid rate of economic growth, and so on. These are, of course, competing objectives. In general, the more resources the nation devotes to national security, the less it will have for social security and vice versa. We could (as some economists have done)[7] conceive of a "social welfare function" which we would attempt to maximize by an appropriate allocation of the nation's resources among the various activities satisfying these objectives.

In fact, for reasons which will become familiar as we proceed but are in any event obvious, this kind of approach to the problem of national security is completely impractical and sterile. We have to break economic problems, like so many others, into manageable pieces before we can make a good beginning at finding solutions. And in fact, in the United States and all other countries, governments and departments of defense are organized to deal with appropropriate parts of the grand problem at many different levels.

As a beginning let us consider economic problems at each of three rather gross levels. National security, from the point of view of an economist, may be said to depend on three things: (1) the quantity of national resources available, now and in the future; (2) the proportion of these resources allocated to national security purposes; and (3) the efficiency with which the resources so allocated are used.

Several parts of the government—including, for example, the Council of Economic Advisers and the Joint Congressional Committee on the Economic Report—are concerned with problems at the first and "highest" of these levels. Of course the quantity of resources existing in the present cannot be influenced by economic policy; but their full and productive employment can be, and so can their rate of growth, and therefore the quantity of resources that will be available in the future. Present resources are the consequence of past economic policies.

Problems at the second level are the special responsibility of the Bureau of the Budget and the Appropriations Committees of Congress, although all executive departments are deeply involved,

---

[7] See Kenneth J. Arrow, *Social Choice and Individual Values*, John Wiley and Sons, New York, 1951, and A. Bergson (Burk), "A Reformulation of Certain Aspects of Welfare Economics," *Quarterly Journal of Economics*, February 1938, pp. 310–334.

and every Congressman is interested. We decide the proportion of
national resources to be devoted to defense when we vote a national
security budget. In effect we are then choosing between more defense and more of other things. President Eisenhower has expressed this choice vividly:

> The cost of one modern heavy bomber is this: a modern brick school in
> more than 30 cities.
> It is two electric power plants, each serving a town of 60,000 population.
> It is two fine, fully equipped hospitals.
> It is some 50 miles of concrete highway.[8]

Problems at the third level—the efficient use of the resources
allocated for defense—are primarily and in the first instance internal problems of the defense departments and agencies, although
for reasons that we will have to examine, the President, other
departments, and the Congress are concerned with the solutions
to some of them. The problems consist in choosing efficiently, or
economically, among the alternative methods of achieving military
tasks or objectives. These alternative methods may be different
strategies, different tactics, various forces, or different weapons.

It is not apparent to many who are unfamiliar with military
problems how wide the range of choice really is. There is typically
an infinity of ways to carry out a military mission, some much
more efficient, or economical, than others. Consider the range of
choice in the following three examples, taken from three different
levels of decision-making within the departments of the government concerned with defense:

a. The provision of some measure of protection to the United
States economy and population against atomic attack. The broad
"pure" alternatives include: (1) widespread dispersal of industry
and population before attack; (2) shelters and underground construction; (3) fighter and missile defenses; (4) full reliance on
an atomic striking force for deterrence or in some circumstances,
to destroy the enemy striking force on the ground. There are, of
course, many ways of implementing each broad alternative, as well
as many "mixes" or combinations of the pure alternatives.

b. Extension of the range of bomber aircraft. Broad alternatives
include the use of: (1) operating bases farther forward, fixed or
floating; (2) air refueling; (3) staging bases forward for ground
refueling; (4) larger aircraft with greater fuel capacity. If there
is time enough for a development program, additional alternatives
would include the use of: (5) high energy fuels, chemical or

---

8 "The Chance for Peace," an address reprinted in *The Department of State Bulletin*, April 27, 1953, p. 600.

nuclear; (6) lighter structural materials; (7) boundary layer control; and many others.

c. The design of a new machine gun. There are many possible performance characteristics: range, accuracy, lethality of bullet, durability, reliability—some of which may have high military worth, some little. Each has its cost in money, development time, and production time; each its "trade-off" against other characteristics.

This factoring of the big economic problem into many subproblems at different levels has some disadvantages, which we will consider at appropriate places. But it makes both the analytical and the decision-making problems tractable, an advantage not to be lightly discarded. The sergeant in the *New Yorker* cartoon understands the point well when he shouts: "I'm telling you for the last time, Harwick. It's none of your business how much it costs the taxpayers. Your job is to fire that gun."

II

DEFENSE AGAINST WHAT?

During the last decade or so the development and accumulation of nuclear weapons—first by the United States, then by the USSR and finally by other nations—have revolutionized the problems of national security. No comparable technological revolution in weapons has ever before occurred in history. The analogy of gunpowder is frequently suggested, but the substitution of gunpowder took place gradually over a period of centuries; and, like the weapons it replaced, gunpowder was used almost exclusively in a circumscribed area known as the battlefield. Nuclear weapons, a few years after their invention, have made it feasible—indeed, cheap and easy—to destroy economies and populations. They will not necessarily be used for this purpose; but the fact that they can be so used profoundly influences the character of the security that is attainable, as well as the policies by which we must seek it. Today, or next year, or within ten years, any one of several nations can unilaterally destroy the major cities of the others, and the latter, if they are prepared and respond quickly, can make the destruction mutual. In these circumstances, problems which once dominated our thinking about defense become unimportant. And while other problems assume new importance, we have scarcely had time to learn what they are, let alone how to think about them.

Because the weapons environment critically influences choice of policy, this chapter will first describe and project the weapon developments themselves, and then attempt to trace their implications for the kinds of war that our policies should be designed to prepare for or prevent. At this point we shall be concerned with the technological possibilities in the absence of any agreement to disarm or adopt significant limitations on the use of weapons.

WEAPON DEVELOPMENTS

Enough is known concerning the development and production of nuclear weapons and the means of delivering them—both here and in the USSR—for a general consideration of medium- and long-term policies. For this purpose we can collapse the next decade or so to the present point in time. Exact estimates of present or near-future capabilities of both the United States and the USSR in terms of thermonuclear weapons and carriers are not here required. The significant facts are plain enough to informed public opinion throughout the world. They may be summarized as follows:

1. The number of urban centers which account for most of the economic strength of a major military power like the United States or Russia is small—certainly not more than a few hundred. Fifty-four United States metropolitan areas contain sixty per cent of the nation's manufacturing industry. Their population of well over 65,000,000, while only forty per cent of the national total, includes a much larger proportion of the nation's highly skilled technical, scientific, and managerial personnel. The 170 metropolitan areas listed by the Census Bureau contain seventy-five per cent of manufacturing industry and fifty-five per cent of the nation's population.[1] The concentration of industry in Russian urban centers appears to be roughly the same as in the United States, although the centers themselves tend to be more compact and therefore easier targets. While the total Russian population is less concentrated than that of the United States (almost half live on farms), the concentration of industrial and skilled labor and management is at least as great. Britain, Germany, and other industrial countries present even fewer targets.

The elimination of fewer than 200 metropolitan areas in either the United States or the USSR (still fewer elsewhere) would therefore, as a direct effect, reduce industrial capital by 75 per cent and the most valuable human resources by about as much. This, in itself, would demote a first-class power to third class, but to the direct effects must be added indirect ones. Because of the interdependence in a modern industrial economy, the productivity of the surviving unbalanced economic resources would be reduced, perhaps disastrously. Radioactive fallout would be likely to inflict serious casualties on populations outside the target cities.

2. How many bombs would be required to "eliminate" a metropolitan area? It depends, of course, upon the size and shape of the area and the size of the bomb as well as upon other factors. But we were told by the Chairman of the Atomic Energy Commission

---

[1] The metropolitan area concept as defined by the Census Bureau is, unfortunately, not a perfectly satisfactory measure of urbanization—because its definition is primarily on a county unit basis. The figures above include, therefore, some capital and population which may be sufficiently far from presumed city targets as not to be vulnerable to the direct effects of urban bombing, except fallout. On the other hand, the arbitrary legal boundaries of cities are much too restricted and even less satisfactory for our purposes.

after one test in the Pacific that a thermonuclear explosion could destroy any city on earth.[2] We know that very much smaller bombs will destroy small cities, as the first primitive 20 kiloton atomic bomb destroyed Hiroshima, a city of 250,000, killing a third of its population; that thermonuclear weapons have been made in the multi-megaton "yield" range; and that the area of destruction from blast increases as the two-thirds power of the yield (thus, a ten megaton bomb would devastate an area approximately sixty times as great as that devastated by a twenty kiloton bomb). We have also been told that the area of intense radioactive fallout from the Bikini shot was 7,000 square miles—that is, an area fifteen times the size of Los Angeles or approximately equal to the total land area of New Jersey.

About the long-term radiation hazards from such fission products as strontium-90 and cesium-137 we know less. The dangers resulting from a large-scale attack would be significant, though they may not affect the number of weapons that "rational" attackers would be willing to dispatch.

In any event, we are clearly entering a one-bomb-to-one-large-city era, which means usually one, perhaps occasionally two or three, bombs per metropolitan area. Barring large-scale passive defenses, total bomb-on-target requirements to destroy urban concentrations in the United States appear to be in the low hundreds, even allowing some to be assigned to economic targets outside cities. A larger number of bombs would have to be dispatched if delivered by missiles with low accuracy or reliability. Against a very effective air defense the number dispatched might have to be several times the number required on target—but we are told that no completely effective air defense is in existence and, as we shall see, it is questionable how effective air defense can be made against surprise attack.

3. Nuclear weapons of the same kind or in their small, light, "tactical" guise [3] may revolutionize war on the ground and at sea as drastically as the strategic air war. Less is evident about "requirements" for nuclear weapons against military targets: the number needed to destroy some highly dispersed and "hardened" military forces could be very large. What is evident is (1) that tactical forces armed with even moderate numbers of nuclear weapons and the means of delivering them can easily and quickly

---

[2] *New York Times*, April 1, 1954. Mr. Strauss was not using "destroy" in a literal physical sense, and he was undoubtedly implicitly assuming no large-scale expensive passive defense measures to reduce vulnerability.

[3] The largest "strategic" thermonuclear weapons may be even more effective against some military targets, e.g., by making huge areas uninhabitable for long periods.

defeat forces which do not possess them; (2) that both the United States and Russia can use such weapons, and (3) that ground, naval, or tactical air forces that have not adapted their deployment and tactics to the new weapons will be hopelessly vulnerable to nuclear attack.

4. While Russia's weapon technology and nuclear stockpile *may* still lag behind ours, it would be rash indeed to expect any such lags to widen. As to technology, the Russians have obviously made tremendous progress in rocket engines and missiles, and quite possibly have more first-rate scientists working on their programs than the United States has in its programs. As to nuclear stockpiles, increases in production rates on both sides depend mainly on a willingness to invest in additional productive capacity. No one believes any longer that a shortage of some crucial specific resource like uranium ore will conveniently (for us) inhibit Soviet production. The Soviet Union is compelled by the strongest of motives to match or surpass the United States programs, and has not hesitated in the past to undertake very large investment programs (for example, in steel) to meet security objectives.

Several implications of these weapon developments for the relative strengths of offense and defense have become fairly clear. These implications may be summarized in the following way.

1. The game is loaded against the defense when small-scale (by World War II. standards) sudden attacks can cause catastrophic and perhaps irreparable damage.

2. Responsible officials of the Air Force and of the North American Air Defense Command have told us repeatedly that a leak-proof defense is not now attainable. Under some, not too unlikely, circumstances of surprise attack, we could fare very badly.[4]

While air defenses can undoubtedly be vastly improved over the next few years, the offense is likely to improve concomitantly. Ballistic missiles present formidable problems for air defense.

3. The superiority of the offense does not necessarily imply that either side can eliminate the enemy's ability to retaliate in force; still less that either side can *guarantee* such elimination. A strategic bombing force is much easier to protect by active and passive measures and by mobility and concealment than are economic and population targets. Such developments as nuclear-powered submarines armed with Polaris and train-mobile Minuteman missiles are offensive weapons with revolutionary implications.

---

[4] We could of course do much better against a *small* attacking force *if we had adequate warning* than we could in less favorable circumstances.

Moreover, the development of thermonuclear weapons, by greatly reducing the number of bombs on target required to cause massive damage to economic and population targets, has enhanced the retaliatory capability of whatever portion of one's striking force manages to escape surprise enemy attack. Unless the attacker is extremely successful, he may fail to prevent effective retaliation.

4. Similar considerations apply to tactical engagements, on the ground and at sea. Nuclear weapons and modern delivery systems give an attacker the ability to compress a devastating attack in space and time. Again we appear to have made much greater progress in offensive missiles than in missile defenses. And here, as in the strategic war, it is hard for the attacker to insure against effective counterattack.

That the superiority of the offense will persist is, of course, not certain. Judgments about the future rarely are. The revolution in military technology which began with the atomic bomb is a continuing, even perhaps an accelerating, one and will certainly take unexpected, unpredictable turns. And the fact that the odds favor the offense by no means implies that attempts to provide any defense are a foolish waste of resources. On the contrary, some kinds of defense measures are essential and integral components of a strategy of deterrence. But the prospects are poor that we will ever again be able to rely on such defenses to prevent great destruction if deterrence fails and an attack is launched.

IMPLICATIONS FOR KIND OF WAR

The weapon developments that have been described could conceivably influence the character of warfare in either of two directions, neither of which can be ignored in our plans. They could increase the violence of war, or they could limit it.

All-Out Thermonuclear War and Limited Local Conflicts

Most obviously, these developments could make war "total" to a degree never before experienced. An all-out thermonuclear war involving nations like the United States and the Soviet Union could easily destroy either or both, at least as powers of any consequence, in a matter of days or perhaps even hours.

There is increasing recognition, however, that the dangers implicit in participation in all-out thermonuclear war may result in a stalemate. In the words of Sir Winston Churchill, a "balance of terror" may replace the balance of power. Nations may become too fearful and cautious to use or even threaten to use their ultimate weapons, except for direct self-protection. This would mean, assuming no change in the objectives of Russia or Red China, a continuation of the cold war, with the Russians and Chinese attempting to win uncommitted areas by political and economic warfare, by subversion, and by limited, local military aggression. To avoid piecemeal surrender, we might determine to engage in defensive or counter-military actions also limited in character.[5]

These military actions, or limited, local wars, may flare up as a result—indeed as an extension—of international negotiation, of internal revolution, or of pawn moves by major powers to test or exploit a weakness. They are the late twentieth century "balance of terror" counterpart of the limited-scale, limited-objectives wars of the "balance of power" century between Waterloo and World War I. We have seen many of these limited wars in recent years: the contest in the Formosa Straits, the Indo-China War, the Korean War (small only in comparison with World War II), the Greek-Albanian-Yugoslav conflicts, the Chinese Civil War, the Indonesian revolutions, the Suez invasion, the Lebanon crisis, and others. While some of these were not of primary concern to the major powers, most of them were. Challenges (or opportunities) like Greece, Korea, and Suez will continue to present themselves.

The recent history of restraint in the use of nuclear weapons,[6] of attempts to confine these conflicts, of negotiated armistices, of ability to swallow frustration where the outcome was completely adverse (as for us in Indo-China and for the USSR in Greece)— all these are significant indications that the war of limited scale and limited objectives is here to stay.

But so is the danger of thermonuclear war, despite its recognized suicidal threat. There are many ways in which all-out war could be triggered by accident or misunderstanding. Either side may resort to a thermonuclear strike to protect some presumed vital interest (for example, on our side, Western Europe), or in frustration or desperation (for example, if the cold war appears to be going hopelessly against it), gambling upon the very great advantages accruing from a surprise first strike. Finally, the very fearsomeness of the threat is an invitation to a calculating, ruthless power to remove it by force if any happy circumstance presents itself—as, for example, the temporary impotence or vulnerability of the opposing strategic air force; or his own temporary

---

[5] See Henry A. Kissinger, *Nuclear Weapons and Foreign Policy*, Harper and Bros., New York 1957, Chapter 5 and *passim*, for an extreme but persuasive statement of this argument.

[6] We would by no means rule out the use of tactical atomic weapons in local wars; in fact, there have been numerous authoritative statements that the U.S. will so use them. But past restraint must be explained in part by the fear that their use would make it more difficult to limit the scale and objectives of the conflict.

invulnerability resulting from, say, a breakthrough in air defense technology. Moreover, in considering the prospects of some power initiating thermonuclear war, we cannot confine ourselves to the Soviet Union and the United States. Within the next ten to twenty years (not too long a period for the weighing of some military economic policies) several nations in addition to the United States and the USSR are likely to acquire a substantial thermonuclear capability. Quite apart from specifically military atomic programs, the widespread use of reactors for power will result in stocks of nuclear materials that may find their way into weapons.

It appears then that in our national security planning we must consider at least two kinds of war—all-out thermonuclear war on the one hand, and limited, local actions of a holding or counter-offensive character on the other.

The relative probabilities of these two kinds of war occurring will depend in part on the policies we pursue. If we prepare to deal with only one, we invite defeat, indeed destruction, by the other. The number of kinds of war which we must consider cannot, therefore, be reduced below two.

War Calling for Prolonged Mobilization

Does the number have to be increased to three? Is there a third kind of war, besides total and local wars, for which we must prepare? It has sometimes been suggested that a third possibility is a large-scale and long war, like World War II, in which strategic bombing of cities is either withheld or, if attempted, is ineffective *on both sides.*[7] Let us call this the World War II type war, although it might differ from World War II in such important military aspects as the widespread use of atomic weapons against military targets.

The question whether this World War II type of war is likely enough or dangerous enough to justify extensive preparations is, as will be seen, a crucial one for economic mobilization policy. We will simply state our views, because to defend them would carry the discussion far beyond its intended scope.

The contingency that strategic bombing would be attempted but ineffective *on both sides* seems to be extremely unlikely, for reasons already explained.

Mutual withholding of strategic attacks on cities for fear of retaliation is a somewhat more serious possibility—but only if the withholding is combined with quite limited war objectives: If the apparent winner presses on for anything like "unconditional sur-

---

[7] If ineffective on only one side, the strategic bombing would be decisive and the war short.

render," the apparent loser would convert the limited war to a total one. But a limited objectives war would be unlikely to be large-scale and long, like World War II. Mutual withholding plus limited objectives define what is essentially a local action.[8]

If a war of this kind did occur, we would have time to mobilize our industrial potential and ought to "win" eventually, just as we did in World War I and World War II, even if we were relatively unprepared at its beginning.[9]

In short, this kind of war appears to be the least likely (of the three) and least important in our preparations. It might become most important if atomic disarmament is achieved. But this has not looked very promising, and effectively controlled atomic disarmament (the only kind that United States policy has contemplated) may no longer be feasible unless completely new ideas for inspection and enforcement are conceived and accepted.[10]

Some British writers have suggested that the contestants might fight a lengthy "broken-back war" to a conclusion on the ground *after* successful strategic bombing on both sides. This would be Phase II of an all-out thermonuclear war. We should not completely ignore it in our planning, yet it is obviously not too important if Phase I is completely successful on both sides, or if one side falls substantially shorter of complete success than the other.

IMPLICATIONS FOR THE IMPORTANCE
OF ECONOMIC STRENGTH

Declining Importance of Economic War Potential
in Its Conventional Sense

The term "economic war potential" has usually meant the maximum *fully mobilized* capability of an economy to supply the men and materials required to fight a war. There are two objections to this concept. The first is its vagueness. What constitutes a "maximum" diversion of resources to war depends importantly upon (a) political and morale factors which in all countries fluctuate with circumstances, and (b) the time allowed for conversion to war production: the longer the mobilization period, the greater the peak war output. There is no single number or simple set of

---

[8] There are other difficulties associated with mutual withholding of city bombing in any war transcending a local action. There may be no practicable way to delimit the restriction: we know that many "strictly military" targets are separated from large centers of population by less than the lethal radius of large bombs.

[9] This is almost a *reductio ad absurdum*. Russia would not allow us to win complete victory while she possessed a nuclear stockpile.

[10] See Eugene Rabinowitch, "Living with H-Bombs," *Bulletin of the Atomic Scientists*, Vol. XI, No. 1, January 1955, pp. 5–8.

numbers which can respect "the" economic war potential of a nation.

Second, and more important, recent and prospective technological developments associated with nuclear weapons have greatly reduced the significance of economic war potential in the sense of maximum fully mobilized capacity for war production. Before the development of nuclear weapons and the means of delivering them on distant targets, the military power of the United States could be fairly well measured by its economic potential. Geography afforded us the time we needed, if pressed, to translate most of our potential into power.[11] Because we were the wealthiest nation in the world with the largest steel and machinery industries, we were also the most powerful militarily.

The development of nuclear and especially of thermonuclear weapons represents a momentous turning point in the cost of acquiring military capabilities. Destructive power has now become so cheap that wars can be won or economies destroyed before there is time for mobilization.

In an all-out thermonuclear war the superior economic war potential of the United States is important only to the extent that it has been effectively diverted to security purposes before war starts. This is true for all our forces, offensive or defensive. It is particularly and most obviously true for our strategic air offensive forces and air defense. For preparedness for full thermonuclear war the United States must learn to rely on forces in being—not as cadres about which much larger, newly mobilized forces will be organized, but as *the* important forces.

Economic war potential also appears to be less than decisive in fighting local wars (Viet Minh could defeat France in the jungles of Northern Indo-China), and of even less importance, as potential, in countering assaults by infiltration, subversion, civil war, and astute diplomacy. In limited wars, too, forces in being seem likely to play a crucial role, useful reserves being mainly those that can be mobilized promptly. Once hostilities have begun, industrial potential cannot be brought to bear soon enough. Even in World War II, the industrial potential of the allies did not save France or count for much in the first two or three years.[12] More recently, in the Korean War, industrial potential was not the force that saved the port of Pusan or shaped the course of the conflict. In all such action—limited in objectives, means, and scope—full indus-

---

[11] Even before the development of nuclear weapons, geography proved an inadequate defense for European countries against Blitzkrieg tactics based on aircraft and tanks.

[12] See C. J. Hitch, *America's Economic Strength*, Oxford University Press, London, 1941, pp. 60–73, 95–110.

trial mobilization is not approached, and economic war potential never comes into play.

In consequence the significance of economic war potential in its usual meaning has been degraded. The nation which can maintain the most formidable forces in being is not necessarily the wealthiest. In peacetime the proportion of national resources that can be diverted to national security purposes is by no means constant among nations. Both in peacetime and in fighting limited wars, countries with less economic war *potential* may support larger military budgets and forces. Russia, for example, a much poorer country than the United States, has supported a larger peacetime military program.

This situation is a particularly dangerous one for the United States. Shielded by geography, we have traditionally (before the Korean War) maintained very small forces in peacetime, and have regarded them as cadres rather than as integrated fighting units in a state of readiness. There is a strong tendency for nations (like individuals) to persist in policies which have been successful long after the external conditions essential to success have vanished, especially when they are pleasant and cheap like this one. The United States will probably maintain a substantial industrial lead over possible enemies for many years, but if we rely upon it as mobilization potential as we did before World War II, we will be inviting irrevocable disaster.

The Importance of Economic Strength Before the Outbreak of War

Without doubt, then, "the nostalgic idea that our industrial power is our greatest military asset could ruin our military planning." [13] This does not mean, however, that economic strength will be any less important in the pursuit of national objectives in the future than in the past. Military power is derived from economic strength, and foreign policy is based on both. Economic strength that is used for national security purposes *in time* is the embodiment of military power. Using it in time demands a new approach to national security problems—which to some extent we have already made.

The essential contribution of economic strength is that it enables us to do more of the numerous things which are desirable from the point of view of national security, but which, in their fullness, not even the wealthiest nation can afford.

---

[13] Thomas K. Finletter, *Power and Policy,* Harcourt, Brace and Company, New York, 1954, p. 256.

What are these desirable things in a thermonuclear era—that is, things that have positive payoffs and that we would like to have if resources were unlimited?

1. Preparations for and deterrence of thermonuclear war. These would include strategic air forces, warning networks, active air defenses, and passive defenses of various kinds including perhaps dispersal, shelters, and large-scale stockpiling of both weapons and industrial commodities. It appears desirable not only to do all these things but to do them in style—to confront the Soviet Union with a variety of strategic air threats, each absolutely invulnerable to any conceivable weapon which might be used against it; to erect a continental air defense system embodying all the latest and most expensive equipment of which any scientist has dreamed; and to buy enough passive defense of all kinds to insure our survival if by any chance an enemy attack still gets through.

2. Preparations for local and limited wars also appear desirable: challenges to fight such wars are almost certain to occur, and it would be comforting to be able to accept such challenges, or to make counterchallenges, if we want to. Sometimes it is argued that limited wars can be handled without ground forces or tactical air power simply by threatening massive retaliation against any and all provocations. If this were true, conventional military forces would be superfluous. The trouble is that the enemy might not believe our threat to launch a thermonuclear attack in the event of minor provocations.[14] Moreover, he might be correct in disbelieving, for we are probably not willing to use H-bombs to cope with minor aggressions—partly to avoid inhumane destruction, partly to retain allies, but mostly to escape the H-bombs that could in turn descend on us. Consequently, without conventional forces, we might have nothing with which to counter local aggressions and be wide open to "nibbling" tactics by the enemy. The net result might also be a heightened probability of thermonuclear war.

Preparation in style also seems desirable. Local, limited wars have taken many forms and have occurred in many places in recent history; future possibilities are even more numerous. We might have to fight in Southeast Asia, the Middle East, or the Balkans, with or without atomic bombs, with native help of varying qualities. We should like to have heavy matériel stocks pre-

---

[14] For a discussion of these issues, see Bernard Brodie, "Unlimited Weapons and Limited War," *The Reporter*, November 18, 1954, pp. 16–21; and William Kaufmann, "Limited Warfare," in W. Kaufmann (ed.), *Military Policy and National Security*, Princeton University Press, Princeton, N.J., 1956, pp. 102–36.

positioned and, in addition, a large capacity for moving men and matériel rapidly by sea and by air to the theater of action. To back up our ready forces for such wars it would be desirable to have trained reserves and facilities for quickly expanding the production of matériel.

3. It would be desirable too (if resources were unlimited) to prepare to fight a World War II type of war. Even though this sort of conflict seems unlikely, it might conceivably occur. Preparations would call for ready forces to fight a holding action (these might do double duty for local wars), and measures to enlarge the mobilization base and to increase its security and the speed with which it can be converted. The accumulation of raw material stockpiles from overseas sources would be desirable, for example, in addition to securing the sea lanes. Construction of new capacity in industries that might "bottleneck" the expansion of war production, support of multiple sources of supply by expensive splitting of procurement contracts, and the training and maintenance of large reserve forces might be undertaken.

4. Cutting across all these areas, it would clearly be desirable to support a very large research and development effort. We are in an era in which a single technological mutation (as in the past, the development of radar and the atomic bomb) can far outweigh in military importance our substantial resources advantage. There are conceivable future mutations of equal importance—invulnerable long-range ballistic missiles, perhaps a high-confidence defense against nuclear weapons. Research and development is most obviously desirable in the context of thermonuclear wars: here certain kinds of technological slippage could break the stalemate, blunt deterrence, and place us at the mercy of the Kremlin. But it is also possible to conceive of developments which would, for example, greatly improve the capability of the United States to fight small engagements in out-of-the-way places. Development is cheap only by contrast with the procurement and maintenance of ready forces. If we tried to develop everything interesting (and possibly significant and therefore "desirable"), we could use all the potential as well as all the actual scientific and engineering resources of the country.

5. Finally, there are substantial opportunities to use economic strength in the cold war itself. Economic warfare, whether waged against our enemies or for our friends, can be expensive. It is widely believed that the Marshall Plan saved Western Europe from collapsing into chaos and perhaps Communism between 1947 and 1950, but at a cost of about 10 billion dollars. The United

States is now spending roughly a billion dollars a year on economic aid to friendly and neutral countries and the Soviet Union is lending over half a billion dollars annually, partly to its satellites and partly to other countries. Britain and Western Europe propose to spend many billions of dollars "uneconomically" on nuclear power plants to reduce their economic dependence on Middle Eastern oil, which is vulnerable both to Arab nationalism and to Soviet power. Economic strength permits a nation to wage the cold war more effectively, to reduce its vulnerability to hostile moves, and to improve its position and power by extending its influence.

These, then, are the desirable things—the things it would be nice to do from the point of view of national security. In the aggregate they far exceed our economic capabilities, so that hard choices must be made. But the greater our economic strength, the more desirable things we can do, and the better we can do them. We cannot prepare for all kinds of wars, but maybe we can prepare for more than one. We cannot develop every technological idea of promise, but maybe with three times Russia's economic strength we can develop enough more than she to keep ahead in the race for technological leadership. We cannot buy perfect protection against thermonuclear attack by any combination of active and passive defense, but perhaps we can afford enough defense to reduce Russian confidence of complete success to the point where she is deterred from striking. Perhaps on top of all this, we can afford a positive economic foreign policy which will preserve our alliances and increase our influence on developments in the uncommitted parts of the world.

At the least, the possession of greater economic strength enables us to do more of these things than we otherwise could do. But it does so if, and only if, we use the strength now, during the cold war, before a hot war starts. For that reason the term "economic war potential" will not be used in the present study. The timely translation of economic strength into military power, the proportion of that strength so translated, and the efficiency of the forces in being, have become of critical importance—as opposed to some theoretical maximum potential which could be translated into military force at some later date. While the traditional concept of the mobilization base is not yet fully obsolete and may even justify a limited expenditure of budget, it is no longer the shield of the Republic.

PART TWO

THE RESOURCES AVAILABLE FOR DEFENSE

III

RESOURCE LIMITATIONS

As noted earlier, Part I is devoted to problems of choice at comparatively high levels, choices among policies that affect (1) the resources at the nation's disposal and (2) the proportion of resources allocated to national defense. Our national security depends first of all upon these choices, for they determine the volume of resources available for defense.

Resource limitations are our starting point because in all problems of choice we strive to get the most out of what we have. To put it another way, we try to use the resources that are available to us so as to maximize what economists call "utility." Resources are always limited in comparison with our wants, always constraining our action. (If they did not, we could do everything, and there would be no problem of choosing preferred courses of action.) As a consequence, resource limitations are often called constraints. We try to achieve the most desirable outcome that is possible in view of these constraints.

We should therefore inquire into the nature of resource limitations as a preliminary step in selecting courses of action. In this chapter we shall discuss specific *versus* general resource constraints, the total resources that are at the nation's disposal, and policies that would influence those resources in the future. In subsequent chapters of Part II, we shall discuss how to choose the size of the defense budget and the major considerations bearing on that choice.

SPECIFIC VERSUS GENERAL CONSTRAINTS

How should constraints be expressed if they are to be most meaningful in appraising a nation's strength and in choosing the scale of the defense effort? What are the effective limitations on what we can do? Sometimes constraints are expressed as the projected supplies of specific items such as laborers in each skill and age bracket, tons of bauxite and mica, board feet of lumber, or kilowatt-hours of electricity. The supplies of individual items like these will be called "specific constraints." Sometimes, however, resource limitations are expressed as projected amounts of money that can be spent, putting a limit on the total effort but not on quantities of specific resources that can be employed. Such an over-all limitation will be called a "general constraint." In which form should constraints be expressed in different circumstances? In which form do they more accurately reflect the real limitations imposed by the physical world?

Different Constraints in Different Problems

In some problems, the constraints unquestionably ought to be expressed as definite quantities of specific products. Consider, for example, the decisions of a task force commander in a naval engagement. He must try to get the most from the particular items that are at his disposal—destroyers that are now in the force, man hours available for maintenance and operations, ammunition on hand, and so on. It is beside the point that, by allocating money in a budget differently, he could have equipped a task force with another aircraft carrier at a sacrifice of so many destroyers. The option of shifting basic resources from the production of one item to the production of another is hardly open at this stage of the game. Hence, in this situation, it is not a budget that constrains the actions of the commander. Limited stocks of specific items genuinely *are* the constraints, and they should be expressed in that fashion.

In other problems, however, the supplies of specific resources are not fixed, and the use of specific constraints is wrong. Consider the problems of the Navy in choosing next year's purchases of equipment. Of course, there will be some specific constraints—the physical impossibility, for example, of suddenly procuring an extraordinarily large quantity of some newly developed fuel or of completing an extra super carrier before a certain date. But one principal constraint will be the budget. Within the limits of this budget it will be physically possible to acquire varying amounts of many items—more training and less electronic gear, more ammunition and less manpower. In these circumstances, it *is* chiefly the budget that constrains: the Navy's supplies of many items are not fixed, and it would be wrong to choose policies as if **they** were.

Let us turn from the problems of naval planning for next year to problems of national policy over, say, the next decade. At first glance, the supplies of many basic resources may appear to be fixed. Manpower seems to be limited to its present size plus annual growth. Ore and petroleum reserves can hardly be manufactured. There is only so much coal to be mined. The acreage of each type of soil is already set. And yet, upon more careful inspection, one sees that the supplies of these resources that will be available in future periods are not really fixed. Medical programs and education can affect the total supply of labor. Through retraining, one kind of manpower can acquire a different skill. More intensive mining can recover a larger proportion of given ore reserves. A shift of resources can yield more metals at the expense of textiles or more titanium and less copper. The use of fertilizers, irrigation, drainage, tractors—these and many other innovations can alter the inventory of land, both in total and in composition.

Thus except in the very short run, the nation can usually get more of one item—even of many so-called basic resources, as far as future supplies are concerned—by sacrificing something else. The more distant the future to which the problem pertains, the less applicable are specific constraints. Where time and technology permit adjustments, the nation is not constrained by fixed supplies of individual resources, and thinking in terms of specific constraints is misleading. The real constraints, the truly "basic" resources, are exceedingly complex and difficult to measure, involving the state of the technological art, stocks of ingenuity and knowledge, institutional arrangements, and incentives as well as the total supplies of capital and people. Probably the most satisfactory way to represent these constraints is by means of some aggregate dollar amount of output that is at the nation's disposal each year. Such an amount, say national income or gross national product (GNP),[1] is a general constraint similar to a budget. It is a rough indicator of the aggregate output that is available annually, an indicator having no implication that the nation must work with specific quantities of individual items.

General monetary constraints are not put forward as perfect indicators of resource limitations even in the long run. Frequently some specific constraints will be operative as well as the general one (as in the case of the Navy's super carrier). Sometimes, too, specific limitations are imposed by decree of higher authority. For instance, the branches of the service, in planning ahead, face not only the general constraint of their budgets but also the specific

---

[1] Gross national product will be discussed in more detail in the next section of this chapter.

constraint of a manpower ceiling set by Congress. Strictly speaking, in problems of national policy as in most others, there is usually a combination of specific and general constraints.

Money Costs When General Constraints Apply

Only by counting the costs that constitute the real constraint can we determine the policies that achieve a specified task at minimum cost. If the stock of magnesium is the real constraint (and the only one), we should be interested in the cost of alternative actions in terms of magnesium. If several individual inputs are limited, we should be interested in the cost of alternative policies in terms of those inputs. If there is a general monetary constraint but specific inputs are not fixed, we should consider cost in dollars.[2]

To some people, dollars do not appear to reflect real resource cost, and their use has little appeal. Let us examine the justification for paying attention to monetary expense. What, in a fundamental sense, is the "cost" of a course of action? It is whatever must be given up in order to adopt that course, that is, whatever could otherwise be kept or obtained.[3] If we examine the problem of planning future programs from the standpoint of the Defense Department, it seems fairly obvious that money costs are pertinent. The Department faces a budgetary constraint. For the most part it does not face a limitation on particular weapons or supplies but can buy more of them by paying their prices. What does the Department give up in order to implement one course of action? The answer is money—or, to go one step further, the alternative weapons or supplies that could otherwise be purchased. The Department could substitute one item for another by paying the price of the one instead of paying the price of the other. Dollar costs do reflect what must be given up in order to adopt a particular policy. They reflect real sacrifices by the Department because the prices of different items show the rates at which they can be substituted for each other.

This is not to say that money costs perfectly represent resources sacrificed by the Defense Department. The prices of goods to be bought in the future are uncertain. One course of action may itself drive up the price of particular weapons or materials, and it is not possible to predict these effects with complete accuracy. The characteristics and cost of some items will change as technology advances. The quantity of some exceptional items may literally be

---

[2] Only by counting costs in these terms can we determine the policies that achieve the most with the given constraints, that is, with the available resources.

[3] That is, the cost is the sacrificed alternative *opportunity*. Hence, economists refer to these sacrificed alternatives as the "opportunity costs" of a course of action.

fixed, or nearly fixed, even if we are looking several years ahead. Nonetheless, imperfect as it is, the money cost of a future program usually shows the sacrifice that would be required of the Department better than other measures of cost. While dollars do not precisely measure the real sacrifices, costs in terms of metals and manpower would be grossly misleading. Saying that airplanes cost so much aluminum and ships so much steel plate does not tell us how one may be exchanged for the other. Saying that each costs so many dollars adheres more closely to the facts, namely, that the services can, in making future plans, trade one for the other.

But even if dollars reflect resource costs fairly well from the viewpoint of the Defense Department, do they do so from the standpoint of the nation? If the economy is a reasonably competitive one, the answer is Yes. The reason is that market prices in a competitive economy reflect not only the approximate rate at which the Defense Department can exchange one item for another but also the approximate rate at which the whole economy can substitute one article or material for another. Suppose that the price of a bomber is $1,000,000 and that of a destroyer $20,000,000. How can 20 bombers possibly entail the same resource cost as a destroyer? In other words, how can the construction of 20 bombers use up materials and manpower that could otherwise have produced one destroyer? Aircraft construction requires different metals, engineers with different skills, and different facilities from those required in shipbuilding. Obviously the set of inputs needed in the one case cannot be directly substituted for the other set of inputs. The specialist in aerodynamics cannot be put to work promptly and effectively on the design of destroyers. The labor force that might be used to build bombers in the Southwest cannot be shifted en masse to shipyards in Philadelphia.

Nonetheless, 20 bombers can use resources that would otherwise make it possible for the economy to produce one more destroyer. It is indirect substitution that makes this possible. If the bombers are ordered, the contractor must recruit the necessary laborers, build any newly required facilities, and buy the materials. In order to attract these resources, he will have to pay about what they could earn in their next-best use. These amounts or prices, in a competitive economy, correspond to the value of the output that the resources could otherwise produce. The sum of these amounts—the cost of the bombers—is therefore the value of civilian, or other, outputs that must be sacrificed.

As the recruitment of laborers and the purchase of materials takes place, a chain reaction is set off. The firms that begin to lose the laborers and materials try to replace them. The prices of aluminum, aeronautical engineers, and other resources used in aircraft production may rise somewhat relative to the prices of other inputs. Consumers of these scarcer resources shift to substitutes. Some workers learn that good jobs are available in aircraft plants and transfer to them, leaving vacancies in their former occupations, which in turn are attractive opportunities to still other workers. As a result of this process, the resources for the bombers are in effect released from myriad industries—perhaps coal-mining in Illinois, hair cutting in New Jersey, shrimp fishing in Louisiana —industries that are far removed from aircraft production.

Now suppose the destroyer is to be constructed instead of the airplanes. Imagine that we have a table model of the economy with figures to represent the various resources, and let us transfer the resources by hand. We do not move the men and materials directly from the aircraft industry to the shipyards. Instead we move them back to their next-best uses in the economy. The materials and men that would have replaced them in those uses are moved back in turn to their next-best uses. Simultaneously, we transfer resources into the production of destroyers, drawing them from other kinds of shipbuilding and related parts of the economy and setting off another sequence of shifts and substitutions.

If it is hard to take these roundabout substitutions seriously, remember that they happen constantly in real life. In any particular year some industries (for example, electronics or plastics) expand, and others (say, railroads or movies) decline. The growing industries, as a rule, take over few of the inputs once employed by the declining industries. Relative prices, reflecting the substitution possibilities among goods and services, lead firms to shift resources much more efficiently than transferring them directly from declining industries to expanding ones.[4]

As a consequence, money costs of *future* defense activities approximate the real alternatives that are foregone—the real sacrifices that are entailed—when one activity or weapon system is selected. This will be true for those problems in which a general monetary constraint is proper, that is, for problems pertaining to dates sufficiently in the future to permit the production and procurement of varying quantities of weapons and matériel.

------

[4] A more complete and rigorous discussion of these points can be found in most textbooks on the principles of economics, e.g., Paul Samuelson, *Economics*, 3d ed., New York, McGraw-Hill Book Co., 1955, pp. 17–21, 34–37, 49–50, 475–525.

GNP AS THE CONSTRAINT ON THE NATION'S ACTIVITIES

So far we have discussed the constraints and costs that are appropriate to defense problems or even problems in general. What about the problem at hand, that of assessing the nation's strength and deciding how much should be diverted to defense? By and large, in dealing with this problem, a general limitation on our efforts, such as GNP, is more nearly accurate and more useful than specific constraints. This problem is not how best to conduct a naval engagement with given weapons—not how to assess the power of a retaliatory attack that could be launched immediately. Instead the problem is how to gauge the strength that is the source of our defense effort and how to determine the share that should go to national security. These questions pertain to the planning of defense policies in future years, not to the planning of tactics for today's mission. There is time for a great deal of adjustment, and the constraint is more appropriately described as a general monetary one. It is more nearly correct to say that a projected $560-billion GNP (1957 dollars) will constrain our defense effort in 1965 than to say that 250,000 short-tons of magnesium, 150 billion ton-miles of transport, and 8 million long tons of sulfur will limit our program.

Moreover, even if particular resources were limited, a list of specific constraints would not be as manageable and meaningful as GNP in debating the above questions. Judgment as well as analysis must play an important role in assessing the nation's strength and deciding upon the share to be devoted to defense. These are questions that must be considered and debated at the highest levels—by the voters, by the administration in power, by the Congress. An electronic computer could take a large number of specific constraints and show a variety of combinations of output that could be produced. (It is scarcely possible, however, for a computer to show *all* of the combinations of output that could be produced with limitations of particular resources. Moreover, it is doubtful that such a tremendous mass of data would help anyone to reach better decisions about the national security budget.) [5] But the selection of the "correct" combination of defense and nondefense outputs depends greatly upon the unarticulated preferences of Congressmen and voters.

---

[5] This is *not* to say that electronic computers are unable to help us find useful answers to lower level problems of choice. On the contrary, they can help in many instances—as will be stressed in Part Three. For in many lower level problems, a suitable criterion can be made explicit, and calculations can point to the preferable courses of action.

That being the case, the resource limitations must be described in terms that the human mind can comprehend. It would be difficult, indeed impossible, for people to debate policy in the following manner: "In 1965 our strength will consist of 900 thousand short tons of fluorspar, 80 million man-years of labor, 15 thousand flasks of mercury (and so on). As the future situation looks to us now, the United States should plan on devoting 20 thousand tons of fluorspar, 20 million man-years of labor, and 2 thousand flasks of mercury to defense." It would surely be more meaningful to hear: "In 1965 our GNP will be 560 billion dollars. As the situation seems to shape up, the United States might plan on devoting 10 or 12 per cent of its GNP or roughly 60 to 70 billion dollars to national defense." For in the end, obligational authority and appropriations will be expressed in dollars, not in commodities. The debate about the scale of the military effort will take place mainly in terms of budgets (and the capabilities various budgets will buy), not in terms of commodities (and the weapons they can produce). Accordingly, as an aid in this debate, the constraint on the nation's activities—our economic strength—is most meaningful if it is expressed as a general monetary limitation.

Statements by government officials show that the debate usually does proceed in terms of a general monetary constraint, not only in appraising over-all strength but also specifically in deciding how many resources should be devoted to defense.[6] Right after the 1955 Geneva conference, former Secretary of Defense Wilson was reported as saying "he was considering whether more might not be spent on defense in the future if the national product and income continued to expand prosperously. To maintain the current level of defense spending in the face of a continually expanding economy, he suggested, would be tantamount to a cutback."[7] Thinking about defense expenditures in relation to GNP is not new. For example, President Truman in his 1952 Economic Report to the Congress stated, "Our total output [GNP], measured in 1951 prices, was more than 90 billion dollars higher than in 1939, and more than 100 billion above 1929. . . . The growth of production during the last few years now enables us to carry the security program without undue impairment of the rest of the economy."[8]

[6] See, for example, *Study of Airpower,* Hearings Before the Subcommittee on the Air Force of the Committee on Armed Services, U.S. Senate, 84th Congress, 2d Session, Part XXII, U.S. Government Printing Office, Washington, D.C., 1956, pp. 1668–72.

[7] *New York Times,* November 17, 1955, p. 11.

[8] *The Economic Report of the President,* together with a Report to the President, The Annual Economic Review, by the Council of Economic Advisers, Washington, D.C., 1952, p. 2.

For other problems, to be sure, other means of describing resource constraints are more pertinent. Suppose the problem is to select policies for industrial mobilization, as in World War II, rather than to choose the scale of the defense effort for cold or limited war. In that case, specific limitations are of the greatest significance. Thus, the programming of production in World War II depended upon the projected supplies of critical materials, skilled labor, and fabricated components (small electric motors, for example).[9] Because they were primarily concerned with the problems of industrial mobilization, previous books on the economics of defense have usually emphasized these limitations on individual resources.[10] But, as stressed earlier, the crucial problem in the nuclear era is not planning how best to mobilize our reserve strength. Instead the most urgent questions have to do with the planning of our forces in being for deterrence and limited conflicts. One of these questions is how much of our strength should be turned into forces in being. And for the purpose of attacking this question, we should think mainly in terms of a general monetary constraint.

The Meaning of GNP[11]

Gross national product, or GNP, is simply the dollar value of a nation's final output over a period of one year—about $440 billion in 1957 in the United States (1957 dollars). It is the total volume of goods and services, valued at market prices, that is at the nation's disposal over the period. Unlike net national income, GNP represents the whole of the nation's output, no portion being already set aside to allow for depreciation. Therefore any consumption, replacement of wornout or obsolete equipment, additions to the stock of capital, military outlays, or other government expenditures must come from GNP.[12] Of course, this measure is a proper constraint only if we are speaking of *full-employment* GNP. If only half the nation's resources are employed, GNP will be rela-

---

[9] See D. Novick, M. Anshen, and W. C. Truppner, *Wartime Production Controls*, Columbia University Press, New York, 1949.

[10] E.g., George A. Lincoln, *Economics of National Security*, 2nd ed., Prentice-Hall, Inc., New York, 1954 ; J. Blackman, A. Basch, S. Fabricant, M. Gainsbrugh, and E. Stein, *War and Defense Economics*, Rinehart & Co., Inc., New York, 1952; *Economic Mobilization and Stabilization*, L. V. Chandler and D. H. Wallace (eds.), Henry Holt and Co., New York, 1951; S. F. Harris, *The Economics of Mobilization and Inflation*, W. W. Norton & Co., Inc., New York, 1951.

[11] For a full description of the concepts and methods used by the U.S. Government in measuring gross national product, see *National Income Supplement to the Survey of Current Business*, prepared in the Office of Business Economics of the U.S. Department of Commerce, U.S. Government Printing Office, Washington, D.C., 1954, pp. 27–158.

[12] For our present purpose, this statement is sufficiently accurate. It is not 100 per cent correct, for a nation could consume more than GNP for a time by drawing on inventories or on foreign balances, credits, or gifts.

tively small, but in those circumstances it is not a true indicator of the nation's capacity to produce. A larger defense program, or more of any program, can then be produced without sacrificing other things—simply by getting idle resources back to work. Thus the constraint referred to here is GNP at a high level of employment.

GNP is not the same thing as the total wealth of the nation—the value of its land, buildings, and equipment. The total wealth of the United States has been estimated to be about 800 billion dollars (as of 1948 and 1948 prices).[13] If the value of people as producers was counted among the country's assets, the figure would be much higher. But an estimate of the country's wealth is not directly pertinent to the problem of planning the national defenses. The assets of an individual or firm can be sold or "cashed in," and the proceeds can be devoted to any purpose that is chosen. Not so with the assets of the whole nation. They cannot be liquidated in order to get resources for defense or for any other purpose. The resources that can be devoted to national security are essentially the outputs that can be obtained each year from the stock of capital and supply of labor. Those are the outputs that make up GNP. If all of GNP is consumed, the capital stock is slowly depleted. If part of it is invested, capital may be maintained or augmented. But GNP is the amount that is at our disposal over a year's time.

If each year's GNP is expressed in current prices, it will reflect changes in the general price level, that is, inflation or deflation. If it is expressed in terms of a constant price level, GNP is an index of the physical volume of final output. When talking about past years, it is often proper to refer to GNP in current dollars, since past defense budgets too are ordinarily in current dollars. When considering future national-security policies, however, there is no reason to introduce the capricious effects of changes in the general price level. Our concern is either with the relationship between the defense budget and GNP or with physical output in "constant" dollars. In discussing future GNP and future budgets, we should think of the amounts in constant dollars.[14]

It should be noted that GNP includes government expenditures for goods and services as though this amount measured accurately

[13] Raymond Goldsmith, "A Perpetual Inventory of National Wealth," *Studies in Income and Wealth*, Vol. 14, National Bureau of Economic Research, New York [no date], p. 18.

[14] Whether to use GNP valued at market prices or by an "adjusted factor cost standard" depends partly upon the precise problem that is being considered. See Abram Bergson, *Soviet National Income and Product in 1937*, Columbia University Press, New York, 1953, pp. 42–54. For the United States (where indirect business taxes are small compared to their amount in, say, the USSR) it probably makes little difference which of the two is used. Unless otherwise specified, we will refer in this study to GNP valued at market prices.

the value of the government's final product. Two major objections to this procedure are widely recognized: (1) This is not a satisfying measurement of the value of government output. The government's services may be worth either more or less than their cost. (2) Part of the government's output, for example, statistical services, may be regarded as intermediate products—that is, as ingredients of private output whose value is already counted. Why, then, do our national income accounts continue to use expenditures to represent the final product in government? The answer is simply that this procedure, rough as it is, appears to be better than the practicable alternatives.

There are other difficulties with the concept and measurement of GNP.[15] There are questions particularly about the extent to which such measurements can reflect ultimate national well-being. But these difficulties need not detain us. Even if it does not measure total satisfaction or welfare accurately, full-employment GNP appears to be a useful index of physical production possibilities— a useful indicator of the flow from which resources for national defense must be diverted.

There is another aspect of GNP that should be kept in mind. Earlier it was pointed out that unique outputs of specific items cannot properly be regarded as fixed constraints. GNP as observed and measured, even with full employment, is not absolutely invariant either. Later in this chapter, methods of stimulating the growth of GNP will be mentioned. But quite apart from long-term growth, there is a certain amount of short-run resiliency—of quick expansion that can be achieved by taking up the slack. For example, at the outbreak of the Korean conflict, the nation was experiencing what one might call normal full employment. Yet in 1951 the 20-billion-dollar increase in annual defense expenditures was accompanied by a 20-billion-dollar increase in real national income, an amount of growth almost triple the amount that could ordinarily be expected. As a consequence, instead of the drastic price-level inflation anticipated by many persons, there was a sharp increase in real production—the military services using more output without reducing the nation's consumption or investment—and only a modest inflation. Part of this increment in output was no doubt illusory—attributable to flaws in the measurements. But not all of it. How did the increase in the defense budget produce this

---

[15] Examples are the difficulties in handling non-marketed outputs and changes in the quality of products. For discussions of these and other points, see *A Critique of the United States Income and Product Accounts*, Studies in Income and Wealth, Vol. 22, A Report of the National Bureau of Economic Research, Princeton University Press, Princeton, N.J., 1958.

effect? Presumably by offering larger lures, causing people to work harder and longer, attracting additional persons into the labor force, bringing more rapid application of technological improvements, and altering the composition of output. Thus, projected full-employment GNP is not an absolutely inflexible limitation on output.[16] Nevertheless, it is a good approximate indicator of the over-all constraint on the nation's activities.

It should be noted too that while GNP is a useful index of resource limitations, it is no simple matter to divert GNP from consumption to defense, or investment. On the contrary, it is a difficult thing to do, particularly in a free democratic society. J. K. Galbraith has pointed this out very forcefully in his book, *The Affluent Society*.[17] Most of the growth of the United States, for instance, stems from increases in consumption and from private investment designed to meet consumers' demands. Interdependence makes it technically difficult for us to give up the use of certain items (even the family's second car) that may appear to be frills; and our emphasis on consumption makes it psychologically difficult for us to sacrifice such items.

Consequently, according to Galbraith, the "minimum" standard of living is always the existing one, and no Administration or Congress that is interested in being reelected is likely to propose any substantial reduction in that standard of living. In this connection, it may be significant that the United States devoted mainly "slack" or growth to World War II and the Korean conflict; in neither instance was the absolute level of consumption (as usually measured) reduced.

We must therefore avoid identifying GNP, or even expected growth of GNP, with economic strength for the cold war. It is an illusion to think that the United States can twist a faucet and convert its mighty GNP into deterrent capability without a change in popular value-judgments. It takes both GNP and willingness to make sacrifices to yield resources *for national defense*.

Determinants of GNP

As mentioned earlier, the truly basic resources include not only the supplies of capital and people but also institutional arrange-

---

[16] For an attempt to allow for the extra capacity that would come to light if expanded defense spending caused the nation to produce under pressure, see Gerhard Colm and Manuel Helzner, "General Economic Feasibility of National Security Programs," National Planning Association, March 20, 1957, published in *Federal Expenditure Policy for Economic Growth and Stability*, Hearings before the Subcommittee on Fiscal Policy of the Joint Economic Committee, 85th Congress, 1st Session, U.S. Government Printing Office, Washington, D.C., 1958, pp. 359–360.

[17] J. K. Galbraith, *The Affluent Society*, Houghton Mifflin Company, Boston, 1958, pp. 161–180 (Chapter XII on "The Illusion of National Security".)

ments, incentives, and the state of the technological art. Such factors are the underlying determinants that one may consider when trying to estimate future GNP or to figure out policies that can increase it. The principal determinants are summarized in the following list.[18]

A. Initial Stock of Basic Resources and Their Use
   1. Manpower
      a. Labor
      b. Number of hours in the work-week
      c. Level of employment
      d. Extent of skill and training
   2. Stock of capital equipment
   3. State of the art and knowledge
   4. Degree of efficiency in the use of resources
      a. Allocation of resources among uses
      b. Methods of organization to make use of our knowledge
      c. Incentives to produce
B. Growth
   1. Increase in manpower
      a. Increases in the labor force
      b. Changes in the work-week
      c. Changes in the level of employment
      d. Improvement in skills and training
   2. Growth of capital stock
   3. Advances in the state of the art
      a. Amount of resources devoted to research and education
      b. Incentives to explore new ideas
   4. Efficiency in taking advantage of innovations
      a. Incentives to introduce innovations
      b. Mechanism for reshuffling resources in response to innovations.

Most of these items and their relation to the nation's potential output are self-explanatory. Thus, the pertinence of manpower, capital equipment (for example, machines, buildings, and other structures), and the state of the art (for example, knowledge of hybrid corn or transistors) is probably clear. The role of efficiency

---

[18] For other lists of growth determinants and discussions of them, see M. Abramovitz, "Economics of Growth," in *A Survey of Contemporary Economics*, Vol. II, Richard D. Irwin, Inc., Homewood, Ill., 1952, especially pp. 132–144; W. Arthur Lewis, *The Theory of Economic Growth*, George Allen & Unwin, Ltd., London, 1955; *Capital Formation and Economic Growth*, A Conference of the Universities-National Bureau Committee for Econmic Research, Princeton University Press, Princeton, N.J., 1955; W. W. Rostow, *The Process of Economic Growth*, The Clarendon Press, Oxford, 1953.

in the use of these resources, however, may need to be clarified. Without suitable incentives and a reasonable allocation of its resources, a nation can fall short of getting maximum output from its manpower, capital, and "laboratory knowledge." If monopoly, governmental restriction, tax structures, or other "institutions" impair incentives or discourage resources from moving to their best uses, the potential GNP of the nation will not be fulfilled.

Such factors can also operate to promote or retard long-run growth of GNP. The institutional framework undoubtedly has much to do with advances in the state of the art. In one environment, inventiveness flourishes; in another, it languishes. Moreover, even after new ideas are conceived, the institutional framework influences the rate at which innovations are made and diffused and the speed with which resources are subsequently reshuffled.[19] If monopolistic restrictions, financial organization, or government policies tend to shelter the status quo, known technological improvements may not spread rapidly, and resources may not shift quickly to what now become their best uses.

One wonders, naturally enough, about the quantitative significance of these various factors. Are some of them, such as incentives and institutional framework, merely high-sounding abstractions that actually exert little influence on the growth of GNP? Does it turn out, upon close inspection, that the rise of GNP is accounted for almost solely by the increase in capital equipment and the labor force? Or does it turn out that the other factors do play a major part in economic growth?

Recent studies have begun to shed light on the answers to these questions. These studies indicate that the rise of GNP in the United States has far outstripped the growth in the quantities of capital and labor.[20] More specifically, they suggest that half or more of the increase in national product must be attributed to rising productivity of the inputs. One researcher concludes that "Of the historic increase in GNP, about half represented the effect of

---

[19] The effects of institutions on the growth of knowledge, the application of new ideas, and the reshuffling of resources have attracted a good deal of attention in recent years. For provocative discussions, see W. Arthur Lewis, pp. 1–200; Yale Brozen, "Business Leadership and Technological Change," *American Journal of Economic and Sociology*, Vol. 14, pp. 13–30; and Yalt Brozen, "Invention Innovation, and Imitation," *American Economic Review*, Papers and Proceedings, XLI, May 1951, pp. 239–257.

[20] M. Abramovitz, "Resource and Output Trends in the United States since 1870," *American Economic Review*, Papers and Proceedings, XLVI, May 1956, pp. 5–23, reprinted by the National Bureau of Economic Research as Occasional Paper No. 52; John W. Kendrick, "Productivity Trends: Capital and Labor," *Review of Economics and Statistics*, XXXVIII, August 1956, pp. 248–257, reprinted by the National Bureau as Occasional Paper No. 53; Jacob Schmookler, "The Changing Efficiency of the American Economy: 1869–1938," *Review of Economics and Statistics*, XXXIV, August 1952, pp. 214–231.

increased resources, and half, the effect of increased efficiency of resource use." [21] According to another inquiry, an index of factor inputs (capital and labor combined) quadrupled between the decade of 1869–78 and that of 1944–53, while over the same period net national product grew to 13 times its original size.[22] Such results indicate that new ideas and their efficient and widespread application may be of overriding importance to growth.

This conclusion apparently applies with as much force to "underdeveloped" countries as it does to the United States:

> The per capita output of the United States rose at a rate of about 1.9 per cent per year (compounded) of which only about one-tenth is ascribed to the rise in the stock of tanglible capital, according to Fabricant.[23] The rest of this remarkable economic growth may be represented as coming from increases in output per unit of input of labor and of such capital.
>
> Such fragmentary data as there are for Latin-American countries indicate the same pattern. In Mexico, for example, the relatively large crop producing sector increased its output 60 per cent from 1925–29 to 1945–49, using, however, only 27 per cent more input; thus output per unit of aggregate input rose by 26 per cent. Farm production in Brazil was 55 per cent larger in 1945–49 than in 1925–29. The input index rose only 30 per cent; and, accordingly, output per unit of aggregate input increased 20 per cent.[24]

Such data do not show just what influence is exerted on economic growth by each factor, but they do suggest that, to achieve rapid growth, an economy needs more than a growing supply of tools and labor. It needs education and investment in human beings, research, and an environment in which inventiveness is stimulated, and a framework in which the reshuffling of resources is permitted. Both new discoveries and untrammeled adjustment afterward seem to be important to rapid growth. On the one hand, inventions cannot be applied unless they are discovered, and, on the other hand, the fruits of inventions cannot be harvested unless they are widely applied and resources are efficiently reallocated. Consider the effects of a single innovation—atomic power. Suppose that atomic power made the cost of electricity 2½

[21] Schmookler, p. 224.

[22] Abramovitz, p. 8.

[23] Solomon Fabricant, "Economic Progress and Economic Change" (a part of the 34th Annual Report of the National Bureau of Economic Research, May, 1954). Tangible capital here consists of structures, including housing, equipment, inventories and net foreign assets, but excluding consumer equipment, military assets and land and subsoil assets [footnote from passage quoted].

[24] Clarence A. Moore, "Agricultural Development in Mexico," *Journal of Farm Economics,* February, 1955; Clarence A. Moore, "Agricultural Development in Brazil" (unpublished TALA paper, No. 54–044, September 29, 1954, University of Chicago) [footnote of T. W. Schultz, author of the passage quoted]; Theodore W. Schultz, "Latin-American Economic Policy Lessons," *American Economic Review,* Papers and Proceedings, XLVI, May 1956, pp. 430–431.

mills per kilowatt hour less than it would otherwise be. It has been estimated that our national income would be increased by no more than 2/5 of 1 percent.[25] Even this growth could occur only if there was considerable readjustment in the economy. And only if "trigger effects" (the impacts of further innovations that emerge as firms try to take advantage of atomic power)[26] were introduced— only then could the projected increase in national income become very impressive. Without the trigger effects, most great inventions—the printing press, the railroad, the internal combustion engine—would surely have made only modest contributions to total production. Hence, not only institutions that stimulate research and inventiveness but also those that facilitate full adjustment by the economy are influential factors in economic growth.

GNP, Past and Future

So much for the meaning of GNP and its determinants. How has this index to the nation's strength read in recent years? How do recent readings compare with those of earlier years? What are the prospects that lie ahead?

In 1957, GNP amounted to $440 billion. Of this final output of $440 billion, $284 billion or 65 percent was devoted to personal consumption, $65 billion or 15 per cent to gross private domestic investment, and $47 billion or 11 percent to national security. (The remainder was net foreign investment and other government purchases of goods and services.)

Compare these figures with the corresponding amounts for earlier years. In 1953, when United States expenditures on the Korean conflict were at their peak, we produced a gross national product of $399 billion and devoted $60 billion or 15 percent to national security programs. In 1929, GNP was only $197 billion, and national security expenditures were less than one per cent.[27]

---

[25] Herbert A. Simon, "The Effects of Atomic Power on National or Regional Economics," chapter XIII in Sam H. Schurr and Jacob Marschak, *Economic Aspects of Atomic Power*, Princeton University Press, Princeton, N.J., 1950. For the assumptions that guided the preparation of these exploratory estimates, see that volume and particularly chapter XIII.

[26] *Ibid.*, pp. 232–234.

[27] All the amounts and calculations in this section are in terms of 1957 dollars. The amounts in 1954 dollars are given in the *Survey of Current Business*, July 1958, pp. 10–11. They were converted to 1957 dollars by using the implicit deflators published in the same source. For more precise measurements, this method of putting the amounts in 1957 dollars would be too rough, but for our purposes the procedure seems to be suitable.

National security expenditures in current dollars for 1941 to 1957 (*Ibid.*, pp. 4–5) were converted to 1957 dollars by using the implicit deflators for federal purchases of goods and services. For 1929 to 1940, inclusive, national security outlays were approximated in the following way: For those years, military expenditures as a percentage of military plus civil governmental expenditures have been estimated (M. Slade Kendrick, *A Century and a Half of Federal Expenditures*, Occasional Paper No. 48, National Bureau of Economic Research, New York, 1955, p. 41). These factors were applied to "federal purchases of goods and services" (roughly equivalent to the National Bureau's "military plus civil" expenditures) in 1957 dollars.

As for future years, the President's Materials Policy Commission has estimated that GNP can rise at a rate of about 3 percent per year, at least for the next few decades.[28] In making the projections, the Commission's staff tried to take into consideration the determinants of GNP that were discussed above. Looking at 1975 (really "a shorthand means of denoting 'sometime in the 1970's' "), the Commission assumed a labor force of 82 million people. This figure rested on an estimate that there would be 146 million people 14 years of age and over, with the labor force constituting, as at present, 56 percent of that number. Of this supply of laborers, 4 million were expected to be in the military service, 7½ million in agriculture, and 2½ million unemployed. Another assumption was that the average work week would decline 15 percent by the middle 70's. Finally, with our institutional arrangements, the probable growth of the capital stock, and advances in technology, it was believed that productivity (average output per man-hour) would rise at a rate of 2½ percent per year. The resulting rate of growth would yield a GNP of $700 billion—over 50 percent greater than that of 1957—by the middle 1970's.

Figure 1 shows the past and projected growth of GNP, and the past allocations to national security, consumption, and private domestic investment. National security outlays, it might be noted, include the programs for atomic energy, stockpiling, and Mutual Defense Assistance, as well as the strictly military programs. As can be seen in the figure, GNP has increased rapidly during the past two decades, and can continue to grow at about the same rate. While personal consumption has not quite kept pace with this rate of growth, national security outlays have risen from nearly nothing to about 10 percent of GNP. Note, however, that national security expenditures constituted a smaller part of the total in 1957 than they did during either the Korean War or World War II. Table I traces these components as percentages of gross national product.

If we merely continue to devote 10 per cent to national security, the absolute amount could reach $70 billion in 1957 dollars by the early 1970's. And if the national security program became 15 percent of GNP (over $100 billion in 1957 dollars), consumption and investment could still expand tremendously. In other words, production possibilities are likely to increase greatly over the next

[28] *Resources for Freedom*, A Report to the President by the President's Materials Policy Commission, Vol. II, U.S. Government Printing Office, Washington, D.C., 1952, pp. 111–12. Most efforts to project GNP have produced similar estimates; see, for example, Committee for Economic Development, *Economic Growth in the United States, Its Past and Future*, A Statement on National Policy by the Research and Policy Committee. February 1958, pp. 42–43.

Figure 1. GNP and major components, 1929–1957; and projected GNP, 1958–1975.

Table 1. Major Components as Percentages of GNP in Selected Years

Compounds	Percentages of GNP					
	1930	1940	1944	1950	1953	1957
Personal consumption	71	68	49	66	62	65
Gross private domestic investment	15	15	4	19	15	15
National security	1	1	46	7	15	11
Other	13	16	1	8	8	9

two decades, easing the constraint on these various activities. If we view this future growth from the vantage point of, say, the early 1960's, we still have considerable latitude in choosing how this extra output is to be used.

ALTERNATIVE POLICIES AFFECTING FUTURE RESOURCES

Future GNP is not irrevocably determined. It does not have to behave in accordance with projections like those shown above.

Quite apart from errors of estimation, GNP may deviate from its projected path on account of either fortuitous events or deliberate policies. In this section, the possibilities of deliberately increasing future resources will be mentioned. They will not be examined in detail, for the primary concern of this study is defense, not general economic growth. But it is relevant not only to take existing resource constraints into account but also to consider at least briefly the means of influencing future constraints.

Even in the short run when the supply of resources is given, government policies can affect the level of employment and the efficiency with which the resources are employed. Monetary-fiscal policy to avoid the unemployment that comes with recession can be of enormous significance. During the thirties, to take an extreme example, the loss of GNP due to unemployment was "some 300 billion dollars—almost equal to the real economic cost of World War II." [29] Recession could severely reduce our strength without being anything like the deep depression of the 1930's. Of course, the actual GNP that occurs when there is large-scale unemployment is not properly a constraint on defense activities, for resources can then be put into defense programs without sacrificing other outputs. Nonetheless, in reducing our economic strength and pulling down the economies of our allies, recession would seriously undermine our national security. Moreover, recession would shrink investment, retard technological advance, and stunt the future growth of GNP, resulting in more confining resource limitations at a later date than would otherwise exist. We should make no mistake on this point—a sharp recession could curtail ominously the economic basis for national security planning. Therefore the government should be willing to cut taxes, expand the volume of money, and reduce interest rates if aggregate demand slumps and serious unemployment develops. We should keep up our guard against overconfidence in "new-era" psychology.

It would be wrong, however, in trying to avoid recession, to invite drastic inflation. Deficits and easy money in *all* circumstances are not the answer. For severe inflation too prevents the economy from functioning efficiently and retards its development. It frequently leads to price controls, which inhibit the market mechanism, because people object to its inequities. Furthermore, violent inflation (or any inflation suppressed by price controls) pushes people into inefficient activities such as barter and efforts to convert monetary receipts into goods immediately. Hyperinflation usually ends with the economy thoroughly disorganized.

---

[29] Samuelson, *Economics*, p. 225.

Thus, among the government actions that are vitally important to GNP and its growth are monetary-fiscal efforts to guide aggregate demand for goods and services—to steer the economy between the Scylla of deflation and the Charybdis of inflation.

Other government policies affect the efficiency with which given resources are used, thus influencing the size of GNP. On the one hand, restrictions on firms and individuals, though stemming from the best of intentions, may distort the allocation of resources and impair incentives. Price controls, price supports, minimum wage laws, tariffs, and subsidies often produce such distortions. On the other hand, failure to intervene in certain situations allows distortions to persist. Examples are situations in which monopolistic groups can restrict entry into occupations or industries, or situations in which firms do not bear certain costs that they inflict on others (for example, by polluting water or congesting highways). In addition to their influence on the efficiency of the private economy, public policies determine the efficiency with which the government's own activities are conducted.

It is inappropriate here to describe specific policies that would yield increased efficiency in the private and public sectors of the economy. We will, however, stress one point. In order to choose the specific actions that constitute preferred policies, policy-makers need analytical assistance wherever it can be provided. They need well-conceived estimates of the prospective gains and costs of alternative courses of action. Without such estimates, advice is bound to consist of generalities and to sound arbitrary, or like an exhortation to do good. To say anything concrete about the merits of, say, a particular subsidy, the costs and gains from alternative arrangements must be estimated. To make recommendations about a particular health program, the costs and effects have to be gauged, albeit roughly. To choose the government investments that will contribute most to future GNP, the impacts of alternative investments must be measured as best we can. Systematic effort to determine preferred courses of action is called "operations research" when applied to problems in military or industrial operations. It is called "systems analysis" when applied to certain broader or longer-range problems, particularly the comparison of weapons systems. It is called "cost-benefit analysis" when such things as water-resource developments are being considered. More and better analysis may be useful in increasing efficiency in shaping many government programs and policies.[30] And increased

30 Roland N. McKean, *Efficiency in Government through Systems Analysis*, John Wiley and Sons, New York, 1958.

effectiveness in shaping these policies means higher GNP and greater growth—a larger resource base for defense and all the other activities that contribute to the national well-being.

In the longer run, when the supplies of capital, labor, and knowledge can be expanded, there are additional methods of increasing future GNP. While this country would hardly attempt to control the quantity of labor, government policies may affect the evolution of the work week and will definitely influence the health, education, training, and mobility of our manpower. This form of investment, that is, in human resources, probably yields a comparatively high return.[31] National policy can also influence the volume of private investment in capital equipment and, more directly, the volume of public investment. Private capital formation depends, in part, upon monetary-fiscal policies because they affect the availability of funds, upon the size and character of the government budget because some public spending competes with private spending and other public spending stimulates it, upon the tax structure because some taxes deter investment more than others. Public capital formation, of course, is determined by the proportion of the budget that is devoted to investment.

Another means of shaping economic development is by devoting more funds to basic research and exploratory development, and, of course, by maintaining a free economy in which the fruits of discoveries can best be harvested. The government sponsors a good deal of research at present, much of it as part of the national security programs, but the payoff to the nation from still more research appears to be high. Such evidence as adding up the direct results of a few outstanding developments tends to support this conclusion.[32] Although it is extremely hard to measure the returns attributable to research, the average annual return on this form of investment has been estimated to be from 100 to 200 per cent.[33] Calculations have been made which suggest the same general range in one sector of the economy, agriculture. The savings in 1950 due to improvements in production techniques from 1940 to 1950 have been estimated at 60 to 300 per cent (lower and upper

---

[31] Theodore W. Schultz, *Redirecting Farm Policy*, Macmillan Co., New York, 1943, pp. 68–71.

[32] For example, see *The Mighty Force of Research* by the Editors of *Fortune*, McGraw-Hill Book Co., Inc., New York, 1956; Yale Brozen, "The Economic Future of Research and Development," *Industrial Laboratories*, Vol. 4, December 1953, pp. 5–8; Allen Abrams, "Measuring the Return from Research," Proceedings of the Fourth Annual Conference on the Administration of Research, University of Michigan, Ann Arbor, 1951; and Zvi Griliches, "Research Costs and Social Returns: Hybrid Corn and Related Innovations," *Journal of Political Economy*, October 1958, pp. 419–431.

[33] This was the estimate of Raymond Ewell of the National Science Foundation—mentioned in *The Mighty Force of Research*, p. vi.

limits) of ten years' research and extension outlays at the 1950 rate of expenditure.[34]

A substantial amount of government activity in this sphere, particularly in basic research, seems to be justified. Research that is profitable to the whole economy may nonetheless be unprofitable to any individual firm, because the gains are so widely diffused. Such research must usually be sponsored by universities, foundations, or government agencies.

There are several ways in which defense policy can itself affect resources available in the future. National-security programs may have by-product effects on the determinants of GNP, for instance, on the employment level or the rate of technological advance, Also, the efficiency of defense activities can influence the resources that will be available in the future by affecting the amount that the nation can devote to investment.

SUMMARY

In the very short run (say in a military situation in which a commander must use the specific forces at his disposal), resource constraints are properly viewed as quantities of specific inputs. In the longer run, in decisions affecting the situation several years hence, the main resource limitations are best viewed as general monetary constraints, and costs are best measured as dollar costs.

In connection with longer-run decisions, the over-all constraint on the nation's consumption, investment, defense, and other activities can be regarded as the nation's capacity to produce as measured by full-employment GNP (gross national product). Only for very sudden and drastic changes in the level and composition of such activities would it be either helpful or necessary to think in terms of specific resource constraints.

GNP in the United States is likely to increase a great deal over the coming decades, offering considerable freedom of choice in determining the amounts to be devoted to defense (and the other categories of expenditure). Moreover, national policies, including defense planning itself, can affect the growth of the nation's resources.

---

[34] Theodore W. Schultz, "Agricultural Research: Expenditures and Returns," in *The Economic Organization of Agriculture*, McGraw-Hill Book Co., Inc., New York, 1953, pp. 114–122. If we look at a longer period, savings in 1950 due to improvements from 1910 to 1950 are from 130 to 230 per cent of 40 years' research and extension outlays at the 1950 rate of expenditure.

IV

DIVERTING GNP TO DEFENSE:
HOW BIG A DEFENSE BUDGET?

Defense expenditures in the late 1950's have set new records for peacetime, outlays for military plus other major national security activities amounting to over 40 billion dollars annually. Budgets of this size, naturally enough, are viewed with considerable concern. Have the added outlays in recent years purchased things that were worth the cost? Or has spending just become a "happy reflex?" [1] How much of GNP should be devoted to defense? Before we take up such questions, or try to show how they should be approached, let us review a few points about the formulation of the budget in the United States.

THE BUDGETARY PROCESS [2]

The annual defense budget is part of the massive document, *The Budget of the United States*, which the President sends to Congress each January. An enormous amount of time, effort, and "bargaining" goes into its preparation.

Consider the military budget for the fiscal year 1960 (July 1959 to July 1960). Part of the work on these estimates was started about two years earlier—that is, in mid-1957. At about that time [3] the departments of the Army, Navy, and Air Force began to plan for the fiscal year 1960. They based their figures on the force requirements and long-range plans tentatively established at various levels in the Executive branch. On the basis of directives from the top levels of the Army, Navy, and Air Force, the lower levels worked up detailed programs showing the physical inputs that would be "required."

---

[1] Senator Paul Douglas has wondered if people are now conditioned so that their mouths water when budget-time rolls around much as Dr. Pavlov's dogs began to salivate when a bell was rung.

[2] For a detailed account, see Arthur Smithies, *The Budgetary Process in the United States*, McGraw-Hill Book Company, New York, 1955, pp. 101–159 and 240–256. We are indebted to Frederick M. Sallagar of The RAND Corporation for several of the points stressed in this section.

[3] The procedures are constantly evolving, and they vary from one department to the next; the statements here depict a sort of "average" procedure that may not be one hundred per cent correct for any particular department over any particular budget cycle.

Next, in the spring and summer of 1958, these programs were modified, costed, and converted into departmental budgets. Early in this period, the Secretary of Defense issued "budget guidelines" to the individual Services. Then the budget offices of the departments issued their "calls for estimates," and the various commands and bureaus prepared budget estimates. During the summer the departmental budget offices sent preliminary budgets to the Secretary of Defense. At this point the Secretary discussed the figures with the President and with officials in the Bureau of the Budget. After some further revision, perhaps on the basis of Presidential ceilings, the estimates were sent to the Budget Bureau.

During the autumn of 1958, these figures were revised by the Budget Bureau and also by the Defense Department. A series of discussions involving officials in the individual departments, the Defense Department, and the Budget Bureau took place. The Secretary of Defense, after consulting with the Chief of Staff and each departmental secretary, officially transmitted the estimates to the Budget Bureau. The latter sent its recommendations to the President. In January 1959, the President, having reached final decisions, submitted the official document to Congress along with his budget message. (Sample exhibits, taken from the budget for the fiscal year 1960, are shown later in the chapter.)

Finally, the stage that we usually read about in the papers was reached. During the spring and early summer of 1959 there were the hearings before the subcommittees of the Committee on Appropriations, the Congressional debates, and the passage of appropriations bills for the fiscal year 1960 by both the House and the Senate. (At the same time, the Services were trying to adjust their programs to make them consistent with the revisions in their budgets.)

Thus, budget formulation is a long and complex process, and the results are influenced considerably by the mechanics and institutions involved. It is a process of bargaining among officials and groups having diverse strengths, aims, convictions, and responsibilities. Also, these participants naturally have various "political" considerations in mind—concerns about the impact of budgetary decisions on the success of rival departments or officials, on the attitudes of voters, on the actions of various groups. The effects, as far as reaching sound decisions is concerned, are not all bad—nor are they all good.

Other notable characteristics of the process are oppressive deadlines and inadequate opportunities for decision-makers to study exhibits. At best, officials can hardly give attention to the issues commensurate with their importance. Both civilian and military administrators have other day-to-day decisions to make, multitudes of them. If we ask ourselves how we would prepare or evaluate this thousand-page document or the hundred-page portion pertaining to the Defense Department, we can better appreciate the awesome nature of this task.

Moreover, there is often severe personal penalty for originating mistakes yet little or no penalty for perpetuating past decisions—except in time of crisis. Consequently there are strong forces against making "new" decisions (in budget formulation as well as in other governmental problems of choice) except when palpable crises occur.

In brief, deciding upon the defense budget is a tremendous task that must be performed under difficult circumstances. We cannot expect to identify or achieve "optimal" solutions; we should have no illusions on this score. Nonetheless, looking at the problem in the right way can aid us in reaching better solutions. It can help officials get better results with existing institutions—and it may point toward institutional modifications that can improve budgetary decision.

BUDGET-FIRSTERS VERSUS NEED-FIRSTERS

To get the most out of the nation's resources, we devote fewer billions to national security if some defense activities are worth less to the nation than they cost, and spend still more billions if extra defenses would yield greater value than the other things that the money could buy. This way of looking at the problem is not universally accepted, however. Some persons apparently believe that the size of the national security program should be determined in the light of cost alone. They name some figure and say "That's all we'll pay, and that's that." Others apparently believe that the program should be planned on the basis of need alone. In Congressional hearings, military leaders are often asked to reveal what they "really need." For instance, Senator Chavez told General Maxwell D. Taylor, "We would like to know what you need and not what the Budget Bureau thinks you should have." [4] As another case in point, Senator Ervin deplored the Defense Department's willingness to cut purchases below our "needs." According to the Senator, this attitude smacked of the economic

---

[4] *Department of Defense Appropriations for 1957,* Hearings Before the Subcommittee of the Committee on Appropriations, U.S. Senate, 84th Congress, 2d Session, U.S. Government Printing Office. Washington, D.C., 1956, p. 93.

philosophy of an old acquaintance who used to say, "Now, good boy, if you want to get along in this world you just have to do without the things you have to have." [5]

Some simply say that the task of determining budget size has to be done one way or the other:

> In general, there are two ways in which the problem of balancing defense needs against fiscal requirements can be approached. One way is to ascertain essential defense needs and then see if the funds can be made available to meet them. The other is to predetermine, as a matter of fiscal policy, a dollar limit for defense expenditures; and thereupon refuse to satisfy any defense needs that cannot be compressed within that limit.[6]

The truth is, however, that one cannot properly draw up defense plans on the basis of either cost alone or needs alone. There is no budget size or cost that is correct regardless of the payoff, and there is no need that should be met regardless of cost.

On the one hand, there is no presumption that the defense budget is now, or should be, near any immovable upper limit. As far as physical and economic feasibility is concerned, national security expenditures could be raised (within a two- or three-year transition period) by, say, $30 billion per year. With appropriate changes in tax rates and monetary policy, this could be done without causing severe inflation.

From existing levels, in other words, outlays for defense activities can be raised if we really want to raise them—if we feel that we need extra defense programs more than other things. There is, of course, a maximal amount that could be devoted to national security. It is less than total GNP, since part must go for subsistence and supporting activities in order to have any security program at all. But there is no magic number like fifty or seventy-five or one hundred billion dollars which we can stand, and above which we can't. To be sure, the larger the budget, the greater the sacrifice, but we cannot say, as some have tried to argue, that taxes amounting to more than 25 per cent of national income must inevitably bring collapse or intolerable inflation.[7] Countries in Western Europe have successfully borne taxes in excess of 30 per cent of GNP.

---

[5] *Study of Airpower*, Hearings Before the Subcommittee on the Air Force of the Committee on Armed Services, U.S. Senate, 84th Congress, 2d Session, Part XXII, U.S. Government Printing Office, Washington, D.C., 1956, p. 1691.

[6] *Airpower*, Report of the Subcommittee on the Air force of the Committee on Armed Services, U.S. Senate, 84th Congress, U.S. Government Printing Office, Washington, D.C., 1957, p. 9.

[7] For example, Colin Clark took such a position, often cited, in "Public Finance and Changes in the Value of Money," *Economic Journal*, December 1945, pp. 371-389.

We shall not try to add to the evidence that much larger programs are economically feasible.[8] We believe that we can take this proposition as our point of departure. There are serious questions, of course (as noted in the preceding chapter), as to whether or not extremely large programs are politically feasible—whether or not United States consumers in the aggregate are ever willing to cut back on consumption. Even if reductions of consumption are ruled out, however, growth of the economy of the United States would by itself permit increases in defense outlays up to about $10 billion per year. If we wished to do so, therefore, we could raise the annual defense budget by $20 billion in two years' time without cutting aggregate consumption, investment, or civil government programs.[9] To repeat, then, the defense budget is not near any absolute upper limit.

On the other hand, there is no particular national security program that we need in an absolute sense. As mentioned in Chapter 2, a list of the "desirable" items that could strengthen our defense would be almost endless. Where does one draw the line (without reference to cost) between what is needed and what is not? There are no clear-cut "minimal" needs, either for defense as a whole or for particular programs. President Eisenhower has emphasized this point:

> Words like "essential" and "indispensable" and "absolute minimum" become the common coin of the realm—and they are spent with wild abandon. One military man will argue hotly for a given number of aircraft as the "absolute minimum." . . . And others will earnestly advocate the "indispensable" needs for ships or tanks or rockets or guided missiles or artillery—all totaled in numbers that are always called "minimum." All such views are argued with vigor and tenacity. But obviously all cannot be right.[10]

Outlays for various programs *can* be cut if we feel that we need other things even more. It is up to us to choose.

In brief, our national security budget is not near any physical limits—GNP minus subsistence, on the one hand, or zero expenditures, on the other. Also, because of growth, large *future* increases could be accomplished without cutting consumption. Consequently,

---

[8] On this subject, the writers agree with many of the general conclusions in the study by Gerhard Colm, *Can We Afford Additional Programs for National Security?*, National Planning Association, Washington, D.C., October 1953, and the subsequent paper by Gerhard Colm and Manuel Helzner, "General Economic Feasibility of National Security Programs," March 1957, published in *Federal Expenditure Policy for Economic Growth and Stability*, Hearings Before the Subcommittee on Fiscal Policy of the Joint Economic Committee, 85th Congress, 1st Session, U.S. Government Printing Office, Washington, D.C., 1958, pp. 356–364.

[9] The hypothetical programs discussed by Colm and Helzner, *op. cit.*, do not imply reductions in aggregate consumption.

[10] "The Eisenhower Tax Program," *U.S. News and World Report*, May 29, 1953, p. 98.

our range of choice is wide. Making the choice should be viewed as a problem of getting the most out of resources, not as one of hunting for a tablet on which the right budget, requirement, or doctrine is inscribed. In formulating defense budgets we should not be "need- or doctrine-firsters"—those who insist upon discovering what we "need" regardless of what we have to give up. Nor should we be "budget-firsters"—those who insist upon discovering what we can give up regardless of how much we value defense activities. Instead let us be deliberate choosers, changing our budgets and reshaping our forces as long as a change appears to gain more than it costs. If taken literally, the questions, "What can we afford for defense?" and "What are our needs?" are the wrong ones to ask in deciding upon the size of the defense effort. The right question is, "How much is needed for defense *more than it is needed for other purposes?*"

HOW MUCH FOR PROGRAMS VERSUS HOW MUCH FOR OBJECTS [11]

In trying to answer the above question, we should probably think in terms of programs—that is, combinations of activities that produce distinguishable products. A governmental program is the counterpart of an industry in the private sector of the economy— and is just as ambiguous, as hard to define, and yet as useful a concept as an industry. There is one important difference, however. In the private sector of the economy, markets reveal prices for industry outputs, even if they are intermediate products. In the governmental sector, there are no markets for most outputs, and the significance of the products, especially quantities of intermediate outputs, becomes especially hard to judge. To facilitate judgments about their value, programs should be aggregations of activities yielding products that can be at least subjectively appraised. In general, we should move toward thinking in terms of programs that perform tasks and yield end-products,[12] speaking rather loosely, rather than actions that yield objects or intermediate products.

Let us illustrate the distinction between a program and an object (we use this terminology because the *Budget of the United States* has made a similar distinction between "programs" and "objects"). Certain activities of the Air Force, the Army, and the

---

[11] For other discussions of some of these points and of related topics, see Arthur Smithies, especially pp. 229–277, and Jesse Burkhead, *Government Budgeting,* John Wiley and Sons, New York, 1956, pp. 110–181.

[12] David Novick, "Which Program Do We Mean in 'Program Budgeting'?" The RAND Corporation, P–530, May 12, 1954.

Navy produce retaliatory striking power or deterrence, and these activities might be grouped together and called a program. In providing deterrence, the Services use missiles, manpower, food, paper clips, and transportation—intermediate items which might be called "objects of expenditure."

Several points about programs and objects should be noted. First, decisions about the size of programs and those about the things to be bought are interdependent. One would not make one of these decisions in complete ignorance of the other. If the desired striking power is increased, different types of equipment may become the most efficient means, and if some equipment innovation appears (for example, more accurate ballistic missiles), a different level of striking power may become the proper choice. But to some extent these choices have to be made separately —by different people or at different times. In making one choice we try to make reasonable assumptions about the other.

Second, just what one means by an "end-product" or a "program" is not unambiguous. The line of demarcation between programs and objects is not clear-cut. Is the Military Air Transport Service a program or simply an activity supporting, say, the Tactical Air program? Or is even the latter merely something to be purchased for a program that might be called "deterrence and fighting of limited wars"? Even such tasks as providing nuclear striking power and providing forces for limited war have interrelationships. Neither is solely a supporting activity of the other, yet each can influence the credibility and effectiveness of the other. It may seem that one is driven to regard every military item and activity as an object purchased for and contributing to *one* program—national security.

Despite these complexities, officials do find it helpful to think in terms of several programs, and there is hope of developing categories that will be even more meaningful. After all, our only chance of pondering the gains as well as the costs of defense budgets is to think in terms of rather broad aggregations of activities. We cannot appraise the adequacy of the defense budget, either subjectively or with the aid of quantitative analysis, by thinking about the gains from such categories as paper clips, petroleum, or personnel. Nor can we go to the other extreme and think in terms of a single national security program. Such an aggregation is too broad; we have no conception of units of "national security" that could be purchased. But there are possibilities between these extremes—aggregations of activities that produce species of end-products such as capabilities for nuclear retaliation or for limited war. Complications and difficulties abound, and yet for some such programs we can make judgments about, or even develop quantitative clues to, their worth as well as their cost.

Perhaps an analogy from a consumer's budget will help clarify those points. An individual cannot judge intelligently how much he should spend on a car if he asks, "How much should I devote to fenders, to steering activities, and to carburetion?" Nor can he improve his decisions much by lumping all living into a single program and asking, "How much should I spend on life?" Yet it is often helpful to ask, "How much am I willing to spend on my car-program—on transportation to work, stores, and recreational facilities?" Although not really an end-item, an individual's transportation is closer to an end-product than fenders or carburetors. While his car program is somewhat interrelated with, say, his recreational program, the interrelationships do not dominate the outcome, and he can get some feeling for the gains from the car, making reasonable assumptions about the other program.

In determining the size of the defense budget, then, we should ask whether various broad programs should be increased or decreased, and we should keep trying to define programs about which we can make sounder judgments. To be sure, attention should also be given to detailed objects of expenditure. They help determine the efficiency with which the programs are carried out, and much of the economics of defense pertains to increasing the efficiency with which resources are employed *within* defense programs. The way the Services use materials and manpower deserves hard scrutiny—even at the highest levels. If Congress, through the review of defense expenditures, can perceive better ways to combine objects of expenditure or discover wasteful purchases that can be eliminated, it should certainly insist upon the increased efficiency.

But the objects of expenditure already get a goodly share of attention at the Congressional level. The annual hearings on appropriations are to a considerable extent about such matters as maintenance costs, the utilization of surplus butter and cheese by the Services, the location of National Guard armories, aircraft fuel and oil, travel costs, and the location of flag officers' quarters. Attention is attracted by things like the 104-year supply of Jeep parts once held by the Services or the 11,000 dozen oyster forks owned on one occasion by the Navy.[13] Here we wish to stress that

---

[13] Paul H. Douglas, *Economy in the National Government*, University of Chicago Press, Chicago, 1952, p. 150. To make matters worse, it turned out that "10,442 dozen of these oyster forks were of such a poor quality that, so the records showed, they were usable only in an emergency!"

the broader problem, the selection of the scale of defense programs, also deserves careful attention. At whatever degree of efficiency can be achieved, the question remains: Should the nation buy larger or smaller national-security programs? Are the last increments to existing programs worth this cost? Would further increments to particular programs be worth more than their cost?

HOW TO APPROACH THE CHOICE OF PROGRAM-SIZES [14]

To the preceding questions, we cannot provide definitive quantitative answers, of course. No analysis can yield solutions to the problem of choosing program-sizes that would necessarily be valid for all Congressmen and voters. Each person's answer depends upon how much value he attaches to deterrence of nuclear war, to the checking of limited aggressions, and to other products of national defense. It depends upon his attitude toward risks and uncertainty—that is, upon whether he is inclined to gamble or to hedge. It depends upon his valuation of side effects or impacts that cannot be made commensurable (in any *generally* valid way) with the main effects of the programs. Nevertheless, we can devise exhibits and analyses that facilitate weighing the gains and costs of alternative program-sizes. In deciding how much (if any) penicillin to buy, a man with pneumonia does not know precisely how much he values good health, how to assess the risks, or precisely what the side effects will be; but it helps a lot to know how much penicillin costs and what effect it has on pneumonia.

It might be reemphasized that judgments or measurements of gains are just as important as measures of the costs (which are really the alternative gains that could be obtained if the resources were put to other uses). We cannot make intelligent decisions on the basis of either alone. In this section we turn first to exhibits of costs and then to the possibilities of appraising gains, in both instances taking the exhibits in recent budgets as points of departure. In doing this, we must regard certain changes, such as more extensive crossing of departmental lines, as being feasible. Crossing departmental boundaries could be achieved either by organizational changes or by the preparation of special exhibits separate from the main budget documents.

Breakdowns of Cost in Recent Budgets

Since 1949 the budgetary presentations in the Department of Defense have been improved. Proposed obligational authority and

---

[14] In various parts of this section the writers are indebted to David Novick of The RAND Corporation.

expenditures [15] have been collected into one document and put into somewhat more meaningful categories than had previously been used.[16] These recent compilations probably make possible more informed judgments about expenditure levels than could be made in earlier years. Nonetheless, the current presentation falls far short of being an effective program budget. Perhaps the best way to demonstrate this shortcoming is to present and discuss briefly a few sample exhibits from a recent budget.

The broad functional budget. To begin with, there is the broad functional budget in which all defense activities are put into one huge program called "major national security." [17] This is indeed an end-product program, but it is *too* comprehensive—embracing all Army, Navy, Air Force, and other national-security missions. To appreciate its cost and significance is almost impossible. Few persons have any subjective "feel" for a national-security capability—that is, for the output that would be provided. And there is little hope of ever devising quantitative measures that would shed much light on this mixture of capabilities. To try to sort out several less inclusive programs would seem to be a more promising approach.

The current "performance" budgets of the individual services. The present budget does classify expenditures into less inclusive categories that have been called programs. (In the Budget for the fiscal year 1960, they are often labeled "appropriation groups.") There are fairly detailed exhibits in terms of both programs and objects. The classification of expenditures by program, however, turns out to be a classification by organization unit (Army, Navy, or Air Force) and account title,[18] though the exhibits for each account title include a few paragraphs purporting to describe the program and its performance. Consider the summary presentation at the front of the section devoted to the Department of Defense.

---

[15] In the U.S. Budget, "obligational authority" is total authority to make commitments during the designated fiscal year, whether the cash is to be expended in that year or later on; and "expenditures" are the estimated disbursements during the fiscal year, whether the obligations were incurred in that year or previously. We shall refer mostly to obligational authority here, believing that it approximates future costs more closely than would the scheduled disbursements.

[16] For comments on the form of earlier budgets and the evolution of the current form, see Smithies, pp. 232–237.

[17] The other governmental functions are international affairs and finance, veterans' services and benefits, labor and welfare, agriculture and agricultural resources, natural resources, commerce and housing, general government, interest, and allowance for contingencies. *The Budget of the United States Government for the Fiscal Year Ending June 30, 1960*, U.S. Government Printing Office, Washington, D.C., 1959, p. M25.

[18] The "account titles" are the major "programs" listed in table 2.

In order to conserve space, Table 2 omits proposed expenditures and shows only proposed new obligations.[19]

Table 2. Budget Authorizations and Expenditures[a] by Major Appropriation Groups or "Programs" (millions of dollars)

Appropriation groups[b]	New obligational authority		
	1958 enacted	1959 estimate	1960 estimate
Military personnel—total	10,982	11,475	11,625
Operation and maintenance	10,237	10,306	10,512
Procurement—total	11,054	14,524	13,348
Research, development, test, and evaluation	2,258	3,464	3,772
Construction—total	2,086	1,369	1,563
Revolving and management funds	130	—	30
Total, Department of Defense........	36,747	41,138	40,850

[a] Source: *The Budget of the United States Government for the Fiscal Year Ending June 30, 1960*, p. 445.

[b] Amounts for these "appropriation groups" are further subdivided into amounts for certain subgroups and for the branches of the Service (Army, Air Force, Navy), but the groups shown here are the basic categories that have been regarded as programs.

Note the nature of these "programs." Few of the items on this list are even remotely like end-product missions, and the dollar amounts are not the costs of achieving capabilities in such missions. Instead, the items are collections of objects used in a variety of tasks; and the dollar figures are the sums of selected costs from all of them. For instance, "military personnel" covers officers and men for all military functions. "Military personnel, Air Force" includes men for the Strategic Air Command, Tactical Air Command, and all other Air Force activities.

How does one choose the amount that should be spent on categories like across-the-board procurement or military personnel? Surely this choice is made by seeking the most efficient way of carrying out end-product programs such as achieving a nuclear deterrence force. And efficiency *within* programs can and should be sought more carefully than by pondering proposed expenditures for total personnel, procurement, and construction. Indeed, the use of these categories is likely to cause inefficiency. Procurement of new missiles or aircraft often has special glamor or appeal, and the Services may find that the best way to get money is to ask for increased procurement authority. Other categories such as military

[19] See footnote 15 for an explanation of these terms.

construction may appear to be relatively remote from operational capabilities and be neglected.[20] As a consequence, vital actions such as the dispersing and hardening of our deterrent force are postponed, and the constraints on specific objects of expenditure (like governmental allocations of specific materials to firms) bring about unbalanced inefficient operations. In short, this classification of expenditures by account titles gives little help either in choosing program levels or in seeking efficiency within programs.[21]

It was mentioned at the outset that current budgetary exhibits include breakdowns of expenditure both by programs (so-called) and by objects. To make clear what these objects are and why they do not convey useful information about end-product programs, Table 3 presents a sample breakdown of authorizations by objects —the one for Army personnel.

Table 3. Object Classification of Obligations for "Military Personnel, Army," 1960 Estimates[a]

Object Classification	Obligations in millions of dollars
01 Personal services: military	2,989
02 Travel	172
03 Transportation of things	49
07 Other contractual services	13
08 Supplies and materials	233
11 Grants, subsidies, and contributions	—
12 Pensions, annuities, and insurance claims	3
14 Interest	1
15 Taxes and assessments	55
Total direct obligations	3,514[b]

[a] Source: The Budget of the United States Government for the Fiscal Year Ending June 30, 1960, p. 460.

[b] The individual items do not add up to this total because of rounding. For "grants, subsidies, and contributions," the amount was less than $500,000.

The amounts proposed for these object classes (such as travel or transportation of things) may aid officials in locating in-

---

[20] A tendency to neglect construction or other investments that do not yield a quick or tangible output is sometimes suggested by the communications underlying budgetary guidelines. For instance, one assumption used in a memorandum sent to the departmental secretaries in connection with the budget for fiscal year 1955 was as follows: "Military public works programs will be limited to those items for which there is an immediate operational requirement" (Study of Airpower, p. 1644).

[21] The budget also contains a further breakdown of these so-called programs (classifications by account title) by "activities." For instance, obligations for Air Force Military Personnel are broken down into amounts for pay and allowances, subsistence in kind, and so on. These categories are again types of objects, and they help little in appraising program levels.

efficiencies; though systematic analysis would be necessary before anyone could be reasonably sure where inefficiency existed. Such a list of amounts can scarcely assist anyone, however, in weighing alternative program levels.

Improving the Breakdown of Costs

The first step in trying to improve our choice of program sizes is probably to put budget figures into categories that more nearly correspond to end-product missions.[22] Officials can make more perceptive judgments about the importance to the nation of these missions than they can make about the worth of categories like those listed above. Moreover, as will be indicated near the end of this chapter, there is hope of devising useful quantitative clues to the importance of end-product missions.[23] Thus, for these programs, there would be both rough estimates of the costs and a chance of gauging the gains.

A budget designed to show the approximate costs of such missions would naturally have to cross departmental lines. Activities that contribute to a broad military capability are seldom confined to one branch of the Service. Air Force activities, Naval operations, and the Army's role in active defense contribute to strategic deterrence, and all three departments also contribute to limited-war capability. The sort of exhibit that might be used to set over-all program levels is illustrated by Table 4. In this presentation, there would be essentially three broad programs: (1) deterrence or fighting of all-out war, (2) deterrence or fighting of limited war, and (3) research and development. Each of these would be divided into component missions. Many of the latter would be interdependent to a great degree (the broad programs to a lesser degree), and the costs of one would depend in part upon the sizes of the others. Some parts, such as a submarine force or a transport fleet, would contribute to both the nuclear deterrent capability and the limited-war mission.

In principle, one always likes to know the incremental or *extra* cost of whatever policy or program he is considering. If he considers two programs and a certain item is necessary for each of

---

[22] One format (using the Air Force as an example) has been suggested by G. H. Fisher in "Weapon-System Cost Analysis," *Operations Research*, October 1956, pp. 568–571.

Another "pro forma budget," also using the Air Force as an example, has been proposed in Smithies, pp. 265–277. In this format, major "programs" include forces in being, support of forces in being, force build-up, and mobilization reserves, with the first three broken down into strategic, tactical, air defense, and air transport portions.

[23] We use the term loosely. At best, as was pointed out earlier, no aggregation of defense activities yields an output that is unambiguously an independent end-product, and *some* "programs" will inevitably comprise leftovers or aggregations that are not very meaningful.

Table 4. Possible Format of National Security Budget

Programs and sub-programs	Proposed force composition (No. military units, where applicable)				Expenditures implied by proposed programs			
	'60	'61 . . . '64		'65	'60	'61 . . . '64		'65

Deterrence or Fighting of All-Out War
   Nuclear Striking Force (AF, Navy)
      B–47
      B–52
      Atlas
      Polaris
      .
      .
      etc.
   Active Defense (Army, Navy, AF)
      Early Warning
      Interceptors
         F–102
         Bomarc
         .
         .
      etc.
      Local Defense
      Nike
      .
      .
      etc.
   Passive Defense (OCDM)
      Dispersal
      Shelters, Evacuation
      Recuperation Planning
Deterrence or Fighting of Limited Wars
   Ground Forces (Army, Marine)
   Sea Power (Navy)
   Tactical Air (AF, Navy)
   Transport, Air and Sea (AF, Navy)
   Military Aid to Other Countries
      (Mutual Security)
   Reserves for Mobilization
      Military Units (Army, Navy, AF)
      Defense Production (OCDM)
Research and Development (AEC, AF, Army, Navy)
   Exploratory
   Weapon Systems
General Administration
Miscellaneous

them, its cost cannot properly be allocated between the two. One can ask several different questions: whether Programs A + B are worth their combined cost (including any unallocable items), whether Program A is worth its incremental cost, or whether Program B is worth its incremental cost. Proper costing depends upon which of the questions is being asked. Since preparing and digesting numerous cost estimates is itself rather costly, however, it is uneconomic to insist on precise estimates. In the budgetary exhibits suggested here, the costs of programs and program-increments would be rough approximations. Joint costs might be allocated among programs according to crude rules of thumb, or sometimes assigned to one program with recognition that others were being aided. Some items used jointly, such as top administration, could be considered as a separate aggregate (called, for the sake of convenience, a program).

These particular aggregations simply represent one set of possibilities. There may be others that would be equally or more useful. It might be better if exploratory development and weapon systems development were explicitly regarded as separate programs, their proposed costs never being lumped together into a single figure. Additional programs might be formulated from the activities in the "all other" or "miscellaneous" category. In a general way, however, Table 4 does indicate the way we should approach the choice of program-sizes and the direction in which our budgetary exhibits should probably be evolving.[24]

Notice that this format would project the costs entailed by these programs, year by year, for several years ahead. This information (for example, about future operating costs, which are sometimes extremely heavy) is essential in making decisions about program levels.[25] Yet conventional budgetary documents do not reveal the future expenditures that are implied by proposed programs. Future expenditures are vitally important whether the new programs are larger or smaller, that is, whether our concern is with initiating new programs or with terminating old ones. For frequently the major impact of either will be felt not in the next year, but in

---

[24] The use of the suggested exhibits would call for, or be aided by, a number of changes in current estimation procedures—for example, increased emphasis on the use of statistical cost factors and a shortened budget cycle, increased attention to costs *during* the formulation of proposed programs (i.e., prior to their translation into budgets), improved cost analysis, and perhaps a better system of accrual accounting. Some of these reforms are discussed in Smithies, pp. 237–265, and in David Novick, "Weapon-System Cost Methodology," The RAND Corporation, Report R–287, February 1, 1956. See also Fisher, pp. 558–571.

[25] Note, however, that only costs which are genuinely entailed should be so shown. R and D programs, for instance, do *not* imply the procurement and operation of the whole menu of weapon systems that are under development.

the more distant future. Expenditures in the first year on a new weapon system, for example, are likely to be a small proportion of the ultimate future cost of procurement and operation. Similarly, the savings from canceling a going program are often mainly or exclusively in future years : in the current budgetary year the costs of cancellation may equal or even exceed any gross savings. The flexibility in the budget in any current year, in either direction, is small compared with the possible impact of program decisions this year on the budgets of future years. The fact that everyone is mainly concerned with the current annual budget is frustrating because that budget has so little "give," and inefficient, because it neglects the larger, hidden part of the budget iceberg.

Actually, what is needed is an exhibit similar to table 4 for each of several program levels. Then the Administration and the Congress could choose among explicit, meaningful programs in deciding upon the size of the defense budget.[26] When only one program level is presented, either additions to the budget or cuts in it must be made blindly—and sometimes with consequences that are worse than they need be. Disproportionate cuts may be made in some budget categories, or supplements may be voted to others which will buy little in the way of military capability without corresponding increases in complementary activities. Adjustment may require frantic and inefficient reprogramming. With a range of alternative levels prepared in advance, adjustments could be made by simply turning to a level that had been consciously considered and whose elements had been balanced.

Charles Silberman and Sanford Parker, in an article entitled "The Economic Impact of Defense," [27] attempted in 1958 to calculate the costs of, and indicate the gains from, alternative supplementary defense programs proposed by the Rockefeller Brothers Fund Report,[28] the official Gaither Report,[29] and others. They conclude on costs: "The Administration's defense program now calls for a rise from $43.3 billion in fiscal 1958 to $45.5 billion in fiscal 1959, with the rate of increase slowing down thereafter. The Rockefeller program would have spending rise to $53.2 billion in fiscal 1961, while the third program, as *Fortune* has called it—a synthesis of the recommendations of experts who worked on the Gaither Report and other studies—would have spending rise to $65

---

[26] Of course, where possible, the indicators of performance discussed below should also be estimated and presented for each of the alternative budget levels.

[27] *Fortune* Magazine, June 1958, p. 102.

[28] *International Security—The Military Aspect*, published by the Rockefeller Brothers Fund, Inc., 1958.

[29] As reported in unconfirmed press stories. The Report itself has not been made public.

billion in fiscal 1963. And still other experts urge programs that would add up to perhaps $75 billion." Unfortunately the Congress and the public must make up their minds about the right size of defense budget with little official information of this sort about the costs or gains of either larger or smaller programs.

Indicators of Performance in Recent Budgets

The next step toward improving our decisions about program-sizes is to get better information about the outputs of alternative programs. Budgetary presentations today do attempt to describe the product that is being purchased. At the beginning of the portion of the United States Budget pertaining to the Department of Defense, there is an informative discussion of force structure and of certain military activities.

Moreover, since 1949, when the Services were instructed to submit "performance budgets," they have classified proposed outlays into the so-called programs that were previously discussed, and have tried to indicate the output or performance that would be purchased. These indicators are not very revealing, however, chiefly because the categories into which outlays are grouped are remote from end-product programs. As an example, consider the paragraphs on the performance of the "military personnel" category—one of the programs mentioned earlier in connection with table 2.

MILITARY PERSONNEL [30]

The following narrative statement covers the active duty appropriations for the Army, Navy, Marine Corps, and Air Force.

1. *Pay and allowances.*—This provides for the pay and allowances of military personnel on active duty including cadets and midshipmen at the three service academies, aviation cadets, and other officer candidates.

The number of active duty military personnel provided for is shown in the following table. The personnel in the civilian components of the Defense forces are described under the pertinent appropriations below.

In addition, provision is made for payment for proficiency advancements to selected enlisted personnel in critical-skill areas. Funds are provided for advancement of 80,000 men by June 30, 1959, and 163,000 men by June 30, 1960. It also provides for the Government's contribution to the Federal old-age and survivors insurance trust fund under the Servicemen's and Veterans' Survivor Benefits Act, purchase of individual clothing for initial issue to enlisted personnel, replacement of clothing issues in Korea, and for payment of clothing maintenance allowances.

---

[30] This excerpt from the narrative statement (in budgets prior to that for fiscal-year 1960, it was entitled "Program and Performance") is from *The Budget of the United States Government for the Fiscal Year Ending June 30, 1960,* p. 459. In the published statement the exhibit includes the "average number" as well as the "year-end number" of personnel.

2. *Subsistence in kind.*—This provides for the purchase of food supplies for issue as rations to enlisted personnel including emergency and operational rations.

3. *Movements, permanent change of station.*—This provides for. . . .

Year-end Number

	Actual 1958	Estimate	
		1959	1960
Defense total	2,599,848	2,525,000	2,520,000
Officers	325,460	318,515	316,045
Enlisted	2,264,290	2,194,091	2,190,911
Officer candidates	10,098	12,394	13,044
Army	898,192	870,000	870,000
Officers	104,220	100,100	100,100
Enlisted	792,271	768,200	768,200
Military Academy cadets	1,701	1,700	1,700

The only parts of the above passage that convey much information are the numbers, and, since personnel are ingredients rather than end-products, even they are not very helpful. Sometimes, descriptions of performance are a good deal worse, constituting merely lyrical pleas for a program. The following example, though it pertains to nondefense (and non-Federal) activities, illustrates the generalities that are sometimes used to describe performance:

> Instead of thinking of money alone . . . citizens should hear children singing in the spring concert, travel with the crippled child in early morning from his home to his special unit, feel that school roofs are tight and walls are safe, see the pupils in the corridors washing their dirty hands and drying their clean ones, accompany in spirit the injured child to the hospital for treatment, and see salmon fishing in Alaska with children in the fifth grade. A top performance budget paints pictures in words that justify the expenditure.[31]

Small wonder that some officials (for example, Mr. John Taber, long of the House Appropriations Committee) prefer a budget in terms of objects to be purchased. (With the latter one can at least try to say something about the internal efficiency of programs.) The advantages of a program budget are considerably reduced if

---

[31] Harold E. Akerly, "For Better Public Relations Use a Performance Budget," *Nation's Schools*, February 1951, p. 37, copyright 1951, The Modern Hospital Publishing Co., Chicago; all rights reserved; cited in Jesse Burkhead, *Government Budgeting*, John Wiley and Sons, Inc., New York, 1956, p. 138.

the indicators of performance are uninformative or downright misleading.

IMPROVING THE INDICATORS OF PERFORMANCE

If activities are grouped into more meaningful missions, however, it seems likely that better subjective appraisals of output can be made and also that better indicators of performance can be provided. There is no hope, of course, of measuring the ultimate "worth" of defense. It is obviously impossible to put a generally valid price tag on the output. The gains from program increments cannot therefore be expressed in the same units as the costs, and the two cannot be compared in terms of a common denominator. But there is hope of describing the product meaningfully, and some ways of describing it are more meaningful than others. Similarly, no researcher can measure the ultimate worth of a new car to a particular consumer. But there is hope of meaningfully describing this product, and what the car will do is a more meaningful description to the consumer than the car's chemical composition.

Changes in force structure. As a first approximation, force structure for each category in Table 4—numbers of B–52 wings, Atlas squadrons, army and naval units of various types—would be much closer to the end-products than the numbers of personnel or pieces of equipment. To some extent, the quantity of wings and divisions in each category suggests what is being purchased. Note that this information is constantly used at present. Officials in the Services and in the Defense Department are as familiar with force structure as they are with their own names. Part of the information is published in the Budget and is fully aired in Congressional hearings on appropriations. Even so, force structure may not be considered systematically *in conjunction with costs* as in Table 4, for costs by such military units have seldom been presented. Long-range planning and also programming have been in terms of military units, but budgeting (that is, translating the programs into costs) has usually been in terms of other categories.

Numbers of wings and divisions, however, do not reveal enough about capabilities. For one thing, force structure per se may not tell much about the kind of capability that it provides. An augmentation of our forces may increase our capability to strike first, but not our ability to strike second. If so, it may help deter minor aggressions somewhat, but as far as the thermonuclear war is concerned, it may produce negative deterrence. Or, additional divisions may increase our ability to fight World War II but not our strength in more likely kinds of conflict. If so, they may produce small gains.

The enemy's response. For another thing, force structure per se does not tell us anything about the enemy's position or about his probable reaction to changes in the structure of our forces. Yet what our forces buy for us is clearly relative to the enemy's capability and his reaction to our decisions. This fact can hardly be emphasized enough. The pertinent question is whether or not we are buying sufficient strength, *relative to potential enemy forces* (when fairly sensible strategies are attributed to him), to deter central war and cope with limited aggressions. We need a higher national security budget if the potential enemy is Soviet Russia than if it is Argentina; higher if we have no allies than if we have reliable ones; higher if the enemy devotes 20 per cent of his national product to the military efficiently than if he devotes 10 per cent inefficiently; higher if the enemy increases his technological and industrial capability in future relative to ours, while devoting the same proportion to military purposes; higher if our strategy draws containment lines in the Eastern Hemisphere than if these are drawn at our own shores. Discussion of the appropriate size of military budgets often misses this essential point of relativity. An increase in the absolute efficiency with which we use resources ("more bang for a buck") creates no presumption that the budget can be cut when a potential enemy is correspondingly increasing his absolute efficiency ("more rubble for a ruble").

Thus when considering program increments or decrements, we must try to take into account the enemy's position and probable response. Are our forces strong enough, and properly designed, in view of his situation and his capabilities? If we add to our forces in a particular way, can he easily counter our move? What deterrent capability (or ability to fight local wars and keep them limited) will we end up with? Will our action yield a better basis for finding mutually advantageous weapon limitations or disarmament measures?

For these several reasons, most simple indicators of performance, including changes in force structure, that would be affected by program increments or decrements are not sufficiently revealing. Fortunately, it is often possible to indicate in more significant terms what program increments will buy.

Changes in designated capabilities. It is possible to make analyses comparing alternative ways of carrying out broad missions such as the strategic deterrence mission. Such analyses seek to answer questions like: Which combination of means yields the greatest deterrent capability for a given budget? Capability may be measured by the destruction that could be inflicted on potential enemies in selected (and not improbable) contingencies even if we received the first strike. Part III will deal with the methods and possibilities of comparing various courses of action in planning defense. Here we wish only to point out that similar analyses can be devised to answer a different type of question: What capabilities are yielded by different program levels? What change in capability result from program increments or decrements? The analyses would by no means point to the preferred program level —but they would give highly relevant indicators of performance.

Analysis could also provide revealing indicators of another gain from portions of the strategic deterrence mission—namely the contribution of retaliatory capability, active defenses, passive defenses, and recuperation planning to the chance of survival in the event of enemy attack. Analysis could give a rough yet informative picture of, say, capital, human beings, and emergency stocks that would survive a plausible enemy attack. These data, in conjunction with program costs, would also help in choosing among alternative program levels.

In addition, analysis of this sort might be able to reveal what different program-levels could accomplish in the limited-war mission (another of the broad programs listed in table 4). Calculations might give clues to the scale and kinds of local aggressions that could be "handled" with alternative programs for limited-war capability. The results would constitute quantitative clues to what we could do in various plausible contingencies. Obviously the outcomes of such conflicts could not be projected with precision. Nonetheless, such clues to our capability would be more revealing than numbers of divisions, tactical air units, and so on.

These indicators of gain would not embrace all possible effects of program changes. There would be spillover effects on other programs. For instance, a change in strategic deterrence capability would have some influence on our prospects regarding limited conflicts. There would also be other impacts not reflected in the suggested indicators of performance—impacts on our relations with neutral or friendly nations, on the basis for trying to reach mutually advantageous agreements with enemy nations, and so on. There would be further indirect effects on our economy. But a budget in terms of broad programs for which such indicators of performance could be provided would help sort out the major implications of alternative budgets. It would facilitate the task of weighing the costs and gains of budget increments or decrements.

As for the research and development program, there is probably no good way of indicating the performance that would be purchased with alternative program-levels. Research and development activities are by nature explorations into an unknown and distant future. Estimating the results of research is even more uncertain than measuring the consequences of, say, future programs for limited war. We can try to estimate the potential gains *if* certain break-throughs or developments can be achieved, and such estimates are valuable clues in shaping research and development programs. Even though estimates of potential payoff are helpful, however, tremendous uncertainties must be recognized. Exploratory research and development often produces quite unpredicted payoffs. Hence, while the output of research and development is of enormous significance to future capabilities, that output is extremely uncertain in both form and magnitude, and there is no way to show what a particular year's program will produce. Judgment on the size and character of the program must be based largely on experience with similar programs in the past, taking both failures and successes into account.

It is partly for this reason that it seems to be appropriate to segregate research and development as a separate program or programs. In a sense it is a supporting activity. But we do not know to what extent it will turn out to support strategic deterrence and to what extent it will support other missions. Moreover, because the program's objective is to acquire knowledge rather than to carry out a well-defined task, research and development should be managed differently from operational missions. It is best, therefore, to regard research and development as a separate program— probably to regard exploratory research and development and what might be called weapon-systems development as separate and distinct programs. But no over-all indicator of performance in these activities (or in Administration and Miscellaneous!) can be provided.

Where meaningful indicators are feasible, they would have to be separate presentations, not just a few numbers in another column of Table 4. But they would be introduced *along with* the breakdown of costs by broad missions. Like that breakdown of costs, the indicators of performance and the underlying analyses would usually have to bear a military classification. These tools could nonetheless be valuable to military planners, to officials in the Department of Defense and the Budget Bureau, and to Congressional leaders.

One aspect of the gains—and costs, for that matter—that merits a final mention is their uncertainty (a subject which will be considered in some detail in chapter VII). When a program increment is considered, one cannot see a particular outcome that is certain and that determines a unique set of gains. What one foresees is a number of potential outcomes, some more likely and others less likely, but all of them quite possible. This uncertainty makes the task of weighing gains and costs still more formidable. Instead of the question being, "What is the worth of this particular increase in capability?" the question is, "What is the worth of this probability distribution of increases in capability (or of this uncertain increase in capability)?" Furthermore, since steps can often be taken to hedge against contingencies, another question arises: "What is the worth of particular attempts to reduce uncertainty?"

Obviously, these questions are hard to answer. Different individuals, given the same information about prospective gains and costs, will answer differently. The main reason is that the answer depends upon one's attitude toward risk. Some people prefer a comparatively safe policy and will give up a great deal in order to reduce the chance of disaster. Others are willing to live more dangerously.

HOW BIG A BUDGET DURING HOT WAR?

If and when local conflicts break out, certain programs are likely to seem more important to us than had previously been the case. If the conflict lasts long, it will be imperative to expand certain activities. Consequently the national-security budget is almost certain to rise. The nature of the problem, however, is still the same. In order to decide how much should be spent on national security, one should think, not just about expenditures for objects, but about the gains and costs of having higher (or lower) programs. The types of gain and cost to be considered, and the analyses that would help one weigh them, are the same.

If all-out war involving unlimited objectives should occur, the choice among alternative budget *levels* would probably not concern us greatly. In the unlikely event that atomic weapons were not exchanged, the war would be similar in many respects to World War II. The budget would probably approach its upper limit— GNP minus subsistence and "necessary" supporting activities.[32] During the first few years of such a war, physical constraints (the difficulty of shifting resources from one activity to another) rather than budgetary ones might limit the diversion of resources to de-

[32] As explained earlier, it is difficult to determine such an upper limit, because it is hard to define "necessities." Someone always insists (quite properly): "Give me the luxuries of life, and I'll do without the necessities." But we can say that at some budget level, the sacrifice entailed by trying to devote more to defense becomes enormous.

fense. In any event, the considerations discussed above would probably not play much of a role in setting budget levels.

In the more likely event that unlimited war led to a thermonuclear exchange, interest in budget formulation would fall off considerably! In those circumstances, it would make little difference whether one thought in terms of programs or of objects; and the exhibits suggested above would have little bearing on the challenging problems of the day.

PART THREE

EFFICIENCY IN USING
DEFENSE RESOURCES

V

EFFICIENCY IN MILITARY DECISIONS[1]

In this part we will assume that the amount of the nation's resources to be devoted to military use has been determined. Our problem is: How can we use these resources efficiently to buy military power, or more broadly, national security? Actually, the solutions to the problems of parts II and III are interdependent to some extent, and, as noted earlier, analyses of the sort to be described in part III are important in appraising the effectiveness of defense programs and therefore in deciding upon their size. However, we must usually tackle these choices—the size of the budget and the effective use of that budget—one at a time, making reasonable assumptions about one choice while analyzing the other.

While the efficient allocation or use of resources has always been the core problem of economic theory, economists have until recently made little attempt to apply the theory to military, or indeed any governmental, expenditure. A possible explanation is the small proportion of national resources formerly devoted to the military sector (indeed to the whole government) in the United States and other Western countries except in wartime. Now with the prospect of United States national security expenditure continuing indefinitely at 10 per cent or more of GNP and total government expenditure (including state and local) at two to three times this level,[2] the efficient use of the very large resources involved has become a matter of primary importance.

---

[1] Also pertinent are the articles in "Economics and Operations Research: A Symposium," *Review of Economics and Statistics*, August 1958, pp. 195–229.

[2] A great deal of what is said in this Part about the efficient use of resources by the military applies equally to many other kinds of government expenditure.

The reason the efficient use of military (and other government) resources is a special problem is the absence of any built-in mechanisms, like those in the private sector of the economy, which lead to greater efficiency. There is within government neither a price mechanism which points the way to greater efficiency, nor competitive forces which induce government units to carry out each function at minimum cost. Because of the lure of profits and the threat of bankruptcy, private firms are under pressure to seek out profitable innovations and efficient methods. In this search they have often used, and are now using to an increasing extent, formal quantitative analysis. But even if they do not, continued progress and increased efficiency still tend to come about, though less-rapidly. After all, *some* firm is likely to discover more efficient methods through trial and error even in the absence of systematic analysis. Subsequently, other firms observing the resulting profits copy the innovation; those that fail to do so (that is, those who make inferior choices of methods) begin to suffer losses, and hence tend to be eliminated by the process of "natural selection." [3]

In government, by contrast, there is no profit lure, and promotions or salary increases do not depend on profits. In most operations, an objective criterion of efficiency is not readily available, and even if it were, incentives to seek profitable innovations and efficient (least cost) methods are not strong. There is scope for "Parkinson's law," [4] personal idiosyncrasy, and uneconomic preferences of officials to take hold, because the costs of choosing inefficient policies do not impinge upon the choosers. [5]

Finally, the process of natural selection, whose working depends upon the degree and type of rivalry, operates only weakly, if at all, to eliminate wasteful governments or government departments. The federal government, for instance, competes only with the political party that is out of office, and survival in this competition depends upon many factors other than efficiency in the use of resources. Thus, there is neither an adequate price mechanism to reveal the cheapest methods of performing public functions nor

---

[3] A. Alchian, "Uncertainty, Evolution, and Economic Theory," *The Journal of Political Economy*, LVIII, June 1950, pp. 211-221. The prevention of mistakes by systematic analysis would be a cheaper path to progress than their correction by natural selection—*if* the analyses always led to correct policies. On the difficulties of correct analysis we will have much to say below.

[4] C. Northcote Parkinson, *Parkinson's Law: and Other Studies in Administration*, Houghton Mifflin Co., Boston, 1957.

[5] For a provocative discussion of this matter, see the paper by A. Alchian and R. Kessel presented at the Universities-National Bureau of Economics Research Conference on Labor Economics in April, 1960.

any force which induces or compels the government to adopt such methods.[6]

THREE GENERAL APPROACHES

What, in these circumstances, can be done? We want efficiency; we want to obtain the greatest possible security from a given budget, both because national security is itself of such transcendent importance, and because the more efficient the use of the military budget the more resources we can have for nonmilitary purposes. But how, in a sector containing 10 per cent of the economy (much more if we include civilian government functions) with no adequate price mechanism and no institutions forcing natural selection of the efficient, can we achieve efficiency?

There are three possible approaches, interrelated and interdependent, which will be considered in this part of the book.

1. The improvement of institutional arrangements within the government to promote efficiency. Extreme proposals have been made which would simulate price and market mechanisms within the government. Less ambitious proposals would improve budgeting and accounting methods (see Chapter 4), attempt to provide more appropriate incentives, and reorganize the apparatus of decision making.
2. Increased reliance on systematic quantitative analysis to determine the most efficient alternative allocations and methods.
3. Increased recognition and awareness that military decisions, whether they specifically involve budgetary allocations or not, are in one of their important aspects economic decisions; and that unless the right questions are asked, the appropriate alternatives selected for comparison, and an economic criterion used for choosing the most efficient, military power and national security will suffer.

It is our conviction that something can be accomplished by the third approach alone—that is, by improved understanding of the nature of the problem—even without greater use of systematic quantitative analysis and with no changes in governmental structure. In formulating policy it does help to ask the right questions instead of the wrong ones. If the alternatives are arrayed, and a serious attempt made to apply sound criteria in choosing the most efficient ones, decisions are likely to be improved even though the

---

[6] In a few government activities, e.g., the Military Sea Transportation Service, simulation of the market mechanism is attempted.

considerations brought to bear are mainly qualitative and intuitive. There are enough responsible and highly motivated persons
involved in the decision-making process—officers, civil servants,
members of the Cabinet, Congressmen, and influential citizens—
to make education in principles worthwhile for its own sake.

What may be even more important, as we shall see, is that any
real improvement in the methods of quantitative analysis or in
government structure to achieve economy is absolutely dependent
upon a firm grasp of these principles. Quantitative analyses that
are addressed to the wrong question or administrative devices that
promote the wrong kind of economizing can easily do more harm
than good.

The role of systematic quantitative analysis in military decisions
is potentially much more important than in the private sector of
the economy. It is obviously more important than in households
because the problems are typically so much more complex. We all
know families that manage well on their incomes, and families
that manage poorly, apparently attaining a lower standard of life
or running into recurrent financial difficulties despite apparently
adequate incomes. Some of the good family managers may rely
heavily on systematic quantitative analysis—on elaborate budget
calculations, the studies of consumers' research organizations, and
so on. But others do not, and in general we find little correlation
between goodness of household management and reliance on systematic quantitative analysis. The overwhelmingly important factors are a firm grasp of principles and good sense or judgment.
The quantitative relations are usually familiar, and simple enough
for a man or woman of average intelligence to work out intuitively
or in the margin of an account book.

In many military problems, however, this is not true. The quantitative relations may involve many different fields of technology as
well as operational factors, and are sometimes so intricate that
elaborate computations are necessary. There is almost never anyone who has an intuitive grasp of all the fields of knowledge that
are relevant. For example, if we are comparing the relative merits
of a high performance fighter and a cheaper fighter with somewhat lower performance, it is easy to see, qualitatively, that the
more expensive aircraft will do better in a two-plane duel, but that
we can have more aircraft on a billion dollar budget and thereby
more interceptions and duels if we choose the plane with lower
unit cost. But the problem is essentially quantitative, and depends
upon fairly precise answers being developed to three questions:
How many more of the cheaper plane can be procured and main-

tained on a billion dollar budget? What are the relative values of numbers and various performance characteristics in interception? *How much* better is the high performance plane in a duel? In some special cases we may be able to assemble a group of "experts," each of whom has a good intuitive grasp of the factors relevant for answering one of these subquestions, and after discussion emerge with a fairly unequivocal answer. But in general, and especially where, as is usually the case, the choice is not between two but among many, systematic quantitative analysis will help—or prove essential.

For a somewhat different reason systematic quantitative analysis is more important in military than in private business decisions. There is, as we have seen, an alternative process for achieving efficiency in private business—competition and natural selection—which would be fairly effective even if the variations in techniques were random. In government this alternative does not exist. Efficient techniques and policies have to be selected consciously; and wherever the relevant factors are diverse and complex, as they frequently are, unaided intuition is incapable of weighing them and making an efficient decision.

Sound analyses, it might be noted, can not only help identify efficient courses of action but can also improve incentives. The existence of good analyses cannot alter penalties and rewards so that "what is good for the chief of each department is also good for national security"; but their existence, in conjunction with rivalry between departments, may increase the cost to decision-makers of making uneconomic decisions. That is, the existence of sound analyses plus rival branches or departments that may make use of the arguments to get their budgets increased can cause each department to veer toward more efficient policies.

The possible utility of improved institutional arrangements for promoting the efficient use of resources by government departments has been the subject of much debate. This has in the past been the province, perhaps too exclusively, of the management efficiency experts. As economists we will not have much to say about government organization and structure. We believe, however, that what we say about criteria and methods of analysis can help in judging the efficacy of alternative organizational forms and that the development of practical institutions which encourage efficiency deserves far more attention than we or other economists have yet given it. It should at least be possible to remove some of the perverse incentives injected by such factors as special constraints, the premium placed on getting budgets raised rather than using budgets more efficiently, and cost-plus-fixed-fee contracts. There must be some way to provide postmasters and depot managers with more appropriate motivations, as well as to improve the government's decision-making machinery.

OPTIMAL, EFFICIENT, AND FEASIBLE POSITIONS

We have so far used the term "efficient" in a vague and general sense to mean "making good use" (including "making the best use") of available resources. Much of the time, though, we have in mind a more precise meaning for this term. We can best define it by contrasting "efficient," "optimal," and "feasible" positions.

In order to reach an *optimal* solution to problems of choice, we must be able to value various "situations" or outputs. Then we can revise our choices and shift resources to get the maximum value that is possible in the face of whatever constraints confront us. Even if we cannot always compare the values of different outputs, however, we can find some positions that yield more of some valuable outputs without yielding less of any others. When we cannot produce more of one output without sacrificing another, we have reached an *efficient* position. Many other situations are *feasible*, of course, by using the resources inefficiently. The differences between efficient positions and the others will be clearer if we consider a simple example.

ONE INPUT, TWO OUTPUTS

Suppose that we are concerned with the allocation of a military budget, fixed at $B billion, between the procurement (and maintenance in a state of readiness) of two forces—say, a strategic bombing force and an air defense force. Suppose further, for the sake of simplicity in this example, that the effectiveness of the strategic bombing force can be measured by a single number—the expected number of enemy targets that it could destroy after D Day—and that the effectiveness of the air defense force can be similarly measured by its "kill potential"—the number of attacking enemy bombers it could be expected to shoot down in certain circumstances.

We can draw a production-possibility curve, as in Figure 2, representing all possible *maximum* combinations of target destruction and kill potential which we can buy with $B billion—maximum in the sense that the fraction of the budget allocated to the strategic bombing force is spent in such a way as to maximize the target destruction potential of the force, and the fraction allo-

Figure 2. Production-possibility curve.

cated to air defense is so spent as to maximize kill potential.[7] The Y intercept represents the target destruction potential that we could achieve by spending all $B billions on the strategic air force, the X intercept the kill potential from spending all on air defense.

An efficient use of resources, in the technical sense, is one which makes it impossible to increase one valuable output without increasing a valuable input or decreasing another valuable output. It is apparent that each point on our curve represents an efficient use of resources in this sense; the curve is therefore a locus of "efficient points." At any point on the curve it is possible to increase target destruction only by moving to the left along the curve; that is, by decreasing kill potential, or by moving to a higher curve (dotted in fig. 2) representing a larger budget ($B + △ billion).

All points such as P' lying below and to the left of the curve of efficient points represent inefficient uses of resources, and are therefore called "inefficient points." They do, however, represent *feasible* uses of a budget of $B billion. We can draw up a plan to spend $B billion inefficiently to achieve a target destruction potential of only 200 and an air defense kill potential of only 500— probably all too easily. But if we did have such a plan, we could revise it, without additional budget, to increase target destruction potential without decreasing kill potential (or vice versa). We can always find several efficient points which are unequivocally superior to an inefficient point.

Note that the points lying above and to the right of the curve on Figure 2 are simply *infeasible* on a budget of $B billion. The

---

[7] The estimation of the points on this curve is, of course, the job of systematic quantitative analysis. The curves in this chapter are purely hypothetical.

efficient points form a boundary between the feasible and the infeasible points.

But which of the infinity of efficient points should our military planners choose? At one extreme there is an efficient point providing no offensive capability, at the other extreme an efficient point providing no defensive capability. While both may be efficient in a technical sense, at least one and possibly both would be disastrous for the security of the United States. Technical efficiency is not a sufficient condition for economic choice.

In principle the answer is easy: We want to choose that efficient point which maximizes the "utility" or "military worth" of the combined forces. In practice, as we shall see in chapter VI, the explicit measurement of military worth frequently presents formidable difficulties. If we abstract from these difficulties for the moment in order to clarify definitions, we can draw curves (called indifference curves) that reflect our preference for some combinations of target destruction and kill potential over others (fig. 3). Combinations represented on a curve to the right and higher (more of both goods) are obviously preferred to combinations on a curve to the left and lower (less of both). We are indifferent among com-

Figure 3.   Indifference curves and optimal point.

binations represented by different points on any single curve; we are willing to sacrifice some defense potential if we can obtain thereby a sufficiently enhanced offensive potential, and vice versa. Indifference curves are typically convex to the origin, which means that the more of one good (for example, offense) we give up, the less willing we are to sacrifice still more, and therefore the larger the increment of the other (for example, defense) we insist upon having in compensation.[8]

The *optimal* use of our $B billion budget is represented by the point of tangency of the original curve of figure 2 with an indifference curve (Point P, fig 3). From this point it is not possible to improve our position (that is, move to a higher indifference curve representing a preferred combination) by any change in allocation or use of resources.

If all portions of the production-possibility curve are not concave to the origin, there may be complications. The shape of this curve depends upon whether the costs of producing the goods measured on the axes are increasing or decreasing. Or, to put the matter another way, the shape depends upon whether the returns per extra dollar expended on the outputs are decreasing or increasing. Returns can usually be assumed to be decreasing, making the production-possibility curve concave to the origin. But there are troublesome counter-examples; for example, returns in terms of defense kill potential might be increasing if we consider extra outlays on plugging gaps in an almost completed radar line.[9] If there are increasing returns and part of the curve has a peculiar shape, we have to look at large reallocations as well as small ones.[10] We may find more than one point of tangency between the production-possibility curve and the indifference curves, or we may find no point of tangency and the highest indifference curve may be attained where the production-possibility curve intercepts one of the axes (that is, it may then be best to spend the entire budget on the item that yields increasing returns).

The frequent difficulty in locating *the* optimal point by systematic quantitative analysis, while unfortunate, should not be regarded as disastrous in all or even most practical problems of military choice. In the first place, decision-makers or their advisers who have thought deeply about a problem are likely to have shrewd ideas about the sector of the curve containing the optimal point, even if they cannot provide a mathematical proof of its exact location. If systematic quantitative analysis can narrow the choice

---

[8] The incremental amount of Y we need to compensate for an incremental loss of X is the slope of the indifference curve at any point. It is the rate at which we are willing to trade one for the other.

[9] Many plausible examples of "increasing returns," however, are really examples of rectifying errors, which can be done by redesigning one's proposal, not solely by expanding outlays along one axis or the other. If I forget to include a bathroom in my plans for a new house, and therefore the addition of a bathroom has a high payoff, is it correct to say that house construction is an example of increasing returns?

[10] Malcolm W. Hoag, "Some Complexities in Military Planning," *World Politics*, July 1959, pp. 553–576.

to a set of efficient points, the burden placed upon intuitive judgment is reduced and the quality of judgment should be improved. Secondly, optima are characteristically flat, like the crest of Half Dome rather than the peak of the Matterhorn. It isn't usually important to find the precise peak or point of tangency. On Figure 3 one can move along the opportunity curve for some distance on either side of the point of tangency without getting far from the highest attainable indifference curve.

In the third place, *the best practical aim of systematic quantitative analysis is to demonstrate that some course of action A is better than some alternative course of action B,* when B is what is proposed, or planned, or will otherwise occur. If B is an inefficient point, systematic quantitative analysis can find several efficient points A, A', A'', . . . which can be shown to be superior to B even if nothing is known about military worth except that certain capabilities, like target destruction and air defense kill potential, contribute to it (see fig. 4).

Figure 4.   Efficient points versus inefficient points.

Let us emphasize once more that this concept of seeking efficient points is extremely important. For while we cannot usually find optimal, or second-best, or even *j*th-best, solutions, it frequently enables us to identify improvements over existing or proposed policies.[11]

---

[11] The difficulties of determining second-best policies have received some well-deserved attention in recent years. See I. M. D. Little, *A Critique of Welfare Economics,* Clarendon Press, Oxford, 1950, especially Chapter VII, pp. 110-120, and Chapter XV, pp. 267-272; J. E. Meade, *The Theory of International Economic Policy,* Vol. II, *Trade and Welfare,* Oxford University Press, London, 1955, Chapter VII, "The Marginal Conditions for the Second-Best," pp. 102-118; R. G. Lipsey and K. Lancaster, "The General Theory of Second Best," *Review of Economic Studies,* 1956-57, pp. 11-32; and M. J. Farrell, "In Defense of Public-Utility Price Theory," *Oxford Economic Papers,* February 1958, pp. 109-123.

TWO INPUTS, ONE OUTPUT

In the preceding example we considered a planning problem that involved the allocation of a single valuable input (a budget) to produce two valuable outputs (target destruction potential and defense kill potential). The extension of this case to three or more outputs raises no new problems, although diagrammatic representation in two dimensions is no longer possible. If there are three outputs, the production-possibility and indifference curves become three-dimensional surfaces; if n, they are n-dimensional surfaces.

Problems involving two or more inputs do, however, require a somewhat different, although analogous, approach. Consider first the simplest of these, where there are two valuable inputs and only one valuable output. We might, as an example, take a subproblem of our first example, namely, the procurement of a strategic air force which will maximize target destruction. Suppose, for simplicity of analysis, that only two valuable inputs are required by a strategic air force—say bomber aircraft and bombs.[12] We will continue to assume, again grossly simplifying reality, that the output or objective of the strategic air force can be measured as a single dimension—expected number of targets destroyed. We may estimate by systematic quantitative analysis and plot the maximum potential destruction with varying numbers and combinations of bombs and bombers (see fig. 5). We estimate, say, that with 400

Figure 5. Substitution between bombs and bombers.

---

[12] We will assume in this example that bombs must be paid for by the Air Force, as if the Atomic Energy Commission managed bomb production as an "industrial fund" or business. It is apparent that military forces should be planned *as if* bombs were costly inputs whether funds are actually transferred or not. See Stephen Enke, "Some Economic Aspects of Fissionable Material," *Quarterly Journal of Economics*, Vol. 68, May 1954, pp. 217–232.

bombs and 400 bombers the best we can achieve, with the best tactical employment of the bomber force, is the expected destruction of 200 targets, represented by point P (that is, we estimate that 50 per cent of the bombers, each armed with a bomb, will be attrited or will miss the target). Similarly, we estimate that it would take 250 bombs and 250 bombers to destroy 100 targets (point P') : the expected attrition rate will be higher with a smaller strike force.

With what other combinations of bombs and bombers can we expect to destroy 200 targets? Of course, with many possible combinations. As is typically the case in military (and other) operations, one valuable input may be substituted for another—within broad limits. There is no necessity to plan to use the same number of bombs and bombers. If the number of bombers exceeds the number of bombs, the aircraft not carrying bombs can serve a useful function as escorts, cutting down the attrition of the bomb carriers. If the number of bombs exceeds the number of bombers, some bombers can carry more than one bomb, attacking targets in sequence; or, alternatively, bombers surviving the first strike can be sent on a second. Of course, as we continue to substitute one input for the other, substitution will become more and more difficult. It will require at least 200 bombs to destroy 200 targets, no matter how many bombers we have at our disposal. Similarly some minimum number of aircraft will be needed to penetrate enemy defenses and deliver bombs on 200 targets, no matter how plentiful the bombs.

The locus of point P, showing the combinations of bombs and bombers which, with best tactical employment, can be expected to destroy 200 targets, is therefore a curve (known in economic theory as an "isoquant") convex to the origin and more or less asymptotic, at both extremes, to lines parallel to the X and Y axes (see fig. 6). The locus of the point P' (expected destruction = 100 targets) will be a curve of similar shape closer to the origin. Other isoquants can be estimated for any given level of expected target destruction—the best tactical employment being assumed for the combination of bombs and bombers represented by each point.

The use of resources is "efficient" in this case with a single valuable output or objective, where it is impossible to increase the output without increasing the use of at least one of the valuable inputs.

In figure 6 every point on each of the isoquants represents an efficient use of resources. It is therefore possible to move to a higher isoquant (that is, destroy more targets) only by increasing the use of at least one valuable input (bombs or bombers).

Figure 6.   Isoquants and exchange curves.

But which of this infinity of efficient points is *optimal?* In order to answer this question, we must have a measure of the relative costs [13] of bombs and bombers. Suppose, again for simplicity of exposition, that the costs of both bombs and bombers are constant, that two bombs can always be exchanged for one bomber. We can now immediately determine the optimal combination of bombs and bombers for any allocation of budget to the strategic air force. If the budget is sufficient to buy 500 bombers (all spent on bombers) or 1,000 bombs (all spent on bombs), the optimal combination of bombs and bombers to procure is represented by point E on figure 6. At this point the "exchange" curve (the straight line A-B) showing the combinations which may be procured with the given budget is tangent to a target isoquant—the highest isoquant which it can attain.

Let us go over the meaning of these curves again in order to make them clear. The exchange curve shows the way the inputs can be exchanged (in buying or producing them) while keeping the total budget constant. The isoquant shows the way the inputs can be substituted for each other while keeping the quantity of output constant. When the two curves are tangent, as at point E on figure 6, no further substitution of one input for the other can increase the output.[14] The only way to increase output in those circumstances would be to get a larger budget.

---

[13] The problems of defining the appropriate measure of costs are postponed to chapter VI.

[14] The slope of the exchange curve indicates the trade-offs possible in buying the inputs. It is the ratio of their marginal or incremental costs—the latter being the extra cost of buying an additional unit of each item. The slope of the isoquant similarly indicates the trade-offs possible in using the inputs. At the point of tangency these slopes, or trade-off possibilities, are equal.

Other points such as C on the exchange curve would be non-optimal. For exchange curves representing different budgets, there would be other optimal points, of course. The expected target destruction so calculated for all hypothetical budget allocations to the strategic air force (the budget being divided among inputs in each case in the optimal manner) was part of the information needed for the construction of the production-possibility curve in our first example, shown in figure 2.

A number of interesting and characteristic relations between inputs and outputs may be "read off" figure 6. Suppose that the price of bombs is higher—one bomb exchanging, say, for one bomber as in the exchange curve AD. In that circumstance, the optimal combination will tend to contain a smaller ratio of bombs to bombers, and appropriate tactics economizing on bombs will have to be used. With a higher price for bombs, the target destruction potential at any given budget level will be reduced, but not by as much if the ratio of bombs to bombers is optimally adjusted as if this ratio is left unchanged. We can also use this diagram to see how much the budget would have to be increased to maintain the same target destruction potential with a higher price for bombs: more bombers and fewer bombs would be purchased with the larger budget.

If the quantity of one input is limited (for example, if no more than, say, 300 bombs may be obtained from the Atomic Energy Commission at any price) the exchange curves become vertical at this point, as in figure 7. Increments of high budgets must all be spent on bombers, and tactics optimally adjusted to whatever bomb/bomber ratio results. Calculations of this kind can be used to estimate how much additional bomb production would be worth—in terms of bombers and therefore also in terms of dollars. In the hypothetical example shown in figure 7, the target destruction that can be achieved with a maximum of 300 bombs available and a budget equivalent to 600 bombers could be achieved with a budget equivalent to 500 bombers if bombs were continuously available at half the cost of bombers. In other words, the additional bombs would be "worth" 100 bombers more than their cost.

The extension of this case to three or more valuable inputs requires nothing more than the abandonment of plane geometry. Here let us turn to the use of economic analysis in the search for more efficient courses of action.

Figure 7. Exchange curves with special constraints.

THE ELEMENTS OF AN ECONOMIC ANALYSIS

The essence of economic choice in military planning is not quantitative analysis: calculation may or may not be necessary or useful, depending upon the problem and what is known about it. The essential thing is the comparison of all the relevant alternatives from the point of view of the objectives each can accomplish and the costs which it involves; and the selection of the best (or a "good") alternative through the use of appropriate economic criteria.

The elements of a military problem of economic choice, whether its solution requires advanced mathematics, high speed computing equipment, or just straight hard thinking, are therefore the following:

1. An objective or objectives. What military (or other national) aim or aims are we trying to accomplish with the forces, equipments, projects, or tactics that the analysis is designed to compare? Choice of objectives is fundamental: if it is wrongly made, the whole analysis is addressed to the wrong question. For instance, we assumed in example 1 above that the sole objective of air defense is the slaughter of enemy aircraft: if in fact one of its major objectives is the early identification of an enemy attack and the provision of tactical warning to United States targets, the force we selected in example 1 is unlikely to be either optimal or efficient.

2. Alternatives. By what alternative forces, equipments, projects, tactics, and so on, may the objective be accomplished? The alternatives are frequently referred to as *systems* [15]

---

[15] Hence "systems analysis," a term frequently applied to complex quantitative analyses.

because each combines all the elements—men, machines, and the tactics of their employment—needed to accomplish the objective. System A may differ from System B in only one respect (for example, in number of bombs per bomber), or in several (number of bombs per bomber, number of strikes, and so on), but both are complete systems, however many elements they have in common. The great problem in choosing alternatives to compare is to be sure that all the good alternatives have been included. Frequently we lack the imagination to do this at the beginning of an analysis; we think of better alternatives (that is, invent new systems) as the analysis proceeds and we learn more about the problem. The invention of new and better systems in this fashion is indeed one of the principal payoffs from this kind of analysis.

3.   Costs or resources used. Each alternative method of accomplishing the objective, or in other words each system, involves the incurring of certain costs or the using up of certain resources (these are different phrases to describe the same phenomena). Costs are the negative values in the analysis (as the objectives are positive values). The resources required may be general (as is commonly the case in problems of long-range planning), or highly specific (as in most tactical problems), or mixed. Some of the difficult problems of which costs to include and how to measure them are considered in chapter VI.

4.   A model or models. Models are abstract representations of reality which help us to perceive significant relations in the real world, to manipulate them, and thereby predict others. They may take any of numerous forms. Some are small-scale physical representations of reality, like model aircraft in a wind tunnel. Many are simply representations on paper— like mathematical models. Or, finally, they may be simple sets of relationships that are sketched out in the mind and not formally put down on paper. In no case are models photographic reproductions of reality; if they were, they would be so complicated that they would be of no use to us. They have to abstract from a great deal of the real world—focusing upon what is relevant for the problem at hand, ignoring what is irrelevant. Whether or not one model is better than another depends not on its complexity, or its appearance of reality, but solely on whether it gives better predictions (and

thereby helps us to make better decisions).[16] In systems analyses models of one type or another are required to trace the relations between inputs and outputs, resources and objectives, for each of the systems to be compared, so that we can predict the relevant consequences of choosing any system.

5. A criterion. By "criterion" we mean the test by which we choose one alternative or system rather than another. The choice of an appropriate economic criterion is frequently the central problem in designing a systems analysis. In principle the criterion we want is clear enough: the optimal system is the one which yields the greatest excess of positive values (objectives) over negative values (resources used up, or costs). But as we have already seen, this clear-cut ideal solution is seldom a practical possibility in military problems.[17] Objectives and costs usually have no common measure: there is no generally acceptable way to subtract dollars spent or aircraft lost from enemy targets destroyed. Moreover, as in two of the cases above, there may be multiple objectives or multiple costs that are incommensurable. So in most military analyses we have to be satisfied with some approximation to the ideal criterion that will enable us to say, not that some system A is optimal, but that it is better than some other proposed systems B, C, and so on. In many cases we will have to be content with calculating efficient rather than optimal systems, relying on the intuitive judgment of well-informed people (of whom the analyst may be one) to select one of the efficient systems in the neighborhood of the optimum. The choice is the subject of chapter VI.

It cannot be stated too frequently or emphasized enough that economic choice is *a way of looking at problems* and does not necessarily depend upon the use of any analytic aids or computational devices. Some analytic aids (mathematical models) and computing machinery are quite likely to be useful in analyzing complex military problems, but there are many military problems in which they have not proved particularly useful where, nevertheless, it is rewarding to array the alternatives and think through their implications in terms of objectives and costs. Where mathematical

---

[16] Bombardiers once bombed visually, using simple models in their heads to estimate the bomb's trajectory in relation to the target. Modern bombsights use mathematical models, requiring high speed computers for solution, to make the same estimate. The model used by the modern bombsight is better only if its predictions are more accurate—a question of fact which has to be tested by experiment.

[17] In private industry this "ideal" criterion is the familiar one of profit maximization.

models and computations are useful, they are in no sense alternatives to or rivals of good intuitive judgment; they supplement and complement it: Judgment is always of critical importance in designing the analysis, choosing the alternatives to be compared, and selecting the criterion. Except where there is a completely satisfactory one-dimensional measurable objective (a rare circumstance), judgment must supplement the quantitative analysis before a choice can be recommended.

THE REQUIREMENTS APPROACH

In the absence of systematic analysis in terms of objectives and costs, a procedure that might be called the "requirements approach" is commonly used in the military departments and throughout much of the government. Staff officers inspect a problem, say, the defense of the continental United States or the design of the next generation of heavy bomber, draft a plan which seems to solve the problem, and determine requirements from the plan. Then feasibility is checked: Can the "required" performance characteristics, such as some designated speed and range, be achieved? Can the necessary budget be obtained? Does the nation have the necessary resources in total? If the program passes the feasibility tests, it is adopted; if it fails, some adjustments have to be made. But the question: What are the payoffs *and the costs* of alternative programs? may not be explicitly asked during the process of setting the requirement or deciding upon the budget. In fact, officials have on occasion boasted that their stated "requirements" have been based on need alone.

This, of course, is an illusion. Some notion of cost (money, resources, time), however imprecise, is implicit in the recognition of any limitation. Military departments frequently determine "requirements" which are from 10 to 25 per cent higher than the available budget, but never ten times as high, and seldom twice as high. But this notion of cost merely rules out grossly infeasible programs. It does not help in making optimal or efficient choices.

For that purpose it is essential that alternative ways of achieving military objectives be costed, and that choices be made on the basis of payoff and cost. How *are* choices made by military planners prior to any costing of alternatives? We have never heard any satisfying explanation. As we noted in our discussion of figure 6, a good or efficient choice depends upon the relative costs of different resources or inputs; there was no "good" bomb/bomber combination or tactic independent of cost. The derivation of requirements by any process that fails to cost alternatives can result in good solutions only by accident. Probably military planners sometimes weigh relative costs in some crude manner, at least subconsciously, even when they deny they do; or they make choices on the basis of considerations which ought to be secondary or tertiary, such as the preservation of an existing command structure, or the matching of a reported foreign accomplishment.

The defects of the requirements approach can be seen clearly if we think of applying it to our problems as a consumer. Suppose the consumer mulls over his transportation problem and decides, "on the basis of need alone," that he requires a new Cadillac. It is "the best" car he knows, and besides Jones drives one. So he buys a Cadillac, ignoring cost and ignoring therefore the sacrifices he is making in other directions by buying "the best." There are numerous alternative ways of solving the consumer's transportation problem (as there are always numerous ways of solving a military problem), and a little costing of alternatives prior to purchase might have revealed that the purchase of "the best" instrument is not *necessarily* an optimal choice. Perhaps if the consumer had purchased a Pontiac or a secondhand Cadillac he would have saved enough to maintain and operate it and take an occasional trip.[18] Or if he had purchased a Chevrolet he could have afforded to keep his old car and become head of a two-car family. One of these alternatives, properly costed and compared, might have promised a far greater amount of utility for the consumer than the purchase of a new Cadillac "on the basis of need alone." Or the exercise might have reassured the consumer that the new Cadillac was indeed optimal. While expensive unit equipment is not necessarily optimal, in some cases it can be proved to be.

THE PRIORITIES APPROACH

Another procedure that seems to have a great deal of appeal, in both military planning and other government activities, is the "priorities approach." To facilitate a decision about how to spend a specified budget, the desirable items are ranked according to the urgency with which they are needed. The result is a list of things that might be bought, the ones that are more important being near the top and the ones that are less important being near the bottom. Lists that rank several hundred weapons and items have sometimes been generated in the military services.

---

[18] Costing in our sense is never simply the cost of a unit of equipment; it is always the cost of a complete system including everything that must be purchased with the equipment and the cost of maintaining and operating it. See the next section below.

At first blush, this appears to be a commendable and systematic way to tackle the problem. When one reflects a bit, however, the usefulness and significance of such a list begins to evaporate. Consider the following items ranked according to their (hypothetical) priorities: (1) Missile X, (2) Radar device Y, (3) Cargo aircraft Z. How do you use such a ranking? Does it mean that the entire budget should be spent on the first item? Probably not, for it is usually foolish to allocate all of a budget to a single weapon or object. Besides, if a budget is to be so allocated, the ranking of the items below the first one has no significance.

Does the ranking mean that the money should go to the first item until no additional amount is needed, then to the second item until no further amount is needed, and so on? Hardly, because there could be some need for more of Missile X almost without limit. Even if only a limited amount of Missile X was available, to keep buying right out to this limit would usually be a foolish rule. After quite a few Missile X's were purchased, the next dollar could better be spent on some other item. Even using lifeboats for women and children first is foolish if a sailor or doctor on each lifeboat can save many lives.

Perhaps a priority list means that we should spend more money on the higher-priority items than on those having a lower priority. But this makes little sense, since some of the items high on the list, for example, the radar device, may cost little per unit and call at most for a relatively small amount of money; while some lower-ranking purchases, such as the cargo aircraft, may call for comparatively large sums if they are to be purchased at all. In any event, the priorities reveal nothing about how much more should be spent on particular items.

Just how anyone can use such a list is not clear. Suppose a consumer lists possible items for his monthly budget in the order of their priority and he feels that in some sense they rank as follows: (1) groceries, (2) gas and oil, (3) cigarettes, (4) repairs to house, (5) liquor, and (6) steam baths. This does not mean that he will spend all of his funds on groceries, nor does it mean that he will spend nothing on liquor or steam baths. His problem is really to allocate his budget among these different objects. He would like to choose the allocation such that an extra dollar on cigarettes is just as important to him as an extra dollar on groceries. At the margin, therefore, the objects of expenditure would be equally important (except for those that are not purchased at all).

The notion of priority stems from the very sensible proposition that one should do "first things first." It makes sense, or at least

the top priority does, when one considers the use of a small increment of resources or time. If one thinks about the use of an extra
dollar or of the next half-hour of his time, it is sensible to ask,
"What is the most urgent—the first-priority—item?" If one is deciding what to do with a budget or with the next eight hours, however, he ordinarily faces a problem of *allocation*, not of setting priorities. A list of priorities does not face the problem or help solve it.

Thus in formulating defense policy and choosing weapon systems, we have to decide how much effort or how many resources
should go to each item. The "priorities approach" does not solve
the allocation problem and can even trap us into adopting foolish
policies.[19]

SOME MISUNDERSTANDINGS

There is some resistance to the use of economic analysis in military problems that is based on misunderstanding.

An economically efficient solution to military problems does not
imply a cheap force or a small military budget. It simply implies
that whatever the military budget (or other limitation, for example, on personnel) the greatest military capabilities are developed. Since military capabilities are plural and not easily commensurate, an efficient military establishment, in the technical
sense, would merely be one in which no single capability—antisubmarine, ground warfare, offensive air, and so on—could be
increased without decreasing another. An optimal establishment
would in addition have the right "balance" among capabilities
—a harder problem for analysis.

From the point of view of the nation, of the military establishment as a whole,[20] and of the Treasury Department, the achievement of efficiency and the approach to an optimal solution can be
a common objective. There is a conflict of interest between the
Treasury, the Bureau of the Budget, and economy-minded Congressmen on the one hand, and the military services on the other
when the level of the budget is in question. The military services
always (and properly) want more; the economizers always (and
also properly) offer resistance, or try to impose reductions. But

[19] For a revealing discussion of priority lists, see *Military Construction Appropriations for 1958*, Hearings before the Subcommittee of the Committee on Appropriations, House of Representatives, 85th Congress, 1st Session, U.S. Government Printing Office, Washington, D.C., 1957, 420–427.

[20] There are undoubtedly sectional interests within the military—particularly commands, services, and staff units—which might suffer from increased efficiency in the establishment as a whole, and have therefore a perverse incentive to prevent efficiency.

once the budget has been determined, there is no longer conflict of interest.

In fact the choices that maximize military capability for a given budget are the same choices that minimize the cost of attaining that capability. As we shall see in chapter VI, the capability-maximizing criterion (given budget) and cost-minimizing criterion (given capability) are logically equivalent and therefore lead to the same choices and the same programs (for any given scale of operations, as determined by either budget or capability). If an Atlas missile system maximizes our strategic air power for a given SAC budget, it also minimizes the cost of providing that much strategic air power.

Some officers object to economic analysis because they think it implies cheap equipment, or the continued use of obsolescent equipment. This is by no means the case except, properly, where the use of cheap or old equipment results in lower system cost. New equipment does tend, on a unit basis, to be more expensive than old; but this does not mean that its use is uneconomic, any more than the use of modern more expensive equipment is necessarily uneconomic in industry. What counts, in the military as in industry, is not the unit cost of procurement, but the total system cost—the cost of procuring and maintaining and operating the whole system in which the new equipment is embedded—of achieving an appropriate capability or objective. This may be greater or less with new, more "expensive," higher performance equipment. In the case of the atomic bomb it was much less, although the bombs themselves are presumably much more expensive. There is no presumption that the substitution of the "expensive" B–47 for the "cheap" B–29 was uneconomic. The problem of the relative worths and costs of quality and quantity is, in the military as in private industry, an economic problem, amenable to economic calculus.

Another misunderstanding is reflected in the question, "What do dollars matter when national survival is at stake?" They matter precisely because they represent (however imperfectly in some circumstances) generalized national resources at the disposal of the military. Unless they are economically used, resources will be wasted, and the nation will have less military capability and a smaller chance of survival. If any one dimension of military power is wastefully planned, that is, at greater than minimum cost, some other dimension will, with a given total military budget, have fewer resources at its disposal and necessarily less capability.

Of course waste can be compensated, within limits, by voting higher military budgets at the expense of non-military objectives, but legislatures are understandably less than willing to raise budgets for this purpose. If they vote a higher budget, they want the still greater military capability that an economic use of the higher budget would make possible.

EFFICIENCY IN THE LARGE VERSUS EFFICIENCY IN THE SMALL

It is convenient in analyzing national security problems (and many others) to distinguish between "efficiency in the large" and "efficiency in the small." (Efficiency in this section will again be used in the general sense of "making good use" of resources—not in the technical sense defined earlier in the chapter.) Efficiency in the large, or at relatively high levels, involves getting the gross allocations right in reference to major objectives—in the case of national security, the allocation of resources between military and non-military uses, and allocations to the Services and the major military "missions" in conformity with national objectives. Efficiency in the small, or at relatively low levels, involves making good use of the resources allocated to each mission and the numerous subordinate jobs within each.

Quantitative economic analysis can be useful in both types of problems, although the type of analysis that is appropriate in the two cases is likely to differ. Typically in decisions at relatively high levels there are important qualitative or intangible factors which make it impossible to define a satisfactory criterion and therefore impossible to devise an explicit model which points the way to *the* right decision.[21] Nevertheless the explicit use of models and of quantitative analysis is not only possible in many such problems, but essential if good solutions are to be found.

Take as an example the division of the budget for the strategic air war between offense and defense. This is a comparatively high level problem, beset by intangibles. On one side is the mystique of the offense—the conviction of military services everywhere that morale depends upon offense-mindedness, and that reliance on defensive measures is self-defeating. On the other side is the morale and resolve of the civilian nation: will it dare to threaten war if it is defenseless against enemy bombs? And in between is that most pervasive of all intangibles—the mind of the enemy. How does it function, and what will deter him?

---

[21] Some lower level problems are in this respect precisely like the high level ones.

Nevertheless, quantitative calculations are essential to a rational solution. Calculations can show that with the expenditure of a tolerable number of billions of dollars annually on an offensive force *and on the defense of the offensive force*, we can with high confidence (say, 90 per cent) guarantee effective retaliation against an aggressor and therefore that a rational aggressor will be deterred. Similar calculations can show how this total deterrent budget should be divided between the offensive force and various protective devices including warning nets, hardening of installations, and interceptor and missile defenses.

At the same time, calculations can show that much larger budgets (beyond the range of practical politics) will provide only partial and uncertain (low-confidence) protection in the event deterrence fails.

Calculations of this kind, whether made explicitly or implicitly, account for the prevalent view, undoubtedly correct in present circumstances (1960), that protected offensive deterrent power has first claim on the national security budget. For what we are trying to do in allocating between offense and defense is to minimize some combination of (a) the chance that all-out thermonuclear war will occur, and (b) the amount of damage we will suffer if it does occur.[22] While we do not know precisely what combination we want to minimize, we can as a first approximation regard it as the product of (a) and (b). We would be willing to reallocate budget from deterrent forces to protective ones like Nikes or civilian shelters only if the expected damage to us if war occurs was reduced by a greater factor than the chance of war was increased.

Of course, we cannot make a complete, explicit calculation of such a product, for we do not have a direct measure of the chance of war. The final stage in allocating funds between deterrent and survival measures is a task for judgment, but judgment's task can be greatly facilitated by calculations showing how accomplishments of the proximate objectives, that is, ability to inflict damage and ability to survive attack, are related to budget expenditures.

If the technical possibilities of offense and defense, as reflected in the budget costs of buying given amounts of deterrent power and protection, were drastically altered by, say, some technological breakthrough in defense, our judgment about the best allocation would also change. Suppose that, both for the Russians and ourselves, the relations were more or less reversed, so that at practical budget levels we could buy a high-confidence, virtually leak-

---

[22] The amount of damage we will be able to inflict on the enemy is implicit in the calculation, since that *is* our means of deterring war.

proof defense; while the similar effectiveness of the Russian defense made the task of providing an effective retaliatory force tremendously uncertain and expensive. We are sure that in these circumstances men of good judgment would assign top priority to providing the curtain of death rays that would kill incoming bombers, missiles, and bombs. On the other hand our strategic bombing forces, in fighting for appropriations for their low-confidence mission, would find themselves in the same difficult, uncomfortable position that Continental Air Defense and the agencies responsible for civil defense now occupy.

Of course *priority* provides no clue to the proportion of the budget to be allocated to the deterrence mission—except when the total budget is small. When the budget is large, the best proportions depend upon the effects of *increments* of budget spent on deterrence and survival respectively (and these effects are calculable).

As we descend to lower levels of decision making, there is frequently a change in the proportion of quantitative and qualitative factors that affords greater scope for explicit analysis. If the problem is not how much to allocate to air defense relative to other missions, but with which of two proposed electronic gun sights to equip fighter aircraft, the relevance and necessity of quantitative analysis becomes obvious. To make a rational choice we must, at the least, have quantitative evidence on accuracy, reliability, cost and availability, weight and the consequences of added weight, and so on. Of course the great majority of problems of military choice are, like this one, lower level problems, which are decided in the first instance at levels in the departmental or military hierarchy well below the top.

The bulk of explicit quantitative analysis so far attempted in the military, chiefly by operations analysis groups, has been directed toward such lower level problems, and this will probably always be true, and it may be desirable. Not only do the lower level problems demand quantitative analysis and appear more "manageable"; they are, in the aggregate, of great importance. Experienced operations researchers report that they frequently discover that some of the systems which they compare are better by large factors—three, four or more—than others seriously proposed, sometimes with enthusiastic advocates. This should come as no surprise to economists who have studied international differences in productivity and costs, or even differences among enterprises within a nation. There are many ways to make any product or achieve any objective, and some are much more efficient than others. In the absence of an adequate economic calculus, highly inefficient ways can be and are chosen.[23]

The usual task of quantitative analysis is the improvement of decisions at relatively low levels in the military hierarchy—efficiency in the small. But while decisions at these levels appear more susceptible to quantitative analysis, and indeed frequently are, such analysis presents peculiar and formidable difficulties. These are associated with the choice of criteria, and will be more fully discussed in chapter VI. What follows here is an impressionistic introduction to the nature of the problem.

In the first place, for a lower level analysis to be more manageable, it must be confined to a lower level context. Many of the things that would be treated as variables in a higher level analysis —specifically, decisions at still higher levels and at the same levels in other branches of the military—must be taken as given. The systems to be compared in the analysis, while "complete" in some sense, must be limited, with only a few elements varying from system to system.

Analyses so confined to lower level contexts, which assume decisions given at higher and collateral levels, are called "sub-optimizations." [24] They attempt to find optimal (or near optimal) solutions, but to subproblems rather than to the whole problem of the organization in whose welfare or utility we are interested. If a consumer tries to solve his transportation problem (Cadillac *vs.* Chevrolet) more or less in isolation, taking other major decisions affecting his income and expenditure as given, he is sub-optimizing. If the Air Force tries to decide between two gun sights for fighters, taking the general organization, size and tactics of fighter defense as given, it is sub-optimizing. If we are taking a Departmental or Service point of view, we sub-optimize when we try to solve a problem at a level lower than that of the Secretary or Chief of Staff. From a national point of view, even problems at the Chief of Staff level, in a context coextensive with the responsibilities of the Service, must be regarded as sub-optimizations.

Sub-optimizations are both necessary and inevitable, and provide scope for productive quantitative analyses of important problems of choice. But they are hard to do well. While analysis appears

---

[23] We are not suggesting, of course, that *all* international or intercompany differences in productivity measure differences in the efficiency of utilization of resources. Where labor is a relatively cheap factor it will usually be efficient to choose methods which result in lower average labor productivity. But the differences do measure the wide range of alternative methods and therefore the range of possible error if economic rationale is lacking.

[24] Sub-optimizations correspond to the partial equilibrium analyses of conventional economic theory.

to become more manageable as we move to lower levels, limit the context, and restrict the scope within which systems vary, three inter-related problems tend to become more formidable the further we move in this direction:

1. The first is the problem of selecting an appropriate criterion —appropriate, that is, to the level at which the decision is being studied—that is consistent with higher level criteria, and ultimately with the welfare of the organization or group in which we are really interested. It is very easy to choose some proximate criterion in a low level problem that is inconsistent with higher level criteria—to take a previous example, maximizing air defense kill potential when an equally important or more important function of air defense is to provide adequate warning.

2. The second we will call the problem of spillovers; and this too we will discuss at greater length in Chapter VI. When we confine analysis within narrow contextual limits, there is always a possibility that some of the consequences may affect—favorably or unfavorably—other parts of the larger organization or group with whose welfare we are concerned. Certain SAC deployments will facilitate, and others will make more difficult, the task of the air defense system in providing warning to and defense of SAC bases. These spillover effects would be missed in an analysis narrowly confined to SAC.

3. Third, there is the problem of choosing the context and the elements that will be permitted to vary in the systems compared. The context need not, and indeed normally should not, be as restricted as the area of immediate decision that provides the *focus* of the analysis. The broader the context the less the danger from inconsistent criteria and the less likely it is that significant spillover effects will be missed. The broader the context, too, the fewer other decisions one needs to take as given, and the greater opportunity one has to explore the interdependence of decisions at different and collateral levels. But breadth of context and any increase in the number of variables have to be purchased by drastically increasing the complexity of the analysis,[25] with all this im-

---

[25] The number of cases to be computed and compared increases as the power of the number of interdependent variables. If we let each variable take four alternative values and have two variables, the number of cases is 4^2 or 16—a back-of-the-envelope problem. If we increase the number of variables to 10, we have to compute 4^{10} cases, or more than a million, and probably need a high speed electronic computer.

plies in terms of research manpower, expense, and time. So we don't want to expand context or increase variables un necessarily.

How large should the context be? How many decisions should be analyzed simultaneously? There are no rules except—be aware of the dangers, and use good sense to reduce them. Some low level problems are "factorable," that is, good decisions don't depend much upon other decisions, and spillovers aren't too important. Where problems are relatively factorable, the context can be kept small and the variables few. One can frequently minimize the cost of one operation without much affecting others. But other problems simply aren't factorable in this sense. Their solution, even if responsibility is fixed at a low level in the hierarchy, has wide ramifications. And any optimal solution must take account of the interdependence of this problem and others. As an obvious and extreme example, an analysis of the location of SAC bases cannot be successfully sub-optimized even at the level of SAC Headquarters. Their location not only has spillovers on air defense, as we have seen, and on our ability to fight local wars in various parts of the world; but it may also affect the whole structure of our alliances. We must either optimize on a fairly grand scale (probably impossible in any explicit quantitative manner), or frankly label our sub-optimization a partial analysis, dealing only with *some* of the factors important to a decision.

Consider another hypothetical example, mentioned above, which demands, in the design of the analysis, some compromises between desirable breadth of context and the need to keep research requirements within practical limits. Suppose the analyst's assignment is to select the "best" of several proposed electronic gun sights for fighter aircraft. How large a context should he assume in the study? How many other decisions should he assume to be given?

At one extreme he might fit the sights into very small systems— say specific fighter aircraft—and "score" them by the number of hits registered in tests on tow targets. Would this give him the right answer? Not necessarily. In the first place the criterion may not be closely related to the real task of fighter aircraft. The sights (or some of them) may be heavy enough to affect the plane's range, or its speed or maneuverability. The number of tubes in the electronic system would affect the reliability and the ease of maintenance of the weapons system. Furthermore, performance in combat situations might not be taken sufficiently into account in comparing the number of hits on a tow target.

To overcome some of these shortcomings, the analyst might enlarge the context slightly and fit each gun sight into a fighter plane in combat (on paper) with an enemy aircraft. Would it be in accordance with higher level aims to put this particular emphasis on victory in individual duels? Again, not necessarily. The best gun sight in a duel of one against one would probably turn out to be an extremely expensive one, making it necessary, with a given budget, to sacrifice numbers (or perhaps the range of the fighter). The electronic gear might cause too many aborts (planes that return to base unable to complete their mission) or keep too many planes on the ground. From the standpoint of numerical superiority, number of interceptions, and other aspects of the whole fighter operation, this gun sight might be a poor choice indeed.

The analyst appears to be driven to larger and larger systems— fitting the gun sights into planes, then the planes into fighter groups, then the groups into relevant military operations. He may even want to ask what tasks or budgets make sense in view of the whole military operation and of political realities. But while larger systems analyses make his criterion problem (or one aspect of it) more manageable, they become more cumbersome and more aggregative. At some point in the process, depending on many circumstances (how much time he has, what research resources he has, what chance he or his organization has of influencing higher or collateral decisions, how important the choice among gun sights is anyway?), he must accept a limited context and a less-than-perfect proximate criterion, try to keep aware, in a general and qualitative way, of its shortcomings and biases, treat effects outside his system crudely, and get on with his inevitable job of sub-optimizing.

KINDS OF MILITARY DECISIONS

Military decisions may be classified by kind as well as by level. For purposes of economic analysis it is frequently useful to distinguish:

> Operations decisions (strategy and tactics)
> Procurement or force composition decisions
> Research and development decisions.

The basic difference among these kinds of decisions, from the point of view of analysis, is the time at which the decision affects the capability of the military forces concerned. An operations decision (how many destroyers to use per convoy) can affect operations and capability almost immediately; in fact, analyses and decisions focused on operations are usually concerned with the near future. A decision to procure something, on the other hand, cannot affect capability until the thing procured has been produced (in the case of manpower, trained) and fitted into operational forces. If the thing is an aircraft carrier or a bomber, the time involved may be many years. Decisions to develop something tend to affect capabilities at an even later date—after the thing has been developed, and produced, and then fitted into operational forces.

An economic analysis, whether quantitative or qualitative, will usually attempt to determine the utility of alternative systems by examining the effect on military capabilities, whenever these occur. The effects of a change in tactics in 1960 can perhaps be fully evaluated in the context of 1960. But to evaluate the effects of a decision in 1960 to develop (or even to procure) a new missile may require projecting the context to 1970 or later. Analyses based on long-range forecasts are, of course, highly uncertain, and this fact drastically alters the form of analysis which it is sensible and useful to make and the kind of conclusions one can draw from it.

In an operations decision, the relevant resource constraints are usually specific rather than general, simply because the time horizon is so short. If the problem involves the tactics of convoying, the escort vessels that have to be used must probably be taken as given—in number, speed, armament, and so on. No budget however large can produce more in the short run. Similarly, SAC's emergency war plans for a retaliatory strike must utilize specific planes carrying specific bombs from specific bases. The fact that the appropriate resource constraints are specific by no means inhibits economic analysis. We have seen that the problem of making economic use of a number of specific resources is fundamentally the same problem as making economic use of a single general resource, although the calculations may be more complicated. In fact, the first large-scale explicit use of quantitative economic analysis in military problems by operations research groups in the Second World War was directed toward problems of tactical operations. Serious attempts to apply the same techniques to longer-range procurement and development problems, in which constraints are more appropriately one or a very few general resources, followed much later.

Analysis focused on a *procurement* decision (for example, which of two missiles to order in 1960) almost of necessity will have to study *operations* in later years—the strategy and tactics with which each missile will be used after it has been introduced into the force. For a valid comparison, each must be used in the most effective way in the context of the appropriate future year. (Similarly, an analysis focused on a development decision may, in order to gauge potential payoffs, study procurement and operations as well.) The analysis of a procurement problem is, however, solely directed toward the procurement decision in the immediate future; its analysis of future tactics is incidental to choice of bomber; it is tentative and leads to no recommendations about tactics. The time to make analyses focused on tactical decisions in 1968 is not earlier than 1967.

VI

THE CRITERION PROBLEM

In the earlier chapter we stated that the selection of an appropriate criterion is frequently the central problem in the design of an economic analysis intended to improve military decisions. Whatever the particular problem, military or civilian, it is fairly obvious that, in choosing among alternative means to our ends, we need to scan the ends themselves with a critical eye. New techniques or types of equipment may be extremely efficient in achieving certain aims, but these aims may be the wrong ones—aims that are selected almost unconsciously or at least without sufficient critical thought.

But to say that we should scrutinize our ultimate ends carefully in deciding upon the best course of action is much too vague. Suppose we wish to choose among various motorcars. Merely to name and list the things we ultimately value (such as growth, approval, security, freedom, leisure, goods) is not very helpful in solving the problem. It is wise to think about such a list, for it may prevent us from making some absurd choice that does not contribute to *any* of these things, but in most situations the list provides little counsel. One reason it fails to do so is the tremendous gap between gas consumption, wheel base, and new seat covers, on the one hand, and leisure, security, and approval, on the other. This gap has to be at least partially bridged in order to reach any conclusions about policies. Another reason is the necessity of trading part of one desideratum for some of another, sacrificing faster "pick-up" for improved fuel consumption or giving up some comforts for a little more leisure.

Similarly, the mere enumeration of objectives in choosing among weapon systems, while it may be pertinent, does not serve as a guide to specific action. The objectives may include target destruction potential, invulnerability to enemy attack, strengthening of alliances, and reliability—all to be achieved "as soon as possible." All of these things would indeed be nice to have. But while good intentions are sometimes reputed to be excellent paving materials, in themselves they do not pave the way to preferred action. In practical problems of military (or other) choice there are always constraints which prevent us from simultaneously achieving all our objectives.

CRITERIA

Hence, in choosing among alternatives, we do more than to list things which it would be nice to have. Explicitly or implicitly we adopt criteria or tests of preferredness. One essential step in the analysis is predicting the consequences of alternative actions or systems—a step which, as indicated earlier, involves the use of sets of relationships called models. Another vital step is distinguishing preferred combinations of consequences from less desirable ones; this step entails the use of criteria. Thus, after having the features of different cars spelled out, the chooser has to decide what is the best combination of features. He may want the car that has maximum acceleration while meeting specific constraints on other aspects of performance and on cost. If so, that is his criterion. Or he may compare the features (including cost implications) of different cars subjectively and reach his decision. If so, the criterion is never made explicit, but is presumably the maximization of some function constrained by the chooser's limited resources.

There are times when the terms "criterion" appears to be a misnomer. For, on occasion, as we have seen, analysis can unravel only *some* of the consequences of alternative actions and exhibit these consequences to decision-makers after the usual manner of consumers' research.[1] (By this term we mean the kind of research that is often done to help consumers choose an item such as an automobile or a refrigerator.) Insofar as this is the case, a partial criterion (comparison in terms of selected consequences) may be used. There is then no problem of devising a definitive test, but there is the closely related problem of deciding *what* consequences the decision-maker should know about. In other situations, however, the analyst may be able (or may try) to trace out all the significant effects and learn enough about the decision-maker's preferences to evaluate those effects. In these instances, quantitative analysis *per se* may be used to pick out and recommend preferred courses of action. Insofar as this is the case, a definitive test of preferredness is necessary, and the criterion problem is the devising of that test. Most of the discussion that follows will relate

---

[1] Consumers' research publications sometimes recommend a single "best buy," using a criterion which may or may not be acceptable to a particular subscriber. But usually they content themselves with describing features and analyzing certain consequences, letting the subscriber supply (a total or final) evaluation and make the choice.

directly to the criterion problem faced in the latter situations, but much of it will pertain, at least indirectly, to the selection of partial criteria, that is, of selected effects that are relevant to the comparison of alternative actions.

The Necessity for Using "Proximate" Criteria

Ideally we should choose that course of action which, with available resources, maximizes something like the "satisfaction" of an individual, the profits of a firm, the "military worth" of the military establishment, or the "well-being" of a group. If possible, we should like to ascertain the total amount of these magnitudes under each of various alternative policies. Then we would pick the policy that promised to yield the most satisfaction, the most profits, the most military worth, or the most well-being, depending on the identity of the person or organization whose choice we were advising. But this prescription usually helps little more than saying that we want the best. Nobody knows precisely how satisfaction and military worth are related to the observable outcomes of various courses of action. We do not have the ability to translate outcomes into such terms. In practical problem-solving, therefore, we have to look at some "proximate" criterion which serves to reflect what is happening to satisfaction or military worth. Actual criteria are the practicable substitutes for the maximization of whatever we would ultimately like to maximize.

In comparisons of military operations or equipment, what is desired is the course of action that would contribute most to "winning" or deterring some kind (or kinds) of war, or even more generally, to achieving national security. Since it will usually be impossible to measure achievements in any of these terms, it is necessary to adopt indirect but workable criteria that appear to be consistent with ultimate aims.

Sub-Optimization and Criteria

The need to use proximate rather than ultimate tests opens the door to the selection of incorrect criteria. But the door is really swung wide open—in fact one might say that the welcome mat is put out—by another fact of life stressed in chapter V: the fact that problems of choice must be broken down into component pieces or sub-problems.

Let us examine this difficulty in somewhat greater detail. A military service (or government department or large corporation) cannot possibly have one man or one committee examine *all* its problems of choice simultaneously and pick each course of action in the light of all other decisions. It is inevitable that decision-making be broken into pieces. The division is almost necessarily along hierarchical lines, some of the broader policy choices being made by high level officials or groups, others being delegated to lower levels.[2]

Similarly, analyses must be piecemeal, since it is impossible for a single analysis to cover all problems of choice simultaneously in a large organization. Thus comparisons of alternative courses of action always pertain to a part of the government's (or corporation's) problem. Other parts of the over-all problem are temporarily put aside, possible decisions about some matters being ignored, specific decisions about others being taken for granted. The resulting analyses are intended to provide assistance in finding optimal, or at least good, solutions to sub-problems: in the jargon of systems analysis and operations research, they are suboptimizations.

Note again, however, that the scope of analysis does not have to, and indeed usually should not, coincide with the scope of authority in decision-making. Take the case of military decisions within the government. Analysis of a problem in antisubmarine warfare may have to be made in the context of a global war involving all services and the national economy, even though it is relevant to decisions within one bureau of the Navy Department. Fortunately no single authority runs the whole executive-legislative-judicial process in the United States government, but this does not mean that individual departments and subordinate units should not, on occasion, take a broad national point of view ("context" and criterion) in making decisions for which it is responsible in the hierarchy. The situation in a private corporation is precisely analogous. The individual division or department of the corporation, in making certain decisions delegated to it, will be expected to take a corporationwide point of view, tracing the full consequences of its actions on all operations of the firm.[3] The sales department is not

---

[2] We must again stress that no connotation of greater or lesser significance should be associated with these terms "higher" and "lower" levels. The lower level decisions may in some circumstances be the more important ones. Choosing the best bomber-missile systems and the means of protecting them, for example, may do more to enhance our deterrent force than allocating more funds to the Air Force to buy inferior systems.

[3] The exceptions in which individual divisions (e.g., those of General Motors and U.S. Steel) are instructed to act autonomously and ignore the possible repercussions of their actions on the profits of other divisions of the corporation, are instructive. In these cases the corporation has deliberately decided that the "spillover" effects on other divisions are less important in the long run than the advantages of fixing responsibility and providing strong, clear-cut incentives. There is probably also a fear that the use of corporation-wide criteria in analysis may inevitably lead to an undesirable centralization of decision-making itself—a sort of "spillover" effect of a different kind. In any event, these exceptions are usually limited to certain kinds of decisions. Divisions of General Motors are supposed to be completely antonomous in buying and selling, but not in financing and therefore not in decisions requiring major capital expenditures. There are useful analogies in all this for the military.

expected to choose actions which maximize sales, or sales minus selling costs, but the total profits of the corporation—sales and other receipts minus all costs in all departments.

Piecemeal analysis and decision making have great advantages, some of which have already been stated. Small problems tend to be more "manageable" in a number of senses. As problems are broken down into smaller chunks, more detail can be taken into account by both researchers and decision-makers. In large firms a degree of decentralization greater than that which is inevitable is usually believed to be desirable so that the "man on the spot" can decide about many matters—and be held responsible for them.[4] In analysis, somewhat similarly, considerable breakdown of the problems of a corporation or a government department may be desirable so that the models used in estimating outcomes can be "on the spot," that is, less aggregative and more precise in their predictions than global or firm-wide models would be.

Finally, better hedging against uncertainty *may* result from breaking big problems into smaller ones. The difficulties that stem from inherent uncertainties will be discussed mostly in the next chapter, but a few words are in order here. If decision making is decentralized to a considerable extent, it may help against the possibility of getting stuck with lopsided views at the top. In civil government it has long been widely recognized that some separation of powers and dispersal of authority are important, partly as a hedging device. And in analysis, a degree of suboptimization *may* mean, for some problems, less risk of tying all analytical results to a "bad" criterion, for instance, one involving a spuriously specific objective in which uncertainty is neglected.

On the other hand, there is a real danger in piecemeal analysis, one whose importance must be reemphasized because it is probably not as widely appreciated as are the difficulties inherent in biting off too big a chunk of the problem. The danger is that the criteria adopted in lower level problems may be unrelated to and inconsistent with higher level criteria. As mentioned before, proximate criteria have to be used in any case; but since problems must be considered one piece at a time, a whole hierarchy of proximate criteria comes into play, and potential inconsistencies are abundant.

---

[4] This not only takes advantage of the man-on-the-spot's familiarity with the details of a problem but also constitutes a more desirable decision-making process anyway, getting more persons in the habit of using ingenuity and taking responsibility. Indeed this is of major importance for the functioning of the economy, and probably of equal importance in the military services.

An an example from the military sphere, suppose that the military establishes a requirement for 90 per cent reliability in the functioning of its weapon systems. Bows and arrows may pass such a test with flying colors, yet hand grenades may accomplish much more at the same cost, even if half of them are duds. Perhaps 90 per cent or 50 or 99 per cent has some intuitive appeal, but this gives little assurance that it is a sensible "requirement," criterion, or test. The point is that even plausible criteria for choosing lower level policies may not harmonize with higher level tests, that is, may not be in agreement with what we really want to do. Earlier we criticized the widespread practice in government of setting "requirements" without looking explicitly at costs. Because problems must be taken up piecemeal, there is danger that requirements will be set without looking .critically at payoffs either. And the achievement of a blindly selected "requirement" (even at minimum cost)[5] is likely to be inconsistent with higher level aims.

In a free enterprise economy we have a price mechanism and a system of incentives which, imperfectly but pervasively, enforce some measure of consistency between the lower level criteria used by individuals and firms in making their economic decisions and certain higher level criteria appropriate to the economy. A whole branch of economic theory, rather unfortunately labeled "welfare economics," is concerned with relations between high and low level economic criteria.[6] Under certain circumstances (the most important being absence of monopoly, free movement of factors of production, "full employment," and no external economies or diseconomies), the maximization of their own preference functions by individuals and of their own profits by firms will lead to an "efficient" use of resources in the economy—in the precisely defined senses that it will be impossible to produce more of any one good or service without producing less of some other *and* that it will be impossible to improve the satisfaction of any one individual

---

[5] Admittedly, if the requirement *has* to be taken as given, it is better to achieve it at minimum cost than at higher cost. Even a "bad" sub-optimization may be better than none at all. It may not make sense in the total context to raise the reliability of hand grenades to a magic 90%, but if it has to be so raised, the fewer resources we use in doing so the more will be available for sensible products.

[6] The classic work in this field is A. C. Pigou, *The Economics of Welfare*, 1st ed., Macmillan and Co., London, 1920. For an introductory and somewhat more modern exposition, see J. E. Meade and C. J. Hitch, *Introduction to Economic Analysis and Policy*, Oxford University Press, New York, 1938, especially Part II. For developments in, and qualifications to, the theory of welfare economics, see Paul A. Samuelson, *Foundations of Economic Analysis*, Harvard University Press, Cambridge, Mass., 1948, pp. 203–253; Kenneth J. Arrow, *Social Choice and Individual Values*, John Wiley and Son, New York, 1951; and R. C. Lipsey and K. Lancaster, "The General Theory of Second Best," *Review of Economic Studies*, 1956–57, pp. 11–32.

without reducing that of another.[7] Since, in general, firms do try to maximize profits and individuals do try to maximize preference functions, there will be a tendency for resources to be efficiently used in the economy to the extent that the assumed circumstances are approximated.

This is an interesting and, within limits, a useful conclusion. It might be regarded as equally plausible, or even more plausible, that the higher level economic criterion would require firms to minimize cost per unit of output (the ratio of cost to output) or to maximize productivity per head or per man-hour (the ratio of output to some one input) instead of maximizing profits (receipts minus costs). In fact both these criteria have been widely used—in some cases appropriately, in others not—as indexes of efficiency in comparisons between firms and countries. But it can be demonstrated that maximizing either of the ratios by firms in choosing methods of production, scale of operations, and so on, would result in an inefficient use of resources in the economy.

SOME CRITERION ERRORS

In the military (and indeed in the government generally) there is no comparable mechanism that tends to insure consistency between high level and low level criteria.[8] Since piecemeal analysis (sub-optimization) and therefore the use of low level criteria cannot be avoided, the prevention of even gross errors in the selection of criteria requires hard thought. In a very general sense all criterion errors involve inconsistency between the tests that are selected in analyzing lower level problems and the tests that are applicable at higher levels. However, some of the mistakes that occur most frequently have special characteristics and can be put into categories.

Maximizing Gain While Minimizing Cost

The consequences of an action fall into two types—(1) those positive gains which we like to increase, or the achievement of objectives, and (2) those negative effects which we like to decrease, or the incurrence of costs. Neither type by itself can serve as an adequate criterion: the maximizing of gains without regard to cost or resource limitation is hardly a helpful test, and the

---

[7] Of course efficiency in this sense does not imply an "optimal" distribution of income from anyone's point of view or an "optimal" rate of growth. Efficiency is not a sufficient condition for an optimum, but it does enable us to identify improvements in many situations.

[8] There are administrative devices—committees, special staffs at higher levels, etc.—which attempt, through cooperation and "coordination," to mitigate the consequences of the absence of such a mechanism.

minimizing of cost regardless of other consequences of the alternative actions is nonsense. Hence both gains and costs must appear in criteria but, as will be seen, they can make their appearance in various ways.

One ubiquitous source of confusion is the attempt to maximize gain while minimizing cost or, as a variant, the attempt to maximize two types of gain at once. Such efforts are made, or at least talked about, in connection with all manner of problems. It is sometimes said, for example, that we should choose new weapons "on a 'maximum effectiveness at minimum cost' basis." [9] Or consider the following criterion, which allegedly guided one military operation: "The Germans' triumphant campaign . . . was inspired by the idea of . . . achieving the unexpected in direction, time, and method, preceded by the fullest possible distraction and followed by the quickest possible exploitation along the line of least resistance to the deepest possible range." [10] In connection with civil-government choices (in India), even the London *Economist* slips. "Above all, in choosing between possible schemes, the Indian planners never admit to using the simple test: which will be more profitable? Which, in other words, will give the maximum increase in the national income for the minimum use of real resources?" [11]

Actually, of course, it is impossible to choose that policy which simultaneously maximizes gain and minimizes cost, because there is no such policy. To be sure, in a comparison of policies A and B, it may turn out occasionally that A yields greater gain, yet costs less, than B. But A will not also yield more and cost less than all other policies C through Z; and A will therefore not maximize yield while minimizing cost. Maximum gain is infinitely large, and minimum cost is zero. Seek the policy which has that outcome, and you will not find it.

It may seem that proposals to use such tests are harmless, since it is impossible to use such a criterion when the analyst buckles down to the comparison of specific alternatives. Nonetheless, this type of criterion error should be taken seriously, for it can lead to some wild compromise criteria. If a person approaches a problem with the intention of using such a criterion, he is confused to begin with; then, when he finds that it will not work, he may fasten upon *any* sort of constraint on gain or cost that converts this impossible test into a feasible one.

---

[9] "Organizing for the Technological War," a staff study, *Air Force*, December 1957, p. 44.

[10] B. H. Liddell Hart, *Strategy*, Frederick A. Praeger, Inc., New York, 1954, p. 240.

[11] *The Economist*, July 30, 1955, p. 400.

Overlooking Absolute Size of Gain or Cost

One common procedure is to pick that policy which has the highest ratio of "effectiveness," or achievement-of-objective, to cost. In that case, the maximizing of this ratio is the criterion. Note that the terms "effectiveness" and "achievement of objectives" mean positive gains, or the achievement of tasks that it is desirable to carry out. To examine this criterion, let us look at the comparison of alternative military weapons. These could be anything from various antitank weapons to different bombers, but suppose it is the latter. Let the ability to destroy targets, in the relevant circumstances, be the measure of effectiveness. Suppose next that a B–29 system, already on hand and relatively easy to maintain, would be able to destroy 10 targets and would entail extra costs of $1 billion—a ratio of 10 to 1—while System X would destroy 200 targets and cost $50 billion—a ratio of 4 to 1. Does it follow that we should choose the B–29 system, the one with the higher ratio? The answer is surely No, for it might merely be a system that would invite and lose a war inexpensively. To maximize the *ratio* of effectiveness to cost may be a plausible criterion at first glance, but it allows the absolute magnitude of the achievement or the cost to roam at will. Surely it would be a mistake to tempt the decision-maker to ignore the absolute amount of damage that the bombing system could do.

Without constraints on either total level of effectiveness or total budget, the ratio of the two may point to extreme solutions, to nearly-zero or to almost infinite effectiveness and cost. Of course, common sense and empty pocketbooks prevent us from paying attention to such a ratio at the extremes. But what is its significance in the middle-ground that is not ruled out by common sense? Does the ratio take on meaning in these circumstances? The absurdity of the choice to which the ratio might lead is then bounded, and perhaps the chances that its prescription will coincide with the "correct" choice are increased, simply because the ratio is partly penned up. But still the ratio does not take on real meaning. In fact, the only way to know what such a ratio really means is to tighten the constraint until either a single budget or particular degree of effectiveness is specified. And at that juncture, the ratio reduces itself to the test of maximum effectiveness for a given budget, or a specified effectiveness at minimum cost, and might better have been put that way at the outset.

Of course, if the ratios did not alter with changes in the scale of achievement (or cost), the higher ratio would indicate the preferred system, no matter what the scale. That is, if the ratio of achievement to cost were 10 to 1 for the B–29 system and 4 to 1 for System X at *all* levels of achievement, then the B–29 system would be "dominant." For it would destroy 500 targets at the $50 billion level of cost, clearly a better performance than that of System X. But to assume that such ratios are constant is inadmissible some of the time and hazardous the rest. In the bomber illustration the assumption of constant ratios would obviously be wrong, because with larger scales of activity, it would be necessary to buy more B–29's instead of merely using the ones on hand. Moreover, whatever one's belief about the constancy of the ratio, the straightforward test of maximum effectiveness for a given budget (or, alternatively, minimum cost of achieving a specified level of effectiveness) reveals just as much as the ratio—and seems much less likely to mislead the unwary.[12]

It might be observed that ratios are sometimes handy devices for ranking a list of possible actions when (1) the scale of activity is fixed, and (2) the actions are not interdependent (more on this point later). Thus the rate of return on stocks and bonds (the ratio of annual net return to the cost of the investment) is a convenient aid in ranking securities. Then, *with a fixed investment fund,* the set of securities that yields the greatest return for that fund can be quickly determined. Note, however, the limited conditions under which this procedure can be used.

Setting Wrong Size of Gain or Cost

As just suggested, a criterion in which the budget or level of effectiveness is specified has the virtue of being aboveboard. The test's limitation, the fact that it relates to a particular level of cost or achievement, is perceivable with the naked eye. This fact indicates, though, that while avoidance of ratio tests is a step in the right direction, our troubles are not over. For if an incorrect or irrelevant scale of gain or cost is taken as given, the test is unlikely to result in good policy decisions.

In choosing the bombing system, let us suppose that the test is minimum cost of achieving the ability to destroy 10 targets. In these circumstances, the hypothetical B–29 system is better than System X. On the other hand, if the criterion is minimum cost of achieving an ability to destroy 200 targets, System X is better.

[12] For examples of ratios used as criteria, see Charles Kittel, "The Nature and Development of Operations Research," *Science,* February 7, 1947, pp. 152–53. For more on the hazards of using ratios as criteria, see Charles Hitch, "Suboptimization in Operations Problems," *Journal of the Operations Research Society of America,* May 1953, pp. 94–95 and *passim.* See also Charles Hitch, "Economics and Military Operations Research," *Review of Economics and Statistics,* August 1958, pp. 199–209.

Clearly it makes a difference which scale of gain (that is, effectiveness) is stipulated, and it would be possible to fix upon the wrong scale.

If the analyst has been instructed to specify a particular level of effectiveness, then someone else has, in effect, chosen this aspect of his criterion for him—for better or worse. If he has leeway, however, and chooses the scale uncritically, he is using what was described earlier as the requirements approach.[13] In other words, he is picking the desired task or level of achievement without inquiry into the sacrifices of other achievements that would be entailed. What he can do to choose the right scale will be discussed a little later. The thing to be noted here is that this sort of criterion error is always a threat in piecemeal analysis.

There is precisely the same danger if the cost (or budget, or resources) is to be stipulated instead of the task. Of course, if the budget is already definitely set by higher level decision, the analysis has to take the predetermined amount as given. But budgets for future years are never "definitely set" in a democracy, and if the analysis is concerned with development or procurement, it is usually the magnitude of future budgets that is relevant. Wherever the budget is subject to change, perhaps on the advice of the analyst, his test should not take as given a budget that is uncritically assumed or stipulated.

Neglecting Spillovers

In economics, impacts of one firm's action upon other firms' gains or costs are referred to as "external economies and diseconomies."[14] For example, an oil well that forces brine into the underground water supply may reduce the fertility of adjacent farmlands. Within firms or governmental units, similarly, the action of one department may affect the gains or costs of operations in other departments. (This would be the case, for instance, if the oil-producing firm owned the farmlands.) The term "spillovers"[15] will be used here, chiefly because it is short, as a general title covering all such effects.

In comparing alternative military policies, it is easy to adopt a criterion that leads to the neglect of spillover effects. For example,

---

[13] Of course, he will presumably minimize the cost of satisfying the requirement—which is, as we have seen, better than choosing uncritically both the task and the method of accomplishing it (the "pure" requirements approach, undefined by any cost considerations).

[14] Or sometimes "divergences between private and social product or cost."

[15] The term "spillover costs" and a helpful discussion of those that arise from congestion are contained in J. M. Buchanan's article, "The Pricing of Highway Services," *National Tax Journal*, June 1952, pp. 97–106.

a classic piece of military operations research may have ignored some impacts on activities other than the one that was directly under examination. In this frequently cited example of successful analysis, alternative arrangements for washing and rinsing mess-kits were compared. As his test of preferredness, the analyst used the minimization of the number of man-hours required to do the job, given a total of four tubs. The optimal arrangement, according to this test, turned out to be the use of three tubs for washing and one tub for rinsing. A hypothetical reaction of the mess sergeant has been reported as follows:

> Yeah, I remember that guy. He had some screwball idea that the mission of the Army was to eliminate waiting lines. Actually I had it all figured out that two was the right number of rinse tubs. With everyone rinsing in one tub the bacteria count would get way past the critical level. But we switched to one rinse tub while he was around because the old man says he's an important scientist or something and we got to humor him. Had damn near a third of the outfit out with the bellyache before we got the character off the reservation. Then we quick switched to three rinse tubs and really made a nice line. "Nothing like a good line to get the men's legs in condition," the old man says.[16]

The purpose of this example is not to disparage this particular piece of analysis, which may have been quite useful. The point is simply to suggest how easy it is, in the comparison of *any* policies, to neglect spillover effects.

Using Wrong Concepts of Cost or Gain

The manner in which cost and gain are defined may seem to be a matter of measurement. These definitions are pertinent in a discussion of criterion errors, however, because wrong concepts of cost and gain may grow out of, or be inextricably bound up with, the adoption of incorrect criteria.

Probably the most important cause of error of this sort is the exclusion of relevant costs from the computation. The costs to be compared are the full system costs of each alternative—all the costs directly or indirectly stemming from the decision. Thus, if we are trying to decide between a missile and an aircraft to accomplish a given mission, it can be completely misleading to compare the manufacturing costs of the competing major equipments. We must also count the costs (except where they are already "sunk") of all the auxiliary equipment, of the ground-handling and support equip-

---

16 From A. M. Mood's Review of P. M. Morse and C. E. Kimball, *Methods of Operations Research*, in the *Journal of the Operations Research Society of America*, November 1953, p. 307.

ment, of the training of personnel, and of operation for some appropriate period of time.

Our major emphasis in this volume is on peacetime preparations for war and on deterring war. This means that we are interested *mainly* in peacetime, not wartime costs. We are trying to make the most of the resources available for national security in peacetime. In principle, the wartime costs are relevant. In practice, we can frequently ignore them. For in the case of general nuclear war, we expect the war to be fought with the forces in being at its outbreak. The major economic problem is to maximize the capability of these forces by using resources efficiently before the war starts—so efficiently that we hope an enemy will never dare start it. In the case of limited war there may well be significant production of weapons and expenditure of resources after the limited war begins (as in the case of Korea), but occasional wars for limited objectives will cost little compared with the year-in year-out costs of peacetime preparedness. It is estimated that the "cost of United States forces in Korea over and above the normal cost of such forces if no action was taking place" was approximately five billion dollars in the fiscal year 1951/52, about 11 per cent of total United States expenditures for major national security programs that year.[17]

Right and wrong concepts of cost and gain can, however, be illustrated by either wartime or peacetime studies. For example, in a World War II study of alternative ways to destroy enemy shipping, the criterion adopted was the ratio of enemy ships sunk (the gain) to allied man-years of effort (the cost).[18] Now our concern in this section is not with the hazards of such a ratio test,[19] but rather with the nature of these concepts of gain and cost.

Neglect of higher level gain. First, "ships sunk" as a measure of gain may have been an unfortunate choice (whether made by the analysts or by "higher authority"), for shipping could be effectively destroyed by actions such as mine-laying without necessarily sinking many ships. The criterion adopted would have prejudiced the case against such measures.

Neglect of valuable inputs. Next, let us examine the costs of these ship-sinking operations. Costs are the consequences that have nega-

---

[17] *Mutual Security Act of 1952*, Hearings before the Committee on Foreign Affairs, House of Representatives, 82nd Congress, 2nd Session, U.S. Government Printing Office, Washington, D.C., 1952, p. 359.

[18] Kittel, p. 152.

[19] The operation that maximized the *ratio* of ships sunk to allied effort might be a trivial operation sinking one ship or a gigantic effort destroying vast quantities of shipping and requiring the bulk of our resources. There is little assurance that the operation picked solely on the basis of this *ratio* would contribute the most toward victory.

tive values, or in other words they are the sacrifices that have to be made in order to conduct the operation. In the above-mentioned study, man-years of effort—which included those used in construction of vessels and equipment, training, operations, and replacements—appear to be a somewhat dubious measure of these sacrifices. One reason is that man-years, while important in wartime (and in peacetime), were not the only items given up. Thus a method of destroying enemy shipping that used comparatively little manpower, even though it required extremely valuable equipment and skills, had a spurious advantage over a method that utilized relatively worthless equipment and much labor. In effect the test ignored inputs other than man-years as if they were free.

In extreme cases, this sort of procedure may be the correct one. Since the cost of one course of action is whatever has to be sacrificed, that cost depends upon what alternatives are genuinely possible. If, for example, the only courses of action that can be considered are different ways for unskilled laborers to use given equipment to carry out a specified task, the only input that has other uses is the labor. The analysis becomes a time-and-motion study, and a suitable test is the achievement of the specified task with the minimum expenditure of man-hours.

In general, however, the use of man-hours, a "critical material," or any other single input to represent cost is likely to be wrong. Other valuable inputs are usually involved. To ignore these other inputs is to pretend that their use involves no sacrifice, whatever the quantity employed. Another plausible procedure—putting a specific constraint on the amount of each input that is to be used— is in most cases equally misleading. Such a constraint pretends that we do not have the choice of acquiring extra amounts of the input. Sometimes the choices open to us are limited in this fashion, but placing specific constraints on all inputs usually shortens the list of alternatives that is truly admissible; hence it distorts the sacrifices entailed by taking the actions that are in fact examined.

What, then, is the right way to measure cost? The answer, in principle, is that the measures in any particular problem should approximate the value of the alternatives that must be sacrificed. In long-run problems (most development and many procurement choices) the almost unlimited possibilities of substitution in the economy make dollar costs—the dollars representing general resources—a satisfactory measure in most cases, and far superior to such practical alternatives as man-hours. Dollars do, even if imperfectly, take account of the value in other uses of different skills and of factors of production other than labor. In short-run and intermediate-run problems the difficulties are greater, and one must usually impose cost or resource constraints of several kinds. In the extreme case of a field commander who has to prepare for an imminent battle with what he has on hand, the amount of each specific resource (men, tanks, ammunition, and so on) he has is fixed,[20] and no more of any one can be secured at any price. In this case each resource must be taken as a constraint on his tactics. In less extreme cases some resources will be fixed and others variable —the latter frequently at "increasing costs" reflecting either higher incremental production costs in the short run or the withdrawal of the additional resources from increasingly valuable uses elsewhere.

The Navy, for example, may have a certain number of warships readily available for an operation in the Mediterranean (those on station there). In a very short-run problem, no more could be made available from anywhere. In an intermediate-run problem, additional ships could be obtained, but only by the very expensive method of "de-mothballing" or by transferring to the Mediterranean ships whose "outputs" are valuable in other areas (increasingly valuable the more are transferred). In a long-run problem, of course, additional ships could be procured for more dollars. Finding satisfactory cost measures and resource constraints in the intermediate-run problems will frequently tax the ingenuity of the analyst. He must try to avoid treating as free those resources that have value in other uses, or as fixed those resources that, at some cost, are variable. (Also, of course, he should avoid the opposite errors.) While perfection is unattainable, the avoidance of the grosser fallacies is not.

"Sunk" costs and salvage values. Consider once again the costs counted in the search for the best way to destroy enemy shipping. These costs included man-years of effort used in the construction of ships, equipment, and submarines—many of which were already built and on hand. Yet the sacrifice entailed by the use of existing equipment was really its value in other operations,[21] not the original or historical cost of constructing it. Only future sacrifices are relevant—not past. In an economic calculus "bygones are forever bygones."

---

[20] Though even here some of his resources may have value for later battles—a relevant alternative use.

[21] This may well be hard to measure quantitatively, but better the roughest approximation of the relevant magnitude than the most precise measure of the irrelevant.

This point was critical in the comparison that we made above of B-29 and X bombing systems, where the B-29's had already been produced and the X-bombers had not. Should the Air Force "be fair" to System X and insist upon costing each bomber from scratch? Never could considerations of equity be more misplaced. Any real cost associated with the production of the B-29's had already been incurred and is unaffected by what is done with them; if they have no alternative use and no scrap value, then the cost of incorporating them into the bombing system is zero. If they have a scrap value or a value in alternative uses that is sacrificed, then that value is the relevant cost. It is only the extra or incremental cost, not historical or "from scratch" cost, entailed by each alternative system that is relevant to the comparison. The analogy with a business firm's view of cost is complete: in deciding whether to replace an old machine with a new one, the production cost or purchase price of the new machine enters into the calculus, but only the scrap value (or alternative use value) of the old machine, however unfair this may appear to be to the new machine.[22] Considerations of fairness, which might be appropriate in courts of equity, are an undependable basis for choosing production methods or weapon systems.

Frequently in comparing the costs and gains from alternative weapon systems during some relevant period, it will be apparent that some of the systems will be worth more than others at the end of the period. An estimate of the worth of the system at the end of the period—its probable contribution to security in following periods—is commonly referred to as the system's "salvage value." If salvage values are substantial and vary significantly from system to system, they should be subtracted from system costs (or added to system gains). If these values are small or appear to be similar for all systems, of course they can be ignored.

Allocation of Joint Costs

In sub-optimizing, the analyst is frequently confronted with the necessity of computing the cost of X, when some or all of the costs of X are also costs of Y and Z. Suppose, for example, that the construction of an airbase is being considered for joint tenancy by three fighter squadrons and various Military Air Transport Service (MATS) facilities and services. Suppose that the total cost of the base is 100, of which 50 is the cost of basic or common facilities,

---

[22] For examples in which business management formally compares alternative policies in terms of incremental costs and gains, see Horace C. Levinson, "Experiences in Commercial Operations Research," *Journal of the Operations Research Society of America*, August 1953, pp. 220–239.

30 the cost of facilities required by MATS only (these might include, for example, costs of extending or strengthening runways for heavier MATS planes), and 20 the cost of facilities required by the fighter squadrons. If the base were used only by MATS its cost would be 80; if only by fighters, 70.

One way to approach the problem (it turns out to be a treacherous way) is to ask: How should the common costs be allocated among the various uses? One cabinet officer attempted to answer the question in this manner: "The Department believes that the costs of multiple-purpose . . . projects should be allocated on a basis which properly recognizes the added costs of including each separable function and a *fair* [23] share of the joint costs." [24] Again we have the unwarranted intrusion of ethical concepts into an economic calculus. In the Twentieth Century, it appears, we must be fair not only to people, but to weapon systems, machinery, and airbases.

If we keep firmly in mind the principle that only the *incremental* costs for which a system is responsible should be counted, problems of the type presented by the airbase offer no great difficulty. Of course which costs *are* incremental depends upon the breadth of context and the precise definition of the system. If the problem is whether to construct the airbase, and if so, whether for joint tenancy, for MATS only, or for the fighters only, we have to cost the base in three alternative systems. In the first (joint tenancy), the cost is 100; in the second (MATS only), 80; in the third (fighters only), 70. The base should be constructed if its value to MATS exceeds 80, if its value to the fighter command exceeds 70, *or if its value to both combined exceeds 100.* If its value to both combined exceeds 100, the base should be constructed for joint tenancy as long as its value to MATS exceeds 30 and its value to the fighter command 20. A businessman launching a multiproduct investment would think along precisely these same lines in maximizing his profits.[25] As long as the use values can be calculated,[26] the analyst can find a unique solution to his problem without allocating, "fairly" or otherwise, the common costs. The question simply doesn't arise.

[23] Italics ours.

[24] Former Secretary of Agriculture Brannan in *Study of Civil Works*, Part 2, Hearings before the Subcommittee to Study Civil Works of the Committee on Public Works, House of Representatives, 82nd Congress, 2nd Session, U.S. Government Printing Office, Washington, 1952, p. 198.

[25] George J. Stigler, *The Theory of Price*, Macmillan Co., New York, 1946, p. 307.

[26] Of course if the use values can't be calculated, the analyst may have a difficult problem on his hands and may have to be content with a "good" or "better" rather than a unique optimal solution. But allocating the common costs won't help him in this case. His fundamental difficulty is his inability to measure military worth.

If a formula for allocating total costs among uses is intended to show how costs respond when one use is eliminated, it can serve a very useful purpose; it is then an attempt to get better estimates of incremental costs. But a formula that is supposed to hand out "fair shares" of joint costs, the shares exactly exhausting the total, is not needed for good decisions and can lead to bad ones. Inability to allocate *all* costs meaningfully among joint products is often a fact of life, not a disgrace or a sign of laziness. The extra cost of adding on a function or a feature can be calculated, or the total cost of the combination of features—but not a meaningful total cost for one feature when undertaken jointly with the others.

APPROPRIATE CRITERIA

So much for potential errors in the devising of tests for preferred policies. What of a constructive nature can be said about the selection of criteria? Clearly, there is no all-purpose criterion, for the appropriate test depends upon what alternatives are open to the decision-maker, upon what aspects of the situation must be taken as given, and even upon what kind of measurements are feasible. Nonetheless a few general observations about suitable criterion-forms can be made.

Maximum Gains-Minus-Costs

If gains and costs can be measured in the same unit, then to maximize gains-minus-costs is certainly an acceptable criterion-form—the equivalent of making the most out of whatever actions can be taken. Suppose the possible courses of action are to put available resources to one of three uses, to be called A, B, and C. Now the gains that could have been obtained by using the resources in B and C are what have to be given up when we use the resources in A. These sacrifices are the *costs* of devoting the inputs to use A, the costs of obtaining the gains from A. When costs are viewed in this way (that is, as gains that must be given up), it is easy to see that maximizing gains-minus-costs is the same as maximizing total gains. If A yields 100 units of gain, B yields 75 units, and C 50 units, A is the use that maximizes gains-minus-costs (100 minus 75), and it is the use that yields the greatest total gain in the circumstances. Note again that this sort of test is possible only when gains and costs are commensurable. It can be used in the comparison of the actions of business firms and certain government measures but only exceptionally in the analysis of military activities.

Either Gain or Cost Fixed

In any situation there are constraints. The decision-maker can borrow additional funds only at higher rates of interest, only a limited number of practical actions are open to him, and there are only twenty-four hours in his day. In many analyses, one constraint is that a particular scale of gain or cost is fixed. This constraint may be imposed when gain and cost are commensurable, as in the case of a firm comparing different ways to use a given investment budget. And it should be imposed, as a rule, for analysis in which costs and gains are incommensurable. In the latter case, naturally it is impossible to maximize gains-minus-costs; what would be the meaning of the ability to destroy ten targets minus one billion dollars? The next-best procedure [27] is to "set" either the costs or gains, seeking the way to get the most for a given cost, or to achieve a specified objective at least cost.

These two criterion-forms are equivalent, if the size of either gain or cost is the same in the two tests. If the test of maximum gain for a $5 budget points to the policy which yields a gain of 10 units, then the test of minimum cost to achieve a fixed gain of 10 will point to the same policy—the one which achieves the gain of 10 at a cost of $5. The two tests also yield equivalent information if calculations are carried out for many different scales of cost and gain. The choice between these two criteria depends largely upon convenience of analysis and upon whether it is gain or cost that can be fixed with the greater degree of "correctness." In some cases it will be immediately apparent which way round the criterion should be stated and the analysis made. For example, the field commander (or his operations analyst), preparing for an imminent battle with a multiplicity of fixed specific resources, will obviously fix the level of resource constraints and attempt to maximize his chances of winning, rather than set some arbitrary chance of winning and calculate the combinations of resources necessary to achieve it. In other cases the preferred way round will not be apparent, and it may indeed make little difference from any point of view which is selected. For example, we can either choose some index of strategic capability we think we might be able to achieve, and calculate the necessary budget, or assume some practical budget and calculate the corresponding index of capability.

This leads us to the big question: How does one determine the right achievement or budget? If the achievement or budget is set

---

[27] Equivalent to maximizing gains-minus-costs in the special case where gains and costs are commensurate and the right level of gains or costs is fixed.

uncritically, the procedure degenerates into the "requirements approach." For example, it might be taken as given that we "need" in the case of a bombing system, a capability of destroying ten thousand targets; and the analysis would seek the cheapest way to achieve that "requirement." What can be done to improve upon this approach?

As a starter, several tasks or scales of effectiveness can be tried, and several budget-sizes can be assumed. If the same system is preferred for all tasks or budgets, that system is dominant. In the bombing-system example, the best bomber (though not the right scale or capability) is then determined.[28] If the same course of action is not dominant, the use of several tasks or budgets is nevertheless an essential step, because it provides vital information to the decision-maker.

Note, however, that the decision-maker, if he is making a quantitative decision or if the qualitative answers vary in the scale, must then himself select the scale of the task or budget. He is presumably helped in reaching this decision by the information about the cost of achieving different tasks or the potential achievements with different budgets. But he has to draw on further information in order to set the right task or budget. He has to ask what task or budget, as the case may be, is consistent with higher-level criteria. Is a capability of destroying ten thousand targets too much or too little in view of the over-all aims of the defense program?

Clearly the analyst will be more helpful if he can answer these questions than if he merely estimates the results for a variety of budgets or tasks. As a matter of fact, he must try to answer these questions approximately if he is even to hit upon a reasonable range of tasks or budgets. He cannot experiment with all possible scales of achievement or cost, as the computations would be too expensive and voluminous to provide any net assistance. Hence the analyst can and should do more than try several tasks or budgets (the procedure which was labeled a "starter"). He should make some inquiry into higher level criteria and into their relationship to possible lower level tests. He may even convert the analysis into a higher level sub-optimization. At *some* higher level, of course, the criterion must be taken as given—that is, to carry out the higher level task at minimum cost, or to get the most out of the higher level budget. But this acceptance of a task or budget as given at some high level is skies apart from setting "requirements" uncritically all the way up and down the line.

---

[28] This may be the decision-maker's current problem—*which* bomber to develop or procure. The decision regarding numbers may be made (and re-made) much later.

Criteria for Deterrence

Suppose that our problem (in 1959) is the design of a strategic offensive force for the middle 1960's to deter prospective enemies from attacking us. Deterrence of World War III is a frequently stated national objective. Our strategic offense force, while not the only force important for deterrence, is generally recognized to be the principal one. But "deterrence" is an elusive and qualitative concept, not too far removed from "military worth" itself. To calculate the relative contributions of alternative weapon systems, base locations, and strategies to deterrence, we require a much more precise and objective proximate criterion. What is a good criterion—one that avoids the pitfalls we have outlined and is consistent with the high level national objective of deterrence? Let us consider some possibilities (all of which have been used in similar studies), beginning with some that, while avoiding the crudest fallacies, are still clearly unsatisfactory.

a. *Numbers or weight of offensive weapons (for a given budget)*. Criteria of this general type are used in a surprisingly large number of cases by military correspondents, columnists, and other "experts" who should know better. Our deterrent force is held to be effective because we have more (or bigger) bombers than the Russians; or thought not to be effective because the Russians allegedly are building more long-range missiles than we. Little thought is required to dismiss such crude counting devices. What matters is not the number of aircraft or missiles on either side, or any other physical measure of their size, but in some sense the damage they are able to inflict. A missile that can carry a small bomb and deliver it within 10 miles of its target presents nothing like the deterrent threat of a missile that can carry a large bomb and deliver it within two miles.

b. *The number or value of enemy targets that can be destroyed (for a given budget)*. This is a criterion that makes a little more sense. It takes into account not only the numbers of our offense bombers and missiles, but also their operational effectiveness, the yield of the bombs they can carry, their ability to penetrate enemy defenses, and the accuracy with which their bombs can be delivered. It is still, of course, an ambiguous criterion, and requires more precise definition. For example, what target system—population, industry, or military bases—should we use to keep score on alternative United States strategic forces? In principle, the one whose prospective destruction would be most likely to deter the Russians from striking. If we are not sure which target system would have this characteristic, we might have to try several, to see whether the same strategic force performed best (or well) against all. Similarly, what kind of air defenses should we assume the Russians will have in the mid-sixties? Here we will almost certainly have to assume several kinds and quantities to test the alternative forces, giving the Russians some opportunity in each instance to adjust their defenses to the composition and basing of our force. But there remains another ambiguity in this criterion —one of crucial importance. Should we count the destruction potential of the entire force (the customary procedure) or the potential of that part of the force that survives an enemy attack? In other words, are we interested in a "strike-first" or a "strike-second" capability? Which is consistent with the national objective of deterrence?

To the extent that we are concerned with deterring a direct Russian assault on us, the essence of deterrence is a strike-second capability. The Russians will be deterred, not by the damage we can do if they refrain from attacking, but by the damage we can do if and after they attack. An American force that can make a devastating first strike but is easily destroyed on the ground is more likely to invite direct attack than to deter it. (It may, however, have some utility in deterring lesser aggression, for example, against third parties.)

c. *The value of enemy targets that can be destroyed (for a given budget) after an enemy first strike.* This is much closer to what we want. It requires us, in allocating our given budget, to reduce the vulnerability of our force whenever money spent on reducing vulnerability (say, on dispersal, on increased alertness, or on underground construction) will increase our strike-second capability more than the same money spent on additional bombers or missiles and the personnel to operate them. In general, this is what deterrence demands. This criterion is probably good enough to justify extensive quantitative comparisons of our capabilities with different kinds of weapons (bombers and missiles), different base systems (continental United States *versus* overseas *versus* on or under the seas; fixed *versus* mobile), and different modes of protection (such as ground alert, airborne alert, dispersal, and underground construction). In making the comparisons we must consider a range of possible Russian attacks, with special emphasis on those that look most dangerous to us, and are therefore most likely to be preferred by the Russians.

But we should be under no illusions that this good, workable criterion is good enough to yield definitive answers. It too ignores several vital elements of this exceedingly difficult and complex problem. For example, it ignores the danger that World War III might break out as the result of an accident or misunderstanding; it would do us little good to deter a rational enemy from attacking only to stumble into hostilities by accident (and some weapons and modes of operating them are more "accident prone" than others). This criterion partly neglects the objective of deterring "minor" aggressions, such as enemy attacks on United States or free-world positions in the NATO area or the Middle East. A strike-second capability would also have a strike-first potential, but it is not obvious that the measures that are optimal for deterring a direct attack are also optimal for deterring an indirect one. This test also ignores a good many interdependencies among different military capabilities: can our strategic offensive forces be designed in such a way as to contribute to our ability to fight limited, local wars or to facilitate the task of air defense? Can it even be assumed that the best force for deterring World War III is also best for fighting it—in the event that deterrence fails?

There is, moreover, the problem of what size the "given" budget should be. The optimal mix of weapons, bases, and protective measures may or may not be similar at different budget levels (this could be tested by trying a number of different levels). But even if the mixes are similar, it is tremendously important to get the absolute level somewhere near right—to have a deterrent force that is good enough, not merely the best achievable on a budget too low to provide deterrence, or one so good that we over-deter World War III and have little left over for other vital capabilities. The fixing of this level requires, of course, a higher level study that focuses on the size of the national security budget and its allocation among the major military claimants—for strategic offense, strategic defense, limited war, and cold war. While rigorous maximization at this level is silly, hard straight thinking in an economic framework can help, and can be helped by quantitative calculations. The size of the budget for the strategic offensive force must not be accepted *uncritically* as "given"; its determination is one of the most important national security decisions.

VII

INCOMMENSURABLES, UNCERTAINTY, AND THE ENEMY

We have seen that at best the problem of determining relevant, correct criteria is troublesome. The complications that are now to be introduced make the problem still less tractable, and indeed affect the very meaning that must be attached to the word criterion.

INCOMMENSURABLES: MEANING, EXAMPLES, AND TREATMENT

Incommensurables, as we use the term, are certain consequences of the alternatives compared—those consequences that cannot readily be translated into the common denominator or denominators that are being used.[1] Thus, if gains are being measured in dollars (as they ordinarily are in a business prcblem), the effects that cannot be measured in money by any objective and generally acceptable method are incommensurables. In principle, these effects are not different from any others. They may or may not be measurable in their own appropriate quantitative terms, in a manner helpful to the decision-maker. (If not, they are "intangible" as well as incommensurable.) Moreover, an *individual* can compare them subjectively with the other effects. Indeed, implicitly the decision-maker does translate these incommensurables into the common denominator when he makes a choice. But they cannot be expressed in terms of the principal or common unit in any *generally acceptable* manner. Of course if no single unit is used extensively enough to be regarded as a common denominator, there is no basis for distinguishing between effects that are commensurable and those that are not. This is often the case in consumers' research, which we regard as the most rudimentary, least ambitious type of economic calculus.

Incommensurable objectives and costs are likely to mar the neatness of any analysis, whether it pertains to problems of business,

---

[1] We saw in Chapter V that it is possible to carry out a quantitative analysis with two or more objectives or common denominators as long as we are satisfied with a set of "efficient" solutions rather than an optimal solution. We will usually assume in this section that a single common denominator is used in the explicit calculus. But see pp. 147–148, below.

the military, other parts of the government, or individual consumers. No matter how industriously the analyst works at devising a single quantitative test, considerations that must be measured in other units (if at all) will still be pertinent to the final decision. It is difficult to find problems of military choice in which such considerations do not have to be given serious attention. We have already seen[2] that in high level military problems incommensurables may severely restrict the usefulness of quantitative analysis. They are likely to dominate any analysis of the optimum size of military budget, or its division among the military services.

Even at relatively low levels incommensurables are likely to be too important to ignore; and in some low level problems they are dominant. In other words, there are military problems at all levels in which a definitive economic calculus cannot be made because of the multiplicity, incommensurability, or nonmeasurability of the objectives or costs.

Consider the importance of such effects in military problems where quantitative analysis can be helpful. In many such problems, cost can be fairly satisfactorily measured in dollars, and the objective as the degree of achievement of some military mission. But suppose that the preferred (that is, minimum-cost) method of achieving the objective is expected to involve the loss of more lives than some alternative method that is more expensive in dollars—even when the costs of recruiting and training the additional personnel required are included, as of course they should be, in the calculations. There are at least two reasons we might be concerned about this. First, the higher casualties *may* affect the morale of our forces and degrade their efficiency in a manner not taken into account in the calculations, making the efficiency of the first method less than it appears on paper. In *principle* such reactions should be taken into account explicitly; in practice, the intangible character of a factor like morale may make this impossible. Second, we are interested in lives for their own sake. We want to win a war with no more casualties than necessary. Fewness of casualties *per se* is an objective in planning any military operation, even if a subordinate one, that is not fully allowed for by including the resource cost of replacements.

Other examples of incommensurables frequently encountered in military problems include the whole gamut of other factors influencing morale; increased capability to fight a war of type B when the major consideration is the capability to fight war A;

---

[2] Chapter V.

impetus to specially promising state-of-the-art advances in choosing the next generation of some type of equipment; the maintenance of a "healthy" aircraft industry or broad mobilization base in selecting contractors (and therefore weapons); repercussions of all sorts on United States foreign relations and hence foreign policy (an extreme example is action that a potential enemy might regard as "provocative"); the effects of some methods of winning a war on the prospects for a tolerable and durable peace.

There are several ways of handling incommensurables in quantitative analysis. One way is just to ignore them: if there is no objective way to make them commensurate, have no truck with them at all. This method is not recommended; the significance of the numbers in an analysis depends upon the importance of effects not encompassed by those numbers, and the recognition of this dependence should not be left to chance. What effects are finally measured in terms of the common denominator must be made clear;[3] what major effects are *not* so measured, though perhaps initially considered as candidates for inclusion, should *at least* be described.

Sometimes it is suggested that, if the analyst works hard enough, *everything* can be put in terms of the common unit. For example, it has been suggested that the saving of a human life can be priced by consulting (1) the values implied by past decisions, (2) the average court award, or legal compensation, for accidental death, (3) the value of a person as productive capital in the economy—the sum of his expected future net earnings discounted to the present, or (4) the cost of saving a life by the cheapest alternative method. Now any of these devices may be useful in particular problems, but none provides a generally valid and appropriate measure of "the" value of human life, and the real meaning of some of them, in the absence of an organized market (like a slave market) to which governments and individuals adjust their actions, is hard to unravel.

It is possible, in some cases, to estimate the values attached to human lives implied in some World War II decisions—the amounts that were in effect traded for lives; but these values differed from one situation to the next and were not necessarily the values that should then have been, or ought now to be, assigned to lives. Court awards provide no generally appropriate value; they are notoriously influenced by adventitious factors. As for the value of a man as a productive resource, it does not reveal our valuation of a life

---

[3] For example, was the performance of the system degraded to reflect high casualty rates or not?

as such. Besides, the value of a person as peacetime productive capital is almost irrelevant in war, when we are willing to sacrifice peacetime values to achieve war objectives. The costs of saving additional lives by other methods may suggest a maximum value in some circumstances, or may be useful in suggesting a reallocation of budget among various policies designed to save lives. It is inefficient, in the technical sense, to spend $10 million per life saved in the design of a bomber system when we can save lives for a small fraction of this by, say, installing seat belts in ground vehicles. Of course people may attach different worths (apart from the diverse values of persons as productive resources) to different lives—those of children, older people, military personnel, civilians, volunteers, or persons who die in particularly brutal or painful ways. But this fact simply reinforces the original proposition, that there is no *generally acceptable* method of valuing human lives.

Suppose that the analyst's problem is the comparison of alternative strategic bombing systems that are to be maintained in a state-of-readiness to deter attack. Some of these systems will, it is estimated, result in higher casualties among crews if and when war occurs. The analyst includes in the cost of each system the expenses of recruiting and training the additional personnel required because of these higher casualties. He also estimates the degradation of each system resulting from high casualty rates. Should he *in addition* include some valuation of the crew lives lost as human lives in his cost calculations? Almost certainly not. In the first place, in an exchange of bombs, the crew lives lost will inevitably be swamped by the lives of civilians and allies lost to enemy attack: if our interest is in lives *per se,* it would be ludicrous to value the dozens in the air and neglect the millions on the ground.[4] In the second place, we are really interested not in the lives lost in any particular operation, but in the war. If we prejudice victory by selecting relatively inefficient (costly) systems because they save lives in a particular operation, we may well prolong the war and lose more lives before we win it, or even lose the war itself.

This is not to say that the attempt to "price" lives in all problems is unhelpful. Nor is it to say that it is hopeless to try to value other effects which appear at first glance to be incommensurables. In specific analyses ingenuity can often go a long way toward measuring such effects in terms of the common unit. We cannot say just

---

[4] The expected destruction of life and property on the ground incidental to the campaign is an important incommensurable which certainly should influence the choice of weapons or strategies.

where to draw the line between effects that should be measured in terms of the common denominator and those that should not. We can say, however, that insistence on the measurement of all effects in terms of a single common unit will not make for the most useful analysis. A Congressional committee was probably justified in concluding its review of an evaluation of federal resource development projects: "Some of the effort to place monetary values on indirect benefits is nothing short of ludicrous." [5]

The analyst is then frequently left, after the prudent exercise of his ingenuity in reducing everything to a common measure, with one or more important effects that defy reduction. We call them "incommensurables." What can the analyst do about them that will be helpful either to himself in making recommendations based on his study, or to the decision-makers directly?

(1) A device that is frequently useful where there are two or more objectives, each of which is measurable but with no common unit of measure, is the calculation of the set of efficient solutions as explained earlier in our chapter on "Efficiency in Military Decisions." This may be enough in itself to identify some system that is preferred to an existing or proposed system—a good practical aim for quantitative analysis. Furthermore, by limiting the alternatives, a calculation of this kind can facilitate the exercise of judgment in selecting, from among the efficient solutions, a near-optimal one.

(2) It will frequently be possible to calculate the value one must assign the incommensurable either in dollars or in terms of the unit measuring the major objective if he is to prefer System A over System B. Thus, the analyst can tell the decision-maker: Bombing System A will give you a target destruction potential of 1,000. If you are willing to take the diplomatic trouble and risks involved in various overseas countries, System B will provide the same potential for $1 billion less (or will increase the potential to 1,500 for the same budget). For System A to be preferred, one must put a value of at least $1 billion on the avoidance of the trouble and risk. Someone must exercise judgment in deciding, but it can be helpful in making this decision to know that $1 billion is at stake rather than $100 million or $10 billion. [6]

---

[5] It is ludicrous by our test of *general acceptability*. Each individual Congressman can decide, for example, how many millions the development of the Northwest region at the expense of the rest of the country is worth to him, but there is no reason to expect the valuations of Congressmen from Oregon and Oklahoma to coincide.

[6] If all the leading alternatives involve significant and different incommensurables, this device is not very useful. The situation would then be like that in which the little boy valued his puppy at $50,000 and, according to his story, sold it for that amount. How? By accepting a couple of $25,000 cats as payment.

The calculation of such break-even points or trade-offs is more difficult than, but far preferable to, the common practice of placing limiting constraints on the solution. For example, instead of trying to calculate the impact of casualty rates (through morale) on crew performance, a frequent practice is simply to rule out all solutions in which casualty rates exceed a certain arbitrary percentage. Or to take another example, some political problems of overseas basing can be swept under the rug, as far as the analysis is concerned, by simply declaring certain countries off-bounds, or by specifying in advance an "intercontinental" solution. Some such constraints on an analysis are necessary and justified. Limitations of time and cost alone prevent the consideration of every conceivable alternative and opportunity. But the selection of constraints must be made with care and discrimination and with knowledge of the havoc they can play with the analysis. Casually selected or arbitrary constraints can easily increase system cost or degrade system performance many-fold, and lead to solutions that would be unacceptable to the person who set the constraints in the first instance if he understood their implications.[7]

(3) In some cases where systems achieve incommensurable objectives, the analyst may be able to design another system which is better at achieving some things and as good, or almost as good, at achieving the others. Suppose for example that he is comparing the capability of a force based overseas in peacetime with that of a mobile force based in the Zone of the Interior (ZI). Suppose that quantitative analysis shows the ZI force to be markedly superior, but that the stationing of troops overseas is believed to be important for the maintenance or strengthening of our alliances. The analyst may be able to design and suggest a third solution, say, a rotation system, which has most of the advantages of the ZI based force without this incommensurable though important disadvantage. The rotation system may be almost as effective (for a given budget) as the ZI based force, and almost as acceptable to allies, while perhaps having some advantages (realistic practice in mobility) possessed by neither of the original alternatives.[8] In many cases the analyst's ingenuity may be more rewardingly exercised in trying to find ways of satisfying multiple objectives than in

---

[7] We know of studies in which an arbitrary limitation on casualties led to solutions in which, at the margin, $100 million was being spent to save a single life. Even if one regards a human life as "worth" this much, the same amount of money could be spent in ways to save many more.

[8] If the new system is better in *all* respects than any of the alternative systems it is said to be "dominant." Pure dominance is almost always unattainable, but it provides a goal for systems invention which may be approximated.

devising common measures for them. It can in fact be argued that the *chief* gain from systematic analysis is the stimulus that it provides for the invention of better systems.

(4) Finally, as a minimum, the incommensurables can be displayed and talked about. Quantitative or qualitative information about them may be helpful to decision-makers.[9] Although by definition they are not commensurable with the other costs and gains, clues to their impact can often be given. A very short essay on the possibilities of negotiating base rights in India might be sufficient to rule out certain alternatives that look attractive in the quantitative analysis. The annoyance to the population of sonic booms cannot be subtracted from fighter defense kill potential, but it will still be helpful to present estimates of the numbers of such booms over populated areas with different basing systems or training concepts. Such effects can be partially traced out, sometimes quantitatively, after the fashion of consumers' research, and presented in an exhibit that supplements the principal estimates. This can be helpful to the decision-maker in the same manner that consumers' research is helpful to the consumer.

UNCERTAINTY

The estimates of costs and gains considered so far are average, predicted, or "expected" outcomes. But we know in advance that, for all sorts of reasons, these amounts may be off the mark. Actual costs of development or production of new weapons never precisely coincide with advance estimates and sometimes differ from them by factors of two to twenty. Times of availability are also very hard to estimate accurately, and as a rule greater uncertainty attaches to estimates of effects or gains than to estimates of cost and availability. The enemy never does what we expect; indeed, he always has greater or less capability than we expect. Every war is full of surprise outcomes. Now while uncertainties of these sorts are pervasive, they are likely to affect some systems in a comparison more than others. The availability of the overseas base system is more uncertain than that of the ZI base system. We can predict the performance of a weapon of which we have a prototype with much greater confidence than the performance of a rival weapon on the drawing board. As a consequence, Systems A and B may offer identical predicted outcomes, yet differ greatly with respect to other possible outcomes. These differences may be a matter of some moment if, say, A's possible results are all thought to be

---

[9] For pure "intangibles" the information would have to be qualitative.

nearly the same as predicted, but B's range from fabulous success to utter disaster. Yet while such differences in the pattern of uncertainty—or, more precisely, in the "frequency distribution of outcomes"—are matters of great concern, it is ordinarily impossible to attach a value or price to them. A price, that is, which would have any *general* acceptability. In some situations and for some persons, to reduce the chance of a bad outcome is worth a great deal. In other situations or for other persons, even a small chance of an extremely favorable outcome carries a high premium.

Types of Uncertainty

It may help to put this complication in proper perspective if we see how pervasive uncertainty is. Perhaps this will also help show that uncertainty is inherent in the nature of things and is not necessarily evidence of lazy or careless estimation. One can sympathize with the general who shouts at his analyst: "Give me a number, not a range": unique numbers are easier to work with and to think about than ranges or probability distributions. But he is probably asking his analyst to falsify the real world in a manner that will make it impossible for him, as a commander, to make good decisions.

Uncertainty about planning and cost factors. Every model uses as inputs certain relations between its elements which are known in the military as "planning factors"—for example, the number of miles a unit can march or drive in a day over specified terrain; the radius of destruction of atomic (or other) weapons of specified power against specified objects; the circular probable error (CEP)[10] of bombing with a given bombsight as a function of, say, speed and altitude; the average number of hours a cargo plane can be used per day. It is apparent that we may attempt from time to time to determine some planning factor, for example, CEP, as a function of bomber speed and altitude, or of other parts of the system. In that case the particular planning factor would be a variable, not a given, in the analysis. But in any particular analysis many planning factors must simply be taken as given; there is never time to calculate everything from scratch. So they are borrowed from other analyses of varying quality, from books of official planning factors assembled and published by the military Services, or from other sources.

This procedure may conceal uncertainties that arise for two reasons: first, the quality of the sources from which the factors

---

[10] The radius of the circle within which half the bombs will fall.

are borrowed varies from fair to bad to biased (they have seldom
been estimated with the particular requirements of this analysis
in mind) ; and second, they are almost invariably "numbers"
rather than ranges or probability distributions, suppressing significant variations in the behavior of the relations in the real
world.[11] Divisions do not always march the same number of miles
in a day, even over "specified" terrain, for any of a thousand
reasons. Even if one has the right *average* value of CEP (almost
certainly an unwarranted assumption), it will be wrong for any
particular strike.

Factors used to estimate costs of specified military forces and
weapons systems are always uncertain, especially when they relate
to the distant future. Cost estimating is an approximate art even
in the most well-run businesses. Wages and material prices are
subject to unforeseeable fluctuations. More important, it is impossible to predict accurately how many men, what kinds of material, and how much time will have to be paid for. On production
items the range of error in cost estimates may be only 10 per cent
or so—perhaps too small to be worth bothering about in view of
other uncertainties inherent in the analysis. But the actual costs
of developing, producing, and operating complete weapon systems
have frequently exceeded cost estimates made prior to development by factors of ten or more, largely because of the technological uncertainty that existed when the costs were estimated. Necessary modifications that double system cost must be regarded as
fairly normal.

Uncertainty about strategic context. Every war, whether all-
out, limited, or cold, is fought in some "strategic context"—at a
certain time and place, with certain enemies and allies, to achieve
certain political objectives. Since the ranking of alternative forces
or weapon systems may depend decisively upon the strategic context, the analyst must make assumptions about it.

In some circumstances (during a war, or in planning for an
imminent outbreak of war at a particular place against a known
enemy), there may be a fairly obvious "best" set of assumptions
to make about the strategic context. Analysts working on North
Atlantic convoy problems during World War II knew where and
when the war was occurring, who the enemy was, who our allies
were, the constraints under which both sides were operating, and
the general political objectives and grand strategy of our side.

---

[11] We are arguing *not* that the use of average values is necessarily wrong, but that the uncertainty this covers up should be recognized.

But when the problem is to choose military forces in peacetime that will give us a capability of fighting future wars, good assumptions about the strategic context may be far from obvious.

Consider the questions that have to be answered about the strategic context in choosing among alternative future bombing systems. First, when will war occur? System A may seem far preferable if the threat is in 1960, system B if the date is 1965. Who will be our enemies and allies? The answer is always less obvious than it seems—if a few years are to elapse (how many could have guessed in 1942, or even in 1947, that Germany and Japan would be among our most valued allies in 1957?). Will our allies make overseas bases available for our bombers, or will they yield to "atomic blackmail"? Will the war be general or local, all-out or limited? What constraints will be imposed—say territorially, as in Korea, or on the use of nuclear weapons? It is apparent that the "best" bombing force will depend critically upon answers to questions of this kind.[12] And, curiously but perhaps fortunately, there is no *authoritative* way for the analyst to get the right answers— or any answers. Of course no single military service can provide answers; decisions about war and peace (and kind of war) are made at the highest level of the government—our own and the enemy's. And just as no Congress can make decisions binding our future Congresses, neither can a President or Joint Chiefs of Staff effectively bind a future President or Joint Chiefs.[13] The analyst must face up to gross uncertainties of this strategic sort, and his recommendations may well depend upon the way he does so.

Technological uncertainty. Technological uncertainty may occasionally be serious in the analysis of current operational problems, but as we try to peer further and further into the future it becomes more and more important and can, indeed, dominate the analysis. Technological uncertainty is the central problem in research and development decisions. There is always some technological uncertainty connected with research and development; otherwise it would not be research and development but production. But because of the interdependence of all factors in an analysis, this kind of uncertainty may influence analyses that are not focused on research and development.

---

[12] It is also apparent that the strategic context will in turn be affected by the forces and weapon systems we choose. Enemies will attempt to force us into the kind of engagements for which we are not prepared. If we prepare only for hot wars, they may choose to defeat us in cold ones.

[13] Except in a negative way. If certain forces having long lead times have not been provided, future Joint Chiefs will not be able to fight certain kinds of wars in certain ways—even if one of them then appears to be in the nation's interest.

For example, uncertainty regarding the A-bomb importantly (and properly) influenced our preparations for the final stages of our campaign against Japan in World War II. Uncertainty about the H-bomb—whether it would work, how soon, and how cheaply —affected not only the nuclear and missile development programs [14] but our strategic concepts and plans for future military forces of all types. Uncertainty about the progress of various missile programs is now (1959) grossly influencing not only missile development but bomb development, aircraft development, aircraft procurement, the composition of our air defense forces, and plans for civil defense. Expert guesses about the dates of operational readiness of important missile systems vary by as much as a decade: no one can be sure which guess is right.

Uncertainty about the enemy and his reactions. Two kinds of uncertainty stem from the fact that the object of military forces is to oppose other military forces—those of enemy (or potentially enemy) countries. A military tactic, strategy, force, or development program is never good-in-itself, but only good-in-relation-to the tactics, strategy, forces, and future weapon systems of an enemy.

First, our factual "intelligence" about an enemy is always less than perfect, and when the enemy country is a dictatorship that ruthlessly and efficiently suppresses information and restricts travel, our ignorance of its military capabilities may be gross. The practice of military intelligence agencies of presenting numbers ("best guesses") rather than ranges in their estimates obscures but does nothing to remedy the incompleteness and unreliability of most of the information on which the estimates are based. As is characteristic of uncertainty, the probable errors of intelligence estimates increase as we look further into the future. How can *we* predict when a Russian missile system will be ready when we know that the Russians, with far more knowledge of their program than we have, cannot make such a prediction with any accuracy themselves? It is unfortunate that our choice of weapon systems usually depends as critically upon enemy parameters as upon our own.

Second, and even more fundamental than our ignorance of his capabilities, is our ignorance of the enemy's "intentions" (in the vocabulary of the intelligence agencies) or "strategy" (in the language of the theory of games). Military forces are used, wars

---

[14] It is widely reported that the intercontinental ballistic missile development program suffered from lack of support in the early years because the guidance problems seemed so intractable. Then the unexpected development of the H-bomb made even very inaccurate ICBM's useful.

are fought, against human beings exercising human intelligence. The best way for us to fight a war, or to prepare to fight one, is likely to depend decisively upon decisions that have been or will be made in, for example, the Kremlin. But no one has ever devised a good method of predicting the decisions of other human beings —even of human beings with whose psychological conditioning and drives we are fairly familiar. With what confidence can we expect the men in the Kremlin to be "deterred" by promises of "massive retaliation"? In what circumstances would they, or anyone else, start a thermonuclear war? What kinds of limitations (for example, territorial or in the use of nuclear weapons) might we be able to impose upon them in limited wars? What are their territorial targets likely to be in cold and limited wars? If they start a war, will they rely on mass or surprise attack (our "best" defense is likely to be very different in the two cases)?

It is easy to spend billions preparing for a kind of war or strategy that the enemy would never choose. Some individuals have special insight into the behavior of the Russian (and other) élites, but it is difficult enough to tell in advance which ones really have insight and which merely have confidence—let alone to assess the confidence that we can place in their predictions.

Statistical uncertainty. Finally, there is "statistical" uncertainty, the uncertainty resulting from the *chance* element in recurring events. This is the kind of uncertainty that would persist even if we could predict enemy strategies and the central values of all important parameters. We know that if we flip a penny a thousand times, it will come down "heads" approximately half the time; but that if we flip it only ten, the proportion of heads may be much higher or much lower. Similarly, we may have a radar sensing system that we expect to identify enemy planes 90 per cent of the time; it will still be possible for the planes to slip through undetected on the one day that counts. In most long-range problems, statistical uncertainties are the least of our worries; they are swamped by uncertainties regarding central values and states of the world. In some problems, however, we cannot rely exclusively on average or expected values.

The Treatment of Uncertainty

What can the analyst do to take account of the proliferation of uncertainties resulting from our ignorance of the future? As with incommensurables, the most important advice is: Don't ignore them.[15] To base an analysis and decision on some single set of best guesses could be disastrous. For example, suppose that there is uncertainty about ten factors (such as, will overseas bases be available? Will the enemy have interceptors effective at 60,000 feet?) and we make a best guess on all ten. If the probability that each best guess is right is 60 per cent (a very high batting average for best guesses from most sources), the probability that *all ten* are right is one-half of one per cent. If we confined the analysis to this best-guess case, we would be ignoring a set of futures with a 99.5 per cent probability of occurring.

So we must design the analysis to reflect the major uncertainties, and this usually means computing results for a number (sometimes a large number) of contingencies. If overseas bases may or may not be available, and some of our systems depend upon them more than others, we must test the systems assuming we have them, and again assuming we do not. If future missile CEP's (that is, accuracies) are grossly uncertain, we must make the computations with at least a high and a low value, and possibly one or two intermediate ones. If our strategic bombers may be required in local wars in the Middle East or Far East as well as for general war, we must test them in all theaters and circumstances that appear likely and important.

The trouble with computing "all interesting contingencies" is a practical one. The number of cases to analyze and compute increases as the power of the factors that are permitted to vary.[16] Unless discretion is used in restricting the cases to combinations that are really significant, we are likely to formulate a problem that is too big to solve—or at least too costly or time consuming to be worth solving. Developments in high-speed electronic computers in recent years are making it possible to compute solutions to more and more complex problems. Nevertheless it is still necessary to cut problems down to manageable size on computational grounds alone, and usually far more important is the effort required on the part of the analyst to assemble the data and structure the models for each of numerous cases. Testing systems in a different kind of war or even a different theater may double the

---

[15] Ignoring uncertainties is a chronic disease of military planners and analysts. There is a great temptation and frequently great pressure to use official planning factors, official intelligence estimates, and the best guesses of higher military authorities.

[16] As noted earlier, if there are two uncertain factors (say, kind of war and CEP) and each is permitted to take four values, the number of cases is only 4^2 or 16. But if ten uncertain factors are permitted to take four values each, the number of cases soars to 4^{10}, which is over 1,000,000.

work of analysis—and therefore either the manpower or the time required to complete the study.

So the practical problem is to design the analysis to reflect the truly significant contingencies but, in order to keep it manageable, only these. This requires practical judgment of a high order; the analyst must know a great deal about his problem—in effect, what is likely to be important and what unimportant in influencing the solution—before he structures it. Sometimes he can cut down on the number of cases that have to be computed by constructing an *a fortiori* argument; that is, if he is lucky as well as skillful, he may be able to show that his preferred system is best (or better than some alternative) when he makes unfavorable assumptions regarding many of the uncertainties, and therefore does not have to bother with computations involving favorable assumptions. But at best he will have to show how things can be expected to turn out under a number of different future circumstances, and usually one of his systems will look best in some contingencies, another in others. How does the analyst then choose the preferred system? What decision does he recommend?

Making Decisions in the Face of Uncertainty

Suppose that we are considering the choice of an anti-ICBM system and are weighing the relative merits of three proposals—1, 2 and 3—in what appear to be the three most interesting contingencies—A, B and C (see below). Contingency A is very favorable to the United States—perhaps the contingency in which we

Illustrative Payoff Matrix

System	Contingency		
	A	B	C
1	100	20	0
2	60	40	0
3	20	10	10

strike first against the enemy's offensive force, so that its attack on us is disrupted and our defenses against it are fully alerted. Contingency B is much less favorable; here the enemy starts with a massive, coordinated attack. Finally, C is a catastrophic contingency—one, say, in which the enemy discovers a way to make a simultaneous attack without any warning against all our defended targets. We "score" the three systems for performance in each contingency by the utility or worth of what is left—100 representing everything, and zero representing nothing.

System 1 is obviously a fair-weather system, which works splendidly if everything is just right, but is almost worthless when the going is rough. In particular, it is easily saturated. System 2, on the other hand, while leaky, is not rate-of-fire limited, and does almost as well (or badly) in case B as in case A. Both 1 and 2 are useless against a C attack. System 3 is a desperate sort of system, which uses all the funds available for burrowing underground. In consequence, even the light attack assumed in A practically destroys the country, while even the heavy, warningless attack of C leaves a little to rise from the ashes.

Which of these three systems do we choose if our choice really is restricted to these three? There is no completely satisfactory and generally accepted theory either of how people *do* make such choices or of how they *should* make such choices.

Maximize expected value. If it is possible to estimate the utilities (that is, the worths) of the various outcomes (as we assumed in the above table), and *if* we can also, at least roughly, calculate the probability of each contingency, it would appear reasonable to choose that course of action or system that maximized expected utility.[17] Thus, in our example, if we attached equal probability to the three contingencies, we should choose system 1. If we believed B to be four times as likely as A, and C to be wholly unlikely, we should choose system 2.

This principle is, within limits, a valid and useful guide in some situations. While attaching utilities and probabilities to outcomes is difficult, we can frequently do it in a rough fashion—yet well enough to narrow the field of choice to good alternatives. Of course there may not be agreement about the utilities and probabilities of the various outcomes. The customer may insist that the analyst let him make his own estimates and draw his own conclusion. But the theory directs our attention to the relevant questions.

Minimax. There is, however, an important circumstance in which it is inappropriate to ask questions about the probability of outcomes. If the contingency depends not upon "nature" or luck but upon the choice of a malevolent enemy, we are not concerned with probabilities. The rational man, it is argued, should assume that the enemy will do his worst and therefore choose the system

[17] L. J. Savage, *The Foundations of Statistics*, John Wiley and Sons, New York, 1954, pp. 1–104 (chapters 1–5).

that will minimize the maximum (worst) the enemy can do.[18] The shorthand expression "minimax" can be used to refer to this strategy. If in our example we assume that the enemy can choose the contingency, it appears that he would choose C, and that the "best" we can do in consequence is to opt for system 3 and guarantee ourselves a survival utility of 10.

There is much in this view that is relevant and important in the analysis of military problems. Where the enemy controls the choice, it is not meaningful to compute probabilities. We should focus our attention instead, as this view does, on the freedom of the enemy to choose, and the likelihood that he will choose something pretty unpleasant, if not the worst. Moreover, the enemy's worst —or "reasonable" worst—is a case on which the analyst should concentrate—not exclusively but heavily. Wishful or lazy thinking too often causes the analyst to dwell on threats that he thinks we can counter, rather than the more dangerous ones that will appeal to the enemy.

Nevertheless, these concepts and rules borrowed from game theory must be applied to actual military problems with a good deal of discretion. War, especially of the modern nuclear variety, is not a two-person zero-sum game; that is, a game in which only two players are involved, the gain of one being exactly equal to the loss of the other. And it is only in such a two-person zero-sum game that even a very intelligent enemy can "reasonably" be expected to choose the course that is worst for us. In non-zero-sum games, what is best for the enemy is not necessarily what is worst for us. To take an extreme case (although not very extreme any longer): if the enemy has an end-of-the-world machine, the worst thing he can do to us is to use it, but this also happens to be the worst—not the best—from his point of view too. We would be foolish to adapt our whole strategy to this contingency, which will have little appeal to him.

In much less extreme cases minimax (as we are using this term) is unduly conservative. If we choose our systems solely for their ability to shore up our defense in the worst case, (a) we may not be able to shore it up enough to matter much (as in contingency C in the example), and (b) we may be sacrificing oppor-

---

[18] The term "minimax" and the general flavor of this argument are borrowed from the theory of games, but we are *not* using the term minimax in the technical sense in which it is used in the theory of games. We are thinking of situations in which we have to choose a system in advance, and the enemy knows of our choice. The classical work on games is John von Neumann and Oskar Morgenstern, *Theory of Games and Economic Behavior*, Princeton University Press, Princeton, N.J., 1944 (2d ed., 1947). For a brief and highly readable volume, see J. D. Williams, *The Compleat Strategyst*, McGraw-Hill Book Co., Inc., New York, 1954.

tunities for major improvements in our capabilities to deal with other contingencies that have some substantial likelihood of occurring. For even if the situation approximates a two-person zero-sum game, the enemy may not act as game theory assumes. A minimax solution is motivated by the idea that the enemy is completely rational, perfectly intelligent, can read minds, never makes mistakes, and so on. Enemies, especially enemy countries, are seldom like that. They are run by bureaucracies that make mistakes like our own. Their intelligence has blind spots. Their leaders are full of prejudices. There is a vast amount of irrational inertia in the determination of policy. Probably no great military leader in history except the conservative Ulysses S. Grant ever worked on minimax assumptions, and Grant had such superiority in resources that he could afford to be (it made sense for him to be) conservative. Great profit can be derived in many circumstances from anticipating enemy mistakes and being prepared to take advantage of them. Minimax forfeits such opportunities.

Any departure from the two-person zero-sum assumptions accentuates the conservative bias of the solution. The contingencies in this kind of analysis are seldom under the complete control of the enemy. In our example the enemy can obviously influence who strikes first, but he can no more decide it than we can (he can decide to strike first, but that is a different matter: we may learn of the decision and preempt him). Nor can the enemy simply will the massive, simultaneous warningless strike that we feared could be so devastating in contingency C. He can will a research and development program in the hope that such a capability will prove feasible; but nature will determine whether the program is a success. In mixed cases of this sort, and *a fortiori* where there is no game at all (that is, where the only "other player" is "nature," as when the uncertainty is statistical), the bias of a solution that assumes a malevolent intelligence at work may be extreme.[19]

So we are left with no generally satisfactory answer. *If* we can estimate the probabilities and the utilities of outcomes even roughly, as sometimes in "playing against nature," expected value seems satisfactory; but if we have to use physical outcomes in lieu of their utilities, or are confronted by an intelligent enemy, we must beware of a bias toward recklessness in applying this technique. *If* circumstances approximate those assumed in the two-

---

[19] Some find more intuitive appeal in a variant of the minimax solution variously called minimizing the maximum "regret" or "loss." It at least gives less conservative solutions in many instances (including our example, where it would opt, not too convincingly, for system 1!). See L. J. Savage, pp. 163–171.

person zero-sum game, we can compute the minimax solution, keeping in mind its conservative bias.[20]

This reference to conservative and reckless biases in various solutions provides some clue to the basic difficulty in generalizing about the behavior of rational men in the face of uncertainty. For while rational men do act in the face of uncertainty, they act differently. There are audacious commanders like Napoleon, and conservative ones like Grant—both successful in the right circumstances. Different people simply take different views of risks—in their own lives and as decision-makers for the nation. Some "insure" and others "gamble." It is therefore most important, whether the analyst calculates a general solution or not, that he present responsible decision-makers with the kind of information provided in the example on p. 136, and let them use their own risk-preferences in making the final choice. The risk-preferences of responsible decision-makers may be very different from those of the analyst.

Designing for Contingencies

But the most important part of the answer to the pervasive uncertainty facing the analyst or the military planner is not greater subtlety in making difficult choices, but *the design of systems to cope with more of the critical contingencies.*[21] A situation like that represented in our example, where each of three proposed systems is good in one contingency and bad in the others, covering only one best, should be a challenge to the analyst and the decision-maker to invent a better system—one that looks good in more than one contingency. Truly dominant systems—those that are better in all circumstances—are hard to find, and require luck, too, but it is rare that a resourceful analyst cannot get closer to dominance than the systems in the example.

The first thing to try in designing a system capable of coping with several contingencies is to mix ideas, concepts, or hardware from the systems designed for each contingency. Mixed systems usually involve extra costs, which can be estimated, but are frequently worth it (we have rarely relied on pure weapon systems). Multiplicity is more frequently justified in development than in procurement and operations (both because uncertainties are greater at the development stage and because the extra costs of mixing or "duplicating" are less). In other cases mere mixing may

---

[20] In some circumstances, e.g., if the intelligent opposition aspect is unimportant but we cannot estimate probabilities, we may want to minimize the maximum regret.

[21] In this respect the problem of dealing with uncertainty is like that of dealing with incommensurables.

be an inadequate or inferior solution. It may be better, for example, to redesign the hardware to serve more than one purpose, combining some of the characteristics of the special purpose hardware previously compared. Or drastic redesign of operational concepts, or the invention of new ones, may be indicated. Protection against warningless attack, for example, may be better secured by concealing some of our targets, or making them mobile, than by burrowing underground. Or there may be superior concepts for burrowing. Whatever the device, the analyst's responsibility is to come up if he can with a system that has no critical soft spots and that still looks very good in the favorable contingencies.

Sometimes the redesign of systems will have a different objective from dominance. Suppose that an apparently dominant system—one that is best against some contingencies and as good as its rivals against the others—is still alarmingly ineffective in the most probable situation. Suppose, in other words, that it is still only the best of a bad lot as far as the principal contingency is concerned. We may wish in this instance to invent a system that is better against this contingency even if it is worse in other less probable situations.

Thus one reason for inventing new alternatives is to find a dominant one, enabling us to choose regardless of the probabilities that particular contingencies will occur. Another reason may be to improve upon the present poor set of alternatives.

Hedging and Insurance

Despite the ingenuity of the analyst, there may remain in an otherwise preferred system some chance of an extremely unfavorable outcome. Sometimes the best he can do (a very useful best) is to calculate the least-cost method of providing some hedge or insurance (complete or more usually partial) against this contingency. This is necessary information for a rational decision whether or not the hedge is worth making.

Hedging in busines operations is frequently a highly organized activity supporting special markets. Hedging is also a typical reaction to uncertainty by individuals. A family planning an automobile trip may buy a new set of tires even though it estimates the chance of a blowout as less than 50 percent. A hedge against even a slight possibility of a fatal accident (or major inconvenience) may be worth the price. Any purchase of insurance is an example of hedging.

The military does not have a futures market in which it can hedge, nor can it eliminate uncertainty by the purchase of insurance from commercial companies. But there are innumerable ways in which it can hedge against loss or disaster, and analysis can define and cost them. Mixed systems can be regarded as one kind of hedge; general purpose systems, another. A hedge against ECM (electronic counter-measures) may be some kind of electronic *counter* counter-measure. The extra cost can be computed in money and resources, or in the degradation of performance in more favorable contingencies.

It is not necessary that the hedge be complete and certain in its operation. We may, indeed, be able to deter the enemy from taking certain actions by what are called "low-confidence" measures—measures with only a moderate (50 percent or less) chance of succeeding. If the enemy action is one that he would not undertake without high confidence, we can sometimes deny him this confidence by a cheap low-confidence measure of our own (if its chances of success are only 30 percent, the enemy's cannot be higher than 70 percent). There are occasions when intermittent patrols make sense—for the military as well as for the police. Fair-weather fighters may be useful even in defense: the enemy may be unable to plan an attack for a time when bad weather is predicted, or the weather may turn out to be good in spite of the predictions of enemy weather forecasters. Low-confidence measures are no general substitute for high-confidence measures, but they are useful hedges in some circumstances—when they are cheap and we have reason to think that the enemy is likely to insist on high confidence from his standpoint.

Reducing Uncertainty

Sometimes an important, or even the most important, conclusion of the analyst is that measures should be taken to reduce some of the uncertainties and that some decisions should be postponed until more is known with confidence.

Knowing when to make decisions may be as important as knowing what decision to make. The costs and dangers of "indecisiveness," of postponing decisions too long, are obvious and widely appreciated. But there are also costs and dangers in making decisions on the basis of incomplete and uncertain information. In recent years we have wasted billions by making premature decisions to produce operational equipment with trivial improvements in capability, when what was needed was a broad program of research and development to buy knowledge of markedly improved hardware. We simply did not know how to design equipment with a capability that would be worth the high costs.

So if the question is what to procure, the best answer may be: nothing but a research and development program, or a test program, at this stage. Do not try to decide until you know more, until you know enough about costs and performance to make useful cost-effectiveness studies. This does not mean doing nothing. One important job of the analyst is to spot the critical areas in which more knowledge is needed, and to devise proposals for getting it.

And if the question is what to develop, the answer may well be in terms of a strategy for buying information rather than a detailed blueprint of some futuristic operational weapon. With technological uncertainty layered on top of strategic uncertainty, it is rarely possible to specify an advanced weapon system far in advance and schedule a development program for it. And it may be a mistake to try. The first step is to determine the critical uncertainties and to undertake a research and development program to resolve them. Only then will we be in a position to schedule the next steps.

DEALING WITH THE ENEMY

As we have seen, many of the crucial uncertainties in any military analysis stem from our ignorance of the enemy and his intentions. Analysts make two very common mistakes in dealing with the enemy—the first is to regard him as stupid, inflexible, and devoid of initiative; the second is to attribute to him diabolical cunning, unlimited flexibility, and boundless initiative. In the cliché of the Pentagon, we insist on picturing him as either 2 feet tall or 10 feet tall. The first kind of blunder is the more frequent, but either one can ruin an otherwise excellent analysis.

How much capability and flexibility, for example, should we attribute to the Soviet Union? We have a fairly firm knowledge of her current industrial capacity and output and of her industrial growth rates. But how many ICBM's, or atomic submarines, or nuclear weapons, or defense radars can we expect them to have by 196–? These are important questions. The design, procurement, and deployment of our own weapons are obviously sensitive to the answers.

The first thing to realize is that we do not and cannot know the answers with certainty. No one can. The Russians do not know themselves. We cannot answer similar questions about our own strength in the 1960's. We should not take the best guesses of the intelligence community as gospel. The best guesses may be wrong, and even if right today, the Russian leaders can change their plans and make them wrong tomorrow. Another common error is to assume that the Russians will put all their potential for expansion into the one capability (say, atomic submarines) that happens to be critical to our analysis. The best thing we can do is to project Russian industrial capacity and the Russian military budget—with margins of error—and then face up to the Russian allocation problem in much the same way we face up to our own.

The recognition of the extreme importance of enemy intentions and enemy reactions in most military problems has led to much work in recent years on techniques to improve our ability to predict enemy reactions (that is, reduce the uncertainty from this source) and to deal with them more effectively. The most important of these are (a) game theory, and (b) "gaming"—sometimes called "war gaming" or "operational gaming."

(a) Game theory has contributed a conceptual framework for thinking about situations of conflict that has proved extremely valuable in many problems. The preceding discussion would have been impossible without constant use of concepts derived from the theory of games—like "strategy," "solution," "dominance," and "minimax." Game theory has been effectively applied to a number of tactical problems in which a conflict or "game" occurs repeatedly (as in the case of duels between fighter aircraft). It has also provided useful insights that have aided in the solution of more complex problems. But for broader military problems, formal game theory solutions have two serious deficiencies. First, most military problems are too complex to permit of practical game theory solution (even simple games like checkers are too complex for practical solution by the theory). Second, and more fundamentally, as we have seen, wars are not two-person zero-sum games—and little progress has been made in solving other kinds of games. Two-person means that there are only two sides, each with a consistent and unambiguous set of values: there is no room for "third forces" or for imperfect and shifting coalitions. Zero-sum means that the gain of one side corresponds exactly to the loss of the other; each side is playing the same game with the same rules and the same understanding of the scoring. But in war there may be no "victor"; the total losses may far exceed the total gains; the two sides may fight for objectives that are qualitatively different, not mere mirror images of each other. When the game theory solution is computed for a problem in which the circumstances do not correspond to the two-person zero-sum assumptions, its relevance depends more upon its intuitive appeal to "rational" men than on the rigorous proofs of the theory. The solution is likely, as we have seen, to be an unduly conservative one.

Game theorists have probably concentrated too much, however, on *solving* games. More emphasis should be placed, not on finding formal solutions, but on simply exploring and studying game situations—particularly, of course, those pertaining to non-zero-sum games.[22] New variants on these actions, possible gambits in tacit bargaining, the manner in which specific steps do influence payoffs, and the probable enemy reactions to specific policies—all these matters deserve intensive study, and game theory is one framework for studying them.

(b) Another means of exploring such questions is experimentation with various gaming techniques. Gaming has almost nothing in common with game theory, which it long antedates. Gaming is an exercise engaged in by human beings (individuals or teams) on two (or occasionally more) "sides"; whereas game theory has so far been a branch of mathematics. Gaming is an extremely flexible device, and can take numerous very dissimilar forms. There are war games that allow great freedom to the participants in making moves, and others that are highly "structured," with rules almost as precise as those of chess.

War games have long been used by military staffs, and were perhaps most highly developed in the nineteenth century by the German General Staff (*Kriegsspiel*). They have been used by the military, however, primarily as training devices, to teach junior officers principles that others have previously learned in actual combat. The possibility of solving problems of strategy by gaming has been considered by military authorities, but usually dismissed as unpromising. Not only is it difficult to reproduce reality adequately on a sand table, but the time and manpower required for a single play of an elaborate war game preclude the numerous plays that are needed to test out several strategies on both sides in various contingencies—the sort of test that could point the way to optimal, or at least good, strategies for blue.[23]

Recent developments have concentrated on speeding up play, a necessary condition for the effective use of gaming as a problem solving device. High-speed computers have been used both to assist players in making moves and to help the umpires trace the consequences of moves.

There is little doubt that the gaming activities of this kind are worthwhile. In particular, there is no doubt at all that the players

[22] Thomas C. Schelling, "The Strategy of Conflict: Prospectus for a Reorientation of Game Theory," *Journal of Conflict Resolution*, September 1958, pp. 203–264.

[23] For an historical account see Clayton J. Thomas and Walter L. Deemer, Jr., "The Role of Operational Gaming in Operations Research," *Operations Research*, February 1957, pp. 1–27.

learn from the game, that they acquire insights that are valid and useful to the extent that the game has been well designed. But there is some doubt that games of this kind are very effective as problem-solving devices. Rapidity of play, which permits numerous plays, is a necessary but not a sufficient condition of a game that will solve problems; and the number of plays is, in any event, still grossly inadequate by analytic standards.

Operational gaming has never really solved the criterion problem, and its attempts to evade it by substituting human beings for explicit objectives have merely obscured the issue. Game theory at least faces up to the problem, although its solution, minimax, appears too conservative except in repetitive zero-sum games. Gaming, while it frees itself from this specific and unsatisfactory criterion, has none to take its place. The blue player is usually told to behave as if he were a blue commander or the blue government; the red player, as if he were a real red. The extent to which the players are rightly motivated is unknown and unknowable.

For this and other reasons the results of repeated war games are difficult to interpret in most cases. One knows the outcomes of the plays, but one cannot determine analytically the relative importance in determining the outcomes of (1) the skill of the players, (2) their motivations, (3) the structure of the game, (4) the assumed values of various parameters, and (5) chance elements. One is left essentially with the intuitive insights that the players and observers believe they have derived from playing.

These insights, however, should not be belittled. While less than totally satisfactory (what alternative approach would give results passing this test?), they can be provocative and suggestive of good solutions which can be tested by more analytic methods. It is terribly important, no matter how it is done, to look at things from the enemy's point of view. Games provide a good stimulus and setting for doing so.

The importance of keeping the enemy's viewpoint in mind was brought out earlier in the discussion of criteria for deterrence. Many persons, leaving enemy viewpoints and responses out of account, have assumed that a large offensive force automatically provides deterrence. If we look at the matter from the enemy's point of view, a large *but vulnerable* Western striking force provides *negative* deterrence (at least as far as thermonuclear attack is concerned). In general, the analyst who looks at problems too exclusively from his own country's point of view, like some conventional military planners, is likely to forget how ingenious and resourceful the enemy may be. The war gamer whose force has been destroyed by enemy initiative is much less likely to make this dangerous kind of mistake.

The Meaning of Criteria

Earlier it was convenient to discuss criteria as though the term referred to definitive tests of preferredness. These reflections on incommensurables and uncertainty, however, make it clear that the word "criterion" sometimes means a partial test—one that provides a significant rather than a nonsensical basis for the comparison of policies and yet not a basis that embraces all the relevant considerations. In many problems, the precise relationship between proximate criteria and the ultimate test will not be known, and hence the former must be incomplete tests.

This is true in business as well as in military and other governmental problems. Consider, for example, an attempt by the managers of a firm to apply the test of "maximum profits from available resources." [24] Let us assume that when the managers consider several alternative courses of action, they can predict expected profits, and also something about the variability of profits, under each alternative policy. In other words, they can say to themselves, "Under Policy 1, profits would be $1 million, plus or minus $200,000. Under Policy 2, expected profits would be $2 million, though there is a chance that they might run as high as $3 million or that losses of $1 million would be incurred." What *is* "maximum profit from available resources" in this situation? It may be defined as maximum *average* profit, but in any event, it will be an incomplete criterion, because its relationship to the ultimate test will not be fully traced out. The ultimate criterion is to maximize something—it is usually labeled "utility"—which *depends upon* expected profits, upon the other possible profit figures, and upon the management's attitude toward risk and uncertainty. But the precise nature of this relationship is not ordinarily known. Hence to show which course of action yields maximum expected profit is to compare the policies in terms of one selected policy-consequence, that is, to apply a partial or incomplete criterion. To compare the policies with respect to other possible outcomes or to variability of outcome is to use other incomplete or partial criteria.

In military problems utility has frequently been labeled "military worth." Let us assume, for the moment, that the military

---

[24] See G. Tintner, "The Theory of Choice under Subjective Risk and Uncertainty," *Econometrica*, IX, 1941, pp. 298–304; A. Alchian, "Uncertainty, Evolution, and Economic Theory," *The Journal of Political Economy*, XVIII, June 1950, pp. 211–221, or S. Enke, "On Maximizing Profits," *American Economic Review*, XLI, September 1951, pp. 556–578.

worth we wish to maximize in a particular military problem is a function of the retaliatory power of SAC, the frequency distribution of results, the size of the federal budget, various diplomatic impacts, and the number of lives saved. We do not know how important some of these effects are in relation to others. Consequently we can devise no complete criterion which points to the "correct" force composition of SAC; the determination of such a force involves value judgments by several of the Executive departments and of Congress. However, we can show what would happen to a measure of SAC's retaliatory power with different force compositions. If possible, we should show data related to some of the other effects (for example, the frequency distribution of results). In any event, it is plain that maximum expected offensive power for a given SAC budget is an incomplete test, and it should be understood that the term "criterion," when it is used in connection with the economic analysis of military problems, often refers to such an incomplete test.

VIII

PROBLEMS ASSOCIATED WITH TIME

Much of the discussion so far has had a static dimension. We have usually spoken of costs and of benefits (or achievements or capabilities) as if they were timeless or, perhaps, concurrent. In fact, every cost is incurred and every benefit is realized at a particular point in time, and we are far from indifferent to the dates of these points. In 1960, 1961 seems far more significant to most of us than 1970. In our illustrative example in the fuller text we had to face up to some of the difficulties associated with time because we were dealing with a real problem. We did so in that example by constructing a simple artifice, dividing the relevant future into three periods—Period I, Period II, and "beyond the horizon"—and ignoring time differences within each period. In this chapter we will consider, in a quite general manner, some of the principal difficulties associated with time and some of the methods of dealing with them. We will discover that, as with other difficulties of systematic analysis, simplifications and compromises with the ideal are inevitable, but that there are better and worse ways to simplify.

In any economic analysis we are likely to begin with certain assets inherited from the past. In a business firm these usually include buildings, machinery, and inventories. In the airlift example used they included not only the 400 C–97 cargo aircraft, but airbases, cargo handling equipment, maintenance depots, spare parts, trained crews, and so on. The production or "initial" costs involved in creating these assets have been incurred in the past; they are "sunk" costs[1]—bygones that are irrelevant in any comparison of the economic merits of alternative means of accomplishing future objectives. The use of some of these inherited assets to achieve any particular future objective may involve "opportunity" costs; that is, the use of these assets may make it necessary to forego valuable opportunities of using them to reach

---

[1] Sunk costs and salvage values were also discussed in chapter V. Because of their importance and their pertinence to the treatment of time streams, we review these topics briefly here.

some other future objective. Thus, the 400 C–97's might have some use (after conversion) as tankers to refuel bombers; if they have, their net value as tankers is a legitimate cost—an opportunity cost —of providing airlift. But their value as tankers (if any) bears no necessary relation to their historical cost of production: it could be considerably greater or much less. In our example it was assumed that their marginal value as tankers (or in any other alternative use) was zero. While this may not have been literally true (they would bring something if sold for scrap), it was probably a close enough approximation for the kind of analysis we were making. The alternative-use value of specifically military equipment is frequently (although by no means always) small enough in relation to other costs that the analyst is justified in ignoring it.

The only costs and benefits in which we are interested in economic comparisons of alternatives are future costs and benefits. The opportunity costs associated with using inherited assets are one category of future costs. Far more important, in most cases, are future production costs, installation costs, maintenance costs, and operating costs.[2] These future costs are incurred at different times in the future. Some of the production costs may be incurred this year; some of the operating costs, ten years from now. We may think of the prospective costs associated with any one of the alternative means of achieving a military objective as a stream in time, whose width at any particular moment is proportional to the costs to be incurred at that date. Similarly, we may think of the benefits or capabilities associated with each alternative system as a stream in time, with width proportional to the capability expected on each date.

Now not only are the total *areas* of the cost streams (or benefit streams) associated with different alternatives likely to differ; their shapes are also likely to differ, and significantly. For example, if one compares the cost streams associated with a least-cost fleet and a least-procurement fleet, he may discover that the least-cost stream is broader (that is, costs are greater) in the early years, when new, more efficient equipment is being procured, and narrower in the later years, after it has come into use. The savings in later years more than counterbalance the additional expenditure in the early years if no discount rate is used, that is, if costs incurred in any year are assigned the same weight or significance. But, in principle, this procedure is obviously wrong. The shapes

---

[2] These are also, of course, opportunity costs. All significant economic costs are opportunity costs. The reason production costs, for example, are significant, is that the productive resources used (or used up) could have been used to produce something else of value.

of the streams do matter. We attach greater significance to costs and benefits this year than to prospective costs and benefits in future years, and in general we attach less significance the more distant the future year. In other words, we discount the future.

WHY DISCOUNT?

Individuals, firms, and governments borrow and lend in markets in which interest (or discount) rates are invariably positive. Consider first the individual or firm. If I have control over funds today I can invest them and obtain 3 or 4 percent more every year. To me $100 today is the equivalent of at least $103 or $104 a year from now or perhaps $150 ten years from now. The government is in an analogous position. Tax income today can pay today's bills. Tax income a year from today is less useful. Today's bills must be paid by borrowing at 3 percent (unless the government prints or otherwise creates money), and next year's tax income used to repay the loan plus interest. So $103 next year is the equivalent of $100 this year.

The principal reason interest rates are positive is that control over funds makes possible capital investments (in factories, machinery, inventories, and so on), and capital investment can be productive. This creates a large demand for present funds, and the demanders are willing to pay for the limited supply that is available. Each borrower must be willing at least to match what the marginal borrower is willing to pay. Each saver can get (at least) that price for the use of his funds.[3] As a result, the price for funds measures their opportunity cost or, in the language of economics, the marginal productivity of capital.

At the same time, this rate on funds measures our marginal time preferences—that is, the rate that we are willing to pay for consumption now rather than consumption later. The reason for this is that each person is free to adjust his savings until another dollar spent on current consumption is as important to him as another dollar saved for future consumption. If the prevailing rate of interest is 3 percent, each of us values the marginal dollar put into consumption now as much as $1.03 for consumption next year. If this were not true, additional dollars would be shifted from consumption to savings. Hence the prevailing rate of interest

---

[3] There is no need for any saver to accept less, even though some people would be willing to save and lend to industrial borrowers at lower—even zero—interest rates.

measures the opportunity cost of funds diverted from either consumption or production.

In most instances, there is an additional factor that affects discounting and makes for a whole structure of rates rather than a unique interest rate. This important factor is the risk and uncertainty associated with different ventures. Risky business enterprises must pay much more than the "pure" rate of interest to obtain control of funds—and it is right that they should. If the risky enterprise does not have a prospect of a higher return than the safe one, the funds should go to the safe one. Or, to view the matter in another way, the future net gains (or gains and costs) of risky ventures should be more heavily discounted than the estimated net gains from relatively safe enterprises.

In comparisons of alternative military systems, the reasons for discounting are precisely the same as they are in the private economy. A $150 cost (or gain) that will occur ten years hence is the equivalent of only, say, $100 now, first of all because resources can be made to grow that much if put to alternative uses. A least-cost fleet may use funds *now* which, if we had opted for the least-procurement fleet, could have been used to finance productive private investment. It should be charged at least a rate representing the market's evaluation of the marginal productivity of such investment.

In fact, it should be charged more than this. That market rate is the *minimum* rate appropriate in comparing military systems. There is the second, and in the typical military case quantitatively more important, reason for discounting future costs and benefits, namely, the existence of risk and uncertainty about the gains and costs. First, the war for which we are preparing may occur before the date at which the cost would be incurred or the capability realized. Second (less likely but conceivably), peace might break out, or disarmament be achieved, before the date in question. More generally, all sorts of things can happen that will completely alter the need for forces of the type envisaged, and they are more likely to happen the more distant the year. The future costs and benefits are prospective rather than real, and may never become real. We live in an uncertain world, and its military aspects are more plagued by uncertainty than most others. Military technology is passing through a revolution—apparently an accelerating one. Concepts, tactics, strategies and alliances are all in ferment. Future weapon capabilities that look attractive today may be useless tomorrow.

WHAT RATE?

The straightforward (but not necessarily the easiest or preferred) way to make costs and benefits at different times commensurate is simply to apply an appropriate discount rate to future costs and benefits, so that all are stated in terms of "present value." [4] This is what a business firm does, at least implicitly, in comparing present and future amounts, preparatory to choosing policies that maximize present value.[5] But what is the "appropriate" rate for this discount calculation? In general terms, the rate should be the marginal rate of return that could otherwise be earned—that is, the rate that reflects the productivity of the next-best opportunity. If the investor can borrow and lend freely, the marginal opportunity will turn out to yield approximately the market rate of interest. If he faces a fixed budget, the marginal opportunity may yield some other rate.[6] If legal or other constraints close off certain opportunities, those investments are simply not relevant and have no bearing on the selection of the rate of discount.

It is often argued that governments should not discount future amounts at as high a rate as do individuals and firms, because governments should take a longer-run view and endeavor to provide more for posterity than the decisions of private individuals would provide. We may indeed want governments to take a long view and to make extra provision for later generations—by increasing *total* public investment (in either defense or other forms) or by stimulating private investment. But, having settled this issue, governments should presumably try to channel the investment funds into those activities that have the highest rates of return. Similarly, an individual who wishes to provide more for his heirs should cut his consumption and raise his total investment, but should channel his capital into its most productive uses.

---

[4] The present value of any future cost or benefit is

$$\frac{a_n}{(1 + r_1)(1 + r_2) \cdots (1 + r_i) \cdots (1 + r_n)}$$

where a_n represents the future value in year (or period) n, and r_1, r_2, r_i, r_n the appropriate discount rate during the ith year (or period). If the r's are equal, the present value $= \dfrac{a_n}{(1 + r)^n}$.

[5] It is usually assumed that businessmen attempt to maximize the present value of anticipated future income streams, costs counting as negative income. Present value maximization is the equivalent in economic dynamics of profit maximization in economic statics.

[6] This brief discussion is greatly oversimplified, but in our judgment, the finer theoretical points do not affect the main conclusions that can be drawn about comparing military systems. For more details and complexities, see Roland N. McKean, *Efficiency in Government through Systems Analysis, With Emphasis on Water Resource Development*, John Wiley and Sons, New York, 1958, pp. 74–95, and Jack Hirshleifer, "On The Theory of Optimal Investment Decision," *Journal of Political Economy*, August 1958, pp. 329–352.

In either instance, this means discounting streams of cost and gain at the marginal rate of return, not at some artificially low rate.

In government, the marginal opportunity depends upon the problem of choice that is being considered. Usually, when we look several years ahead, leaving the resources in the private economy is a pertinent alternative, one that may be taken to be the marginal opportunity. In other words, the government can repay debt or refrain from borrowing or taxing instead of making the purchase under consideration. As a consequence, the rate the government has to pay to borrow funds—on the order of 3 per cent—is a suitable minimum rate. If leaving the resources in the private economy is not an admissible alternative—if the problem is to allocate a given budget—the marginal opportunity and yield may be something else.

As suggested previously, however, we usually have to add an appropriate risk premium to this minimum rate. We should allow to some extent for the chances that the future benefits we expect may never be realized, that the costs may not have to be incurred, and that the estimated amounts may turn out to be wrong. But we do not know and cannot hope to learn precisely how risky any particular military investment is.

Some investments are certainly riskier than others. The probability of war (or peace) breaking out before realization of the anticipated benefit or cost is probably similar for all military systems; but some systems will be more vulnerable than others to uncertainties about technological advances, future strategic situations, and enemy capabilities and intentions. Advanced weapon systems, such as a future hypersonic long range bomber, appear to be among the riskiest enterprises of the modern world. Airlift systems appear to be much less risky. Technological advances in economical air transportation occur more slowly than in offensive and defensive weapon systems, and it seems likely that we will be able to use a lot of economical air transportation for something important through the 1960's even if technological or political developments rule out the danger of limited warfare in the vicinity of Bangdhad.

Perhaps, therefore, an appropriate discount rate (pure interest plus risk premium) for a military investment like that in airlift capacity would be similar to a rough average in private enterprise —say 6 to 8 per cent per annum; while the appropriate rate for an advanced weapon system might be higher—say 10 per cent or more. Twenty per cent would be an extremely high discount rate to use: it reduces a cost or benefit anticipated 5 years hence to almost a third its nominal value, and one anticipated 10 years in the future to about a sixth. If risks are *really* high enough to justify a 20 percent discount rate, investments whose payoffs are in the distant future can rarely be justified unless the nominal payoffs are spectacular.[7] The appropriate discount rate during World War II appeared to be even higher than 20 percent because immediate results were so much more important than distant payoffs; so we required that development and procurement be justified on the basis of payoff during a very short period.

It is pretty clear that a rate as high as 20 or even 15 percent per annum could not be justified in present circumstances (1960) by the probability that war will intervene. If we really thought that war was sufficiently imminent to warrant discount rates of 15 to 20 percent, we would be spending much more than 40 billion dollars annually on military programs. Discount rates as high as these are appropriate only for systems with high risks of obsolescence. Of course *if* our assessment of the probability of war increases, we should both increase military expenditures and use a higher discount rate in choosing *among* alternative purchases.

WHAT VALUE FOR FUTURE INPUTS AND OUTPUTS?

We have said that future gains and costs should be discounted—that distant amounts should be weighted less heavily than present ones. Whatever the prices of individual inputs and outputs, a hundred dollars now is worth more than a hundred dollars ten years from now because (1) it can produce something, or "grow," in the meantime, and (2) we prefer a unit of satisfaction now to one ten years later. All this is not to say, however, that the price or value of *particular* objects will be lower in the future than at present. We may well expect the cost of certain inputs or the value of certain outputs to rise.

Thus, in addition to discounting cost and gain streams, a private investor must also do his best to estimate the future prices of inputs and output. He may reason that the cost of petroleum will be higher in 1970 than in 1965 because the more easily accessible supplies will be exhausted. Or he may expect the worth of an "advertising capability" to go up because of the growth of his competitors. Clearly, the future values of such items and therefore the *undiscounted* amounts of future costs and gains, are ex-

---

[7] Expenditures on research and exploratory development projects, however, which are cheap and may lead to spectacular payoffs in a decade or two, can be justified at 20 percent or even higher discount rates. However, we are not arguing that all uncertainties can or ought to be reflected in discount rates.

tremely important. We must not fancy that proper discounting can make up for their neglect.

Similarly in the comparison of military systems, we should discount future amounts, but the undiscounted gains and costs of certain defense capabilities may be greater in 1970 than in 1965. Careful discounting does not by itself assure that the streams of costs and accomplishments are being handled properly.

This fact becomes especially important when we start taking into account the interdependence between our policies and the enemy's future actions. Suppose that an enemy is expected to have no ballistic missile capability in the early 1960's, a gradually increasing but less than decisive capability until 1965, and, after 1965, the ability to annihilate us if we have no defense. In these circumstances, anti-missile capabilities are clearly worth more to us in 1965 than in 1960. In fact, the appropriate value in the current year is zero—if the enemy cannot attack with missiles and if there are no by-products from an immediate capability like effective training for next year. On the other hand, some anti-missile capability in 1965 and later would be, on this supposition, of enormous value.

Consider a hypothetical comparison of two weapon systems. Suppose that our expected budget for defense against ballistic missiles is "given" during the next few years, and that we want to develop and procure antimissile defense systems that will optimize, in some sense, our capability over time to shoot down incoming missiles. System A, adapted from a system developed primarily for defense against bombers, promises to give us some immediate capability but has little growth potential. System B cannot possibly provide a defense for several years, but promises a comparatively effective defense beginning, say, four years hence when it becomes operational. In choosing between the systems, we must assign reasonable values to capabilities in different years before we discount. Or it might be more practical to reformulate the problem, stipulating a reasonable time-path for our capabilities and discounting only the cost stream to seek the most efficient system for achieving the stipulated capability.

Thus, when we urge the discounting of future amounts, we mean that command over general resources now is worth more than command over the same amount of resources next year—not that specific objects are worth more now than in the future. We emphasize this fact because we do *not* wish to encourage the built-in tendency of governments to undervalue future outputs (see the concluding section of this chapter). To repeat, before discounting streams of cost or gain, one must take pains to assign realistic values to future inputs and outputs.

SOME PRACTICAL DODGES

As a practical matter, we must abstract from some of these complexities. It is impossibly difficult in most comparisons to determine the appropriate future budgetary constraints, the proper list of alternatives and the yield of the marginal opportunity, the degrees of riskiness of various opportunities, and finally the appropriate discount rates. In these matters, as in others, we must simplify reality to a considerable extent. We seek to simplify reality enough to make systematic thought and calculation feasible yet not so much as to make the results inapplicable. Some crude approximations are usually justified, if we are careful to avoid distortion and bias. Needless to say, judgment must enter into this procedure of devising "practical dodges."

The Time Horizon

In comparing alternative weapon systems, it is never practical or desirable to estimate benefits and costs for all eternity and to determine and apply appropriate discount rates to these streams. It is always necessary to cut off the analysis at some point, ignoring or crudely lumping costs and benefits thereafter. Our ability to foresee the future becomes so limited after, say, ten or fifteen years, that for purposes of comparing weapon systems it seldom pays to try. If we did use appropriate discount rates, with appropriate allowance for risks, the comparisons would, in any event, be little affected by the distant years. The simple and straightforward thing to do is to omit them.

If a fairly early date is taken for the time horizon of the analysis, it may be desirable to lump net benefits beyond the horizon by crediting each system with some crudely calculated "salvage value" instead of simply ignoring them.

The Rate of Discount

Because of uncertainties about future costs and capabilities, it is not worthwhile to devote an inordinate amount of time to refining one's estimate of "the" proper discount rate. Historical studies show that projections of cost and performance of weapon systems, particularly those made at early stages of development, have often been wide of the mark. For systems analysts to put great effort into determining "the" discount rate would probably be less productive than other uses of their time.

Moreover, because of uncertainties about future budgetary constraints and hence about marginal opportunities and their yields, the discount rate that may later be appropriate is inevitably in doubt at the time choices must be made. The best estimate may simply be a rough average rate of return in the private economy, like 6 or 8 percent. This rate would include an average allowance for risk. Special degrees of risk associated with particular weapon systems should be pointed out by the analyst but would have to be allowed for subjectively by the final decision-makers.

Indeed, for certain classes of problems, we can make a stronger case for using an average rate of return from the private economy. At the time many weapon systems are being compared, future budgetary constraints have not been set, and we can reasonably argue that the relevant options are to buy the weapons or to leave the resources in the private economy. This choice being open, the marginal opportunity is simply investment in the private economy. Hence the rate of discount that reflects what could otherwise be earned by the resources is the rate of return that could be obtained in private investment.

We can also assume, with some justification, that this rate is consistent with time preferences in the economy—with the rate of return in consumption, so to speak. That is, we can assume that future budgets fixed by the government will be consistent with time preferences as reflected by interest rates in the private sector. Individually we do not have the opportunity to adjust government outlays so that another dollar spent on government activities is as important as another dollar saved for future consumption. But the task of our governing officials is to act for us in determining budgets, and they are able to do so in the light of prevailing interest rates. For this reason, too, we might well use an average discount rate from the private sector in analyzing long-range problems of choice.

Sensitivity and Break-Even Points

In short-range problems of choice—those in which narrower resource constraints exist—the average rate of discount from the private sector is less satisfactory, even if it is the best estimate that we can make. Also in many problems, whether long-run or short-run, the risk premium may be especially troublesome. The preferred procedure may then be to regard the discount rate as "variable" and test the results for sensitivity to the rates of discount.

This procedure also yields a "break-even rate of discount"—that is, a rate of discount that makes the two leading systems equally attractive. Below this rate, one system is preferred. Above this rate, another system is best. To show such break-even points is often a useful device, especially when uncertainties are great and judgment must play a major role in reaching final recommendations. By means of this device, the analyst or policy maker can see the range of discount rates within which one policy is clearly preferred and may be able to judge that the proper rate lies within that range.

The Stipulated Capability

In view of the uncertainties, it may appear to be more straightforward and appropriate in many problems to stipulate a desired capability over future time than to do any discounting of capabilities. Indeed in many instances it may appear to be the only feasible method of handling time paths for gains or capabilities. If the enemy threat were an increasing one, so usually would be our desired capability to counter it. The stipulated capability would presumably avoid "soft spots" if our intentions were defensive; it might point toward a maximum at some particular point of time if our intentions were to take the initiative. The general considerations which cause us to discount the future might be taken into account partly by attaching little or no weight to capabilities after some arbitrary cut-off point or horizon. Also, of course, the cost streams would still be discounted to seek the lowest-cost means of achieving the stipulated capability.

Period Costing

The most common technique for comparing the costs over time of alternative systems is to add to the initial or investment costs the costs of operating each system for some fixed period, usually four or five years. Thus, one speaks of the "four-year system cost" or "five-year system cost." An end-of-period salvage value may or may not be subtracted. This is obviously a crude approximation to discounting. In effect, the discount rate is assumed to be zero during the period, rising abruptly to 100 percent at the end. But in many problems such crude devices may be completely adequate. If we are merely interested in choosing a best or better system, we can test the sensitivity of the choice to the length of the period (lengthening the period is equivalent to reducing the discount rate). If there are no great differences in the ratio of initial to annual operating cost among the various systems being compared, choice will not in fact be sensitive to the length of the period or the discount rate. Frequently, however, such differences are important—especially where some of the systems make much more extensive use of inherited assets.

Multiple Period Costing

A variant of period costing is costing over two or more periods. This increases the flexibility of the method and makes it possible to deal with more complex problems. If we are interested in an extensive future period, over which the "stipulated capability" is increasing substantially, or new systems become available to satisfy it at later dates, or both of these complications confront us simultaneously, we *may* be able to divide the future into a conveniently small number of periods, each approximately homogenous, and aggregate stipulated capabilities and costs by periods. Of course, we still have the problem of applying appropriate discount rates to the more distant future periods *as a whole*.

Lowering One's Sights

Some of the difficulties associated with time simply cannot be resolved by any kind of quantitative economic analysis. This does not mean that quantitative economic analysis has no useful role to play in connection with such problems, but it does mean that its role is subsidiary and that it must address itself to the practical problem of finding a better alternative rather than the best.

Consider, for example, the vexing question of whether to skip a generation of weapons. Sometimes vast savings in resources are possible if one skips—but at the cost of a lessened capability during the intermediate years. If we are interested in offensive or defensive weapons, there are cases where greater numbers cannot be made available or where no degree of quantitative superiority can compensate for inferiority in crucial weapon characteristics (for example if the enemy has an effective electronic counter-measure against which existing weapons possess no counter counter-measure).

At the end of World War II, the British government took a calculated (?) risk and decided to skip a generation of bombers, concentrating its resources on the development of the then advanced V-Bombers. This enabled it to cut its military budget substantially in the early post-war years, but would have left it without a modern bomber force if another war had occurred. It justified this course of action by arguing that the probability of war was low in the immediately following years. The United States Air Force was faced with a decision in the early post-war years whether to develop air-breathing missiles (like the Navajo and Snark) or whether to skip immediately to long-range ballistic missiles (Atlas). It decided to develop the air breathers. The Russians, faced by a similar choice, apparently made the opposite decision, putting their effort into the more advanced system.

Quantitative economic analysis could not have determined an optimum in a generally acceptable way in any of these cases. It could not have predicted the probability of war in the "soft" years; or the extent to which that probability would itself be affected by the softness; or the way in which the government or nation should value enhanced risk for a few years as compared with budgetary savings. But it might have been able to facilitate choice. At the very least it could have estimated quantitatively how much our capability would have been reduced for how long, and how much money would "really" have been saved. It might have been able to do something even more useful—to show how capability might have been shored up inexpensively during any soft period. Some cheap modifications of wartime bombers, for example, might have made them an effective fighting force for an unexpected emergency. Alternatively, surplus B-29's or B-50's might have been turned over to our allies as military aid and kept operational during the soft years (in fact, some were). In the missile case, air-to-surface missiles might have been a more attractive alternative than the long-range air-breathing surface-to-surface missile. Or quantitative analysis might have demonstrated that the lack of the air-breathing missiles would have had only a marginal effect on our capability, given the improved bombing aircraft that were to be operational during the soft years. Frequently, we can demonstrate that system A is better than system B even when we cannot show that system A is optimal. At a minimum, we can produce evidence relevant to the choice between A and B. And with a little ingenuity, we can often suggest a modification of A, system A', that is demonstrably better than A.

UNDERVALUING FUTURE OUTPUTS

We conclude with a final warning about the valuation of future outputs. There is a marked tendency on the part of the military services, the government, and the Congress to undervalue future capabilities. The primary responsibility of the military services is the operation of today's forces. Perhaps significantly, they always have emergency war plans, but seldom long-range war plans. Moreover, the policy of rotating service personnel at short intervals (usually three years or less) means that officials are always trying to make a recognizable mark in the very near future—later someone else will be in their jobs and responsible. Governments, similarly, have short tenure in most democracies, and many political officials have even shorter tenure. The next election always appears much more significant than the election 12 years hence—when, in any event, no rewards will be showered by the electorate on a party responsible for prescient decisions 12 years earlier. Congress (as well as an administration) is notoriously interested only in *this year's* budget and its relation to possible tax relief. The result is that within research and development almost all the resources are used in developing weapon systems with a predicted combat capability in the relatively near future; that measures that promise significant savings over a period of years are rejected because they involve somewhat higher expenditures the following year.[8] In fact, it has for this reason been almost impossible to get approval for the purchase of high performance cargo aircraft. Here let us simply point out that this bias in past and current decisions presents opportunities for quantitative economic analysis to demonstrate large gains in efficiency. In many cases, unfortunately, they will be easier to demonstrate than to sell.

---

[8] Interesting exceptions are many water and other natural resource projects which are approved in spite of the fact that they promise rates of return as low as 2½ percent. This is the opposite error: they should be required to earn at least 6 percent. In this case local benefits and log-rolling play an important role in reversing usual attitudes.

CONCLUDING OBSERVATIONS

The purpose of this book has been to explain a *way of looking* at military problems which we and others with whom we have been associated have found fruitful in insights and productive of solutions. Essentially we regard *all* military problems as, in one of their aspects, economic problems in the efficient allocation and use of resources. We believe that this way of looking at military problems goes far toward reconciling the apparent conflict of views between the officers and officials who are responsible for defense and the officials and Congressmen whose primary interest is economy—except in determining the over-all size of the military budget, where conflict between these points of view is inevitable.

While we have strong views (or prejudices) on the substantive solutions of many of the military-economic problems which we discussed, we have tried to subordinate them in writing this book. We are concerned more with how to look at military problems and how to go about solving them than with the substantive solutions themselves—which are, in any event, dependent on current circumstances and technologies and hence ephemeral. One of our aims has been to focus attention on the new problems which have become important as a result of the revolution in military technology since the development of atomic weapons. But we have tried to avoid taking sides on current controversies regarding military strategy except where the issue is too fundamental to be evaded, like the desirability of protecting our deterrent capabilities or of making preparations for localized, limited warfare. That more of our illustrative examples have been taken from Air Force rather than from Army or Navy problems in no way reflects our views regarding the relative importance of the three Services, but is the result of historical accidents that have given us greater familiarity with Air Force problems.

The book is in no sense a text in how to do military "operations research" or "systems analysis." The treatment is nonmathematical, and problems of designing detailed models of military reality have been avoided. We hope, however, that operations researchers have found here the economic concepts and analysis which are essential to their craft, and that military decision-makers have found material which will enhance their understanding of operations research and their ability to use it.

INDEX

O

Objectives, economic analysis, 81
Obligational authority, 15n.
Operations decisions, 95–96

P

Parker, Sanford, 58
Performance budgets, 52
Performance indicators, 59, 61–65
Period costing, 159–160
Planning, military, 67–97
Priorities approach, economic
    analysis, 85–87
Procurement decisions, 96–97
Production-possibility curve, 73
Program·changes, 62–65

Q

Quantitative analysis
    and time problems, 160–161
    incommensurables, 124–129
    uncertainty, 129–143

R

Radiation effects, 9
Requirements
    and economic analysis, 84–85, 118
    selection of, 104
Research and development
    decisions, 95
    defense role, 18
    discount rate, 155n.
    in defense programs, 64
Resource constraints
    and GNP, 27–38
    and money costs, 24–26
    general, 23–24
    policies affecting, 38–42
    specific, 21–23
    (see also Gross National Gross
        Product)
Resource use, and efficiency, 104–105
Retaliation, military strategy, 10–11
Rockefeller Brothers Fund Report,
    58–59

S

Silberman, Charles, 58
Spillovers, 93, 109–110
Sub-optimization, 92–93
Substitution, resource use, 25–26
Systems analysis, 40, 81–82

T

Technology, 3
Thermonuclear war, 11–13, 15
Time problems
    and stipulated capability, 159
    and value of future capabilities,
        161–162
    costing for fixed period, 159–160
    cut-off point in time, 157
    determining appropriate discount
        rate, 153–155
    moderating capabilities, 160–161
    multiple period costing, 160
    reasons for discounting, 151–153
    role of uncertainty, 152
    testing rates of discount, 158–159
    use of average discount rate,
        157–158
    value of future inputs and outputs,
        155–157
Truman, President Harry S., 28

U

Uncertainty, 65, 152
    and contingencies, 140–141
    and enemy reaction, 133–134
    and military decisions, 136–140
    defined, 129–130
    hedging and insurance, 141–142
    kinds of, 130–134
    reduction of, 142–143
    statistical, 134
    strategic context, 131–132
    technological, 132–133
U.S.S.R., 10

W

War
    economic potential for, 14–19
    ideal preparation for, 17–19
    limited, 11–13
    mobilization for, 13–14
    thermonuclear, 11–13
    World War II type, 13–14
War gaming, 144–146
Weapon developments
    defense implications, 10–11
    influence on warfare, 11–14

Z

Zero-sum games, 138–140

rived from Bronson and from neighboring Alachua County, but by the time they got there, there was no one left to save. The town was empty. As for the burning, they just watched.

A week had passed since the bells of Rosewood rang in the new year. Now those bells lay smoldering among the twisted steel and blackened ruins, the charred carcasses of cats and dogs, the smoking soot of a place that would never exist again.

By sundown, the white men were gone, back down the sandy Florida roadways to their own towns, to their own homes and families.

And the black men, women and children of Rosewood, they were gone, too. Simply gone.

$\mathscr{A}$ WAKENING

Old News

It was a Friday afternoon, payday, and a steady stream of men and women was shoving its way through the front doors of Lundy's Liquor Store, looking to cash their checks and maybe pick up a pint or two, something for the weekend. Each time the glass doors swung open, the springtime sounds of the city rushed in, sharp hoots and shouts from the pedestrians pushing past on the sidewalk outside, the blare of horns and the blast of radios from the sedans surging up Tangerine Avenue toward the east, toward the purple twilight above downtown St. Pete.

The liquor store's safe was stuffed with cash, and Arnett Doctor was working the counter, manning the register, bagging bottles, making small talk with the customers. He was a tall man, with piercing eyes and a strong body, solid save for a belly gone soft with middle age. On his hip, tucked beneath his light cotton shirt, was a pistol, a snub-nosed .357 Magnum, what the people on the street called a "spoiler." Wearing a pistol was part of the job in a place like Lundy's. Doctor knew as well as anyone how liquor and cash made for a deadly

Sarah Carrier, with son Sylvester and daughter Willie

combination. He knew too how poverty could make it even worse, and plenty of the people passing through the doors of Lundy's were poor.

Doctor had grown up with half of them. The rest he knew at least by face. Most lived within a mile or so of the store, many in the public housing project just down the street. Jordan Park, it was called, a tangle of beige two-story buildings sprawled across twenty-six acres of bare dirt and broken glass. When the first tenants had moved there in the spring of 1940, Jordan Park was hailed as a place of hope, like so many such projects across America. There were fresh lawns to water, bright beds of gardenias and hibiscus to weed. Now, forty-two years later, the grass and the flowers, along with the hope, were gone, and Jordan Park had become one of the bleakest, most violent neighborhoods in the state of Florida.

Doctor counted himself lucky never to have lived there. His mother had spent her life working two jobs, sometimes three, just to keep herself and her children out of a place like that, out of the projects. Cleaning white families' homes, cooking and caring for white women's children, that's what Philomena Doctor had done for longer than Arnett could remember, since long before he was born. Most of what he had, he owed to his mother, but even more, most of what he *was,* he owed to her. She loved more fiercely than anyone he had ever known, but she could hate just as hard, and Arnett was the same way, with the same hair trigger, the same volcanic temper, the same river of hurt that ran so deep inside it was hard to understand where it came from.

Much of it came from the simple fact that he was black, born in the '40s, come of age in the '50s and '60s, all in the Deep South, enough right there to fuel a lifetime of fury. For his mother, born before World War I, black and a woman besides, it was unimaginably worse. She had given up a lot in her life— to be married, to have children, then to be divorced and have to raise a son and daughter by herself. But it wasn't the things she lost that hurt Phil Doctor half as much as the things she never had, the things she always swore should have been hers had circumstances been different. And for that she blamed only white people. She cursed the white man. Warned Arnett from the time he was a baby that he could never trust a white man or woman. He might share his days with them, she said, he might work for them or beside them, but he must never allow them to come close enough to hurt him. And that is what they would do, she assured him time and again. They would hurt him, use him, take his life if he let them. She had seen it before.

He had seen it, too, early on, back in Lacoochee, the small sawmill town where he was born, an hour into the central Florida forests and open cattleland north of Tampa. Arnett was just a boy then, but he would never forget the lynching. And that's what it had been, though the authorities never called it that. The body was found by the railroad tracks out toward the river, not far from the sawmill where half the town worked. It was a black man, middle-aged, dead, hit by a passing train, probably drunk. At least that was the way it was officially reported, the way the white world put it to rest.

But the blacks knew better. Arnett's mother and father, their kinfolk and friends, every black person in the town of Lacoochee knew better. Arnett was only ten at the time, still too young to know many things, but even he knew better than to believe this was anything but murder.

The man was a friend, a neighbor. His name was Wallace Jordan. He lived with his wife and a house full of sons three doors down from the Doctors. Some of his boys were Arnett's playmates. Jordan drove deliveries for a grocery store in town, a white man's store, and word was he had glanced the wrong way at the storekeeper's wife one afternoon, not something a black man in a place like Lacoochee could dare to do, not in the 1950s. By that evening Wallace Jordan's beaten, mutilated body had been driven to the edge of town, already a corpse by the time it was dumped on the Seaboard tracks.

Arnett never understood how someone could get away with something like that, how the grownups, his own mama and daddy, could talk about it behind closed doors, then go on as if nothing had happened. Things like that weren't supposed to happen in America. People weren't supposed to die like that with nothing done about it, no questions asked, no questions answered.

But black people had been dying like that in this country. Arnett learned this as he grew older. Even in a city as serene as St. Pete—a town known among Florida's blacks as a better place than most to make a life, the town to which Arnett's mother chose to take him and his sister Yvonne after deciding to leave her husband, a resort town, a lovely town—even there black people had died the way Wallace Jordan went down. More than once, for sure, but the death most remembered, though there were those who would rather forget, was the hanging of John Evans.

He was a common laborer, hunted down by a mob of whites in the winter of 1914, captured and hanged without trial for a murder no one bothered to prove he committed, strung up from a light pole in the center of the city while a taunting crowd of fifteen hundred men and women emptied their weapons into his swaying corpse. The police were nowhere to be seen until the next morning, when they arrived to cut down and dispose of John Evans's bullet-shredded body.

That was a dark stain on St. Petersburg's past, but it was old news by the time Phil Doctor arrived with her two kids in the summer of 1957. There was a lot of old news in this town. The local chapter of the Ku Klux Klan was no longer as bold as it had been in the '20s, when the hooded throngs, including many of the city's most prominent citizens, routinely staged proud parades up the sands of Pass-a-Grille Beach, the glow of their torches glimmering off the waters of Tampa Bay.

By the '50s, the KKK hoods had faded away, replaced by coats and ties and respectable titles like the White Citizens Council. But like almost every city throughout the South, St. Petersburg remained a divided place. Its nicest neighborhoods, its best beaches, the front rows on its buses and trolley cars, the box seats in its baseball field, Al Lang Stadium, where the New York Yankees and St. Louis Cardinals—Mickey Mantle and Stan Musial—sharpened their skills each spring, even the bright green downtown benches built for the retirees who spilled out of the city's apartments each morning to roam its sun-bleached sidewalks, they were all understood, if not clearly marked, to be for whites only.

Arnett wove his way through that world each day, shining shoes in the afternoons with his mother's brother, his Uncle A. T., their pockets filling with nickels and quarters. Evenings Arnett would fetch tubs of drinks and barrels of ice for the black acts that played the Manhattan Casino, a cavernous club above a warehouse down at the heart of 22nd Street, the main artery through the black section of the city, St. Petersburg's Harlem, so to speak. In its heyday, in the late '50s, the Manhattan was jammed each evening with five hundred, six hundred, seven hundred sweat-soaked couples jitterbugging and lindy-hopping to the likes of Billy Eckstine and Buddy Johnson, Brook Benton and Floyd Rawlings, Louis Armstrong, big stars with big wallets, most of them happy to lay a five-dollar tip on a kid clever enough to find them something cool to drink on those sweltering South Florida nights.

Mornings Arnett would head downtown, wending his way through the whites-only sections to get to the beach, the black beach, a stretch of sand they called South Mole. It had no buoys, no lifeguards, not even a way to get to the

Arnett and the other boys were taken to jail. The girls, including one to whom Arnett quietly passed his revolver before the police moved in, were allowed to go home. That was the last Arnett ever saw of that gun.

The first his mother learned of his whereabouts was watching that evening's six o'clock news. The broadcast began with footage of the arrest. It showed a line of black teens being led into a paddy wagon. At the front of the line was Arnett, and Philomena just about had a seizure when she saw him. She didn't even know her boy was *in* the goddamned NAACP.

When Arnett finally got home late that night, after officers of the organization's adult chapter had gone downtown and negotiated for the boys' release, Philomena attacked him, whipping him with a belt, beating his back, his chest, his legs, sobbing and shaking, cursing, swearing that he was going to die, just the way Wallace Jordan had died, just the way so many had died.

Arnett didn't flinch. He had seen his mother like this before, and he would see it again. He would see it when he went into the Army in '63, shipped off to the Pacific, then to places he couldn't tell her about, couldn't tell anyone about, because the U.S. wasn't supposed to be in those places, not yet. But Arnett was there, and his mother knew it, knew he was risking his life for the sake of the white man, because this war—if it was a war—would be like all the others, a white man's cause with black men doing more than their share of the dying.

Arnett didn't die. He killed, though he couldn't talk about it, but he didn't die. Twelve years after he enlisted he came home, world-traveled, trained in intelligence, versed in foreign languages, and more comfortable with whites than he had ever dreamed possible. The Army had done that, but his mother didn't give a damn. All she cared about was the fact that he was alive and back beside her, her only son.

He had a wife now, too, but it was not going well. Thelma was her name, and they were at each other all the time. Arnett had married her after she'd told him she was pregnant. It was the right thing to do, he figured, and so he did it right, a military wedding, raised sabers and all. A baby daughter was born five months later, but she was too small to survive. They hardly had time to name her—Patrice—before she died, six hours after she was delivered.

The marriage was a mess. Arnett and Thelma fought constantly. It was better when he had been wearing a uniform. At least that had kept him away from the house. Now he was home all the time, having to face her, and worse, having to face her parents. Arnett still had his temper, and it was getting the best of him again. More than once he threatened Thelma's mother and father, warned them to stay out of his business, that his troubles with his wife were between him and her. Finally, one night, he told them he'd kill them if they didn't keep away. Them and Thelma too. In a fit of rage, he pulled a gun. Waved it. Soon after that he told Thelma he wanted out, that he was filing for divorce. "Do it," she said, "and I'll see you in hell or in prison."

She saw him in prison. The day after the divorce was granted, Thelma's family filed assault charges with the state's attorney's office—aggravated assault—and Arnett wound up doing time. It wasn't hard time, he would say years later. When you do hard time, he would explain, you do it on their terms. Real time is done on *your* terms, and that's how Arnett insists he did his. Three years, all told. He saw the insides of jails in St. Pete and Clearwater, was sent to prisons in Avon Park, Lake Butler, Zephyrhills, Largo. He was all over the state during those three years, serving cafeteria food to inmates in one place, putting on a coat and tie in another and going outside the gates to help run a Special Olympics. He took college classes, too—a couple of business law courses and one in logic. They were behind bars, but they counted.

When he finally came out, in the summer of 1981, came home to St. Pete, Arnett Doctor fit no profile. He was an ex-con who spoke with the polish of a professor, a veteran who had carried a carbine in the jungles of Asia and now packed a sidearm on the streets of St. Pete. He had put his life in the hands of the white man, both in the Army and in prison, and he had survived without scars, without bitterness, though trust remained an issue. His mother made sure of that. The worst hurt he had to show for his life up till then, besides the loss of sheer time, was the feet he tore up during boot camp back in '63. The pain still jerked him awake most nights, the tangle of tendons and tissue stabbing like needles beneath his skin. Sometimes it got so bad he could hardly stand, which was why he had taken to carrying a cane.

The cane was there that Friday afternoon, propped in a corner behind the counter as he made change for his customers. He had been at Lundy's a year now, had worked his way up to manager and was looking to leave soon, to start his own business, maybe something janitorial. He was thirty-nine and in a hurry, a man with connections and some catching up to do. He didn't need any more trouble in his life, which is why he recoiled when he saw a white man appear in the door.

White people didn't come to Lundy's. They didn't come to this *neighbor-*

hood unless they had business, and the business they had was normally something to do with drugs. But this man was not looking for drugs. He was looking, he said, for a man named Arnett Doctor.

"Who wants to know?" asked Arnett. The man looked harmless enough, with a thick brownish beard and unruly hair that hung almost to his shoulders. He wore a checked flannel shirt, wrinkled khaki trousers and sneakers. He reminded Arnett of some of the holdover hippies he had seen when he came out of the service. But this man was no hippie. His deep voice was thick with a southern twang, the voice of a cracker. Educated, but still a cracker. And that set Arnett on edge. His mother had warned him about all white folks, but crackers, she said, they were the worst.

The man introduced himself, said his name was Gary Moore, said he was a reporter for the *St. Petersburg Times*. He extended his hand. Arnett hesitated. He shook the hand, but he didn't speak.

"I was told you might be able to help me out," said the reporter.

"And how's that?" asked Arnett.

"Well, I've been investigating an incident that happened up in Levy County."

Arnett felt his chest suddenly swell. He could hear his heartbeat thudding inside his head, the pounding of his pulse.

"Actually," the man continued, "it's something that happened back in 1923 . . ."

Arnett's hands were clenched now, his knuckles straining against the skin.

". . . at a place called Rosewood."

A Wall of Darkness

A rnett had been to Rosewood before. Once.

It was the summer of 1962, a year before he left to join the Army, and he was with his buddies, Bobo and George. They used to run together, the three of them, cruising the streets of St. Pete nearly every night in Bobo's '57 Buick Roadmaster. The car was a dream, silver and gray and snow white on the outside, black crushed velvet inside, with an engine that got cooler the faster and farther it was driven. Weekends they would take it out of town, hit the highway and open it up, toward Lakeland, Orlando, Ocala, any place that offered bright lights, cold drinks and warm women.

They were always looking for women, and they always came armed, because the kinds of clubs they walked into, a man would be a fool to enter without a weapon. Clubs like the One Stop Inn over at Plant City. Arnett would never forget the night the three of them stopped in there, met some young ladies, danced a while, had a few drinks, finally got up to leave and found themselves facing a crowd of locals, eight or nine of them, blocking the door, making

Philomena and Walter Doctor

it clear they objected to some city boys walking in off the street and hitting on their women.

Arnett didn't blink. He pulled out his piece, a .38, and just the sight of that pistol was enough to part the crowd. The locals backed away, let Arnett and his buddies leave the same way they'd come in, with their new lady friends in tow, and so the night was counted a success, although Arnett and Bobo and George never did go back to the One Stop Inn.

They were headed for Tallahassee that June afternoon in '62, when, about two hours north of Tampa, Bobo suddenly yanked the wheel and turned the car toward the coast.

"What the hell are you doing?" Arnett asked as the Roadmaster lurched left onto a narrow two-lane highway, just past a small sign that read Otter Creek.

"This place you been telling us about for so long," said Bobo, "I want to see it for myself. Rosewood. That's where we're going."

Arnett hadn't told his friends much about Rosewood, nowhere near all that he knew, and he knew nowhere near as much as he wanted to. Still, what he had told them was more than they could believe, and who could blame them? Who could believe there had once been a town up here in this godforsaken swamp country, a busy town filled with black people, three hundred of them at its peak, at the turn of the century, land-owning people with their own homes and businesses. Hard to believe there could have been anything at all out here in the middle of nowhere. Harder still to believe it could have been here one day and be gone the next, swept away overnight, the houses burned to the ground, the land seized, the people driven into the bogs, never to return, and nothing done about it, not after forty years, no mention of it in any history book, as if none of this had ever happened, as if the place had never existed.

Crazy, that's how it sounded to Arnett's buddies. As far as they figured, the place never *had* existed. This was just another one of Arnett's stories, and Arnett could *tell* a story. Sometimes it sounded crazy even to himself, even now, even after a lifetime of hearing the whispers, of hiding as a child around doorways and under windows, listening through walls to the words of the grownups, hearing them talk in hushed tones, late at night, after they thought the children were asleep and it was safe to speak, to speak about Rosewood.

Arnett was six when he first heard of it. It was Christmas day, 1949, and it was cold, bitter cold. They were living in Lacoochee then, he and his sister and his mama and daddy, living in the only house he had ever known, a company house back in what they called the quarters, across the Seaboard tracks, hard against the piney woods, in the crowded corner of town where the black sawmill workers lived. Dirt lanes and two-room huts, no electricity, no plumbing, outhouses out back, wood-burning stoves in the kitchens—that was the quarters.

Arnett's father was what they called a stacker up at the mill, pulling the fresh-cut planks of cedar and cypress as they were sliced off the logs, piling them to the side for the wagons to pick up and haul across the yard to the trains. He worked six days a week, every week of the year but Christmas, because Christmas they shut down the saws. And so Arnett's father was home that wind-whipped afternoon when Philomena came out on the porch and called the kids inside, hollered to Arnett to go find his sister and come on in the house.

They had a tree up, and there was a fire going in the fireplace. As he came in the door, Arnett could see his father was agitated, but then his daddy was always on edge around Christmas, because Philomena always got so sad that day. She'd sink into a tailspin and wind up back in her bedroom, stretched out on the mattress, crying and calling out her grandmother's name. *Mama, Mama*, she'd wail, and Arnett never knew why. All he knew was his father would follow her in there, close the door, and that's where the two of them would stay, for hours sometimes, until it was close to dark and finally his daddy would come out, drained and deathly quiet, and they would sit down to dinner, the three of them. Sometimes Arnett's mother would join them and sometimes not.

But this day it was different. Arnett's father was not so much sad as he was angry. He was facing Philomena as Arnett and his sister walked in.

"Why do you want to *do* this, Phil?" he said. "Why you want to tell them about this now? Just leave it alone. Why don't you leave it *alone?*"

She wouldn't even look at him. He grabbed his jacket, stormed out the door and slammed it behind him. Arnett's mother motioned the children to take a seat on the floor. He could feel the cold coming up through the bare wood. Arnett could see small slivers of light in the cracks between the planks, daylight shining up from beneath the house. He wished he was back outside with his friends, playing cowboys, showing off the new Hopalong Cassidy holster and cap guns he'd unwrapped that morning. But his mother wanted him here, told him and his sister to take off their coats, that she had something important to talk to them about. Arnett fixed his eyes on the tree, staring at the shiny tinsel as his mother began to speak.

"I want to tell you about something," she said, "and I want you to listen carefully. This is very important."

The fire spit and crackled behind her as she wiped her eyes with a handkerchief. His mother was still slim then, and strong. She could carry a washtub under one arm and a load of firewood under the other. She could carry Arnett if she had to, and his sister, too.

"I want you to know who you *are,*" she said, narrowing her eyes. "You are *not* like everyone else. You are special. Your ancestors were special people, people of importance. Your granddaddy owned land, a lot of land, just like Mr. Cummer."

Arnett never doubted anything his mama told him, but this was hard to believe. The Cummers owned all of Lacoochee. That sawmill was theirs, along with untold thousands of acres of woodland around it. The houses where most of the men who worked at the mill lived, those belonged to the Cummers. The commissary where the mill hands and their families shopped, that belonged to the Cummers, too. The Cummers themselves lived in a mansion up at the other end of town, across the tracks, a huge three-story home like something out of the movies, set back behind moss-hung oaks, surrounded by hundreds of acres of private woods loaded with fish and game, patrolled by armed guards who arrested anyone caught trespassing. Before they took you to jail, these guards would give you a good beating just to make sure this wouldn't happen again.

Arnett had been up on that Cummer property. He'd been inside the Cummer house as well. His Aunt Becky did laundry and cleaning for the Cummers, and sometimes she would bring him along with her. His father did yard work there, too, and occasionally he would bring Arnett with him. But Arnett's mother never set foot in that house or on that land. She wanted no part of the Cummers.

That world always seemed so far away, even when Arnett was right there, inside that big house. He never met the Cummers, just watched them come and go like white shadows. He never dared to even dream about such a life, but now his mother was telling him his own people had once had something like that—their own land, their own businesses, their own big houses with living rooms and lamps and sofas. Not just two rooms and a kitchen, like the shotgun shacks they lived in now. They owned pianos, his mother said. And organs. They had horses and buggies, and on Sundays they rode to church like royalty.

Royalty. That's what Arnett's mother said her people had been. The Goinses and the Carriers, the two families her father and mother came from, they were the most important people in the town of Rosewood, she said. Her great-uncle, Martine Goins, he was the best businessman in those parts, the way she described him, a man respected by blacks and whites alike. He ran a turpentine operation so big it had housing for some of the men who worked there, quarters just like the Cummers', quarters right there in Rosewood.

That's where she was from, Arnett's mother said. Not Tampa or Gainesville, cities Arnett knew his mother had lived in back before he was born, places he had heard of. No, she was from Rosewood. And so, she was now telling him, were many of his aunts and uncles, and more than a few of his neighbors right there in Lacoochee. They were all from this place called Rosewood. But they could never go back, none of them, his mother said, because there was nothing left to go back to.

And then she began crying, her pride giving way to pain as she told Arnett and his sister, in scattered, sketchy detail, how the town had vanished, in shouts and gunshots and flames.

She was there, she said, at the white woman's house that winter morning in 1923, one village away from Rosewood, in a place called Sumner. Her parents were gone that month, working at a lumber camp near a little spot known as Otter Creek, and so Philomena and her younger brothers, A. T. and George, were staying with their Grandma Sarah, Sarah Carrier. "Mama," that's what Philomena called her. Every morning Sarah walked to Sumner to do house-work and laundry for white folks, and that New Year's morning she brought Philomena with her.

Not long after they arrived, as they were hanging clothes on the line outside this white woman's house, Sarah and Philomena saw a man slip through the back door. It was a white man, but it was not the woman's husband.

They had seen this man before. He was an engineer with the railroad, and he was known to be the woman's boyfriend. Her lover. Most of Rosewood knew it. Most blacks in Sumner knew it. Grandma Sarah knew it. She had seen the man come and go from this house more than once. She never said a word, never even looked up as he passed. She knew better than that.

Normally the man came and left in silence, but this day there was a commotion, some banging and yelling from inside the house. Then the man burst out the back door, hurried across the yard, stepped over the fence without opening the gate, and rushed up the railroad tracks, on foot, toward Rosewood.

Some time passed, a half an hour or so. Philomena and Grandma Sarah were just finishing up their work when the white woman burst out her door, screaming that she'd been attacked, that a black man had beaten her. It wasn't to protect her lover that she lied, said Arnett's mother. The man had just beaten her bloody. It was to protect herself from the beating or even worse she might get from her husband if he knew.

Men came, his mother said. Dogs too. A mob formed. Grandma Sarah tried to step in, to tell them this was wrong, to tell these people what had really happened. But they pushed her away, told her to shut up, her and her little pickaninny, shut up and get on home.

And so the whites would never know, would never *hear* of the notion that it had been one of their own who had done this. It had to be a black man. And so it was.

After a week, Arnett's mother said, it was over. The town was gone. No one ever came back, she said. Not then, not ever. And that, she explained, was why she cried every Christmas, because for her the holidays meant nothing but memories of that week, of Rosewood, of what she had lost and what they, Arnett and Yvonne, had lost, too. She was eleven years old when it happened, she told them. Just a girl, she said. But she would never feel like a child again.

It was dark by the time Arnett's mother was done. Time to take a bath and go to bed. Christmas Day was done.

Arnett hardly slept that night, his mind was swirling with so many questions, his six-year-old chest heaving with so many feelings. He heard his father stumble in late, drunk, but the next morning it was as if nothing had happened. His daddy was up and joking like always, his mother was in the kitchen, breakfast on the table, and Arnett's friends were outside, hollering for him to come and play.

Arnett never heard much more from his mother about Rosewood than what she told him and his sister that Christmas. It became their annual ritual, Philomena sitting the children down on Christmas Day and telling them the Rosewood story. It was always the same, nothing new added, and no questions allowed. None. Arnett's mother spoke, and the children listened.

Every other day of the year, the subject was taboo. Arnett got more than one whipping for mentioning it to a playmate or comparing notes with a cousin. Over the years he was able to squeeze a few tidbits out of some of his relatives, the older ones, like his Aunt Beauty and Aunt Sweetie, who were willing to answer a question or two with a promise not to tell his mother.

But Arnett was never able to learn as much as he wanted. His aunts were eager to talk about what the town had been like before it was destroyed, about their deep family lines, both the Goinses' and the Carriers', about their roots up in the Carolinas and the Indian stock they had come from, about what they had made of themselves by the turn of the century in this hamlet in the woods. But when it came to details of the attack itself, Arnett knew only bits and pieces, and the things he knew raised more questions than they answered. He didn't even know where Rosewood *was*, not until Bobo took that turn that Saturday afternoon.

"It's on the map, man," Bobo said, pointing at a tiny dot over near the coastline. Arnett had never searched a map, never dreamed the place might still exist. But sure enough, there it was, in tiny letters along State Route 24, halfway up the coast. He moved his finger down the map, inland, southeast to Lacoochee, and he measured the distance. About eighty miles.

And now Bobo was slowing down, because there was a sign up ahead on the side of the road, a green metal sign with simple white lettering:

ROSEWOOD

They came to a stop, looked around. Nothing but stands of short scrub pines to the right, second growth come up since the logging crews cleared out. But to the left was thicker forest, the trees larger, older. That's where Rosewood was, back in that forest.

Up ahead, down a dirt lane, under the trees, they could see a few scattered homes, some made of cinderblock, the rest of wood, all small, with roofs made of tin.

Bobo turned there, onto the dirt. Arnett could hear the sand and shells crunching beneath the tires. An old white woman was sitting on a porch swing. When she saw them, she got up and went inside, shut her screen door behind her.

The road forked, and they followed it to another house. Nothing there but some dogs and a dead end, the forest gathering together into a wall of darkness.

They turned back toward the highway, past a house unlike the others, a large, ghostly Victorian place, with stained glass windows and latticed porches, set back among some oaks and fruit trees. It, too, had dogs in the yard, and Arnett and Bobo and George were not about to mess with any dogs, not in a place like this. It was the turn of the '60s, civil rights clashes brewing in cities like Selma and Birmingham, with marchers and megaphones, Freedom Riders and federal troops, newspaper reporters and TV cameras. But back in places like this, there was none of that. Places like this were where black men's bodies still bobbed up from riverbeds and nobody blinked an eye.

Just before they got back on the highway, they passed a small store, no more than a hut, with a couple of gas pumps and four or five white men sitting on stools out front, playing checkers. Arnett watched the group look up, staring at this car of black men, probably the only black men between there and the Gulf of Mexico. He saw a shotgun leaning by the door. And he decided he had seen enough. Fifteen minutes later, he and Bobo and George were back on Route 19, hurtling north to Tallahassee.

Arnett never told his mother about that trip. It had been twenty years now since that day, and he still wouldn't dare to tell her about it. No matter that he was about to turn forty, a middle-aged man. If she knew he had ever been to Rosewood, she would beat him like a child. And if she knew he was considering going up there *again,* and with a white man, no less, well, Arnett could not even imagine what she might do.

But he *was* considering it. He left the reporter that afternoon with the promise he would meet him in the morning at the liquor store, and they would leave from there. He spent the rest of the evening on the telephone, calling his boss to get the day off, calling some friends to let them know where he was going, in case something happened and he didn't come back.

He did not call his mother. His mother would be damned if her boy was going to take a trip like this.

But Arnett would be damned if he didn't.

THREE

"If That Ain't Country"

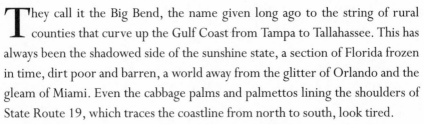

They call it the Big Bend, the name given long ago to the string of rural counties that curve up the Gulf Coast from Tampa to Tallahassee. This has always been the shadowed side of the sunshine state, a section of Florida frozen in time, dirt poor and barren, a world away from the glitter of Orlando and the gleam of Miami. Even the cabbage palms and palmettos lining the shoulders of State Route 19, which traces the coastline from north to south, look tired.

Hand-scrawled signs nailed to roadside pines hawk fresh-picked corn and okra, pecans and "p-nuts." Plywood placards appear, mounted on twisted oaks, their warnings scribbled in bright red letters:

PREPARE TO MEET THY GOD

Towns pop up along the way, places like Perry, where the Flat Creek Gun Shop shares its front lawn with the Pisquah Missionary Baptist Church, where the Rebel Room Bar & Grill is right up the road from Grady's Feed and Hound Supply.

And Cross City, the hub of Dixie County, where flatbed trucks and railcars

Lelland "Beauty" Carrier and her sister Ruby

loaded with fresh-cut timber rumble past the B&B Ammo store and the Lost in Time Lounge.

And Chiefland, where Elnora's Beds for Less furniture shop and the Bent & Dent discount food store flank VFW Rebel Post 5625.

And Otter Creek, nothing but a flashing orange light in the heart of Levy County, Hershel's Quick Stop grocery on the right and a BP service station on the left. There is no need to slow at Otter Creek, no drop in the speed limit, and most of the traffic shooting south—the RVs and campers with lawn chairs and bicycles strapped to their roofs, out-of-state plates screwed to their bumpers, vacationers bound for Sarasota, retirees headed to Clearwater—they keep going. The few vehicles that stop here are turning inland toward Gainesville, twenty-five miles to the east on Route 24, or out toward the coast, twenty miles west.

Route 24 is the road that runs through Rosewood, two lanes of lonely asphalt slicing straight as a razor into thick hardwood hammocks and marshy swampland, past scattered patches of scrub pines and palmettos and bare stretches of briars and weeds, not a soul in sight save for a smattering of tin-roofed shacks and tree-shaded trailers, rickety roadside stands selling smoked mullet, and rotting outdoor tables stacked with sacks of boiled peanuts.

Traffic is sparse. Small brown lizards skitter across the blacktop as packs of turkey vultures, their tar-like feathers gleaming in the midday sun, alight on the sandy shoulders, picking at fresh road kill, undisturbed by the occasional passing of a pickup truck or logging trailer rumbling east, back toward Otter Creek and beyond.

Now and then comes a car headed west. A couple bound for a cheap weekend bungalow. A family with fishing gear stowed in their trunk. Maybe a van full of college kids, University of Florida frat boys and their dates, cutting classes and taking a road trip to the coast.

Halfway there they pass through Rosewood, but few of them notice. There is little to notice. A couple of rusted gas pumps, a half dozen small cinderblock homes stuck back beneath the pines and palms, a tiny trailer park, and a lone, two-story, tree-shaded house set off down a dirt drive. All just a passing blur.

Ten miles beyond, the road runs out in the fishing village of Cedar Key, a tiny island community ringed by coves and bayous, a town that has tried a long time to tout itself as a tourist resort. Twice a year, during its annual art festival in mid-April and its seafood festival in October, when the narrow lanes lining

the waterfront are jammed with thousands of camera-strapped visitors, it actually feels like a booming resort. The rest of the time, the place is quiet, sleepy,
the way Key West was half a century ago.

That's how the locals like to think of Cedar Key, as the best of Old Florida.
And it does have that air of serenity, its hourly rhythms as gentle as the gulf
water lapping at its waterfront wharves. The island's main street is quaint, a
collection of small shops and boutiques anchored by the old Island Hotel, a
weathered wooden structure built back before the turn of the century. Pelicans
perch on worn pilings down at the west end of town, where a string of pierside
cafes feature the day's bounty, pulled fresh from the holds of Cedar Key's small
fleet of fishing boats.

Some new condominiums have recently risen along that waterfront, a
hopeful sign for the chamber of commerce but not for the residents who have
been driven off the island by ballooning property values and rocketing tax
rates. More than a few of Cedar Key's fishermen now commute to their boats
from the shacks and trailers sprinkled back up along Route 24, including the
handful of homes that make up what has become of Rosewood.

Visitors curious about the area's history can stop in the Cedar Key Historical Society Museum, a homey, coral-colored house a block off the waterfront,
where a smattering of pamphlets and scrapbooks, old snapshots and newspaper
clippings tell a sanitized version of how this place came to be, how Seminoles
fleeing the white settlers to the north arrived on these islands in the first part of
the nineteenth century, how the U.S. Army moved in during its war with the
Indians in the 1840s and drove the natives out, and how the town took root
with the construction of the first trans-Florida railroad, which ran from the Atlantic coast harbor of Fernandina Beach across the state to Cedar Key.

When that rail line opened in 1861, Cedar Key was poised to challenge
Tampa as Florida's premier Gulf port. But the Civil War delayed those plans, as
Union troops blockaded the island and tore up the tracks. The museum doesn't
mention that more than a few local fishermen made good money during the
war by trimming their schooners for speed and slipping out through the bayous
at night, skirting the Union ships and carrying contraband to the Confederate
forces. Nor does it make much of the fact that some of the local folk fought on
land as well. To this day, there are people in Cedar Key who recall with pride
how a band of their boys ambushed a raiding party of black Union soldiers on

the island's Number Four bridge in February of 1865, recapturing most of the booty the Yankees had seized from the surrounding woods and farmland, including a hundred head of cattle, a dozen horses and about fifty slaves.

Two months after that skirmish, the war was over. By the end of the year the tracks were rebuilt, and the boom Cedar Key had been awaiting began. Wharfs and warehouses went up as steamers arrived from Mobile and New Orleans with goods headed east and south. Ships came up from Havana with cargo headed north. Hotels were built—three of them—along with a string of saloons, dance halls and gambling houses. The island's narrow gas lamp–lit streets were jammed with sailors and fishermen, as well as lumbermen who were now sweeping through the surrounding swamps and forests, cutting cedar and cypress for the sawmills that had sprung up along the tracks. The loggers worked all week, sleeping in remote inland swamp camps, then roared into Cedar Key on weekends, wearing six-shooters and bowie knives, looking for some fun and maybe a good fight. The watermen were glad to oblige, and Cedar Key soon built a reputation to rival the deadliest western frontier towns. Shootouts and "bushwhackings," as the local newspaper called them, were common items in daily news columns. Murders were so routine they hardly rated more than a brief mention.

It was during this time, soon after the Civil War, that a young freelance magazine writer named John Muir arrived in town—on foot. He was at the end of a trek he had begun seven weeks earlier, a thousand miles away, in Indiana. His aim was to chronicle the post-war conditions in the South, and his notebooks were filled. His most recent entries described the "watery and vine-tied land" along the Gulf Coast. He hadn't planned to stay in Cedar Key when he arrived in October of 1867, but he fell sick, so sick he wound up slumped beneath a tree in town, where he was ignored as just another drunk until a passerby finally stopped, shook the body to see if it was alive and discovered the man needed a doctor.

Muir had malaria, a common condition in those parts at that time. He spent that winter bedridden on the island, pondering the wilderness he had passed through, sketching his impressions of the land he had seen as well as the people he had met. He moved on in the spring and eventually settled in California, where he helped create Yosemite National Park and founded the Sierra Club. It was not until 1916, two years after his death, that John Muir's journal of that

1867 journey through the South was finally published, with its descriptions of the "traces of war not only apparent on the broken fields, mills and woods ruthlessly slaughtered, but also on the countenance of the people."

For the people of Cedar Key, however, the years just after the war were the best of times. But the boom was brief, lasting hardly a generation. By the mid-1880s, a rail line was opened to Tampa, sucking the shipping away from Cedar Key and turning the place into a relic. By the 1890s the hardwood in the hammocks between the island and Otter Creek was nearly gone, logged out by the voracious timber companies. A pencil factory, built on the island by a German businessman and fed for twenty years by cedar from those swamps, was now barely running, all but a handful of its employees laid off and most of its machinery inert and seized solid with rust. The final blow was a hurricane that hit the coast in 1896.

The people of Cedar Key were used to hurricanes, lived through a couple every year, boarded up their windows, lit their lanterns and sat out the storm. But this one brought with it a tidal wave, a wall of water twenty feet high, sweeping over the island like the hand of God. And when it had passed, it had taken half of Cedar Key with it. One out of every two buildings had vanished. The island's fleet of sponge boats was smashed to splinters. The population, too, was in pieces. The year before that storm, fourteen hundred people inhabited Cedar Key. The year after, fewer than seven hundred remained. The rest had been washed away by that wave, or had seen all they owned obliterated and had simply picked up and left.

Almost a century later, there are still roughly seven hundred people living in or around Cedar Key, many of them fishermen lounging down at the docks beside their tired boats, bitching about the size of their catch, about the price of gas and the government bureaucrats bound to run them out of business with their laws and regulations. Over at the L&M bar, a block away from the Island Hotel, neon beer logos glow in the windows as they do each day beginning at noon. The stools inside are sprinkled with locals, some watching the TV, others waiting their turn at the pool table. A Confederate flag is draped on the back room wall, the words *The South Will Rise Again* stitched on its border. A David Allan Coe tune is punched up on the jukebox:

> *. . . thirteen kids and a bunch of dogs,*
> *House full o' chickens and a yard full o' hogs,*

He spent the summertime cuttin' up logs,
For the winter.
Tryin' like the devil to find the Lord,
Workin' like a nigger for my room 'n board,
Coal-burnin' stove, no natural gas,
If that ain't country, I'll kiss your ass. . . .

This is, indeed, the Deep South, which did not surprise Gary Moore, the reporter from the St. Pete *Times,* who wandered into Cedar Key in early 1982 while working on a travel story. "It was a way to kill a weekend, to get out of town," recalls Moore. "I just went along the way looking for things. I didn't know anything about Rosewood."

But he knew about places like Cedar Key. There were plenty of them all over the state—tiny towns, insulated pockets of people who had been able over the course of the past century to resist change, to keep things pretty much as they had always been, small hamlets that were somehow able to stand still in the face of the force of time. There was mystery around these places, and menace, the gothic stuff of countless southern novels.

But Moore was no novelist. He was a journalist, and he became intrigued by the fact that there was not one black face to be seen in Cedar Key—this in a town whose population had been one-third black at the turn of the century. It was black labor that had laid the tracks through the swamp into Cedar Key, and many of those men had chosen to stay, settling with their families in the woods between Otter Creek and the coast, hunting, fishing, cutting lumber and tapping turpentine for their living. At the turn of the century, there had been a black school in Cedar Key. Black churches, too. And now there was nothing.

When Moore began asking around, no one said much, not at first. Most simply shrugged, a few pointed toward the section of town where the blacks used to live, a place the locals still called "Nigger Hill," back toward the middle of the island. But no one would say where the "niggers" had gone, not until one woman—Moore visited her in an old church, which was now the woman's home—finally mentioned "the massacre."

And that was how it began, one story giving way to another, a light piece on weekend getaways turning into something deeper and darker. Moore could hardly believe what he heard as some of the townspeople began to talk. Images of torture and immolation, of unholy terror and unspeakable fear, of murder and mutilation, body parts severed and stored in Mason jars, still pulled out with a queer sense of pride sixty years later by those into whose hands they had passed.

So much sounded like myth, so much was mere memory, massaged over decades into odd and outsized shapes, pieces that didn't fit, facts that were flawed, truth faded to fable by the passage of years. Still, a story emerged, began to take shape, of something hideous that had actually occurred in those woods up the road from Cedar Key.

And that is what eventually led Gary Moore to Lundy's Liquor Store on that Friday afternoon in the spring of 1982, to ask Arnett Doctor to go with him, to go up to Rosewood.

Ground Zero

Arnett was worried sick as he climbed in the passenger's side of Gary Moore's car that Saturday morning. It was a sunny day, cool, with puffs of clouds rolling in from the coast. Arnett wasn't sure if this thing might not be a con, that somehow someone might still be out to get him and his family sixty years after the fact. But he figured he'd done all he could to cover himself. His friends knew where he was, and if worse came to worst, he had that .357 tucked in the waistband of his slacks.

It wasn't himself he was worried about, it was his mother. Her health had been so bad lately, and it was getting worse every day. Blood pressure, diabetes, glaucoma, gout. Arnett could count on one hand the number of sick days his mother had taken during all the years she'd worked for her living, but now it seemed she was sick all the time. And it was all because of the eating.

In the course of just a couple of years, Arnett had watched his mother balloon before his eyes, from one hundred and sixty to two hundred pounds. Then two-thirty, two-forty, twice what she had weighed when she married Arnett's

The old Wright house

father. And there was no sign of it stopping. Every day she got bigger, and her
health was caving in under the load.

It was hard to watch, hard for Arnett to think that this was what it had
come to, that his mother had worked her entire life, from the time she turned
ten until she was almost seventy, worked countless hours at thankless jobs, and
this was what she had to show for it, a body literally feeding itself on bitterness.

She had washed other people's clothes and cleaned other people's homes
for decades before she finally found her first clock-punching job, on an assembly line in an eyeglass factory there in St. Pete. She spent ten years at that, then
moved onto another line, this one inside the windowless walls of a missile
plant. Arnett never knew exactly what his mother did there—"Defense work,"
she called it—but he knew she never sat down. Eight hours a day she stood in
one spot, sticking the same parts on the same pieces, coming home at night dog
tired and aching, her legs still sore when she rose the next morning to go back
out to the bus stop and do it again.

It wasn't until she was in her sixties that she found the first and only sit-
down job of her life, copying and filing forms for a job-training company up-
town, which is where she was when she decided it was time to retire. No to-do
about it, no company luncheon. Her last day of work was the same as her first,
and when it was done, she punched out, rode home, and opened the refrigerator.

Watch TV and eat, that's all she had done since she quit working—that and
attend the monthly meetings of the Quest Federated Social Club, a group of elderly black women who gathered at one another's homes to plan their annual
ball, a grand affair at which hundreds of black women from Tampa and St. Pete
would convene to see which of them would be crowned Miss Black Federated
Woman of the Year. One year—her children say it might have been the happiest night of her life—that crown was placed on Philomena Doctor's head.

Those Federation meetings and church. Nothing else could get Phil Doctor
out of the house. Nothing else mattered. Food and her God was all she needed.
And family. She never missed a family gathering, no matter when or where it
was. A christening, a wedding, funerals, holidays. Relatives were like religion
to her, and that's how she raised her children. There wasn't an aunt or uncle
alive or dead that Arnett and Yvonne didn't know at least by name. Most of
them they knew better than that. Arnett had slept in their beds, broken bread

at their tables, bowed his head and held their hands as they lifted their voices to the Lord.

Arnett never knew of a family that prayed like his. Every day of the week they prayed, and not just at mealtime either. When he was grown and on his own, he'd stop by his mother's house to see how she was, middle of the afternoon, and there would be an aunt or two sitting on the sofa, TV on in the corner, and one of them would say, "All right, now, let's have a prayer," and they'd switch off the set and all kneel down together, right there on the living room carpet. Then one of them would get up and go fix him something to eat.

These days that's all Philomena did was eat, and it was killing her. Still, she remained the most powerful person Arnett had ever known, a matriarch who ruled with an iron hand. Every time the family gathered, cousins by the dozen, aunts and uncles by the score, it was Aunt Phil—"Sissy" to her siblings—who held court. Without question. Without dissent. Any decision to be made, whether it was which Bible verse would be read aloud, or who would read it, or when the potato salad should be served, Sissy made it and the others obeyed.

Part of it was her age—once Aunt Beauty passed away, Arnett's mother was left as the oldest female in the family line. But beyond her seniority, it was the sheer force of her will that made Phil Doctor so hard to resist. And the fuel for that force was resentment and rage.

Some of it came from her marriage, Arnett knew that. She had left Arnett's father when Arnett was fourteen. Twenty-four years she and her husband had been together, and she never married again. But long before the breakup— right from the beginning, in fact—there had been a seam of rancor in their marriage. Because Philomena Goins had always wanted to be a singer, and Walter Doctor had made her quit.

She was in her early twenties when they met, during the Depression, and already she was making a name for herself in clubs in Tampa and St. Pete, black night spots where acts like Count Basie, Duke Ellington, Louis Armstrong and Ella Fitzgerald would stop in on their swings through the South. Arnett's mother said she had once shared a microphone with Ella Fitzgerald, a memory Arnett would share as fact all his life, with anyone who would listen.

His mother lived for the sounds of jazz and swing, could hush a whole room with the sweet sadness of the blues, make it feel like Billie Holiday herself was caressing that microphone. Everyone who heard Phil Goins sing could feel it.

They all said she was bound for great things. But when she became a wife, her new husband would have none of it. There were children to raise, a house to keep. And so, beyond serenading herself as she cooked in the kitchen or sharing her voice with the choir on Sundays, the singing stopped.

Arnett knew some of his mother's pain had to come from the career she gave up for a marriage that didn't last. Some of it came, too, from the pride she then had to swallow to keep food on the table. But he knew just as well that beneath it all was what had happened at Rosewood. Everything about his mother, from her seething sense of injustice, to her manic fear for the safety of her children, was rooted in Rosewood.

Arnett hardly heard a word Gary Moore spoke as they drove north that Saturday morning, past the well-heeled retirement resorts of Palm Harbor and Port Richey, Spring Hill and Crystal River, across the Withlacoochee River into the rural woodlands of Levy County. The trip took two hours, and all the way all Arnett could think of was his mother and what it might do to her if she knew where he was.

And then they were there, taking the same turn Bobo had taken twenty years before, off Route 19 onto 24, into the same woods, past the same swamp and the same shacks, finally slowing at the same green sign, across the road from the same cinderblock homes that had been there in 1962. The store was still there, and the pumps. But the store's door was locked and no one was in sight.

The woman was still there, too, sitting out on that same porch swing. Only this time she didn't run inside when they approached. She stayed put as the car crunched to a stop and Moore stepped out. It was only when Arnett emerged that the woman moved, finishing the conversation from behind her screen door as Arnett kept his distance.

This day there were no dogs at the old Victorian house, so they tried there, knocking on the door and getting no answer. Arnett noticed how full the fruit trees had grown, heavy with pears and plums. Pecans, too. There were grapes dangling from an arbor, and beehives off across the side yard, a bank of boxes neatly lined along a pine rail fence. Those hadn't been there twenty years earlier.

They climbed back in the car and turned down a dirt drive Arnett had not seen before. The road, pitted and pocked by recent rains, took them deep into the woods behind the big house, under canopies of old oaks, and finally into a clearing, an open yard where the vines and thickets had been hacked back enough to allow some trailers to be parked.

Out of one of them stepped a small, skinny white man wearing no shirt, no shoes, just a pair of pants and a ball cap, his graying hair hanging in long wet strands, a blue-and-white can of beer in his hand.

The man recognized Moore, offered him a beer. He offered one to Arnett, too, which was surprising. If Arnett had ever seen a redneck in his life, he was looking at one now. But the man seemed pleasant enough, polite even. Moore said he was back again to look around if that was all right, and he'd brought an assistant with him. To sidestep suspicion, that's how Moore introduced Arnett, as his assistant.

Arnett noticed a raised mound of earth grown over with weeds, cutting through the woods, stretching out of sight in a hard, straight line. "That's what's left of the railroad," said Moore. "The tracks were pulled up fifty years ago."

Moore pointed toward a structure off in the distance, beyond a barbed wire fence, back beneath the trees. It was a shack, wet and rotten, sagging with the weight of time, draped in moss from the overhanging oaks. "That over there is where the depot was."

And now Arnett understood where he was standing.

This was ground zero, the place where his mother's Rosewood had stood. That rotting depot had been the center of town, the spot where the trains stopped on their way to Cedar Key. The dirt drive they had just driven down, that used to be the main road through town. The deserted railbed was the path the dogs and the mob had followed the morning they charged up from Sumner.

Arnett approached the shack, stepping over shrubs and briers. He poked at the rubble with his cane, hit something made of metal, bent and picked it up. It was a rust-flaked rod of iron, pointed at one end, pounded flat at the other. A railroad spike. And there was another. And another. The rails were long gone, but the spikes were still there, scattered like seeds.

Moore watched Arnett, studied his face, let the silence sink in. Then he pointed off to the left, deeper into the woods, toward a thicket of palms and palmettos.

"Over there," he said, "that's the graveyard."

Both white men stayed put as Arnett walked that way, pushing through chest-high brush, bending beneath low-hanging limbs, picking his way through thorns and brambles that tore at his trousers. He could hardly see more than a few yards ahead. Sunlight shone down in thin shafts around him. He was sweating. He could hear the buzz of insects, feel them lighting on the wetness of his neck.

Then he stepped on something solid. He bent down, brushed back some leaves and there it was—a headstone, small and smooth, the size of a writing tablet, the shape of an arch. Its inscription was worn away, nothing Arnett could make out. Just a simple piece of carved granite, lying flat in the soft, loamy soil, fallen over or knocked down God knew how long ago.

There were a half dozen more just like it scattered through the brush, some grown over with a thin carpet of soft green moss, the inscriptions unreadable on every one. And then, behind the fronds of a palmetto, Arnett saw one stone still standing, a small obelisk, maybe two feet high. This one he could read:

MARTIN GOINS
BORN JUNE 15, 1842
DIED DEC. 16, 1905

Martine Goins, Arnett thought to himself. Not Martin. Martine. This was his mother's great-uncle's grave, the man she had mentioned so many Christmas mornings. Uncle Martine. The stone had a tiny flower etched on its face, a rose.

Arnett could feel the soft ground sinking beneath his feet. He stepped back, realized he was standing on the bodies of his family, and for a moment he felt dizzy, faint. Then he steadied himself, stepped onto harder ground and circled the stones, seeing if there were any he had missed. There were not. This was it, a plot about ten feet on each side, grown over by forest, smothered by time.

When Arnett got back to the trailer, he asked the man in the ball cap about the cemetery.

"I didn't even know it was there," the man said, "'til my girls found it one day, playin' back in the woods."

It was getting to be mid-afternoon, time to leave. As they walked to the car, Moore mentioned to the man that Arnett had relatives who used to live around here.

"Is that right?" asked the man. Arnett said nothing.

"So who were your relatives?" the man asked.

"Some of them are buried back there," said Arnett, nodding toward the woods. "The Goinses—they were my family. And the Carriers, Sarah Carrier and Sylvester—she was my great-grandmother and he was my great-uncle."

The man stopped walking. He knew those names. He narrowed his eyes, and pointed his beer can at Arnett.

"So I guess you probably want your land back, right?"

Arnett had no idea why the man would ask that. "I'm just trying to gather some information," he said.

"Unh huh," said the man, squinting and taking a sip from his can. "Information."

By the time they pulled back onto Route 19, the sun was setting. A pickup passed with two white men in the cab and a rifle in the rack. The men stared at Arnett as they went by. Then they slowed, allowed Arnett and Moore to come alongside, and the one in the passenger's seat let loose a rebel yell, a shrieking war whoop.

It was a sound Arnett knew well. He had grown up with that sound in Lacoochee. He heard it from packs of white kids whenever he walked home from the candy store or the movies and he had to go through their part of town to get back to his. That sound was a warning. It was wicked. And it was not a game.

Arnett could still hear it as the reporter let him out in the parking lot of Lundy's. It was evening, Saturday night in the city, and the night was young. The traffic on Tangerine was heavy, the pace picking up by the minute. But for Arnett, the evening was over. He headed home, one hand gripping his cane, the other squeezing a piece of iron tucked in his pocket—a rusty railroad spike.

The Death of a Dog

It was a family secret that was stirred that spring of 1982, a secret that had been kept for sixty years by a family that included everyone touched by Rosewood, black and white, children and grandchildren, the living and the dead. Over the better course of the century, through twelve presidents, from Warren Harding to Ronald Reagan, the whites of Levy County, as well as the blacks who had fled, had kept their secret among themselves, some out of fear, some out of shame, and all, as the years went by, with the rooted belief that the thing was behind them, done with, a bad memory at worst and at best simply something to be forgotten.

Even those charged with remembering such events—the people who write history—even they had forgotten about Rosewood. There was no mention of it in any book on Florida's past, no record in any account of the region's racial relations. It was as if the historians, like the families themselves, had chosen to leave Rosewood behind, keeping the secret by joining the silence.

But it was far from a secret at the time it took place. Newspapers throughout Florida followed the events of that New Year's week in 1923. After the

(January, 1923, newspaper headlines)

shootout at the Carrier household, the story leaped to the top of every front page in the state.

5 DIE SUMNER RACE RIOT

That was the *Gainesville Daily Sun*'s lead story on Friday, January fifth.

SIX DIE IN RACE CLASHES,
ACCORDING TO TELEPHONE REPORT FROM ROSEWOOD

That was the *Tampa Tribune*'s headline the same morning.

MANY DIE IN FLORIDA RACE WAR,
HUNDREDS OF WHITES BATTLE NEGROES AMBUSHED IN CABIN,
FOUR WHITES, 20 BLACKS DEAD

That was the *Miami Daily Metropolis*'s banner. The *Jacksonvile Journal* headlined its story in starker, simpler terms:

BURN TOWN OF ROSEWOOD

Eyes beyond Florida were fixed on Rosewood as well, with newspapers across the nation trumpeting the "race war" in this tiny Gulf Coast village. That's what the *Chicago Tribune* called it, taking its information from the wire reports out of Cedar Key. The *Washington Post* did the same, referring to a "negro desperado" whose gunfire from inside his home had sparked the battle. The *St. Louis Post-Dispatch* described "two negresses" dead after an attack on a "barricaded hut" inhabited by a "band of heavily armed Negroes." The *New York Times* ran its version of the story on page one, under a bold black headline:

KILL SIX IN FLORIDA
BURN NEGRO HOUSES

The nation's black newspapers weighed in with their own versions of the attack, including the *Afro-American* in Baltimore, which published an elaborate account evoking images of the siege at the Alamo:

FLORIDA MOB USES TORCH,
NUMEROUS INSTANCES OF HEROISM
AS MEN DEFEND HOMES AGAINST SAVAGES

Rosewood, Fla., Jan. 9. (Crusader Service)—Eighteen white and colored men and women are known to be dead and many others wounded in a savage mob battle that has raged here since the evening of January 5th, following an attempt by a mob of lawless whites to take the law into their hands in the case of a colored man accused of attacking a white woman.

Hearing that the accused man, Jesse Hunter, was hiding in the village of Rosewood, whites from the neighboring towns invaded the Negro section and attempted a house-to-house search. They were met with a hail of bullets at the first house they came to. The inmates, recognizing the belligerency and lawless composition of the howling mob did not wait to ask for an explanation of their visit. They opened fire and prepared to sell their lives dearly. They might not have committed any crime but they knew a lawless mob when they saw one.

Two whites were killed outright at the first shower of lead. Four others were wounded, one probably fatally, and the whites retreated to await reinforcements from the surrounding lawless elements.

At this point Negroes from other houses came to the aid of the besieged brothers and a rude barricade was thrown up and loop holes made for rifle fire. Negro ex-soldiers put their knowledge and experience gained in France to use in the service of the Race and an effective defense was soon organized.

The whites, reinforced, came back, 600 strong, and a battle royal developed. In spite of their reinforcements the whites were persistently beaten back by the little determined band within the rude improvised fort. Robbed of their prey and not anxious to face the lions at bay the most cowardly part of the white mob set itself to the safer task of destroying the undefended Negro residences and the village church and lodge buildings.

In the meantime, within their improvised fort the little colored group put up a defense that will bear comparison with many of the bravest feats of the colored soldiers on Flanders fields, and forged another link in the long chain of evidence going to show that the Negro has at last decided he can fight his own battles just as bravely and as effectively as he has ever fought the battles of others.

Finally, their ammunition almost exhausted, the little band decided to emulate the action of the "Guards at Cahill" and with clubbed muskets, made a rush through the besieging forces and, breaking through, sought the refuge of the surrounding woods.

The vacated house revealed the bodies of two victims of the mob, one being that of an old woman.

Another colored woman, apparently 40 years of age, was shot and killed on the same day not far from here. At Bronson, a few miles from here, a colored man was found on the roadway, his body riddled with bullets. On a lonely road an-

other colored victim, a farmer, was found strung to the limb of a tree. Two Negro women were attacked and raped between Rosewood and Sumner. The sexual lust of the brutal white mobbists satisfied, the women were strangled. An older colored woman was severely maltreated on the same stretch of road and forced to submit herself to the most shameful sexual degradation.

Race feeling is running high as a result of these actual attacks on colored women and the alleged attack on a white woman. Negro farmers have armed themselves with rifles and shotguns and are grimly determined to protect their women and sell their lives dearly if it comes to that. The situation may culminate in violent race warfare worst [sic] *than the terrible night at Rosewood.*

Leaders are urging colored people throughout the State to sell their property and move northward. Every colored home here was set on fire by the mob and burned one by one. The church and hall also were destroyed.

It was no coincidence that these cities—Chicago, Washington, St. Louis, Baltimore and New York—perked up at news of a "race riot" down south. Each of them had been rocked in recent years by bloody racial clashes on their own downtown streets, attacks that left dozens dead, almost all of them black. They called them riots, but in truth they were large-scale lynchings, sanctioned wildings in which mobs of whites ran rampant through urban black neighborhoods while the authorities looked the other way or in some cases helped out.

It was the end of an era, the turn of the '20s, the climax of a forty-year period that had begun in the post–Civil War South with the backlash against newly freed blacks, had spread north with the onset of World War I and had burst into open combat among white and black workers competing for jobs in overcrowded cities. Those four decades, from Reconstruction through the wake of the first World War, would come to be called the "lynching era" in America. Blacks would continue to be burned, shot and hanged for a half-century more, through the end of the '60s, but the number of deaths during that time would come nowhere near the three thousand men, women and children murdered by mobs between the 1880s and the 1920s.

"The good work of Judge Lynch," as some southern newspapers of the time heartily described it, had been a way of life in America since its creation. The term came from a Virginia magistrate named Charles Lynch, who made a habit in the late 1700s of hanging Tory conspirators without the trouble of a trial. During the next century, as the nation moved west, lynching became the baseline of frontier justice, with the victims mostly Mexicans, Asians and immigrants from southern Europe. Not until their slaves were freed did southern whites have more than an occasional need for the noose, and not until federal troops were withdrawn in 1877, leaving the South to govern itself, were they fully free to use it, which they did with a vengeance.

Beginning in 1883, when the Civil Rights Act of a decade before was repealed, southern blacks who had enjoyed a brief postwar taste of political power and financial success were slammed back into virtual slavery by frustrated, embittered whites. From then until the turn of the century, the nation averaged more than one hundred and fifty lynchings a year, the vast majority of them in the South, some in full view of crowds that numbered in the thousands. The displays were meant to both horrify and delight, to put the fear of God in the hearts of blacks while filling the whites with a sense of power and pride, something they were losing each day as the nation's economy shifted from fields to factories and the curtain of hard times began falling all across Dixie.

Among southern whites, that curtain fell hardest on the working class, the rustic farmers who had become known by a variety of terms over the course of the past century: *rednecks, hayseeds, hicks, piney-wood folks, clay-eaters,* and, most commonly, *crackers.* The poorest of them, with hardly enough acreage to feed their families, were called crackers because of the corn they pounded to make their meals. Those who could afford a little livestock and a couple of slaves preferred to believe the term came from the sound of the whips they used to herd their cattle. For the slaves themselves, who spat the term with disgust, it stemmed from the sound of those whips on their own backs.

Along with their upper-class neighbors, many of these poor and middle-class whites depended on cheap black labor for success. Not only did they lose that labor after the war, but they were forced to compete against it as blacks began growing their own crops on their own land, selling their own harvests at market in quantities and at prices that often outdid the whites. And so, besides protecting white womanhood, which most mobs claimed was their calling— the cry of "rape" guaranteed an enthusiastic posse—or simply asserting the racial superiority they believed had been given them by God and taken away by government, working whites had purely financial reasons as well to reach for the lynching rope.

They called it "whitecapping," the use of terrorism and torture to drive blacks out of their businesses or off their land, and it was openly condoned by officials like North Carolina governor Daniel Russell, who proclaimed in 1900 that for a black man "to get above his ordained station in life is to invite assassination." If they didn't die, whitecapped blacks at the very least lost all they owned to mobs who drove them away, then stepped in and seized the abandoned property at discount rates.

It happened in Tennessee, where a lynch mob chased twenty black families off several hundred acres of land assessed at twenty dollars an acre, then bought the property at auction for less than a fifth that price. It happened in Texas, where a father and his three sons refused to leave their land and were finally hanged, all from the same tree, for the crime of harvesting the first cotton in the county that year—with no one left alive to pay the taxes, their property then went up for sale. It happened in Mississippi, where a white man who owed a black farmer $1,200 led a mob against the black man, running him and his family off their farm forever and erasing the debt in the process.

There were hundreds of cases like these, along with a litany of whippings, knifings, shootings, skinnings, hangings, beatings, burnings, tarrings, dismemberings and desexings too numerous and too often unrecorded to count. The charges, phrases found in official records of the time, ranged from "insulting women" to "annoying white women" to "saying hello to white girl" to "bumping into white girl while running to catch a train." In Paducah, Kentucky, a black rape suspect was lynched by a mob which then murdered a black onlooker for "expressing sympathy" for the first. In Waco, Texas, a mob pulled a retarded black youth charged with killing a white woman from a courtroom, burned him alive, then sold his teeth as souvenirs. In Brooks County, Georgia, a mob enraged by the murder of a white planter stormed the countryside for a week, killing ten blacks, including a pregnant woman who was hanged by her ankles, doused with gasoline and set afire—but not before her unborn baby was cut from her stomach and trampled underfoot. The coroner in that case labeled the victims' deaths, both baby and mother, as coming "at the hands of parties unknown," a phrase repeated in hundreds of official reports written and read by men who not only knew the names of the mob that had done the deed, but were often among them.

"The life of a Negro isn't worth as much as that of a dog," wrote a black minister, venting the despair of the times. "He may be shot down, murdered, strung up to a tree, burnt to death by any white ruffian, or band of law-breakers and murderers with impunity. . . . If he goes to law, there is no redress."

For a time, northerners were able to comfort themselves with the belief that lynching was a southern problem. But it would soon move their way, as Mark Twain predicted in an essay he wrote in 1901 titled "The United States of Lyncherdom." Prompted by the murder of a white girl in his home state of Missouri, a death that led to the lynching of three black men, the burnings of five black homes and the routing of thirty black families who were driven into the woods never to return, Twain warned that this was nothing less than a sickness, "a mania, a fashion; a fashion that will spread wide and wider, year by year, covering state after state as with an advancing disease."

Twain's essay was not published until 1923, the year Rosewood was torched, and by then his forecast had come true. Five years after Twain died in 1910, a combination of the intolerable violence faced by blacks in the South and a devastating boll weevil infestation that wiped out what work was left in the fields caused a northward exodus that came to be called The Great Migration of 1915. Hundreds of thousands of blacks moved north that year, many finding jobs in factories that were gearing up for war in Europe. Agents from those factories swept through the South, tossing leaflets to blacks in the fields, luring them north with visions of wealth and true freedom. Many who knew those promises were too good to be true still made the move. "To die from the bite of frost," wrote one reader of the black *Chicago Defender* newspaper, "is far more glorious than at the hands of a mob."

But the mood of the mob was moving northward as well. That same year, 1915, saw the premiere of a motion picture that would run for a record forty-seven weeks at the Liberty Theater in New York and would continue playing to sellout audiences across the country for the next decade. It was called *The Birth of a Nation,* based on a book titled *The Clansman,* which had been written ten years before. Its portrayal of noble Ku Klux Klan horsemen saving the South from the sinister Negro was "like writing history with lightning," gushed Woodrow Wilson, a southerner himself—a Virginian—who, now that he was president, showed little interest in the subject of lynching.

By the end of that same year, the Klan, which had disbanded during Reconstruction, was resurrected with robes and torches in an eerie ceremony atop Stone Mountain, Georgia, outside Atlanta. Much of the reason for the group's resurgence was a response to the emergence of a stronger, less subservient, more militant black man in America, what many were calling "the New Negro." For decades there had been scattered voices urging black men to fight back if attacked, voices like T. Thomas Fortune's, an early black activist who declared in the mid-1880s, "To be murdered by mobs . . . is not to be endured without protest, and if violence must be met with violence, let it be met. . . . If the white scamps lynch and shoot you, you have the right to do the same."

It was easy for Fortune to talk; he was settled safely in the North. Most southern blacks of the time still leaned toward the accommodationist words of Booker T. Washington, who urged patience and cooperation with whites. But by the turn of the century, patience had run out. Washington was now called "cowardly" for refusing to openly condemn lynching, and a new wave of black leaders was pushing him aside, men like W. E. B. Du Bois, whose defiant attitude was reflected in a 1915 editorial published in New York's black paper, the *Amsterdam News*: "Lynching would cease in short order if the Colored people of this country resented the lawless murdering of friends, relatives and compatriots as they should—with rifles and sword."

The image of black men armed with rifles was unthinkable for most whites, especially in the South, but it became a reality when more than three hundred thousand black men enlisted in America's armed forces as the U.S. finally entered the war in Europe 1917. By the time those soldiers came home a year later, most of America's cities, north and south, had become cauldrons of suspicion and resentment against blacks. There had been a dozen large-scale outbreaks of violence, capped by a riot in East St. Louis, where rage over black workers brought in to replace striking whites touched off a day-long attack in which thirty-nine blacks were killed and more than ten thousand men, women and children—"truckloads of quivering, bandaged blacks," as one local newspaper account described them; "an exodus of weary, weeping people," as another put it—were chased across the river into St. Louis, never to return.

Nine whites died as well during that attack, and so it was called a riot, a term with clear meaning for black people of the time. If they chose not to resist a mob, their deaths were called lynchings; if they fought back, it was called a riot. Either way they were likely to die, and so now, as never before, blacks were beginning to fight back.

They fought back in Houston, where late in the summer of 1917, a black soldier was shot and killed by a sheriff's deputy. Several days later two black military policemen were beaten by white Houston policemen, prompting more than a hundred soldiers from the highly decorated 24th Infantry, a black unit that had gained fame during the Spanish-American War and was now training in Houston for action in Europe, to grab their weapons and march on the city. It was the white southerner's worst nightmare come true, armed black men on the attack, and before it was done, seventeen whites lay dead, along with two blacks. Sixty-four of those black soldiers were subsequently court-martialed. Thirteen were immediately hanged, and forty-one were imprisoned for life.

That set the stage for the summer of 1919. Cities were swollen with wartime workers who were now left with no war and no work. Bolshevik conspirators were rumored around every corner, organizing labor unions, inciting strikes, fomenting a revolution like the one taking place in Russia. Dispossessed and disgruntled blacks were said to be a prime target of the radicals, and so they became targets as well of fearful, frustrated whites in a climate of racial tension more charged than any the nation had yet seen. With the heat of summer, the tension exploded.

By the end of that "Red Summer" of 1919, twenty-six race riots had left dozens dead on the streets of cities from Chicago to Washington, Knoxville to Omaha. The last of these occurred in remote Phillips County, Arkansas, where a group of black farmers meeting to set the price of their cotton was fired on by railroad officials representing the region's white planters. The blacks fired back, and the result was a slaughter. More than two hundred black people, "many of whom had no idea what the trouble was about," according to an NAACP field report, were, in the words of that same report, "hunted down in the fields and swamps to which they had fled and shot down like animals."

That same summer, a nationwide anti-lynching movement began to stir. The NAACP, which had been created in 1909 in direct response to the problem of lynching, issued a flood of studies and reports detailing the number and nature of the atrocities. By the fall of 1921, a federal antilynching bill made it through the U.S. House of Representatives and onto the floor of the Senate before a filibuster led by Southern Democrats finally killed it. No such law would ever come that close again, but lynch mobs could no longer simply be ignored.

By 1922, the number of lynchings nationwide had dipped to a relatively low total of fifty-seven, almost all of them in the Deep South, where the Klan had reached an all-time peak in membership of three million—some estimates put that figure even higher. Most of these new Klansmen were the same poor and middle-class whites who had been desperate for a sense of power and place ever since losing their hold over blacks a half century earlier. Now, with the "New Negro" rising and society beginning to respond, the rural southern white felt even more cornered, more defensive and desperate than ever, more help-less in the face of blacks who no longer knew their place. The Klan gave these men back some of their pride, and lynching gave them their power.

And so, though the tide was turning, though the number of lynchings that were prevented in 1922 actually outnumbered those that succeeded, blacks in the Deep South, especially in the rural South, still knew there would likely be no one to turn to if a mob attacked. And no one could know when or why such an attack might come.

The people in Rosewood had no way to know, no reason to imagine that when they went to bed that New Year's Eve of 1922, they would wake up to face a crowd of armed, angry white men. Florida had had its share of lynchings during the previous year—a hanging down in Key West, another in Mayo, one out in Kissimmee. Word of those killings might have reached Rosewood. Maybe, maybe not. Surely they knew of the lynching just up the road in Perry. It hadn't been a month since that happened, just before Christmas, three black men killed, one burned at the stake, all after a white schoolteacher was found dead on a lonely stretch of dirt road.

There had to have been talk of those Perry deaths down around Rosewood. The folks in Rosewood knew the people up in Perry. The two towns' baseball teams would often play each other, hooking up for Sunday doubleheaders at one team's field or the other's. They had to know what had happened in Perry, but the men and women of Rosewood had no reason to think it would happen to them.

Not until it did.

And no one else would ever know what it was like, no one but them. Only they could say how it looked from inside their homes, the mob surging up and down their small streets as they hid behind locked doors. Only they could say how it looked from the woods, where they crouched as the sky above them turned orange from the flames of their burning town. Only they could describe what it was like to huddle in boxcars, bringing with them only what they wore, leaving behind all else that they owned, leaving it forever.

Only they could tell that story, but they had no voice. And those who had voices did not speak for them. The day after the attack on the Carrier house, as hundreds of vigilantes poured into Rosewood from across the state and be-yond, Florida's governor, a banker named Cary Hardee, wired the Levy County sheriff from Tallahassee, asking if help might be needed, perhaps the national guard. The sheriff telegrammed back that the situation was "under control," and so, as the town continued to burn and the death toll climbed, the governor took the afternoon off and went hunting.

By the end of that week, in newspapers outside the state, the surge of stories about Rosewood began to subside. It was left to Florida's press to sum up the affair, and although the *Tampa Times* called the attack "a foul and lasting blot on the people of Levy County," such criticism was the exception. The state's general feeling was reflected by an editorial published in the *Gainesville Sun* on Sunday, January 7, the last day of the attack on Rosewood:

> *Let it be understood, at the very beginning of what we shall here write, that the racial trouble at Sumner or, more properly, Rosewood, was no "Southern Lynching Outrage." It was caused by the shooting down and killing of two officers of the law and the wounding of another. These law officers were shot down by negroes, barricaded in a house where a brutish beast was supposed to be sheltered and this brute had criminally assaulted a white woman. . . . Preach and admonish and warn as you may, however, the crime of rape will never be tolerated for one single moment. Congressmen may rave and froth and pass laws as they please but the time will never come when a southern white man will not avenge a crime against innocent womanhood. . . . Let it be understood now and forever that he, whether white or black, who brutally assaults an innocent and helpless woman, shall die the death of a dog.*

A month later, a grand jury composed of local farmers and merchants, all white, was convened in the county seat of Bronson. Twenty-five witnesses were called, including eight blacks. After three days of investigation, the jury declared the evidence "insufficient" for indictments. None were made, and the case was closed. The alleged rapist, Jesse Hunter, was never found.

And so it was finished. The town was gone, and its memory soon vanished as well. Like the remains of a rock thrown into a pond, the record of Rosewood faded from a single splash, to scattered ripples, to stillness.

It was the last act of an era, the closing chapter, the final "race riot" of its time. It would also be the one that was forgotten, the only one not detailed and documented on library shelves. And perhaps there was a reason for that, because unlike the others, the story of Rosewood did not end in its ashes. Six decades after it happened, in that spring of 1982, those ashes began to stir, and it soon became clear that this was one story that was far from finished.

PART TWO

THE *Survivors*

Sweet Potatoes

L ate on a weekday morning, the section of Jacksonville called Lerner's Circle is deserted, like a toy village without people, block after block of squat
bungalows painted the bright colors of fruit—lime, grape, raspberry, lemon—
their stucco walls blistering in the North Florida sun. The yards are small,
some carefully mowed, edged and embellished with ceramic lawn ornaments,
others untended, sprinkled with junked automobiles and rusted appliances.

At the end of one lane, beneath the shade of a bent cabbage palm and an old
oak, sits a small cinderblock house, painted pink, the color of bubble gum. Beside it runs a culvert, wastewater trickling from an open pipe into a ditch
strewn with bottles and beer cans. Insects and sunlight dance off the surface of
the green, oily pond.

The home's yard is unmowed, children's toys strewn across the sawgrass—
a plastic machine gun, a water pistol, a pair of skates, a go-kart, all circled by a
sagging chain link fence. Next to a side door sits a bag of trash torn open by animals, its contents—chicken bones, soiled diapers, a half-eaten piece of fish—
spilling onto the dirt driveway.

Minnie Lee Langley

A young woman, gold hoop rings dangling from her ears, lets herself through the fence gate and knocks on the front door, hollering into an open louvered window, a window protected by steel bars. All the windows in this house are barred.

"Minnie!" she calls. "Minnie Lee, you in there?"

No answer.

"I *know* she's in there," the woman says, pushing through the knee-high grass to another window. "She's got to be here. Nowhere else she *could* be."

The woman is a neighbor. She and her mother live two doors down. They keep an eye on Minnie, check in now and then to see if there's anything she needs. This morning they're going out for some shopping and think Minnie might like to come along.

"This is not like her," says the woman. "She's always up by this time of the morning."

The woman taps on a window at the back of the house, and finally, a voice answers. Small, faint, it asks who's there, says to come on around to the front, she'll be there in a minute. And in a minute she is, a tiny face framing a pair of bright, wet eyes, peeking around the doorknob, squinting in the morning sunlight.

It's dark inside, hot and cluttered. A half-eaten pastry sits on the small kitchen table, beside a can of roach spray. Brown sodden newspapers are spread on the linoleum floor by the refrigerator, soaking up a leak. The living room coffee table is covered with vials of medicine. A tube of analgesic cream is by the TV, and half-used bottles of rubbing alcohol are everywhere—on the kitchen counter, atop the refrigerator, on an end table near the sofa where Minnie takes a seat, her thin little body hardly making a crease in the cushion.

She is the color of dark chocolate, her limbs skeletal, her fingers long and gnarled, the nails an opaque, milky yellow. She is wearing a faded pink bathrobe, her tiny feet floating in a black pair of oversized bedroom slippers. Her gray hair is short and wiry, pulled on one side into a small knot held by a rubber band. On the wall above her hangs a plaque:

GOD SEES US AS WE CAN BE, BUT LOVES US AS WE ARE

Beside her sits an ashtray filled with cigarette butts. "Lord yes, I smoke," she says, picking a stray butt off the floor and dropping it in the dish. "Not as much as I used to, but I do. If you're gonna drink that coffee, you *got* to smoke."

The door is still open, and now a figure appears, a man, his face pressed to the screen.

"*Yo,*" he shouts, yelling into the darkness, "can I get a *dollar* from anybody in there?"

Minnie screws up her face, turns her head away, her tiny chin thrust toward the ceiling. "*Hah!*" she says. "I'd like to throw a dollar in a *hole* as give it to you. That's if I *had* a dollar."

The man moves on, and Minnie gets up to shut the door.

"He wants that *dope* is what he wants," she says.

The walls around her are decorated with crucifixes and religious paintings. The Last Supper. The Virgin Mary. A book is propped on a shelf by the window: *You Can Live Forever In Paradise On Earth.*

Minnie decides she'd like to sit outside. It's a nice day. She pushes some toys off the porch sofa, sending a lizard skittering across the cement floor. A small cockroach creeps across the wall behind her as she sits down and sighs.

The toys, she says, are her great-grandsons'. "My children," she calls them, the two little ones living with her right now. They are brothers, Charles and Matthew, one five years old and the other four. Minnie took them in nearly three years ago, after their mother, Minnie's granddaughter, committed suicide. "That hurt me," says Minnie, her eyes welling up. " 'cause I loved that child. She was the oldest grandchild I had."

Minnie has six grandkids, all of whom spent the better part of their childhoods in her care. "Oh, I'm *still* taking care of the children, I sure am," she smiles. "I love my children, I *love* 'em."

She has two of her own, her daughter Dorothy, born in 1930, and her son Anthony, whom she adopted when he was an infant. "He's growed up now, with his big-mouth self," she chuckles.

Anthony was three months old, says Minnie, when she took him in. "This girl where I was working, she was giving that baby *away*. Her husband was in the service, and she was fixing to give her child up. When I heard that, I asked her to give that baby to *me*. She said all right, and that's the way that come along. Went down and had papers drawn up on it, and that was it. He was mine."

Minnie twists a thin wedding band on her left hand. Her husband Clifford gave it to her when they were married in 1936. He died from a heart attack in

'56, the year they bought this house. "That's right," says Minnie. "I moved in here as a widow."

Clifford worked at a filling station most of his life—"Firestone," says Minnie. "Changing tires, changing oil." They met at the start of Franklin Roosevelt's first term and married near the end of it. "Just about the time we started putting in for the Social Security," she says.

Her daughter Dorothy was six by then, born to Minnie and a boyfriend named Curtis Telfer. "I liked him," she says of Curtis, "but he had too many sweethearts, too many outside girls. I wouldn't take him for no husband."

Clifford Langley was a different story. He was loyal, and he raised Dorothy as if she were his own child. "He was a good man, yes *goodness,*" says Minnie, her eyes welling up again. "Couldn't find another one like him in a hundred years."

Minnie stopped working in 1980, after more than thirty years on the assembly line at a brush and broom factory. At her peak she turned out fifty boxes of fiber brushes a day. "Fifty-four brushes to a box," she says with pride. For that she was paid seventy-five cents an hour when she began in the late '40s. When she retired, her hourly salary was $3.75.

These days Minnie spends most of her time tending to her great-grandsons. She watches a little television in the afternoons—"'The Young and the Restless' and 'Guiding Light,' that's it." And she spends her Sundays at the nearby Community Faith Baptist Church. "I can't *live* without Him," she says, glancing up at the late morning clouds.

This is as much as most of Minnie's neighbors know about her. Few know anything of Rosewood. Those who do know only what they have heard on television or read in the newspapers. The young woman who has come this morning to fetch Minnie for shopping has never heard of the place, not until now.

"I never talked about it to nobody," says Minnie. "Never told my own children about it. I always said to them, 'I don't want y'all to come up like I come up.' But that's all I told them. Not a word about Rosewood."

She closes her eyes, shakes her head.

"We ain't had no problems back there, not with the white folks, not with no one. Ain't had a *bit* of problems. I don't understand *why* them peoples did us like that."

Minnie was born in Rosewood on the Fourth of July, 1913. Her mother was named Daisy, Daisy Mitchell, but Minnie never knew her. Daisy died during that birth, leaving Minnie and her brother Ruben in the care of their grandmother, Emma Carrier. Emma became "Mama" to Minnie and Ruben Mitchell. Their father Theodore was gone by the time Minnie was born, off making a living diving for sponges, sending home what money he could. Emma occasionally took Minnie to visit him, down the coast at a place called Crystal River, a half day's trip from Rosewood. Minnie would sit by the clear water and watch her father work, see him take deep gulps of air then dive to the river bottom, coming back up after what seemed like forever with a sopping piece of coffee-colored sponge in his huge, hard hands. "Big old pieces," she says. "As big as I was. *Bigger*."

The last time Minnie saw her father was the summer she turned nine, the summer before the attack. "I don't know when he died," she says. "Don't know if he *is* dead. I ain't seen or heard of him since this stuff happened."

The Rosewood Minnie recalls was a happy place, "A good place to be a child," she says. She remembers planting and watering and weeding sweet potatoes with her grandmother, digging them up at harvest time and storing them in piles covered with pine bark to keep them from rotting. Sometimes Emma went to white people's homes in Sumner, to cook in their kitchens and milk their cows, and Minnie would come along. When Emma went down to the Rosewood depot to sell fresh eggs to the trains passing through, Minnie would come along. Before her granddaddy James had his stroke, he trapped for a living, and it was up to Minnie and the Carrier kids to clean what he caught.

There were seven Carrier children and grandchildren in the home, all older than Minnie and Ruben, so Minnie learned early how to hold her own. "Oh, I could fight," she says. "I beat every one that come my way, every one. They was *scared* of me."

She was in second grade at the Rosewood school the winter of the attack, and she remembers the day it began, standing out in the yard with her grandmother, watching "a gang of crackers" charge past with some hound dogs, then seeing them come back to her grandmother's house, pulling her uncle Aaron from inside and talking about hanging him with some rope. It wasn't much later that her cousin Sylvester showed up at the door.

"He told us to come over with him, 'cause he felt like them crackers was going to come our way again and he couldn't take care of both houses. So we went. We didn't carry no clothes or nothin'. We just went. We didn't think we'd be staying long."

Sylvester had been threatened by the mob that afternoon, says Minnie, when they came across him down at the depot. "'Don't let sundown catch you here.' That's what they told him," she says. That is what brought Sylvester to Emma Carrier's door, says Minnie, and that is how both families wound up in Sarah Carrier's house the night of the shootout.

The children were just getting to bed that night, says Minnie, when she heard voices calling from outside the house. "I could hear them out there hollering, 'Sarah! Come on out here! Come on out here, Sarah, you hear me?'"

She heard a blast of gunfire from outside. Then an explosion of shooting. The next thing Minnie knew, her Aunt Honey rushed into the children's bedroom covered with blood and crying. "They done killed Mama! They done killed Mama!" Minnie didn't know it was Sarah who had been shot. She thought it was Emma, and she rushed downstairs, stumbling in the darkness, searching for her grandmother.

"Then Cuz' Syl' grabbed me. He said, 'Come here, baby, let me save you.' And he pulled me back with him, into the wood bin under the steps. Both of us climbed in there, and I got down between his legs and he put his gun up over my shoulder.

"Then they kicked in the front door, *boom,* and that's when my cousin let them have it. Shot two of them dead, right there."

In Minnie's memory, more men died by Sylvester's hand before the night was through: "He could see them crackers running across the yard, and every time he'd see one, he'd shoot them, *BOOM, BOOM!*"

Before long, white men were "piled up on the porch," says Minnie. When the mob pulled back, she says, Sylvester told everyone in the house to leave, out the back and into the swamp. Minnie wound up with some of the other children and her Aunt Beulah, Emma's daughter, the one they called "Scrappie."

"She stayed with us out in those woods for three days, feeding us berries and cabbage root. It was so cold, Jesus it was cold. And we was about naked. We ain't had no clothes. But Scrappie wouldn't let us build but a little bitty fire, because she didn't want them to find us."

By the second night, says Minnie, they could see the flames from Rosewood lighting up the evening sky. "Like Judgment Day," she says.

The third night was when they got word to make their way to the tracks, that someone was sending a train to pick them up. "Captain Bryce," she says, "he sent word through a man that worked up at the turpentine still in Wylly to bring us over and put us on that train and it would take us to Gainesville."

She doesn't remember much about that ride, says Minnie, other than they were fed some fresh fruit and the trip took three hours. When they reached the station at Gainesville, they were met by a cousin who told them Emma was safe in Sumner but Grandpa James was dead, shot to death by the white men.

Emma soon joined them, living with the children in a small shack in the black section of the city. "But she ain't never gotten well," says Minnie. Emma had been hurt in the gunfight, shot in the hand and wrist, but it wasn't those wounds that killed her, says Minnie. "She just took sick over what happened, and she never did get well."

The children went to work, including Ruben, who was left with one eye after the attack. "He found work picking up paper," says Minnie. As for herself, she washed dishes in one white woman's home and helped another milk cows and churn butter. All the children pitched in to put dinner on the table each evening, with Minnie's oldest cousin, thirteen-year-old Lonnie, acting as the father, leading the group in prayer. Late at night, while the others were asleep, Minnie would get up and feed her grandmother her medicine.

But it did no good. Emma died the following summer, in 1924, just after Minnie's eleventh birthday, and the children were on their own. A young aunt came to help out, but left after a few months. "Aunt Rita," says Minnie, with a small smile. "She liked a good time." Another aunt, Ethel, had her own family there in Gainesville. She had no room for the Carrier kids, but she did bring Minnie and her cousins food when she could.

And so they survived. Minnie moved to Jacksonville in 1926 and found work caring for babies in private homes. Four years later she gave birth to Dorothy. Six years after that she married Clifford and she never looked back, never talked about Rosewood to a soul, never had a need to, not until the newspaper reporter from St. Petersburg came to her door in 1982, she says, "right here at this house," and asked her what happened at Rosewood.

"I told him," she says, leaning forward and stretching her thin, bony arms. "I told him everything. He sent me the story he wrote, but I didn't read it."

"Then the '60 Minutes' people came here after that," she says, "right here in my driveway, taking pictures and stuff. They asked if they could carry me down there to Rosewood, me and Lee Ruth. That's all of us that was left. I knowed I had some cousins somewhere, but I didn't know where they was, didn't even know if they was still alive. Ruth was the only one I knowed was alive."

Minnie took that trip, she and her daughter Dorothy, in the fall of 1983.

They drove down to Rosewood, met the television people there, reporter Ed Bradley and his crew. Met Lee Ruth Davis, too, and two other Rosewood survivors as well. One was a man named Sam Hall, who had come down from his home on the Georgia coast. Minnie remembered Sammy Hall as a boy in Rosewood, but she hadn't seen or heard of him since. The other was Lee Carrier, a cousin of Minnie's, settled up in Pensacola now. She hadn't seen Lee Carrier either, not since they were children.

They spent the day with Ed Bradley, walking the grounds of what had once been their home, walking around the yard of the old Wright house, too, the only place still standing from back then, a looming Victorian house. They relived some of the events that had happened sixty years before. They each told their story. Then, at the end of the day, they all went back home.

"I told them everything," says Minnie Lee, standing and stretching before going back in the house.

"Everything you need to know is there on that TV show," she says, pulling open her screen door and moving back into the darkness. "Just watch it."

SEVEN

Hard Dirt

A. T. Goins watched it the night it was broadcast, two weeks before Christmas, 1983. He sat in the den of his St. Petersburg home with his wife Anna Maude and listened to Ed Bradley describe how forty people were killed in the "mass murder" at Rosewood.

Though he hated to admit it, A. T.'s eyesight was even then just about gone, blurred by the glaucoma that had crept up on him in recent years. But he could still make out the figures on that television screen, and he was transfixed as he watched an old white man in a cowboy hat, a man named Fred Kirkland, recall a mob he said grew to as many as fifteen hundred men, and then explain almost casually what drove them toward the slaughter. "Satisfaction," the white man said, chewing on a toothpick. "I reckon that was it."

A. T. could see his cousin, Lee Ruth Davis—"Mossy," they called her—standing by a fencepost, musing about the house and land her family had owned and how they had lost it all, how they had to start over again with nothing. Lee Ruth lived in Miami now, had settled there not long after the attack, but she and A. T. had stayed in touch over the years, meeting up at holidays and funer-

---

A. T. Goins

als and other family affairs. The same with Lee Carrier, who was up there now on the TV screen, too, talking about Rosewood.

A. T. was amazed to see Sam Hall, limping with a cane across the lawn of the old Wright house. A. T. hadn't seen Sammy since they were both boys, before the attack, and now there he was, so crippled he could hardly make his way from one side of that yard to the other. It made A. T. feel his own age, seeing Sam Hall like that. It made A. T. realize how long it had been.

And by God, there was Minnie Lee Mitchell, as feisty as ever. A. T. hadn't seen her either since the massacre, didn't know she was still alive. They were about the same age, Minnie and A. T. They used to tussle together all the time. She was nothing but a tiny thing, no bigger than a minute, A. T. recalled, but she would not back down from anyone. She had the spunk of somebody twice her size, that's what A. T. remembered most about Minnie Lee. And now there she was, sitting on the porch of a house up in Jacksonville, her little head swallowed by a red knit cap, wrinkles all over her face, telling Ed Bradley how her cousin Sylvester killed all those white men that winter night, "just dropped every one that come to the door."

Lord, A. T. thought to himself, Sissy must be beside herself right now. He knew his sister Philomena had to be cursing all these people at this very minute. He knew how she felt about this whole Rosewood mess, how she squashed Lee Ruth every time she tried to bring it up. And now here it was, going out on the television for the whole country to see.

A. T. felt pretty much the same as his sister, though he wasn't the type to get as upset as her. He never wanted any part of Rosewood after they were all carried away on that train, never talked about it to anyone, not even to Anna Maude. Thirty years they were married before she heard of it, and that wasn't from him. It was from Philomena, who finally saw fit to tell her. Up to then, Anna Maude had always thought A. T. was from Gainesville, and that was the way he wanted it.

It could drive a man crazy thinking about something like that, that's the way A. T. felt. Wondering how things might have been different if it hadn't happened, wondering what life would be like if their family had been able to hold onto their houses and land and make it all grow into something even bigger and better—a man could lose his mind worrying over thoughts like that. And there was the shame of it, too. What man would want to admit that he'd run like a scared animal into the woods, run away from people who had come to burn his home and take his land, run like a rabbit rather than taken a stand? A. T. knew it didn't make sense to think like that, he knew he was just a little boy at the time, only eight years old, but he still felt shame just the same. And so he just didn't think about it. No sense to it, he figured, no sense thinking about things that can't be changed. Just leave it behind. That's what A. T. said when some of the others, like Lee Ruth, got all agitated and tried to stir things up. Just leave it behind.

That's what A. T. had done, and he'd made out all right for himself. It hadn't been easy, shining shoes all those years, twenty cents a pair in the beginning and some of those people so stingy they wouldn't budge from that chair till you made change for their quarter. Some Saturdays A. T. would stay up and shine shoes all night, clear through to dawn, do as many as four hundred pairs of shoes and have them all lined up and waiting for his customers to pick up and wear to church.

That's how A. T. did it for years, and by the time his daughter Annette graduated from high school, he had saved enough to send her to college. Now she was a Ph.D. herself, married to a college president up in Mississippi. A. T. and Anna Maude had Annette to thank for helping them with this nice house they lived in now, a house by a golf course, the same course A. T. caddied on fifty years earlier, in the 1930s, when he first came to St. Pete. Of course he wasn't allowed to *play* on that course back then. No blacks could play that course back then.

By 1983 there were blacks teeing up right alongside whites. But not A. T. His body wouldn't let him. His bones ached day and night with arthritis, and his eyesight was just about gone from glaucoma. He was happy enough just to be able to take his afternoon walk around those fairways, watch the sun set over those sand traps, then come back home to his hibiscus bushes and his lemon trees and his poinsettias. He did love his trees and flowers, had a way with them. Anna Maude marveled at how A. T. could make blooms come up out of nothing but hard dirt.

Some of that had to have come from Rosewood. Their yard was full of fruit trees back then. Pear trees, peach trees, mulberry trees. A.T.'s grandmother Sarah had them all growing outside her windows, and they all bore fruit, all except one, a plum tree, which was her "whippin' tree," the place she'd go to strip branches whenever one of her grandchildren was due for a spanking. Sarah would pull off two or three of those branches, braid them together and just burn their butts up. A. T. never would forget that. Some days Mama Sarah would come home from work, hear about one of the children's transgressions, and she'd just sink into a chair. "I'm too tired to whip you right now," she'd sigh, "but don't think you ain't gonna *get* that whipping." And she always kept her word, even if it meant sometimes saving up two or three into one.

A. T. adored his Mama Sarah, loved staying in her big house when his own mama and daddy were off working for the lumber company. "Harvesting" the logs, that's what the company called it, and the men they sent into those swamps to do it were black men, just like A. T.'s daddy. Five in the morning until five at night they worked, wearing boots and overalls and big-brimmed hats, wading by the dozen into waist-high swamp water, carrying axes and long crosscut saws, saws that were seven feet long, making as much noise as they could so the gators would move over and the water moccasins would move on, seeking out the oldest, biggest trees, virgin cypress and cedar, trees two to three thousand years old, six feet wide in the trunk, some wider than that, notching each one with their axes, then bringing it down with the saws, two men pulling at each end, and once it was down they'd cut off the branches and tie on the ropes and snake the beast back through the thick forest to the train that would haul it to the mill.

It was a hard way to make a living, but A. T.'s daddy did it. George Washington Christopher Columbus Goins, that was his name. His wife was Willie Retha Carrier Goins, one of Sarah Carrier's daughters. When George Goins went to work in the woods, his wife Willie came with him, the two of them living in the logging camp, wherever it was. When they began having children, they'd bring the baby along until it was big enough to stay with Willie's mother. Philomena was their first child, born in 1911. Three years later came A. T.— Arnett Turner. Next came Harold, who lived only two years before he died from the fever. Another brother, George, was born December 24, 1918— "Our Christmas present," A. T. called him. Finally came a baby sister, Vera, born in 1921.

A. T. could hardly remember his parents being home, his daddy was away working so much. It was Sarah's house A. T. would always recall as his own, with its hard wooden floors, rugs in the living room, a piano *and* an organ. It seemed like everybody in the family could play that piano but A. T. He never did have any musical ability, never had any interest in music.

But put a ball in his hands and he became an artist. That's all A. T. cared about: playing ball with his cousins, all those Carrier kids. His great-uncle James had a bunch of boys, and every morning they'd all be out there on the "hard ground," out front of Mama Sarah's house. She'd warn them to stay in that yard, not to go past the fence, but they always did. They knew they'd get a whipping when she found out, but they always did.

What they loved most was to hunt rabbits. A. T.'s Uncle Sylvester kept three dogs in a pen out back of the house. He had a deer dog they called Rattler, a bird dog named Kate and a rabbit dog named Trixie. The boys would take Trixie with them and sneak off into the woods, keeping their eyes peeled for rattlesnakes. Rattlesnakes were the main reason Sarah wanted those boys to stay out of the woods, but to A. T.'s cousins, killing rattlers was as much a game as hunting rabbits.

Trixie would always let them know when a snake was around. She'd stand dead still, bark, then begin walking slowly, in a wide circle. Somewhere inside that circle, in the thick brush, was a snake. The dog would never get within striking distance, but the boys, they would close in, each of them carrying a stick, until one of them spotted the serpent, usually coiled, poised to strike. Then they would kill it, simply beat it to death. They had to kill it. If they didn't, Trixie would not hunt. She would not move on until she saw that that rattler was dead.

A. T. never was much for killing snakes, but when it came to catching rabbits, he was a star. His weapon was a sawed-off broom handle with an iron nut attached to the end. The nut was huge, the size of a baseball. A. T. would find them up by the railroad tracks. Once Trixie flushed a rabbit, the boys would give chase, sprinting behind until the animal hit a clearing. Then they would all heave their weapon of choice at it, mostly rocks and crude spears fashioned from tree branches. A. T. had his club, which he would aim, then hurl, the iron nut leading the stick through the air toward its target. The nut was lethal, and so was A. T.'s aim. By the time the boys returned home, they would have a sack full of rabbits, as many as a dozen, most of them victims of A. T.'s good eye and strong arm.

The boys often returned with just as many gophers, flushed from holes where the rabbits tried to hide, and it was all good eating, the rabbits parboiled then fried just like chicken, the gophers simmered and stewed like beef. Even when he was grown and moved to the city, A. T.'s favorite dish was always gopher stew.

He never did forget how well they ate in Rosewood. Grandma Sarah's smokehouse stayed filled with the ducks and turkeys Sylvester shot in the forest, as well as hams from the hogs they raised. The hogs roamed free through the woods, fattening themselves on whatever they could find, along with the corn and slop they knew they could get at the house. There was no worry of losing them, because A. T.'s Papa Hayward, Sarah's husband, had his mark on each one of them, branded them just like cattle.

They kept a chicken coop out back, and it was A. T.'s job to feed the hens and gather the eggs. He hated that job. As far as he was concerned, chickens were the nastiest creatures on earth, eating anything they could find on the ground and leaving a mess wherever they went. When it was time to have one for dinner, Mama Sarah would carry it in a few days beforehand and keep it in a back room of the house. "Got to let it clean itself out," she'd say.

There was a garden behind Mama Sarah's house, and A. T. remembered it thick with peas and beans. There was a stable, too, for the mule Papa Hayward used for plowing. He used that mule to grind cane, too. A. T. loved to help his grandfather grind and cook that cane. They'd take one of the big iron pots Sarah used for washing clothes, clean it out with hot water, then cook the thick, sweet syrup until it boiled. There wasn't a morning A. T. could recall from his boyhood that didn't begin with a plate of Mama Sarah's hot biscuits, bathed in that home-cooked cane syrup.

That was how the morning began the day the white men came. A. T. was out in the yard that day with his cousins. It was cold, but not too cold to play. When A. T. saw the gang of white men coming up the railroad tracks, he thought it was strange. They were carrying guns, and they had dogs with them, too. But they went right past the house, and so A. T. and his cousins went back to playing. It was not until late that morning that Sissy and Mama Sarah came home and said something had happened over in Sumner.

Still, A. T. didn't know what was brewing, not even the next day when his Uncle James and Aunt Emma and all their boys, and Minnie Lee, too, and her brother Ruben, all of them arrived at Mama Sarah's house, and Uncle Sylvester said they'd be staying there for a couple of days. Even then, the boys went out in the yard and played. But they did not even think about going past the fence. They could see Mama Sarah was more serious than ever about that.

Then came Thursday night. It was around bedtime, the way A. T. remembered it. The moon was shining just as bright as could be, and the kids were all upstairs, horseplaying and staying awake though they were supposed to be getting to sleep. They were making enough noise that A. T. didn't even hear the shouts from outside. The gunshot, though, he heard that, and then it seemed like all hell broke loose, the children diving on the floor, bullets flying through the windows, Aunt Honey rushing into the room with blood all over her, Ruben with blood all over him too. The funny thing was, A. T. didn't feel frightened at all. In fact, the first thing he thought about was his suit.

It was his Christmas present from his daddy, a brand new dress suit. A. T.'s parents had come home Christmas Eve from Otter Creek, where they were staying at a logging camp. They had A. T.'s baby sister Vera with them, and they carried her back with them when they returned Christmas Day after having dinner with the family, leaving Philomena, A. T. and little George with Sarah.

Now, with the window shutters and glass shattering around him, with his aunt and his cousin crying and covered with blood, all A. T. could think was to get downstairs and find his suit. Which was what he did as soon as the shooting stopped. While the other children all rushed toward the back door and out to the woods, A. T. reached the bottom of those steps and turned toward the living room. Then he tripped over something. A body, a dead man. Then another, a woman. And now he was afraid. He left the suit behind and hurried out the back to catch up with the others.

He could hardly remember the next two days and nights. It all seemed like a blur. They stayed in the woods, and it was cold, he remembered that. Too cold to sleep, so they sat up and shivered, leaning close to one another for warmth. He remembered sipping swamp water to quench his thirst.

When they finally got on the train, he thought they'd be coming back. He had no idea this was the last time he would see his grandparents' house. He didn't know what was happening when they got to Gainesville, couldn't understand why his Aunt Rebecca, who lived there with her husband and children, refused to take them in, turned them away, told them she didn't want anything to do with this mess.

A. T.'s mama and daddy got to Gainesville after a couple of days, gathered their children together and left for Tampa, where they found a place to live. They brought Papa Hayward with them, but A. T.'s grandfather was never the same man after what happened at Rosewood, after he'd come back from his hunting trip that week to find nothing left. His wife Sarah was dead. So was his son Sylvester. And his brother James. He had lost his house and his land, lost everything he'd ever lived for, everything he had. He rarely spoke from then on. When he did talk, it was only to himself. If no one was there to stop him, he would wander out of the house and off into the city streets, sometimes without any clothing. Buck naked. No one had to tell A. T. what had happened. His grandfather had lost his mind, gone crazy with grief.

Hayward Carrier died in Tampa in 1925, two years after the attack on Rosewood. A. T.'s mother, Willie, died four years after that, but his daddy George never stopped traveling during all that time, moving from logging camp to logging camp, roaming across the better part of the state, and sometimes he took one or two of his children with him, to fix his meals. That's how A. T. learned to cook, alongside his sister Philomena. Mornings, it was A.T.'s job to get up and fix his daddy's lunch bucket for him, and he'd cook dinner at night, too, after Philomena grew old enough to leave home. When A. T.'s brother George was big enough, A. T. broke him in so they could alternate days, one getting up with their father before dawn while the other slept in.

After A. T.'s mother died, his father remarried and moved to Gulf Hammock. A. T. went to Lacoochee to live with his Aunt Beauty. He was sixteen then, big enough to work for a living, which he did, at a crate factory up in Gulf Hammock, making wire baskets for the people who picked beans and peas on the surrounding farms. A. T. earned a dollar and a quarter a day and was glad to have it, times being as hard as they were.

And they got harder. A. T. worked his way through the Depression digging ditches, laying down sewer pipes, pulling up weeds from the side of the road, any job he could find. Most of them he found down around St. Petersburg. Sometimes he was paid money, sometimes he was simply paid with pieces of paper, scrip redeemable for groceries at neighborhood food stores. Those were hard times for A. T., but then they were hard for everyone. He realized that, so week in and week out he just did the best he could to survive. And weekends, well, weekends were wonderful, because that was when A. T. could play baseball.

He had adored the game from the time he first watched the grownups play back in Rosewood. They had a strong club, the Rosewood All Stars, resplendent in their pinstripe uniforms. Black ball teams would travel down from Perry or Chiefland and play them on weekends. There'd be a big picnic, just about the whole town would walk over to the ballfield to watch, and almost invariably the Stars would come out on top.

A. T. was too little to play with the men back then, too little even to play with the big boys, but he would watch, especially when they went out at night to play a game they called "fireball." There was always plenty of turpentine around, and occasionally a group of the Rosewood kids would grab a bucket, soak a ball in it overnight, and then, the next sundown, they'd head over to the ballfield, carrying some small cans of turpentine gum with them, enough to place one at each base, including home plate, and a couple out around the pitchers mound.

Then they would light the cans. And then they would light the ball. And then they would play, a boy at every position, the infielders' faces glowing from the flames of the flickering cans, the outfielders invisible in the darkness, the pitches lobbed toward home plate, tracing an arc of light against the night sky, the batter swinging, connecting, sending a missile toward the woods, a small flaming comet, the runners circling the bases, stopping only if that flying ball of fire suddenly stopped, because that meant it had been caught and it would be coming back in in an instant because the only way to play fireball was to catch and throw in one motion, get that ball in and out of your hands fast enough so you didn't get burned.

It was a country game, fireball. Nobody had heard of it in St. Pete, where A. T. arrived in 1932. He was eighteen years old by then, big enough to try out for one of several black semipro teams in the city. He was small, five-foot-eight and no more than 130 pounds, but his right arm was like a whip. That and his pinpoint control earned him a spot as a pitcher, and soon he was on the roster of St. Petersburg's best black ballclub, the Florida Stars.

There was a time, during the 1920s, when that team traveled the entire east coast, playing in cities as far north as Philadelphia and Boston. They were called the Sunshine Babies back then, but the Depression did them in. By the time A. T. joined them, the club had changed its name and was playing only in Florida. Still, there were dozens of black ballclubs in cities across the state eager to take them on. Sarasota and Bradenton. Lakeland and Miami. Jacksonville, Sanford, Gainesville. A. T. and his teammates would travel by car, arrive around lunchtime, the hosts would have a homecooked meal waiting for them and then the teams would play a doubleheader, with the winners pocketing sixty percent of the gate.

The Stars offered the same deal when they played at home, and that was where A. T. had the best moments of his life, because that was where he took

the field against some honest-to-God legends, members of the fabled Negro
League professional baseball clubs that criss-crossed the country during the
Depression. Teams like the Homestead Grays and the Newark Eagles, the Indi-
anapolis Clowns and the Chicago American Giants, the Atlanta Black Crackers
and the Birmingham Black Barons. They all stopped in St. Pete during their
Florida swings, they always made a point of playing a game or two against the
local club, and so, during his stint with the Stars in the late 1930s and early
'40s, A. T. Goins played against some of the best hardball players on earth,
black or white.

Cool Papa Bell and Buck O'Neil, Josh Gibson and Satchel Paige, they all
visited St. Pete during that time. Willie Mays's father, "Cat" Mays, he came
through one year with the Black Barons. Not a bad center fielder, as A. T. recalled, though nothing like his son would turn out to be.

One of the strangest sights A. T. ever saw was the Zulu Cannibal Giants,
who took the field dressed in grass skirts and wearing red wigs. They looked
like clowns, he never would forget that. And he never forgot how those boys
could hit the ball. Skirts or no skirts, they put a whipping on the Stars that afternoon.

A. T. pitched against most all of them, but the moment that stood out above
any other occurred the night he played right field against the Grays, and Josh
Gibson came to bat. Gibson—they called him "the black Babe Ruth"—had already hit a home run the day before that was still rising when it cleared the left-
field wall. Rather than see that again, the Stars walked him to get to Buck
Leonard, a monster in his own right. And Leonard proceeded to hit the hardest, longest home run A. T. ever saw. The ball was a pellet as it passed directly
over his head. He didn't bother to move. He simply looked up and watched as it
cleared the wall behind him, cleared the towering oak tree standing beyond
that wall, cleared the street behind the oak, cleared two front yards beyond the
street and finally landed in a vacant lot halfway down the block, a distance of
some five hundred feet from home plate.

People around St. Pete still talked about that home run forty years after it
happened. A. T. still talked about it. He'd take a friend to the south end of the
city, to where that ballpark still sits, Campbell's Park, its sea-green cement out-
field walls now covered with graffiti, the infield swallowed by weeds and
sparkling with bits of broken beer bottles, the wooden bleachers caved in and
rotten, the old stadium gone to seed like the neighborhood around it, and he'd

point toward home plate. Then he'd point the other way, toward a house that now sat on that once-vacant lot where that ball had finally landed that memorable night. And no one would believe him. No man could hit a baseball that far. But Buck Leonard did it. A. T. knew he did it, because A. T. was there.

He married Anna Maude in 1940, Annette was born three years after that, and a year later A. T. was drafted into the Army. They found a spot on his lung during his physical, sent him home to get it checked out, and that's when he learned he had tuberculosis. He wound up in a sanitorium just outside Orlando, where he stayed for nearly two years—twenty-two months, two weeks and two days, to be exact. A. T. could recite those numbers the way a ballplayer recites his batting average.

They weren't sure he would survive when he went into that hospital, but he did. He never played baseball again, though, and his days of hard labor were behind him. When he came out, in the autumn of 1946, A. T. began shining shoes, and that's what he did for the next thirty years, until his eyesight got so bad he finally had to put away his brush.

Yes, he had had a life, and a good one when it was all added up. He was never one for feeling anger, never saw much sense in confrontation. He understood what those marchers were all about in the 1950s and '60s, protesting and demonstrating for civil rights, but that was never his style. He would fight if he had to, but he was never one for the front lines. His way was quiet, gentle, minding his own business, tending his own garden. Nothing like his nephew Arnett, Philomena's boy.

Now there was a fighter. Arnett was like a son to A. T. The boy was named after him, but they were as different as fire and water. A. T. had watched Arnett get in and out of trouble his whole life, always stirring things up. That's the way it was with this Rosewood business. Ever since he was a boy, Arnett had been poking around with questions about Rosewood, and A. T. would shoo him away, ask him if his mother knew what he was up to, nosing around again about that mess.

A. T. was amazed when that newspaper story came out in the summer of 1982. There had never been a word written about Rosewood his whole life, not a word, and suddenly there was this big Sunday spread in the St. Pete paper. Sissy warned him it was coming out and told him not to believe a word of it. The white man who wrote it, he had talked Arnett into going with him up to Rosewood, that's what she said. The man had even tried talking to Sissy herself, she said, till she got sick of his questions and threw him out of her house. Then she got on the telephone and warned everyone in the family not to speak to this man.

The newspaper story came and went, with not much made of it. But about a year later, A. T. got another phone call from his sister, and this time it was about television. She said "60 Minutes" had come to her house, trying to get her to talk about Rosewood. She hadn't given them the time of day, slammed the door in their face, she said. But they went ahead and did their story anyway. Sissy called to warn A. T. it was coming on that Sunday and God knew what it was going to say.

Now it was Sunday, now it was on, and Sissy had to be beside herself. That's all A. T. could think as he sat next to Anna Maude, watching Minnie Lee and Lee Carrier and Lee Ruth and Sammy Hall there on that TV screen, all of them talking about Rosewood. Sissy *had* to be upset now.

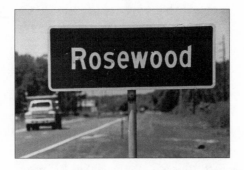

No Ear on Earth

" **L** ies, lies. Nothin' but goddamn *lies!*"
Arnett watched his mother almost leap out of her soft chair, cursing the television set as she saw these people acting like they were the only ones left, talking about her family as if it were theirs, telling her story as if it belonged to them.

Who the hell did they think they were? Sam Hall, he wasn't even *there* when the shooting started. The Halls lived clear across Rosewood, at the other end of town. Lee Ruth? She wasn't there either. She didn't see one person die. She didn't have to sleep in the woods like they did. She was over at the Wright house, hiding in a bedroom with the rest of them till the train came and carried them away. As for Lee Carrier, he should have known better than to get himself drawn into this mess, all these outside people using Rosewood for their own purposes, using *him.* And this Minnie Lee Langley woman? She was nothing but a damn baby at the time, and anyway, where had she *been* all these years? Nobody heard a word from her for a *lifetime,* and now she shows up, putting on this poor pitiful face for the television people, running her sad, sorry mouth about how

Rosewood today

it was like this and it was like that, when she didn't know *what* it was like.

Lies, that's all this "60 Minutes" show was to Philomena. Just like that newspaper story had been nothing but a mess of goddamn lies. She'd given Arnett a beating after that story came out, slapped him like a child for going up to Rosewood with that man. She thought that was the end of it, and it was, until Arnett called one day about a year later and said, "Mama, Ed Bradley is going to be coming to St. Petersburg to talk to you about Rosewood."

"Who the hell is Ed Bradley?" she asked.

"He's a black guy, Mama," he said, "a reporter for the '60 Minutes' TV show."

"He ain't coming *here,*" she said.

"Mama," said Arnett, "this is a *black* man. His last name is Bradley. *Bradley,* Mama. He might be kin to us."

"He ain't no kin to *me,*" she said. "The only Ed Bradley I know is my cousin Ed Bradley."

"Where is *he* at, Mama?"

"He's *dead,*" she said. "And I don't want to see no other Ed Bradley."

Three days after that conversation, Philomena answered her doorbell and faced two white men. One was the newspaper reporter, Gary Moore. The other said he was a producer from "60 Minutes." They had come to ask Philomena if she would be willing to go back to Rosewood with them, to join several other survivors for a taping there.

"No way," said Philomena. "No way in hell am I doing something like that. And you can leave now. Just leave."

When Arnett arrived from work that evening, Philomena was on him before he could sit down.

"Those goddamn sons of bitches came to my house today," she said.

"Who, Mama?"

"You *know* who," she said. "Those damn '60 Minutes' people you was talking about."

"'60 Minutes'?" said Arnett. "'60 Minutes' was *here?*"

She nodded. "And I threw their asses *out,* too," she said.

"Mama, tell me you didn't do that."

"The hell I didn't."

Arnett covered his face with his hands. But Philomena wasn't finished. "*You're* the one started this goddamn shit, you and Lee Ruth," she said. "Now get your ass out of my house. Pick up your shit and get out."

Philomena spent the next several days calling every family member she could, warning them they might be contacted by these television people and forbidding them to take part in the project. But now, as she watched the screen on this Sunday evening, she saw it had done no good. She couldn't stop them all.

Arnett saw it, too, and he hardly knew what to make of it. It had been a year since he had gone up to Rosewood with that reporter, and the subject had become more forbidden than ever. Once that newspaper story appeared, Philomena seemed doubly determined to quash even the briefest mention of Rosewood. It was as if she owned the thing, and she would not allow another soul to touch it.

But Arnett had become just as determined to learn more. Once he sensed the scope of what actually happened that week, what had been a lifelong shadow for him became a burning obsession. He was consumed with Rosewood now, with the need to know who had been there, what they had lost, where they had gone and where they were now.

But the more he learned, the more he felt lost. In the past year he had talked to dozens of relatives, anyone with the least connection to Rosewood. He had begun making a chart, a family tree of sorts, each branch leading back to that town. It was a delicate business, tiptoeing around his mother, trying to find some factual footing in the fog of hearsay, myth and memory, pulling threads of recollections from relatives still reluctant to speak. And when they did, so much of what they said bumped up against what someone else had told him.

So many stories, and how to tell which were true? Everyone had his own truth. If there was one thing Arnett was learning, it was this, that everyone had his own truth about Rosewood.

There were some who said Sylvester Carrier never died in that gun battle, that it was another man they found in that shot-up house, that Sylvester slipped off through the woods that night, his eerie laughter echoing through the trees. Others said he escaped hidden in a coffin, was carried right through that crowd of whites and got away to Texas, then Louisiana, where he lived until the 1960s, mailing cryptic postcards home every couple of years. Arnett's mother said she had some of those cards, though Arnett had never seen one.

Some said Sylvester's wife Gertrude was alive even now, living in Gainesville, where she was married to a minister. But no one knew the minister's name. They said Fannie Taylor was alive, too. Arnett had heard talk about her even when he was growing up in Lacoochee. Four years after the attack on

Rosewood, Cummer and Sons closed its sawmill in Sumner, having already shifted its operation south to Lacoochee. The story was that Fannie and James Taylor moved with the company, that they lived in Lacoochee during the late 1920s until Fannie got in some more man trouble and they were forced to leave. At least that's what Arnett heard. And now he was hearing that Fannie Taylor was still alive, after all these years, staying up around Cedar Key somewhere, though again no one could say exactly where.

The identity of Fannie Taylor's assailant was another misty subject. If he was a white man, why in the world would he have fled to Rosewood, to a town full of black people? That question had nagged Arnett all his life. The answer, he was told, came from the fact that the attacker, whose name no one seemed to know, was a Freemason, a member of the secretive white brotherhood that had met behind locked doors for centuries, swearing allegiances to one another in ceremonies closed to all but themselves. By the turn of this century, there were as many black Masonic temples in Florida as white ones. Before the Civil War, black Masons—freed men—had been a key link in the Underground Railroad, their lodges providing havens for runaway slaves. By the time of the Rosewood attack, Arnett was told, there were white and black lodges that recognized one another, that honored their Masonic bonds like blood. Though they were segregated by race, the brotherhood knew no such bounds—or so Arnett was told. If a Mason was in distress, white or black, his brother was bound to help him.

That, Arnett was told, was why Aaron Carrier opened his door to this white man, why Sam Carter carried the man away, and why neither of them betrayed the man's identity, even in the face of torture—even, in Carter's case, in the face of death. Aaron Carrier and Sam Carter were high-ranking Masons, which apparently meant even more to them than the fact that they were black.

This was hard for Arnett to believe, but then there was so much that was hard to believe about Rosewood. How to believe the tales of the death toll, so many numbers so wide apart, the newspapers at the time saying just two white men died on the front porch that night, while Minnie Lee insisted the white men dropped like flies? The St. Pete *Times* story quoted a white man saying he saw nearly twenty black bodies, including babies, buried in a single mass grave. Ed Bradley stated on TV that a total of forty people died in the attack. Some of the family told Arnett the number was closer to a hundred.

What to believe? Who could believe any of this could have happened in the first place without it becoming a matter of record, something that could be looked up at the local library? Arnett had tried that. He had gone and searched through every text he could find on Florida history. Nowhere was there a mention of Rosewood. Not a single sentence. Yet it had been front-page news at the time it happened. Arnett had seen that for himself, on microfilm in the library's reference room, the headlines in huge black letters stripped across the top of nearly every newspaper in the state. But then nothing. For the next sixty years, nothing.

Now Arnett realized what he was up against within his own family. Now he began to understand the reticence of his relatives. It was more than simple fear that seized their souls, more than the pain of what they had lost or the trauma they had lived through that made them reluctant to even talk about what took place. Now, for the first time, Arnett began to fathom the utter helplessness his family had experienced, not just during that attack but after it as well. In a nation of laws and justice, there had been no law to protect them, no justice to give them back what they had lost. Now Arnett began to sense not in his mind but in his gut, the utter futility his family had felt, the brutal fact that they had had absolutely nowhere to turn for help or for hope, that there was no ear on this earth to hear their pleas, that not only had it been impossible for them to fight for themselves, unless they were ready to die, but that there had been no one to fight *for* them, not even the government supposedly sworn to keep them safe.

That is what it meant to be black in that place in that time. Arnett realized this now, more than he ever had before. As much as he had struggled with and had to swallow in his own lifetime as a black man in America, he realized now how much more his elders had faced. Why should they be expected to believe now in the government that forsook them then? He wouldn't blame them if they gave up on God himself. But none of them had done that. God was all they had had when this thing was over, faith was all they had had to carry them through, faith in something beyond this earth, certainly not in anything on it.

Arnett felt ashamed. He had come to believe that his sense of outrage was somehow stronger than theirs, that his uncles, his aunts, even his mother, they were afraid, meek, weak. But now he knew better. Now he knew they were, in every sense of the word, survivors. When he looked at them now, he felt awe, not anger. And he knew he was going to have to go beyond all of them if he was going to even begin to embrace the extent of this thing. He could not trust them to tell him the story. He could only trust them to tell him *their* story. Neither could he trust the accounts of the institutions ordained by society to record its history. The newspaper reports he had found from that time gave wildly different accounts of what happened, as did the modern journalists who had now come sniffing after this thing. As for the historians, they had never even known or bothered to include Rosewood in their records.

And so, by the end of that December, 1983, broadcast, Arnett understood that nothing he heard could be taken at face value. There was some truth to every story he was told, but no single version had the whole truth to it. The town of Rosewood had been burned, and people—*his* people—had been killed. He knew that much. But how many had been killed, how many were still alive, what they had lost, and what, if anything, they might be owed were questions he realized could not be answered by others—not by his family, not by reporters, not by historians. If he was going to answer any of these questions, he realized, he was going to have to answer them for himself, by himself.

He would continue to talk to the family. He promised himself that. These people were old. Some were dying, and when they died they would take their stories, their own truths, with them. He needed to have those stories, he knew that. But he needed more. He needed facts, numbers, records, the hard stuff of tangible truth. And if those records did not exist after 1923, after Rosewood was effectively erased from written history, then he would go back to before that time, to find clues in this vanished town's past that might help build a bridge to the present.

He would have to sidestep his mother, whose wrath loomed at every turn. He would have to sneak into his relatives' homes, gently probing for whatever their memories might offer. But he also began slipping off to libraries and courthouses, politely asking clerks to pull dusty volumes from backroom shelves, then scanning hundreds of columns of handwritten words and numbers, taking note of any entry connected to the place that had once been Rosewood. Census reports, tax books, property records, deeds, any document related to the inhabitants of that town, that's what Arnett was after. His job, his personal life, it was all going to take a back seat now. If it took him years, nothing was going to come between him and this search.

And it would take years.

NINE

Smoke and Fog

It was a wet morning in the spring of 1987 when Arnett Doctor pulled into the parking lot of the Levy County Courthouse in Bronson, the county seat, twenty miles east of Rosewood, ten wooded miles from Otter Creek. The drive up had been unremarkable, open fields flecked with hay bales and palmettos, ringed by barbed wire and shrouded in mist, clusters of black cattle grazing among flocks of white egrets. Much of that farmland had been sectioned off and sold in recent years, developed into neighborhoods of curving cul-de-sacs and split-level homes inhabited by commuters to Gainesville. But Arnett had seen no suburbs as he passed the green open fields. This part of Levy County was still country, rural and apart, as it had been for centuries, as it had been when Rosewood was a town.

Just south of Bronson, he crossed the Waccasassa River, its waters dark and still, lily pads floating on its unmoving surface. Farther north flowed the storied Suwannee, where Stephen Foster had set his antebellum music about the heart of the southland, his lyrics inked in slave dialect, "Way down upon de Swanee Ribber . . ." In the late 1970s, the federal government set aside thousands of

Downtown Cedar Key, 1920s

acres of Levy County swampland along the Suwannee as a wildlife refuge, and its forests had grown thick with bald eagles, osprey, hawks and ducks, its waters alive with alligators, tortoises, snakes and an occasional manatee wandering upstream from the Gulf.

As Arnett had approached Bronson, he saw swamp ponds swollen by recent rains, the black water rising to the edges of the road, threatening to cover the highway itself. He hadn't been back up this way since making the trip with the reporter five years before. He had spent countless hours since then at libraries in Tampa and St. Pete, studying turn-of-the-century Levy County census reports, taking the information he could find—names, ages, heads of households, occupations, the ability to read or write, whether homes were owned or rented—and using it to construct a skeletal picture of what Rosewood would have looked like in 1923.

Much of the information was sketchy at best. There were names and data that conflicted with what Arnett's relatives had told him. There was information that conflicted with itself. The 1910 census listed "Harod" and Sarah Carrier with a nineteen-year-old son named Sylvester. But in the 1920 census, Sylvester, now married, was listed as age twenty-seven.

That kind of confusion, Arnett knew, had to be at least partly due to the fact that each census was taken by a white man, going door to door on foot in a black community of which he likely knew little, a community he probably had never seen before, asking questions of men and women who were bound to be as uncomfortable with his presence as he was with theirs and who were likely to give him incomplete or downright incorrect information, all of which wound up on the official record, to be taken as truth for all time.

But there remained much that *was* true, much that was familiar to Arnett as he scanned the aged pages of handwritten script. He followed his finger down column after column of names and felt a surge, like the touch of a spirit, each time he came to a name he knew, white or black. It was as if these people, of whom he had heard so much for so many years, were suddenly alive again.

There, on the 1900 census, was the name of the head of the 296th household visited by census taker J. Asakiah Williams—Edward Goins, Arnett's great-grandfather, outlined by government categories: A black male, age fifty-two, married, date of birth unknown, number of years married unknown, place of birth North Carolina, occupation turpentine farming.

And there, on the 1920 census, this one recorded by a man named Alfred

Dorsett, was the name of Dorsett's neighbor down the road in Sumner, the head of the household of the eighth home on the first page: C. P. "Poly" Wilkerson, age thirty-nine, listed along with his wife, two daughters and three sons.

Ten pages later, one hundred homes into the list, up the road in Rosewood now, was the name of Lexie Gordon, a black female, widowed, age fifty-two.

And around her name were all the others, the Bradleys and the Halls, the Colemans and the Carriers, the Davises and the Carters, the Edwards and the McCoys, the Goinses and the Gordons. There was no way to tell exactly where the Rosewood households began and ended on the list, sandwiched as they were between Sumner on one side and the small settlement of Wylly on the other, with no indication where Alfred Dorsett left one town behind and walked into the next.

The entire census for that area for that year listed 638 people—344 blacks and 294 whites—spread among the three communities. Studying the order of households listed, knowing what he had learned from family members about their memories of who lived where in relation to whom, Arnett was able to guess roughly where on the list Rosewood began. From that, he figured there were close to thirty households in the town in 1920, a total of about two hundred men, women and children.

There was other information Arnett was able to glean from the census reports. In 1910, Rosewood's population was nearly seven hundred, and almost one-fourth of those people were white. By 1920 the whites were gone, all except John Wright and a handful of others. It was hard to say exactly why the town had shrunk so severely in such a short time. One reason had to be the depletion of lumber in the surrounding forests, slowing business at the sawmill in Sumner. There was also the departure of Arnett's great-grandfather, Ed Goins. He was listed on the 1910 census as a Rosewood resident, along with about forty men who worked for him. But by 1920 he was gone, along with most of his employees.

Arnett had heard stories over the years about why Ed Goins had left Rosewood, that he was harassed for years by lawsuits from whites who owned their own small lumber and turpentine operations in the area and began filing complaints against Goins and his workers for everything from trespassing to damaging timber. From what Arnett understood, Goins finally decided to move, taking most of what he owned out of his turpentine business and leaving the remains to his sons. Arnett also heard that Ed Goins had, at one time, owned or

leased more than two thousand acres of land around Rosewood. Arnett had always wondered what happened to that land. He still wondered as he read those
census reports.

There was no denying Rosewood was a town in decline by 1923, Arnett
could see that. But it was still a town, nonetheless, with families living in homes
they owned, on land that belonged to them. And this was something the census
did not tell him—how much land these families owned. For that Arnett needed
to see property records, and to see them he had to go to Levy County itself, to
the courthouse in Bronson. Which was how he wound up taking that drive in
the spring of 1987, a drive that carried him past a sign just outside the city limits:

CAUTION
SMOKE AND FOG AHEAD

And then he was there, a string of stoplights to slow the traffic bound south
toward Ocala or north to Gainesville, a couple of service stations, a bank, a
diner, a bar with its door ajar, two men in white T-shirts and ball caps leaning
on a pickup parked on the gravel outside, sipping coffee in silence as Arnett
drove past.

The courthouse was a block off the highway, beside a Methodist church
with a message printed in letters on the signboard out front:

EXPECT GREAT THINGS FROM GOD

An American and a Confederate flag hung side by side by the courthouse
door as Arnett went in and asked a woman seated at a desk where he might find
property records. She asked what he was looking for, and Arnett lied, told her
he was doing a study of the county, a history project. He said he needed to research property records from the turn of the century for his report. She
paused, looked him up and down, then pointed him to a room at the back,
where an old white man approached as he stepped through the door.

"Findin' what you're lookin' for?" asked the man.

"Well, not really," said Arnett. "I've been over in Putnam and Alachua, looking at old property records for a report I'm doing on the growth of these areas,
and I'd like to see those same records for Levy County."

"Aw, well," said the man, stroking his chin, "records that far back aren't out

here. They're in the back, but you got to get permission from the supervisor to
go back there, and he's off. Won't be in till next week."

"Mmmm," said Arnett. "I really need this today. I drove all the way up from
St. Petersburg."

Arnett studied the skin around the man's neck and ears. It was raw and red,
scaly, flecking off in spots.

"Is there any way I can get a look at those papers?" Arnett said, reaching in
his pocket and pulling out a bill, a fifty. "I'll be happy to pay for it."

The man looked at the money, then glanced back toward the room. No one
else was in sight.

"All I really need," Arnett continued, his fingers rubbing the bill, "are the
records from, say, 1910 through 1925. If I had those, I'd be in good shape."

The man again looked toward the rear room. Then he reached out and took
the money. "Hold on," he said, and he disappeared into the back.

Arnett waited. The woman from the front room peeked in, asked if he was
doing okay. Arnett smiled. "Fine," he answered, "just fine." Ten minutes later,
the old man emerged, a stack of photocopies in his hands.

"If you tell anyone I gave this to you, I'll call you a liar," he said, passing the
papers to Arnett. "I never did a thing for you. I never saw you before."

Arnett nodded, took the material and left. He was sweating. He couldn't
believe he was actually sweating. It wasn't until he was beyond the Levy County
line that he pulled over at a coffee shop and took a good look at what he had.

He was stunned. There, on the pages of deeds and tax rolls, were his people's names, next to columns of acreage owned and taxes paid. There was Sarah
Carrier's name beside two acres of land she bought in 1901. And her husband
Hayward's name beside another half-acre. There was Lexie Gordon buying a
small piece of property in 1913. And Ransome Edwards, the grandfather who
raised Arnett's uncle Willie Evans, he had two acres. The Hall family was down
for twenty. Emma Carrier had herself an acre. And Ed Bradley, Lee Ruth's
uncle, he owned three.

But the numbers that took Arnett's breath away were Ed Goins's. The deed
books were full of transactions with Arnett's great-grandfather's name beside
them. Starting in 1907, Ed Goins began leasing land right and left. By 1919
there were thirty-one leases in the Rosewood area with his name on it. The
man was a magnate, that's how Arnett felt as he gazed at Ed Goins's name listed

alongside the Cummer Cypress company itself, making the same kinds of deals as them, paying the same kinds of taxes.

Then Ed Goins moved away, and his leases expired. The 1921 tax rolls showed him owning a single sixty-five acre plot of land. That year's list was the last that showed any black families in Rosewood owning property. Their names were absent on ensuing lists. Gone. Other names had replaced theirs, the names of white people. Their land had been sold for delinquent taxes, sold, Arnett was certain, to some of the same people who had burned the town down.

But none of the names meant a thing to him. He'd never heard of them. None but one: John Wright, the man who had risked his reputation to save Lee Ruth and her family, who had hidden them in his house till the train came. There was John Wright's name, listed on page after page of the 1927 tax rolls, as the owner of acres of property that formerly belonged to the people of Rosewood.

That was a hard one for Arnett to understand, another twist, one more question with no clear answer.

The old man in the courthouse had been careful. He had picked and chosen what he passed to Arnett. He hadn't pulled everything, but he had pulled enough for Arnett to get a hint of what his people had had. And that was plenty.

Arnett closed the folder of papers, climbed back in his car and pointed it south to St. Petersburg. He'd gotten what he came for, and now he had to get home. There was work to do, a lot of work.

Soul Food

None of his family knew where Arnett had gone that spring of 1987, none of them knew about the documents he had been collecting and studying for the past four years. And when they drove up to Gainesville that summer for the third annual Rosewood Family Reunion, they were not surprised by his absence. He had skipped the first two gatherings as well.

The reunions, spurred by the "60 Minutes" broadcast, had begun in the summer of '85, in Lacoochee, where scattered remnants of the clans connected to Rosewood came together for the first time, the families of the families of the families who had been there. It was a modest event, about fifty people, all told. They rented a tent, set it up in the yard beside the New Bethel A.M.E. church, borrowed tables from the church basement and piled them with steaming pots and laden platters of food, good honest soul food, potato salad and corn bread, fried chicken and collard greens, ribs and ham and gopher, cakes and pies, all cooked in kitchens back home, loaded into bright Buicks and Chevys along with the children and the grandfolks and driven halfway across the state in some cases, the cars arriving Sunday morning, raising dust as they came down

Bernadina "Honey" Carrier

the dirt drives that crisscrossed the section of Lacoochee called Mosstown, where the oaks hung heavy with the green-gray strands that had once provided a living for some of these families back when the moss was pulled from those branches and hung on fenceposts to dry in the sun, to be sold as stuffing for sofas and car seats in upholstery factories up north.

But no one stuffed sofas with moss anymore. Now the grassy beards just waved in the breeze as the traffic streamed past, the vans and station wagons parking in a long line on the sweet green grass of the church lawn, the children spilling out before the engines were even cut off, the older folks moving more slowly, stepping gingerly into the sunlight, some carrying canes, others lifted down into wheelchairs, each of them assessing the scene, narrowing their eyes and taking stock before moving cautiously toward one another, toward faces grown ancient since last they had met, some faces not seen since they had been children, back in Rosewood.

This is what Aunt Beauty had wanted all those years, for the families to come together like this, not just her family but *all* of them, everyone who had sprung from those roots, who had come into this world by way of Rosewood and who had scattered like seeds after the massacre, who had gone on to spawn children and grandchildren and, by the time Aunt Beauty was getting near the end of her life, great-grandchildren. They were all from Rosewood, and Aunt Beauty wanted them to know it, to acknowledge it, to both mourn it and to celebrate it.

Aunt Beauty was the one who would raise the subject whenever her family came together, especially at funerals. Always, it would be after a Sunday service that she would rise to speak. She would pull the grownups and children alike into a group, right there in the church, ask those who were not linked to Rosewood to please step outside, and then she would begin, always the same way, in a soft, almost scolding tone, saying what a shame it was after all they had been through that the only time they seemed to come together these days was for weddings or births or funerals, that the devastation their parents and grandparents had suffered at Rosewood was not something to be forgotten, something fearful, something shameful, but that it should be a reminder of who they were, both then and now, of their connections to one another and to those who had passed on, of what they owed to the memory of the clan and the community they had once been.

It was a speech Arnett heard all his life, growing up in Lacoochee, spending as much time down the lane at Aunt Beauty's house as he did at his own. His mother was a powerful woman, with a will no one could match, but as long as Lelland Carrier Gordine, his Aunt Beauty, was alive, *she* was the matriarch of this family, the trunk that controlled the branches that had spread among the Carriers and the Goinses. As vivid as Arnett's mother's memories of that slaughter might have been, Aunt Beauty's were even stronger. She was twenty-seven when it happened, a grown woman, taking it all in, seeing her brother and mother lying dead on that living room floor as she hurried the young ones out into the night-darkened woods. She could have become even harder and an-grier than Arnett's mother. She had every right. But Aunt Beauty was not made that way. Her spirit was different. There was a light in her that refused to grow dim, a glow that infected everyone who came near her. Arnett sensed that glow, could actually feel himself get warmer whenever his Aunt Beauty was around.

When he was still small, he would help her sometimes at bathtime, watch-ing in awe as Aunt Beauty prepared herself, undressing before his eyes, unashamed of her body, the hugest, most massive body Arnett's six-year-old eyes had ever beheld, two hundred and fifty pounds of flesh draped on a five-foot-two-inch frame. They used tin tubs for bathing, galvanized basins filled with water carried in from the outside pump and heated on their wood stoves. The tubs were numbered, from a size one, big enough for a foot bath, to a size two, which could hold a healthy adult, to a three, which was big enough for both Arnett and his sister to bathe in at the same time. A number three tub was like a small swimming pool to the children, but Aunt Beauty's body filled that number three tub from one side to the other, her flesh pressing against the tin in all directions, threatening to burst the whole thing open, flooding the kitchen with gallons of displaced bath water. That's what Arnett imagined each time he watched his Aunt Beauty bathe, and he was amazed each time she emerged, her skin wet and glimmering, ready for drying and powdering and perfuming and, finally, dressing. It was a production, and when she was done, you could smell that powder and perfume all the way up the street and there would be no doubt about it, the entire neighborhood would know that Aunt Beauty had taken her bath.

She sang like an angel, just like Arnett's mother. She was in charge of the choir there at the A.M.E. church and she ran the Sunday school as well. She was a loving, laughing teacher but a stern disciplinarian, too. She busted Ar-

nett's behind more than once, and she busted his mother's, too, when Philomena took to speaking in a way Aunt Beauty thought sassy. That was a sight for
Arnett, to see his mother, a full-grown woman, spanked like a child by his
great-aunt.

Arnett was away in the Army when Aunt Beauty died in 1970. And when
he came home, he could see that his mother had taken hold of the family reins,
her grip growing tighter with each passing year. There were other family members now pushing to do what Aunt Beauty had asked, to reach out and find the
remnants of Rosewood, the relatives who had been lost over the years, but
Philomena would not hear of it. Maybe it was anger, maybe it was fear, maybe it
was the power that came from holding those reins. Maybe it was all those things
and more, but they fueled Philomena's will and allowed her to almost single-
handedly quell the voices urging that the family be found.

Those voices had remained mere whispers until that newspaper story appeared and the "60 Minutes" segment was aired. Neither piece had much effect
on the public—an editorial or two was written and then the subject receded
without notice, just as the stories written at the time of the attack had faded
into silence. But the effect on the families was explosive, stronger than the grip
of any one woman, even Arnett's mother. For better or for worse, and no one
knew which it might be, the silence had been broken. They were a family. Despite the fear and the fragmentation, they were a family, and they extended further than many of them had imagined. Now they felt a need to reach out more
than they ever had. And so a gathering was arranged, a reunion of Rosewood
survivors and descendants.

It was Annie Bell Lee and her sister Altamese, two of Arnett's many
cousins, who picked up Aunt Beauty's old address book, tattered and thick with
names and numbers smudged and yellowed over the years, and began writing
letters and making phone calls. The two women understood what a delicate
business this was, emotional surgery of sorts, probing the edges of the pain,
dread and shame that had silenced so many for so long. Annie Bell was too
young to feel ashamed or afraid, but she knew the hurt, discovering at age ten
that her grandparents' home had been torched in Rosewood and that some of
the people who had lit those flames had been among her neighbors in Sumner,
where she was born two years after the attack.

Annie Bell was living in Lacoochee when she learned about Rosewood, and
fifty years later, in the spring of 1985, as she sat at her dining room table writ-

ing letters and making phone calls to people she had never met, people with the same blood running through their veins as through hers, she was still there. Lacoochee, they decided, was the place to hold the first gathering, and so they came, on a weekend in July, each wearing a nametag, all of them hugging and kissing and crying, praying at a memorial service for those who had "gone on," eating outside under the tent, and laughing, and remembering. Some stayed away, out of fear or discomfort, or, in cases like Sammy Hall's, because they were dead. Sam Hall had passed away the year before.

Though the flush of reunion was buoyant, there was a tension as well, a holding back. The remembering was careful, controlled, the conversations about the attack itself no more open or revealing than those Arnett had overheard at smaller family gatherings over the years. His mother was there, policing the scene like a sergeant at arms, with a trail of lieutenants behind her, Rosewood survivors like her cousin Eloise King, blind and in a wheelchair, and her cousin Berthina Fagin, who'd driven down from Deland, near Daytona Beach, and Arnett's Uncle A. T., all of them backing Philomena at the hint of an uprising, which there was when Lee Carrier stood up at one end of the tent, the rest of them chewing on their food and chatting about the children, and he stopped them all in mid-bite and mid-conversation with a pronouncement.

"Do you all know what *really* happened at Rosewood?" he said, sweeping the room with his eyes as the place fell silent. "Because I *know!*"

Philomena and Eloise were on him in a second.

"Ya'll let that *alone*," hissed Eloise.

"You shut *up!*" shouted Philomena, and that was the end of it.

Arnett didn't see that showdown, but he heard about it many times over the course of the next year. When the family gathered in Deland in 1986, there were no incidents. But by the following summer, when the group, now grown to more than a hundred, came together in Gainesville, some of the second generation, the children of the survivors, men and women Arnett's age, knowing Rosewood was right down the road, arranged an outing, a Sunday afternoon drive to the site itself.

The idea was appalling to Philomena. Dorothy Hosey, Arnett's aunt, a survivor herself, four years old when the town was attacked, had no interest in going. Arnett's Uncle A. T. stayed behind, too, as did almost all the rest of the men, women and children, gathered at the motel where they were all staying, on the west end of the city. When a van and two cars finally pulled away that afternoon, headed for Rosewood, they carried a mere dozen people, including, surprisingly, Philomena's baby sister, Vera Hamilton.

When it came to the subject of Rosewood, Vera had always stood by Philomena. At the time of the attack she had been but an infant, not yet two years old. She had no memory of Rosewood. The night of the shootout at the Carrier house, she was with her parents at the logging camp in Otter Creek. It was not until six years later, when she was living in Tampa, that she heard a word about Rosewood. That was when she was visiting her Aunt Beauty in La-coochee, and a cousin named Jimmy Robinson drove her and a couple of the kids up to the town where her Grandma Sarah used to live, the grandmother she had never met, who had died before Vera was born. That's all Vera had been told, that her grandmother had died.

Vera thought she was going to see a town, but when they got there, all there was was woods. They walked back to a clearing, and Cousin Jimmy showed them where their grandma's house used to be. There was nothing but ashes, and a corroded bedstead, and two washtubs, crust-orange with rust as well. There were some crepe myrtles, and it being springtime, they were blooming, pink and white. But there was no house. Just sand, hard white sand.

The place had burned down, that's all Vera knew. That's all Jimmy said. It wasn't until seven years later that Vera was finally told about the massacre. She was a mother by then, with a two-year-old daughter named Juanita. Vera had left school when Juanita was born, still a child herself at fourteen, and Philomena took her in, gave Vera a bed in her home in Lacoochee, where, for the next fifty years, through three husbands, two children, five grandchildren and one great-grandchild, Vera stayed, working for ten of those years at the Pasco Packing plant down in Dade City, the largest citrus packing plant in the world.

Pasco. The company had started out picking and packing whole oranges and grapefruits during the Depression, shipping crates of tissue-wrapped fruit to buyers up north. But soon it shifted focus, finding its niche at the start of the war in sectionized fruit and canned juice, selling millions of khaki-colored containers of orange juice to the military, including the Air Force, which believed the vitamin C helped its fliers' vision during night missions.

It was just before the war that Vera went to work for Pasco, rising each morning at dawn to meet one of the dozens of schoolbuses sent out from the plant into the surrounding countryside to pick up the workers, fifteen hundred workers a day by the mid-'40s. Vera would arrive on her assembly line at seven A.M., walk past the plant manager's office, where a framed motto hung on the wall—*A Quick Nickel Beats a Slow Dime*—and she would spend the next eight hours standing by a conveyor belt peeling grapefruits, seven grapefruits to a tray, fifteen cents a tray.

On a good day she could do a hundred trays, but it was hard. The hot fruit, steamed to make it peel easier, burned her hands as she picked it up. The juice soaked her skin, stinging and swelling her fingers as the acid seeped into the nicks and cuts made by her slicing knife. Her shoulders ached, her feet, wrapped in plastic, ankle deep in sloshing liquid, went numb from cold in the winter. Sweat burned her eyes in the suffocating heat of summer. There were fifty women on the line alongside her, six more lines ahead of them and six behind, the building as big as a gymnasium, the fruit rolling past from dawn to dusk, another shift ready to come on when that shift was done, grapefruits by the millions, peeled, sectioned and canned around the clock.

Vera spent a decade at Pasco before she left to get married. For a time, she ran a "jook"—a juke joint, a private club—out of her house over by the railroad tracks, just up the road from where Philomena and her husband and kids, Arnett and Yvonne, lived. Vera had the best blues and jazz in town on her jukebox, Erskine Hawkins, Louis Jordan, Lionel Hampton; she even had a couple of country records in that box, "Mule Train" by Frankie Laine. "Something to suit everybody and something to suit me, too," that's what she used to say. Vera served good homecooked food along with the liquor, and she enjoyed it all, the music, the laughter, the dancing, even the trouble her husband and some of the fellows had to break up when the hour got late and the words and the fists would start flying.

Her "shop," that's what Vera called the place. She could have stayed there forever, but she and her husband had to tear it down in the early '50s, needed the lumber to build a bigger house, and so Vera left the bar business and went to work for a family on the white side of town, cleaning and ironing, stirring feed for the chickens, and gathering eggs. She did that for ten years, switched to another family for another ten, then closed out her working days at the Holiday Inn over by the new interstate west of town, where she cleaned rooms until she retired in 1983.

That was the year the "60 Minutes" show came on about Rosewood, and Vera was beside herself when she saw it. She didn't understand why she was so upset, sobbing the way she did that night. She wasn't there when it happened, never even knew her Grandma Sarah. But she did have a photograph hanging on the wall right above her television set, an old-fashioned tintype, brown and faded, of Sarah Carrier, strong and stern, seated on a chair, surrounded by her children, thirteen-year-old Sylvester standing behind her left shoulder, staring straight into the camera, and a young girl, Willie Retha—Sylvester's sister, Vera's mother, Arnett's grandmother—standing beside him.

Vera never knew her grandma and uncle, but they had always been real to her, and so had the grief she felt every time she thought of them. It was always there, all her life, the thought of what she had lost, the family she had never known, the home she had never had, the course her life had taken and how it might have been different if this hadn't happened. That's why she sided with Philomena every time the subject of Rosewood came up. She agreed there was danger in going too far with this thing, that it could do more harm than good to get into it. Because it just hurt too much.

And yet, when the families met that summer in Gainesville, something pulled Vera toward that van. Though she knew her sister would hold it against her, wouldn't understand how she could betray her, Vera climbed in, along with Lee Ruth and Lee Carrier and Eva Jenkins and Lillie Washington. And Willie Evans, who was blind in both eyes and had no way of seeing the place where the white men had run him and his grandparents out of the home in which he had spent the first sixteen years of his life.

Willie stayed in the van when they got there. He didn't explain why. It's just what he wanted to do. The others climbed out and walked slowly up the drive to the old Wright house, the big Victorian Arnett had seen both times he'd been there. A couple named Doyal and Fuji Scoggins lived in it now, retirees from down in Clearwater who had bought the place in the late '70s, who knew nothing about Rosewood or John Wright until the story surfaced in the early '80s, who tended their fruit trees and grape arbors and beehives, selling jars of honey to passing motorists.

Doyal and Fuji Scoggins were there to greet the group when it arrived, offered them iced tea, asked if they'd like to come inside and see the place. Some did. But most stayed outside, strolling around the yard, looking into the forest, *feeling* the place because that's all they could do was feel it. There was nothing left to see other than this house, nothing left of Rosewood but the swamp around them.

Vera was upset. She thought she would be able at least to see the place where her cousin had brought her nearly sixty years earlier, the spot where her Grandma Sarah's house had stood. But that had long been reclaimed by the swamp, swallowed by six decades of trees and vines and water.

Vera did go in the house to use the bathroom, but as soon as she stepped through the door and saw rifles mounted on the wall in the living room, she recoiled. All she could think was that one of those guns might have fired the bullet that killed her grandmother. It would have done no good to tell her the weapons were antiques, single-shot muskets that hadn't been fired in more than a century, part of Doyal Scoggins's collection. Vera wouldn't have heard that, and no one tried to tell her. She pushed past the others, out to the van, and soon they were all headed back to Gainesville, silent but for the sound of soft crying from the back seat, Vera's tears.

It hurt, more than any of them imagined it might. There was nothing happy or healing about that trip. It was haunting at best, horrifying at worst. But mostly it just hurt.

And that is why Arnett was met with such caution when he arrived at the following summer's reunion in Orlando in 1988 armed with dozens of packets of photocopied documents, the deeds and censuses and newspaper reports he had been collecting for five years, one packet for each family, passing them out in the motel lobby as the relatives arrived to register, asking everyone to take the papers back to their rooms, read them over, and maybe they could all talk about it later. He didn't give a packet to his mother, but someone else did. And at the picnic that afternoon she called him over, pulled out the papers and slapped him across the face.

"What the hell is *this?*" she said, shaking the sheaf in his face.

"It's something I think we should look at, Mama," he said.

"The *hell* we will," she said, and she began tearing the papers, ripping them apart until the ground around her was littered with shreds. "*Nobody* is gonna do a damn *thing* with this," she said, as her cousin Eloise rolled up in her wheelchair.

"Boy," said Eloise, her wizened face turned toward him, her small blind eyes squeezed shut, "you don't know what you're doin'. You wasn't there. You don't under*stand*. Those crackers will *hurt* you, boy, they'll hunt you down, hunt *all* of us down."

"Arnett," his mother said, her voice softened, "I want you to stop doing this."

Arnett said nothing. He didn't argue, didn't fight back. He just left, got in his car and drove home. When his mother came back the next night, he sat her down and told her there would be no more sneaking around, no more hiding.

"Mama," he said, "I can't stop now. There is no way I'll *ever* be able to stop now. I'm going to keep this all to myself as long as you're alive. I'll honor your wishes. But if God sees fit to call you before he calls me, rest assured that I'm going to pursue this with every fiber of my being."

He bent down and kissed her on the cheek.

"Once you're gone, Mama, there is no other survivor that can stop me from doing what I want to do. I'm *going* to go after it."

She heard him. She realized, finally, what this thing had come to mean to her son, that he was as driven now to bring their family's past to light as she had been to hide it. In a strange way, for the first time, she saw something of Sylvester Carrier in her boy, the defiance, the drive, the will to stand his own ground, all of it more likely, she was certain, to lead to self-destruction than to any kind of success. She wouldn't be surprised if this thing killed him just the way it killed Sylvester. But she knew there was nothing she could do. And so, at last, she surrendered, gave her boy her blessing and told the family so, told them to talk to him, answer his questions, share as much of themselves as they could and put the rest in the hands of the Lord.

The next two years were like a whirlwind, Arnett crisscrossing the state, sitting in tiny kitchens and cluttered living rooms with the old ones, the survivors, looking at photographs and letters he had never seen before, hearing stories that had been held back for generations, stories of life in Rosewood that were darker and went deeper than the safe, sanitized accounts he had heard so far. Some of the stories were sad, some were ugly, but Arnett was eager to hear them all because they were the truth, and he needed the truth. He had no idea what he might do with it, but he needed the truth.

He needed to know about the bad blood between the Carriers and the Goinses, about the feud that developed between those families long before the destruction of Rosewood. It was a rivalry rooted in race, the Goinses being a light-complected clan come to Florida from North Carolina, where their African forebears had arrived in the early nineteenth century. They had become indentured servants, mating with the local Lumbee Indians, producing a line of blue-eyed, even blonde-haired blacks, including Martine Goins, whose success and respect among the white men with whom he did business around

Levy County was earned largely by the fact that he looked like a white man himself. It was not until Martine left Rosewood, passing the turpentine business to his darker-skinned brother Ed, that the problems with their white rivals began.

The Carriers, on the other hand, were black as pitch. Their ancestors had come straight from Africa, shipped into slavery in South Carolina. Sarah Carrier had been a Robinson before she married Hayward Carrier, and her roots too went right back to bondage. She had been born a slave, a fact that apparently made her unique by the time she was a grandmother in Rosewood. Arnett's relatives told him the name they used to call Sarah when they were children, a name some used with respect and others with disdain. "Slave Woman," that's what they called her.

They were up against one another in every way, the Goinses and Carriers, competing for control of this small community. The Goinses had their turpentine business, the Carriers their logging. They went to the same churches, the men were Masons together, they even married among one another. But there was always tension among them and sometimes it burst into violence. An argument here, a fistfight there. One memorable Christmas, it came down to murder.

It was Arnett's great-uncle Charlie Goins who pulled the trigger. He was one of Ed Goins's ten children, a brother of Arnett's Grandpa George, a man known for his quick temper. George Goins had married a Carrier, Arnett's grandmother Willie Retha, and Willie Retha's cousin Elias had a problem with George Goins. He didn't like the way this man spoke to his cousin, and finally he told him so, told George Goins he would beat him if he showed disrespect for Willie Retha one more time. Charlie Goins got wind of the threat, shoved a pistol in his pocket and walked across town to the Carrier house. It was Christmas week. Elias wasn't in, they told him. He'd gone over to church, to rehearse with the choir for their Christmas pageant. So Charlie Goins walked to the church, looked through a window, saw Elias Carrier there with the rest of them, singing a hymn, and he shot him. Just like that, right through the church window, he shot him dead.

No one ever saw Charlie Goins in Rosewood again. He left that night, wanted for murder, and no one ever caught up with him. But Arnett knew he survived, because he showed up one Christmas, thirty years later, at the Doctors' house in Lacoochee. He was the lightest-skinned black man Arnett had ever seen, light enough to pass for white, which is how he had managed to get a room in the only hotel in town, a white hotel. Charlie Goins had a pocket full of money, Arnett remembered that, and he passed some out to all of them, a roll of coins each for Arnett and his sister and some paper bills for their parents. Arnett was impressed. His uncle Charlie was clearly a man who had made it. Nice clothes. Pockets of cash. Living in hotels, even ordering room service. He didn't look like a murderer.

That was the only killing Arnett heard of in Rosewood—the only one before the massacre. But he learned there were other petty crimes that occurred, arrests made and jail terms served. He learned that Sylvester Carrier himself served a prison sentence along with his father Hayward, that the two of them spent the summer of 1918 working on one of the state's notoriously brutal road gangs for stealing cattle and changing the brands, a charge the family swore was a setup by whites, another dose of bitterness to shorten Sylvester's temper and sharpen his trigger.

It was hard hearing these stories, of pettiness and anger among his own people, of jealousy and rage. But in the end Arnett found them all beautiful, because they were the truth. Now he was able to see these people, these names he had known all his life, not as myths or legends but as living, breathing human beings, and the town itself, it was no longer an imagined Eden, a place of bucolic perfection. It was real, with shadows as well as light, and that was more gorgeous than any fantasy.

It was also more gut-wrenching. By the end of 1990 Arnett was literally falling apart from the stress, his weight dropping by the week, his vision beginning to blur. He was thirsty all the time, drinking two gallons of water a day and still wanting more. He was working on Rosewood every spare minute he had, but he was working sixty, sometimes seventy hours a week with his own business as well, a janitorial service he had started soon after leaving the liquor store.

He had begun with a contract on one building and was now handling a dozen high-rises and office buildings in the Tampa Bay area. He had more than fifty people on his payroll, and he followed behind them all, staying up until two or three in the morning, checking trash baskets, cleaning toilets, filling paper towel holders, walking the stairwells to make sure the steps were swept, climbing up and down forty-floor buildings, doing the right side one night and the left the next because there were just too many steps to walk them all in one evening.

He had turned forty-seven that year, too young to even think of retiring, but some days he could barely walk anymore. His feet were already bad from the Army, and this work was only making it worse. His body was betraying him now, and he knew some of it had to do with Rosewood.

The thing was eating him up. By that summer's reunion the doctors were telling him he had to slow down, but he couldn't. These people, the survivors, they were old. Some were dying. Some were dead. Lee Carrier had passed away. Sam Hall, whom Arnett never met, he was gone. So many were gone now, with nothing to show for what they had been through, no justice, not even the simple satisfaction of acknowledgment. With each death, Arnett grew angrier. These people were *owed*. That is what it came down to. This thing had affected all their lives, steered the courses of generations, but the survivors themselves, the ones who had actually gone *through* it, they were the ones who were owed first and owed most, because they were the ones whose suffering had been greatest. And they were dying now, dying every year, dropping like leaves off a tree, taking their memories and their grace and their pain and their strength with them. And it just wasn't right. That's how Arnett felt. It just wasn't right. The unfocused rage that had always been a part of his soul now became *out*rage. Someone needed to pay for this. He had no idea who or how, but someone needed to pay.

That's what he was feeling that New Year's Eve of 1990. New Year's was always a hard time for him, its promise of renewal and hope eclipsed by the fact that this was the day it began, the massacre. And that his own birthday, January fifth, was the date Sylvester and Sarah Carrier died in a hail of bullets. Arnett sometimes felt like it was some kind of cruel joke. Other times he was convinced God had piled it all together for a purpose, these January days and all that they meant. He had no idea what that meaning might be, but before this month was over—January of 1991—he would have one more date to deal with. The day his mother died.

It was a Monday, Martin Luther King Day, and she called him that morning, asked him to come over and take her to the parade. He was too busy, he told her, he had too many contracts to check over. Next weekend, Mama, he said, I'll come over next weekend and we'll go out. She sniffed a little bit, but then she was always trying to make him feel guilty. He didn't think anymore about it, was out at one of his buildings until well after midnight, and when he got in, the light on his answering machine was blinking. He punched the button, and it was his niece Gretchen's voice—Yvonne's daughter—sobbing, saying something had happened to Grandma. The next message clicked on, and it was Gretchen again, still crying, saying she was so sorry, that Grandma was gone. And all Arnett could do was stand there and say no. No, No, No, over and over again.

He didn't cry, not yet. He got in his car and drove over, walked in the door and they were all there, Yvonne, her kids, Aunt Vera, Uncle A. T., the whole family. And Arnett came in like it was just another day, hugging everybody, asking how they were doing, seeing his sister break down in tears and telling her to take strength in Jesus, trust in God, moving toward his mother's bedroom even as he spoke, saying he had to go in there, had to see Mama, half of him knowing she was dead, the other half holding out, still believing she was alive in that room.

But she wasn't. Her body was gone. It had happened after dinner, they told him. Fried fish, that's what they'd eaten, fried fish. She'd finished her meal, gone to the bathroom for some Alka-Seltzer, and she never came out. They found her in there, on the bathroom floor. The paramedics tried to bring her back, but she was gone, dead.

It was just words now to Arnett, just noise. He hardly heard it. He closed his mother's door behind him, locked it and sat down on her bed, in the darkness, sat there all night. In the morning he went to her closet, pulled out her housecoat, put it on and sat down again.

He stayed there for four days, sitting, sleeping, rolling on the floor and screaming. They called an ambulance, but he wouldn't let them in. He spoke to the medics through the door, assured them he would not harm himself, and so they left.

Finally, the day of the burial, he came out. The church was wall to wall with people, hundreds of people, a hundred more standing outside. The relatives were there, all of them. Of course. This was a funeral. This was family.

Arnett stepped to the casket, leaned in and put his lips to his mother's, kept them there until he had to be pulled away.

They buried her under an oak, on a knoll by a pond. And when it was done, Arnett drove home, alone. There would be time later for the others, for Rosewood. But right now he needed time for himself.

PART THREE

*M*OVEMENT

ELEVEN

The Fire This Time

It was May of 1992, one day after a Los Angeles jury had acquitted four white policemen in the beating of Rodney King, and Michael O'McCarthy's car radio was crackling with reports of sniping and looting on the streets of L.A. He was a continent away, steering his small white Toyota into a section of Dade County called Liberty City, a bleak grid of broad streets lined with palms as tall as any in Miami but not tall enough to mask the utter poverty beneath them.

This was not a good day to be a white man in a black place anywhere in America, but that's what O'McCarthy was, hunting among this neighborhood of decaying projects, paint-flaked bungalows and sagging shotgun flats, searching for the home of a woman named Lee Ruth Davis, the address scribbled on the scrap of paper clutched in his hand.

He was surprised his hands weren't shaking. Miami had become a foul stew of racial strife during the past decade, tension among Anglos, Latinos and blacks boiling over into combat on inner-city streets, drug wars and gang battles turning backyard barbecues into drive-by death traps, the Mariel boatlift

---

Lee Ruth Davis

upping the ante in the Cuban community, Haitians flooding in as well, facing off with the Cubans, and, always, the dead-end desperation and simmering rage in the black sections of the city, block after block of short-fused dynamite ready to blow with the slightest spark.

They had blown time and again during the previous decade, beginning with an explosion right there in Liberty City in the summer of 1980, after an all-white jury acquitted four white deputy sheriffs in the beating death of a black insurance agent, touching off three days of rioting that left sixteen dead, four hundred injured and more than one thousand residents behind bars. Smaller flareups continued through the '80s, culminating in 1989, on Martin Luther King Day, when the shooting of two black men by a white police officer set off another three days of rioting, this time on the streets of a ghetto called Overtown, to the east of Liberty City. Football fans tuning in for news from the Super Bowl, played that week in Miami, were treated to footage of flak-jacketed police squads patrolling the sidewalks of Overtown and Liberty City, searching for snipers in darkened windows.

It had been three years now since that outbreak, but as O'McCarthy hunted for Lee Ruth's house number, the L.A. updates spilling from his radio gave him every reason to expect it to happen again, here, at any minute. He saw Miami cops on every corner he passed, called out in force in case the lid blew. But they were small comfort. If the shit came down now, in this place, O'McCarthy would have no way out. No white man would.

O'McCarthy had been in situations like this before, but never when he was sober. He'd always had liquor or dope or both to lean on in the past, but now he was straight, no dimmer switch for the fear. And still he kept driving. No way was he turning back from this one. When he had called Lee Ruth the night before, introduced himself over the phone, told her he'd like to meet her, to talk about Rosewood, she said he was welcome to come on over, told him he was *more* than welcome. As a matter of fact, she said, she had been waiting her whole life for him to show up.

The fact was, O'McCarthy had been waiting his whole life for her as well. He would turn fifty that year, Lord willing, and he wanted more to show for it all, more to share with his young son, than memories of modeling gigs and unsold movie scripts, soft news tips peddled to tabloid TV shows like "Hard Copy" and "A Current Affair," the stuff of his life at the moment.

There had been a time when he felt he was at the heart of something that mattered, back in his counterculture days, when he was rubbing shoulders with the Black Panthers, going underground with the IRA, getting laid in Paris and Belfast and writing about it all in radical magazines and books, reporting from the front lines of what looked at the time like an honest-to-God revolution. But that was before the booze wore him down and turned him into a lush, just another leftover from the sad, sorry '60s, holed up in Hollywood, trying to sell his life as a movie and finding no takers, peddling himself and his stories like a carny barker until he finally gave up and came back to the South, the place he'd been running from since the day he was born.

Purebred cracker stock, that was Michael McCarthy—he didn't add the "O" until he was in his forties, marketing himself as a model and needing a gimmick to set him apart from every other McCarthy in the book. His father, an Atlantan by birth, spent the happiest years of his life, including the year Michael was born, killing Japanese in the Solomon Islands. The old man went to his deathbed forty years later, still cursing niggers and Jews. O'McCarthy's mother, born on the side of a steep wooded slope in rural Georgia, left her husband during the war and moved her kids to Miami, where she waited tables in a shrimp shop and fretted that her little boy Michael was getting too friendly with the son of the black woman who kept house for them, a boy named Aubrey. O'McCarthy would never forget the day his mother came home, found him out on the porch with Aubrey, both of them playing the same harmonica, and she snatched the thing away as if it were poison, pushed Aubrey off the porch, told him to get on home and yanked little Michael, all of four years old, into the house, where she washed out his mouth as if there were dirt in it.

He never forgot that, and he never forgave it. He grew up hating the hate he saw in his parents, and he dealt with his hate the same way his father did, by drowning it in liquor. If there was one thing he owed to his father, one legacy the old man left him, it was the bottle. Before O'McCarthy was out of his teens, he had become a drunk, just like his old man. When he was fifteen he quit school, ran away from home, got caught stealing hubcaps and wound up in the state reform school in Marianna, north of Tallahassee, where he was routinely beaten, whipped with a steel strap by "men with taut grins and white Baptist faces, hard Christian men serving the state, steeped in the doctrine of original sin and the swift application of salvation and retribution."

That's how O'McCarthy described it twenty years later, in the mid-'70s, in an essay he wrote for a book about what it was like to grow up in the Deep

South, what it did to a person, black or white. What it did to O'McCarthy was drive him as far away as he could get, clear across country to California, where, on a warm, clear night in the fall of 1962, in an alcoholic haze, with his Jamaican girlfriend asleep back in his apartment, he held up a filling station for six dollars and seventy-four cents and wound up spending the rest of the decade behind bars.

It was there, at San Quentin and Soledad, in cell blocks jammed with Mexicans and blacks, surrounded with books by Trotsky and Marx, that Michael O'McCarthy became a dyed-in-the-wool revolutionary, "the Lenin of western America," as he likes to remember himself. Or another favorite phrase: "the white Eldridge Cleaver."

He rubbed shoulders with Cleaver and Huey Newton, became pals with George Jackson and spearheaded the formation of a racially integrated prisoners' union, the first of its kind in California. He swears he survived two attempts on his life—a stabbing and a shooting—arranged by prison authorities, he has no doubt. The assassination attempts, and that's what he calls them to this day, were like a badge, earning him the respect of his black prison mates. He points with pride to the page in Jackson's collection of prison letters, *Soledad Brother*, where his name is mentioned as a white soulmate, as close to the Black Panthers as any son of the South would ever get.

O'McCarthy was out of prison by the time Jackson was gunned down on the yard at San Quentin in 1970, during an alleged escape attempt. That death only added fuel to O'McCarthy's fire and pages to a manuscript he was writing with some friends on the "police state" of America. But the book, published in 1973 under the title *The Glass House Tapes*, went nowhere, and O'McCarthy dove deeper into the bottle than he'd ever been.

Somehow he was able to keep it going for another ten years, developing documentary-style scripts on subjects ranging from the death penalty in Florida to uranium mining in Virginia, while ingesting insane amounts of cocaine, mushrooms and booze. In 1981, a year before Arnett Doctor took his drive up to Rosewood, Michael O'McCarthy's photo popped up in *Rolling Stone* magazine—bushy hair, beard, backpack and peace button—for his part in organizing a hunger strike among a group of L.A. Vietnam Vets.

But that was his last hurrah. Not long after, his string finally ran out. He was picked up for a DUI in West Hollywood and tossed in the drunk tank, the first time he'd been behind bars since emerging from prison in 1969. The shock pushed him into AA and, finally, out of Hollywood. In 1987 he moved back to Florida, found an apartment in Coconut Grove and cashed in on the one thing he had left—his good Irish looks. Somehow his body had not betrayed him. He had aged well, a little gray in the temples but that only added to the corporate cachet his clients were looking for. Soon O'McCarthy's fortysomething face was on TV screens and billboards all over Florida, hawking pizzas and fabric softeners, telephone companies and banks. He even did a little stand-up comedy on the side. Met a flight attendant from Costa Rica, had a baby boy, and now he was a family man.

But he couldn't shake the part of him that needed to make news. Or find news and make it into a movie. He was still sniffing around for stories, something true-life, with a nice edge to it. Something like serial killer Aileen Wuornos, a Florida prostitute who was arrested in January, 1991, for the murders of seven men. O'McCarthy perked up at that one, tracked down a cop who had investigated the case, signed him to a book-and-movie deal and now he was back in the business.

A month later, he was up in Gainesville, poking around for something on the grisly deaths of five University of Florida undergrads. He wasn't sure what he was after—a book, a movie, maybe a tip for one of the tabloid TV shows, anything he could dig up. He got on the phone with a producer friend in Hollywood, told him where he was, what he was up to, and the friend asked if he'd ever heard of a place called Rosewood, said it was right down the road if he remembered right. O'McCarthy had never heard of the place, never heard of the story, but it sounded like it had potential. So the next morning he rented a car and drove on down to Levy County.

It was a wet, eerie day—primordial is the way O'McCarthy recalls it. Dark sky, a steady rain, old oaks and thick moss, all of it sodden and dripping. He came to the sign for Rosewood, saw nothing but mud and trailers, and so he drove on to Cedar Key. Went to the library and asked if they had anything on the shelves about this massacre. The two librarians, both elderly women, looked at each other, then eyed him, then hesitantly pulled out a tattered newspaper clipping, the *St. Petersburg Times* story from 1982.

Before O'McCarthy was halfway through it, he was on fire. This was a story that encompassed his entire life, a parable of the breed to which he belonged, the strain of white working-class southerners that produced his parents, a tale of the twisted blend of religion and violence that created the Messianic Baptists who ran that Marianna reform school. When O'McCarthy read the account of the mob ravaging Rosewood, all he could see were the faces of the men who had beaten him at that school. He saw the death of George Jackson, too, lynched on the yard at San Quentin just as surely as Sam Carter was lynched under a tree in this Gulf Florida swamp. There might have been fifty years between the two, but to O'McCarthy they were the same story, the murder without penalty of black men in America. He'd done all he could about the death of Jackson, but there was still something O'McCarthy felt he could do about this. So many things: stir up some social justice, assuage some of his family ghosts, and maybe get a movie deal in the bargain.

He called back his producer friend and was told that the story, optioned a while back by the St. Pete reporter, Gary Moore, had been shopped around L.A. for a couple of years with no luck. Everyone in town had passed on it, the producer told O'McCarthy. It was old news, they said, a period piece. By the time O'McCarthy hung up the phone, he knew he had to have some kind of modern hook, something to bridge those seventy years, to carry the story into today's world. Something like a lawsuit.

He spent the rest of that summer calling, writing and faxing every civil rights agency he could think of—the NAACP, the ACLU, the Southern Poverty Law Center, Klanwatch, Jesse Jackson's Rainbow Coalition—trying to find anyone who would take on this case, take on this cause, help him find survivors and pursue restitution. They all either turned him away or passed him along to someone else. Most had never heard of Rosewood. The few who had said there was nothing to be done, not now.

"Your objectives are laudable," the NAACP's national deputy executive director wrote O'McCarthy that October, "and we believe the truth should be pursued. Unfortunately, our limited resources both in financial and staff terms rule out our active participation."

He called Moore as well, who was then living in Seattle. O'McCarthy described his idea for a film, built around current-day courtroom testimony of aged Rosewood survivors. Moore backed off, telling O'McCarthy no such testimony had ever occurred. Moore was interested in fact, not fiction.

So O'McCarthy was left with nothing but names, the names he'd read in Moore's story. He had no faces, no flesh and blood, no survivors. He had no addresses, no phone numbers; Moore wasn't about to share that information, though O'McCarthy did his best to pull it out of him.

A year came and went, and O'McCarthy kept modeling, kept developing movie deals, kept passing tips to the tabloids and kept trying to track down one living person connected to Rosewood. Finally, that summer, after all the long-distance phone calls and faxes, he found what he was looking for in his own backyard, there in the Miami telephone directory—Lee Ruth Bradley Davis, of Liberty City.

And so, on this bright morning in May, as Los Angeles burned, Michael O'McCarthy pulled up to a faded green cinderblock house, parked his Toyota at the curb, and walked in to see if Lee Ruth Davis was ready to make a deal.

TWELVE

Eat What You Kill

The thing smelled like a hustle. It didn't take Steve Hanlon long to figure that out. If there was one thing Hanlon had learned after twenty-five years of practicing law, it was how to smell a hustle, and the voice on the other end of the line, such a smooth voice, so polished, so prepared, a voice you'd hear on the radio, a voice trying to sell you something—the voice alone was enough to set off Hanlon's alarms.

And then there was the man's name. O'McCarthy. Now why in hell would someone stick an "O" on a good Irish name like that, hang it out there like a stolen hood ornament? Hanlon was Irish himself, a "recovering Catholic," as he liked to put it, and if he had a nose for hustlers, well, he had an even better nose for Irish hustlers. It didn't surprise him one bit when this man said he was in the movie business. Of *course* he was in the movie business.

Still, the guy could tell a story. Hanlon had to give him that. He could tell a story, and that's what kept Hanlon from simply hanging up.

On the face of it, the tale was preposterous. Two women, elderly, poor, black, the sole survivors of a town that was wiped off the map seventy years

Rosewood, January, 1923

ago, and now they wanted to bring a lawsuit against the state of Florida, a life-time after the fact. Preposterous. But then that was Hanlon's job, to pursue the preposterous. That's why the largest law firm in the state had hired him, put him in charge of its new pro bono division, set him up in a swank suite in its Tallahassee high-rise headquarters and given him carte blanche to call on any of the firm's four hundred attorneys for some free, non-billable hours. Go out and represent the poor, he was told when he was hired. Go out and represent the preposterous.

And so he had. In the three years since he had joined the hallowed Florida law firm of Holland and Knight, he and his colleagues—they called themselves the Community Services Team—had tackled almost two dozen cases, ranging from civil rights transgressions to consumer fraud. With Hanlon at its helm, the team had filed a class action suit on behalf of several hundred low-income women in the Tampa area who had unwittingly signed a form during their pregnancies allowing doctors from the University of South Florida to perform medical experiments on their high-risk fetuses. Hanlon's group had filed a housing discrimination suit against a Miami apartment complex that had turned away thousands of prospective black tenants over the course of the 1980s. It had filed a civil suit on behalf of a lesbian couple who had become fos-ter parents to a six-year-old boy only to see the boy removed from their home by state authorities after it was revealed they were gay.

These were David and Goliath cases, the huddled masses versus the powers that be, high-profile battles guaranteed to make headlines if not money, and ei-ther one was fine with Hanlon. By the time he arrived at Holland and Knight, he had made plenty of both.

The headlines had come first, back in the mid-'70s, when he moved south from his home town of St. Louis to join the staff of a nonprofit legal services team in Tampa, representing the underprivileged of that community. He was paid twelve thousand dollars a year, a salary his law school classmates would have laughed at, but he was making a reputation as well, as a gladiator for the underprivileged. Rent disputes, food stamp cutoffs, tenant complaints, mi-grant worker rights—whatever walked in the door, Hanlon took it, and those being the Carter years, the glory years of legal services, there was plenty walk-ing in the door.

But Hanlon and his partner, a fellow named Robert Shapiro, weren't con-tent to just take what came to them. They were out to stir the pot themselves.

Each morning they'd open their small rented office there on the east side of the city, across the street from a bar, with spent bullet casings from the night before sprinkled on the sidewalk outside, and they'd look out their window toward the distant skyline of downtown Tampa, turn to each other and ask, "Who should we go after today?"

They went after them all. They took on church and state. They battled the bishop of the Roman Catholic diocese of St. Petersburg over back pay for a former nun. They forced a local school system to allow a teenage girl to play football with the boys. They represented a woman whose charges of sexual harassment against a community college president eventually led to the man's dismissal. All those cases were covered by local and state newspapers and television, of course, and when Hanlon stepped into the arena of racial issues, challenging Florida's functional literacy test as being culturally biased against black students, he was given a national stage, arguing his case against "funky lit"—as the black kids called it—on "Nightline" and the "Donahue" show, as well as in front of the U.S. District Court in Tampa, which handed down a four-year injunction against the test while a new one was devised.

This was heady stuff, the kind of law Hanlon had imagined practicing when he was fresh out of the University of Missouri Law School in the late '60s, he and his wife camped in a small St. Louis apartment, the two of them young and poor and happy, surrounded by neighbors just like themselves, Jewish couples, Italian couples, black couples, all of them fresh and full of faith, talking politics and the war late into the night over potluck dinners and bottles of cheap wine, gorging themselves on *The Greening of America* and *The Making of the Counterculture*, quoting Baldwin and the Berrigan brothers, believing they were all going to go out and make a difference, that every one of them would make some change for the better in the dominant culture.

The dominant culture. Hanlon adored that phrase from the moment he first heard it. He was still using it long after he had become part of that culture himself, after he left his little office in Tampa to join the corporate world. It was the looming specter of his kids' college years that did it, he says, prompting him to set social justice aside and start earning a serious salary. It was a tough decision, he says, but his daughter had her heart set on Yale, his oldest son on Swarthmore, and there was no way he could afford that on the thirty grand a year he was making in Tampa at the time. So in 1980 he shaved his beard, left legal services, signed on with a large corporate firm and stepped into the world of lean, mean billing machines, where a man eats what he kills.

Hanlon ate plenty. He spent the rest of that decade "rearranging the assets of the upper class," as he puts it, and watching his own income swell to three hundred thousand dollars a year. By the time his two kids had gotten their diplomas, and the third was about to get his, Hanlon was deep inside the belly of the corporate beast. And he was miserable. Not miserable enough, however, to go back to making a tenth of the salary he was now earning.

It was a quandary, comfort calling from one side and conscience nagging from the other. Hanlon had always said there was no thrill in life like walking to the courthouse with a poor person. He had shared that quote with more newspaper reporters than he could count, shared it so often it began to sound canned. But he meant it, he really did. He needed that feeling, just as much as he needed his six-figure salary. He wanted to have it both ways, and eventually he figured out how. In 1989 a couple of lawyers with Holland and Knight, knowing Hanlon's sense of social commitment, approached him about running for office. He laughed. Politicians spend more time raising money to keep their seats than making real changes, he said. But he countered with an idea of his own. Pro bono, he said. Let's talk about pro bono.

The legal profession has long considered pro bono work—from the Latin *pro bono publico*, meaning "for the public good"—as part of its social duty, giving a voice to those who would otherwise have none. Not all lawyers buy into the notion, by any means. Traditionally, most law firms have always left it up to the attorneys themselves to volunteer whatever hours, if any, they would like to work for causes in the community. A few firms, however, have long required their attorneys to participate in a measured, accountable, obligatory pro bono program. Hanlon's idea was to turn Holland and Knight into one of those firms.

The firm, chaired by a former American Bar Association president named Chesterfield Smith, a maverick of sorts who made a name for himself in 1974 by publicly calling for Richard Nixon to resign, considered Hanlon's suggestion. Holland and Knight, whose clients included most of the largest corporate interests in the state of Florida, surprised Hanlon by agreeing to create a division that would likely wind up turning many of those clients into defendants. By the following year, the Community Services Team had been created, with Steve Hanlon as its quarterback—its well-paid quarterback.

He brought the same game plan to Tallahassee that he had used in Tampa, a laid-back, what-me-worry demeanor comfortably cloaking a strategic, calculating mind. His weary, heavy-lidded eyes, his unruly salt-and-pepper hair—more salt than pepper—his unknotted neckties and wrinkled shirts, his loafered feet propped on his cluttered desk, a framed portrait of Sir Thomas More gazing down from the wall behind him—a gift from the nun he represented in that back pay dispute—all of it was meant to disarm the most skeptical onlooker.

And almost always, it worked. Hanlon knew how to play an audience, be it a jury or a television camera, and he understood how thin the line between the two had become. He constantly referred to the "court of public opinion," where the outcry of newspaper readers and TV viewers on an issue could affect judges and politicians just as much as any attorney's well-reasoned argument. Hanlon had turned to that court more than once in his career. That's what all those headlines had been about. That's why he went on "Nightline" and "Donahue."

And that's why he was willing to hear this O'McCarthy character out. So what if the guy had an angle? Everybody has an angle. All Hanlon cared about was the question of whether this was the kind of case he wanted to take. It sounded crazy, which he liked. It sounded implausible, which was true of almost every case he represented. It sounded like it couldn't possibly be true. But there was only one way to find that out.

He buzzed his secretary and asked her to book a flight to Miami.

THIRTEEN

Tiny Island

Arnett Doctor felt lost, dead in the water. It was May of 1992, more than a year since he had buried his mother, and months since he had finished mourning and begun throwing himself headlong into Rosewood, into *doing* something about this thing.

But nothing was happening, nothing was moving. He had called or written every black attorney he knew of in the state of Florida. Tampa, St. Pete, Orlando, Miami, even Atlanta—he'd gone to them all, sat in their waiting rooms, his briefcase perched on his lap, watching the doors open and close, people coming and going, shadows crawling across the carpet, until finally a secretary would emerge and tell him he'd have to try another time, that Mr. Jones or Ms. Williams was just too busy to fit him in today.

They were all too busy, even the ones who saw him, who listened to his story and looked politely at the papers he pulled from his case. They nodded with interest, agreed how awful this was, but they all wound up saying the same thing. They had no time for it, and time was money, and Arnett had no money,

Arnett Doctor

so, well, they hoped he understood. It was very nice meeting him, they would say, and they would wish him the best of luck as they showed him to the door.

Arnett could not understand it. These were black people, his people. The Rosewood story was *their* story. That was how he saw it. He had no doubt when he began looking for a lawyer that they'd be lining up to take this case. Righteousness. Outrage. Injustice. The eternal themes of the black man in America, they were all there, right in his briefcase. How could anyone turn away from that?

But they did. Most didn't even bother to take a look. Business, they told him. This was about business, and that meant money, in this case at least fifty thousand dollars up front, for a retainer. That's the number he kept hearing. Fifty thousand dollars. Arnett had twelve thousand to his name, his entire life savings, all he had to live on now that he wasn't working anymore.

He had left his job in October, when the doctors told him he had a choice: He could quit working or die. The circulation was gone in his feet. His legs were shot. He could hardly haul himself up the steps of his own house anymore, much less climb the stairs of those skyscrapers. His strength was sapped, and his weight was dropping like the autumn temperatures outside. By Christmas his body had shrunk from 230 pounds to 170. He was so weak he could barely pull himself out of bed. He could hardly even breathe anymore.

Grief. That had to be part of it, he figured. The madness he'd gone through with his mother's death had given way to an emptiness that lasted for months, a kind of walking coma. From that January of 1991 through the spring and on into the summer, he did nothing, saw no one, left his business to his employees and went off alone, north of the city about twenty minutes, to a little fishing spot on a creek off the Hillsborough River, a quiet place he'd been escaping to for years, whenever he needed to be alone.

Now he went there for days at a time, set himself up on an empty dock, tossed out his line, leaned back and watched the wildlife go past. Turtles and egrets. Deer and wild hogs. And gators, lots of gators. Sometimes he'd grunt those gators up, just the way his Uncle Ernest had taught him back in Lacoochee. He'd make a high-pitched, screechy sound, the sound of a baby alligator in distress, and the grown females would rise up from the river bottom, swim straight toward that sound like a fish to bait.

Grunting gators. For Uncle Ernest, it had been a way of catching dinner. He'd skin the creatures, chop up that meat, sprinkle it with salt, pepper, a little vinegar, slice up some onions, garlic, cloves, a few tomatoes, wrap the whole thing in aluminum foil and bake it in the oven. That was some of the best eating Arnett ever tasted, though food was the last thing on his mind as he sat on the dock that spring. All he wanted was to watch those animals. There was something soothing about them, the way they slid through the water.

But the monkey, that was something else again. There was nothing soothing about the monkey.

Arnett had heard about the monkey long before he actually saw it. A park ranger had told him about it. There was a small wooded island out in the river, about twenty-five yards offshore, and one day the ranger happened by, pointed at the island, and told Arnett an ape lived out there, a chimpanzee of some sort. Right, said Arnett. The ranger shrugged, left, and Arnett went back to baiting his line.

A few weeks passed, and one morning Arnett was sitting out on the dock's edge, nearly asleep, when he heard a commotion in the treetops out on that island, a violent heaving among the branches. And then he saw it, hanging among the cypress and myrtles and weeping willows, leaping from limb to limb. A monkey, small, maybe two feet tall. It couldn't have weighed more than twenty, maybe thirty pounds, but it was shaking the trees like something twice that size. It was going berserk.

Arnett couldn't imagine where it came from. The zoo, maybe. Maybe the circus. How it got onto that island was anyone's guess, but it soon became clear how badly the thing wanted to get off. Arnett began looking for it every time he came out to fish, and sooner or later it would always appear. There was a tide to the river, and when it was low, the monkey would climb down from the trees and creep out across the mud, tiptoeing toward the edge of the water on all fours, as if it were looking for some way to get across, to reach the shore. But there was no way. And the tide would rise. And the monkey would retreat from the riverbank, back into the trees, back to life on its tiny island.

That was the way the summer went, Arnett spending his days by that creek and his nights at home, in his small pale blue bungalow, with its fruit trees—plums and papayas, bananas and oranges—shielding it against the surrounding squalor, the decayed trailer park a block down the lane, the half-naked Hispanic kids playing in mud puddles in the street out front, the pawn shops and prostitutes and pink rent-by-the-hour motels over on Hillsborough Avenue, where the Saturday night shouts and gunshots were loud enough to keep Arnett awake, the Cuban flea markets and sandwich shops selling their *empanadillas* and *alcapuras* in the shadows of billboards pointing the way up the interstate to Busch Gardens, or down to the dog track, or out to the new gambling casinos at the Seminole Reservation.

Arnett would shut all that out, blockade himself in his tiny office, no bigger than a closet, pull the shades, turn his TV up and pick through the piles of papers he had amassed on Rosewood. Mountains of paper, hundreds of pages of notes, interviews, records, charts, old newspaper clippings, everything that remotely had anything to do with what happened to his people. Sometimes he'd fall asleep right there in that room, in that chair, with those papers all over his lap.

Another reunion was approaching, down at Deland this time, and Arnett wasn't sure he even wanted to go. His mother's death had taken so much out of him, and so many others were dying now, too. They'd lost eleven family members since the summer before, including a couple of survivors. Leroy Smith, from Tampa, one of the oldest—he was eighteen years old when the attack happened—Leroy had passed away that year from a brain tumor. And Eloise King, Philomena's right hand, she had just died that very week. In fact, they were going to bury her the following Wednesday, three days before the reunion, right there in Deland.

That was the reason Arnett finally decided to go, because of Eloise's funeral. And after they put her in the ground, he did what he'd done just about every day lately, grabbed his tackle box and poles and went off to do some fishing. The family could use some extra food for the weekend, and he'd heard there was a nice spot just up the road, on the St. Johns River, where a man could catch more fish than he could carry. Bluegill, shell cracker, speckled perch, all good eating, great on the grill. His cousin Albert Edwards saw Arnett loading the trunk, asked if he could come along, and so they both went.

Albert was a big man, bigger than Arnett, about the same age, with a bad shoulder that left his right arm hanging limp at his side. His father was Earl Edwards, another Rosewood survivor who had passed away. Arnett had never met Albert until the family's 1986 reunion. There was no mention of Rosewood at that gathering, and now, as they pushed their boat out into the river, settled back and began baiting their poles, Arnett was shocked to discover Albert knew nothing at all about the massacre. Here it was, the summer of 1991, and this man, a direct descendant, knew nothing at all.

"You're kidding me," said Albert when Arnett mentioned that he was thinking of finding the family a lawyer. "You mean these reunions we been having are because we were all chased *out* of that place?"

"They killed us, man," said Arnett. "They came in and killed our people, burned the houses down, took our land and refused to give it back."

Albert's face was flushed.

"*All* our people?" he asked.

"Yes," said Arnett. "Your father, too. Your father and his family had to leave their land."

"My family owned land in Rosewood?"

"Five and a half acres," said Arnett. By then he had memorized every name and number on those pages of property records stacked back in his house.

Albert had never heard of any land owned in Rosewood. He'd never heard of the massacre. His father, like so many others, had mentioned the place only as the town he came from, nothing more. Not until this moment did Albert realize there was more to these reunions than spare ribs and cole slaw.

"Those crackers," Albert said, staring at the water and shaking his head. "Those goddamned crackers."

"Yeah," said Arnett, "but I think there's something we can do about it."

"Go get some *guns* is what we can do about it," said Albert.

"No," said Arnett. "I'm thinking about a lawsuit. A class-action lawsuit." Arnett paused, tugged on his line. "If we did sue," he asked, "how much you think we should ask for?"

"I don't know," shrugged Albert. "Millions, probably."

"I don't think so," said Arnett, smiling now. "I'm thinking more like billions."

"*Billions?*" Albert snapped back his neck. "Are you serious?"

"Hey," said Arnett, "have you ever heard of the Japanese-American Reparation Act? Just a couple of years ago. They gave those people twenty thousand dollars each, a billion and a half dollars in all. A billion and a *half*. And all they did was intern those people, put 'em in prison camps. They *killed* us, man. They eradicated us, burned our property, terrorized us, took our land, took away our whole *livelihood*. That's got to be worth at least a hundred times more than what they gave those Japanese."

Arnett paused, gazed at the ripples around his fishing line.

"I think five billion would be more like it."

"Five billion?" said Albert. "At that rate, everybody in this family would be a millionaire."

"So?" said Arnett. "That's the idea, to break the whole cycle of poverty in our entire family, the cycle that goes straight back to Rosewood."

Now it was Albert studying the ripples.

"If I'm not mistaken," he said, "we'd have to go through some white people to get anything out of this."

"That's right," said Arnett.

"Uh huh," said Albert, giving his reel a spin. "I can see trouble down the line any way this thing goes."

And that was it. The fish began biting, and the men stopped talking. They came back with a cooler full of bass and bluegill, and everyone ate well that weekend. Arnett didn't mention the lawsuit, not yet. But he wasn't surprised when Albert pulled him aside on Sunday, as everyone was saying their good-byes, and told him he was going out and buying himself a rifle. "Just in case there comes a time I might need it," he said.

And so that summer and fall came and went. By the winter, even with his body falling apart, Arnett had begun looking for a lawyer. His weight loss and weakness kept getting worse, and now he figured it was the stress added to the grief that was doing him in. He hated hospitals, had never trusted a doctor since the time he was a soldier. He had always blamed those Army doctors for letting his feet go so bad in boot camp. But now, as Christmas turned to New Year's, he couldn't even get out to take care of his yard.

Finally, one afternoon in early January, on the verge of fainting, he had a friend drive him to the hospital, where they pricked his finger, checked his blood sugar level, read the result and rushed him straight into the emergency room, put an IV needle into his left wrist and the thing popped back out like a bullet, his blood pressure was so high. He wouldn't know it until a day later, when he woke up in a hospital bed, but Arnett had gone into diabetic shock.

He should have known. Lying there in that hospital bed, he thought about his mother and her diabetes. Uncle A. T. had it. Aunt Vera, too. Come to think of it, almost all the old folks at the Rosewood reunions had diabetes, every one of those families. *That* was their legacy, Arnett smiled to himself. That was something they'd been allowed to keep.

So now he had insulin to carry him through his days, and his days became better. He had the energy to write letters and make phone calls, to drive to those lawyers' offices. He was eager, hopeful, certain his story would light a fire under the first attorney who heard it.

But January turned to February, and February to March. Winter turned to spring, and the doors kept closing. And now it was May, 1992, and Arnett felt the way he'd felt the summer before, dragging himself home each night to that back room and those piles of papers. And those kids out on the street. And the gunshots from over on the Avenue, everything the same as it ever was. And he felt lost. Dead in the water.

FOURTEEN

Original Sin

B y the time Steve Hanlon returned from Miami after spending a day with
Lee Ruth Davis, and from Jacksonville, where Davis sent him on to see
her cousin, Minnie Lee Langley, he was pumped. These two women and the
story they shared represented everything Hanlon liked to think he believed in,
both about himself and his profession.

He always told people there were two ways in which he ultimately measured every case he took. One was what he called its "wonderfulness scale"—
how inspiring, noble, dramatic, even romantic a situation and its circumstances
were. And the other was its "impossibility index"—the odds against winning
the case, which, being a man who relished a challenge, Hanlon preferred to be
high, very high. These two graceful, elderly women with their mixture of beautiful and horrific recollections of this vanished village were off the chart on
both counts.

Hanlon had always been a self-confessed bleeding-heart liberal, embracing
that label like a badge of honor in a time and a profession where it had become
an object of ridicule. Issues of race had always been close to his heart, even

Walter H. Pillsbury

though he was raised in a suburban, middle-class world as white as milk, a world of cul-de-sacs and country clubs, of Catholic nuns and Jesuit priests, a world where he and his buddies would choose up sides for pickup baseball games by counting, "Eeny, meeny, miney, moe, catch a nigger by the toe," and none of them even knew what a nigger was. Hanlon's father, a prestigious St. Louis attorney and a liberal Democrat, applauded the Supreme Court's *Brown v. Board of Education* decision the day it was passed in 1954, to the chagrin of his Republican clients and friends, yet he continued to use the phrase "a nigger in the woodpile," and meant no harm by it.

Young Steve Hanlon had no idea what that expression meant. He was thirteen at the time, and the only black person he had ever met was his grandmother's maid, Mildred. He never even knew her last name. Holidays he would sit in his grandmother's kitchen with Mildred and listen with fascination as she talked about her family, about how her daughter was studying to be a nurse. He'd watch how Mildred swelled with pride when she talked about her girl and it would make him swell with pride, too. There were marches and protests going on all over the country by then, demonstrations for civil rights, a bus boycott in Montgomery, Martin Luther King making newspaper headlines. But Mildred didn't talk about any of that, not there in that kitchen, nor in Hanlon's family car when he grew old enough to drive it and would often carry Mildred home to her apartment in a black section of the city Hanlon had never seen before.

That was when he began to think about race. He and his buddies, their hair slicked back in ducktails just like James Dean's, would listen to black music on the radio—Chuck Berry, Jackie Wilson, the Isley Brothers—and they'd talk about how unfair it was that you had to hunt so hard to find those songs in the record stores and then you'd turn around and see some white guy doing a lame imitation of the same stuff and his watered-down sound would be everywhere. It just didn't seem right.

By the time Hanlon had finished high school and gone on to spend a year in the seminary, he had formed a personal philosophy about racism in America. To him it seemed much like original sin—an apt analogy for a former altar boy. White people in America, he believed, would never escape the taint of their treatment of blacks during the first two centuries of this nation's history. It was a sad, sorry fact that could neither be changed nor denied. It could only be acknowledged, with amends made whenever possible.

Hanlon carried that conviction with him into college, where he and his classmates at St. Louis University would take weekend excursions across the river into East St. Louis, sampling the delights of that city's Harlemlike Saturday night scene. His racial sensitivities were further galvanized in law school, where his favorite professor was an outspoken liberal who had actually had a cross burned on his lawn back when he was teaching at the University of Mississippi. By the time Hanlon emerged from law school in the spring of 1966, his heart was set on doing wonderful, impossible things, and he vowed that some of those things would involve racial justice.

He learned a lot during his legal services stint in Tampa during the 1970s, both about black culture and about the most effective ways to take racial cases through the legal system. He continued handling a few civil rights cases even while practicing commercial litigation in the '80s, and what he saw during that time was the increasing uselessness of federal courts for rich and poor people alike. As far as he could see, the field of commercial disputes had evolved into six-year paper wars in which only the lawyers came out ahead. Everyone else, plaintiffs and defendants alike, were simply financing the furniture and artwork in the attorneys' offices. That, figured Hanlon, was why, by the end of the decade, there was already a movement away from the courtroom, toward mediation and arbitration.

As for poor people, the thrill of walking toward the courthouse doors had been dampened by the fact that now, when those doors were reached, they were almost impossible to pry open. The federal court system had been dramatically altered during the decade, first by Ronald Reagan, then by George Bush. By 1990, the federal benches were filled with phalanxes of judges who were white, conservative, and male—three strikes against Hanlon's clients. Blacks. Females. The elderly. The disabled. AIDS patients. These were the people Hanlon represented, and it became rapidly, painfully apparent to him that they were simply not wanted in those courtrooms. He was facing barrages of pretrial hindrances now that he had never encountered before—federal preemption, the abstention doctrine, webs of technicalities and piles of paperwork that made actually getting a case onto the courtroom floor almost anticlimactic.

And so, by the time he came to Holland and Knight, he was looking for alternative arenas for his civil rights cases. One was the state courts, where he had more control over the agenda. Another was the state legislature.

He considered both options as he mulled the story these two women had told him. Their details differed, as did the specifics in the old newspaper clippings O'McCarthy had shared with him. But the basic, essential facts were clear. A town had been burned, people had been killed, the government knew about it and did nothing to stop it, and that's just not supposed to happen in America. To Hanlon it was that simple. *All those in favor of burning towns, raise your hands. All those against . . .*

Simple. Everything else was just details, tangential material, mere static. The fogginess of the facts—exactly how many people lived in this town, how many homes were there, how many businesses, how much land, who owned what, who lost what, how many people were killed—those were for the journalists and historians to sort out. The essential facts were clear, and these two women, the only survivors left, were living witnesses to those facts—powerful, compelling, heart-wrenching witnesses. Hanlon's favorite kind.

As for Michael O'McCarthy and his movie deal, that meant nothing to Hanlon. O'McCarthy had both Lee Ruth's and Minnie Lee's signatures on contracts for the film rights to their stories, signed for a thousand dollars each, and that was fine with Hanlon. Let this guy go and make his movie. All that mattered to Hanlon was making a case, and he had a pretty good idea which direction he would take this one. If there was ever a situation made for the court of public opinion, this was it, and there was no forum more sensitive, more *answerable*, to public opinion than the legislature.

The Florida House of Representatives and the Florida Senate, they would be both the target and the arena. A claims bill filed against the state of Florida itself, for damages done to these two women, these two American citizens, seventy years ago—that's how Steve Hanlon shaped the case as he began drafting a memo that summer of 1992 to send around to his colleagues. The first step would be finding a sponsor for the bill, a champion, a man or woman willing to carry a cause layered with controversy into the political thicket of a southern state legislature. And there was no mistake about that. This was, as ever, even at the tail end of the twentieth century, the South, with all the pride and pain, stain and shame, hope and hurt that that implied, especially when it came to matters of race.

Wonderful. Impossible. Steve Hanlon was pumped.

FIFTEEN

A Delicate Dance

O n the face of it, it would have been hard to find two men on the planet more unalike than Miguel De Grandy and Al Lawson. One was Cuban-American, born in Havana, raised in Miami, urbane and even-keeled, respected by friends and foes alike, a compact presence at five-foot-eleven inches, and a Republican. The other was African-American, with rural roots, from a panhandle farm family, a fiery man, outspoken and quick-tempered, courting controversy at every turn, a looming giant at six-foot-eight, and a Democrat. There were no two more improbable allies to be found on the floor of the Florida legislature, but Steve Hanlon needed them both. If the Rosewood claims bill he had in mind was to become anything more than a notion, these two men would have to make it so.

There were reasons Hanlon believed they could. Despite their differences, both were members of a minority, politically as well as racially. On the crowded floor of the Tallahassee statehouse, the black and Cuban-American caucuses were little more than upstart seedlings among the implanted, overwhelming forest of their non-Hispanic white colleagues. Both De Grandy and

Miguel De Grandy and Al Lawson

Lawson knew what it was to be outsiders. They also understand dispossession. De Grandy's family had lost all they owned when Castro took power in Cuba. Lawson's family, with its roots in slavery, owned little to begin with. If these men could not relate to what happened at Rosewood, no one could—which was what Steve Hanlon was counting on when he contacted them both in the fall of 1992.

Hanlon knew he had no hope if this bill were presented as strictly an African-American issue. The Florida legislature was too thick with born-and-bred good old boys, North Florida lawyers and Big Bend businessmen who proudly referred to themselves as crackers with neither shame nor apology. To ask them to pay for the sins of their fathers, to compensate a pair of elderly black women for damages done seventy years in the past, was like asking them to turn their backs on those Confederate flags flapping outside their county courthouses. Hanlon knew he needed to broaden the issue, to pull in moderate Democrats and even Republicans with concerns that went beyond mere moral obligation, and he knew he could do it with the Cuban-Americans by plucking that chord of dispossession, of people run out of their homes and off their land, losing everything they owned, including their sense of place, of belonging.

That was the story of almost every Cuban-American family in Florida, and that was why almost every one of them had voted Republican for the past thirty years, ever since the aborted invasion of the Bay of Pigs, when John Kennedy's scheme to retake the Cuban expatriates' homeland unraveled into a laughable travesty. Kennedy had destroyed their hopes, let them down, and they never forgave him. Kennedy was a Democrat, and so, for that reason alone, from 1961 onward, almost every Cuban in Florida could be counted on to vote Republican.

Miguel De Grandy's parents certainly did. Theirs had been one of the more fabled families on the island, a clan of stage stars—singers, dancers, actors. De Grandy's grandmother was known as the Shirley Temple of Cuba, the island's most famous child actress in the 1920s. His grandfather was a tenor featured on opera stages across Latin America. His mother was a soprano and, when television arrived, she became a staple on variety shows and Spanish soap operas. De Grandy's father, also an actor, was a favorite among the Cuban-Jewish community—"Jubans," they were called—for his role as Tevye in Spanish versions of *Fiddler on the Roof.*

Miguel was born one month before Fidel Castro took power in 1959. His

family fled to Mexico, where they became thespian gypsies, traveling by bus
from town to town, staging comedies, dramas, musicals, whatever could pull in
a crowd and a check. In 1963 they moved to Miami, where Miguel grew up
among a transplanted Cuban middle-class community that would transform
the face of southeast Florida, both economically and politically. By the time he
graduated from law school in 1981, a year after the Mariel boatlift, he was
among the generation of "Yucas"—Young Urban Cuban-Americans—who
were replacing their parents not as adjuncts to American society, but as Americans through and through, here to stay, to make it in this country on this country's terms.

De Grandy's first job was as a prosecutor in the Dade County state attorney's office, one of a hundred and fifty young lawyers working for a hard-driving
boss named Janet Reno. Seven years later, at the age of twenty-nine, he made
his first run for political office, campaigning against a fellow Cuban-American
for a state House seat. When all eight thousand votes were counted in that election, the two men were tied. A recount gave the seat to De Grandy's oppo-
nent—by one vote. That story was front-page news across the state, as was De
Grandy's election a year later, in 1989, when Florida's fabled U.S. Senator
Claude Pepper died and a state legislator ran for his open seat in Washington,
opening a seat in Tallahassee, which De Grandy filled.

He arrived as one of a mere seven Cuban-Americans on the floor of the
Florida House of Representatives, and like his Hispanic colleagues, though Republican by party, he was far from conservative, especially on social issues. Hispanic rights were of course his priority, but he also sponsored a bill for
homeless assistance in Dade County; he pushed an environmental amendment
that killed plans to build a jetport near the Everglades; and, in probably his
most visible act, he sponsored a bill to allow breast-feeding in public. That got
him national headlines, as well as a tour on the talk show circuit. ·

So he and Steve Hanlon had at least one thing in common—they had both
been on "Donahue." They also both knew how to use the press. By the time
Hanlon called him in the fall of 1992 about Rosewood, De Grandy was chairman of the Cuban-American caucus, savvy enough to understand exactly why
this attorney was approaching him to help sponsor a bill aimed at black people,
and skeptical that such a piece of legislation stood more than a snowball's
chance in hell of passage.

But he went ahead and met with Hanlon, had lunch, took the inch-thick package of material Hanlon left him—copies of sworn statements from these two women, assorted newspaper clippings, excerpts from the "60 Minutes" program—looked over it all, and when he was done he still felt this thing was politically hopeless.

But he felt some other things as well. He felt depressed. He felt ashamed. He felt the same rage about these people's uprooting that his own people had felt about theirs. And, though he was convinced the bill was a long shot, he felt there was no way he could turn it down. When he called Hanlon back to say he'd give it a go, he also suggested the obvious choice for a co-sponsor—Al Lawson.

Lawson was chairman of the legislature's black caucus—no more a position of overwhelming power than De Grandy's. The caucus numbered nineteen members at the time, up from the ten who had been there when Lawson arrived in '82, and they were generally considered a cautious group, struggling to find their footing, rarely willing to stick their necks out on any issue that might offend their white colleagues and hurt their careers. Their timidity was no secret. One state newspaper columnist wondered in print "if they would ever stop begging for political crumbs and take their rightful place in the political buffet line." One of the caucus's own members criticized them as a group that was "just happy to be here." That member was Al Lawson.

Lawson was not the most beloved leader the black caucus had ever had, but he had, during his decade in office, pushed the group to become bolder, fighting for money to shore up the state's two leading historically black universities, Florida A&M and Bethune-Cookman, which had begun to decay from neglect. Under Lawson's leadership, the group had pushed the state government to do more business with minority firms, and it had put pressure on the state to hire blacks in key positions. Issues like these were unthinkable when Lawson arrived in Tallahassee in 1982. But then so was his arrival itself.

He came out of a district that was seventy percent white, a North Florida panhandle region of farmers, loggers and fishermen that hadn't elected a black to the state legislature since Reconstruction. These people were, in Lawson's own words, "poor, rural, redneck." He could pronounce each of those terms with an odd sort of affection, the way only a poor black who has grown up among poor whites in the poor Deep South can.

Only those who have lived it can fully comprehend this curious coexistence, the blend of fondness and fear, of endearment and revulsion that evolves from black and white lives shared on the same land, under the same conditions, flowing from one generation into the next, the bond of something close to affection that develops even in the context of rooted resentment, rivalry and racial dis-ease. The fact that the people who burned Rosewood were essentially the same people who elected Al Lawson could not be explained simply by the passage of time and the shift of circumstances. There is a delicate dance that has gone on between poor blacks and whites in the South for well over a century, an intricate *pas de deux* that continues to this day. Some partners are clumsy, some are smooth, toes get stepped on, faces are slapped, punches are thrown and guns sometimes pulled. The tune changes, but the music never stops. And neither does the dance. And Al Lawson was a man who learned to dance early and to dance well.

He was born in a place called Midway, a dozen miles west of Tallahassee, on land his father's family had bought out of slavery. Lawson's great-grandfather Eugene had come down to Florida from Alabama before the turn of the century, found work as a miner, digging what they called *fill-o'-de-earth*—phosphate. Day and night Eugene Lawson's life was defined by the land—on it, in it, under it. Land was holy to him, like religion. His father had taught him that. To own a piece of land was to have a small part of heaven right there in your hands.

And so he bought some of that north Florida soil as soon as he could. Even when he couldn't afford to do anything with it, when he had to go under it to earn his living and feed his family, he still bought land. And his son Solomon bought some more. And by the time Al Lawson was born, the family had a couple of hundred acres to its name.

Lawson's father built a house on that land, farmed as much of it as he could plant and plow by himself—about forty acres—selling what he grew off a truck he drove to the market in town. But when Al was four, the house burned down. The family had no insurance, the corn and tomatoes his father grew couldn't cover the cost of rebuilding, and so Al's father found better-paying work in town, hiring on as a maintenance man over at Florida State University. They were poor, dirt poor, but they rebuilt their house, and they still had their land. They would never give up their land.

The little town of Midway was a black island in the white sea of Gadsden County, a poor county lorded over by a handful of millionaires whose families had made their fortunes buying Coca-Cola stock back in the early part of the century. The place was all tobacco farms by the early '60s, with white schools and black schools. The black schools would let out early during harvest time so the children could get out in the fields and help pick those leaves. "It was almost still like slavery," says Lawson, who was one of those children.

He was always big for his age, strong, and so he went into the fields earlier than most—he turned eight the summer he first started picking in 1956. A dollar a day, that's what they paid him. He was allergic to tobacco, bad enough that his parents sometimes had to take him to the doctor when his rashes flared up. But worse than the rashes was the coughing. That happened whenever the cropdusters flew over. They didn't bother getting the workers out of the way. They just dumped those clouds of pesticides right on the pickers, sent them all home that night with their lungs full of poison. Some would complain, say this stuff was making them sick, and the boss would say, Fine, go ahead and quit, there's plenty of others waiting to take your place.

Years later, Al Lawson would visit some of the older folks, his neighbors, people he had worked beside out in those fields, and they'd be lying in their bedrooms, hooked up to oxygen tanks because they could no longer draw a breath on their own, and he knew, he had no doubt, it went straight back to those tobacco fields. He often wondered why he'd gotten out healthy and they hadn't. Fate is all he could figure. Just fate.

The thing was, he never felt as much anger as he might have, as so many did. He saw racism every day, had a white boss in those tobacco fields who liked to pair the pickers up during water breaks, pick out two of the biggest, strongest men and make them go at it, fight each other just for a show, for his amusement. The boss would sit back under a tree and watch until it was time to get back to work. Al Lawson was young, but he was big, and more than once he was forced to join one of those contests—that, or lose his job.

It was humiliating, demeaning. So was going to the doctor and having to come around through a back door, sit in the waiting room for hours, watch white people come and go until there weren't any white people left, and then the doctor would start seeing the blacks. Lawson's parents always taught their children to love everybody, even those who did you wrong, because hate was something that ate you up inside, that hurt you just as bad as it hurt whoever you hated.

But sometimes it was hard for Al Lawson not to hate. It was hard not to hate the colored and white bathrooms they had all over Quincy, where the Midway kids went to high school. Or the water fountain at the truck stop Lawson and his buddies would walk past every day on their way home from basketball practice, a fountain with a dipper hanging on a hook for the black people to draw their drinks with. One day Lawson stopped at the fountain, started to take down the dipper as usual, looked at how filthy the thing was and said, no, he wasn't doing this anymore, he was going to take his drink straight from that water cooler just like the white people. And when he bent to take a sip, an old white man sitting on a bench nearby stood up, said, "You trying to be *funny*, nigger?", walked into the store, came back out with a pistol, fired it into the air, then pointed it their way. Al and his friends took off running, found a police officer, told him what had happened, and the cop just laughed. Shrugged his shoulders and laughed.

It was hard not to hate after things like that, but when Al got home that day, when he came home every day, it was as if he'd been out in a foreign world and now he was stepping back into the real one, a warm haven filled with family and friends, familiar faces, comfort, protection. This was home, and this was *his*. Even with all the ugliness outside, this was a beautiful place, and it belonged to him, him and his family. Every year that passed, he understood better why his father held onto that land at all costs, even when there was nothing to do with it but to have it, simply to have it.

That was the chord that struck deepest when Lawson learned about Rosewood. That visceral, inviolable link to the land that meant so much to his people, and the soul-stripping devastation that would be wrought if that land and that link were lost. Until he learned about Rosewood, he could only imagine what a loss like that might be like.

But it would be a long time before Al Lawson learned about Rosewood. Meanwhile, he made his way through high school, continuing to grow until he was pushing seven feet tall, won a basketball scholarship to Florida A&M, entered college in 1966 wanting nothing more in life than a good job, a nice home, a nice new car every couple of years, maybe a Cadillac. That's how he arrived, but he left wanting a lot more.

He had never paid much attention in high school to anything beyond sports and his studies. The civil rights movement was something the folks in Midway read about. They watched it on television the same way they watched footage from the war that was heating up over in Vietnam—as something happening someplace else, far away. There were NAACP meetings down at the church, but they were always hush-hush affairs. Al Lawson always wondered what was going on in those meetings, but he never wondered enough to join them.

It wasn't until he got to Florida A&M that his eyes were, as he says it so simply, opened. Suddenly he was learning there were black leaders out there besides Martin Luther King, black organizations besides the church and the NAACP. Stokely Carmichael. Eldridge Cleaver. SNCC. CORE. The Muslims. Even a country boy couldn't help learning these things at that time in that place.

Even a jock couldn't help it, and Al Lawson was a jock, running track and playing basketball, putting up numbers gaudy enough to draw professional scouts. By the time he graduated in 1970 with a degree in government, the offers were good enough that he took one, signing with the Indiana Pacers of the American Basketball Association, an upstart league on the last legs of its quirky existence. Lawson played with and against the likes of Julius Erving and Moses Malone, Rick Mount and George McGinnis. He played *for* Wilt Chamberlain during a brief, bizarre stint with the San Diego Conquistadors, a team as destined for obscurity as Lawson's own short career.

By the mid-1970s he was back in Tallahassee, coaching basketball, getting a graduate degree in public administration, selling life insurance to some of the professional athletes he had played against, and building a base to launch a political career. In 1982 he made his move, running for a state seat from a district of Gulf Coast counties that flanked the one in which he was raised, down along North Florida's Apalachee Bay. The voters were predominantly blue-collar and white, loggers and oystermen who were used to seeing black candidates on their ballots and who had always voted for someone else.

But that year came a shock. Out of a five-candidate primary election emerged two choices for the final runoff race, and both were black: Al Lawson and a woman named Bette Wimbish. While Wimbish, with years of local and state government experience and connections behind her, took a polished, refined approach to the campaign, aiming at the more elite among the electorate, Lawson went door to door, pounding the pavement, rubbing shoulders with the common man, white or black, eating more raw oysters and barbecue at more shucking houses, flea markets, picnics and pig-pickings than he could count.

He touted himself as the poor man's choice, and there were more poor men in those counties than rich ones. He even met with some of the Klan, at a campground back in the woods, where he parked his car pointing out the way he'd come in. He half-jokingly asked if they wouldn't mind taking a bite of some of that fried chicken before he did, just to make sure they hadn't put something evil in it. He glanced kind of nervously at the hunting rifles they had propped against their pickups. And when it was over, he came away with enough of their votes and the votes of people just like them to push him over the top. No one expected Al Lawson, a man with no political experience what-soever, to beat a veteran like Bette Wimbish. But he did, thanks largely to hair-sprayed women in polyester pantsuits and burly white men in fishing caps and wading boots—"Rednecks For Lawson," as the newspapers called them.

And so here he was, ten years later, reelected twice, keeping his con-stituents happy the way any politician does, by tending to their interests, fun-neling state money their way, pushing laws that protected their livelihoods, getting himself named to committees that mattered to his people, which, with all those shrimpers and farmers back home, was why he had focused on the state's Committee on Natural Resources, of which he had risen to chairman.

Keeping himself in office, that was Al Lawson's priority, just like every other legislator around him. Yes, he had pushed his black colleagues to be more aggressive on black issues, but he understood their caution as well, their sense of self-preservation, and their ambition. No one was more ambitious than Al Lawson, and no one understood better than he the juggling act of balancing his conscience as a black man with the demands of a white constituency. He was no good to anyone, black or white, if he didn't keep his seat. And so, although he had been urging his colleagues to step out front on issues of race, he was still prudent enough to pick his battles. And this Rosewood thing, at first glance, did not look like a battle worth fighting.

Lawson had no doubt that something like this could have happened in Florida in the 1920s. He *knew* things like this had happened back then. He had studied about them back in his undergraduate days at Florida A&M, about all the lynchings, and the riots, and he wasn't surprised. There wasn't much that could surprise him after what he'd experienced himself during the time he'd grown up, and those were "modern" times.

But politically this thing was dynamite, and it had all the looks of something that would blow up in his hand. There was no question how an issue like this would divide the people in his district, as well as polarize the entire state.

Florida had more than it could handle at the moment in terms of racial problems, from its seething inner-cities to its poverty-riddled rural areas. Did it
need to dredge up something that happened seventy years ago? And besides,
this thing happened halfway down the coast, five counties south of Lawson's
own district.

The issue looked like a loser all the way around. But like De Grandy, Lawson took home the package of stuff Steve Hanlon gave him and he read it, read
about a somewhat independent, relatively prosperous community of property-
owning black people—a community much like the one he was raised in, the
one in which his family still lived. These two women, and all those who had
died before them, had lost their community, lost all they had, and that hit too
close to home for Al Lawson to turn away. If he stepped into this fight, he had a
lot more to lose than Miguel De Grandy. So did his colleagues in the black caucus. No matter how it was packaged, this was a black issue. It would be their
fight, and the price would be theirs to pay.

When Lawson called back Steve Hanlon, he couldn't speak for his colleagues, but he could speak for himself, and his answer was yes, count him in.

And so, as the year moved toward its end, the Rosewood claims bill began
to take shape.

SIXTEEN

Road Kill

It began as just another winter morning for Arnett, his legs cold and numb as he rolled out of bed. This had become his daily routine now, rubbing his calves to get the circulation going, to get a glimmer of feeling back, knowing that what he'd be feeling the rest of the day would be pain. It was the diabetes, and there was nothing he could do about it, nothing but live with it, throw on a bathrobe, cut on the heat and wade into another day. The newspaper was out on the porch, as always, and he'd get to it soon enough. But right now he needed to wake up, get warm, have a little breakfast.

And then the telephone rang. Odd. Kind of early for a phone call.

"Arnett?"

It was one of his cousins, the daughter of one of the survivors.

"Arnett," she said, "have you seen it?"

"Seen what?"

He moved to a chair, sat down, still kneading one of his legs, trying to get the blood moving.

"The story in today's newspaper, did you see it?"

Cummer and Sons sawmill, Lacoochee

No, Arnett said, he hadn't read the paper yet.

"Well you *better* get it and read it, because Lee Ruth is in there, and Minnie Lee Langley, and they've got themselves a lawyer, saying they're the only survivors of the Rosewood massacre. *The only ones left.* That's what it says right here."

Arnett listened, tried to keep himself calm. He couldn't afford to get worked up these days, not with his blood pressure the way it was.

"Let me look into it," he said.

"Well, *somebody* better damn well look into it," she said, "because this Minnie Lee woman knows damn *well*, and so do you and so does Lee Ruth, that my father was there, and your mother, and all the others, and I don't know what kind of *shit* these two are trying to pull, but they're not going to get *away* with it."

Arnett tried settling her down, told her not to get excited, said he'd take care of it. Then he hung up and dialed his Uncle A. T. over in St. Pete.

"Yeah, I saw it," said A. T., his voice as soft and steady as ever.

"You okay?" asked Arnett.

"Why *sure* I'm okay," said A. T., sounding like the question made no sense at all. And really it didn't. Arnett had never seen his uncle upset, not once in his life, not about anything.

But Arnett's sister, Yvonne, she was another story. No sooner did he finish with Uncle A. T. than Yvonne was on the line, and Arnett could have sworn he was listening to his mother, raging from the grave.

"What the *hell* does Lee Ruth think she's doing?" Yvonne yelled. "I'm going to write that bitch a letter and I'm going to give her a piece of my *mind*. This is *crazy*, Arnett. Do you hear me? *Crazy*."

And then Aunt Vera called from up in Lacoochee. And Eva Jenkins from over in Orlando. And Lillie Washington from Gainesville. And on and on, the phone ringing and ringing until finally Arnett pulled the plug, fetched the paper off his porch and sat down in blessed silence to read this story himself.

And there it was, dateline December 29, 1992, from the Associated Press, out of Miami:

> *Two survivors of a racial rampage that destroyed the all-black Florida town of Rosewood 70 years ago will ask lawmakers to reimburse them for property loss and memorialize the New Year's Day massacre.*

That was the lead. Arnett read on.

> *. . . . Lee Ruth Davis, 77, of Miami, and her cousin, Minnie Lee Langley, 88* [sic], *of Jacksonville, say they are the only people left who witnessed the violent chaos. . . .*

Now he couldn't help himself. He could feel his pulse racing, his blood pressure rising, that familiar, lethal feeling of fury. He read the rest of the story in a blur, set it down, shut his eyes, collected himself. Then he called Lee Ruth.

"*Hey*, honey!" sang the voice at the other end of the line. "How you doin'?"

Arnett had always been Lee Ruth's favorite cousin, almost like a son. And he'd always adored her right back, lived under her roof for a time when he was in the Army, stationed at Homestead, near Miami.

"I'm doin' fine, Ruth, just fine," he said. She sounded the same as always. Bright, upbeat, unbothered by a care in the world. No different today than yesterday or last month or last year. No mention of any lawyers, or newspaper stories. Or lies.

"Ruth," said Arnett, "I been getting phone calls all morning from family members about an article in the newspaper today concerning Rosewood."

Silence.

"You and Minnie are quoted in here as saying you're the last two survivors."

Now Lee Ruth spoke.

"I ain't said *no* such a lie as that."

"You didn't say that?"

"No, I didn't say any such a lie as that. I told that reporter I don't know where they all *live* at, that's all I said. Now Minnie *Lee* might have said that they was all dead, I don't know. But Arnie, I could never say that there was only two survivors, because I *know* where you all are at."

She had already gotten other phone calls that morning, Lee Ruth said. Ugly calls. Upsetting calls, from various members of the family. Arnett's sister was the worst of them, she said. Lee Ruth said she almost didn't pick up when Arnett rang, but she was glad she did.

Arnett didn't push her any further. It was pretty clear Lee Ruth had played this thing halfway at best. Maybe she hadn't come right out and claimed she and Minnie were the only ones left, but she hadn't pointed to the other survivors either. She had let the reporter *believe* there was only Minnie Lee and her. If she hadn't lied, well, she certainly had not told the truth—the whole truth. Maybe that was her decision, maybe it was Minnie's, maybe it was their lawyer's. All that mattered to Arnett now was calling this lawyer, the name there in the newspaper story, an attorney named Manny Dobrinsky, with the Miami office of the law firm of Holland and Knight.

It took Arnett a while to get through, and Dobrinsky sounded skeptical to Arnett, cautious. After several phone conversations and a couple of days, he told Arnett he would talk with Holland and Knight's Tallahassee office. They were the ones who would have to make any decisions about representing any additional survivors, said Dobrinsky. And so, a week into the new year, Arnett got a phone call from a man named Steve Hanlon.

If Dobrinsky had seemed cautious, Hanlon sounded downright disbelieving. When Arnett told him he was a direct descendant of a Rosewood survivor, that his mother had been in that house at the time of the attack, Hanlon chuckled. When he asked Arnett where his mother was and Arnett answered that she was dead, Hanlon said nothing. When Arnett said the only reason any of this was happening at all was *because* his mother was dead, Hanlon remained silent.

Arnett could hear doubt in that silence. But he kept talking, and Hanlon kept listening. And when Arnett was done, Hanlon said, "Look, can you prove this to me? Can you arrange for me to meet face-to-face with these people? Can they bring documents with them, birth certificates, deeds, something to show me they're who they say they are?"

"You got it," said Arnett. "Name the time." Hanlon checked his calendar, saw he had a partner's meeting coming up in the middle of the month down in Tampa, asked if they could all meet sometime that weekend, and Arnett said that would be fine. He suggested Sunday, the seventeenth, the day before Martin Luther King Day. At the New Bethel A.M.E. church, in the town of Lacoochee.

And so that Sunday arrived. Hanlon and his wife Fran got an early start, driving north from Tampa on Interstate 75, passing rest stops marked by newly installed signs:

THIS AREA PATROLLED
BY 24-HOUR ARMED SECURITY.

A recent spate of carjackings and killings across South Florida had the whole state on edge, fanning the festering image of the Sunshine State as a feeding ground for madmen and murderers. Racial violence was in the air that month as well, after the shocking New Year's Day attack on a black man in Tampa by three whites who kidnapped and robbed the man, then doused him with gasoline and set him on fire, leaving his body to burn in a wooded field on the outskirts of the city.

Like everyone else in America, Steve Hanlon was disgusted by the torching of Christopher Wilson, and he couldn't help thinking how it connected to Rosewood, a modern-day mirror of the same sort of hate that swept through that town back in 1923. Hanlon was thinking about that that morning, as he and his wife approached the Interstate exit toward Lacoochee.

Lacoochee had made its own lurid splash four years earlier, in 1989, when *Esquire* magazine published a story about a grisly murder that had taken place there a decade before. A rancher searching for some of his lost cattle in the summer of 1979 had come across the charred remains of a human body in a stand of trees near the Withlacoochee River, just east of town. Two local white men, members of a biker gang, were subsequently arrested and sentenced to death for raping, then beating and burning a white woman they had met at a party—it was her blackened body the rancher had found. Nine years later, the pair were freed from death row after a key witness recanted her original testimony under questionable circumstances. That brought on *Esquire*, whose writer found the essence of Florida's seedy side on the streets of Lacoochee. "The town that eats road kill," he called it. "In Lacoochee," he wrote, "roads are dirt, cars are dented, teeth are missing."

A pretty fair description. This was a place beyond decline, with its best days far in the past. A century earlier, the town of Lacoochee had sprung from the fields beside the Withlacoochee River, the rich soil producing orchards thick with oranges and strawberries. Fortunes were made from that fruit, and opulent homes were built on the banks of that river. But a freeze in 1895 so devastated the crops that the fields were abandoned, as were most of the homes. Not until the early 1920s was Lacoochee reborn, when the grandsons of a Canadian timber tycoon named Jacob Cummer moved their largest sawmill operation from a small Gulf Coast town called Sumner south to Lacoochee. Some sources say that move was made in 1922, others say 1923. None give a reason for it. None mention anything about a place called Rosewood.

By the late 1920s, Lacoochee had established itself as one of the busiest logging towns in the nation, boasting the largest electric sawmill in the South. More than two thousand employees worked the 83,000 acres of timber owned by the Cummer and Sons Cypress Company. The company's saws turned twenty-four hours a day. The town's main street had a thirty-room hotel, two movie houses, four churches, two bakeries, two drug stores, three barber shops, a pool room, a couple of gas stations and public boxing matches every Saturday afternoon on the town square. Housing was plentiful, with the company renting homes for twelve dollars a month and rooms for fifty cents a week. A company store was provided for mill employees, and a company doctor was available as well.

Timber, specifically cypress, was Lacoochee's lifeline. Its homes were built from cypress. The furniture inside those homes was fashioned from cypress, as were the sidewalks outside them. Even the town's heat came from cypress—the fine wood was so plentiful Lacoocheeans used it to feed their fireplaces.

Those were Lacoochee's high times, the 1920s and '30s, but the Depression took its toll, and by the early 1940s—around the time Arnett Doctor was born—better-paying wartime jobs elsewhere, coupled with forests thinned out from twenty years of logging, drained off the town's work force, and Lacoochee began to wither away. Businesses closed. The mill downsized. Finally, in 1959, Cummer and Sons closed up, and the town became what it has remained to this day—a decayed, hollow shell of its former self, a company town without the company.

Its main street now runs past little but boarded-up buildings. The mill is a massive ruin, its sloped tin roof, the size of a football field, rusted and riddled with holes, its windows shattered by rocks and gunshots, pigeons fluttering in and out of its interior darkness. Across a muddy dirt lane, in a field where the company homes once stood, now sit rows of beige concrete duplexes—government-subsidized housing inhabited by families from Haiti, Cuba, Mexico and Vietnam. In one way or another, through migrant field work or government assistance, these families have wended their way here, to Lacoochee.

There are still whites and blacks here as well, among the town's population of about three thousand, almost every one living in poverty. And there remains racial tension among them, sporadic outbreaks of violence. A beating here, a shooting there. And the occasional cross-burning, most recently in the fall of 1993.

This region—Lacoochee, Dade City, all of Pasco County—was once known as the heart of Florida's Klan country. A 1965 series of investigative newspaper articles examining the extent of Ku Klux Klan activity in Florida featured a segment on the Dade City area, including a photograph of the La-coochee Klavern, a decrepit, tar-papered shack perched beside a remote two-lane highway. The chapter's treasurer, according to the story, had recently emptied the group's bank account and skipped town.

One of Steve Hanlon's partners in the Holland and Knight offices up in Tal-lahassee, a woman named Martha Barnett, was from Dade City. She never said much about the place, just that it was *real* country. And now, on this January morning in 1993, Hanlon was driving through it, past Dade City's small, quaint downtown district with its dress shop and department store, and on toward the north side of town, where the looming water tower of the Lykes Pasco citrus processing plant threw its shadow over rows of brick buildings inside which hundreds of workers cranked out the FLORIDAGOLD line of cartoned orange juice and frozen concentrate. Hanlon had heard of this plant, recalled that at one time it was said to be the largest such factory in the world. He had never heard of Vera Hamilton—not yet—but these were the same buildings in which Arnett's aunt had spent the 1940s peeling grapefruits.

Fifteen minutes north on Route 301—the same roadway on which that Klavern had been photographed nearly thirty years before—Hanlon slowed, took a right onto a narrow asphalt lane called Cummer Road, and then he was there, in Lacoochee. He passed the abandoned mill, the government housing, and turned down a dirt lane into a tree-shaded section of small homes, some solid and neatly-tended, others no more than shacks, with trash and animals sharing space on rotting porches, each inhabited by a black family. The whites, as ever, lived on the other side of the tracks, but in this case their homes were no better than the blacks'.

Hanlon followed the directions Arnett Doctor had given him, turned one corner, then another, and finally came out from the shadows of the overarching oaks and up to the sunny, front lawn of the A.M.E. church—a lawn covered with lines of parked, empty automobiles.

In front of the church stood a single figure, a tall black man wearing a white dress suit, his hair shaved close around his large, blocky head, a goatee framing a polite smile, one hand leaning on a walking cane, the other raised in a gesture of welcome.

"Hello," he said, approaching Hanlon and his wife as they climbed from their car. "I'm Arnett Doctor."

An impressive man, thought Hanlon. Pleasant. Polite. Low-key, even. But there was nothing low-key about the number of cars parked out on that lawn. The sheer size of this gathering was more than Hanlon had expected. And when he stepped into the church itself, packed wall-to-wall with nearly two hundred people, including a television news crew from the ABC affiliate in St. Petersburg and a reporter and photographer from the St. Pete *Times*, Hanlon recoiled. This was *definitely* more than he'd expected.

He pulled Doctor's sleeve, leaned toward his ear with the eyes of the entire room upon him. "You didn't tell me we were going to have *television* here," he hissed, hoping his whisper hid his distress.

"Well," said Doctor, smiling like a cat enjoying his first bite of canary, "we want to ensure that our efforts are known."

Hanlon drew a deep breath.

"Well," he said, forcing a tight smile as he turned toward the audience, "I just wish you would have let me know."

And so they walked side by side up the red carpeting to the front of the church, this odd couple, facing what would become a familiar task over the coming months—answering the many questions of these hopeful, expectant people. But first Hanlon had some questions of his own, such as who these people were.

Arnett turned toward the families and asked the survivors among them to please stand. Seven elderly men and women rose from their seats, and Arnett introduced each one. Willie Evans. Arnett Goins. Dorothy Hosey. Eva Jenkins. Lillie Washington. Vera Hamilton. And Berthina Fagin. All the survivors but four—Lonnie Carroll, who was in a nursing home, Thelma Hawkins, who was sick in bed in her home just next door to the church there in Lacoochee, and Lee Ruth Davis and Minnie Lee Langley, who simply hadn't shown up.

Hanlon looked out at the scene, at the sunlight washing through the windows of this old church, at the dozens of black faces gazing up at him, some with suspicion, some with hope, young faces, old faces, the oldest of them, the seven survivors, up on their feet, gripping the pews in front of them to stay steady, all waiting to hear what he had to say, this lawyer from Tallahassee.

And Hanlon had no doubt now, no question about the truth of what this man Arnett Doctor had first told him on the telephone. He felt none of the skepticism he had harbored right up until the moment he had entered this church. These people's validity was no longer an issue for Steve Hanlon. He was looking at the truth, and the truth, two hundred pairs of anxious eyes, was looking right back at him, waiting for him to speak.

And he did. Two survivors. Twenty-two survivors. It made no difference how many they were, he told them. As long as they could pull together and stand united, his firm was willing to represent them all, from now till the end of time. That's what he said. But they had to be *together*, he said, and they had to be happy. There was a lot of work ahead of them, a lot to do, but he and his firm were ready to do it, he said. They were ready to spend time, money, whatever it took, and there was but one condition—that everybody stay *happy*.

Everyone in that church knew what this man meant with his "happy" talk. He was talking about Lee Ruth and Minnie Lee. He was talking about deception, about the families' anger. He was telling them they had to put that anger aside, work out their differences and make some sort of peace with Lee Ruth and Minnie Lee, that they didn't stand a chance if they went into this thing fighting among themselves. The fact was, and most of them knew it, they didn't stand much of a chance anyway.

By the time the afternoon was done, after Hanlon had finished fielding questions, after Arnett had delivered his message from the pulpit, speaking for and to the gathered families, raising the issue of compensation, not just for the survivors themselves but for everyone in that room, for children and grandchildren, for "all the generations who have suffered," as he put it, and after Hanlon had dealt with the reporters, facing their cameras and notebooks, after all of that, Hanlon and his wife climbed back into their car, watching the Rosewood families climb into theirs, and the lawyer smiled.

Keep it simple, he thought to himself. That had always been Steve Hanlon's cardinal rule. But it was going to be tough keeping this thing simple. If there was one thing that had become abundantly clear to him by now, it was that there was nothing simple about the subject of Rosewood.

SEVENTEEN

Three More Names

None of the Rosewood family members were surprised when Minnie Lee Langley and Lee Ruth Davis missed that Sunday afternoon meeting in Lacoochee. Most figured the two women had stayed away from fright, that they were avoiding the wrath of their relatives, which may have been so. But Minnie Lee and Lee Ruth had another reason as well to skip that gathering—they were scheduled to appear on national television the following day, as featured guests on the "Maury Povich" show.

After six months of striking out in Hollywood, Michael O'McCarthy had finally scored in New York. He had left the legal side of things to Steve Hanlon, as well as the task of hunting down other survivors, if there were any. "I didn't give a fuck *who* he found," recalls O'McCarthy. "He could go find *all* of them, for all I cared. I was going on with what *I* was doing."

For the previous half a year O'McCarthy had not been doing well. Los Angeles was still reeling from the Rodney King riots, and so were the Hollywood dealmakers who showed him the door each time he ambled in with his tale of this mass lynching in Florida. "They told me, 'You've got to be fucking *crazy*.

Wilson Hall

The last thing we want to make right now is a movie about white people killing niggers.'"

Finally he had turned to television, calling the Povich people in New York and pitching the Rosewood story as a natural for Martin Luther King Day. When a Povich producer called back and said they liked the idea, O'McCarthy leaped. He booked Minnie Lee and her daughter on a flight from Jacksonville to New York, arranged for Povich to do a videotaped interview with Lee Ruth in a Miami hospital, where she had been admitted with stomach pains, and he caught a red-eye flight himself from L.A. back to the east coast, arriving in New York the night before the taping, just in time to get himself a haircut before taking the stage with Maury and Minnie Lee. "The ball was rolling," recalls O'McCarthy. "Hollywood wasn't biting, but the ball was finally rolling."

The broadcast, on Monday, January 18, 1993, was vintage talk-tabloid-television, opening with taped footage of the Cedar Key waterfront, moody shots of the highway to Rosewood, images of rural shacks and the thick palmetto forest of Gulf Hammock. Povich's grave voice-over described the murder of "nearly one hundred women, children and men" that January week of 1923. Then the cameras cut live to the program's New York studio, where Minnie Lee Langley, dressed in a bright red suit, and Michael O'McCarthy, with his hotel haircut ("Just horrible, man. The guy gave me whitewalls. I looked like Jack Nicholson playing Hoffa"), sat on the stage with Povich, facing a studio audience encouraged to react audibly to each revelation.

They gasped as Minnie Lee described the shooting of Sarah Carrier. They grumbled as she told how the children hid in the swamp, wearing nothing but nightclothes. They shook their heads as Minnie detailed her escape by rail. They drew their breaths as Lee Ruth appeared on a video screen, propped in a hospital room chair, wearing a bathrobe, plastic tubes running from her nostrils, telling Povich her account of the rampage. "They was killing everything breathing that was black," she said.

Finally, after fielding questions from the audience, Povich turned to Minnie Lee and asked how she felt about white people today. "Well," she said, pausing for several long seconds. "*Some* of 'em is real nice." Another pause as she stared hard at her lap. "Too *good* to be white." And the audience erupted into laughter and applause.

More than two million Americans watched that broadcast, including one with more than a passing interest, a man named Wilson Hall, the owner of a small nightclub in a north Florida hamlet called Hilliard, above Jacksonville, just seven miles from the Georgia state line.

Actually it's generous to call Wilson Hall's place a nightclub these days, and he's the first to admit it. "Yes," he says, pulling a chair across the plywood floor and taking a seat at one of the room's three tattered booths, "it's been hard staying open anymore. The drug peoples, that's what did it, with their guns and their fussing and shooting. They done drove all the *decent* people away."

A juke box by the back wall blinks red and orange. A pool table in the corner is bathed in the glow of the shaded lamp above it. Other than that, the room is dark, even at midday. The neon beer signs in the tiny front windows are turned off, and the bar, its refrigerator stocked with food Hall cooks for himself and his wife, is locked behind a wire cage door.

He calls his place the "705 Club," after its address on Oxford Street, the only paved road in or out of the black section of Hilliard. Most of the town's population of twenty-five hundred live on the other side of the tracks, where Hilliard's main street features a hardware store, a taxidermist, and the Dixie Motel. The rest live here, in an assortment of small clapboard houses, some saved by aluminum siding, others decaying into shacks. There's a ballfield and a swimming pool just down the way from Hall's place, both built a few years back for Oxford Street's children. The pool is bone dry and abandoned. The ballpark is grown over with weeds, stray dogs asleep on its infield dirt.

It wasn't always this way, says Hall. When he first bought his place in '84, the front dirt parking lot was clean, not littered with broken glass and torn lottery tickets like it is now. Back then he didn't need the barbed wire fence that encloses his long, gray stucco building. "Had to put that up when the cars kept driving around back, dealing their drugs and shooting their guns. I walked out there once, and one man had a gun stuck in another man's mouth, robbing him. Can you believe it?"

Wilson Hall didn't used to have to hire security guards at thirty-five dollars an hour each, but the town began cracking down a few years ago, closing a half dozen other clubs in the area for drug and disturbance violations and threatening to close Hall's if he didn't do something about the "bad elements." Never mind that the county sheriff himself had a healthy little cocaine business of his own going on the side, for which he is now doing time in federal prison.

Hall shakes his head and chuckles at that one. He's eighty-one, but still built like a block of granite. Stout, barrel-chested, strong enough that he doesn't bother hiring bouncers on the rare nights when he still opens his bar for business. He can take care of trouble himself, just like he takes care of his forty-four-year-old wife Stephanie, who lives with him here at the club. He takes care of his eighty-six-year-old sister Margie, too, who lives just up the street in the same rickety, tin-roofed cottage she's called home for the past thirty-six years.

Margie was one reason Wilson moved here from Chicago in the spring of 1984. The other was that this remote, wooded corner of Florida reminded him more than any place he'd ever seen of the town where he was born and raised, a little village over on the Gulf side of the state, he says, a place called Rosewood.

Wilson Hall was seven years old when he last saw Rosewood, but not a day has passed since then that he hasn't thought of it, of the forty acres of land his granddaddy started with just after the Civil War, and the hundred his daddy added to it, clearing the trees, pulling the stumps, growing sugar cane and sweet potatoes in that soil, building the biggest smokehouse in all of Levy County, bigger than the nightclub Wilson owns today. "People would bring ten cows to my daddy to butcher, and he'd take some of that meat in payment, smoke it and sell it in his store."

Charles Bacchus Hall, that was Wilson's daddy. He ran the only general store in Rosewood other than the one owned by a white man named John Wright. Charles Hall's store took up the first floor of the family's two-story house. They had a corral out back, with pens for their animals and a grinding machine to squeeze the juice from their sugar cane. Come cane season, farmers would arrive from miles around, hauling wagonloads of sugar stalks to Charles Hall's grinder. Wilson's earliest memory was riding the back of his daddy's mule as it circled that machine, turning the gears of the grinder as the farmers fed the sweet stems into the machine.

Charles Hall was a blacksmith, too, along with Sam Carter. He was a Mason as well—"Thirty-second degree," says Wilson, "just about as high as it got." Sundays Charles Hall preached at the AME church, says Wilson, and he was a principal for a time at the Rosewood school. "Everything that needed doing, my daddy did," says the son, still swelling with pride more than seventy years after his father died.

That was in the winter of 1920, when Charles Hall took sick to bed and never got back up. After that the family had to shut down the store. Wilson's mother Mary went to work over at the sawmill in Sumner, "dogging" logs—rotating the tree trunks with metal tongs each time the saws sliced off a plank. "Lord, she was strong," recalls Wilson. "She worked for a while on the railroad, too, stripping crossties."

With their mother off working, it was left to Wilson and his brothers and sisters to tend to the house and themselves. They each had their duties, and Wilson's was cooking. His mother taught him how to make fried chicken and bread pudding, grated potato pone and sweet potato pie. Seventy years later, he was still using her recipes. When his club was thriving, he'd throw open the doors at holidays and lay out a spread for his customers, treat them to a free feast. But it's been a couple of years now since the last one.

"People have changed so much," says Wilson. "You do a favor for someone now, not only do they not do one for you back, but they expect *another* from you. And they gets *angry* with you if they don't get it. It's not like it used to be, no, not at all."

That was the thing about Rosewood, says Wilson. "Everybody helped everybody there," he says. "You didn't want for nothin'. You didn't *need* for nothin'. If I didn't have no flour or bacon, I came to your house. If nobody was home, I'd come in and take what I need and leave a mark, and you'd do the same with me. That's the way it was, the way it *should* be."

But it all ended that cold January night in 1923, when Wilson's mother shook the children awake a little past midnight. "Get *up*, we got to *go*," Wilson remembers her saying. "I can hear 'em comin'." The family didn't know about any shootout earlier that evening at the Carrier house. Sarah Carrier lived clear at the other end of town. But everyone knew about the killing of Sam Carter early in the week, they knew trouble had been brewing ever since then, and now they could see car headlights bumping up the road through the woods, coming straight toward their house.

Mary Hall and her children barely made it out the back door before the white men got to the front. Wilson remembers slipping through the corral, under the fence and into the woods. They spent two nights there before making their way to Wylly, then boarded a train that was stopped and searched twice on its way to Gainesville. "Women and children were safe," he recalls. "They were looking for *men*." He remembers lying on the floor beneath the railcar's bench seat, watching mud-covered boots go past. "Mama didn't want us to look in those white men's faces, no how," he says.

Wilson turned eight that April in Gainesville, in a two-room shack behind an ice house near the railroad station. That's where he and his mother and brothers and sisters lived for the next seven years, finding work wherever they could, all of them. "Gathering trash, cleaning yards, shaking pecans out of trees," says Wilson. "We picked up some coins any way we could."

He was big for his age, and at thirteen he got a job sparring at a local gym, five dollars a session. He'd bring that money home to his mother, never told her where it came from, because he knew she'd never approve. She was a devout woman, and boxing, well, that was the devil's work. One day, the Jewish man who owned the gym came to her door and told Mary Hall he wanted to turn her boy into a professional prizefighter, that Wilson was a better boxer than the men he'd been sparring against. She sent the man on his way, then sliced a switch off a nearby tree and gave Wilson the worst whipping of his life. "That," he says with a smile, "was the end of my boxing career."

When he was fifteen, he moved to Miami, where he lived with his older brother Steve and found a job cleaning and maintaining cars for a local cab company. People would ask where he was from, and he'd say Rosewood. They'd say they never heard of the place, they'd ask where it was at, and then he'd tell them about the attack. "No one ever believed me. They couldn't believe nothin' like that ever happened. Pretty soon I just stopped tellin' the story. It wasn't worth the bother."

But he never stopped thinking about it. And he never felt anger. Nostalgia, yes, but never anger. "What could I do with anger? Where could I put it? A black man in the 1930s and '40s didn't have no place to put any anger. And my mama explained to me early that I didn't have no reason to be angry, that I didn't have no one definite to be angry *with*. There was no one individual to put a finger on. I didn't have a name, I didn't have a face. So I just pushed the bad part to the side. Not to where I ever forgot about it, but to where it didn't worry me."

He moved to Chicago in 1945, after getting a telegram telling him another older brother, Charles, was dying, and he wound up staying. He made a good life for himself there, working as a janitor for the Universal motion picture company, cleaning the two warehouses the company used to produce its newsreels. He bought a home, moved his mother up with him when she took sick in 1950, and that's when he found out what had happened to Dosha and Sammy. His mother wasn't real specific, but she knew Sammy had settled in a place in

Georgia called Brunswick, out on the Atlantic coast, and Dosha had moved with her husband to a little Florida town called Hilliard, someplace just below the Georgia line.

Wilson decided to find Sammy first.

It was August of 1955 when he climbed in his DeSoto with a buddy and headed south. That same month a fourteen-year-old boy named Emmett "Bobo" Till was lynched near the town of Money, Mississippi—pistol-whipped, shot through the head, strangled with barbed wire and dumped in the Talla-hatchie River for calling a white woman "baby." Wilson Hall drove through that very county mere days after the killing, stopped for gas at a small service sta-tion and was turned back to the road by a raised shotgun. "The same thing hap-pened again just before I got to Brunswick," he says. "That stuff was everywhere then, it was all over."

Sam Hall had been working in Sumner the week of the attack on Rose-wood, says Wilson, and wound up cut off from his family. That was the first thing Wilson says Sammy talked about when Wilson arrived at his door. "He told me that was the worst mistake he ever made, the only thing in his life he was sorry about, that he left Mama with us little children out in those woods. He felt bad about that, right up to the day he died."

It was two years after finding his brother that Wilson took a train from Chicago to Miami, got off in Hilliard and bumped into a local church deacon who took him straight to Dosha's house, there on Oxford Street.

"She came to the door, and this deacon says, 'You know this man here? Be-cause he *think* he know *you.*'

"She eyeballed me up and down and said, 'No, I don't know him.' Said, 'He kind of *favors* one of my brothers, but I don't got no brothers this large.'

"Then she looked hard at me and said, 'Who *are* you?'

"I said, 'I'm Wilson.'

"She weighed about three hundred pounds, and she musta' jumped high as my waist. '*Wilson! My baby brother!!*' She damn near killed me, but I wiggled out of that."

And he visited her every year thereafter. Bought some land in the process. Then he bought his club. And finally, in 1984, the year Sammy died, Wilson Hall moved to Hilliard. His mother was dead by then. All Wilson's siblings were dead by then, too, except Dosha, Margie, and their baby sister, Mary, who lived down in Jacksonville. They all watched Sammy on that "60 Minutes" show in 1983, but none of them heard of any Rosewood reunions after that. They didn't know about any Arnett Doctor. And he didn't know about them.

Dosha passed away in 1991, leaving Wilson, Margie and Mary as the last living Rosewood Halls. None of them saw the story in the newspaper about Lee Ruth and Minnie Lee's lawsuit. But by the time the "Maury Povich" show was rolling its credits that Monday afternoon in January of 1993, Wilson Hall was on the telephone. And before that month was out, Steve Hanlon had three more names to add to his list of Rosewood survivors.

PART FOUR

THE *C* LAIM

EIGHTEEN

"Attention White People"

The auditorium was filled, aisle to aisle and front row to back, every seat taken, the room pulsing with the grassroots black power of the state of Florida. Black mayors and black city councilmen, black school commissioners and black board members, black principals and black professors, black businessmen and black businesswomen, black ministers, deacons and elders, the NAACP, the Urban League—they were all there, more than three hundred leaders of every black social, political and religious organization between Pensacola and Key West, gathered on this sweltering Saturday in September of 1993 on the campus of Florida A&M University in Tallahassee to see for themselves what this Rosewood matter was all about.

It was Al Lawson who had issued the call, and now he stood on the stage, surveying the scene, beholding a sea of curious but suspicious faces—not unlike the faces Steve Hanlon had stood before in Lacoochee eight months earlier. Lawson knew a moment of truth when he saw one, and this was most assuredly such a moment.

Skepticism about Rosewood, about the validity of this claim by the scat-

The lynching of John Evans, St. Petersburg, 1914.

tered survivors of a sketchily documented racial attack seventy years in the distant past, had soared since the start of the year. What had begun as a noble crusade had rapidly dissolved into a quagmire of doubt and dissension, beginning
with the very filing of the claims bill itself, which was late. Lawson and Miguel
De Grandy had stumbled out of the starting blocks by missing the January 1 filing deadline for that year's legislative session, and only the forgiveness of
Florida's House Speaker Bolley Leroy "Bo" Johnson had saved the bill from
a stillborn death. Johnson's leniency was surprising on the face of it, considering his white North Florida background and his brittle relationship with Al
Lawson.

Bo. The name itself fit the timeworn tradition of the shrewd, savvy political
kingpins who have long carved up and controlled small chunks of the Deep
South as if they were their personal fiefdoms. Bo Johnson was bred to inherit
that tradition, born into a family of local politicians up around Pensacola, raised
on a steady diet of after-dinner cigar smoke and deal-making among his father
and grandfather and their friends. Sometimes, after the smoke cleared, there
lingered the scent of scandal. The scent was there when Bo's father Leroy, who
held local office up near the Alabama border during the '60s and '70s, died in
1984—not a week after he was arrested on a murder-for-hire charge. A police
informant had taped Leroy Johnson offering $10,000 to have a political critic
killed. Six days after his arrest, he dropped dead of a heart attack.

By then, Bo Johnson was nearly a decade into his own career as a state legislator, well on his way to the most powerful seat in the House, and—not coinci-
dentally, according to his critics—also amassing a personal fortune in real
estate. By 1993, his net worth had ballooned from $28,000 the year he was first
elected to the House, in 1977, to more than $800,000—not bad, said skeptics,
for a man whose annual salary as Speaker was $31,000. Johnson claimed that
his wealth came from astute real estate deals. Doubters said those deals were
steered by political clout. They pointed to a bridge-building bill he pushed
through in 1984, the same year his father died. Was it coincidence, they asked,
that the proposed bridge over Pensacola Bay would bring a new highway—and
rocketing property values—directly through waterfront land owned by Bo
Johnson's family? A decade later, Johnson would shake his head about the
"grief" that bridge deal brought him. But it also brought him nearly half a million dollars when he sold the property in 1991.

Bo Johnson admitted early on in his career that he was from the Old Testament school of politics, where friends are rewarded and foes are punished, where favors are remembered and betrayals never forgotten. When he became Speaker in 1992, he wasted no time acting on that edict, passing out the key positions of House committee chairmen to his buddies—an all-male group led by a disproportionate number of North Florida lawmakers. In the process, Johnson removed several veteran chairmen, including Al Lawson, who wound up in a shouting match in Johnson's office after he was stripped of his chairmanship of the Committee on Natural Resources.

"It was a slap in the face," says Lawson, whose wounds were still fresh when Rosewood came into his life. His war with Bo Johnson made even his colleagues in the Black caucus reluctant to support *any* Al Lawson–sponsored legislation, much less a bill laced with the racial controversy of Rosewood.

"They didn't want to do anything to piss off the Speaker," says Lawson of the caucus. "They went, 'Omigod, *Rosewood?* You don't get along with the Speaker *now*, and you think he's gonna let *you* lead this damn thing?' They knew where I stood with him. *Everybody* knew. Word had gone out among every lobbyist in the state, 'If you've got an issue, *don't* bring it to Al Lawson, 'cause he's not going to get anything out of there for the next two years, not as long as Bo Johnson is the Speaker.' Still, the way I saw it, what did I have to lose? I'd already made the decision this was a horse I was going to ride."

As the 1993 legislative session convened, it quickly became clear that Lawson and De Grandy were riding that horse virtually alone. The only reason the Rosewood bill was even allowed to continue breathing was because Bo Johnson recognized the volatility of the topic and the public stink that would surely be raised if it were dismissed on grounds of mere tardiness. Better to let it die a natural death than kill it, and the bill indeed looked doomed when eleven *more* Rosewood survivors surfaced even as Lawson and De Grandy were trying to get the legislation on its feet. Here they were, seeking compensation for two women who were supposedly the only survivors left alive, and suddenly there were eleven more people creeping out of the woodwork, people Lawson and De Grandy hadn't even known about. How many *more* would there be?

What little credibility the bill might have had took a nosedive. Even Lawson's black colleagues began publicly bailing out. Cynthia Chestnut, a caucus member from Gainesville, told the *Miami Herald* she had serious reservations about this bill. "I have no idea of the cost, of what this bill would entail," cautioned Chestnut. "A claims bill takes money from the general revenue fund.

That's money for education, health and everything else. You have to have good supporting data to get that money."

That theme became the drumbeat among Rosewood's doubters—the lack of good supporting data, the fact that there was scant evidence to support the reliability of these people's claim, the haze of speciousness that infected this whole affair.

By early April, as the legislature moved toward the end of its session, it was clear the 1993 Rosewood claims bill was defunct. Lawson knew that. He and De Grandy were already looking ahead to the next year's session. The original bill, on behalf of Minnie Lee Langley and Lee Ruth Davis, had been obsolete even before it was filed. So much had changed since the start of the year, so much had been discovered, not the least being the fact that there were thirteen survivors now, not two, and each of them would hopefully bring a wealth of evidence and information to bolster a new bill. Rosewood's opponents wanted more supporting data? Lawson and De Grandy would *give* them supporting data. Between that spring and the end of the year, they planned to amass more information than anyone could imagine—along with a bigger, better bill, nothing so flimsy as the piece of legislation they filed the first time around.

And so Al Lawson proposed that spring that the state fund a study to determine what exactly happened at Rosewood. It wouldn't cost much, maybe $50,000 or so. The governor, Lawton Chiles, liked the idea. "There should be a full accounting and investigation into the incident," said one of Chiles's spokespeople, putting the pressure on Bo Johnson to come up with the money. There were murmurs of protest that spending even that small sum on Rosewood—a sliver of the state's $35 billion budget that year—would be a waste. But it was worth it to Johnson, who announced in July that the money had been found and the investigation would be launched.

"At the least," said the Speaker in a prepared statement, "this study is sure to teach us something about our past so we can use the knowledge to guard against anything like it in the future."

That was Johnson's public posture. But there were those who believed his real reason for relenting was less lofty. "That's one of the easiest ways in the world to kill something," says Lawson. "Send someone to go off and study it, and hope the thing just fades away."

But Rosewood was not going to fade away. Lawson believed it, and Arnett Doctor and Steve Hanlon were going to make sure of it. Even as the state began putting together a research team of university history professors, Doctor and Hanlon were pulling together the Rosewood families, healing the rifts, bringing Lee Ruth and Minnie Lee into the fold as well as the newcomers—Wilson Hall and his sisters. Hanlon told them all they had no hope if they did not form a united front.

Doctor reminded them that Lee Ruth and Minnie Lee had done a brave thing by stepping forward, that despite their neglect of the others, these two women were the catalyst for all that was happening now. The message to Minnie Lee and Lee Ruth was that they needed the families as much as the families needed them, that there was even more at stake now than there had been when they first filed their claim. The bill that died that spring was in essence a test run, what the golfers A. T. Goins once caddied for down in St. Pete would call a mulligan. A free swing. The state was now giving the Rosewood families a chance to tee it up one more time, and they were preparing themselves to make the most of it.

While Hanlon worked the halls of Holland and Knight, gathering the firm's legislative resources, the families convened in Orlando to elect a committee, a group of four family members to represent them with the law firm and the legislature. The chairman of that Rosewood Advisory Committee was a natural choice—Arnett Doctor. He would be the spokesman for the more than four hundred survivors and descendants of Rosewood, and he took to the task with relish, spending the spring and summer of 1993 talking to every reporter who would answer his telephone calls, speaking to every group that could find a place for him on its calendar.

And they answered those calls, and they opened their calendars. A year earlier Arnett Doctor couldn't get the time of day from these people, but now they were throwing open their doors to him, and he burst through with a vengeance, wearing his dark purple suit with the gold Lion of Judah pin on its lapel—a family award, he explained to those who asked. "For leadership," he would add, swelling with pride. The NAACP asked him to address its state conference in Fort Myers in April, and he did. He made more television appearances than he could count. The TV news people loved him, this strong bold black man with a hint of anger in his eyes, articulate, almost poetic, with a heart-rending tale to tell, and he told it with such a perfect blend of empathy and outrage.

Arnett Doctor made for great television, and he made great copy, too, feeding the newspaper reporters the kinds of quotes their editors savored. He knew how to tell a story, and if it needed some embellishment here and there to dress it up just a little, well, he was glad to gild the lily. If it took hype to get this story in the papers, Arnett Doctor would give them hype. He would make the people who inhabited Rosewood, as well as the place itself, as mythic as he had imagined it when he was a little boy. Sylvester Carrier was no longer simply a crack marksman; Arnett turned him into a Winchester-wielding superman who, with a slug from his .30-.30, "could drive a nail into a tree one hundred and fifty feet away." There were no longer just two white men shot dead by Sylvester that fateful night; Arnett solemnly told reporters his uncle was "responsible for nineteen deaths." The town of Rosewood was no longer a tidy village of twenty to thirty homes; Arnett fudged the figure to "sixty or seventy," and, in a rush of excitement, he described the place as a "Black Mecca . . . what Atlanta is today."

All these depictions were dutifully rushed into print. No matter that they weren't quite true. That wasn't the point, not to Arnett. The point was to keep this subject in the public eye, to make people aware of Rosewood, to stir the pot while the state did its study. If there was backlash, arguments, debate, so much the better. Anything to keep Rosewood in the news.

And there was backlash. Letters of protest began flashing on editorial pages of newspapers across the state, questioning the validity of this claim and asking why, even if it were true, people today should pay for a crime that took place seventy years earlier. Even the Ku Klux Klan climbed into the act, sending two of its members to Rosewood to do some research of their own. They wound up at Doyal Scoggins's doorstep, on the porch of the old Wright house.

"Two guys in a pickup truck," recalls Scoggins. "They were very polite. I had no idea they were Klan till they said so. They started asking if I knew anything that had not been in the newspapers. I think they wanted somebody to say this had all been an invented story. After about ten minutes, they left."

The Klan then issued its own press release, picked up by the Associated Press and printed in newspapers across Florida. "Things can always be fabricated," said a man who identified himself as H. Jobes, one of the pair that had visited Scoggins. "I don't think it did happen. I can't in my mind believe that these people have such great memories after all these years."

Fliers began appearing around Levy County and on the fax machines of news organizations throughout the state. "ATTENTION WHITE PEOPLE," the notices blared, and they went on to alert Florida citizens that their tax dollars were being spent on a sham. "It's like being sued without due process and YOU are the victims of this scheme," the leaflets proclaimed. There was a phone number at the bottom of each one. Those who dialed it heard a recording by a group called the "Collective Action Network." At the end of the recording, another number was given. Dial that, and a man named John Baumgardner answered from his home in a small town south of Gainesville, where he still lives today.

Baumgardner is a forty-one-year-old "housedad," he says, home-schooling his two children while his wife works. He is also the former Florida Grand Dragon of the Invisible Empire Knights of the Ku Klux Klan, a position he held at the time those fliers went out in the summer of 1993. He directed that campaign, he says, as well as a subsequent demonstration at Rosewood, in which twenty Klansmen outfitted in robes and hoods paraded along Route 24 near Doyal Scoggins's house, waving at passing motorists.

Baumgardner says there were about six hundred members among the state's twenty or so Klan chapters at that time. "But only about a hundred of those were hard-core, active people," he says. Those figures are all about the same today, he claims, although the Florida Klan technically disbanded in 1994 in the wake of a successful lawsuit brought against the national organization by the Southern Poverty Law Center after a lynching in Alabama. Some saw the splintering as a sign of the Klan's decline, but Baumgardner says it's actually made the group stronger. "It's harder," he says, "to kill a snake with many heads."

Baumgardner says he is now retired as Grand Dragon, but he still edits and sends a monthly newsletter titled the *Florida InterKlan Report* to those six hundred names on his mailing list, and he still quotes Bob Dylan and Che Guevara on his newsletter pages—unlikely touchstones for a Klansman.

"Hey, I was a hippie in the Sixties," says the bespectacled south Georgia native. "I was in the SDS, a left-winger. 'Don't trust leaders, watch your parking meters.' I've *always* been a radical. I've never believed solutions are found in the middle of the road. Solutions are found out on the edges, on one side or the other, and I've been on both."

He can't quite explain how he came to the Klan thirteen years ago—"I've been asked that a hundred times, and I don't know the answer"—but he says racial hatred was not a reason. He says he's more concerned about homosexual-

ity and crime than race, and he says the Klan should be, too. He says he trea-
sures his memories of the black nanny and black cook who helped raise him in
Georgia. "I considered those people part of the family," he says. "I loved 'em."

The Florida Klan's opposition to Rosewood, says Baumgardner, was focused on the claim, not the claimants. "Even if this thing occurred," he says,
"and I'm not convinced we'll ever know what happened, we just thought it was
a shame that the state would pay money to these people without knowing exactly what took place. To us, it was an issue of justice, not race. What's right
and what's wrong? That's what this was about."

That was the question Al Lawson hoped every person in that Florida A&M
auditorium was asking themselves as they listened to him speak that Saturday
afternoon in September. The state's study team had finally been selected and
they were there, four history professors and one graduate student, beginning
their research that week by interviewing the survivors themselves. The setting
for those interviews, Florida A&M's Black Archives Research Center and Museum, provided a powerful backdrop, its rooms filled not only with testimony
to the achievements of African-Americans, but also adorned with artifacts of
slavery, segregation and Jim Crow, evidence of what the museum's curators
label "The Black Holocaust."

Signs for "Whites" and "Coloreds," pulled from old bathrooms and water
fountains, are mounted on the walls. Glass cases display vintage Florida postcards from the 1930s, '40s, and '50s, images of black cartoon figures eating
watermelon, stealing chickens, being swallowed by alligators—keepsakes
white tourists could pick up along with a sack of oranges, something to give the
folks back home a chuckle. Mid-century magazine ads, sheet music, toys and
souvenirs abound with the unabashed language of the time: "coons" and "niggers," "mammies" and "Sambos," "black crows" and "pickaninnies."

All artifacts now, remembrances of things past. But for the Rosewood survivors, those were pieces of their lives on those walls and under that glass,
painful yardsticks by which the years since their childhoods could be measured.
Some broke down. Others pulled back. Minnie Lee refused to talk to the study
team member who wanted to interview her, a young white man, until Steve
Hanlon drove over from his downtown office and calmed her, assured her these
people asking all these questions were good people, decent people, that they
weren't going to hurt her. No one here was going to hurt her.

The survivors were in the auditorium that Saturday morning, all but Lonnie

Carroll, who lay in the nursing home in New Smyrna, and Lee Ruth Davis, who had passed away the month before. The stomach pains that had brought Lee Ruth to the hospital in January had turned out to be cancer. Her death added the element of urgency to the bill, the fact that these men and women were all in their twilight years, that time was not on their side. Sympathetic editorials in newspapers around the state noted Lee Ruth's death, the sadness of the fact that she would not be alive to see her day of justice, if indeed that day was to come.

They sat in the front row that morning, the survivors along with Arnett Doctor, who, at Al Lawson's request, stepped forward and introduced them, one by one. As they stood, slowly, with both effort and grace, eleven ancient figures, each turning to face these hundreds of strangers, Al Lawson could see the awe that washed through the room. He felt that awe himself. The sheer sight of these living, breathing beings, the power of their presence, was so much stronger than words, or debate, or doubt.

And Lawson knew right then and there that he would have what he hoped for, that when this crowd dispersed that day and went back to their classrooms and congregations, to their boardrooms and businesses, they would bring with them a commitment to make the Rosewood claims bill black Florida's top priority come 1994.

Now it was up to him—and the families, and Miguel De Grandy, and Holland and Knight—to put together that bill.

And it was up to the study team, they all prayed, to back up the bill with its blessing.

NINETEEN

Doc Willie's Little Girl

It was autumn now and Tallahassee was teeming with college students, the massive campus of Florida State University swarming with tens of thousands of undergrads, a sea of Seminole-shaded shorts and tank tops—garnet and gold—spilling from tree-sheltered dorms and Georgian frat houses, sleepy-eyed students hustling to make it to another Monday morning class. A half-mile south, on a smaller scale, wearing their own school colors of green and orange and scurrying to their own labs and lectures, were the students at Florida A&M.

Downtown it was getting toward lunchtime, the sandwich shops and cafes surrounding the high-rise state capitol building doing a decent business with lawyers and bankers and the occasional tourist, but counting the days until January, when the 1994 legislature would convene, when politicians and staffs and lobbyists from across the state would converge and the cash registers would truly begin ringing.

Steve Hanlon was counting those days, too. He had been in over his head the first time around with the Rosewood bill. He admitted it. He knew the court system inside out, could litigate with the best of them in front of any

William Walters ("Doc Willie") in Lacoochee, 1940s

bench, federal or state. But the labyrinthine rules and procedures of the legislature, not to mention the webs of personal and political relationships among the
men and women sitting in those House and Senate seats, could be grasped only
with time and experience, and Hanlon had had neither.

He was new at this, and that's why the first bill had fallen apart. Lawson and
De Grandy were happy to sponsor it, but they had more than Rosewood on
their agendas. It had been up to Hanlon and his crew to write the thing, then
nurse it through the elaborate maze of hearings and committees that would finally culminate in a vote. They had gotten no further than filing the first time
around, and Hanlon took the blame for that. He simply wasn't ready. But then
neither was the bill.

This time would be different. The smoke had cleared in terms of the number of survivors. No more surprises there. As for the veracity of the claim itself—the facts surrounding the 1923 attack—the state's fact-finding team
would return with its results in December, and Hanlon could only hope those
results would be positive. If not, the whole thing was over. Close the books and
go home.

But assuming that first hurdle was cleared, that the study team's report supported the claim, Hanlon had to prepare his plan of attack, and he knew he
needed help, more than he had thought he might need it the first time around.
That's why he asked one of his partners in the Tallahassee office, an attorney
named Martha Barnett, to join him for lunch on this autumn afternoon.

While Steve Hanlon was a relative newcomer to Holland and Knight and an
oddity of sorts in his role as head of the pro bono division, Martha Barnett had
been with the firm for twenty years—nearly half her life—representing the
moneyed, powerful clients who had made Holland and Knight the most moneyed, powerful law firm in the Southeast. From the environmental tangles
faced by Florida's phosphate mining industry to the franchise squabbles troubling Kentucky Fried Chicken, from antitrust legislation to tax laws, the
twenty-six attorneys staffing Holland and Knight's Tallahassee headquarters
were there to roam the corridors of the state capitol two blocks away, to shep-
herd and shape the state's laws as best they could to suit the interests of their
corporate clients.

They were lobbyists, Holland and Knight's best and brightest, scurrying up
and down the halls of the sixth and seventh floors of the Barnett Bank Building
there in downtown Tallahassee. And the best and brightest of them all—the

best of any lobbyist in the entire state of Florida, according to some observers—was Martha Barnett.

She rolls her eyes at that accolade, shifts with discomfort at newspaper articles that describe her as "tough." She looks anything but tough, camped behind
her walnut desk in her homey, tasteful office, surrounded by photos of her family—her husband and two children, and her parents. A pink "I Believe Anita
Hill" button sits on a side table. A personal secretary is stationed at a desk outside her door, screening calls and visitors. Barnett is forty-eight years old, but
she still looks like the high school cheerleader she once was, her round brown
eyes bright as a doe's, her straight dark hair trimmed shoulder-length, her tan
suit, white stockings and print scarf as comfortably elegant and impeccably
arranged as her office furniture. She could easily be one of the local television
news anchors with whom she has done so many interviews.

Some say that's part of the reason for her success as a lobbyist, that the good
old boys over at the Capitol are charmed and disarmed by a woman, especially
one as youthful and attractive as Martha Barnett. Her low-key, relaxed demeanor doesn't hurt, and neither does her accent, the lilting Deep South twang
that tells the Big Benders she's one of them—which, in a sense, she is.

That's what she was chatting with the firm's new receptionist about that
Monday afternoon in September of 1993, making small talk while waiting for
Hanlon to get off the phone so they could leave for lunch. She wasn't sure exactly what Hanlon wanted from her, just that it had something to do with this
Rosewood bill he'd been working on. She didn't know much more about the
case than what she had seen in the office memos Hanlon had been circulating
for months. She had read a couple of newspaper articles, and she knew Hanlon
had missed the boat the first time around. But she was too busy with her own
legislation to pay more than passing notice. Now he wanted to pick her brain a
little bit. That was all she knew as she stood by the elevators, waiting for him to
get off the damn phone.

"So where are you from?" asked the receptionist.

"Oh, a little bitsy place called Dade City," said Barnett, watching the elevator doors open and close. "Small town, simple Florida. You know."

Hanlon walked up.

"Now don't you listen to her, Joanie," he said. "Next thing you know she'll
be telling you she's just a li'l ol' country lawyer. And then you better hold on to
your wallet."

Barnett grinned, cocked her head.

"Steve Hanlon," she said, "you don't even know how small-town I really *am*. Dade City's where I *say* I'm from, but I actually grew *up* in a little place you never *heard* of."

"Mmm, hmmm," smiled Hanlon. "And where might that be?"

"A place," said Barnett, "called Lacoochee."

Hanlon nearly fell over.

"Martha," he said. "Do you know where half the Rosewood survivors are from?"

She shrugged, shook her head.

"They're from Lacoochee. They all moved to *Lacoochee*."

"You're kidding," she said. "Steve, I spent the first nine years of my life there. My dad *died* in Lacoochee."

"Did you ever hear of a man named Arnett Doctor?" asked Hanlon.

Now it was Barnett's turn to almost fall down. What she had heard and read of Rosewood till now had not mentioned a word about Lacoochee. And nowhere had she seen the name Doctor.

"Arnett *Doctor?*" she said. "My father *delivered* Arnett Doctor. I grew *up* with Arnett."

"Just a minute," said Hanlon. And he reached for the phone.

Arnett Doctor. Martha Barnett couldn't believe it. Arnett and her big brother Will had been good friends growing up in Lacoochee, as close as a black and a white boy could be back then. Martha was the tot, four years younger, trailing behind the big boys whenever they'd let her. Arnett used to hoist her on his back when the summer sun baked the schoolyard sand so hot it burned her bare feet. "Baby Martha," he called her.

They all went barefoot back then, the black kids who lived across the tracks in Mosstown and the quarters, and the children like Martha and her brothers, who lived on the same side of town as the Cummers, the white side of Lacoochee. Martha had grown up with the Cummer kids, eaten plenty of meals at their dinner table and they at hers. It was the Cummers who had brought Martha's father to Lacoochee in the first place, to be the mill town's doctor.

Doc Willie, that's what his patients called him, black and white alike. William Walters. He wasn't Cummer and Sons' first doctor, but he would be its last. The company brought him down from Jacksonville in the late 1930s to set up his office in a long wooden building there by the sawmill. He was still

there when the mill closed in 1959, and he kept his office open for his Lacoochee patients until the day he died in 1983. Even after he moved his family
down the road to Dade City in 1957, Doc Willie still made the daily trip to his
old wood-framed office along the dirt drive at the edge of the Mosstown section of Lacoochee.

Martha Walters just about grew up in that office, its wood floors and walls
rough-hewn and smooth, carved from some of that sawmill cypress. Her
mother Helen was there just about every day, too, to take care of the records
and paperwork. Helen Walters never liked the fact that her husband kept separate waiting rooms for the whites and the blacks, but that was the way of the
times and there was nothing she could do about it. She could, however, see to it
that the blacks had a few more comforts, something to compensate for the separation. She got them a brand-new TV, for example, while the snowy set in the
white waiting room went wanting for repairs. And when color television came
along, she bought one for the blacks long before the white patients got theirs.
"That was just her way," says Martha. "You know, social equity."

Social equity was not a major concern for young Martha, though she saw in-
equity all around her every day. The black children she played with went to a
different school from hers. When she went to the movies, the black kids had to
sit up in the balcony while Martha stayed on the floor level with her white
friends. The only black people she saw when her family went out for a meal
were the cooks and waiters who served them. She and her brothers would play
with kids like Arnett, but always outdoors. The only times black children came
inside her house were when they were with an adult like Arnett's Aunt Rebecca,
who cleaned and washed for the Walters just as she did for the Cummers.

When Martha went into her black friends' homes, it was always with her father, who made his house calls at night. Martha loved to tag along, and she was
always struck by the size of the homes, so small compared to hers, so crowded,
even with hardly any furniture. And always the smell of cooking, something
frying. Night or day, the air in those homes was thick and sweet with the smell
of fried fat. To this day, when Martha Barnett passes a frying pan, it takes her
right back to one of those Mosstown cabins, her daddy in a back bedroom with
his medicine bag while Martha sat in the front room playing on the floor with
the kids, the hum of crickets and the croak of frogs drifting through the open
windows, the air inside warm and soft and safe.

Martha knew almost every family in Mosstown, and they all knew her, Doc

Willie's little girl. Even when the Walters moved to Dade City when she was nine, Martha kept coming back to Lacoochee, making the rounds with her dad. It wasn't until she began high school in 1961 that her visits became less frequent. That was the year the Freedom Riders came south, young protesters rolling into Georgia and Alabama and Mississippi, beaten by mobs in Birmingham and Montgomery, their bus set afire in Anniston, just a taste of the clashes and killings to come.

But Martha Walters knew about none of that. She was a Pasco High cheerleader—a co-captain. She was on the yearbook staff, the student newspaper, an officer in the arts society, head of the Beta Club. "That was my whole life," she says. "I was the typical middle-class kid."

She knew that some of the boys she dated were in the Klan, just like their fathers. To this day she says she wouldn't be surprised if her own brothers had been in the Klan, though she has no doubt her father was not. Back then Dade City had the largest Klan membership in the state. It was almost like a club, as socially acceptable as the Kiwanis. If some of those boys Martha dated were Klansmen, they didn't talk about it, they were never ugly or racist, at least not around her. They were nice boys, good boys, nothing like the "rednecks," as Martha calls them, the ones who swaggered down Dade City's main street, hooting, shouting "nigger" this and "nigger" that, taking weekend joy rides into the black sections of town, heaving beer bottles and jars of mustard at black homes, then driving off into the night, their drunken laughter trailing behind with the exhaust fumes from their hot rods.

Martha Walters knew about them, but she didn't know about the murder of Medgar Evers, or the bombing of Birmingham's Sixteenth Street Baptist Church, or the beatings at the base of Selma's Edmund Pettus Bridge in the spring of 1965. That was the spring of Martha's senior year at Pasco High, and all she knew about the world beyond Dade City was that she wanted to become a part of it, to leave this little town behind and make something more of herself than the nurses or teachers or housewives the women in Dade City were allowed to become.

So she went to college at Tulane, shared classrooms for the first time with blacks and Jews. The only Jewish people she had ever known until then were the Weitzenkorns—Otto and his wife Elaine, who ran a little department store back home. Theirs was the only Jewish family in Dade City. Martha worked summers for them as a clerk.

Now she was surrounded by Jewish students from cities like Chicago and New York, and black students come all the way from Africa. She shared classes with Asians and Europeans, young men and women with wondrous accents and urbane ideas. This was New Orleans in the late 1960s, more than a world away from Dade City, where everything was simply, rigidly black or white.

Martha got married in 1969 and graduated that year with a degree in American Studies, after writing her senior thesis on race relations in America. She watched her husband, a Marine, leave for Vietnam, then she entered law school at the University of Florida, thinking she might make a career working for the rights of underprivileged children. She came out with an offer from Holland and Knight, and she took it, joining the firm in 1973.

Twenty years later she was still there, among the shining stars of Holland and Knight's more than two hundred partners. She billed her clients a top rate of two hundred and eighty-five dollars an hour, a fee they were happy to pay for the services she provided. She was a busy woman, which was part of the reason she hadn't paid much attention to Rosewood. Another was that the case had nothing to do with her, no connection to any aspect of her life.

Until now.

"Arnett?" Hanlon asked, keeping his eyes on Barnett's as he spoke into the telephone. "Hey, this is Steve Hanlon. Listen, do you know a woman named Martha Barnett?"

Silence. Hanlon knotted his eyebrows.

"*Walters*," whispered Barnett. "My name was Martha *Walters*."

Hanlon nodded.

"I mean *Walters*," he said. "You know a woman named Martha Walters?"

Barnett could hear a small yelp on the other end of the line. She reached for it, excited, amazed. Arnett sounded pleased, but not particularly surprised. She exclaimed what an incredible coincidence this was, and he chuckled, as if it were the most natural thing in the world. Wasn't he amazed? she asked him.

No, Arnett told her, actually he was not amazed at all. "This is growing beyond us now," he said. "It's in bigger hands than ours. It's in God's hands. If it was time for you to be a part of this," he said, "then you would be. And it looks like it's time."

Martha Barnett didn't know about all that, but she did know one thing. This was personal now. And she was absolutely going to be a part of it.

TWENTY

Satisfaction

~~~~

There are things Maxine Jones remembers about her father, and there are things she simply knows. She remembers her father was always around the house when she was little, fixing things, horsing around with her and her brothers. But she knows he never lived there, not before she was born and not after. She remembers her mother would cook dinner for the family then carry a covered plate up the street to the room where her father lived. They took care of each other like that, Maxine's mother and father. Sometimes they even acted like they were in love. But they were never married, Maxine knows that. Her mother eventually took another man for a husband, but even then she kept carrying dinner up the street to Maxine's father. And sometimes he would come down and join them for a meal at their house, sitting at the table alongside Maxine's mother and stepdad, just like family.

Maxine remembers how awfully old her father was. It always seemed that he should have been her grandfather, he was that old—fifty-five when she was born. He died before she was grown enough to ask many questions, but she knows his name was Unis McCloud, that he was born in 1898 up around Geor-

Maxine Jones, William Rogers and Tom Dye

gia, and that his parents were slaves, a fact which astonishes Maxine to this day, that a woman as young as she is can say that her grandparents were slaves.

Maxine's father owned his own home for a while, there in the St. Petersburg neighborhood where Maxine grew up. But he got behind in his taxes is the way she remembers it, and he had to give the place up, go back to renting a room. Maxine remembers helping him the day he moved out. She was six or seven at the time, and they were hoisting a wardrobe down the stairs when one of the doors swung open and its mirror shattered.

"Oh Daddy," Maxine said, "you're going to have seven years bad luck."

"Baby," her father told her, "it can't get any worse than this."

Maxine's father was a painter by trade, and sometimes she would go with him on jobs. He didn't have much education, quit school in the third grade, could sign his name and that was about it. But he always told Maxine she was going to be something more, she was going to be something special. She was going to be a teacher, he told her, and she believed him. Maxine believed everything her father told her.

He died when she was twelve, but by then Maxine was already on her way to making her father's vision come true. She was always near the top of her class, came home every afternoon and went straight up to her room to read. She devoured books as if they were candy. Her family didn't live far from 22nd Street, the heart of black St. Petersburg, and there were plenty of kids in Maxine's neighborhood who spent their afternoons and evenings roaming over to those bright lights and loud sounds, seeing what kind of trouble they could get into, what excitement they could find. But Maxine wasn't interested in any of that. The swirl of 22nd Street may as well have been on the other side of the world as far as Maxine cared. Her life was bounded by her books, her school, the church, the playground, her mother and brothers and sisters, and, for the time he was alive, her father who lived up the street.

Maxine Jones is forty-two years old now, an associate professor of history at Florida State University. Of her nine brothers and sisters, and her parents, and their parents, Maxine was the first in her family to graduate from high school, the first to attend college. And now she has become the teacher her father told her she would be.

Her specialty is African-American history. She has written books on the subject, of course, and she keeps a file cabinet full of folders in her tiny office tucked at the end of a narrow hallway in the high-rise history building on the FSU campus. Each folder contains clippings on a topic she might like to write about someday, newspaper and magazine articles that have caught her eye over the years. She never picks up a newspaper or magazine without a pair of scissors by her side.

One of those files is marked ROSEWOOD. She began it in 1982 with a single clipping, that Sunday story in the *St. Petersburg Times*. "I remember saying, 'Hey, this is something I might be interested in.' It didn't shock me. I know my black history, and there's *nothing* that shocks me. But it piqued my interest. I thought it might be something I'd get around to someday, but then I've got a file cabinet *full* of things I might get around to someday."

She fidgets when she talks about Rosewood. She taps a pencil on her desk, squeezes her eyes shut, chooses her words with care. She is an exceptionally tall woman, six-foot-two, dark-skinned, a commanding presence. But she seems to shrink when she talks about Rosewood. And she winces.

"It was not," she says, pausing and drawing a deep breath, "anything like the experience I thought it would be."

Jones remembers the flush of excitement she felt in the summer of 1993 when she first heard that the state was forming a fact-finding team to investigate the circumstances surrounding the attack on Rosewood. She had followed the demise of the first claims bill, adding the clippings to her folder. Now she had a chance to actually become involved, and she leaped at the opportunity. She could think of no one better suited for this study than herself, and the state's Board of Regents, which selected the team, apparently agreed. When the academic political smoke had cleared, after a month or so of behind-the-scenes elbowing and jostling among history departments across the state, five names emerged to form the group, with Maxine Jones's at the top.

It was an impressive lineup, but not without controversy. Besides Jones, there was Bill Rogers, sixty-four, a venerable elder statesman among Florida's historical scholars and an authority on the Old South. From Gainesville came David Colburn, a fifty-one-year-old professor of history at the University of Florida and an expert on the state's racial and civil rights history. Representing Florida A&M was forty-one-year-old Larry Rivers, whose current research focus was slavery in Florida and who was the only black member of the team besides Jones. And then there was Tom Dye, a doctoral student at Florida State who had spent almost a year researching Rosewood's history after stumbling across the subject while writing his master's thesis on the fishing industry in Cedar Key.

There had been some questions about selecting Dye. Compared to the others, he was just a kid, still in his thirties, not even done yet with his dissertation. There were full professors across the state, department heads with pages of publications and awards on their resumes, who had been passed over for this team, and here was a *student* in line for a slot. But Jones, the team's director, and the others insisted Dye be included. He knew more about Rosewood than any of them, and more importantly, he knew his way around the docks and fishermen of Cedar Key. His in-laws had a summer home there. He had spent years in those woods and wetlands, as well as along that waterfront. The team would need someone like that when they began poking around down in Levy County itself.

By the time they first came together that August, the group was well aware of the political freight they were taking on, the firestorm of controversy that was certain to swirl around their findings, and the impact those findings would have on real lives. Before they even began, Florida State's dean's office sent over a public relations expert to give them a crash course in dealing with the media. But there really was no way to prepare for what lay ahead of them. "This was so different from anything any of us had ever done," says Maxine Jones. "We were used to studying history, not becoming a *part* of it."

They faced an ungodly deadline as well. The state had to have the report by December, for the start of the 1994 legislative session. That gave the group four months to conduct the kind of investigation that, under normal academic circumstances, would take three or four years to complete.

But then there was nothing normal about Rosewood. The team soon learned that as they launched their study in late August, beginning with a day trip down to Gulf Hammock, an excursion intended to give them a feel for the place. The outing in itself was odd for scholars more accustomed to searching among library shelves and sifting through archival collections than climbing over barbed wire fences, hacking through briers, swatting at swarms of mosquitoes and dodging the occasional rattlesnake—which pretty much summed up their visit that day to what was left of Rosewood. They scrounged around the woods behind Doyal Scoggins's house, came across a pile of old bricks, one of which Maxine Jones took home with her, "as a souvenir." Other than that, the highlight of the day was the barbecue lunch they stopped for on their way through Chiefland.

Their real research began with the September gathering of Rosewood survivors and their families at Florida A&M University. Tom Dye used his connections with the Tallahassee Radisson, where he once worked, to get a discount rate for hotel rooms for the families. Minnie Lee Langley, for one, had never stayed in a place like that. She'd worked in some, but she'd never stayed in one.

The team spent two days interviewing the survivors over at the A&M campus, sitting down one on one, taping the witnesses' remembrances of the town and their accounts of the attack. The details were vivid, the emotions palpable. Maxine Jones had never experienced anything quite like it, nor had her colleagues. "We knew then that we were dealing with something special," says Jones. "Not just tombs and cobwebbed documents, but living breathing human beings."

Documents, as the team soon found, were maddeningly scarce. Through September and October, Jones and her colleagues fanned out in search of any records they could find related to Rosewood, any shreds of paper that might shed some historical light on this extinct little village.

Larry Rivers flew up to the Tuskegee Institute in Alabama to search the NAACP records stored there, especially the lynching files, and was disappointed to find only one reference to Rosewood, in a tiny newspaper story. Newspaper stories were the last thing the team needed. They had dozens of those already. What they were after, like any good historians, were primary sources, official records and reports. And what they found, which did not entirely surprise them, was that when it came to a black community in the rural Deep South in the early part of this century, nobody seemed to bother much with records and reports.

Still, the team's job was to find what it could. Tom Dye went to Washington, D.C., where he waded into the Library of Congress, sifting through west Florida post office records, federal marshal's reports, Masonic society listings, the congregational records of black churches that existed in that region of the state at the time—he even rode a bus to a distant annex building where old state health department records were stored, hoping to find some reference to Rosewood. His efforts yielded a few scattered sightings of the town's name on this list or that, but nothing that helped sharpen the picture of what the place was like at the time of the attack or of the attack itself.

For that, the team searched closer to home, hoping the state's archives collection in Tallahassee would give them more than the census and property records they already had. Tom Dye's previous research on Rosewood, culled mostly from records stored in the Levy County courthouse, established the basic history of the village, its beginning in 1845 with the opening of a post office, its growth during the next half century, the existence of the black-owned M. Goins & Brothers' Naval stores company, which did a big business after the turn of the century distilling turpentine and rosin from the surrounding pine forests, the decline of the town's population by 1920, and the general layout of the village in terms of homes and churches at the time of the attack in 1923.

Unfortunately, the archives yielded hardly anything beyond what the team already knew. The state of Florida did not even begin keeping an archives until the late 1960s. "History," sighs Jones, "was apparently not a top priority down here."

The archival material concerning Rosewood was spotty at best. There was, for example, no correspondence from Governor Cary Hardee concerning Rosewood, no letters that might have fleshed out and verified newspaper accounts of the telegram he sent to the Levy County sheriff during the week of the attack. In fact, none of Hardee's correspondence during his term as Florida's governor from 1921 to 1925 could be found in the archives. "If those papers exist," says Jones, shaking her head, "they're in someone's attic or basement."

The county's grand jury records of the time were gone, destroyed in a fire. The attorney general's records for that year made no reference to Rosewood. The archives did contain old state prison records, which revealed the arrest of twenty-five-year-old Samuel Carter in 1900. The charge, according to the hand-written one-line entry on the brittle, yellowing ledger book page, was *assault to murder*. Carter was sent to prison that November, according to the entry, and was released in October of 1901—twenty-one years and three months before he was lynched in Rosewood.

On another page, written in the same florid script, were the names of Sylvester Carrier, age 26, and his father, Hayward, age 50, both *brown*, both from Rosewood, Fla., and both sentenced on April 2, 1918, to six months in prison for *fraudulently changing marks*—cattle rustling. They came back home that fall, September 20, according to the record.

As for the 1923 attack, however, there were no records at all. No sheriff's papers. No state militia entries. Nothing from the national guard. Nothing from the governor's office. All the team had to go on were newspaper accounts and the survivors' testimonies. And if those testimonies were to be trusted, the team felt it needed to hear the other side of the story as well, the white side. Which was what Tom Dye and Bill Rogers spent most of that autumn trying to find.

They were the natural choices to try penetrating the close-knit circles around Cedar Key, Rogers with his country lawyer demeanor and his seer-sucker suit, and Dye with the boyish eagerness that had served him so well during the months he had spent researching his thesis. "I had really gotten close to the guys down there," recalls Dye. "They took me out fishing, shared their beer with me, shared their *homes* with me. I figured I'd just put the beat-up ball cap back on, wouldn't shave for a couple of days, and could go back on down there and get right in some doors."

He figured wrong. The previous year had seen Cedar Key overrun with newspaper, magazine and television reporters nosing around about Rosewood, hunting for evidence of racism past and present, and the town was sick of it. Cedar Key felt it was getting a bad rap, along with a bad name. Dye himself had become something of a celebrity around the Florida State history department when he popped up in a *Washington Post* story that summer, quoted as an expert on Rosewood. A copy of that story was still tacked on the department chairman's door when the fall semester began. "I guess it *was* sort of a big deal, for a graduate student to be quoted in a national newspaper like that," admits Dye. "Shit yeah, I was flattered."

The people of Cedar Key were not. Doors that had once been opened to Dye were slammed in his face when he and Rogers came knocking that fall. "They treated me like I was a traitor," he says. "I understood how they felt, people being stigmatized for something they weren't even connected to. But I was hurt, too. I felt like I'd lost some friends."

The best Dye and Rogers were able to turn up was a tape recording Dye had discovered at the Cedar Key Historical Society Museum during his thesis research, and an interview Rogers was able to finagle with an old man in a nursing home in Chiefland.

The tape was a cassette, unlabeled, tossed in a drawer in the museum's back storage room. It contained an interview done in the early 1980s by a local historian with an old fisherman named Jason McElveen, who died not long after the tape was made. Most of the recording consisted of McElveen's memories of logging and fishing around Cedar Key during the first half of the century. But at one point the old man suddenly turned to the subject of the "riot" at Rosewood, and Tom Dye realized he was listening to an eyewitness account of the slaughter he had heard only rumors about until then. The scratchy voice, hardly intelligible at times on the dusty tape, told a tale of carnage tinged with the bluster of a braggart:

> It jus' rolled on three days. We surrounded the mill with guards and tried to keep the niggers working. We knew if we could keep them niggers in the mill we could keep 'em straight. But we knew if we let 'em out of there the farmers would get 'em. Every nigger had jumped up and run out of there whether it was a coon dog or what.

> So that rolled on for three days. In three days they sent word that the one we wanted would be in a certain building, an old school building right beside the depot. Said that they had 'im and that if we thought we could, to come get 'im. That be just about like throwing gasoline on fire, to tell a bunch of white people that.

> So it turned my blood red and all of the others. A bunch of us gathered up and went up there. I didn't have anything but a twelve-gauge gun, a pump gun. Plenty of buckshot. And most of them had the same thing. So we went up to the niggers and come back about midnight, and everything was quiet when we got back.

> The next day, they went up there and buried seventeen niggers out of the house. I don't know how many more they picked out the woods and the fields 'round about there. It was stated several times that there were ten more.

> But Ol' Man Sumner was the yard man around there and he done the burying. They jus' laid 'em in a row and plowed two furrows with a big field plow. Plowed two big furrows there and put the niggers in the trench.

> There's no marker or anything. Don't know who they was or why they was. They said there was twenty-six in there. After that, for the next four or five years, they picked up skulls and things all around there, in the woods and up the creek.

The volunteers manning the museum wouldn't think of letting Dye borrow the tape when he returned that fall, but they reluctantly allowed him to listen to it again in the back room. He had a recorder of his own in his pocket and used it to surreptitiously tape the tape. "I guess it was a little dishonest," he admits, "but it was the only way to get the information."

McElveen's account became part of the team's final report, as did Dye and Rogers's encounter with Fred Kirkland, the same man who had appeared on the 1983 "60 Minutes" broadcast. A former Levy County game warden who knew the Gulf Hammock swamps like his backyard, Kirkland had been an old man when he appeared on "60 Minutes." Now he was ancient, living in a nursing home in Chiefland, where Dye and Rogers arrived on a late October afternoon.

They asked a nurse where they might find Mr. Kirkland, and she pointed toward a ring of rocking chairs set out under a tree on the side lawn, four or five old men rocking silently in the shade. "That's him right there," she said, pointing to a huge, white-haired figure filling one of the chairs.

"He must have been six-three, six-four," recalls Dye. "You could see he had been a big, powerful man at one time. Now he was bent over a little bit. Big hands, big thick glasses. His eyes were real bad. Cataracts. And he was a little hard of hearing. You had to talk real loud to him."

Dye let Rogers do the talking. The professor was at his porch-sitting, iced-tea-sipping best among old folks.

"Why, are you Mr. Kirkland?" asked Rogers, sidling up to the circle.

"Why, yes I am," said the big man.

"Well, Mr. Kirkland, I am so *happy* to meet you. I'm Professor Rogers from Florida State University, and I understand you used to be sheriff here in Levy County."

"Well, yeah, sure," said Kirkland, puffing up with just a little bit of pride. He motioned toward an empty chair with one of his huge hands. "Sit down."

They chatted for a while about this and that, then got around to the subject of Rosewood. Rogers asked if he could use his tape recorder, and Kirkland said he'd prefer not. So the professor simply took notes. The old man said he knew James Taylor, was there the day it started, when Taylor's wife was "raped by a nigger," as Kirkland put it. When Rogers asked him about the lynching of Sam Carter, Kirkland backed off.

"I'm not gonna talk about that," he said. "We got this one boy. We got him. That's all I'm gonna say about it."

"Fine," said Rogers, and he moved on to the shootout at the Carrier house.

"I don't want to talk about that part of it," said the old man.

Rogers nodded. Then Dye stepped in.

"Well," he asked, "how did everybody feel when it was all over?"

The old man looked off in the distance.

"Well," he said. "After it was over, James Taylor said he was satisfied."

"What do you mean?" asked Dye.

"Just that," said Kirkland. "When it was all over, James Taylor was satisfied."

They chatted a while longer, then bid Fred Kirkland goodbye. The old man smiled and leaned back in his rocker, with his friends, quiet again in the October afternoon.

Backwoods Folks

So this was what the historians had. A sheaf of seventy-one-year-old newspaper clippings and a smattering of official documents. They had a dead
man's voice on a dusty tape and the coy recollections of an old man in a nursing
home. They had the testimonies of the survivors, filled with vivid, wrenching
details—but those details diverged as often as they overlapped.

All in all, Maxine Jones and her colleagues were on shaky ground, far from
the solid footing of fact to which they were accustomed. Still, it was November
now, the deadline approaching for the report to be written, and if this was all
they had, well, it had to be enough. And they felt it was—not nearly enough to
satisfy their own standards as historians, but enough to give the state what it
had asked for, an objective basis on which to judge the validity of this claim.

"We would have liked to have had a lot more, of course," says Jones. "But we
had the basics. It would be impossible to recreate exactly what happened, but
we felt we had come pretty close. Especially considering the constraints of
time."

The attack on Rosewood occurred, there was no doubt about that. It lasted

Sumner baseball team, 1922 (Ernest Parham, second from right)

a week, and at least eight people were killed—six blacks and two whites. That much was documented, as was the fact that property owned by blacks in Rosewood prior to 1923 was vacated that year and acquired by local whites soon thereafter. The state government was aware of the activity that week in Rosewood, and although it had time and the resources to respond, it did not. Nor was an effort made to protect or restore the property that was destroyed and the land that was subsequently sold. These, concluded the team, were facts. Finally, the failure of the grand jury to issue a single indictment was evidence of nothing less than "the abandonment of the American justice system," as the team described it in their report.

But even as they began shaping that report in November, the five historians were nagged by the fact that so much of it—especially the description of the town of Rosewood as it existed at the time of the attack, and the specifics of the attack itself—was based almost exclusively on the testimonies of the Rosewood survivors, who were all children at the time, whose memories could well have shifted over the course of seventy years, and who were the claimants in this bill, a fact which might affect their objectivity—or at least be conceived that way.

Total objectivity. That was what was missing from the reconstruction of what happened that week. The witnesses found by the team so far, black and white alike, had reason to be biased, as did the newspaper accounts of the time, which were almost entirely second-hand elaborations of sketchy wire service reports. Few, if any, of the journalists who wrote those articles were actually at the scene. Most of their information came from the Levy County sheriff's department or was relayed through rumors and word of mouth among the area's whites. These "facts" were then filtered through the interpretations of each newspaper's editorial staff, which—black journals as well as white—all had their own social, political and racial agendas.

Just one detached, disinterested witness, one man or woman who was there, who was neither among the attacked nor the attackers that week, but who simply saw what happened and who now, seven decades later, could recount it, clearly, lucidly, unburdened by the yokes of fear, shame or guilt—that is what the study team needed. That is what the Rosewood families themselves would need, when their claim faced the scrutiny of a skeptical legislature.

And that, remarkably, is what fell into Maxine Jones's lap late that month. She won't say who gave her the man's name—"It's a small, small world," is all she will offer. That, and the fact that the man's name came from "a friend of a friend," via Jacksonville, who pointed Maxine down to Orlando, where an eighty-nine-year-old widower named Ernest Parham lived by himself on a tree-shaded street in a quiet neighborhood called College Park. Ernest Parham had never talked about Rosewood to anyone—"No one ever asked," he says—until David Colburn, prompted by Maxine Jones, drove down from the University of Florida on a Wednesday afternoon two weeks before Thanksgiving and knocked on the old man's door.

Ernest Parham answers that same door today, a couple of years older but still remarkably fit. The tiny lawn in front of his house, mowed smooth as a putting green, Parham cuts that himself. The Buick parked in his carport, sparkling alabaster in the midday sunlight, he washes it by hand every week. Waxes it, too. The small, cozy living room into which he hospitably invites visitors is immaculate, kept that way by Ernest ever since his wife Sophia passed away seven years ago. He offers a cup of coffee, tea, maybe a glass of something cold, then settles his soft ninety-one-year-old body into a seat.

His cheeks are pink and his thinning hair is snow white. His eyes smile calmly through a set of wire-rimmed glasses. He moves without effort, rising several times from his easy chair to fetch an old photograph or a scrapbook, nothing hurried or labored about his movements or his speech, everything about him as steady and serene as a monk. His light cotton shirt and khaki slacks are perfectly pressed and creased, fitting for a man who worked almost fifty years in the laundry business. He owned his own company by the time he retired in 1976—Acme Cleaners and Laundry, "the biggest in Orlando at the time," he says, not boasting, simply stating a fact. He sold the place to a nephew that year, and he remembers the specifics of the deal as if it were yesterday. He remembers the specifics of his entire life that way, including the details of what he witnessed that winter's week in 1923, when he was living in a small Gulf Coast village called Sumner, just down the road from a place called Rosewood.

He was twelve when his family moved to Sumner from Cedar Key in 1916, after Ernest's father, a logger, "took tuberculosis" and died. Ernest's mother and stepfather owned the Island Hotel in Cedar Key for a time, and Ernest and his two brothers made good money carrying bags for the steady flow of "drummers"—salesmen—who stepped off the Seaboard train every night looking for the best room on the island. The boys were disappointed when their parents told them the sawmill company up the road in Sumner had hired them to come run the hotel there. Cedar Key was like a city compared to where they were headed, but Ernest and his brothers made the best of it.

"Sumner was strictly a sawmill town," says Parham. "About three hundred and fifty people. Those who worked for the Cummers, blacks and whites, lived in furnished homes provided by the company. Down toward the train depot there were farmers and lumbermen living in homes of their own. There was a post office, two grocery stores, the hotel, and that was about it."

Ernest and his family lived in the hotel, and when Ernest got a little older, he went to work in the commissary owned by the Cummers. The other store in town, a much smaller operation, was run by a man named Poly Wilkerson.

"A big, blustery fellow," recalls Parham. "He was the quarters boss for the Cummers for a time, but they let him go, I presume because he was carrying liquor into the quarters to sell to the black people. At least that's what I was told. There were several other incidents, too. Walter Pillsbury, the general superintendent, finally let him go and hired Clarence Williams, the deputy sheriff, as quarters boss, and Wilkerson was real upset with the mill people after that."

Parham shows no trace of emotion as he tells his story. Occasionally he lifts his hand, ever so slightly, to make a point. But other than that, he simply measures his words and speaks.

"One day Wilkerson came up to the hotel," he continues, "where Clarence Williams stayed. It was a Sunday afternoon, and he called Clarence Williams out. He told him he was gonna kill him.

"Well, Clarence came out. And Wilkerson drew his gun. But Clarence drew his at the same time, and he poked his gun right in Poly Wilkerson's stomach, and he said, 'Well, now. You pull your trigger, and I'm gonna pull *mine*.' And Poly Wilkerson backed down.

"Now that was not the only incident like that that involved Wilkerson, but it was the only one I actually saw."

Though the blacks and whites worked and lived alongside one another in Sumner, their lives were lived apart, says Parham. "My mother's cook had a boy, and we played with him, but that was it. We never played with black kids from the quarters. We called them 'nigras,' and if you were upset with them, you called them 'niggers.'"

As for the blacks in Rosewood, they seemed a world away. "They had a very good baseball team, that's something everyone knew. We used to go up there to watch them play. Whites would come and watch as well as blacks. Sumner had its own team, a white team, but we didn't play Rosewood. You just didn't do that in those days. Or you weren't *supposed* to. The fact of the matter is we used to slip off sometimes and go up to Rosewood to play them, and they would let us win. But they were better than we were, no question about it."

It was in the summer of 1919, after he turned fifteen, that Ernest Parham got to know Rosewood well. That was the summer he began driving his stepfather's ice wagon, making a circular route that took him to houses throughout Rosewood as well as Sumner. He rarely went inside the homes—one of his stepfather's black employees actually hauled the blocks of ice off the wagon, while Ernest did the driving—but over the course of the next couple of years, Parham became familiar with almost every family living in Rosewood. And he respected what he saw.

"These were very progressive black people. They had their gardens and their homes, and they kept them in real good shape, above the average for blacks at that time. No one lived in that settlement but black people, except for Mr. Wright, who had a store there. He was the only white in that area that I knew of."

Parham pauses, takes a sip of water, then goes on.

"They were high-type people, houses kept up real good, white picket fences around some of them. They didn't have lawns. The yards were dirt, and they swept them with big brushes. They had flowers, too, and some fruit trees.

"Some grew vegetables and sold them to people around the mill. Some of the men in Rosewood worked at the mill, and some of them worked at a turpentine still over at Wylly. Almost all of them worked somewhere, and they worked hard and seemed to do fairly well for themselves. The families that stood out, as I recall, were the Bradleys and the Carriers. Sarah Carrier, Sylvester Carrier's mother, was educated, I think, because she had a piano in the front room. They kept that house looking very good, a two-story house. As I said, these were high-type people."

And that, as Parham sees it, was the root of the trouble that erupted that week in 1923.

"Basically there were no problems at all between the people in Sumner and the Rosewood people," he says. "None at all. There was a local Klan group in

Sumner, plenty of Klan people in town, and *they* had no problems with the blacks. The blacks took care of their own business, stayed on their property, and the whites stayed on theirs.

"But there was a certain amount of jealousy among what you called the 'outback' people, the whites who didn't live in the town itself. They lived out in the woods. There was some resentment among those backwoods folks because of the fact that the Rosewood people were more aggressive than they were, selling vegetables and such in Sumner. To tell the truth, they just didn't like to see black people doing better than they were.

"And there was a lot of them that didn't think too much of Sylvester Carrier. He was not as polite as the rest of the blacks. He worked away from Rosewood a lot. Where, I don't know. He'd come home and be there awhile, and then he'd be gone and you didn't know where he was. He was aloof, distant, and there were some who didn't like that attitude. It wasn't the Cummer people who didn't like it. It was those white people who were more out in the woods who didn't like it. The outback people."

Parham stops, takes another sip of water.

"All I can say is they didn't think too much of Sylvester Carrier. They felt like he was *uppity*."

And so arrived that New Year's morning, 1923. Parham remembers how cold it was. "Awfully cold," he says. "There was frost that morning, and we didn't have frost that often."

Normally Ernest would have been off to school. He was eighteen, in his junior year at Cedar Key High, and he drove the school's bus, picking up his classmates on the way in each morning and dropping them off on the way home to Sumner each afternoon. But this being the holidays, Ernest was working at the commissary that morning, punching in at five-thirty, as always. It was mid-morning, as he recalls, when he first heard of the "rape situation."

"Everyone coming into the store was talking about it. First they were saying Fannie Taylor had been attacked. Then somebody said they were pulling bloodhounds together. All day long, I kept getting updates like that."

By the time Ernest locked up at seven, it was dark. His boss, the commissary manager, had left hours earlier to join the group that was following the dogs. "Johnson was his name," says Parham. "Albert Johnson."

Ernest walked on over to the hotel, where he saw Clarence Williams's car parked out front. Someone said the deputy sheriff had gone to Rosewood, so

Ernest decided to bring him his car. "The keys were in it, sure," he says. "You never took a key out of the car in those days."

Parham took a short cut to Rosewood, a dirt road, then circled back onto the "hard road," the highway of crushed limestone that eight years later would be paved and labeled Route 24. There, about a hundred yards from the western edge of the village, sitting on the running board of another man's car, was Clarence Williams. In the distance, in the darkness, Ernest could hear the barking of dogs and the muffled voices of men. He gave Williams the car keys and walked toward the commotion.

"It was a group of about twenty-five, maybe thirty men, not a mob yet," recalls Parham, "in front of Sam Carter's house."

Ernest Parham knew Sam Carter, says Carter often came to shop at the Cummer commissary. "Sure I knew him. He was a large fella, a blacksmith, very humble, like most of them were in those days. I remember the thing about him is he was always immaculate. He wore overalls, what we called a 'jumper' in those days. They'd be blue when you bought them brand new, but they bleached out to almost white after you washed them. And Sam Carter always stood out that way, in this bright white jumper."

Parham pauses a moment, taps the arm of his chair with his fingers.

"When I got there they had him stretched up, trying to make him talk. It was his wagon tracks they'd followed, and they assumed he had picked this black man up, which I'm reasonably sure he had.

"They had him stretched up there and he couldn't talk even if he wanted to. Someone said let him down, and when they did, he said, Yes, he'd tell them where it was. And this one fella who had a hold of the rope, he also had a double-barreled shotgun, and he said, 'Now if the hounds don't pick up that trail, I'm gonna kill you.'

"There'd been some drinking. You could smell it. And this fella with the shotgun, he had been doing some drinking. It was obvious by the way he acted.

"There's no need telling you who he was. I knew him, but he still has family around. I'm sure there are others can tell you who he was. But I won't."

The rope was untied from Sam Carter's neck, and he led the mob about a mile into the woods, says Parham. There were no homes in sight. The only light came from their lanterns.

"They got to where they couldn't go any further. The bloodhounds ran around but couldn't pick up the trail. So this fella stepped up, called Carter a black so-and-so, and then he pulled the trigger. Just like that. Held the shotgun right against his head, and he pulled both triggers."

Parham taps his fingers again.

"I'd never seen a man shot before."

He folds his hands together.

"You could hear the gasps. I think most everyone was shocked. Mr. Pillsbury, he was standing there, and he said, 'Oh my God, now we'll never know who did it.' And then everybody dispersed, just turned and left. They was all really upset with this fella that did the killing. He was not very well thought of, not then, not for years thereafter, for that matter."

Clarence Williams, the only arm of the law within reach, was still up the road at the time, says Parham, waiting beside his car.

"There wasn't a whole lot Clarence could do about this group," says Parham, "and he knew it."

The next morning, "Rosewood was all anybody was talking about," says Parham. The mill was still operating, people were still going to work, black and white. "But there was a lot going on, people coming in from up in Taylor County and Gilchrist County, rushing into the store, getting shells, buying ammunition. We had to finally hide the guns and shells 'cause the people weren't paying for them."

It went that way Wednesday as well, and Thursday, too, strangers streaming into the store, looking to buy weapons. There was no word of anything actually happening in Rosewood, not until Thursday night.

"It was late," says Parham, "probably close to about ten o'clock. It couldn't have been after that because the electricity was always cut off at ten. The hotel was one of the few places in town with electric lights, and they'd flash 'em a couple of times just before ten, from up at the mill, to let us know they were cutting them off. And I know the lights were still *on*.

"We were sitting in a circle around the living room fireplace, there by the lobby. Clarence Williams came up and took a seat. The fire was popping and crackling, like it would, and Clarence sat down and said, 'All hell is taking place up at Rosewood.' He said something about a group getting set to go up to Sylvester Carrier's home.

"And it wasn't much after that, the lights were still on, and in comes one of the fellas that was stayin' at the hotel, and he had four bullet wounds through his arm. He was all bandaged up. He didn't stand around and talk too much. He was headed up to his room. But he did say there'd been some men killed over in Rosewood."

That was all Parham saw that night, but the next morning there was a crowd at the door when he came to unlock the commissary.

"Lots of unfamiliar faces, people I'd never seen before, coming in and asking for shells and guns. We sold them to those who could pay. Sold a lot. That Friday was a busy day."

Parham didn't see what was happening at Rosewood. He was too busy behind the counter. But he heard reports all afternoon from the people passing through his store.

"Word was they were shooting the whole town up, setting fire to houses, shooting people that ran out, just shooting everything they could, which was more or less the elderly men and women."

By the time he closed the commissary that Friday evening, Parham understood that Rosewood had been essentially emptied, that most of the townspeople had fled to the woods, those who hadn't been killed. He went home to the hotel, and not long after, W. H. Pillsbury, the mill superintendent, burst into the lobby.

"He said he wanted as many of us as had guns to come with him. He'd gotten word that these out-of-town people were going to come try to burn the quarters in Sumner, burn down the black section of town. 'We got to stop this mob,' he said. 'They're coming this way.'

"Well, every one of us had guns. That was the way it was back then. You carried a pistol from the time you were fifteen years old. You didn't necessarily carry it on you, but you had it in your car or someplace nearby. Guns were just a part of the way of life in those days."

Parham grabbed his gun and joined the group.

"It was a cold night. Gosh, it was cold. We all went out to the edge of town, the east end, closest to Rosewood. There was a spur at the railroad track there, and we lined up across the road right at that spur, about twenty of us.

"We could hear them coming. They were talking loud. You could tell they'd been drinkin'. It was dark, about nine-thirty. Mister Pillsbury had us lined up from one side of the road to the other, and when they come up to that spur, about a hundred feet away from us, he called out to them, told them that the first man sets foot on that rail, he would personally shoot him. He said he had orders to shoot anybody that came across that track.

"Well, that stopped them. There was a lot more of them than there was of us, and this one fella that killed Sam Carter, he was heading it up.

"They stood there and talked it over among themselves a few minutes. I didn't know what was going to happen. I don't think anyone did. Then they turned and went back. And they didn't come our way anymore."

In the meantime, says Parham, some of the women and children of Rosewood were hiding in Sumner, taken in by sympathetic whites.

"Most of us had taken in some of them. Liza Bradley, she worked for my mother, and she was at the hotel the day after the shootout. When word came about what was happening, she stayed with us. I don't know about her family, but Liza stayed with us. We protected her.

"I know the Pillsburys—they lived right close to us—they did the same. The rest, I don't know. I guess they were out in the woods."

It was W. H. Pillsbury, says Parham, who arranged for the Bryce brothers to bring a train from Cedar Key to pick up refugees from the swamp.

"Mr. Pillsbury was good friends with the Bryces. They were conductors on the train. Everybody thought they *owned* the trains, because they always had a good amount of money, and everyone knew they lived in good homes up at the other end of the line. They were fine people, well-to-do, but they didn't own the train."

Nevertheless, the Bryces were able to bring a train through that weekend, says Parham, and that, he says, is how most of Rosewood's population wound up in Gainesville.

"By the end of that weekend, all the homes in Rosewood had been burned down. There wasn't anything left. After that, every once in a while, when we'd go up to Gainesville for one reason or another, we'd see one of the Bradleys sitting around the courthouse square and they'd come over and talk to us, wonder how things was down home. But they were afraid to go back. In fact, none of them ever did go back."

Ernest Parham left Sumner in 1925 and wound up in Orlando, where he went to work for a laundry company, the same company he eventually owned. Two years after he left, the sawmill in Sumner burned down. By then, most of its workers had already moved to another Cummer mill town, a place called Lacoochee.

"I don't really know how it burned," says Parham, "but you know sawmills had a habit of burning when the timber got all cut out. Just like orange-packing houses would catch fire after all the citrus was frozen."

A pause, and a small smile.

"Funny how that happens."

Now and again over the years, Parham would hear tell of this person or that who had been involved in the affair up at Rosewood. One was a man named Elias Roland.

"He was a high school boy at the time, just like me," says Parham. "That night they killed Sam Carter, he went up and cut off one of Carter's ears. I didn't see him do it, but he was showing it around town for a couple of days, till he finally got rid of it because he wasn't sleeping at night.

"The last I heard of him, they said he was in a bar in Cedar Key and a man shot him, killed him. That was sometime in the early thirties."

Another name Parham heard was John Wright's. Some said Wright was often seen in Gainesville during the years after the attack, talking to some of the Bradleys and other residents who had fled Rosewood, trying to convince them to move back. Wright had bought some of the Rosewood land that went up for sale after it was vacated, and some said his purpose was to return it to its original owners. But no one took him up on the offer, if indeed the offer was actually made.

In any event, John Wright's life was never the same after the attack. When word got out that he had harbored some of the blacks from Rosewood, he was vilified. "Nigger-lover" was one of the kinder things he was called. There were threats on his life, and he took to arming himself wherever he went. At home, they said, he kept a pistol on every table. His wife Mary died eight years after the attack, and they said Wright developed a drinking problem after that. He was drinking the night he died, they said. It was the dead of winter, he'd been at a bar over in Cedar Key, he was nearly passed out and so some locals carried him home in their truck, dumped him off in front of his house and drove off. He never made it to the door. The next morning he was still there, on the ground, dead of exposure.

They buried John Wright in the old Shiloh Cemetery, back behind Sumner, in a grave with no markings. No headstone. Not even a wooden cross, like most of the graves around it. Just a mound of broken clam shells under an old moss-hung oak.

A final name Ernest Parham kept up with, for personal reasons, was W. H. Pillsbury's. Six years after the attack on Rosewood, Parham married Walter Harlow Pillsbury's oldest daughter Sophia. By then, Pillsbury was three years dead.

"He had moved down with the rest of them and taken over the operation in Lacoochee," says Parham. "But it was hard. That group down there did not get along well with him because of their animosity about what happened at Rosewood. A lot of the people that were involved had moved to Lacoochee, white people, and they resented Pillsbury, called him 'nigger-lover' and stuff like that. He never fit in down there, and so the company retired him. He went home to Jacksonville, and he died not long after that, in 1926."

Parham has a photograph of his father-in-law, taken when Pillsbury was a young man in Jacksonville, before he came to work in Sumner.

"He was born up in Michigan," says Parham, opening the frame that holds the photo. "He was Indian, though I can't honestly say what tribe."

The man in the photograph looks stern, strong, tall. He is wearing a dark wool suit and a white shirt, its starched, stiff collar rising to his chin. His black hair is thick, combed straight back. He resembles, in size and stature as well as facial appearance, another Native American of the time, the athlete Jim Thorpe.

"He was a tough man," says Parham, running his fingers across his father-in-law's photo. "He *had* to be tough."

He shuts the frame and sits back in his chair with a soft sigh.

"It was an awful thing, all of it," he says. "You can just imagine being burnt out, run off your home, for no reason whatsoever. None of them had anything to do with it. I doubt very seriously if Sylvester Carrier had anything to do with hiding the man. He could have, I don't know, but I doubt very seriously if the man who did the raping was in Sylvester's home that night."

Parham has no doubt that Fannie Taylor was raped. The story that she had a white lover is, in his opinion, just that. A story.

"I doubt very much that she had a lover," he says. "Because James Taylor and Mrs. Taylor seemed to me to be very nice people. They came from a good Cedar Key family. At least *he* did. Where she came from, I don't know. But some of James Taylor's sisters were in my class in school. I knew that family, and they were good people.

"Besides, if it was a white man, why would he run to *Rosewood*? And why would Sam Carter help him get away?"

The theory of Masonic loyalty brings a another small smile to Ernest Parham's lips.

"I think it was a black man," he says, lifting that right hand ever so slightly. "I really do."

Then he leans back and lets out a deep breath.

"But really, it's going to always be just like Walter Pillsbury said when this fella shot Sam Carter."

One more tap on the chair.

"We'll never know."

TWENTY-TWO

Special Master

It was three days before Christmas, and Richard Hixson was lacing up for his early evening run, a five-mile loop that wound through the hilly tree-shaded Tallahassee neighborhood where he lived alone with his pet Pomeranian, Jennifer, in a brick two-story ranch overlooking the Florida State campus, just a few minutes from his office at the State Capitol.

His nightly run was like a sacrament to Hixson. Sometimes it seemed like the only thing that kept him sane, and this was one of those times. The fact-finding report he'd been waiting weeks for had finally landed on his desk that day: *A Documented History of the Incident Which Occurred at Rosewood, Florida, in January 1923.* Ninety-three double-spaced pages, benignly bound with a powder blue cover, along with more than four hundred additional pages of appendices, including charts, graphs, statistics and verbatim transcriptions of every interview conducted by the study team over the course of the previous four months.

Hixson had skimmed those pages that afternoon, and could already see the minefield of issues contained in them, questions that would have to be an-

Richard Hixson

swered during the legislative hearing session that lay ahead, a hearing Hixson knew would be unlike any over which he had ever presided.

Richard Hixson had pretty much seen and heard it all during his ten years as "special master" for Florida's House of Representatives, a position in which he acted as an appraiser of sorts, a quasi-judge whose job was to provide an initial assessment of the two dozen or so claims bills filed each year with the legislature. In each case, the special master's job was to listen to evidence by witnesses and attorneys, then recommend to the House whether and why it should award the claim, and if so, how much that award should be. The hearing was in essence a gateway, the first hurdle a claims bill had to clear on its journey to the floor of the legislature.

The vast majority of those claims bills—roughly ninety percent—were personal injury cases, lawsuits against the state that had already been tried in a court of law. A teenager run down by a school bus; a woman drowned at a public beach; a young girl decapitated by a state highway sign blown off an overpass by a gust of wind—these were the kinds of cases in which the state, or more precisely, one of its agencies, had been sued for negligence and taken to court.

The question of whether the suit ended there, with a jury's verdict, or whether it went on to the legislature as a claims bill depended on dollars and cents—how much money the jury awarded the claimant. If the verdict was for $100,000 or less—$200,000 in the case of a group claim—the state simply paid. If the jury awarded more than those amounts, the case was passed up to Tallahassee, where it became a bill for the lawmakers to consider, to decide for themselves whether the case in question warranted the payment they were being asked to pull from the state's coffers. In those debates, practical concerns could often become as critical as legal or moral issues.

"Unlike a trial," explains Hixson, "a government agency can step up in this situation and talk about the consequences of the payment it's being asked to make. For instance, a school board that's been sued can come in and say, 'Hey, wait a minute, if we have to pay a million or two million bucks here, we're not going to be able to fund certain programs out of our budget.' There are impacts with judgments like this, government agencies are affected, as is the public, and that's something the legislature has to consider.

"To tell the truth," says Hixson, brushing a lock of thick brown hair away from his eyes, "the members of the legislature don't particularly like having to do this. It's different than any other part of their job. Essentially they have to look at these things like jurors, and they don't enjoy that."

Hixson had played the role of judge to the legislators' jury ever since the position of House special master was created in 1983. Before then, Florida had always hired private attorneys to come in and conduct each claims hearing. Deciding it would be both cheaper and more consistent to have a hearing master on staff, the House had turned to Hixson, who already had a reputation among Florida's legal circles as something of a boy wonder.

A Clearwater native, he had come out of the University of Virginia's law school in 1973, clerked for a federal judge in Tampa for two years, then spent five years in the state's Attorney General's office, where he was put in charge of the civil litigation division. His rise was meteoric, to say the least, a tousle-haired kid of thirty suddenly in charge of fifteen of the state's most seasoned attorneys. In 1981 he became staff director of the House Judiciary Committee. Two years later, when the House went looking for a special master, it didn't look far.

That Christmas of 1993, Hixson was forty-three, still working for the Judiciary Committee. He was a government employee, but when he stepped into the master's role, he was no longer an advocate of the state. In fact, he often became its critic.

"I was basically an independent appraiser," he says, and the costs of the cases he appraised were sometimes dizzying. The teenager run down by the school-bus won a $5.5 million verdict in a Dade County courtroom. The family of the young girl killed by the highway sign was awarded $9 million by a Palm Beach jury, the largest judgment against the state in Florida's history.

"Of course these cases were appealed," says Hixson, "but in Florida, jury verdicts are pretty sacrosanct, and appellate courts are reluctant to change them."

So they wind up in Tallahassee, where the hearing master decides what size *he* thinks the verdicts should be. He looks at precedents, studies similar cases across the state, listens to the testimony of witnesses and the arguments of attorneys, searching for a footing to make his own judgment. Often, that footing remains slippery.

"Take the decapitation case," says Hixson. "Here you had the wrongful death of a child, and that's pretty much the same situation in Pensacola or Miami or Tampa. You have a dead child and grief, which are basically the same anywhere.

But when I began going into other jury verdicts dealing with deaths of children, the awards were all over the ballpark. They ranged from $127,000 all the way up to that nine million. You look at the variety of these judgments, and it's very disconcerting. You try to figure out what makes one jury come back with one figure and another come back with one so completely different, and you can't. You'd like to think there's a better, more consistent way of addressing these issues, but there isn't."

As troubling as such personal injury claims can be, they at least have the basis and context of prior court proceedings to help guide the hearing master. But besides these "waiver statute" claims bills, as they are called, the state faces about four or five claims each year that have not been considered in any court of law. These "equitable" claims arrive in Tallahassee untried, untested. And they are, says Hixson, the most difficult to decide.

"They can come from almost anywhere," he says. "Basically you've got someone who has been aggrieved by some form of state action for which there is no legal remedy, no legal redress. There's no court the person could walk into, and so they come here, to the legislature."

The first question in any such case, says Hixson, is whether the claimant could have brought his case into a courtroom. If he could have and did not, says Hixson, "that's his fault, not the state's."

"Some people simply let time expire without taking their claim to court," he says, "and then they show up at the legislature, trying to bring a suit here after they've had the opportunity to bring the suit into court and simply didn't do that."

Most of these equitable claims involve situations in which years have passed since the case could, if possible, have gone to court. A schoolteacher asking for retirement benefits not paid when he was teaching in the 1930s; a man who charges that his property was improperly seized by the sheriff's department back in the '60s; a woman who was committed by the state to a mental institution when she was a child in the 1950s. In each of these cases, the hearing master's first question is whether the claimant could have taken his case into a courtroom at the time it occurred, and whether he could have received a fair hearing if he had done so.

"That," says Hixson, "was one of the first questions that came up with Rosewood."

There were others as well, all tumbling through Hixson's head as he took off for his run that December evening. Who was in charge of enforcing the law that week in Rosewood? Did they respond? If not, why not? How many people were killed or injured? How many people lost property? How much did they lose? How did the grand jury arrive at its finding?

All these questions would have to be explored, as well as the issue of payment if the state was indeed found to be at fault. Payment, however, was a question still far down the road.

"I wasn't even thinking of the compensation part," says Hixson. "I wasn't going to even begin looking into the issue of who would get what until I was satisfied about what had *happened*."

That satisfaction would not come from the study, but the study was the starting point. "Without it we could not have gone forward," says Hixson. "The study was the line in the sand, the demarcation of issues and facts against which the witnesses' words would be measured."

And the attorneys' words as well. Hixson already knew who would be representing the claimants. He had watched Steve Hanlon in action years before, down in Tampa, and he knew Martha Barnett as well. As for who would represent the state, the special master had no idea.

That was one more question to ponder as he jogged off into the night.

TWENTY-THREE

The Eleventh Hour

How much? And how many?

Ever since the legion of Rosewood survivors and descendants—more than four hundred of them—had surfaced at the beginning of the year, those two questions had hovered at the edges of the public debate, beating their wings like two bothersome birds. How much money would the state be asked to pay, and how many claimants would be asking?

For almost a year, Steve Hanlon, along with Arnett Doctor, had been able to keep those questions at bay. With all that had been written and reported about the attack itself and the impending bill, there had been no mention yet of specific numbers, no reference to what exactly might be the price tag of this claim. One reason Hanlon had sidestepped such questions was a simple matter of strategy, a lesson he had learned during years of courtroom litigation.

"You never mention numbers in your opening argument," he says. "You want the jury to hear the story first. You want them to identify with your people, be angry, be upset. *Then* you hit them with a number."

The jury in this case was essentially the entire population of Florida, four-

---

Steve Hanlon

teen million men and women, represented by their legislators, which meant there was the media to consider as well—another reason, according to Hanlon, to keep money out of the matter for as long as possible. "As soon as you mention money," he explains, "that's all the press is going to focus on, the only thing they're going to cover."

But beyond simple strategy, the fact was that even if it had wanted to, the Rosewood group—the attorneys, the families, and the bill's two sponsors—had no numbers to share. As late as Christmas Day, with the fact-finding team's report freshly in hand and the final draft of their bill due to be filed at the end of that week, they still had not decided on the amount and terms of the compensation they sought. Their focus up to that point had been on shaping the language and issues of the bill, understanding full well the implications of this claim, not just for Florida but for the entire nation. There was no doubt the debate would be fierce when the bill arrived before the legislature. Its ramifications, in terms of the volcanic issue of reparations, were immense. This proposed law was bound to open some of Florida's—and America's—deepest, most sensitive wounds, picking at the raw nerve endings of the nation's racial history.

The Rosewood group realized this, and so they had spent months trying to anticipate every possible issue, hoping to address and clarify each one, in preparation for the hearing process, where their claim would get its first taste of scrutiny.

The language of the bill was no small matter. The distinction, for example, between the terms *compensation* and *reparation* was enormously important. Compensation, as Hanlon made painstakingly clear to every reporter he faced, is a strictly judicial term, involving payments for specific losses or damages identified and measured through legal procedure. Compensation is what is paid each time a lawsuit is won in court or a claims bill is passed by a legislature. Reparation, on the other hand, is a much broader "extra-judicial" concept, extending beyond the strict bounds of law. Reparation involves payments to make amends for more general wrongs and injuries, such as the devastation done during a war or the suffering inflicted by a system such as slavery.

The Rosewood bill sought compensation, not reparation. But that distinction was already becoming lost in the clamor of alarm that had begun rising around Rosewood that summer and fall, fears about the door this claim would open for every group with a historical grievance against the government. Native Americans whose ancestors had been slaughtered and whose land had been seized. African Americans whose forebears had suffered as slaves. What, critics asked, was to keep tens of thousands of these people from stepping through the door opened by Rosewood and draining the nation's treasuries with claims of their own?

The answer—and Steve Hanlon knew it would need to be stated again and again in the coming months—was that the losses suffered by Native Americans and slaves, as grievous as they were, were suffered under circumstances that set them far apart from Rosewood. America was at war with the Indians. And slavery, as heinous as it was, was legal. The people of Rosewood, on the other hand, were United States citizens, entitled to the same personal and property protections as any American—protections they did not, according to this claim, receive. And so they were seeking compensation.

Beyond that issue, the Rosewood group also knew it would face the argument that the attack on the town, as horrible as it might have been, was not extraordinary, that this was, after all, the lynching era in America, that there were literally thousands of cases all across the country in which people—full-fledged United States citizens just like the residents of Rosewood—were killed and their property taken. Were all those families, too, now entitled to step forth and claim compensation?

Steve Hanlon knew this was a stickier question to answer, because even if in principle the answer was yes, in practical terms he realized the bill would be torpedoed if the lawmakers saw it as a precedent for a torrent of claims just like it from every corner of the country. Again a distinction had to be made, and Hanlon and his team were ready to make it. In every other case of lynching that they knew of, whether it was an isolated killing or a large-scale "race riot," the incident took place over a relatively short period of time—a day or two at most—and the authorities could conceivably claim that they did not have adequate time to respond before the deed was done. The attack on Rosewood, on the other hand, lasted an entire week. The nation watched while it happened, as did the governor of Florida and local law enforcement agencies in and around Levy County. That fact alone, Hanlon was prepared to argue, set Rosewood apart from any other lynching in American history.

As for the veracity of the claim itself, the questions surrounding the circumstances and actual extent of the attack on Rosewood, the fact-finding team's report was a godsend, better than anything Hanlon or the Rosewood families could have hoped for. Not only did its detailed, day-by-day description of the events of that week support the claimants' own accounts, but its conclusions included precisely the points Hanlon intended to make during the hearing.

"Rosewood was a tragedy of American democracy and the American legal system," wrote the study team. "By their failure to restrain the mob and to uphold the legal due process, we can only conclude that the white leaders of the state and country were willing to tolerate such behavior by white citizens."

This was a gift that could not have arrived at a more appropriate time. With Christmas lights twinkling outside the Capitol building, the spearheads of the Rosewood claims bill—Arnett Doctor, Steve Hanlon, Martha Barnett, Al Lawson and Miguel De Grandy—came together in a House committee room to answer the only questions left before the bill would be launched.

How much, and how many?

Doctor had actually begun toying with numbers back in October, during a weekend stay at Hanlon's Tallahassee home. The two had become surprisingly close friends over the previous months, considering Doctor's initial suspicions about this white man from a conservative law firm, a firm founded by a politician whose name was synonymous in the Doctor household with racism itself.

Spessard Holland had been the governor of Florida when Arnett Doctor was born in 1943 and became a U.S. Senator for a quarter century thereafter. He was a man who was proud of his Dixie roots—both his father and grandfather fought for the Confederacy. A self-professed "hopeless reactionary," Holland had dug in his heels against the civil rights movement and Great Society reforms of the Fifties and Sixties. In a household like the Doctors', he was considered as close to an antichrist as a human could get.

"He put the black man through hell," says Arnett. "That's all I knew about Spessard Holland. He used the word 'nigra' like you would chew chewing gum. When I heard the name Spessard Holland, it was like hearing the name Theodore Bilbo up in Mississippi. The racist Bilbo. In our house, Spessard Holland was in that same category."

In truth, Spessard Holland, who died in 1971, was more complex than that, more multi-dimensional than most of his political colleagues in the mid-century South. He was an avowed segregationist, but unlike most Dixie legislators, for whom "separate but equal" meant "separate, period, and the equal be damned," Spessard Holland truly believed that blacks deserved the same protections and benefits of the law as whites. He backed that belief by fighting for thirteen years to get the U.S. Senate to pass a constitutional amendment outlawing the poll tax, one of the South's most precious weapons to keep blacks from voting. When the 24th Amendment finally became law in 1964, it bore Spessard Holland's name, to the confusion of many of his critics.

His critics would have been surprised, too, to learn that twice in his life Spessard Holland personally prevented a lynching. The first was in Lakeland in the mid-1930s, when Holland, who was a state senator at the time, happened upon a mob at the city jail while driving home from his law office. Two men inside—white men—had been imprisoned for killing a pair of police officers who had tried arresting them for drunkenness at a party. By the time Holland came upon it, the mob had reached the men's cell and were banging on the bars with bricks. The senator pushed his way through the crowd and was able to quiet the mob by promising to prosecute the prisoners himself. True to his word, he helped convict both men, getting the death sentence for each.

The second case, in the early 1940s, happened in Quincy, the same town where Al Lawson would eventually attend high school. Three black men had been captured and accused of raping a young white woman, then cutting her throat and leaving her for dead. When Holland, who was now governor, got word that a mob was forming in Quincy, he ordered the prisoners transferred to the Tallahassee city jail. The mob followed, and were met outside the jail by the governor himself, who ordered the crowd back while he talked to the prisoners. The three men told Holland they were indeed guilty, that they expected to die, but they begged him to protect them from this horde. Again, Holland talked the crowd down, promising full and fair prosecution, and again he kept his word. The three prisoners wound up dying in Gainesville State Prison's electric chair.

But none of that mattered to Arnett Doctor. He didn't know any of these things, and he didn't care. The only truth he knew was the truth he got from his parents, and that was the truth that counted. His parents had told him Spessard Holland was a dyed-in-the-wool racist, so that's what he was.

Nevertheless, Doctor eventually warmed to Steve Hanlon. It took some time, but he came to trust Hanlon, then to actually like him. At least once a week throughout that summer and fall, the two men met either in Tampa or in Tallahassee, and they found they had a lot in common. They were about the same age. They both liked to fish. They even shared the same medical condition: glaucoma. Doctor had begun taking early morning walks for his diabetes, and when he was in Tallahassee, Hanlon would join him, the two of them rising early, before six, and hiking the hills at the edge of town, talking about themselves, their families, and about Rosewood.

That weekend in October, for the first time, they talked about money. Hanlon had been telling Arnett and the families for months to "start dreaming." Don't think about dollars and cents, he had told them, but just about what they'd like to include in this claim. Education. Scholarships. Maybe a memorial. Things like that. A list had evolved, and most of those items had become part of the bill Hanlon and Barnett were drafting. A college scholarship fund for students descended from Rosewood. Money for scholars to study the attack on Rosewood and other such incidents in Florida history. Inclusion in history books, so no one would ever forget that this attack took place. These were all now part of the claim.

But no one had been allowed to mention money. Arnett wouldn't permit it, on advice from Hanlon. Now, though, Hanlon was asking Arnett to name a figure, privately, to give him something to begin batting around with Lawson and De Grandy, "to get a sense of the size of the ballpark," as Hanlon put it. Martha Barnett had said she knew of very few waiver statute claims bills that came in for more than a couple of million dollars and almost no equitable claims for anything higher than a half-million or so. But then again, there had never been an equitable claim like this one.

"Twenty-six million," said Arnett.

Hanlon coughed. He'd asked for a nice round number, and Doctor had given him one.

"Twenty-six million," Arnett said again. "We've identified twenty-six families that were living in Rosewood at the time of the massacre and that have family members still alive today, either survivors or descendants. That's a million dollars for each family, for each estate."

Hanlon listened.

"Look," said Arnett, "*any* number I give you is going to be too low, as far as I'm concerned, as far as most of the families are concerned. But twenty-six million. I think that's fair."

When Hanlon called Lawson with that figure, Lawson exploded. "He went through the ceiling," says Hanlon. "He said I was out of my mind. He would never submit a number like that. So now we had a read on where Lawson was."

De Grandy was just as shocked.

"He told us one million dollars was doable, two million at the most," says Hanlon. "Anything higher than that, and he was going to back out. He wouldn't have anything to do with it."

And so Arnett spent the next two months talking with the committee, meeting with family members, shuttling back and forth between them and the law firm, trying to whittle down the figure as best he could. By that December evening, when Doctor and the lawyers walked into the committee room to meet with Lawson and De Grandy, they had hammered the amount down to $270,000 for each family—a total of just over seven million dollars. That figure would be divided in various amounts among the fifty-six claimants named in the bill, with survivors each receiving a full share while descendants split theirs.

The mood in the committee room was initially merry, the good news of the study team report still filling the air. But then it was time to talk dollars, and the bubble burst. Lawson and De Grandy waited to hear what Hanlon had now. When he laid seven million on the table, Lawson didn't blink. But De Grandy backed off. No way was he going beyond two million. He had said it before and he was saying it now. Bring the number down, or he was gone.

Lawson understood his colleague's position. De Grandy was a Republican up for reelection. He couldn't afford to be labeled tax-and-spend, and that was the word already going out about this bill.

What Lawson didn't know was De Grandy had no intention of running for reelection. He was about to be married, and had decided to return to private practice in Miami after the upcoming legislative session. His personal political stakes were not a factor in his position. He simply didn't believe the bill would survive at seven million. And he was also playing hardball with Lawson for control of this thing. One of them would be lead sponsor, the man who would run this train, and De Grandy intended to be that man.

Doctor didn't know or care about any of that. All he saw was that here, at the eleventh hour, one of his patron saints was about to turn his back on them all. He was furious. He felt betrayed.

Hanlon and Barnett just watched. They were here for their clients. This was as low as their clients would go. Seven million.

Lawson tried convincing De Grandy to stay in. If the bill's got to be cut, he said, let the legislature do it. *We* shouldn't cut the thing, he said. Make *them* cut it. We owe it to this family, he said.

But De Grandy shook his head. He was sorry, he said, but he could not back this bill for that amount. Then he left the room.

"Hit him."

Hanlon could hardly believe what he was hearing. Then Lawson said it again.

"Hit him. Don't let him get away with that shit. *Hit him.* Go with the seven million."

Barnett, unlike her partner, was not surprised. She'd seen enough back-room legislation to know how it worked. Lawson was ready to force De Grandy's hand. The black caucus, he said, the same group that had basically abandoned this bill the first time around, now had its honor on the line.

"We've been stepping out on this thing," said Lawson. "We've been saying what a great harm was done here. We can't ask for an outrageous amount, but we can't ask for peanuts either. That would be an insult. Anything less than what you're asking here would be an insult."

And so they hit him. Lawson phoned De Grandy and told him they were going ahead with this bill whether De Grandy was in or out. The family, said Lawson, refused to reduce the amount of their claim any more than they had. De Grandy listened, considered, then played his own card. There was no love lost between the Cuban and black caucuses; they were in the midst of a battle to decide where the state should place a new law school—at predominantly black Florida A&M University or at Florida International University in Dade County, whose population was sixty percent Hispanic. If De Grandy was not out in front on this bill, the Cubans were going to bolt. Lawson knew that, and he knew he needed them.

So when De Grandy told him he'd stay in at seven million *if* his name was listed at the top of the bill, as lead sponsor, Lawson said fine. He knew his black caucus colleagues would be irate if an outsider wound up with top billing on this, of all things. The *Rosewood* bill, with a *Cuban* leading the way? Unthinkable. Unthinkable, too, that Al Lawson would step back and let someone else take the lead. That wasn't like him at all. He admitted it himself. He had never been a man who would give up credit if he could claim it himself.

But this was different. That's what Lawson told the black caucus, and that's what he told himself. This was bigger than who got to be the hero. This was more important than politics, he said, though the fact was that this decision, like anything that passed through a legislator's fingers, had indeed become political. It was politics that lost Lawson the lead sponsorship of the Rosewood bill, and it was politics that gave it to De Grandy.

And so another call was made, announcing a press conference for Thursday, December 30. That morning, with Arnett and the family's committee members standing beside him and Hanlon and Barnett watching from the back of the room, Al Lawson announced that the Rosewood claims bill had been filed. It would seek seven million dollars for fifty-six family members, "a small penance," said Lawson, for the state to pay for its role in this "shameful" chapter of Florida history.

"For those who say that's a lot of money," he told the roomful of reporters, "it's really not. If we were in a court of law and the state had to pay restitution to these families, it would be an amount you couldn't add up on paper."

The next day, newspapers across the state ran those words, along with photos of Lawson and Doctor and details of the historic bill. Missing from the rostrum was the proposed law's lead sponsor, Miguel De Grandy, but he had a valid excuse for not being there. He had had to fly home to Miami that day for a wedding—his own.

TWENTY-FOUR

One Last Matter

It was early February now, a week into Florida's 1994 legislative session, bill after bill—more than three thousand proposed bills—already cascading into committees while the Rosewood group sat on the sidelines, awaiting their turn at the end of that month, when their hearing before the House special master was scheduled to begin.

Steve Hanlon was ready to go. He had his arguments prepared and his witnesses lined up, ranging from a psychologist who had interviewed several of the survivors and would testify that each showed symptoms of post-traumatic stress disorder, to an economist whose specialty was translating "value of living" losses from years into dollars and would testify that the amount the survivors were asking in this claims bill was a pittance compared to what his calculations would yield in a court claim. And finally there were the survivors themselves, four of whom Hanlon planned to put on the witness stand.

Choosing those four had been a fairly simple process of elimination. Mary Hall would do little good, since she was only three years old at the time of the attack and had no memories to share. The same was true of Dorothy Hosey,

Willie Evans

who had turned only four that week. Then there was Margie Hall, who was fourteen in 1923. While the others were too young, Margie was now too old. She had begun slipping into senility; her recall was shaky at best. Lonnie Carroll, who was twelve when the massacre occurred, was incompetent, bedridden in the New Smyrna nursing home where he had lain for the past eight years and where he would lie for the rest of his life. As for Lillie Washington, Berthina Fagin, Thelma Hawkins, Eva Jenkins and Vera Hamilton, doubts had already begun stirring about whether those women's names would still be on the bill by the time the hearing was done, since none of them were actually living in Rosewood at the time of the attack, although each had been born and raised there.

That left four: Willie Evans, who was sixteen at the time of the attack and who, unlike Margie Hall, had lost none of his memory; Wilson Hall, who was seven at the time and could speak vividly of what the town had been like before it was destroyed; Arnett Goins, who was eight and was upstairs in the Carrier house the night of the shootout; and finally, Minnie Lee Langley, who was downstairs that night, in the actual line of fire, huddled between Sylvester Carrier's legs. Minnie was nine at the time.

So Steve Hanlon was set, and Martha Barnett, too, was busy. While Hanlon would carry the ball through the critical phase of the hearing, it was Barnett who would usher the claim from that point on, carrying it into the maze of the legislature itself. She was already working the one hundred and twenty members of the House, making phone calls, dropping by their offices, getting a read on where each of them stood on the issue of Rosewood, leaving packets of news clippings and the study team's report, urging them all to give it a read, sowing her seeds now so she'd have a head start when this bill finally arrived on the lawmakers' desks.

She was doing the same with the forty-member Senate. She couldn't afford to wait until the hearing was done to begin her work. The entire legislative session lasted but sixty days, and they were already ten days in, with two more weeks to go before the Rosewood hearing would even begin. The clock was ticking. Barnett had to start now, not knowing what Hixson's decision would be, but assuming—praying—it would give her the boost she needed.

Just before Valentine's Day, Hanlon and Barnett arrived at Richard Hixson's office for a meeting. There were still a few things left to go over. Hixson told them the Senate's special master, an attorney named David Kerns, would be sitting in on the proceedings. Since this bill had been filed with the House and would begin its passage there, Hixson would take the lead, with Kerns essentially looking on and weighing in with any questions he might have.

Hixson stressed, as he had during several meetings he had already had with the Holland and Knight team, that this was an "evidentiary" hearing, that it was not the kind of adversarial proceeding they were used to in court. Hixson had never handled an equitable claims bill with the stakes as high as this one, both in terms of money and moral issues, and he wanted to make the rules of this hearing process absolutely clear.

This was not about lawyers arguing with lawyers, he explained. This was an arena in which each side would simply present the evidence it had to support its position. But they all knew it could never stay that simple, that there was no way to keep a lawyer from being adversarial. It was in his blood. It was what he was trained to do. Asking a lawyer to make a case but not to argue was like asking a boxer to step into a ring but throw no punches.

Which raised one last matter that was still unresolved. Who, Hanlon and Barnett wanted to know, would the other boxer be? Who was going to represent the state?

They'd been asking the state that question for weeks, pestering Pete Antonacci, the state's deputy attorney general, about how the AG's office was going to handle this case. Each time Barnett had called, Antonacci had told her the state was staying out of it. There would be no defense. Hixson could have his hearing, write his recommendation, and the legislature could vote on this thing. But the state was not getting involved.

"'Get a life,' that's what I told them," recalls Antonacci. "We had *never* defended ourselves in one of these types of claims, and we weren't going to start now."

Hixson had gotten the same response, and he didn't like it any more than Hanlon or Barnett. There *had* to be a defense. That's how Hanlon and Barnett felt. The hearing, Hixson's decision, the very bill itself would all lack legitimacy if the state stayed out of it. Even if they won, under these circumstances, if the bill were passed, it would appear that the skids had been greased, that the law was a gift. They didn't want a gift. The essence of this claim was the issue of responsibility, the assertion that the state had shirked its duties seventy-one years before. Hanlon and Barnett were not about to let it happen again. They were not about to allow the state to sidestep yet another responsibility it owed to the people of Rosewood—the duty of answering to these charges now, today.

Hixson had his own reasons for dismay. If the state had no representation in this case, Hixson would wind up in the uncomfortable position of being the only voice critiquing this claim. He would appear to be representing the state, and that was not the role of the special master. That was not his job.

Barnett left the meeting and immediately phoned the Attorney General's office yet again. Antonacci took the call. "No way," he repeated. "We are *not* going to do this, especially not at the eleventh hour like this. That's ridiculous. Forget it."

Hixson then made a few calls of his own. He met with the chairman of the Judiciary Committee—his boss, Robert Trammell—and with the House Speaker, Bo Johnson. The entire process was in danger of losing legitimacy, Hixson told them. The state had to defend, he said. Al Lawson weighed in as well, as did Miguel De Grandy.

Finally, Johnson paid a visit to the AG's office. He closed the door behind him, sat down with Antonacci and Antonacci's boss, Florida Attorney General Robert Butterworth, and said, "Boys, this is how it is. . . ." The state was holding this hearing, Johnson said. And the state was going to *be* at this hearing. Period. End of meeting.

"It didn't take thirteen seconds," says Antonacci.

Bob Butterworth now had some phone calls of his own to make. All right, he said, he would fight this thing. But he was not going to fight it halfway. There was going to be no charade here, he said. If they wanted him to play, he was playing to win. He was going all-out, putting his best man on the case. And so, a scant ten days before the Rosewood hearing began, Assistant Attorney General Jim Peters's telephone rang.

Remarkably, Jim Peters had never heard of Rosewood. At least that's what he says today.

"Not a word," he says. "I didn't know where it was. I didn't know *what* it was."

It's hard to get Peters to open up about his experience with this case. But then he's not the type to open up easily about anything. His answers to questions are as clipped as his haircut, which resembles the actor Steve McQueen's in his prime. In fact, Jim Peters looks a lot like Steve McQueen did, from the laser-beam squint of his eyes to the ropy leanness of his forty-nine-year-old body. The barbell sitting on his cluttered desk is more than a bookend.

"Nautilus, swimming, and rowing machines, I do them every *day*," he says. "That's good stuff. Keeps you from going crazy."

He seems, at first, an impatient man, edgy, at least with an inquisitor. Maybe it's because he is so accustomed to being the inquisitor himself. Maybe it's just the way he is. Or maybe it has something to do with Rosewood.

"This is something I'd just as soon *not* revisit," he had said when first asked to sit down and talk about this case. "There are some things you just have to put behind you," he said. "You just have to get on with life."

Nonetheless he agreed to meet, and after a short time he loosened up a bit. He never stopped twisting the pen gripped in his right hand, and his left eye had a nervous tic to it, but a disarming openness began to shine through the cracks of his military demeanor as he explained some of the souvenirs arrayed on the walls of his cramped, cluttered office in a nondescript corner of a non-descript building located off a parkway just east of downtown Tallahassee.

There is a black-and-white photo, for example, perched on his windowsill. The two men in the picture, one in a sleeveless T-shirt with a Harley-Davidson tattoo on his bicep, thumbs hooked in his belt loops, the other a steely-eyed blond with a thousand-yard stare, are standing by a river. They look like killers, which a jury concluded they were, when the two were sentenced in 1980 to die in the electric chair.

Their names are Earnest Lee Miller and William Riley Jent—the two bikers found guilty of the murder down in Lacoochee, the one in which the woman's charred body had been found in the woods near the Withlacoochee River, the murder written about in *Esquire* magazine. When they were released from death row in 1988 on new evidence, Jent and Miller sued the state's attorney who had put them there. It became Jim Peters's job to defend the state, and he did it well. The suit was dropped, though Miller and Jent still wound up walking. "Yeah," says Peters, flashing a tight smile toward the photo, "I like to keep mementos of some of my fun cases."

He's not your run-of-the-mill, off-the-assembly-line attorney. He came to law late, after earning an M.B.A. degree and working for the Florida state government's consumer protection office. That job was actually what he did between weekends, when he turned to his true passion, racing sports cars. He's got a poster of the Sebring raceway front-and-center on his office wall. MG's, he says, that's what he's into. He actually worked for a sports car dealership for a time before he decided, at the age of twenty-eight, that law school might give him a step up in life. He didn't have the pedigree or credentials of a white-collar attorney. Basically he was a working stiff. But he wasn't intimidated either. "These guys put their pants on one leg at a time, just like I do," he says. "That's the way I approached it. If they could do it, so could I."

So he got his law degree from Stetson University down in St. Pete and went to work for the attorney general in 1977, at age thirty-one. Seventeen years later, he was one of two hundred and fifty assistant attorney generals in Florida. Twelve of those assistant AG's were in the state's civil litigation division, and Peters was the senior attorney among them, the best, as Bob Butterworth had said, they had.

Steve Hanlon, for one, was elated when he heard Jim Peters would be doing this case. Hanlon and Peters had locked horns several times over the years and Hanlon had nothing but respect for an attorney he considered much like himself.

"I don't generally have many good things to say about most lawyers these days," says Hanlon. "I think we have a profession of people, too many of them, with seriously unresolved adolescent conflicts, just horrendous individuals. We don't have trial lawyers anymore. We have litigators who don't really go to court at all. They write memos, file frivolous motions, and accuse each other of being assholes. They're a bunch of yuppies, firing off faxes to each other. I can't stand these kids. I don't even want to be in the same room with them.

"When I heard it was Jimmy who would be doing this hearing, I said great, now here's a *real* lawyer. This is gonna be two old guys who love to try cases, rolling up their sleeves and going kick-ass against each other. This is gonna be fun."

That was hardly the non-adversarial approach Richard Hixson was urging, but Jim Peters's attitude was the same. He was a fighter all the way, a man who had been known to fling a chair across a courtroom in a fit of anger, to get in a witness's face and scream, a passionate man if not always a prudent one. And he was, beyond all else, a loyal man, the state's man, whether prosecuting a case or defending one.

Jim Peters might never have heard of Rosewood, but he knew Levy County. One of the oddest cases he had ever been involved in had come from down

around there, in the early 1980s, when the state's Department of Law Enforcement had used an undercover agent to bust a Big Bend cocaine kingpin named
"Bubba" Capo.

"The godfather of Dixie County," smiles Peters. "That was Bubba Capo."
The FDLE got its bust by having its agent order several thousand pounds of
mullet from one of Capo's fishing partners, a man named Buck Sheppard. The
government had no intention of actually buying the fish, and after the bust,
when Sheppard found himself holding a couple of tons of mullet stored in
frozen lockers across north Florida, he sued the government for the price of
the fish.

"They popped Bubba," chuckles Peters, "and Buck comes right in and says,
'Hey, wait a minute, what about these *mullet?*' The Great Mullet Caper, that's
what we called it."

Again Peters defended the state, and again he won. Poor Buck Sheppard
wound up with nothing to do with his fish but eat them.

Peters knew Levy County, and he knew the members of the black caucus,
too, as well as Miguel De Grandy, all of whom he had represented when Florida
went through a laborious reapportionment process after the 1990 census. Jim
Peters went to an NAACP conference in Atlanta that year to help shape the redistricting requests of Florida's black legislators.

"I *knew* these guys, okay?" he says, rankled again at the wounds incurred by
Rosewood. Peters won't admit the wounds even exist. Like a good soldier, he
saw—and still sees—his role as the state's advocate in those hearings as nothing
more nor less than his duty. Some saw that role as thankless. They say Peters
was a straw dog, a sacrificial lamb set up to take a hit for the higher-ups. But Peters will hear none of that. He won't complain that he had only ten days to prepare for the most visible—and volatile—case of his career. His upper lip
remains stiff.

"It was never a question of sacrifice," he says. "It was my *job.* We're trench-
level lawyers here, that's all. We do what we can with what we've got. We do it
all the time."

At the end of the interview, as he walks toward the door, he almost relents.
Almost, but not quite.

"It was a draining experience," he says of the Rosewood hearing. "But it
doesn't *matter* how I felt about it. It was my job, and I did it."

PART FIVE

REDEMPTION

TWENTY-FIVE

Like an Ant

Tallahassee's Old Capitol building is an impressive sight, sabal palms flanking the front steps like tropical sentries, bold red-and-white-striped awnings overhanging each of the antebellum structure's eighty-two windows, staving off the rays of the relentless Florida sun. Tour guides gather visitors inside, beneath the stained-glass glow of the rotunda, and tell of the building's history, how it began as two log cabins when Florida was but a territory in the 1820s, how those lodges were replaced by a simple brick structure when Florida achieved statehood in 1845, how running water was first installed at the turn of the century and how extensive renovations took place in 1923, overseen by then–Governor Cary Hardee, producing the stately whitewashed edifice that sits at the center of the city today.

The guides point out proudly that this was the only Confederate capitol east of the Mississippi not seized by Union troops during the War of Northern Aggression. They do not mention that Tallahassee, being part of the cotton belt, was the center of Florida's slave trade, and that rumors persist that some of those slaves were auctioned off the back steps of this very building.

Minnie Lee Langley

Nor do the guides speak of the two dozen lynchings that occurred in Florida during Cary Hardee's four-year term, including the attack on Rosewood, which took place the same year that the silver-domed cupola, frosted glass skylights, double-curved staircases and marble wainscoting were added to embellish this seat of the state's law.

The Old Capitol is now used only for occasional bill-signings and, every four years, to swear in the state's governor. The actual business of lawmaking now takes place behind it, in the *new* capitol building, a twenty-two-story monolith of steel and cement, constructed in 1977 to house the offices and chambers of Florida's House and Senate. Day and night a constant stream of legislators, lawyers and lobbyists pushes through its ground floor glass doors, nodding to the pair of security guards stationed inside.

But on the last Friday of February, 1994, there were guards stationed outside those doors as well, and at the rear of the building, and up on the third floor, where the Rosewood hearing was scheduled to begin. At eight-thirty that morning, a full hour before the hearing was set to start, packs of reporters and camera crews were already punching the elevator buttons, asking which way to Room 317.

Richard Hixson had never seen anything like it. The most media attention any of his hearings had ever had was a disciplinary proceeding a few years back, on sexual harassment charges brought against a representative named Fred Lippman. But that was nothing like this. This was national. All the networks were here. Cable, too. Magazines and wire services.

Hixson had reserved the largest hearing room in the building, knowing there would be a crowd. But the room was hardly large enough. By nine o'clock, all seventy seats were filled, and three dozen more onlookers, mostly television camera crews, stood shoulder to shoulder, squeezed along the room's mahogany-paneled walls.

Hixson had not asked for the extra security. That was mainly Martha Barnett's doing. But he was glad the guards were there, for the same reasons Barnett was. This hearing was open to the public, and Hixson had imagined what kind of maniac might show up to make a point, maybe make a name for himself. Arnett Doctor had received enough threats during the previous months, both through the mail and over the telephone, that the FDLE had provided periodic patrols past his home in Tampa. Al Lawson had also gotten several "hate calls," as he put it. Probably just cranks, Lawson said, but Hixson believed they could not be too careful.

Most of all, Hixson was concerned about the witnesses, the survivors. He knew how frightened these elderly men and women were, simply appearing in a setting like this. This was the very thing they had avoided for more than seventy years. This was why they had kept their silence for so long. They did not want to be hurt again by the law, the government, the white people who had punished, then forsaken them so long ago. Hixson wanted these people to know they were safe. He hoped the guards would give them that feeling, but he couldn't be sure. In fact, he realized armed guards might well have just the opposite effect, that they might seem more a threat than a comfort. The sight of white men with guns meant something to the people of Rosewood that no one else could possibly fathom. If there was one thing Richard Hixson understood, it was this.

The witnesses were already upstairs when Hixson arrived, waiting in a private room, along with about a dozen family members. They had all gotten to town the day before, Wilson Hall driving over from Hilliard with his wife and his sister Margie, A. T. Goins coming up from St. Petersburg with his wife and daughter, Willie Evans traveling from Sanford with his son Donnell, and Minnie Lee Langley arriving from Jacksonville with a niece and one of her grandsons.

They stayed at the Radisson, meeting briefly with Steve Hanlon in the afternoon. "This is going to be a long process," he told them, "but I want you to keep in mind, to always remember, that *you* are not on trial here. *They're* the ones who are on trial."

Most of the family took their meals in their rooms that night, avoiding the reporters who had found their way to the hotel and were roaming the lobby. Minnie Lee spent the night at Hanlon's home. She had been hospitalized just the month before with double pneumonia, and she was still weak. There remained a tinge of tension between her and the other survivors. They would always consider Minnie an outsider, not truly a member of the family circle. They had forgiven the claim she and Lee Ruth had filed without them, but they had not forgotten it.

As far as Steve Hanlon was concerned, however, Minnie Lee was going to be the star of this show. He planned to put her on the stand first, to set the stage for the others. If he had a key witness that first day, it was going to be Minnie, and so he took special care of her. His wife Fran made dinner, and when the meal was done Minnie turned to Hanlon and told him he better not leave this woman, because he'd never get cooking as good as this anywhere else.

And now, Friday morning, they were all here, Willie Evans huddled in his wheelchair, and the others, Minnie Lee and A. T. and big Wilson Hall, each perched on the edge of a cushioned waiting room seat, lost in their thoughts, shaking just a little, listening to the hum of the crowd on the other side of the wall, watching Arnett crack open the door every couple of minutes to take a peek and each time he did, hearing the cascade of clicking camera shutters snapping like a swarm of cicadas.

Jim Peters stopped in, introduced himself to the family and survivors, then left to go over his opening statement one last time. Miguel De Grandy came through, told the family how proud he was and what an important day this was, not just for them but for the entire state of Florida. Then he, too, left to go over the remarks he would make as the bill's lead sponsor.

Al Lawson was not there. This time it was *he* who had been pulled out of town by a personal matter. His father, who had battled lung cancer for years, had suddenly died the day before, apparently of a stroke. Lawson had left almost immediately for Midway, where his father was to be buried that weekend.

Before he left, however, Lawson had issued a statement to the press, returning a volley from Jim Peters's office, which had issued a prehearing statement of its own, claiming that Governor Cary Hardee could not be held responsible for trusting the word of the Levy County sheriff after Hardee sent the telegram offering help toward the end of that horrible week. If the sheriff told Hardee that no help was needed, the governor had no reason to doubt him. If anyone was negligent, Peters argued, it was the local authorities, not the state.

Lawson shot back, likening Hardee's lack of response to a modern-day Florida governor sitting back and doing nothing while a hurricane bore down on the state's coast. "How," asked Lawson, "is a governor not responsible when you have a major disaster that you *know* is about to occur, and he does nothing?"

But all the statements and counterstatements were mere preamble. Now it was time for the hearing to begin. The witnesses, surrounded by their relatives, came through the door and the room exploded with flashing camera strobes and the whirr of motor drives.

They took their seats in the front two rows, a mahogany and metal railing separating them from the long hearing table, where the two special masters sat in the center, facing them. Across from the masters, with their backs to the audience, sat the attorneys, Peters and Hanlon. Stationed at one end of the table was a court stenographer, and beside her, the empty seat that awaited each witness.

Hixson called the hearing to order, introduced himself and David Kerns and the attorneys, then invited Miguel De Grandy to step up and make his opening remarks. De Grandy was brief, addressing the main fear of most of his colleagues.

"I have heard that to compensate the victims of the Rosewood massacre would open a Pandora's box," he began. "I have heard arguments, for example, that need we not compensate the Indians for the taking of their lands if we compensate the victims of Rosewood?

"I submit to you that however wrong people may believe those acts were, we were a sovereign nation at war with another sovereign nation and we owed them no legal duty as we owe to our own citizens.

"I have heard," he continued, "that if we compensate the victims of Rosewood, must we not compensate every black citizen in the state of Florida for the crimes committed during slavery? As atrocious and repugnant as you and I and every member of the legislature find slavery to be, there was a time when it was legal. When a human being could be considered property, there could be no deprivation of human or civil rights of that individual.

"There came a time in this country when we as Americans became enlightened. It took a civil war to reread what was written hundreds of years ago, to realize that all citizens *are* created equal and that all citizens are entitled to due process and equal protection of the law.

"And so today, the citizens named in the Rosewood bill come to us as a legislature, either personally or through their descendants, to seek justice—justice not because of the color of their skin but because of their condition as proud, free and equal citizens of this nation and of the great state of Florida. I am convinced as a legislator that when we as a body evaluate the facts and weigh the equities, we will be compelled to find that their cause and their claim is just.

"Thank you, Mr. Hixson."

Then it was Steve Hanlon's turn to speak. Relaxed, conversational, he sounded as if he were chatting with friends in the living room of his own home.

"This is a good day for Florida," he said, addressing the audience as much as the hearing masters. "The old bromide 'Better late than never,' if it was ever applicable, is applicable here today."

Hanlon outlined the briefs both he and Peters had filed, noting that although they might differ about details, he doubted there was any disagreement that this town was attacked, wiped away, and that his clients suffered serious harm. It was the extent and complexity of that harm that Hanlon then honed in on.

"The damage these folks suffered," he said, "is similar to the damage that Holocaust victims suffered and that has endured with them throughout their lives, down to the present day. The Rosewood massacre, from my clients' point of view, is *not* some long forgotten, ancient, unfortunate chapter in Florida's sometimes violent and racially troubled past. It is, and I am convinced you will be convinced of this, a deep, dark present reality in my clients' lives today, tomorrow, and the next day, as it has been for this entire period of time. It has brutally disrupted their lives, and it has changed those lives in ways we will never really fully understand."

The issue, said Hanlon, was not the actual property that was destroyed, the buildings that were burned or the land that was lost.

"The real damage was the loss of that *community,*" he said. "It had its ups and downs, economically, just like everybody else did, but this was a remarkable African-American community, an intact, industrious, self-sufficient community.

"To lose the continuity of that community and be scattered throughout the state and the nation, as these people were, is the core of this damage claim. Literally, as I have said before and I will say it again, the property damage is a pebble on that beach. We will present testimony from an economic expert next week that the amounts sought by the claimants here are remarkably low in terms of the true value of these claims in any American courtroom today."

Hanlon made a point of referring to the Japanese Reparations Act, which had become the basic model for this bill. Then he came to his conclusion.

"Governments which come forward and acknowledge problems in their past, as the United States government has done before and is doing right now with radiation experiments, are *good* governments. It's difficult, but ignoring the problem and pretending it did not exist and hoping it will just go away instead of creatively devising a remedy, which is really what I am urging you to do here in this case, is a serious mistake.

"We *can* devise a remedy here," he said, turning to Hixson and Kerns, "and you *can* make findings about the uniqueness of this situation which will not open the Pandora's box that people have expressed concern about.

"Thank you."

Now it was Jim Peters's turn. He stood, walked around the table and faced the family, the two dozen Rosewood relatives filling the room's front three rows.

"Notwithstanding our differences," he said, "this really *is* a good day for the state. Notwithstanding our differences, I was pleased to be able to meet the claimants today."

Then he turned toward the hearing masters.

"Make no doubt about it, this is a claim about a societal wrong, one of too many such wrongs. I recall approximately fifty or sixty lynchings, violence in which towns were affected, included in the team report, and I will admit that this was a sorry damn period in Florida's history, no doubt about it. Deaths of innocent citizens occurred, property was destroyed, and families were displaced by violence. We should be ashamed of that, and we are.

"I respectfully disagree, however, that insofar as entertaining a claims bill process, Rosewood is really that unique. Whatever damage and trauma were visited upon the claimants—and we'll have the opportunity to prove that later—I respectfully submit that that damage, that trauma, is no greater than the damage or trauma that *other* families of any race who were lynched or murdered or felt that the state's law enforcement powers didn't do justice to them have suffered. It's sad, it's sorry, it's tragic. But I disagree that Rosewood is really unique."

Then he turned back and spoke directly to the families.

"With my apologies," he said, "and I met some of you this morning—Ms. Langley, Ms. Jenkins, Mr. Hall, Mr. Goins, Mr. Doctor, Mr. Evans—I respectfully submit to the special master that you are asking too much of the claims process, too much of the state of Florida, to come forward after over a generation, seventy-one years, and ask this from the state, based upon what we all have to concede is hearsay evidence—family stories revisited in good faith, no doubt—and in the absence of the state officials and county officials who are either implicitly or expressly accused in this claims bill of these wrongs. On behalf of the state, I would say that's not fair.

"The passage of time," he continued, "has precluded the state from being able to respond to your assertions—made in good faith, I am sure—as to what happened.

"I can't," said Peters, turning back toward Hixson and Kerns, "speak through the lips of dead officials."

Then he, too, concluded.

"As a matter of fairness to the claimants, I request that what evidence there is, as flawed as it is, be objectively reviewed today. I welcome the opportunity for the claimants to have a fair hearing. And I am certain this forum will enable the state to have the *same* fair hearing, notwithstanding the emotional appeals with which I sympathize in this case.

"Thank you."

Hixson thanked both attorneys, then asked Hanlon to call his first witness. Gingerly, with gentle pats on her back from family members as she made her way down the front row of seats, Minnie Lee walked to the witness chair. She had on a bright red dress—the same dress she'd worn on the "Maury Povich" show—and her hair was tucked beneath a wig of short silvery curls. Her hands trembled slightly as Steve Hanlon helped her into the seat. He held her shoulder and leaned toward her ear.

"Are you ready?" he whispered. "Are we gonna *get* 'em?"

Minnie nodded slightly, pursed her lips and stared straight ahead. She was sworn in, then Hanlon began, first asking her age, where she was born, who her parents were, her grandparents, what kind of house they lived in, what kind of town Rosewood was. The pace was leisurely, the questions and answers painting a portrait of a serene village, which made it all the more startling, as Hanlon hoped it would, when the subject turned to the night of the shootout at the Carrier house.

"Well," said Minnie, wringing her hands, "I was upstairs with the other children. We was *all* upstairs under the bed."

"Why," asked Hanlon, "were you and all the children upstairs under the bed?"

Minnie paused. For sixty years she had told this story to no one. Then, once she did tell it, it seemed like it never stopped. Lawyers. Television people. Newspaper people. Those college history professors. Everyone asked her to tell the story. Now they were asking again. But this time, she knew, was the one that would matter the most.

"People were shooting at the house," she began, drawing a deep breath, "and they told us to go, brothers and sisters, told us to go under our bed."

It wasn't long after that, she said, that one of her aunts ran up the stairs to say Sarah Carrier had been shot. The hearing room fell dead silent. No clicking of cameras, not even the rustling of reporters writing their notes. They had all stopped writing. They just listened. The only sound was the drone of the air conditioning and Minnie Lee's voice.

"She told us Mama is *dead*, they done *killed* Mama. So we got up, and I crawled up from under the bed, and I went down looking for Mama. I couldn't find Mama, and then Syl grabbed me and said, 'Come on baby, let me save you.'"

Hanlon paused, steering the pace, working the drama.

"Then what happened?" he asked.

"I went in the wood bin with him."

Another pause.

"Then what happened?"

"This old cracker comes looking . . ."

A ripple of titters ran through the audience. Hanlon loved it. It wasn't often that the term "cracker" came up in a setting like this. Hanlon milked it for all it was worth.

"When you say this old *cracker* comes looking through," he said, "are you talking about Poly Wilkerson?"

"Yes," said Minnie Lee. "*All* the crackers come up there looking in, saying 'Come on out of there.'"

"Were there a *lot* of crackers there?"

"Yes, a lot of them out there."

Another pause.

"What happened then?"

"'Come on out of there,' that's what they said. Syl got up under the wood bin, put the gun on my shoulder, told me to lean this way. I leaned over, and then Poly Wilkerson, he kicked the door down. And when he kicked the door down, Cuz' Syl let him have it. He shot him."

"Did he kill him?"

"Yes, he killed him, right in the door."

"What happened next?"

"Another one jumped up there, and Cuz' Syl killed him, too."

Hanlon then turned to the escape, the image of frightened children fleeing into the swamp.

"After Cuz' Syl shot Poly Wilkerson and the other man," he asked, "what happened next? Did you all get out of there?"

"Yes, we had to leave. We wasn't going to let nobody kill us in there."

"Was the gunfire still coming?"

"Yes, it was still coming."

"What did you all do?"

"Jumped and hid, jumped down on the edge of the porch and hid underneath the thing until we can get out of there."

"The *back* porch?"

"Yes."

"How long was it before you ran out of that house?"

"About fifteen minutes."

"About fifteen minutes?"

"Yes, until it got quiet with the bullets."

"It was January of '23?"

"Yes."

"Was it cold?"

"Oh, yes."

"How were you dressed?"

"Naked."

"You don't mean *naked?*"

"We didn't have no clothes."

"Did you have a nightie on?"

"No, we had a gown on, that's all."

"Just a little gown?"

"Mmm-hmmm."

"Now, who all got out of there?"

"All the children did."

"Okay, who was 'all the children'?"

"Twelve of us, about twelve."

"About twelve children?"

"About twelve or thirteen of us was together."

"Did you have an adult with you?"

"Not then."

The reporters were writing now, taking down every word.

"Were you walking through any swamp?" asked Hanlon.

"Yeah. We had to go through the swamp. With the crackers down there shooting, we couldn't walk on no road."

Three days and nights, Minnie said, they hid in the woods. Her Aunt Beulah found them the first night and stayed to take care of them as best she could.

"Did you get some clothes on by this time?" asked Hanlon.

"No, we didn't have no clothes. She covered us with weeds and leaves and stuff. But we didn't have no clothes."

"Did you see these crackers keep coming by those three days?" asked Hanlon.

"Yes. Those crackers were on the road just like an ant."

Another wave of light laughter ran through the room.

"Just like an ant?" asked Hanlon.

"Yes."

Hanlon then took Minnie through her escape by train to Gainesville and through her life over the course of the next half century. Her eyes moistened several times, and Hanlon would stop while she wiped them.

"Did you ever talk about this to anybody?" he asked.

"Unh-unh," she said, shaking her head. "I ain't *never* talked about it."

"Why not?"

"It hurt me. It was just building up in me to just think about how my folks went down and how they killed them and everything. Took everything we had."

Again she wiped away a tear. This time Hanlon did not pause.

"Have you ever talked about this with anybody where you didn't cry?" he asked.

"I don't talk about it to *nobody*."

"Do you talk to your daughter about it?"

"No."

"You have a daughter, don't you?"

"Yeah. She never heard me say a word about it, not to nobody. Never mentioned it to nobody."

"Why not?"

"It *hurt* me. It hurt me because I loved my grandmother and all my grandparents. They was nice to me, would see we were going to school and being clean. Yeah, I *loved* my grandparents. I really do. I love them up until now. I really love them. And I don't want . . ."

Minnie took a breath.

"I *didn't* want nobody to hurt them. Them crackers . . ."

Hanlon glanced over at Peters as he asked the next question.

"I think one thing Mr. Peters is going to ask you and that people would want to know is why didn't you come forward until now to file a claim against the state?"

"I didn't know how to file no claim," said Minnie, lifting her chin. "I am going to tell you, I didn't know *how.* And I wouldn't try to file no claims because I am scared those crackers might come up there and find me and *kill* me up there."

She shook her head.

"I ain't filed no claim. I ain't *tried* to. I just went to work for my living."

Perfect. Steve Hanlon couldn't have asked for anything more perfect than the testimony Minnie Lee Langley gave on the witness stand that morning. By the time she stepped down, Hanlon could see that Hixson and Kerns were both mesmerized. The entire room was entranced. Jim Peters's cross-examination of Minnie Lee was cursory, half-hearted at best. There was nothing he could take her to task for, little he could question without appearing to be a heartless villain.

It was the same with A. T. Goins, who testified next. A. T. talked about the white man his sister Philomena saw rushing from the Taylor house the morning of the alleged rape. He described bumping into dead bodies as he came downstairs to search for his Christmas suit the night of the shootout at the Carrier house. He told of his uncle James coming out of the woods two days later, being seized by the mob, and having to dig his own grave before he was shot to death. And he talked about his life after Rosewood, shining shoes and storing quarters so his daughter could go to college. Again, there was little for Peters to confront.

When Willie Evans was wheeled to the witness table, sunglasses covering his sightless eyes, one hand gripping his cane, his wavy white hair swept back as if the wind were blowing through it, the image alone was as powerful as his testimony. And when Wilson Hall took the stand and described what a heaven on earth his village had been before it was burned—"All we needed was God," he declared, "and God was all around us"—a chorus of *Amens* and *That's rights* burst from the family members.

Then Hanlon brought on his psychologist, a black University of Florida professor named Carolyn Tucker, who detailed the symptoms of post-traumatic stress syndrome shown by each Rosewood survivor she had interviewed, their lifelong struggles with "flashbacks," "emotional numbness," "hypervigilance," and submerged feelings of "stress, fear, terror and helplessness"—all terms Tucker said come straight from the texts.

Finally A. T. Goins's daughter Annette took the stand, testifying to the effects Rosewood had on her father's relationship with her and her mother, how it affected his friendships, how he protected himself and overprotected her throughout their lives. She was never allowed, for example, to spend the night at a friend's house when she was a girl, and she never understood why until she learned about Rosewood. "Even in college," she said, "I couldn't go home with people, like roommates. I could visit, but I couldn't stay for weekends, like roommates do."

There was nothing Jim Peters could do, not on this day. When the session concluded late that afternoon, the hallway outside was filled with hugs and hallelujahs. The family had won, that's how they felt. It was as good as over. Even Steve Hanlon felt that way. He had never seen testimony as compelling as what he witnessed that afternoon. "The greatest day in court in my life," he said.

Jim Peters stopped Hanlon on his way out to acknowledge how strong the survivors' testimonies had been. "Riveting," he said to Hanlon. "Absolutely riveting."

But it was not over. Jim Peters knew it was far from over. This had been Hanlon's day, no doubt about it.

But it was only the first day.

Ambush

Saturday morning, newspapers throughout Florida displayed the drama of the Rosewood hearing across their front pages. By now most of their readers were familiar with the story of the attack; thousands of words had been written about it over the previous year. But Arnett Doctor and Steve Hanlon had been the sources of almost all those stories, making a point of shielding the family members from the press. And so, for most Floridians, this morning gave them their first look at the actual faces of the Rosewood survivors themselves.

The power of those photographs—the frailty of Minnie Lee Langley, the tears of A. T. Goins, blind Willie Evans being wheeled toward the witness stand—was as strong as the headlines and stories that surrounded them.

Jim Peters hardly glanced at the papers. He had more important things to do. He had taken all the punches that first day, and now he was preparing to punch back. Already the answering machine in his office was filling up with phone messages from Levy County, angry calls from white residents demanding that their side of the story be told. By the time Peters arrived at his desk Monday morning, more than a dozen messages were on the machine.

Willie Evans

As it stood, Peters had just two days to counterattack. The hearing's second session was scheduled Tuesday, with the final session set for Friday. Tuesday was a wash as far as Peters was concerned; the only witness scheduled to testify that day was the economist Hanlon had lined up to calculate the claimants' losses— a mere nuisance, in Peters's eyes. He would cross-examine the man and be done with it. His entire focus was on Friday, when he planned to thrust at the heart of the claimants' case, the study team's report. That was his primary target from the beginning.

But now, with those messages on his machine, he realized he might have more ammunition than he thought. Most of the calls were probably dead ends, he knew that. But if there was one voice on that tape that could lead to an actual witness, it was worth extending the hearings to track it down. And so that's what Peters planned to ask for on Tuesday, an extension. Meanwhile, he began returning those calls.

Tuesday's hearing paled compared to the opening session. Gone were the survivors, who had all returned to their homes over the weekend. Gone, too, was the national press; they had gotten the story they came for. What remained were a sprinkling of reporters from state newspapers and television stations, a handful of Rosewood family members, and a couple of dozen curious onlookers, all gathered into a room much smaller than the one Hixson had reserved for the first day. And still there were empty seats.

The session lasted a mere hour and a half. The economist, a man named Stan Smith, whom Hanlon had flown down from Chicago, explained how his company calculates what it calls the "loss of quality of life" for victims of catastrophes. Those calculations, Smith testified, had been used by his company in nearly a hundred court cases, including an ongoing case in California, where four thousand people in a neighborhood near a toxic waste dump site were suing for damages—"A Love Canal–type situation," explained Smith.

In that case, Smith explained, as in every other, he used a formula he had developed himself—based on a combination of property value, wage growth rates, interest rates, ages of each individual and rates of life expectancy—to arrive at a dollar figure for losses suffered over time. In the case of Rosewood, he said, he applied his formula to each survivor listed on the claims bill, as well as to the deceased head of each Rosewood household from which there remained no survivors. His results ranged from a high of $3.1 million for Mary Hall to a low of $423,000 for a deceased Rosewood resident named Queen Pollard, whose offspring were listed on the bill as descendants. Smith's combined calculation for the entire list of Rosewood claimants totaled more than $55 million.

Hanlon felt his point was made. The $7 million his clients were asking was a pittance, he said, and Peters hardly bothered to argue. His cross-examination, again, was cursory. What mattered now was time. His phone calls had already turned up one witness willing to testify, a woman named Margaret Cannon, whose father had been a Levy County deputy sheriff at the time of the attack. There were surely more, but Peters needed time to follow up on them all. And so, after the economist had finished his testimony and Hixson had begun wrapping up the day's proceedings, Peters dropped his bombshell.

"I have another . . ." He paused to pick through his papers. "I have another problem that I can't quite put a finger on right now."

Hixson looked up. So did Hanlon.

"I have received probably a dozen telephone calls from north Florida since the media coverage began," Peters continued. "I'm attempting to make a responsible effort to cull out folks who might have something to say of personal knowledge, and I may be needing to amend my witness list after I meet with these folks."

Hixson paused, said he would decide on Friday, but left Peters with some encouragement. "If we need to take a few more people the following week," Hixson said, calling the day's session to a close, "we'll accommodate you."

Arnett was irate. He saw this as nothing but a stall tactic. Martha Barnett was alarmed. The longer this hearing lasted, the fewer days the bill would have to wend its way through the legislature, and each day was precious at this point. Hanlon, for his part, figured Peters was grasping at straws. The guy was desperate. Let him do what he wanted. This thing was in the bag, that's how Hanlon felt. So he wasn't particularly upset or surprised when Hixson opened Friday's hearing with the announcement that the State's Attorney had submitted a new witness list for that day's proceedings and that Peters had also asked that the hearing be continued for an additional week to contact possible witnesses. Both requests were granted, and then the day's fireworks began.

Peters went straight for the study team's throat, first by getting Eva Jenkins, one of the claimants who had spent her childhood in Rosewood, to acknowledge that a photograph of a burning shack, included in the study team's report and identified as a Rosewood home, was no such thing.

"There was nothing like that home in Rosewood," said Jenkins, studying the photo and shaking her head. "That looks like an *outhouse*. That's not a Rosewood house. No house *like* that in Rosewood."

Doubt. The more doubt Peters raised, the better. When the study team itself took the stand following Jenkins—all of them except David Colburn, who was in Spain at the time—they looked uncomfortable, nervous, out of their element, which they were. Maxine Jones's jaw was clenched as she walked toward the witness table. She hadn't expected anything like this. She thought the team's work had been finished when they turned in their report in December. She was stunned when they were called actually to testify.

And now, as she watched Peters leaf through his copy of their report, its pages bristling with bright yellow Post-It notes, she was terrified. It was clear her work—*their* work—was about to be attacked, lacerated, dismissed as shoddy, sloppy, incomplete. Page by page, paragraph by paragraph, Peters intended to do just that, dissecting the team's methods, their sources, even their choice of words.

He began with the photograph of the burning shack, asking them to respond to Eva Jenkins's assertion. Bill Rogers answered that the photo had been found in a news magazine from the time, that the magazine had identified the shack as a house in Rosewood, and that the team had assumed that identification was correct. "We were really pressed for time," noted Rogers. Peters nodded. *Assumed*. He liked the sound of that word.

Peters spent a full fifteen minutes asking the team to explain its use of the word "posse" in reference to the mob that captured and killed Sam Carter. He noted the legal definition of the term, the fact that men must be legally deputized to become a posse, and he pointed out that there was no indication in the report that anyone was deputized in this case, or that there was even an officer of the law present at the lynching of Sam Carter or at the gun battle at the Carrier house.

"How do we know," said Peters, poking a finger at the report, "if that was a posse, or maybe just a bunch of mad white people?"

It went on like that for more than an hour. Several times Tom Dye almost came out of his seat. He had a temper, and his colleagues knew it. That's why Rogers and Larry Rivers had put Dye between them when the team took their seats at the witness table, so they could hold the kid back. It was Rogers, with

his cool, courtly, southern gentleman demeanor, who took the lead in respond-
ing to Peters. And it was Rogers who answered when Peters stunned the room
with a question no one expected to hear.

"What," Peters asked, focusing on the night of the Carrier house shootout,
"if there was a living witness in Levy County today who could testify under
oath, with cross examination, that he—he and another white gentleman—
were *asked* to come to the Carrier household, because they were trusted, that
they were told that a black prisoner was in custody in that house and that there
were arrangements made to hand over the suspect to them to put in safekeep-
ing because there was trust between the Carriers and these two gentlemen,
who were then killed? What if that person was here to testify? Would that
change your conclusion?"

The wave of shock that ran through the room was almost palpable. Even the
unruffled senior professor looked at a loss for words. When his answer came, it
was halting, almost confused.

"It would be new evidence," said Rogers.

"New material," he added.

He paused.

"It would be important."

Peters had hardly made a dent in his dog-eared copy of the report. He had
hours of questions still left for the study team to answer. But when Hixson
looked at his watch, then dismissed the professors, explaining that there were
other witnesses to get to that day, Peters only mildly protested. He sailed
through the remainder of the session, throwing a few jabs at Arnett Doctor,
who had little to offer as a witness beyond his mother's memories and the
things he had learned about Rosewood from talking to his relatives—all second-
hand information. As was the testimony of Margaret Cannon, who followed
Doctor to the stand to share the story her father had told her years after the attack of how he had been summoned to Rosewood toward the end of that week
and had helped some of the women and children hiding in the woods get
aboard the train that would take them to Gainesville.

That was fine as far as it went, but what mattered most to Peters was the
bomb he had planted that morning. The fuse was now lit, and it was his turn to
open the next day's newspapers with an apparent upper hand.

An ambush. Innocent whites lured to their death. That was the stunning
scenario replayed by reporters, the revelation that the destruction of Rose-

wood might possibly have been brought on itself. That was what Peters's inference boiled down to, and he backed it up by blasting the study team's report in interviews with the press. The document might be fine for historical purposes, said Peters, but it "ain't worth a damn," he said, for determining whether the state should pay this claim. As a matter of fact, he said, the claim itself was hugely inflated, an overblown sack of unsubstantiated exaggerations.

"We're dealing with the *myth* of Rosewood," he told reporters. "I use the word 'myth' not to denigrate the tragedy, but a lot of this myth is just not true. There were deaths at Rosewood, but there was *not* a seven-day reign of terror."

The professors' protest that it was "highly unlikely" that black people in a southern town in 1923 would invite aroused whites to their home in order to shoot them was lost in the furor over Peters's charges. So was Steve Hanlon's attempt to remind reporters that what he called "the core issue here" remained unchanged.

"These people were entitled to police protection and didn't get it," said Hanlon. "Even if the men were invited to the Carrier home and shot, you can't burn down the town and run around shooting people. That's not the remedy."

But Hanlon's words were buried far beneath the headlines and Peters's accusations. All anyone wanted now was to see who this "surprise witness" would be and hear what he had to say. And so Jim Peters packed his gear for a drive down to Levy County to meet the family he was counting on to win him this case.

The family of Poly Wilkerson.

TWENTY-SEVEN

"He Didn't Have a Holster"

Jim Peters headed out that Monday afternoon, after a brief hearing session
in which he put a psychologist of his own on the witness stand to counter
Carolyn Tucker's opening-day assessment that the Rosewood survivors were
suffering from post-traumatic stress disorder. After a quick hour, with Steve
Hanlon's short cross-exam, the psychologist was dismissed, the day's session
was adjourned, Hixson announced they would reconvene Friday, and Peters
rushed home, where he changed into a pair of jeans, grabbed a bag of quarters,
tossed a video camera into the back seat of his white Miata and pointed the car
south on Route 19, toward the green swamp air of Gulf Hammock.

On the seat beside him sat a list of more than two dozen phone numbers,
Levy County callers he hadn't been able to contact yet. Since the hearing's first
day, messages had continued flooding into his office, every caller claiming to
have the true lowdown on Rosewood, and Peters was determined to follow up
on each one. "A living witness," he says, "that's what I wanted."

Short of that, he'd take what he could get if it brought him as close to the
truth as a man named Herb Wilkerson claimed he could take him. Wilkerson

R. L. "Pink" Wilkerson, the brother of Poly Wilkerson, in 1924.

had been cautious when Peters first returned his call. He said he was the grand-son of Poly Wilkerson, that his father James—Poly Wilkerson's son—was a boy at the time of the massacre, that James knew the whole story of what happened that night at the Carrier house, and that he might—*might*—be willing to testify.

The family was upset about what they'd been reading in the papers, said Herb. The stories these black people were telling was not the way it happened at all. He gave Peters a quick sketch of the account his daddy had always told him, how his granddaddy was lured to his death that night, murdered by those black people. But like he said, he wasn't *sure* his daddy was willing to come up to Tallahassee to testify. Their family were private people, Herb said, and they just didn't know if they wanted to be dragged into this mess.

So Peters asked if he could at least come down and meet them, there at their home. Wilkerson hesitated, then said he didn't see why not. When Peters asked for directions, Wilkerson paused again. "Just give me a call when you get down here," he said, "and I'll tell you the way to the house."

It was nighttime, darkness swallowing his headlights, by the time Peters reached the intersection of Routes 19 and 24, a place called Otter Creek. There was a tiny grocery store there, with a pay phone outside. Peters pulled into the gravel lot, got out and dialed Wilkerson's number. Herb answered, said he wasn't far from there, not far at all, but it was getting late and he'd rather they meet in the morning. So Peters found a motel, got to chatting with the desk clerk, said what he was doing, and the man got excited, gave him a few more names to add to his list, people he ought to call if he wanted to know what *really* happened at Rosewood.

First thing the next morning, Peters pulled up to the front porch of a place just off the highway, a tidy, gray woodframe house tucked back among the trees. An aged man, big, with thinning white hair and thick eyeglasses, sat in a rocking chair. He couldn't see too well, he said, as he introduced himself.

"James Wilkerson," he said, extending a large, heavy hand. His son Herb emerged from the house, offered Peters a seat, and they chatted a while, long enough for Peters to feel comfortable asking if the two men might be willing to make a sworn statement right now, this morning. They said they would. Then, as he sat on this porch, at the edge of this swamp, in the middle of this forest, miles from anything resembling a town, Jim Peters realized he needed a notary public.

"Just a minute," he told the Wilkersons. "I'll be right back." And he sped off, back to the grocery store, where the clerk behind the counter shook his head, said he knew of no such thing around those parts, then said Wait a minute, there might be someone over at the phosphate mine, just down the highway a little bit.

Peters floored it, pulling into the company's dirt drive and up to a trailer just as a man was locking up for lunch. Yes, said the man, one of the women working there had a notary's license, but she had just left to go home. Peters asked what kind of car she was driving, which direction she'd gone, then he shot back on to Route 19, raced south, spotted the woman's car up ahead, pulled alongside and waved her over. Ten minutes later, they were both in the Wilkersons' front yard, Peters with his video camera loaded and ready to roll, and the woman, slightly disheveled, standing on the grass, set to swear in the state's witness.

The tape is strange, almost surreal, the sounds of swallows chirping in the treetops as the notary stands awkwardly on the lawn, looking straight at the camera and identifying herself. She is Pamela L. Owens. This is Tuesday, March the 8th, 1994. Sworn testimony is about to be given by Mr. James E. Wilkerson.

Then the lens turns toward the old man. He sits, short-sleeved, in the sun, where his rocking chair has been moved so the camera will have better light. The roar of trucks sweeping past on the highway occasionally interrupts the old man's answers. His voice is gravelly. It quavers slightly, not from nerves but simply from age.

He was born in 1915, he says, in Sumner. His father was named Poly Wilkerson. His name is James. He was the youngest of his family's five children. They called him "Monkey" when he was growing up.

He was seven years old the week the trouble started in Rosewood, he says. He remembers it was a Thursday, early in the afternoon, when "a colored woman come to my daddy's house."

"I was in the yard playin'," he says. "My mother told me to leave."

He doesn't know exactly what transpired that afternoon—"Nothin' but what I was told," he says. But he knows his father met with the woman. Then she left. The family had dinner that night, he says, and then he went to bed. The next time he saw his father was the following evening.

"He was laid on the cooling board in our house, in the hallway." His father was dead, James says, with three loads of buckshot through the head. He had been killed early that morning, he says, but the body wasn't driven back until that night. "By three niggers," he says.

Actually, says Herb, it was a hand-pumped railroad utility car that was used to carry his grandfather's body back from Rosewood. That's part of the testimony the younger Wilkerson gives on the videotape, once he is sworn in after his father is finished. Again Peters remains behind the camera, his voice guiding the interview.

Herb Wilkerson was born in 1941, he says. His grandparents' names were Poly and Mattie. Poly was a "deputy," he says, "a quarter boss" in charge of the "holding cell" at Sumner. "He had the authority," says Herb, with a bit of pride, "to arrest anybody and put them in that holding cell."

Herb says he grew up asking his grandmother Mattie again and again to tell him about Rosewood. "She always told me she'd tell me when I got bigger," he says. "I think it was a bad memory for her."

When he was a teenager, says Herb, he finally heard the story, how his grandfather went to Rosewood that night to bring back the suspected rapist— "To get him out and avoid anyone else getting harmed," says Herb—and how both his grandfather and a deputy from Otter Creek, a man named "Doc" Andrews, were bushwhacked on the steps of the Carrier house. Andrews, says Wilkerson, "took a load of buckshot in the chest." His grandfather took three loads, "in the side of his face."

"But that's not what killed him," says Herb. "He fell backwards, and his neck went over the edge of the front porch, and it broke his neck, and that's what killed my granddaddy."

His grandfather's pistols were still in his pockets when his body was laid out in the hallway of their home, says Herb. "He didn't have a holster," he explains. "And those pistols had never been fired. That's what my grandmother told me."

Herb Wilkerson's grandfather was buried that Saturday, he says, nearing the end of the tape. Jim Peters asks who attended the funeral. As Wilkerson begins to respond, he is cut short by the sound of a screeching cat. Wilkerson is startled. He glances off camera, in the direction of the shriek.

And then the tape is done. Seventeen minutes of testimony from father and son.

Jim Peters had dozens of phone calls yet to make and two days to make them, but he doubted he'd get anything stronger than what these two men had given him that morning.

He just hoped it would be strong enough.

TWENTY-EIGHT

Hands Unknown

W hile Jim Peters was pouring quarters into the pay phones of Levy County, the Rosewood forces were busy back in Tallahassee, mounting yet another offensive of their own. Arnett Doctor, doing what he had learned to do best, began working the reporters. He called a press conference to cry foul about Jim Peters's tactics, claiming the state's attorney was simply stalling, using the clock to kill the bill.

"If he can postpone it long enough or get enough extensions," Arnett announced, "then time will run out and, for all intents and purposes, this claims bill will die."

Martha Barnett realized how critically true that might be. Assuming the Rosewood claim made it out of this hearing with Hixson's recommendation, it would then have to weave its way through a tangle of committees, each of which would have to approve the bill before it could finally arrive before the legislature for a vote.

The problem was that most of those committees had already finished their scheduled hearings for that year's session. They were done. Of the three thou-

Ernest Parham

sand bills filed that January, almost every one had already either been passed or killed by committee. The few that remained to be heard would need special arrangements by the Speaker, and there was no guarantee he would give them. Which was why Barnett went to talk to Bo Johnson that week.

"I wanted to know that we'd be given a chance," she says. "That's all we wanted, was a chance for a fair hearing. And he assured me we'd get it. He made no commitment about his own stand on this bill, but he assured me he was not going to let the clock run out on us. He told me he'd made that message clear to his lieutenants, the committee chairmen.

"He did not want the House of Representatives to be criticized for killing the Rosewood bill on procedure. No matter how long this hearing took, he told me, we were going to get into committee. After that we were on our own, of course, but he assured me we'd get that. We'd get a fair hearing."

Meanwhile, Al Lawson made a move of his own. Jim Peters's suggestion that the Rosewood massacre might have been triggered by the victims themselves had stirred more outrage among the black community than Lawson had seen during his entire career in public office. He wasted no time using that anger to put Peters's feet to the fire.

"We *had* to put him on the spot," says Lawson. "We respected Jim Peters. Still do. But he was bringing up all *kinds* of stuff. We just had to make him back up and think. What are you gonna do? He was putting the heat on us, we had to put the heat on *him.*"

So Lawson called in some of those chips from the meeting he'd staged the previous September with the state's black leaders. He sent out word for them all to respond. He asked for a backlash, and he got it. The strongest, most visible blow came from the state chapter of the NAACP, whose president, T. H. Poole, fired off a letter to the attorney general, with copies sent to the press, calling Peters's tactics "totally indefensible" and his accusation "absolutely ridiculous."

"This position," wrote Poole, "is an affront to the memory of the victims of the Rosewood Massacre in particular and the African-American community in general."

Meanwhile, Steve Hanlon sat back and smiled. He was far from alarmed about Peters's counterattack. In fact, he had little doubt that the bomb Peters planted was going to blow up in his hand.

"I actually thought of going up to him and saying, 'Jim, I don't know if you want to go down that alley.' Going out and getting some witnesses to try to prove that black people egged this on, well, when the headlines came out about that, I think it incensed the average American here in this state, black *and* white. And I think it really put the pressure on Jim. I think it really turned things bad for him."

Still, Hanlon was not about to simply wait for his counterpart to self-destruct. Peters was rooting around for new witnesses, so Hanlon got together with Barnett to do the same. Was there anyone they had missed, anyone they could put on the stand to counter whatever Peters might manage to pull together? They talked it over with Arnett, combed through everything they had, searching for a jewel they might have overlooked. Nothing.

Then they picked up the study team's report. Nothing there, either. They had read the thing more times than they could count, all ninety-three pages. But the appendix, that thick stack of census data and genealogical charts, lynching statistics and interview transcriptions, they had only cursorily looked at that before now. They had assumed all they would need was contained in the main body of the report. And most of it was. But now, as they looked again at the appendix, really *looked,* they realized they had a bomb of their own right under their noses, buried deep in those pages—on page 351, to be exact. The testimony of a man named Ernest Parham.

Hanlon and Barnett knew Parham's name from the main body of the report, where he was mentioned several times. But somehow, through sloppiness or sheer oversight, they had missed the man's significance, the fact that here was an eyewitness to the attack from the attackers' point of view. Hanlon and Barnett's focus had been almost entirely on the survivors. They had never considered the need for this witness. But they needed him now.

Hanlon immediately called Maxine Jones, who had hardly slept since she and her colleagues had been raked over the coals four days earlier. It wasn't Peters's assault on their report that had kept Jones awake. That was upsetting, having her capabilities questioned, her abilities as a historian impugned, but it was Peters's suggestion that the people who lived in Rosewood might have caused their own destruction that tore at Jones's gut. That accusation swept beyond who she was as a historian and cut to the core of what history itself was, what *black* history was in this country.

"My stomach was in knots," says Jones. "I just could not believe that Jim Peters was doing precisely what so many whites have done throughout this nation's history, which is rewriting it in their own terms, either ignoring the victims or making the victims at fault. That didn't sit well with me. It just ate me up that this was happening *again,* that black history was being rewritten yet again at the expense of the victims."

Jones gave Hanlon David Colburn's phone number, since Colburn had been the study team member who had interviewed Ernest Parham. Colburn then called Parham and asked if he'd be willing to meet with this attorney. Parham said sure, and Hanlon caught the next flight down to Orlando. When he returned to Tallahassee that afternoon, it was with a promise from Parham that he would be at the capitol Friday morning, ready to testify. No, Parham told Hanlon, he didn't need a hotel room. He'd just as soon stay with his brother, who lived up around there.

True to his word, Ernest Parham was there that Friday morning as Richard Hixson called the fifth session of the Rosewood hearing to order. Jim Peters had his videotape in hand. His interview with the Wilkersons had indeed been all he was able to bring back from his three-day sojourn to Levy County. He began the morning by asking the masters to view it. He also offered to bring James Wilkerson himself up the following week to testify in person. Finally, he noted that the study team was not off the hook, that he had eighteen pages of interrogatories he expected them to answer in writing.

Hixson said he'd look at the tape later. The study team questions would be taken care of as well, he said. But right now they had a witness to hear. And so Ernest Parham, wearing a light tweed sportscoat, a soft sweater vest and a neatly-knotted necktie, was called to the witness chair.

Again, Steve Hanlon began nonchalantly, asking Parham his age, and how he spent his time these days. Parham responded just as casually. He talked about his yardwork, about the occasional hand or two of blackjack he played with friends, and the baseball games he enjoyed taking in every now and again.

Then Hanlon turned to Parham's boyhood, beginning with his birth in 1904 in a town called Oxford, then on to the death of his father in Cedar Key in 1912, his mother's remarriage, and the family's move to Sumner in 1914. Hanlon asked about the hotel in Sumner, and the company commissary where Parham went to work as a teen. Then he asked Ernest Parham to recount what happened that week in 1923.

Still casual, totally relaxed, Parham described that first day, the rush of customers charging into the store to ask for shotguns and ammunition. His manner was so low-key, so matter of fact, that by the time he came to the events of that evening, when he drove the deputy sheriff's car over to Rosewood, no one was prepared for the impact of what they were about to hear, what no witness in this hearing had described until then, what few people in that room, or anywhere, would expect to hear in their lifetime—an eyewitness account of a lynching.

"What time of day was it now?" asked Hanlon.

"This was approximately eight o'clock," Parham answered.

"Pretty dark out in January?"

"Pretty much, yes."

"When you were there by Deputy Williams's car, did you know—could you *hear* a crowd ahead, a quarter mile, a half mile away?"

"Yes."

"Did you know something was going on up there?"

"That's right."

"What did you think was going on up there?"

"Well, I assumed it was the group which was following the dogs."

"Did you say anything to Deputy Williams then?"

"Yes. I told him I had driven his car up and told him where it was."

"Did you then go up ahead to where the crowd was?"

"Yes, I did."

"Did you have a sense, when you were back there with Deputy Williams, that there was anything wrong going on up where that crowd was?"

"Why, sure."

"Why did you have that sense? What was going through your mind at the time?"

"Well, at the time I really didn't know *what* was going on up there, but I knew that there was a crowd up there."

"You heard a lot of noise?"

"Of course."

"So you wanted to go up and find out what was going on, is that right?"

"Right."

"And you did that?"

"I did."

"And you walked up there?"

"That's right."

"When you got up there, what was going on?"

"Well, they had Sam Carter strung up on a tree limb."

The room tensed. Richard Hixson leaned closer, as if he weren't sure he was hearing this. He hadn't expected to hear this.

"Now Sam Carter," said Hanlon, "who was he?"

"Who *was* he?"

"Yes, sir."

"Well, Sam Carter was a black man that lived in the neighborhood, and this was across the street from—across the *road* from—his home."

"Did you know Sam Carter?"

"Yes, I did. Not personally, but I knew who he was."

"What did you think of him?"

"Well, he was a very fine fellow. Everybody thought real well of him."

"When you say he was strung up, was there a noose around his neck?"

"That's true."

"And a rope over the limb on the tree?"

"That's true."

"And was he pulled up in the air?"

"Well, he was pulled up, but his tiptoes was still on the ground as I came up."

"And the deputy sheriff was still sitting back about a quarter to a half-mile away?"

"That's right."

"Did he ever come up to find out what was going on here?"

"Did he find *out?*"

"Yes."

"Well, now, that I couldn't say."

"Well, while you were there, did you ever see the deputy get off of the running board of that car and come up to see what was going on with that crowd?"

"No, I did not."

"When you got up there to where the crowd was, and you saw Sam Carter hanging there kind of on his toes with the noose around his neck, what was the next thing you saw or heard?"

"Well, I happened to walk right into it, and they had Sam strung up and they was asking him questions."

"What were they asking him?"

"Asking him where he put the fugitive—the black man—out of his wagon. Apparently he had refused to tell them up to that time. And I understood later that they had strung him up about three times, and then they let him down, and he would not tell them. So this particular time when I walked up, I didn't realize I was right into it. And this particular fellow had him strung up, and he was choking, and this fellow was beating him on the chest trying to make him talk. And I said, Well, how can he talk when you're *choking* him? So he let him down. And when he let him down, he kind of fell to his knees. And then he got up, and he said, Yes, he'd tell them."

"Now, was there a man there that had his hand on the rope?"

"That's true."

"Did that man have anything else in his hands?"

"Well, he had a shotgun."

"When he let him down, did he say anything to Sam Carter?"

"Yes, he said, If the dogs don't pick up the trail where you put this fellow out, I'm going to shoot you."

"What happened next?"

"Well, we went about a mile from there, following through the woods, following this man Sam Carter and the fellow who had the gun, to where Sam Carter said, This is where I put him out of the wagon."

"And then what happened?"

"Well, the dogs did not pick up the trail. So he shot him."

Richard Hixson almost came out of his seat. It had been one thing to hear the survivors, who were small children at the time, describe the chaos, confusion and killing that swept through the Carrier house the night of that attack. But this was different. None of those children could name their attackers, none of them knew who was shooting to kill them. They were inside the storm. But this man was outside it. This man was a witness to murder. He watched a killer, and he watched a killing.

Hanlon went on.

"Was Mr. Pillsbury there?"

"I was standing beside him."

"What was Mr. Pillsbury's position?"

"He was general superintendent of the Cummer Lumber Company."

"Were you surprised when this man shot . . ."

"Well, we were *all* surprised. Had no idea. We thought it was just threats. We had no idea he was going to shoot him."

"Did the crowd disperse after that?"

"It did, yes."

"Do you know if the deputy sheriff came up and did anything?"

"I did not see him."

"Was there a coroner's verdict the next day or two?"

"Yes, there was."

"And what was the coroner's verdict?"

" 'Killed by hands unknown.' "

"And what was your reaction when you heard that?"

"Well, we were surprised."

"How many people were in that crowd?"

"At the time of the shooting?"

"Yes, sir."

"About twenty-five or thirty."

Richard Hixson did not move back from the edge of his seat for the remainder of Parham's testimony, which went on for two hours more. Beyond compensation, there was now a new aspect to this claim, to the state's responsibility in this matter, and that was the issue of criminal investigation. The fact that there was a witness to murder here, and that the murderer—or murderers— might possibly be out *there,* was something Hixson had not considered until now.

When Parham mentioned that the Florida Department of Law Enforcement had recently sent two agents to his home to interview him, Hixson jolted. And when, near the end of Hanlon's interrogation, Parham again mentioned the inquest conducted the day after Sam Carter was shot, Hixson stepped in.

"Let me understand something," said Hixson. "The very next *day* you heard there was an inquest?"

"Yes," answered Parham.

"But no one talked to *you,* no law enforcement official?"

"Right."

"You witnessed a killing, right?"

"Right."

"And no one talked to you from law enforcement over all these years, until two weeks ago?"

"No."

"You were never contacted by a state attorney, a deputy sheriff, a police-man, *nothing* in regard to this killing?"

"No."

"Not until two weeks ago?"

"That's right."

And that was that. Three hours had gone by like three minutes. Not only had Ernest Parham's testimony bolstered the families' claim for compensation, with his depiction of Rosewood as a healthy, viable community, but he had added the dimension of murder, something neither the claimants nor the state had considered. It was possible that the men who committed this crime and other killings that week might still be alive, and if they were, it was the state's duty to pursue charges against them.

It had been only three years since the conviction in Mississippi of Byron De La Beckwith, the man who murdered Medgar Evers back in 1963. That case had reminded the nation that there is no statute of limitations on murder. Medgar Evers was dead almost thirty years before his killer was brought to jus-tice. It didn't matter that that killer had become a frail old man. Neither, knew Richard Hixson, did it matter in this case that it had been more than twice that long since the killings at Rosewood occurred. Though there was little chance that any of the assailants were still alive, if the possibility existed that they were, then the state was bound to pursue it.

Hixson watched Jim Peters's videotape that afternoon. And, a week later, he listened to James Wilkerson share from the witness stand the same story he had told on the tape, the story his mother had told him from the time he was a little boy.

And then it was over. The study team's responses to Peters's questions, said Hixson, had yet to be completed and would have to be dealt with by whatever House committee cared to look into them. There was no more time to wait. Friday morning, March 18, the final session of the Rosewood hearing was ad-journed. The special master's report was due on the Speaker of the House's desk Monday afternoon. That gave Richard Hixson three days to write it. One weekend, really.

He had a lot of running to do.

TWENTY-NINE

A Moral Obligation

R ichard Hixson had no doubt he was going to recommend that the legislature pass the Rosewood claims bill. He had been as thunderstruck by the
emotional impact of the survivors' testimony on the hearing's first day as
everyone else who was there to witness them. Beyond the drama of the stories
told by Minnie Lee, A. T. Goins, Willie Evans and Wilson Hall, Hixson was ut-
terly convinced of their sincerity.

"I'd read the testimonies in the report," he says, "but reading the words is
one thing, and seeing them spoken is another. There's nothing quite the same as
seeing living, breathing human beings tell their stories. How a person says
something—not just *what* he says, but the *way* he says it—goes a long way toward judging a witness's credibility. It's like old Justice Potter Stewart put it:
'You know it when you see it.'

"You could see it in each of these people. There was a dignity to all of them,
a grace, and an obvious honesty. When they were talking about their lives, they
spoke as adults, but when they went back to describe Rosewood, they began to
speak as *children* would speak. The terms they used changed. Even the way they

Arnett Doctor and Al Lawson

spoke, their inflection. It was as if they were *there* again. You can't coach something like that."

Hixson thought about that that weekend. And he thought about motive.

"There was no doubt in my mind that these people were not here for money," he says. "I truly don't think they cared about compensation. I think they simply wanted the truth to be known about what happened to them. That was very clear to me that day. You can get a sense of people who are trying to tell you what they think you want to hear, to better their case. But that was not the case here. I truly think they didn't care whether they got fifty cents or a hundred and fifty million dollars. It didn't matter."

As for the factual basis of the claim, the doubts surrounding the details of the events that took place that week, Hixson was convinced, despite the flaws that might exist around its edges, that the heart of the study team's report was reliable. It was true. The town had been savaged; people were killed—at least eight, perhaps more; the state was aware of the events as they transpired and did not respond to prevent them; and after the attack, the state neither pursued prosecution—beyond the cursory grand jury investigation—nor did it protect and attempt to restore the property to its owners. It was the issue of law enforcement and prosecution, raised most of all by Ernest Parham's testimony, that hit Hixson hardest.

"You try to be detached and objective," he says, "to simply listen carefully and show no visible reactions. But sometimes it's hard. The point when Mr. Parham began describing the lynching was one of those times. It came in a such a manner that I wasn't quite sure I was hearing what I was hearing. I had *expected* the other witnesses' descriptions, the survivors', to be about what they were about. But Mr. Parham was so low-key, so reasonable. He was just going along, and I was just making notes, and then, suddenly, he was describing this killing. I remember rising up in my chair and saying, 'Wait a minute, are you telling me you observed a *murder?*' That was one of those moments you never forget. It will always stand out in my mind."

Parham's reference to the inquest of Sam Carter's death was supported by a copy of the coroner's verdict, dated January 2, 1923, produced by the study team:

In the peace of God then, we the Jury, after the Examination of the Said Sam Carter, who being found lying Dead, find that the said Sam Carter came to his Death by being shot by Unknown Party so say we all.

Incredible, thought Hixson, as was the fact that no charges were ever brought by the state for the other killings that occurred that week—the deaths at the Carrier house the night of January 4, and the deaths of Lexie Gordon, James Carrier and Mingo Williams. Nor was there any investigation into acts of arson or theft.

Ernest Parham testified to the study team and at the hearing that he would rather not identify the man who shot Sam Carter. Nor did he name the other members of the mob he saw that night. Some of them might still be alive, he explained—though he doubted it—and he said he would just as soon not disturb them or their families after all these years. What would be the point? But of course, he added, that was only if the choice were his. If the law required, he said, he would certainly name everyone he could remember. Hixson was determined that the law require it, that an order for a criminal investigation be included as part of the Rosewood bill. "Regardless of how anyone feels about compensation," he explains, "no one would think a crime should be left unprosecuted."

The issue of the passage of time, the question raised by Jim Peters as to why these victims had waited seventy years to file this claim, why they had not pursued their case at the time, when the crimes occurred and the accused could defend themselves, was, in Hixson's opinion, no issue at all.

"Civil rights laws were effectively on the books beginning after the Civil War," he says, "but they were never given any real meaning as far as claims and causes of action, by Supreme Court decisions and such, until you saw the Warren Court come forward beginning in the 1950s. Those laws *certainly* had little meaning back in the 1920s."

"And besides," he adds, "these people were *children* at the time."

There was, concluded Hixson, undeniable damage suffered by the people who survived the attack on Rosewood as well as the descendants of the survivors and the dead. The state, he concluded, had been negligent and now had a "moral obligation" to compensate the victims.

And so, the final issue Richard Hixson had to grapple with that weekend was the same one faced by the claimants themselves when their bill was written.

How much? And how many?

The Rosewood bill as filed was by far the largest equitable claims bill Hixson had ever faced. No such claim in the history of Florida came close to the seven million dollars the Rosewood claimants were asking. Hixson knew the legislature would never seriously consider, much less pass, this bill for that amount. Most House members he had spoken with, as well as his boss, Robert Trammell—whose Judiciary Committee would be the Rosewood bill's first stop on its journey through the legislature—had made it clear this bill would almost certainly sink if it stayed at seven million. Hixson had to somehow slice that figure down to an amount the legislature could swallow, while still honoring the claimants with an amount of compensation that adequately reflected and respected the damage they had suffered.

He began by dividing the claimants into two categories—the actual survivors, and the descendants of victims or survivors who were now deceased. For those descendants, the only tangible loss from the attack on Rosewood was the property that their forebears had owned. The precedent Hixson looked to to compensate such a loss was the same model Hanlon and his colleagues had used to write their bill—the Japanese-American Reparation Act of 1988. That law directed that each Japanese-American citizen who lost his home and land during the internment that occurred during World War II would be given an apology and twenty thousand dollars by the federal government.

Using that figure and the fact that there were roughly twenty-five households identified in Rosewood at the time of the attack, Hixson came up with a round number of $500,000. He recommended that a fund of that amount be included in the bill, from which payments would be made to each family that could prove its relatives lost property during the 1923 attack. Those payments would be $20,000 apiece, with the state authorized to increase that amount up to $100,000 for each claim in which the value of the lost property was shown to be higher than twenty thousand.

As for direct compensation, Hixson decided it should be paid only to the survivors, with survivors defined as people who were physically present—actually living in Rosewood—at the time of the attack. That meant that Lillie Washington, Berthina Fagin, Thelma Hawkins, Eva Jenkins and Vera Hamilton were out as survivors. They would now be considered descendants.

To decide the amount of compensation for each survivor, Hixson again searched for a precedent, a similar situation, something that could give him a fix on how much to award in a case like this. But there was no other case like this. Rosewood was spectacularly unique, not only in the annals of Florida's legal history but in the nation's legal history as well. There was no model to which Hixson could turn to answer the issue of money. "This was the most difficult question I faced," he says. "What number do you come up with, and how do you defend it?"

He decided to go back through every claims bill he had ever judged, looking hard at those that involved injuries to children. "Because that's what these people were," he says again. "They were *children*."

He finally found what he was looking for in a claims bill from the early 1980s, filed by the guardian of a young girl in Tampa who had been removed from her home by the state when she was three years old. The reason she had been removed was physical abuse. For the next five years, until she was eight, the girl lived in a series of foster homes where further abuse occurred, causing permanent physical and psychological damages. The girl was twelve when the bill was filed and the claim came before Hixson. It charged that the state social services agencies responsible for monitoring the girl's care in those foster homes had been derelict in their duties. The claim asked for fifty thousand dollars, which Hixson approved. When the bill then went before the legislature, the lawmakers not only passed it, but they tripled the amount of compensation to one hundred and fifty thousand dollars.

"That happens," says Hixson of the increased award. "It doesn't happen often, but it happens."

One hundred and fifty thousand dollars. That was the figure Hixson decided to write in for each of the Rosewood survivors. By Sunday afternoon, Hixson had finished the basic draft of his report—"The guts of it," he says—including the stipulation that a college scholarship fund be established for Rosewood families and descendants.

Monday morning—March 21, the first day of spring—it was done, the House special master's final report, fifteen single-spaced pages ending with the conclusion that "a moral obligation exists on the part of the State of Florida to remedy this matter" and recommending a total payout of $2.1 million. The report was addressed to the Honorable Bo Johnson, with copies made for Al Lawson and Miguel De Grandy, Steve Hanlon and Jim Peters.

Hanlon rushed to Hixson's office to pick up his copy, sat down right there to read it, and by the time he turned to the last page, he felt like a hole had been blown through his gut. On the one hand, he was awash with elation. This was a victory, a tremendous step toward winning the claim in the legislature. In Hanlon's opinion, Richard Hixson had shown the wisdom of Solomon. But the family. Hanlon could only imagine how they were going to respond. And Arnett. He didn't even *want* to imagine what Arnett might do.

He didn't have to. Arnett showed up with Martha Barnett while Hanlon was on his way out of the building. Hanlon handed him the report and held his breath. Arnett read it, standing there in the hallway, and when he finished, he exploded, his voice careening down the Capitol corridors.

"Take it, *take* the goddamned thing," he shouted, thrusting the paper back at Hanlon. "This is *your* goddamned bill now, not mine. You do what the hell you want to do with it. I'm *finished.* I'm *through.*"

And he stormed out.

But he wasn't finished. Hanlon was in De Grandy's office that afternoon, talking to some of the newsmen who had already gotten their own copies of the report, when he got a phone call from his office telling him he might want to know that Arnett was over there, that he had prepared a statement blasting Hixson's decision, and he was getting set to fax copies out to the press.

"Put him on the phone," said Hanlon.

Arnett came on the line.

"Look," said Arnett. "I'm not gonna take this. *We're* not going to take this. We've watched this thing get chopped down and chopped down, and now we've got people getting cut *out. My family.* Aunt Vera and Eva and Lillie Washington, what am I supposed to say to *them?* How am I supposed to tell them they don't *count?* We've already compromised, we've compromised more than we should ever have to. This isn't about money, it's about justice. And *respect.* This is an insult. That's what it is, an *insult.* Two million dollars? People get more money than that for spilling a cup of coffee on themselves at a *McDonald's.*"

Hanlon heard him. He understood. But the first question he asked was whether that fax had gone out.

"Not yet," said Arnett.

"Okay," said Hanlon. "Now listen. I know how you feel. We all do. But I'll tell you this right now. If you send that thing out, we're dead. We can all just go home. And you can tell your uncle he's not getting his hundred and fifty G's. If that's what you want, if you want to go back to him, to all the survivors, and tell them you've taken that away from them, that you've taken away any justice they might ever hope to have, then go ahead. If you want to live with that, go ahead. Do it."

The line was silent.

Hanlon went on.

"Or you can suck it up, Arnett. You can praise what Hixson's done here, and we can all go forward and we can *win* this thing."

The line was still silent. But Arnett had listened. He hung up and began calling the family. The survivors were fine. Richard Hixson had been right. Money was not the issue for them. Two hundred and seventy thousand dollars. A hundred and fifty thousand. Either was fine with them. But the younger generations, the descendants, some of them were as furious with Arnett as Arnett had been with Hanlon.

For many of them, it *was* the money. This had become something that could make a difference in their lives, more money than most of them had ever imagined having. They *hadn't* imagined it at first, hadn't believed it could actually happen when this whole thing began. But once they heard the numbers, saw them in the newspapers, had neighbors and friends asking about it, as if they'd won the lottery, it had become real. Arnett had warned them, and Steve Hanlon, too, that there was a long road ahead and a lot could happen, but still, it seemed real.

And now, just like that, it was gone. Just like that, something they felt was theirs had been snatched from their hands, taken away, *again,* just the way it was taken away in Rosewood.

And they blamed Arnett.

"That was when it started," he says. "The whispering. The finger-pointing. I'd sold them out, that's what some of them started saying. I hadn't stood my ground. I'd given up. That's the way they saw it. No matter that I didn't have anything to *give* up, that the state held all the cards. Some of the family were telling me I should've negotiated, when I had nothing to negotiate *with.*

"Take it or leave it, that's what I ended up telling them. We're going to try to get the most we can out of this for the *survivors,* if no one else, that's what I said. This started with the survivors, the ones who were *there,* and that's who we are all responsible to in the end. If in the course of pursuing justice for them, we can get any benefits at all for ourselves, the direct descendants, then that's gravy. That's what I told them. That's what I told everyone."

That, essentially, is what Arnett wound up telling the reporters that Monday afternoon. And when Tuesday's newspapers came out, with Hixson's decision in the headlines, and quotes of gratitude and praise from Steve Hanlon and

Martha Barnett, Arnett Doctor was right there as well, weighing in with his own kind words for the special master.

Steve Hanlon's work was essentially done. It was up to Barnett now to carry the ball into the legislature. And Richard Hixson's work was done as well. He came home that Tuesday evening exhausted, slumped into a chair and punched the button on his answering machine. He always had two, maybe three calls waiting when he got home from work. Rarely were there more than that.

But this night, the tape was filled. And the calls were ugly, strangers' voices telling Hixson how they felt about what they'd read in that morning's newspaper and how they felt about him. Some of the calls came close to threats, but only one really disturbed Hixson—the one that mentioned his dog, Jennifer. How would someone even *know* about Jennifer?

There had been a newspaper story written just the week before about the hearing and about Hixson, and about the thirteen-year-old Pomeranian he'd inherited from a friend, how he'd fed his pet carryout ribs and Chinese food till it had gotten too fat to join him any more on his evening runs. That was Jennifer. That must have been where this caller learned her name.

His colleagues at the Capitol were amazed Hixson still kept his number in the book. He'd never thought twice about pulling it, getting an unpublished listing. But he was thinking about it now.

THIRTY

Good Friday

The waning weeks of a state legislative session resemble a battlefield in the times of trench warfare, an ugly landscape littered with the carcasses of lobbyists and laws, some mortally wounded, moaning with the last gasps of life, others nothing but corpses, limp casualties to be tossed aside or simply stepped over as weary waves of survivors rise again and again, day after day, over the top and into the breech, a blizzard of bodies and bills, lawmakers and lobbyists alike surging down corridors, shoving into committee rooms, launching salvos of faxes and phone calls, cornering one another in offices, in lunchrooms, on the toilet if that's what it takes, anything to get a minute or two to bend a vote their way.

So many votes, on so many bills. That spring of 1994, more than three thousand proposed laws washed through the halls of the Florida capitol. Some stood out more than others, foaming whitecaps bursting above a roiling sea of more mundane matters.

There was a bill to castrate convicted rapists, and one to ban nudity on public beaches. There was a proposal to pay women on welfare to use birth con-

---

A. T. Goins with daughter Annette Shakir

trol, and another to bar protesters from blockading abortion clinics. A bill to allow prayer in public schools was filed alongside a bill to allow paddling as well. There was a bill to punish people who spread lies about Florida oranges. And a bill to clean up the Everglades. And a bill to build more prisons. And one to ban assault weapons. There was a bill to honor the Florida State Seminoles for winning the 1993 national collegiate football crown and a bill to designate Collier County the "Purple Martin Capital of Florida."

This was the tempest into which the Rosewood claim was tossed that first day of spring. Compared to the $700 million asked to clean up the Everglades, the $300 million it would take to build the proposed prisons, or the $821 million insurance subsidy plan that was at the heart of the Governor's massive health-care proposal, the $2 million asked by the Rosewood claimants was a mere speck in a sandstorm—one two-hundredth of one percent of the $38 billion proposed budget on the table that March.

Not that two million dollars was irrelevant, especially in committees, but on the basis of money alone, Rosewood would not seem a priority. Beyond that, the bill had already gone through the scrutiny of a hearing master, which typically meant a rubber stamp from the legislators. "Members have told me that in the past," says Richard Hixson, "that their policy is generally to vote whichever way the master's recommendation comes down, favorable or unfavorable."

But this case was clearly different.

"I was stunned by how many members came to see me about this, to ask, 'How could you *write* this?'" says Hixson. "I'd say, 'Read it. Just *read* it.' And they did. Almost all of them actually read the report, which is not always the case."

And they talked about it.

"They weren't talking about anything *else*," says Al Lawson. "With health care, the prisons, the environment, all those things in the air, all you heard people talking about was Rosewood."

Martha Barnett had more than a little to do with that. From the day the bill was filed in December, she had been sowing Rosewood's seeds, planting the issue with every lawmaker she could corner, beginning with the governor himself, Lawton Chiles. Chiles, who was hand-picked by none other than Spessard Holland back in 1970 to fill Holland's vacated seat in the U.S. Senate, had a long history of support for civil rights issues. But at the time the Rosewood bill was filed, there was no telling which way he might lean.

Late that January, one of Barnett's partners at Holland and Knight hosted an evening cookout. "Nothing fancy," says Barnett. "Blue jeans, real casual." Among the four or five couples there were Lawton Chiles and his wife Rhea. "Naturally the subject of Rosewood came up," says Barnett. "Everybody wanted to know about it, Mrs. Chiles in particular. The governor was pretty quiet, but she was asking a lot of questions."

Two weeks later, before Hixson's hearing had even begun, the governor issued a letter to the president of the Senate and the Speaker of the House endorsing the Rosewood bill, saying he would sign it if the legislature passed it.

So Barnett had a bit of momentum as she hit the capitol corridors that March, joining the mob scene that began each morning at eight. "I made a list, mostly of leadership people" she says, "and every day I'd mark six to eight names and say, Okay, these are my Rosewood contacts today. I couldn't wait until the committee meetings were scheduled. I had to lay a lot of groundwork beforehand. If I was lucky, I'd get ten, maybe fifteen minutes with each person, just enough time to touch base and maybe do a little educating."

In his own less polished but just as determined way, Arnett Doctor became a self-styled lobbyist, a daily presence in the halls of the capitol. Holland and Knight footed the bill for his room at the Radisson, and each morning he would rise at five, take a short stroll, grab a whirlpool, get dressed, be at the door to the hotel's restaurant when it opened at six, and swallow his breakfast while rifling through a stack of the state's newspapers, scissors in hand, clipping every item he could find about Rosewood. Then he'd head over to the capitol, where his day, like everyone else's, began about eight and lasted till midnight, when he would return to the hotel, catch a few hours' sleep, rise the next morning and do it all over again. Nobody knew who he was at first, this tall, intense black man stalking the halls of the capitol. But they learned.

"I had to be there," says Arnett. "They needed to *see* me. I needed to be on the scene, physically present, every *day*. Even if I didn't talk to them, if I didn't talk to *anybody*, I was going to be *seen*, to remind them of Rosewood, to let them know they were not going to be able to just forget about this. They were going to have to face it. They were going to have to deal with it. I was there to be a reminder, a committed African-American individual, in the flesh, in their faces, every day."

They noticed. There was no way they could not notice.

"Arnett was squaring off against *everybody*," says Al Lawson. "People were coming up to me and saying, 'Al, keep this guy Doctor away from me, get him

off my *back.'* Arnett definitely tested people's patience, but he was also a reminder of the personal side of this bill, that this thing was about living breathing people. That was important."

In the early going, Martha Barnett was hardly more welcome than Arnett.
Mostly she got cold shoulders and the waves of impatient hands, which didn't
put her off in the least. That was what she expected. She smiles even now, re-
calling the brushoffs from conservatives like Everett Kelly, from down in
Tavares, and Fred Dudley, from Cape Coral.

" 'Martha, I love you,' they'd say to me, 'but there isn't any way in the *world*
I'm voting for this bill.' All of them were against it at that point. They just
couldn't see spending money on something that happened seventy years ago.
They just didn't want to open that can of worms. The best I'd get was, 'Let's
wait and see what the master says. I always go along with the master.' "

More disturbing to Barnett was the lack of support, or even interest, shown
by the black caucus. If there was one base of strength Barnett thought she could
count on, it was the black leadership, but when she arranged a breakfast meeting with the group a week before Hixson's hearing began, to go over their plan
of attack, a mere four members showed up.

"Four out of nineteen," says Barnett. "I was shocked. I couldn't believe it."

So Al Lawson had to weigh in again, gathering the group and delivering the
message that had become almost a mantra during the preceding year. "I told
them it was time," he says. "Till then we'd always been Democrats first and
blacks second, and we went along with the Democrat agenda whether we believed it or not. We were afraid to step on toes, and they knew that. They figured the caucus was in their pocket, that blacks didn't even need to be
consulted. And they were basically right.

"I said if we don't change and focus on an issue like this, then we're failing
the people who *put* us here, we're failing the NAACP and the purpose of reapportionment, which was to make a difference in our people's lives instead of
just getting by and going along. If there was ever a time for us to earn respect as
a force to be reckoned with, it was now."

By the time Hixson's report was issued, the black caucus was on board. And
they had to be, because what Barnett had been told by so many of the lawmakers she'd met with—that they would take the master's recommendation and
vote his way—turned out not to be so. The day the report came out, the voices
of opposition were loud and harsh.

"This is a very, very sad part of Florida history, just as the Civil *War* is a very, very sad part of United States history," said Charlie Williams, an insurance salesman whose district included Levy County and the man who would spearhead the fight against Rosewood if it made it to the Senate. "We can't just back up and make everyone whole who's been hurt by injustices," he said.

"I simply don't want today's taxpayers to be responsible for something that happened decades ago," said George Crady, a fifty-two-year-old veteran legislator from Yulee, up near Wilson Hall's home in Hilliard. Crady was one of the first people Martha Barnett had talked to about the Rosewood bill and now he had become one of its chief critics.

Randy Mackey, a real-estate developer from Lake City, who would also become one of the leaders of the opposition, was as succinct as possible. "I'm not supportive of giving the survivors of Rosewood *anything*," he said.

Dozens of voices echoed the same feelings. Beryl Burke, an attorney and female black caucus member from Miami—one of two blacks on the crucial twenty-four-member Judiciary Committee—tried to counter by arguing that, far from asking too much, the Rosewood families had already sacrificed more than they should by watching their claim sliced to $2 million. "When it comes to minorities," said Burke, "we always seem to be looking for an avenue where, instead of giving people what they rightfully deserve, we try to justify just a little bit here and there."

But Burke's words were lost among howls of protest from many of her fellow legislators. So were the sentiments of newspaper editorials across the state, which generally supported the bill even as their readers overwhelmed the letters to the editors pages with complaints against it.

"For the state of Florida to compensate survivors of Rosewood for something that happened seventy-plus years ago," wrote a reader of the *Orlando Sentinel,* "is comparable to reimbursing my family because our family home was burned down a hundred and thirty years ago by Quantrill's raiders during the Civil War. Sounds dumb, doesn't it?"

"Rosewood wasn't the bleakest chapter in Florida's history," wrote another, "because before Rosewood were the Indians of Florida. Maybe Florida should make Rosewood a reservation for the survivors like they did for the Indians. Just a thought."

One reader linked the killings at Rosewood to the recent spate of murders on Florida's interstate highways:

If that bill is justified, then I propose that the same legislature enact similar bills to compensate white victims of black crimes, such as the British man who was shot and killed at the rest stop on Interstate 10, or the German family whose wife/mother was brutally murdered in Miami. These crimes, or "massacres," were committed by blacks on whites. Is the state only responsible for protecting blacks or other minorities?

This was going to be a dogfight, no doubt about it. And the toughest road-block was the first one, two days after Hixson submitted his report, when the Rosewood bill went before Robert Trammell's Judiciary Committee, generally regarded as the most conservative committee in the House. Trammell, a North Florida attorney and former college basketball coach, had already made it clear he was against this bill. Normally that would have been enough to kill it right there. Committees basically belong to their chairmen, which is why Martha Barnett went to Trammell the day before the Wednesday hearing—the sixth time she had seen him in the past month—to plead her case yet again.

"I told him I knew he was going to vote against it," she says. "Fine. But I asked him not to leverage his power with the other members. I asked him to let them vote on their own, to at least give us a chance to make our case."

Trammell told her he would, which guaranteed only a fair hearing, far from success. Tuesday morning's newspapers proclaimed the Rosewood bill was already in "deep trouble." By that afternoon, Al Lawson could count only eight votes among the two dozen Judiciary Committee members. Miguel De Grandy, who was himself the lead Republican on the committee, had only three of the five Republican votes he knew they needed to win.

Late that night, with a committee roll-call sheet clutched in his hand, Lawson stalked the blue-carpeted aisles of the House chamber, cornering Judiciary members and reminding them, in no vague terms, that they were each up for reelection that fall, and they might want to think twice about risking the wrath of the black voters in their districts. Even Robert Trammell had to think twice about that proposition. "He had thirty-seven percent blacks in his district," says Lawson. "I reminded him of that."

One card Lawson knew he now had, which he would not have dreamed of a year earlier, was the support of Bo Johnson. The two had been forced to spend hours together during the previous months, arranging the logistics of this touchy bill's strange path, and the animosity between them had faded. Martha

Barnett had helped as a peacemaker of sorts—she and the Speaker had always been on cordial terms. And it didn't hurt that Bo Johnson's chief of staff, Theresa Frederick, was African-American, providing Johnson with some perspectives on the issue that went beyond the purely political.

Johnson had helped nurse the bill through Hixson's hearing, had waited for the results of that hearing to decide how he personally felt about this bill, and had been convinced by those results to back it with everything he had. He had his doubts about this thing when it was first filed more than a year earlier. He still had his doubts when the hearing began. But now he was a believer. And so, the night before the Judiciary Committee was scheduled to meet on Rosewood, with the eyes of the nation watching, with "Dateline" and "60 Minutes" on the scene, and *The New York Times* and the *Wall Street Journal* and the *Washington Post,* with Florida's national reputation on the line, the Speaker took Al Lawson aside and told him he was going to "try to help turn some people around for you."

When the committee convened the next morning, not only were its twenty-four members present, along with an audience of reporters and Rosewood family members, but two wild cards were in attendance as well, and they weren't there just to watch.

One was Elaine Bloom, a college fund-raiser from Miami Beach who, as Speaker *pro tempore,* had voting rights on every committee. The other was Peter Wallace of St. Petersburg, chairman of the powerful Rules Committee and the Speaker-designate, next in line to succeed Bo Johnson at the helm of the House. True to his word, Bo had sent in his troops—Bloom to cast her swing vote if it was needed, and Wallace to remind the members by his mere presence that he would be the man passing out committee memberships next year.

It was going to be close. The members were caught in a tight squeeze, with their chairman pushing from one side and the Speaker's office pushing from the other. Steve Hanlon and Jim Peters testified first, summing up the cases they had made before Hixson. Then came De Grandy. Then Lawson put a fresh spin on the claim, explaining that it was not so much an issue of race as of property rights. "I was not being sincere," he admits now, "but I had to get the Republican members to see this thing in a different light, one they could relate to."

Martha Barnett stepped up and chided the state for its "collective amnesia." "The simple truth," she told the committee, "is that the whole world knew what happened at Rosewood."

Committee member John Cosgrove, an attorney from Miami, agreed. "We have the power today to right a wrong," he said. "This is, in effect, from the people of Florida, a public confession."

The vote was by voice, *yeas* and *nays,* and when it was done, Arnett Doctor, sitting near the back of the room, had lost count. He had to ask Steve Hanlon the total. Fourteen to eleven, in favor of the claim. Bloom's vote hadn't been needed, but she had cast it anyway.

Arnett leaped from his seat, let out a whoop, and Trammell quickly called for the next item on the committee's agenda. In the hall outside, Arnett was beside himself, hugging Hanlon, high-fiving De Grandy and holding court with a small circle of reporters.

"We buried them," he crowed. "We *buried* them."

But Martha Barnett knew better. Next up was the Appropriations Committee, where the focus would be simply and solely on money. Stung by their defeat in the Judiciary, the Rosewood opposition was already shifting its strategy. If they couldn't outright defeat this bill, they would gut it, strip away its payments and reduce it to something symbolic—a formal proclamation of regret and perhaps a plaque.

"I object only to the money," said Robert Trammell the day after his Judiciary Committee passed the bill on to Appropriations, of which he was also a member. "But a recognition that something terrible happened," he added. "I could support that."

Trammell said he might allow the property payments and perhaps the scholarships, but the direct payments to survivors had to go and he was going to do his best to amend them out. Daryl Jones, the member of the black caucus who would lead the Rosewood fight if the bill made it out of the House and into the Senate, called Trammell's suggestion "totally unacceptable." Pulling the payments from the bill, he said, would render it meaningless. De Grandy preferred the term "hollow" and threatened to use a rare parliamentary ploy—a "point of personal privilege"—to withdraw the bill entirely if the money was siphoned out. That would leave the legislature to answer to the kind of public indignation expressed in an editorial published that week in the *Tallahassee Democrat,* after Trammell announced his intentions.

"This is ill-advised, and almost insulting," wrote the *Democrat.* "It would transform an overdue but heartfelt gesture to a mockery of an apology."

Stepping in to help Trammell lead the fight was fellow Appropriations member Allen Boyd, from Monticello, up near the Georgia state line. The forty-eight-year-old Boyd was born in Georgia, grew up on his great-grandfather's hundred-year-old farm and still listed farming as his profession. Levy County was in Boyd's district; just like the black caucus was defending their people, well, these were *his* people he was standing up for.

Like Trammell, Boyd was a big backer of the school prayer bill written by Randy Mackey, another Appropriations member who had already come out strongly against Rosewood. Al Lawson decided it was time to take all three of them—Trammell, Boyd and Mackey—to task for their piety.

"These people say it's going to make kids more morally fit to pray in schools," Lawson told reporters. "But the same people who are talking about what's morally right are the people who are voting against Rosewood."

Lawson had his staff do some hurried homework, then distributed a list of what he called "frivolous" items passed by the legislature in recent years—a million dollars for a tennis center in Tampa, a quarter-million for a Florida Sports Hall of Fame in Lake City, another quarter-million for a stock car racing promotion—all of which were close to the hearts of conservative whites and all of which the black caucus had supported. Now, said Lawson, those same whites were turning their backs on Rosewood.

"The issue is race," he said flatly. "A lot of racism is still prevalent in this state. What's wrong with our race relations in Florida is this thing right here."

If money was the issue, he continued, why had the state approved more than fifty million dollars in claims over the previous decade with none of those bills facing the heat Rosewood was getting?

He got no answer, but he was feeling that heat. They all were. The day before the Appropriations Committee was scheduled to hear their claim—the last day of March—the Rosewood forces were still at least three votes shy of the number needed to pass the thirty-eight-member committee. Taking a cue from Lawson, Alzo Reddick, a college administrator and black caucus member from Orlando, stepped up and made the same threat Lawson had made on the eve of the Judiciary vote. If Rosewood went down, Reddick promised, the state's black leadership would target the reelection campaign of every legislator responsible. "The process of politics," he proclaimed, "allows for retribution as well as repatriation."

Something was stirring here, a boldness neither Florida's House nor its Senate had ever seen from its minority members. The call to arms issued to the black caucus at the beginning of the session was finally being answered.

But the fact was that it might be too late. The Appropriations Committee seemed dead-set on gutting the bill at best and simply voting it down at worst. Martha Barnett had met with every member, she had counted the votes, and it looked bleak. That Wednesday afternoon, the day before Appropriations would decide Rosewood's fate, she went to see John Long.

Long was the Appropriations Committee's chairman, arguably the most powerful position in the House. It was the Appropriations chairman who held the purse strings, who was responsible for putting together the state's multibillion-dollar budget and who essentially decided how every one of those dollars would be spent. Long was an even-tempered man, forty-eight years old, highly respected by his peers—a *Miami Herald* poll of the legislature conducted that spring rated him third among the state's 120 representatives.

When he wasn't in Tallahassee, Long worked as an assistant school superintendent down in Pasco County, which included the schools of Lacoochee and Dade City—a fact both Martha Barnett and Arnett Doctor reminded him of each time they ran into him, which was as often as they could. Barnett had been knocking on John Long's door for weeks, and each time she did, he told her to come back later. Talk to me when the hearings are over, he told her in February. Talk to me after you get past Judiciary, he told her in March.

Now it was almost April, nine days until the 1994 Florida legislative session would draw to a close, fewer than twenty-four hours until Long's panel would meet to decide whether the Rosewood bill would finally move out of committee and onto the floor for a vote by the entire House of Representatives. Now, Barnett told him, it was time to talk.

This time Long did not send her away. He invited her in, told his staff to hold his calls, and asked Barnett to take a seat and tell him everything she knew about Rosewood. An hour later, she was done. An hour with John Long. The man had more lobbyists lined up outside his door than any legislator in the Capitol. If they got five minutes with him they were lucky, and Martha Barnett had just been given an hour.

Long was glad to give it. Now that this issue had reached his doorstep, he needed to know the specifics. He hardly cared about the money aspect of this bill—"In terms of dollars and cents," he said, "it wasn't much at all." He did care about who, beyond the actual survivors themselves, would be receiving payments—"We didn't want everybody in the world just cashing in on this." But his major concern was the same as the Speaker's—that this was a highly volatile issue with moral, not just monetary implications for the entire state. Personally, he was ready to vote for the bill. But he knew his committee was not so inclined, at least not the majority. As soon as Barnett left, he put through a call to Bo Johnson.

The next morning, when the Appropriations Committee convened at eight A.M., Chairman Long made the unusual announcement that the Rosewood claims bill, scheduled to be heard that morning, would be postponed until that evening, after the full House finished its business. He and the Speaker were buying time for Barnett and her people to do what they could.

Meanwhile, Al Lawson decided the time had come to put pressure on the top. The black caucus was scheduled to have lunch that day at the Governor's Mansion, where Lawton Chiles was scrambling to salvage his health-care package, which was being shredded to ribbons by a hailstorm of amendments— nearly two hundred revisions had been attached to his proposals, which were up for a floor vote that evening.

Still, Chiles was upbeat as he took a seat that afternoon with eleven members of the caucus and about a dozen other guests. The meal was served—roast beef, asparagus, potatoes and cheesecake. A brief prayer was given, then Chiles turned to Lawson as the group began to eat.

"Well," said the governor, "what can I help you with?"

Lawson began slowly, politely, acknowledging the support the governor had given the Rosewood bill so far. Chiles had promised he would sign the bill if it passed the legislature, and Lawson told him the caucus appreciated that. But, he continued, at this point they needed more.

Heads turned. The eating stopped.

"It's getting to be mighty upsetting," said Lawson, his voice turning shrill, "that we've got Democratic members that are attempting to gut this bill in Appropriations. We've got a better shot at getting *Republican* help on Rosewood," he said, "than we do with Democrats."

Lawson had told no one he planned to lay down this gauntlet. The governor was stunned.

Lawson went on, telling Chiles they needed him to do more than simply follow the legislature's lead, that he needed to send his people out to help muscle this claim through that committee. If the governor *didn't* step in and do something, Lawson warned, he could not guarantee that the caucus would continue to support his health-care package. As a matter of fact, he said, they might just vote *against* it.

Chiles was dumbstruck.

"It was," said Lieutenant Governor Buddy MacKay, who was there at the table, "like watching a slow-motion accident."

Chiles finally gathered himself enough to speak.

"You're picking the wrong way to solicit my help," he said, scarcely bothering to conceal his rage. "I came out for Rosewood before anybody *asked* me, and now you're talking about shooting the one friend you've *got*. I don't like somebody coming and putting a gun in my ear and saying you're going to go vote with the *Republicans*."

"*I* don't like the tone of your *voice,* Governor," replied Lawson.

"I don't like hearing the tone of what *you've* said," shot back Chiles.

By then Lawson's black caucus colleagues were by his side. Cynthia Chestnut suggested the group walk out, which prompted MacKay to step in and play peacemaker. He half-jokingly asked that grace be said again and everyone start over. "You're all friends of ours," he said.

"I'm beginning to wonder," huffed Lawson.

Les Miller, a caucus member from Tampa known for a temper not unlike Arnett Doctor's, held court with reporters after the luncheon, reciting a list of black issues he claimed had been abandoned by his white colleagues in recent years, issues that ranged from creating a law school at Florida A&M to providing incentives for minority-owned businesses.

"When we want something, we can't get anyone to budge," said Miller. "We're not here to be ping-pong balls for the leadership of the House. We're tired of playing games, tired of being used, tired of being pawns."

No one knew what Chiles was going to do. On the one hand, he had nothing to lose by fighting for Rosewood. "He's not going to get those North Florida crackers' votes anyway," said one veteran Tallahassee lobbyist. But then there was the matter of the governor's pride. "You just can't push him," said that same lobbyist. "Lawton gets his *back* up if you threaten him, even if he agrees with you."

By late that afternoon, though, it was clear that Chiles had decided to help. MacKay, along with Chiles's chief of staff, Tom Herndon, were dispatched that afternoon to call on Appropriations Committee members. And once again Peter Wallace, the Speaker-designate, was on the scene, roaming the House floor, collaring each member of the committee in their seats. The press and the public watching from the glass-enclosed galleries above the chamber, looking down on the rows of cushioned seats, wooden desks, mounted microphones and computer monitors from which the 120 House members made their speeches and cast their votes, could see that Wallace was taking some sort of count, though most had no idea what it was about. Martha Barnett knew. It was about Rosewood. But she had no idea how it was going.

The House was scheduled to adjourn at five, which was when the Appropriations Committee would then meet on Rosewood. But the largest, most tangled issue on that year's legislative agenda, health care, was now on the floor, and the debate had just begun. It dragged on till six. Then seven. Barnett and Hanlon and Arnett went out to grab dinner, a cellular phone in hand in case the session adjourned while they were eating and they had to rush back.

At eight they returned, and the debate was nowhere near finished. Member after member rose to speak, amendment after amendment was read. Some were shouted down, others voted in. Nine o'clock. Then ten. Exhaustion was setting in. Impatience. Tempers were short. All Barnett and her crew could do was sit and watch. And wait.

Close to midnight there was a small commotion down in one corner of the chamber. It was the black caucus, huddled around Lawson. Another knot of members came together over by the Speaker's chair. Messages were relayed from one group to the other and back. At twelve-thirty, the fourteen black House members abruptly stalked out of the chamber, walked off the House floor and into a side room. Eventually they were coaxed back. Then, suddenly, the press corps came tumbling out of its upstairs gallery, rushing down toward Bo Johnson's office. Martha Barnett grabbed one reporter and asked what was up. He wasn't sure, he said. But the Speaker had called a recess to make a statement to the press. Something about Rosewood.

Johnson wasn't about to go into the details, but the fact was that the caucus was holding the health bill hostage again. So far that night, they had voted with the governor, stalemating the Republicans each time they tried to shoot down the bill. But the caucus's primary concern was Rosewood. The next day was Friday, when most of the legislature traditionally left early to get a head start on Easter weekend, before returning for the session's final five days. It was clear this health-care debate was far from over. The messages relayed down on the floor between the Speaker and the caucus had begun with the Speaker's suggestion that the Rosewood hearing be put off until Monday. The members were fried. They had no gas left for a late-night hearing on Rosewood. They wanted to go home.

But the caucus said no way. Beyond the Appropriations hearing, the bill still had to get through a House vote and then through the Senate and *its* committees. There was no time to do all that in a week. No, they said, the Speaker's suggestion was out of the question. They wanted their hearing *tonight*. And if they didn't get it, they said, they were ready to vote with the Republicans on health care.

So now Johnson was in his office, the reporters pressed wall to wall. He told them what was going to happen the rest of the night, that the health-care bill was going to take up the time they had left. Then he turned to John Long, who had an announcement to make "of great importance to many members of the House." The Rosewood bill, said Long, which was originally set to be heard tonight, had now been rescheduled for first thing the next morning.

The question of a quorum was raised by one of the reporters, who noted the imminence of Easter. Johnson nodded, then said he had informed every member of the Appropriations Committee that they were free to go home *after* the Rosewood claim was heard. Any absences, he said, had better have a good excuse, meaning any members who wanted to stay on that committee had better be there in the morning or be able to tell Bo Johnson why they were not. Even the most seasoned capitol-watchers were stunned.

"People were out in the halls going, *Whew, SHIT!,*" says Martha Barnett. "It was an extraordinary act of power for a Speaker to take."

And it was good enough for Barnett. As long as they had a quorum for that meeting, she was happy. De Grandy was not so pleased. His vote count of the committee came out almost dead even; they couldn't afford the absence of even one of their supporters, excused or not. Al Lawson was satisfied; he knew both the Speaker and the Governor were already leaning on those committee members to bring some swing votes Rosewood's way.

As for Arnett Doctor, he saw the entire situation as a plot, a deal among all sides—John Long, Bo Johnson, Peter Wallace, *all* of them—to sabotage this bill. Arnett had been walking these halls for the past sixteen hours. His legs were killing him. He'd heard promise after promise put off time and again.

Now it was being put off again. He didn't even wait to hear an explanation this time. He shoved his way out the door and stomped off into the night.

But he was back the next morning. They were all back. And when John Long called the Appropriations Committee to order at half past nine, thirty-seven of its thirty-eight members were in their seats—Daniel Webster of Orlando had been excused for religious reasons. There was little debate to speak of.

"If you search your heart and you search your conscience," proclaimed black caucus member Josephus Eggelletion, a schoolteacher and barber from Lauderdale Lakes, down near Miami, "I think you will agree this incident is like no other in the state of Florida."

Eighteen of Eggelletion's committee colleagues agreed, casting their votes with him in favor of the bill. Twelve disagreed, voting against it. And six— most of them North Florida legislators caught between constituencies furiously opposed to this claim and pressure from the House leadership to support it—simply abstained.

"God bless America," crowed Arnett, as a crowd of reporters again closed in around him.

And so the Rosewood claims bill had clawed its way out of committee. Monday it would face the full House. Passage there, wrote most reporters, would virtually assure endorsement from the Senate. Martha Barnett wasn't so sure, but she relished the opportunity to find out.

Meanwhile it was time for everyone to take the weekend off.

It was Good Friday.

THIRTY-ONE

Amen

Monday, the morning after Easter, the final week of the 1994 session of the Florida state legislature began. For the families and survivors of Rosewood, soaked in the spirit of resurrection and renewal, this was their day of reckoning.

Two dozen of them were seated up in the House of Representatives' glass-enclosed East gallery, gazing down on the floor below, along with the portraits of past Florida Speakers of the House hanging high on the wall that surrounds the elliptical chamber.

Lording over the gently curved rows of blue-cushioned legislators' seats was the Speaker at his rostrum, flanked by the flags of Florida and of the United States. Mounted behind and above him was a slab of black blank glass, an electronic toteboard that, when switched on, lit up with seven columns of names, each of the 120 members of the House. Every time they cast a vote, pushing a button at each of their seats, the board would light up like a Christmas tree, red dots beside the members who have voted no, green beside those voting yes. Voice votes, the traditional thunder of shouted *yeas* and *nays,* with exaggerated gestures of thumbs up or down, were saved for the floor debates, the verbal tornado of procedures and amendments that preceded a verdict. But when it was time for that verdict, the voting was done silently, with the push of those buttons, the lights on the board flashing instantly and simultaneously, the totals tallied by a clerk at a computer, all in a matter of nanoseconds—lawmaking in the age of fiber optics.

At precisely ten A.M., Bo Johnson gaveled the session to order and the torrent began, the day's first bill announced by the clerk, amendments read aloud, then argued, struck down or adopted by the yells of the lawmakers, amendments to amendments dispensed the same way, a dizzying swirl of points of procedure and parliamentary convolutions, all somehow finally leading to a vote. And then on to the next bill.

There were dozens of bills scheduled ahead of Rosewood on that day's docket. Proposed laws on biomedical waste, bail bond agents, the moving and storage industry, motor vehicle registration, recreational boating, animal control regulations, insurance rates, public library funds, helmet laws for kids on bicycles—the lawmakers plowed through them all that morning, broke for lunch, then carried on into the afternoon, while the Rosewood families watched and waited.

Finally, near two, the agenda shifted to the day's list of claims bills. First up was the case of a motorcyclist permanently disabled after being hit by a bus in Broward County in the winter of 1987. A jury had awarded him $380,000—$280,000 over the state limit. He was here to ask that difference. The House voted to pay him $100,000 instead.

Next came a woman from Hernando County whose car had been pinioned by a government dump truck and a road grader in a three-way collision in 1988. She too now had lifelong injuries. A jury had awarded her $432,000. She was also asking $280,000 from the state, and she too received a positive but diminished verdict from the House—for $180,000.

Then, at two-thirty, the clerk announced the next item on the agenda, House Bill #591, "A bill," she read aloud, "to be entitled 'An act relating to Rosewood, Florida.'"

It was literally a defining moment, not just for the Rosewood families gathered up in the gallery and the lawmakers down on the floor, not just for the fourteen million people of Florida, but for an entire nation struggling perhaps more than ever with the uniquely American tendrils of shame, guilt, reparation and resentment that are rooted in race. W.E.B. Du Bois's words, spoken near the time of the Rosewood attack—that "the problem of the twentieth century is the problem of the color line"—had come to seem even more true now, at the end of the century, than they were at its beginning.

The civil rights laws and social programs of the 1950s and '60s were being retrenched in an atmosphere of white backlash; the principles of affirmative action and equal opportunity established and enacted in the '70s and '80s had become besieged both in the workplace and on college campuses, where cries of reverse discrimination were as loud from whites as complaints of racial exclusion had long been from blacks; the 1992 race riot in Los Angeles had shocked the nation into realizing the extent of rage and desperation simmering in its inner cities; and the warlike violence on those streets, graphically mirrored in wildly popular rap music and embraced by a new generation of young blacks and whites alike, seemed to overshadow any rays of hope and peace breaking through the gathering thunderclouds of anger and hate.

The time seemed anything but ripe for Rosewood.

And yet it had made it this far. No one had listened three years before, when Arnett Doctor had reached out for a lawyer. The legislature had hardly paid heed a year earlier, when the first Rosewood bill was filed. Even the second bill was not taken seriously until Richard Hixson delivered his verdict. But now, today, an entire nation was watching—squadrons of reporters from national publications and networks crammed into the press gallery—because the issues defined and decided in this debate would doubtless be echoed in courtrooms and legislative chambers across the country for years to come.

Down on the floor, however, there was no inordinate sense of drama. The room was not hushed. The lawmakers were not riveted to their seats. It was business as usual, small clusters of four and five House members huddled in various corners of the chamber, murmuring about one issue or another, others roaming from seat to seat, leaning over a colleague, mumbling earnestly even as someone rose to make a statement or a speech. The commotion, the din of ceaseless movement and chatter, like the background bustle in a busy restaurant, would continue throughout the debate, a noisy curtain of sound surrounding the statements being made for the record. To the casual observer, it would appear that few of the men and women on that floor were paying attention. But they were. This was how they always did business, and the business at hand was what finally to do about Rosewood.

After rushing through the reading of several minor amendments—a string of procedural items recited like a 78 r.p.m. chant—Bo Johnson called on David Thomas, a Republican from Venice, down the coast below Sarasota. Balding, roundish, bespectacled, the forty-eight-year-old ophthalmologist rose to strike the first blow against a bill he considered "dangerous."

"What do we *know* concerning the incident that occurred at Rosewood," asked Thomas, turning to his colleagues. "The report is fairly short," he said, tapping a copy of the study team's paper. "You can read it in an evening. And it will stay *with* you the rest of your life.

"The appendix," he continued, "is longer. Not as interesting. But every bit as crucial, as is the special master's report."

Then he zeroed in on his target, the assertion that the state had been derelict in its duty to protect Rosewood's residents. "Law enforcement has been painted ugly with a broad brush," he said, "and that's just not true."

He pointed to Margaret Cannon's testimony that her father, the deputy sheriff, had helped women and children out of the woods and onto a train. No one, added Thomas, should forget the white train conductors who carried the refugees to safety. He acknowledged the neglect of the county sheriff, Robert Walker, but noted that Walker resigned within a year after the Rosewood incident, perhaps, suggested Thomas, from shame. Thomas said he felt shame himself. Everyone in the state of Florida, he said, should feel shame. "We ought *never* be done with this issue," he said, "because it is an ugly part of our history. We ought to own up to it permanently."

But, he continued—and this would become the crux of the day's debate—money was not the way to make amends.

"I've heard people say we ought to pay these people and be done with it," said Thomas. "But I don't agree. I think that's an inappropriate way to handle this.

"Forgiveness," he continued, "is a two-way street, and we ought not *buy* our forgiveness with a series of compensatory pecuniary actions for this small, select group.

"It's enough," he said, "to have an admission of sorrow and a *recognition* of that admission."

And that, he said, was why he was now bringing the Thomas Amendment before the House. It would strike all cash payments from the Rosewood bill—payments he warned would set a dangerous precedent. Instead, his amendment would create a permanent exhibit at the state library in Tallahassee, as well as a monument at the site of the massacre.

The Speaker then opened the floor to debate on Thomas's proposal, and Cynthia Chestnut seized her microphone.

"Dr. Thomas talks about 'buying forgiveness,'" she proclaimed. "Every claims bill that comes before this *House* is about 'buying forgiveness.' There is no amount of money that can be paid to bring back the lives that were lost here. There is no amount of money that can restore the property that was lost.

"What we have before us today," she said, "is to only *begin* to try to make amends. And making amends does *not* mean simply establishing a marker or building an exhibit."

Al Lawson rose next, giving Thomas credit for helping move the bill out of the Judiciary Committee. That was an important step toward this day, said Lawson, but now that this day had come, it would be shameful to shrink the significance of this claim by hacking at its contents. The Rosewood bill, said Lawson, was about much more than money or monuments. It was about healing, he said, not just for the Rosewood families, not just for Florida's blacks, but for black people looking on from across the nation.

"This removes a dark side of Florida history," said Lawson. "And it gives the African-American hope that this legislature, this body, will try to erase some of the dark shadows that have been hanging over people's heads for so many, many, many years."

Ben Graber, a Democrat from Coral Springs, near Miami—like Thomas, a doctor—then rose and seized on the issue Lawson had raised, the idea of healing.

"We have something we call closure in our society," said Graber. "It's important to a society, but it's *more* important to individuals.

"If this had occurred five hundred years ago, and nobody could trace the relatives, I could understand a marker or a statue. But we *do* have relatives right here," he said, glancing up toward the gallery, "as well as some of the actual individuals who were directly harmed.

"When harm is done to somebody in our society," he continued, "and society stands by, for whatever reason, while that person suffers, some compensation is needed for closure. I think the amount of money appropriated here is really small, but it's not the amount that counts. It's the fact that these people need to know that society is saying, Yes, we do understand you are hurt, and, Yes, we are going to give you closure by saying we're sorry."

Graber concurred with Chestnut's assertion. "There's no way you can fully compensate for this type of tragedy," he said. "But we *can* try to compensate for people's feelings. We *can* try to allow people to close."

Josephus Eggelletion stood next, tapping his copy of the report the same way Thomas had tapped his, and disagreeing totally with Thomas's conclusions.

"I've read this report five times," said Eggelletion. "Eyewitness reports indicated that police officers stood back and allowed this to occur. That is *crucial*. That is *compelling*."

He stopped, drew a deep breath, gathered his thoughts. He spoke from no notes.

"I will tell you this," he continued. "There comes a time in everybody's life, and in the history of a state, when we have to stand tall as humans, to recognize our faults and our shortcomings and to do what we have to do in order to right a wrong.

"And this," he finished, "is a great wrong."

Tom Warner, a Republican from Stuart, east of Lake Okeechobee, chided Thomas, not for opposing the bill but for fiddling with it. "We should either vote this Rosewood bill up or vote it down in regard to the compensation," said Warner. "If the state of Florida has done something wrong, then we should do something right by these people. I *don't* think it's the right thing to do to gut the bill and replace it with a highway marker."

Stephen Wise, a community college administrator from Jacksonville, disagreed, and he raised a startling specter to make his point. "If you look at the Holocaust and what's happened with that," said Wise, invoking the slaughter of World War II, "we *have* that kind of memorial in Washington, D.C. I think we need to put together the same kind of permanent exhibit here, so people will not forget what took place in this dark hour of our history."

A memorial, argued Wise, like the Holocaust Museum in Washington, should be enough. Money, he maintained, was not necessary.

That brought Elaine Gordon bolting from her seat. Gordon had not planned on speaking that day. Her vote had been with the bill from the beginning, simply because she felt it was the right thing to do. Hardly any black people lived in her North Miami district—fewer than ten percent. But she understood and identified with the issue of displacement and dispossession. The people she represented were mostly like herself, transplanted northerners, mostly from New York, many of them Jewish.

When she learned about Rosewood—the details of the women and children hiding in the swamp, the train coming through at night, the evacuation to Gainesville—Gordon, who had grown up in the Bronx, moved to Florida with her husband in 1964, and in 1972, at age forty-one, was elected to the state legislature, couldn't help but think of her own cousins, who had escaped from Poland in 1944 by hiding in the forest, burying themselves beneath the soil so the dogs leading the German search parties could not pick up their scent, staying in those woods for three days and nights until they were able to finally escape, first to Belgium and then to New York, where Elaine Gordon's family took them in. Now, as she heard the Holocaust invoked as an argument against the Rosewood claim, she could not help but rise and respond.

"Members," she began, "there *were* reparations made to the German Jews whose property was taken without due process. There isn't *just* a memorial. The German government, recognizing what they owed to the survivors because they denied them the opportunity of being able to have their descendants inherit their property, their goods, their *mementos,* their *jewelry,* their *paintings,* acknowledged that recognition by paying compensation. There is not just a memorial. There is ongoing reparation that the German government is paying to those people for the taking of their property and goods without due process.

"And *that,*" said Gordon, "is what's going on here."

The final response to Thomas's amendment was made by Miguel De Grandy, who, in lawyerlike fashion, picked his adversary's argument apart, point by point.

The first point was the assertion that Margaret Cannon's father, by helping the refugees board the train, was proof that the state had provided protection.

"The testimony Representative Thomas refers to," De Grandy began, noting that it was not eyewitness testimony and not even necessarily true, "is that *after* the destruction, *after* everything that occurred, *one* deputy sheriff went to the woods and found some black people and helped them get on the train to go to Gainesville.

"Think about this," he said. "If it's true, what message was law enforcement sending here? The message was *Get out of town!* We will *help* you get out of *town!*

"To me," he continued, "that is far from compelling evidence that the authorities in charge did anything affirmative to protect these people's rights. On the contrary, this was evidence of a continuing *failure* on the part of the authorities to do their duty, which was to protect the lives and property of the citizens of Rosewood, to protect their right to remain in Rosewood, as *we* have a right to live and remain anywhere *we* want to live."

As for the issue of compensation, De Grandy was curt.

"I have yet," he said, noting the dozens of claims bills he had seen during his five years in the legislature and referring specifically to the landmark decapitation claim, "to see a case where a person has a DOT sign fall on their head and gets a memorial erected. They get *compensation*."

Finally, he addressed the question still bothering many of the members on the floor, the question of the floodgates of other claims this bill might open.

"We have talked a lot about precedent," he said. "Think about this. What type of dangerous precedent are we going to set if we were to pass Dr. Thomas's amendment and gut this bill? I would submit to you that it would set a very *dangerous* precedent if we were to violate the notion of equal protection under the law and treat these individuals any differently from the way we've treated everybody else who has ever come before this legislature with a claims bill.

"I agree with Representative Warner," he concluded. "If you feel for some reason that the claim is not proven, then vote against the bill. If you feel the evidence shows that the claim has been proven—which I think is clearly the case—then vote for it. But to do what Representative Thomas is asking, to gut the bill, *would* set a very dangerous precedent."

Thomas was then allowed a final comment.

"What we're saying with this bill," he warned, "is that we can take a horrible part of the history of Florida and buy off a handful of residents and forget it.

"I beg of you," he concluded, "that that is wrong."

Then came the vote, a loud chorus of *yeas* to adopt Thomas's amendment, followed by a louder chorus of *nays*. The volume decided the verdict. The amendment was defeated. The bill had withstood its first charge of the day, and now George Albright, an attorney from Ocala, rose to pick up the spear dropped by his Republican colleague.

Slim, blond, thirty-eight, Albright had served in the House for six years. He nodded toward his black caucus colleagues, told them what a pleasure it had been working with them over the previous years. Then he explained why he could not support this bill.

"I have a problem," said Albright, "with trying to interject our views of 1994 civil rights on acts of the past."

His amendment, hardly different from Thomas's, proposed to spend ten thousand dollars planning a "Rosewood Memorial Park" on state forest property not far from the site of the massacre.

"I think the issue here," he concluded, "is that we memorialize this, use it as a historical footnote, and go forward. But if you open this door, ladies and gentlemen, rather than closing anything, you'll be opening up something that will *never* be closed."

This time it was Les Miller who could not keep his seat. The slim, fiery, forty-two-year-old from Tampa was clearly furious as he rose to face Albright. As a member of the black caucus, he said, he was "appalled, hurt, and disgusted" by what he had just heard.

"But as I have sometimes lost my cool on this floor," he said, turning toward the Speaker, "I will try *not* to do that today."

He drew a deep breath.

"The whole crux of this bill," Miller began, "is that law enforcement, the governor, and other state officials knew what was being done in Rosewood and they turned their backs, closed their eyes and did absolutely *nothing.*

"These things happened many times in the state of Florida," he acknowledged, noting the dozens of lynchings that occurred before Rosewood. "But there were *none* like this. This lasted one week. One *entire week.*

"I've had people ask me," he continued, "I even had one member ask me *today,* 'Why didn't the people of Rosewood try to get law enforcement to help them?'

"Ladies and gentlemen, can you *imagine* what rights a black person in the South actually had in 1923? Can you imagine what rights they had to go to police officers in a situation like this and ask for help?

"The answer is absolutely zero. *None.* Null and *void. Nada.* Those rights weren't there. They just *weren't there.*

"So, Representative Albright," he said, turning again to his counterpart, "if you truly have respect for the judgment of the members of the black caucus, if you have respect for the judgment of Representative Miguel De Grandy, if you have respect for the judgment of the people who support this bill, you will withdraw this amendment."

De Grandy, a bit impatient now, took the floor again.

"Please," he implored his colleagues, "vote against this amendment and let's get on to the merits of the bill itself."

But Bill Posey, a realtor from Rockledge, just north of Cocoa Beach, was not about to miss the chance both to stick up for Albright's amendment and in the process, to share a bit of his own family's history.

"Everyone," he began, "has heard the cliché, *Your name is mud.*"

That quieted the room. Heads turned to hear where in the world *this* was going to lead. Posey paused, allowed his colleagues to wonder a moment longer, then launched into his parable.

"After Abraham Lincoln was assassinated," said Posey, "we had literally a lynch mob of elected, empowered officials that went out to convict somebody for the murder. You may know that a number of people were hung in connection with the Lincoln assassination. A lot of other people were punished.

"One of them that was *wrongly* punished," he continued, "was Dr. Samuel Mudd. He lost everything as he sat in a prison in Key West before he was finally released—sick, old, worn out, a waste of life."

Posey paused again, then delivered his kicker.

"Dr. Mudd," he said, "was a *relative* of mine."

Another brief pause.

"But I don't ever expect to be compensated for what the federal government did to *him.*"

It might not have been the day's most persuasive argument, but it was doubtless the most original.

Albright followed with his closing remarks, warning his colleagues of the "Pandora's Box" they were about to open. But the debate, for all intents and purposes, was over. Albright's amendment, like Thomas's, was shouted down, and the Speaker quickly moved the unamended bill onto the floor for discussion.

The only question came from Victor Crist, an ad executive whose Tampa district bumped up against Arnett Doctor's neighborhood. Crist wanted to know whether people who were hurt, killed, terrorized and even run off their property in urban high-crime areas might not qualify for compensation under this bill, loosing an avalanche of inner-city lawsuits against the state.

"No sir," answered De Grandy. "In a case where you have a high-crime area and the state does not have adequate notice that something is going to happen, the state cannot be held responsible. In other words, if someone in your city— and I live in Dade County, where there's high crime—gets mugged, and there's no police officer there because they were all on other calls protecting citizens, or writing their reports, or taking people to *jail,* the state cannot be held responsible. The state cannot be held responsible for not being everywhere at all times.

"But that's what makes Rosewood unique," he continued. "There was more than plenty of time for the authorities to respond.

"And there is no *question,*" he concluded, "that if this were a *white* town threatened by a *black* mob, there would have been adequate protection of those citizens."

Now it was time. No more questions. No more debate. No more witnesses or testimonies or studies or reports. Al Lawson and Miguel De Grandy had been working toward this moment for over a year now. Steve Hanlon had been at it for almost two. For Arnett Doctor it had been twelve years since the spring afternoon when Rosewood was first reawakened in his life. And for the survivors, for literally a lifetime, this had been a moment they dared not imagine, much less hope for.

Bo Johnson's voice shifted into a staccato, rapid-fire monotone as he announced that it was time to vote on House Bill 591.

"The clerk will unlock the machine," Johnson droned, "and all members will proceed to vote."

Two seconds passed.

"Have all members voted?"

Three seconds more.

"Have all members voted?"

One more time.

"Have all members voted?"

And again.

"Have all members voted?"

A final pause.

"The clerk will lock the machine and announce the vote."

Not a full second later, the clerk read the totals aloud, reciting the figures as rapidly as Johnson had requested them.

"Seventy-one yeas," she declared, "forty nays, Mister Speaker."

A smattering of applause swept across the floor. Nothing eruptive, but a polite acknowledgment among the lawmakers that this had been something historic. Several of them turned toward the gallery, saluting the survivors, who wept and hugged one another as cameras flashed all around them. Arnett Doctor thrust his arms in the air, like a heavyweight after a knockout. Wilson Hall stepped away from the celebration to answer some questions from reporters.

"They really don't have enough money to make up for my losses," he said. "How do I know what I really would have been? What could have happened? This was all stripped from me." Still, he added, this bill was a good thing, a healthy thing. "Sure it makes things better," he said. "If not for me, then for my grandkids."

The black caucus members too were elated. There was still rancor and rivalries among them, just as there were and always would be among the Rosewood families. But this was a day for coming together, and the caucus—for the first time, in the eyes of many—had done that. The *Tallahassee Democrat* called it "a great day for Florida politics," praising the caucus for its perseverance and boldness, for the fact that it had "stopped playing politics and started practicing it," that its members had been "steely-eyed and steady handed" at their luncheon showdown with the governor, and, all in all, for the fact that the black caucus had "finally grown up."

Even as the victors celebrated, however, one of the vanquished was holding court himself, reminding reporters that this fight was not over yet. Charlie Williams, the state senator from Live Oak, whose district included Levy County itself, cautioned that there were still four days left in this session, and this bill had yet to begin its trip toward Senate confirmation. Williams admitted it was going to be tough to block it, but he was going to do his damnedest to try.

"It's a sad part of Florida history," he had said back when the House fight began, "but I'm just opposed to paying that money when we have so many other pressing needs in education, prisons, transportation and other things."

Now, with the bill out of the House and on its way to his doorstep, he was more strident. "When will it ever *stop?*" he proclaimed. "If we can go back seventy-one years, why not a hundred? Why not a hundred and *fifty?*"

Charlie Williams had to take that stand. He had no choice. His constituents were the people in Cedar Key and Bronson, Chiefland and Sumner, the towns being dragged through the mud of this whole mess, places that would forever be linked with the evil done three generations ago. Most of the families in these places had never heard of the Rosewood massacre until the reporters started showing up. Their relatives had nothing to do with this assault that had occurred long before they were born. But now it was all they were hearing about, and they were sick of it.

Farmers and fishermen, outdoor folk, blue-collar Christians, simple people with simple values—those were Charlie Williams's constituents. Of course Charlie had made a bit more money over the years than most of them, selling insurance, but he had remained a farmer all along. Matter of fact, he still listed hay and tree farming as his primary occupations on the biography they passed out in his Senate office, still kept his hand on his land down in Suwannee County. He was a Baptist deacon, too, and that counted for a lot with the people who voted for him, his friends and neighbors, hand-clapping, back-slapping Baptists just like him.

Charlie had to fight this battle to the bloody end, and really, he had nothing to lose. The folks back home would thank him in the end, for at least sticking up for them, even if there was no way on God's green earth that this bill would be beaten now.

And there wasn't. Martha Barnett was still worried, but then that was her job. The first thing she did that Monday afternoon, once the House had passed the bill, was pay a visit to Robert Wexler, chairman of the Senate Finance and Taxation Committee, which, along with a special claims committee, would be hearing the Rosewood bill the next day. Wexler was charged with appointing the members of that claims committee, and when Barnett arrived at his door, he just smiled.

"You don't even need to talk to me," he said. "I'm *for* you one hundred percent."

Not only that, he said, but Barnett was welcome to help select the claims committee herself if she'd like. "Tell me who you want," said Wexler, "and we'll put those people on."

So it was not surprising when the Rosewood bill breezed through both those committees that Tuesday without a single dissenting vote. Wednesday was a bit more sticky, with Fred Dudley sitting on the Appropriations Committee. Dudley had been dead-set against the bill from the beginning, just like his constituents back home in Cape Coral. Though many of his Republican colleagues still disagreed with the bill, his was now the only voice besides Williams's still shouting out against it.

"It's money being paid out to people, that's all it is," spat Dudley on the eve of the Appropriations hearing.

But it was no use. Dudley tried the same ploy on Wednesday that Thomas and Albright had attempted in the House—striking the cash compensation and settling for a scholarship fund. But his amendment was voted down by the committee, eighteen to nine, and when the bill itself was put on the table to decide if it would go to the full Senate on Friday, it passed by that same two-to-one spread.

Coupled with the votes it had gotten in Tuesday's committees, the bill now had a majority of the Senate's forty members already on record in favor of it. Friday's final vote would be a formality—"As long as nobody bolts on us," cautioned Daryl Jones, who, along with Matt Meadows from Fort Lauderdale and Jacksonville's Betty Holzendorf, were the black caucus members guiding the bill through the Senate.

Jones needn't have worried. Friday morning the members of the Senate settled into their brown cushioned seats for the last time that spring. Two months of sixteen-hour days had finally come to this. Upstairs, the press and the public filed into the galleries, passing a floor-to-ceiling mural displaying various figures from Florida's march through history—a band of Spanish explorers, some Seminole Indians, a Confederate soldier with the flag of Dixie . . . and a black female laborer standing beside a crate of oranges.

Just as portraits of past Speakers were mounted on the wall ringing the House chamber, so did paintings of past Presidents of the Senate surround this room. At ten A.M., the sitting president, Pat Thomas, gaveled the session to order, and at 11:20 the Rosewood bill came up for debate. When Daryl Jones rose to speak, it was with a set of notes Martha Barnett had helped him prepare—"talking points," as she calls them, "a list of issues and ideas with bullets beside them," something she routinely puts together for each legislator making a speech on a bill for which she has lobbied.

With his notes and bullet points in front of him, Jones addressed the nearly silent room. The Senate is always more controlled, more mannerly, than the clamorous House, but as Jones spoke, the room was unusually hushed.

"This is your chance to rectify an atrocious wrong," he began, "to provide justice where there has been none.

"The simple truth," he continued, "is the whole world knew what happened in Rosewood, but we have buried it in our collective amnesia."

Martha Barnett especially liked that last phrase. She had used it herself in her speech before the House Judiciary Committee.

"It would be a sad day for Florida," Jones concluded, "to once again turn its back on the victims of Rosewood."

Charlie Williams weighed in one last time, pulling every point he had ever made about Rosewood into a single statement.

"How long do we have to pay for the sins of our forefathers?" he asked. "There are other pressing, pressing needs for our state, and this is 1994, not 1923. I can't go back to my eighteen counties and justify spending two million—plus or minus a hundred thousand—of their hard-earned tax dollars on something that happened seventy-one years ago!"

Fred Dudley tried one last time to amend the bill, but was beaten back by a vote of twenty-nine to eleven. "I'll just have to be the one to tell you 'I told you so' next year," he said, "when we've got some lawsuits to defend."

That was the last gasp. Jim Hargrett of Tampa wrapped things up. "Let's stop playing with this issue," he said. "This bill is sort of like a suture on an open wound. It brings it together so healing can begin."

At 12:28, in an atmosphere of anticlimax for all but the Rosewood families themselves, the Senate cast its vote.

Twenty-six in favor, fourteen opposed.

It was over. Only the governor's signature remained to turn the bill into law. That would come in a month.

Meanwhile, after an eruption of cheers, tears and shouts of "Praise the Lord," the family members, three dozen of them, gathered around Arnett Doctor in the foyer outside. Mama Dot. Willie Evans. The Halls—Wilson, Mary and Margie. They each clasped hands and bowed their heads as Arnett led them in prayer, his voice echoing off the rotunda above as he gave thanks for them all.

A crowd collected, including the press, looking on in silence from a distance as the relatives' heads remained bowed and Arnett recited the names of those who had passed on. Dozens of names. The ones who had died at Rosewood—Sarah and Sylvester, Lexie and Lord God, Sam Carter and James Carrier. And the ones who had passed on in the decades since. Beauty and Sweetie, Philomena and Lee Ruth. Family, all.

And then they said Amen.

And then they went home.

PART SIX

COMING HOME

THIRTY - TWO

Nothing But Scars

It had been ten months now since the sparkling May morning when Lawton Chiles took a seat in the Senate chamber of Tallahassee's Old Capitol building and signed the Rosewood bill into law. The members of the black caucus were there for that historic moment, beaming as they gathered behind the governor. Miguel De Grandy was there as well, standing by Chiles's right shoulder as Arnett Doctor, resplendent in a bone-white suit, leaned over his left. Looking on were fifty members of the Rosewood families, half of them dressed in the same white clothing as Arnett—symbolic, they explained, of the innocence of the Rosewood victims. The other half were clad in scarlet, for the blood that was spilled that week.

The governor proclaimed that "the long silence has been broken, the shadow has been lifted." He vowed that "this blind act of bigotry" would never be forgotten. Then he passed out souvenir pens to each of the seven survivors in attendance. Arnett accepted for the eighth, bedridden Lonnie Carroll.

Rosewood survivors at the Governor's signing of the Rosewood bill
(1-r, front row: Minnie Lee Langley, Wilson Hall, Margie Hall Johnson,
Willie Evans, Mary Hall Daniels and A. T. Goins)

"*Thank you,* Jesus," declared Minnie Lee Langley that morning, glad that this day had finally arrived. Glad, too, that the whole ordeal was now over.

But for Guy David Robinson—along with his colleague Frank Beisler, and their boss, Greg Durden—the ordeal had just begun. The day the Rosewood bill was signed into law, Durden, as chief of the state's Attorney General's Office of Civil Rights in Hollywood, near Fort Lauderdale, was charged with enforcing it, which meant finding, verifying and finally paying all qualified Rosewood claimants. Durden knew it was going to be a sticky, lengthy process—but he had no idea how tangled and inflamed it would actually become. Nor did Robinson, a thirty-four-year-old former running back at the University of Alabama who had just joined Durden's staff that month as an assistant attorney general when Rosewood was dumped in his lap.

Robinson had been aware of Rosewood long before he was assigned to it. He'd read about it in the papers, and he was struck by the shock of a group of people being so suddenly and completely severed from their past, having it just swept away. He couldn't imagine what that must feel like. He knew all there was to know about his own family. His father and mother were both from a little town called Wildwood, in the center of the state, just south of Ocala. He had dozens of aunts and uncles and cousins in Wildwood. He knew the place inside out, knew the neighbors, knew his kin, drove up from his office in Hollywood as often as he could, just to visit, just to keep in touch. Family.

Robinson had heard all his family's stories, every one, about every aunt and uncle and grandparent and great-grandparent, all the way back to slavery. But when his relatives heard he was working on Rosewood, they told him a story he had never heard before.

It happened to one of his aunt's families sometime during the Forties, they told him, though no one could say exactly when. The Strongs was their name, and they owned some property up around the middle of the state, though no one could recall just where. The story was that the Strongs were run off that land. Chased off by the Klan, so everyone said. Lost all that they owned and never came back. Just like Rosewood.

"I couldn't believe it," says Robinson. "We were just sitting around talking and this story came up. I looked over at my mom, and she just nodded her head. 'Yeah,' she said. 'that happened.' I was stunned, really shocked. I'd *never* heard this story."

It was easy to see why this assignment became more than just a job to Guy

Robinson. Not only was he black, but now he had learned there were skeletons in his own family's closet, bones that lay not far from Rosewood's. Frank Beisler, though—it would be hard to find a man whose background was further removed from Rosewood than his. A former Marine, a former cop, and a former undertaker, Beisler was from New England, German Catholic, the son of a professional hockey player. He'd come to Florida in the late '80s after banging up his fifty-year-old body training SWAT teams in Virginia. He'd hooked up with the Attorney General's office as a paralegal in 1991, and, in the summer of '94, at age fifty-five, he joined Greg Durden's staff as an "investigator." Like Robinson, he was given Rosewood as his first case. Unlike Robinson, he had never heard of the place. "I thought a Rosewood was a flower," he says.

But he learned. He spent his first week reading everything the state had on Rosewood. Depositions and affidavits. Transcripts of interviews. Transcripts of testimonies. The study team's report. The state's review of the study team's report. Correspondence between the state and the attorneys, correspondence between the study team and the state. Newspaper and magazine articles by the dozen. Ten hours a day he pored over the papers at the office, then he took them home at night, the same as Durden and Robinson had already been doing for three months, the three of them retracing the steps already made by the study team, taking nothing for granted, and, hopefully, taking those steps further. "We were starting over again from step one," says Robinson. "We *had* to, to make sure."

The law signed by the governor and handed to Durden and his staff was essentially as Richard Hixson had recommended. A $1.5 million fund had been established to pay $150,000 each to people who could prove they were Rosewood residents at the time of the attack—survivors. It also created a $500,000 fund to reimburse the families of Rosewood residents who lost property during the attack. A fund to provide twenty-five college scholarships a year was created for minority students, with preference given to Rosewood descendants. And the Florida Department of Law Enforcement was directed to begin a formal criminal investigation of the attack.

Claimants were given until the end of the 1994 calendar year to file an application with the Attorney General's office. Durden's staff, in an effort to toss the net as widely as possible, to contact anyone who might qualify for a claim, placed public notices in newspapers across the state, including black publications. Wire services picked up the notices and ran them in papers across the country. Responses came in from as far as California. Calls came from over-seas, from Japan, France, Australia and England, the foreign press wanting in-formation, interviews, maybe a live sound bite.

Durden's office wound up mailing out more than four hundred applications to possible property claimants. Follow-up correspondence with each of them began filling the drawers and shelves of Robinson's office, hundreds of letters and documents mailed back from dozens of families, any piece of paper anyone could find that might boost their connection to Rosewood.

Robinson and Beisler began drawing family trees. When the limbs outgrew their desks, they began taping them up on the wall. It wasn't long before the wall was covered, floor to ceiling, plastered with paper, more than thirteen hundred names, each one claiming a piece of what the government had to give.

As the number of branches grew, they began to tangle. Family lines began criss-crossing, zigging and zagging, looping and turning on themselves with un-explainable gaps. Some names appeared on several trees. Some children were listed with no biological parents. Aunts and uncles were claimed as parents. Grandparents were claimed as parents. Friends and neighbors were claimed as parents. Some children changed parents every few years. The word "family," so neatly stated in the legislation, became blurred in the convoluted reality of Rosewood's households and of those of the generations that followed.

"This legislation was lacking in how it defined 'family,' " says Robinson. "It didn't give us a lot to go on. As you get into a place like Rosewood, or into many African-American communities, especially back in that time, you see a lot of situations where children are not raised by their biological parents. I saw it in my own family. My father was raised by a married couple he called 'Mother' and 'Father,' and it wasn't until he was a teenager that he learned his 'Mother' was really his aunt, that he was born in North Carolina and was given away by his real mother when he was a toddler. He bounced around among several rela-tives during his early years, then wound up with this aunt down in Wildwood.

"That's similar to a lot of situations we found in Rosewood. Some of the families were structured traditional family units. But there were others where you had cousins living with uncles and aunts and calling them parents."

Tracing those twisted lines three and four generations forward to deter-mine the legitimacy of each property claim became a dizzying nightmare. Al-most every day Robinson got another call or letter from one of the families, and another couple of names went up on the wall.

The survivor claims were simpler to sort out. The four witnesses who testified at Hixson's hearing—Minnie Lee Langley, A.T. Goins, Willie Evans and Wilson Hall—qualified automatically by dint of the scrutiny they had already undergone. The remaining four survivors named in the bill—Lonnie Carroll, Dorothy Hosey, Mary Hall Daniels and Margie Hall Johnson—had to apply like everyone else. In all, Durden's office received twenty-two survivor applications, and Frank Beisler was dispatched to personally interview each one at their home.

Several were easily dismissed. Two came from white people. Others were blacks who told Beisler they had been infants at the time of the attack and had no proof other than family lore that they ever lived in Rosewood. "I got a lot of 'My mother told me we were there,'" says Beisler. "They were sincere, but they had nothing to support it."

Just as sincere was a man named George Davis, whom Beisler visited in Tampa. Davis was seventy-seven years old, living in a nursing home. He was five, he told Beisler, the night his house was set ablaze. A white man pulled him out of the burning building, he said. The man had a rifle in one hand as he lifted Davis with the other. Davis's pants were on fire, he said, as the man carried him to the front yard, where he put out the flames and bandaged the boy's leg. "He told me this man kept his gun lying on his lap while he took care of him," says Beisler.

When Davis was done with his story, he pulled back his bedsheet and showed Beisler his right leg. "Nothing but burn scars," says Beisler, "from the knee down to the ankle."

Beisler has no doubt Davis's story was true. "That's my gut hunch," he says. But his hunch was all he had. Davis had no documents, and none of the verified survivors knew who he was. There was nothing to support his claim but his scarred leg and Beisler's instinct. And that was not enough.

"It killed me having to turn him down," says Beisler. "There were several like that, people I just knew were telling the truth. But they had no proof, no support, so there was nothing we could do. Some who had proof weren't living within the line of the law. They were living *near* Rosewood and were run off their property, lost their homes, but they weren't living *in* Rosewood, so we had to turn them down, too.

"It was tough," says Beisler. "I'll tell you. It really hurt me, in my heart."

In the end, the survivor applications, along with Beisler's reports, were reviewed by a three-person committee that included Robinson, a vice-president of the state NAACP, and the director of the governor's Commission on African-American Affairs. They wound up approving the claims of the four outstanding survivors named in the bill—Carroll, Hosey, Daniels and Johnson. And they approved one more, a wild card, a name never mentioned in the dozens of depositions taken from Rosewood family members, a name not included in the study team's report, a name found nowhere on Guy Robinson's wall. Amidst all the clamor and chaos of the previous two years, this woman had sat quietly at her home near Palm Beach, watching the goings on from a distance and waiting to see how things would shake out. Then, when it was time, she surfaced.

Her name was Robie Mortin, and her house was less than an hour's drive north of Hollywood.

THIRTY-THREE

Wildflower

S he lives literally on the other side of the tracks. Start on the Atlantic sands of Palm Beach and go west, across the sparkling harbor of Lake Worth, with its multimillion-dollar yachts and condos. Pass the mere million-dollar estates on the harbor's west bank, through the neighborhoods of fenced lawns and swimming pools behind them, then cross over the Florida East Coast rail line and you're there, in Riviera Beach, which, despite its deceptive name, is home to the poorest people in Palm Beach County, many of whom work in those mansions by the sea, and almost all of whom, like Robie Mortin, are black.

Her place is right on Old Dixie Highway, U.S. Route 1, the traffic whooshing within a few feet of her front door. It's a small house, a cottage, really, with a chain link gate out front and a rainbow of tropical plants engulfing its tiny front yard. The inside, too, is green and lush with foliage, a jungle of limbs and leaves crawling up the living room's louvered windows, bending over the leopard print pillows and throws arranged on the sofa and chairs.

Robie takes a seat in one of the chairs, filling it from arm to arm. She's a stout woman, broad-shouldered, her biceps and forearms as thick as her son

---

Robie Mortin

Geffery's, who is home on this Monday afternoon, taking a lunch break from his job at a nearby plumbing supply company. Geffery is thirty-seven, a big, beefy man. He's the youngest of Robie's five children. She's been married twice, is widowed now, living alone in this rented bungalow since her husband Johnnie died seven years ago.

Her physique says something about the work Robie did for most of her life, cleaning and loading laundry in some of those palaces across the tracks. She won't give too many details—she says she plans to write her own book someday—but among her employers were the Pulitzers. "Worked for them eighteen years," she says. "Started out a laundress, and wound up doing *everything*. Cooking, cleaning. And parties, a *lot* of parties."

The Fords, the Kennedys, the Waterburys, they all dropped by, knew Robie by name, she says. Once a year, she says, the Duke and Duchess of Windsor would visit and stay for a week. "But I'm not going to tell you what they were like," says Robie. "That'll be in my book."

She's happy to talk about Rosewood, though, and when she does, Geffery comes out from the kitchen and takes a seat. It wasn't until eight years ago that he first heard of his mother's birthplace. "And that was just tidbits," he says, his voice deep but soft, a gentle baritone.

"I didn't know the whole story," he says, "until this stuff all came up with the legislature. When we were growing up, my mother never told us a *thing* about this."

"Of *course* I didn't," says Robie. "I didn't want my children to grow up hating people. Hate destroyed Rosewood. Why should I let it destroy *me*? Or *them*?"

Geffery nods.

"My parents never taught us to hate," he says. "I've never had that feeling in me. And I'm glad now that she never *did* let me know, because it would have set something off in me that I don't even want to *think* about.

"It hurt me so much when I learned about this," he continues. "To realize that my mother could have been so much more, that *I* could have been more than what I am today."

He squeezes his hands together and shakes his head.

"I watched my mother and father struggle their whole lives . . ."

Robie cuts him off. She'll have none of this. No regrets. No pity. No whining.

"You've got to *live* in this world," she says. "You've got to go *on*. It's like my grandmother said. 'Don't look back. Pick up what you got and *go* with it.'"

Robie was startled when she saw the "60 Minutes" broadcast in 1983. "It was like a bolt out of the blue," she says. But even then she didn't tell her children that that was *her* story on that TV screen.

"I was trying to figure out who and what everybody was going to *do* about this thing," she says. "Personally, I couldn't see any sense in revisiting it. I had put this all back in my mind, and that's where I kept it."

Minnie Lee and Lee Ruth were Robie's cousins. They'd come up together as children in Rosewood, and they'd kept in contact for a while afterward. But they had lost touch over the years, so Robie knew nothing about the reunions or the family friction, or even the claim itself—not until she read about it in the newspaper. And even then, when she saw that Minnie Lee and Lee Ruth were filing their bill, Robie kept her silence.

"Frankly," she says, "I didn't believe anything would come of it."

But she began clipping every story she saw, everything that was printed about Rosewood. She dropped each clipping in a bag, and by the winter of '93, the bag was stuffed.

"It was clear to me about then that they were fixin' to do something about this thing, so I said it's time to make a move."

She went to a local attorney, a black lawyer named Richard Ryles, dropped the bag of clippings on his desk and told him she was from Rosewood. "I didn't have a birth certificate, nothing like that," says Robie. "But I had my memory."

That was enough to convince Ryles. He took her case and, heeding his client's wishes, they both sat back and watched that spring's legislative fireworks from afar. Robie had no desire to get involved, not yet.

"Really, I didn't care if the thing passed or not," she says. "I couldn't care less about the money. I could *use* it, but I certainly didn't *need* it. I've never wanted for anything in my life, and I've never needed *anybody's* help. I am not, and I never have been, a welfare, state-assisted person. I never wanted to take one dime from the state. I did for *myself.*

"Whether I got anything out of this or not didn't matter to me," she says. "All that mattered to me was letting them know who I *was,* that I was *there.* And there was no rush for that."

Even when the bill became law, Robie felt no rush. She didn't write Durden's office for an application form until August. But when she received it, she sat with it for days before filling it out, letting the pages stay blank while she called up memories she had suppressed for a lifetime.

She thought about the mother she never met, who died when she was eighteen months old. She thought about her father, Nathan Robinson, who worked at the sawmill in Sumner. When her mother died, he gave Robie to her grandmother to raise. Polly Carter was the woman's name, Sam Carter's mother.

"Uncle Sammy," that's what Robie called Sam Carter. She remembered the wagon rides he gave her, their trips to the beach, the times they'd go wildflower picking in the woods. Robie's father lived just two miles away, on the other side of town, but Robie remained with Polly and Sam Carter and Sam's wife Katie. They were the people who raised her, brought her up as if she were their own.

Robie was at her father's house the day it began, visiting him along with her older sisters Sebie and Esther, who had come down from Chiefland for the holidays. None of them knew anything was wrong until their father rushed in the door Tuesday afternoon and told them to dress warm and dress fast. He was taking them to the Sumner station and putting them on the train to Chiefland. He didn't take time to explain. There was no time. It wasn't until they got off the train that the girls learned Sam Carter had been lynched the night before. It wasn't until late that week that they learned the whole town of Rosewood was under attack. And it wasn't until two years later that Robie saw her father again.

He had escaped the same way as Robie's grandmother Polly—on foot. Polly showed up in Chiefland a day after the girls got there. She was wet, shivering, half dead after hiking through the woods. She had walked all night to reach Otter Creek, where a mailman hid her in the back of his car and drove her to safety. Robie's father had gone east, too, but apparently he had kept going. No one knew where. Not until two years later, when Robie moved to the Riviera Beach area with her sister Esther, was she reunited with their father. They ran into each other in church. Five years later he died, and according to Robie, her father isn't the only Rosewood native buried in Riviera Beach.

"Omigod," she says nodding her head toward the north end of town, "the cemetery up there is *full* of them."

Once she was ready, Robie sat down that August with a granddaughter and filled out the Attorney General's affidavit in a single five-hour session. She got it notarized and mailed it back that same day. A month later, the last day of September, a skeptical Frank Beisler arrived to interview her.

"I had doubts about her at first," says Beisler. "*Extreme* doubts."

He came prepared, peppering Mortin with questions only someone who knew Rosewood inside out could answer. How far was Junior Hudson's barn from the rail depot? What buildings were between the depot and the Rose-wood jook? Who shot Elias Carrier the night of the Christmas pageant? Beisler even tried a trick question, mentioning in passing how hard the chairs must have been in the Rosewood school's classroom.

"No," Robie corrected him. "They didn't *have* chairs. They had *benches.*"

Beisler knew that.

"She was amazing," he says. "Every question, no hesitation, no thought. *Bang,* she had the answer. I couldn't trip her up."

Beisler came away a believer. With confirmation from Minnie Lee and some of the others that Robie Allenetta Robinson had indeed been among them at Rosewood, a ninth, and final, survivor, was added to the Attorney General's list. That fall, along with the eight others, Robie received a check from the state for fifty thousand dollars. The following January, again like the others, she was given a second check, this one for a hundred thousand.

Robie hasn't really done much with the money. She's looking at buying her own home, a place not more than a mile from where she now rents. It needs a little work, but at $38,000, "it's a steal," she says. "Hardwood floors. A nice place, something I can really make my own."

She bought herself a new car, too, a '95 Cutlass Supreme, to take the place of the old '79 Chevy that used to sit out in her carport. And she's thinking about taking her granddaughter on a trip to Greece. She points at a pair of paintings of the Parthenon hanging on the wall above her sofa.

"Greece is the beginnings of civilization," she says. "That's the beginnings of who we *are.*"

She chuckles.

"Or at least who we'd like to *think* we are."

Other than those three things—the house, the car and the trip—Robie doesn't plan to spend a dime more on herself. Whatever's left, she says, will go into a trust fund for her children.

"Why should I change?" she asks. "I was doing fine before all this happened, and I'm doing fine now."

Geffery pats her knee as he heads back to the kitchen.

"You can't teach an old dog new tricks," says Robie, "and I'm one *happy* old dog."

THIRTY-FOUR

Family

It would seem they would all be happy, the dozens of Rosewood families that had endured so much and come so far, who had kept their feet through decades of fragmentation and fear, hard times and hurt, who had finally reached out and reunited, joining hands and gathering strength, then turning to face the most powerful of foes—the state of Florida itself—and against all odds, had emerged victorious, standing on those steps of the Capitol building that golden morning in May, the warm glow of glory, justice and redemption washing over them all.

But the glow faded fast, replaced by rancor. And rivalry. And resentment. All because of the very thing the government had tried to keep out of the Rosewood bill.

Money.

There were signs as early as July, when the 1995 Rosewood Family Reunion was staged down in Micanopy, just outside Gainesville. The press flocked to the scene, reporters from across the state and beyond, descending on that quiet hamlet, recording the hugging, the hand-shaking, the Saturday picnic and the

Willie Evans

big Sunday dinner, the talk of a Rosewood museum, of a family quilt, and a monthly newsletter. It was a feel-good story, great footage to cap off the eleven o'clock news, a nice piece for the feature front of the morning papers.

No one paid much attention to the fact that there were almost as many journalists there as family. Sixty—that's how many survivors and descendants showed up that weekend. Thirteen hundred names were on that wall down in Guy Robinson's office, and sixty came to Micanopy.

They all knew why. Those who had come and the ones who had stayed away, they all knew that a battle was already brewing, a backlash among factions within some of the families themselves, kin turning on kin. Finger-pointing. Name calling. And worse. Now that the law was spelled out, now that the hard figures were set in stone, now that there was nothing left to imagine, no lottery-like prize to dream of, now that it was clear who would get how much and who would have to fight for what was left, the hand-holding and praying subsided, replaced by outstretched fingers and raised fists.

The first targets, incredibly, were the survivors.

Dorothy Hosey was so overrun with relatives—some she hadn't seen in years, some she didn't even recognize—calling her on the phone, knocking on her door, asking for cash, *demanding* it, cursing her if she refused—that she went into hiding. She bought a new house, which she had planned to do from the beginning, leaving behind the bullet-riddled, roach-infested east Tampa housing project she had lived in for so many years. But she told no one where she had moved, and she discarded her phone number as well. Not even Arnett Doctor knows Mama Dot's number now. No one does. She has, in essence, carefully and with forethought, disappeared, like a political exile.

Mary Hall Daniels has moved as well, from her small Jacksonville apartment into a house whose address she too has kept a secret. Her number, like Dorothy's, is unlisted, but her daughter Alzada has permission to share it with people Mary knows.

"I *had* to do it this way," explains Mary, speaking by phone from her new home, north of the city. "It seemed like everybody in the world started calling me after I got this money. People I don't even *know* called me up, telling me they were my relatives. And it's funny, you know? Because everybody *knew* where I was living before. They all knew my telephone number. But none of them ever came to visit me, none of them stopped by. None of them called. People walked right *by* me, which was all right. It never bothered me, because I *had* my friends. I knew who they were, and I know who they are now. But the rest of them, the ones who been trying to get to me now? Forget it. *None* of them knows where I live."

Even if they did, there's nothing any of them could get from Mary. She's put every cent she received from the state into her new home and a car, and she's happy.

"All the money that God blessed me to have, it's all gone," she says. "The house, my new furniture, and a new car, I paid it all off with cash. I don't want to be owing anybody *anything.* I'm right back where I started from, living off my same social security. The only thing different is I'm in my own home now, and that is *so* pleasant.

"It's true," says Mary. "If you wait on the Lord, He'll make a way for you."

Mary's brother Wilson hasn't had to hide. No one would be foolish enough to face off against Wilson Hall, though he's heard more than a few unkind words over the past year.

"It's the younger ones that are talking," says Wilson. "The nieces and nephews. They're looking at me now like I cheated them *out* of something, like I got something *they* should've had.

"But I don't worry about them, 'cause I've never been close to them anyway. They live different lifestyles, those younger ones. They're in a different *world* from mine."

Wilson's world has been, and still is, centered on his wife, his sister up the street—Margie—and his club, which, he says, has been completely remodeled with the money he got from the state.

"You wouldn't *recognize* the joint," says Wilson, speaking by telephone from the bar of the *new* 705 Club. "That old, smoky, rundown place that was here, man, this place is like *sunshine* compared to that."

The club is half again larger, says Wilson, with a brand-new kitchen. "Shiny stuff," he says. "Even a new cooler box." The booths are gone, replaced by tables and chairs and a bar that runs the length of one wall. "Fifteen tables," says Wilson, "and thirty-five stools at the bar. With mirrors all the way around."

The dirt lot out front is paved now, lined off for parking, with signs posted on all sides: NO DRUGS, NO LOITERING, NO LITTERING.

"Those signs are *inside,* too," says Wilson. "Ain't gonna be none of that kind of trouble around here no more."

He now has the cash to pay the security guards required by the city, and he's bought a new mini-van for his wife Stephanie, who teaches special education at a school across the state line in Georgia. "She needs something with some room in it," says Wilson, "to carry those kids around."

As for Wilson's sister Margie, nothing in her life has changed. She is still fighting leukemia, still making regular trips to the hospital for radiation treatment. "She had a bad spell of the sickness not too long ago," says Wilson, "and it's taking effect on her."

Wilson's the one who drives Margie to the clinic for her treatments. He's the one who pays the home nurse who sits with Margie each day. He helps her sign any papers she needs to keep her affairs in order—"For social security and such," he says. And he's the one making sure the money Margie was paid by the state is safe.

"Right now she's just sitting on it," says Wilson. "She says she's saving that money to take care of her sick days. What she don't realize is her sick days are *here*."

While folks around Hilliard have left Wilson alone, there have been a few pecking at Margie's windows. "Not relatives so much as some of her neighbors and friends," says Wilson. "People think she's got a house full of money, and they try to get in there any way they can."

Willie Evans doesn't have to worry about his windows. He's got a new security system installed in his house in Sanford, the same house he bought back in 1968, the year he had to quit work because his eyesight was gone. Twenty-two years of sawing cement and bricks, the dust and chips flying in his face eight hours a day, had done him in. It had been tough work at the start, when they paid him fifty cents an hour, and it was just as hard when he retired, at sixteen dollars a day. But he still wishes he could have hung on a couple more years. "To when the money started gettin' *really* good," he says.

It was the fall after the Rosewood bill had been signed—a September evening—when Willie sat out front of his home, with its tin roof, its pink trim around the windows and the pink pillars holding up the porch, and talked about the difference in the generations he was seeing these days. He made his point by talking about mullet. Fresh mullet. "That's *west* coast mullet I'm talking about," he cautioned, "not that east coast stuff." He said he often picks some up when he pays a visit to one of his friends.

"The older people," said Willie, "they *love* you to bring them something when you go to see 'em. They just appreciate it so *much*.

"But the younger ones," he said, "they see me bringing that fish, and they ask me where's *theirs* and why didn't I buy *them* some. They're *expecting* it, see? I tell 'em, 'Go catch your *own* damn fish.'"

It was raining that September night, a light drizzle dripping off the sagging roof of Willie's porch. It was dark out, but he still had his sunglasses on. He always puts his sunglasses on when he steps outside. That's been his habit ever since he went blind. He keeps the TV going almost all the time—"More for company than anything else," he said—though there are two shows he never misses. "'Wheel of Fortune,'" he smiled, "and 'The Price is Right.' I just *love* that 'Price is Right.'"

Word had come that afternoon from the Attorney General's office that Rosewood survivors would soon be receiving early payments of $50,000 apiece, rather than waiting until January for the full $150,000 each. Arnett had pushed Greg Durden's office for that, saying these people were getting old, and some might not still be around in January. Willie would be turning eighty-seven on Christmas Day, but he waved away any notion that *he* might be checking out anytime soon.

"Got a little arthritis in my left knee," he said, "but then that's been worrying me about forty-five years now, so I don't pay it much mind."

He's got one child, his son Donnell, who lives up in New York, where he works in warehousing at the World Trade Center. A framed high school graduation photo of Donnell's daughter Libra sits on Willie's bureau, though he can't see it. It's inscribed, *Your one and only granddaughter.*

Willie's wife Edna passed away in 1992, and he's lived alone since. His neighbor Edlina James does some cooking for him, and Meals on Wheels takes care of the rest. Three days a week—Sundays, Tuesdays and Wednesdays—he spends at church. Willie's always been a churchgoing man. His grandmother Julia raised him that way back in Rosewood. They went to the AME church there, and Willie goes to the AME church now—the St. James AME there in Sanford, just across the street from his house.

When he mused that September evening about how he might spend the money he had coming to him from the state, Willie talked about fixing up his porch—"The termites been eatin' it up real bad," he said, poking at the rotting wood with his cane. He talked about maybe giving the house a new paint job as well. And he said he was definitely going to give something to the church.

When he answers his telephone eight months later, he still has the TV going. "Yes," he says. "Matter of fact, 'The Price is Right' is just comin' on."

His front porch is fixed now, says Willie, and the house has been painted. "Outside *and* in," he says. It was Arnett who insisted Willie put in the security system, though Willie says he really doesn't see the need.

"I ain't had nobody come here bothering me at all," he says. "Nobody's bothered me about my money. 'Course hardly anybody knows where I *am*."

His only splurge, he says, was the new living room chair that now sits in front of his television. "It's one of them—whatcha call it—one of them *Lazyboy* chairs," he says. "You know, that lift you up, stretch your feet out, lay you back. It's real nice."

And he certainly did give some money to his church. "Fifteen thousand dollars," he says, proudly. Ten percent. The standard tithe. "I *believe* in tithing," says Willie.

As for his health, the arthritis is still the only thing bothering him. "It causes me some misery," he says. "But I can live with it. You *learn* to live with things like that."

Up in Jacksonville, Minnie Lee Langley's health problems have been a bit more serious than Willie's. There was another bout with pneumonia and she's had some recent surgery for a blocked artery in her left leg. But she says she's getting better, and she's lost none of the defiance that has carried her through all these years. Ask her what she's done with the payment she received from the state, and she almost spits into the telephone.

"You got your womens mixed *up* when you go and ask me about my *money*," she says.

Her daughter Dorothy is more forthcoming. Minnie never gave a thought to leaving her home, says Dorothy, but she has fixed it up with a new living room suite, a new refrigerator, new cabinets for the kitchen, and, most notably, says Dorothy, a new washer *and* dryer.

"She washes all the *time*," says Dorothy. "She always has. She's got a lifestyle that doesn't change too much. But she was getting too feeble to keep going outside and hanging things up, so she went and got herself a dryer."

Minnie won't talk about how she does or doesn't spend her money, but she knows what money has been doing to some of the Rosewood families, and she's happy to explain why it's done nothing to her.

"I ain't never been crazy about money," she explains. "I worked all my life, I worked *hard,* and I made what I needed. I made money, but money ain't *never* made *me*. It would never *change* me. Not money, not *nothin'* gonna' get between me and the Lord.

"Them people that's having trouble with all this," she says, "they don't know nothin' about family, about *being* family. I don't even *know* none of those people."

Minnie knows A. T. Goins, but it would be hard for her to get in touch with him, even if she wanted. His daughter Annette has moved into a place near his home in St. Petersburg, and when the phone rings at A. T.'s house, it's either Annette or her mother, Anna Maude, who answers.

"He can't come to the phone right now," says Anna Maude, answering a recent call. "He's feeling depressed today."

The next day Anna Maude answers again.

"He can't talk right now," she says. "He's out in the yard."

Could she call him in?

"No, I can't. The person you need to talk to is my daughter, Annette."

When Annette answers her phone, she says she needs to talk to her own attorney before she speaks to anyone about her family. Furthermore, she says, she has power of attorney for her father. "And I would appreciate it," she says, "if you don't try to call my father anymore."

Frank Beisler, who visited each of the survivors' homes during the Attorney General's investigative process, is amazed at the disputes that have arisen among some of the Rosewood families. But none bewilders him more than what has happened to A. T. Goins.

"When I went to interview him, what I saw was a gentle man, just a nice guy," says Beisler. "He told me all he wanted out of this money was to pay off his newspaper bill. His *newspaper bill,* that's it. And he can't even read, because his eyes are so bad. He said he likes to keep the paper around for friends when they come to visit.

"And now here are these people trying to beat the shit out of this man for his money," says Beisler. "Unbelievable."

You have to go through a lawyer, too, if you want to speak to Lonnie Carroll, but that's because Lonnie is unable to speak for himself, as he has been for the past ten years, ever since he had a stroke and was put in a nursing home there by the ocean in New Smyrna Beach.

That same week last September that Willie Evans sat on his porch and talked about his life, Lugenia Carroll and a dozen or so of her family and friends gathered in the living room of her little house on Hickory Street there in New Smyrna and talked about Lonnie. They set out a nice spread of food—barbecued chicken, collard greens, cornbread, rice, potato salad and iced tea—pulled up every chair they could find, and spent a couple of hours sharing stories.

Lugenia and Lonnie have had that same place—a white cinderblock bungalow with plants hanging on the porch—ever since Lonnie's brother Aaron died there in 1966. "A. C.," they called Aaron. This little tree-shaded neighborhood, just off the main drag in New Smyrna, was where both Aaron and Lonnie wound up after leaving Rosewood. Lonnie and Lugenia married here in 1944. Lugenia said Lonnie told her all about Rosewood when he first met her, told her about his father James, who was shot dead that week, and about his mother Emma, who left Rosewood with bullet wounds in her hand and wrist and died a year later. Aaron never did like to talk about Rosewood, said Lugenia, not the way Lonnie would.

Lonnie was a logger, said Lugenia, "following that wood," she said, wherever it took him. Mostly he worked in the forests around Palatka, halfway between Gainesville and the Atlantic. He was a big man—six foot, two hundred pounds—strong enough to earn some extra money boxing on the side. "Four dollars a fight," said Lugenia, "that's what they paid him."

Toward twilight the talk turned to the claims bill, to the money that was starting to come to the survivors and to the property settlement that had yet to be worked out.

"Lord," said Lonnie's cousin, Rose Edwards, whose father Hubert was a deceased Rosewood survivor, "I just hope this money doesn't destroy our people."

Then it was time to take a drive over to visit Lonnie. The trip was short, just a couple of miles, out of the crowded little neighborhood of Hickory Street, onto the main drag, up over the Intracoastal Waterway and down to the oceanfront, the resort section of New Smyrna Beach, where condos and small seedy motels are painted various shades of pink and aqua. The place where Lonnie lives, the Ocean View Nursing Home, looks like just another motel, painted coral and turquoise, with sand sweeping across its parking lot.

Inside, the halls were crowded with elderly men and women, black and white, parked in wheelchairs, some speaking with one another, a few speaking to themselves, most just sitting in silence.

Lonnie was in his room, in darkness, the shades drawn. A transistor radio sat on the bureau, tuned to a soul station, the voice of a singer named Babyface crackling from the little box:

"I'm gonna keep on searchin' till I find you, baby...
Please tell me where, where, where is my love."

Lonnie was on his back in bed, his mouth open, his eyes closed, his chest rising and falling as he breathed.

Lugenia leaned over him, put her hands on his face and began rubbing it— his cheeks, his forehead—pressing the skin till he knew she was there.

His mouth closed, the lips pressed tight, and his eyes opened. They were white, his eyes, as white as milk. Lonnie is completely blind.

He groaned, moved his head slightly from side to side. The rest of his body remained inert. Then he shut his eyes again, and his mouth fell open, and he lay back as he was when Lugenia arrived, as he has lain every day for the past decade.

For the first seven years Lugenia came to see Lonnie every day. But then she got sick herself, began bleeding out of her left ear and found out she had a brain tumor. Now one side of her face is paralyzed, and though she can hear fine, she has trouble speaking, because half her mouth is paralyzed too.

But she still visits Lonnie at least once a week. That's the way it was that September evening, as she kissed his face and left him in his room. And that's the way it is today. Lonnie's money has paid for a new sofa, a new bed, a new Frigidaire for the house, a chain link fence out front and some air-conditioning that's getting put in any day now, says Lugenia. She's also getting $300 a month from Lonnie's claims payment, to help pay the bills. Other than that, the money is paying for Lonnie's care.

"Nothing's changed too much," says Lugenia. "We're just goin' on living."

It was understandable in a way, say Frank Beisler and Guy Robinson, to see the conflicts that arose around some of the survivors and their families. The money, after all, was a significant sum. But the property payments—Beisler and Robinson were initially amazed at the infighting that grew among some of the families over those. Still, it didn't take long to understand.

The half-million-dollar pie created by the state to pay Rosewood's property claims could be sliced only so many ways. The more slices there were, the smaller each slice. Thirteen hundred names added up to some very thin slices—a fact that did not escape some of the claimants, which Beisler and Robinson discovered as they went about the business of verifying those claims.

"People were purposely leaving other people out," says Beisler. "Their own relatives, their own family. We found that out after digging and digging into this thing. There were a couple of *ministers* who filed papers conveniently leaving family members off their trees. I'm talking about their own sisters and brothers. Now I'm *sure* they knew their own sisters and brothers were alive."

Then again, adds Beisler, there were those on the flip side, qualified descendants who turned down payments to which they were fully entitled.

"We've got a whole drawer full of people who are eligible for property payments who just don't *want* them, for whatever reason," says Beisler. "I've had several people tell me, 'Look, I wasn't *at* Rosewood. Those are my *ancestors*. I'm not entitled to that money and I don't want it, period.'

"And there are some who told me they didn't want anything to do with this money because they were afraid it would start a battle in their family."

There was a small eruption in March of 1995, when Greg Durden arranged a meeting at a church in Orlando with all families whose property claims appeared at that point to have merit. The intent was to have the families themselves help comb and complete the trees that had been drawn by Beisler and Robinson. Seventy people showed up, representing sixteen families. At one point Durden said he'd had complaints from some family members that they were not being kept updated on what was happening with these property claims.

Arnett, sitting in the front row, took the comment as an affront to him and the Committee. He was irate. He told Durden he wasn't about to sit still and listen to accusations from unnamed sources. Durden told him he could leave if he'd like. Arnett shot back that he wasn't about to leave. "This is *my* family that you're talking about," he said. An echo of *Amen*s came from around the room.

But that was about the last sign of solidity the families would show. The complaints Durden had heard continued, and soon the situation had deteriorated into a case of every family for itself.

"It hasn't been pretty," says Beisler.

And it shouldn't be surprising, says Arnett's sister, Yvonne. Through all of this, Philomena Doctor's first child had kept her silence. From that weekend in 1982 when her brother came back from his trip to Rosewood and told their mother he wanted to know more about this thing, through the ensuing decade of shouting and tears, from her mother's death in 1991 through the twisting journey that finally led to the passing of this law, Yvonne Doctor had kept her silence.

And this—the acrimony that was now tearing some of these families apart—was why. This—more than fear, pain, trauma, anger or hate—was why Yvonne's mother had so fiercely forced her family to keep this matter to themselves. Yes, the damage done that winter week in 1923 was immeasurable. But Philomena Doctor knew just as well the further damage that would surely be done by using the ghosts of Rosewood to unleash the evil of greed.

"My mother understood people," says Yvonne, speaking from her home in St. Petersburg, the same home in which her mother died. "She knew human nature. And she *knew* what was going to happen if people went and tried to do something about this."

Like Robie Mortin—only for much longer—Yvonne Doctor watched from the sidelines as the Rosewood forces, led by Arnett, fought their way toward Tallahassee. Yvonne respected what her brother was doing, even though she disagreed with it.

"Whatever my mother said to Arnett, I don't know," says Yvonne. "But till her dying day, her wishes to *me* were to keep this quiet."

Yvonne respected those wishes, long after her mother was dead. Not until the day the Florida Senate voted on the bill did she show her face, sitting with the families in the gallery. It was important to her to be there that day, because that day was not about money. It was about justice, acknowledgment, a tribute her mother would have appreciated, a tribute her mother and those who died before her deserved.

But after that day, Yvonne watched it all dissolve. It even washed up on her own doorstep, there in St. Petersburg.

"When it hit the papers that this law had passed," she says, "they all started showing up here, faces I'd never seen, coming to my door, asking questions, wanting to find out how they were connected so they could make a claim.

"I'd open the door and see this *stranger* standing there, and I'd say, 'God, I can't believe this. What wind blew *you* here?'

"There's one cousin I haven't seen in over twenty years, and she lives right here in this city—*she* showed up."

It's not everyone, cautions Yvonne, who has been stained by this catfighting.

It's not everyone who's guilty of greed. The older generations, she says, and some of the younger ones, too, those who have been showing up at funerals and baptisms for years, who have come together at holidays, who have sent cards on birthdays and presents at Christmas to nieces and nephews and grandsons and granddaughters, who have been family—actively *been* family—long before any of this talk about a claims bill began, those people's concern all along has been that this be a good thing, a healing thing for the family, that the beauty of this bill was what it represented, not what it repaid.

They are hurt, many of them say—some say they are embarrassed—by what they have seen. Yvonne has no doubt her mother is watching, and that Philomena feels the same.

"I don't think she's happy about this, not at all," says Yvonne. "The fact is," she says, "it's turning out just the way she was afraid it would."

THIRTY-FIVE

Sylvester's Shadow

W hen the dust had finally settled on the Rosewood property payments, when the names were drawn up, the figures computed and the checks finally mailed in June of 1995, the money hardly seemed worth the bloodletting it had caused.

Out of four hundred property claim applications, fewer than seventy claimants actually wound up with a check from the state. And those checks were not life-changing. The largest were for five thousand dollars, to each of the four children of Fred Edwards, who had owned two acres of land in Rosewood at the time of the attack. The smallest were those received by the eight surviving sons and daughters of Galvester Nada Bradley, who was one of Rosewood resident John Bradley's twelve children. By the time the math was done, John Bradley's eight surviving grandchildren each got a check from the state for $104.17.

It was worse than anticlimactic. Even after a year's effort, the Attorney General's office, like everyone else who had waded into the subject of Rosewood, was left with a sense of incompletion. Tens of thousands of state dollars sat unclaimed. Hundreds of acres of Rosewood property were unaccounted for.

Rosewood family reunion, Washington, D.C., 1993

"Add it up," said Guy Robinson, scanning the 1922 Levy County tax rolls and reading aloud. " '250 acres unknown . . . 400 acres unknown . . . ' There's a *lot* that hasn't been accounted for."

Just as bewildering were the number of property shares that wound up unclaimed. Among John Bradley's family, for example, almost $12,000 of the $20,000 award went uncollected, with no heirs surfacing among the families of ten of Bradley's twelve children. It was the same story, more or less, among each family that applied. By law, every one of those unclaimed dollars were returned to the state's general fund, from which they were originally drawn.

"As of right now," said Frank Beisler in June of 1995, "there's about a hundred and seventy grand going back to the state."

By then, the buzz among the Rosewood families had shifted from property claims to Hollywood. Not Hollywood, Florida; Hollywood, *California.*

Ever since the Rosewood story had broken nationally, calls had begun coming in to Arnett from producers and motion picture companies, people sniffing around about a possible Rosewood project. Maybe a full-length film, maybe a TV miniseries. Rumors began flying. Louis Gossett, Jr. was supposedly interested. Maybe John Singleton. Quincy Jones. Spike Lee. The families—Arnett and the Advisory Committee—hired an entertainment attorney in Orlando, a man named Greg Galloway, to represent them, to sort rumor from fact and to get them a deal.

As for Michael O'McCarthy, he was out of the picture. That 1993 "Maury Povich" broadcast had been his parting shot. When Arnett and the other family members surfaced, O'McCarthy, who had his contracts with Minnie Lee Langley and Lee Ruth Davis, found himself dealing with people who had little interest in dealing with him. The families' rift with Minnie Lee and Lee Ruth apparently extended to O'McCarthy as well. After a single phone conversation that spring with Arnett Doctor, Michael O'McCarthy heard no more from the Rosewood families. He tried selling what he had with just Minnie Lee and Lee Ruth, but no one was interested. This was no longer just two women's story. And so, as the legal gears he had helped set in motion began to turn, O'McCarthy found himself on the outside looking in. "I guess," he said in a *Los Angeles Times Magazine* story published the autumn after the bill was passed, "I was the wrong color."

Six months later O'McCarthy denied at least the spirit of that quote, saying it was taken out of context. He is living in South Carolina now, still modeling, still making movie deals, still selling stories to "Hard Copy" and "A Current Affair." "I do think I deserve credit for what I had to do with Rosewood," he says, "and I haven't gotten it. But that's all right. I remain very proud that I had the opportunity to help even the scales of justice in my home state of Florida. That's my reward, period. If I die today, I'll know I've done some small thing to make my nation better, period. And that's enough, man. That's it."

Far more than O'McCarthy, a man who feels he has not gotten proper credit for his role in the Rosewood story is the reporter who first wrote about it and has continued researching the subject ever since—Gary Moore. Moore's path has wound far from St. Petersburg since he left the newspaper there not long after his first Rosewood story was published in 1982. Over the ensuing decade, he roved from Central America to Seattle, finally settling in Tupelo, Mississippi, where he lives today, not far from where he was born and raised. He teaches a course in computers, but Rosewood remains the focal point of his life. An eight-hundred-page manuscript sits on his desk, the sum of fourteen years spent digging like an archaeologist into every detail of that 1923 town, from the bricks that formed the chimneys of those houses to the names and ancestry of every man, woman and child who inhabited them. He has tried getting his book published, tried getting it made into a movie, all so far to no avail. Like O'McCarthy, Moore has found himself pushed aside by the course of events, standing offstage while the spotlight falls on others. "This story is an endless locus of bitterness," he says. "Reality itself becomes a labyrinth, and you find yourself falling into it. . . . I just couldn't begin to express to you the subterranean aspects of this thing."

Steve Hanlon wouldn't bother trying. Side streets and alleys, layers beneath layers, they don't interest him. Keep it simple. Stay on track. That's his mantra. Always has been, always will. His current cause is a case against the public housing authority in St. Petersburg, on behalf of a three-year-old boy suffering from lead poisoning. But he's still involved with the Rosewood families, helping them sort out the financial and legal affairs that continue to linger. He looks back on what was an ordeal for so many with the fondness of a mother sorting through baby photos. He keeps a postcard from Jim Peters in his desk. It arrived from England not long after the Hixson hearing was finished. "London By Night," the card is titled, completely black on its front, with an inscription on the back:

Have come to the Queens' Asylum and infirmary to have the track marks re-
moved from my carcass. Doc says the scars should heal. You do good work. Let's try
it again in another lifetime.

                                                                        P.

Martha Barnett, too, has moved on, lobbying her way through Florida's
1995 legislature, a group quite different both in content and in spirit from the
'94 body that passed the Rosewood bill. The right-wing wave that swept America in the fall elections of 1994 washed over Florida as surely as it did through
every state in the nation. Lawton Chiles barely beat back a brutal challenge
from George Bush's son Jeb for the governor's seat. In the Senate, for the first
time since Reconstruction, Florida's Republicans became the majority party. In
the House, the Democrats held on, but by the barest of margins, and a core of
them—including most of the strongest opponents to the Rosewood bill—were
more conservative than their Republican colleagues.

Miguel De Grandy bowed out of the whole scene, choosing not to run for
re-election, returning instead to his private law practice in Miami. Bo Johnson
chose not to run again as well; he's back in Milton, selling real estate. Charlie
Williams was re-elected, despite embarrassing many of his colleagues by declaring at a public rally that the school prayer bill he had pushed in the '94 legislature was defeated by "South Florida Jewish members who don't believe in
Jesus." And Al Lawson was back again, too, though he and his black caucus colleagues were barely heard from in an environment whose terms were largely
dictated by the Republicans' national Contract With America—a contract that
would have no room at all for an item like Rosewood.

"There is no doubt in my mind," says Martha Barnett, "that the Rosewood
bill would not have stood a *chance* of passing this year's legislature. If it hadn't
made it last year, it would never have made it."

Arnett Doctor agrees. He's back in his home in Tampa now, still working
the phone day and night, but he's not calling legislators anymore. He's calling
movie producers, though he can't give any details. "Big things are brewing," is
all he'll say about that. "Big, big things."

He's calling for money, too, trying to raise $600,000, he says, to build a
memorial park—the same sort of project Arnett's legislative opponents tried
to put in the bill instead of money. The memorial he has in mind would be built

near Rosewood, on land to be donated by a Levy County resident—a *white* resident. Arnett has a blueprint of the place, drawn by a team of students and professors in the school of architecture at Florida A&M. He unscrolls it on the floor of his office, pointing at the outdoor gardens, the benches and fountains, the museum itself, as if the blue-inked structures are real. "It's going to happen," he says. "Make no mistake about it. It's *going* to happen."

He still keeps his shades drawn, even in the middle of the day, as he has for the past two years. He still freezes each time he hears a car engine slow in front of his house. He hasn't gotten one of those odd late-night calls in months, but he feels no safer now than he did that Saturday in 1982 when he first drove up to Rosewood, with a pistol in his slacks. "They're out there," he says, stroking his goatee. "I *know* they're out there."

He still keeps a gun in every room, as he has for the past two years. There's a Winchester .22 rifle propped in the corner of his office, a shotgun back in the bedroom, a Colt .32 revolver and the old .357 Magnum tucked away in various drawers, along with a new Beretta .25 automatic pistol he bought for his girlfriend Loretta. "I'm not paranoid," says Arnett. "Let's just say I'm *protected.*"

But despite the wariness and the weaponry—steel-edged shadows of his great-uncle Sylvester—Arnett has softened. His fuse is longer, and he's more philosophical about those who stand against him. A year ago, when the government seemed to him to be dragging its feet in paying the survivors, he was furious. "What they don't have the backbone to say," he had declared one afternoon, driving to the coast to visit Lonnie Carroll, "is 'We don't *mind* if we're giving money to the Japanese, or if we give it to the Hispanics, or to the whites, but we don't want to *give* it to the goddamn *niggers.*'"

Today, though, he is a different man. Ask him how he feels about the amounts of money everyone has received, especially the property claimants, and he sounds like one of those senators up in Tallahassee. "I think," he says, "that the fact that the state of Florida has seen fit to pay at *all,* that they would reach into their pockets at *all,* speaks volumes about the state of mind of our elected legislators and how far we've come in the past seventy-three years."

Unlike his sister, Arnett is convinced his mother is looking down on all this with a smile. "Yvonne's entitled to her opinion," he says, "but I think my mother is *ecstatic* about what has happened."

He won't say how much he personally received from the state for his share of his mother's property claim, but it couldn't have put a dent in the twenty thousand dollars he figures he has spent over the past decade pursuing this dream of his. And that, he says, doesn't bother him. "At this juncture, quite honestly," he says, "I'm not in the complaining mode."

As for his dream, it's hard to say exactly what it is, because Arnett's dreams seem to shift with time and circumstance. At first he just wanted to find out what happened at Rosewood. Then he wanted to bring his family together, to make it whole again. Then rose the idea of justice, of making somebody pay for the damage his relatives had suffered.

Now he dreams of that memorial park.

And the movie.

And he has begun dreaming as well about his Seminole Indian roots, something he stumbled across during his research on Rosewood.

"That's right," he says. "My great-grandfather on my *father's* side of the family was a *war* chief in the Seminole Nation."

Arnett pulls a copy of Florida's statewide Seminole tribal membership voting list from a cabinet, and there indeed, among the columns of names, more than a hundred names to a column, among the Gophers and Tigers and Cypresses and Youngbloods, are the Doctors. Nathan Dean Doctor and Minnie Billie Doctor. Toka Carrie Doctor and Susie Osceola Doctor. Two dozen Seminole Doctors, and Arnett intends to track down every one, to trace his connections to them all, and theirs to one another.

"These are my *people*," he says, the late afternoon light slanting through his windowshades. "These are my *relatives*. This is where I came from, *too*."

He folds the list and puts it back in the cabinet.

"That's going to make me feel more complete than I used to feel," he says, closing the drawer. "It's going to make me even more aware of who I am," he says, as his telephone rings.

He lets the answering machine take the call, his recorded voice filling the room.

Hello! . . .

Better it is to be of humble spirit with the lowly, than to divide the spoils with the proud. . . .

After the beep, please leave your telephone number. . . .

Thank you, and God bless.

They still say there are bodies buried back in this swamp. Blacks and whites alike, they still believe there are piles of bones sleeping deep beneath the sand and mud, covered by the thick canopies of oaks and palms and palmettos that have risen like a green cathedral since the day the dead were dropped into the ground.

How many dead is hard to say. The Florida Department of Law Enforcement began combing this forest the same summer the Attorney General's office began counting survivors. A team of state agents pushed through the shrubs and briers, swatting at clouds of mosquitoes and sand flies, stepping over sluggish creeks and black bogs, picking through the eighty acres of dense woodland that was once called Goins Quarters, searching for the mass grave so many told them was here.

They talked to old Fred Kirkland, and he said there were thirty-five women and children dropped into a well a couple of days after the attack on the Carrier house. They listened to Jason McElveen's account of a mule-pulled fire plow dragging dirt over the bodies of twenty-six more. And there was the testimony of a man named James Turner, who was just a fourteen-year-old boy at the time but would later become Levy County sheriff. Turner said he was led to an open grave a few days after the attack and was shown a pile of bodies too tangled to count. He guessed there were at least seventeen, all of them black.

Turner and McElveen are long dead. Fred Kirkland is too old to tromp through those thickets. And even if he weren't, he told the agents, there was no way he could find that well after all this time. Eighty acres, and it's been almost eighty years.

The agents did get Kirkland's help in identifying suspects. Ernest Parham helped as well. As did Gary Moore, the newspaper reporter whose notes and tapes included interviews done in the early 1980s with many white and black witnesses who have died since then.

Moore shared his notes, and the Levy County sheriff's office lent a hand. Court records were pulled, death certificates were gathered, and state agents fanned out across the county, from Chiefland to Cedar Key, interrogating witnesses as well as possible suspects, old men and women not many steps from the grave, each of them struggling to recall details of neighbors who had long ago gone to theirs.

The result—discounting the crowds of the curious who came to Rosewood that week to simply watch as the town burned down, the throngs who arrived in their Model Ts to witness the torching as if it were a carnival, the two to three thousand onlookers Fred Kirkland says filled the village's streets by week's end to witness the smoking ruins—setting all those people aside, the state arrived at a final list of sixteen suspects, men who were witnesses to and possibly involved in the killings that took place in Rosewood that week.

Only one was listed as an actual murderer—a man named Bryant Hudson. He was twenty-five at the time. Four witnesses named Hudson as the man who shot Sam Carter that night by the edge of the woods. "Hudson," states the FDLE report, "is the only suspect identified as having committed a homicide." Records show Bryant Hudson died at a Veterans Hospital in Lake City in 1931, from injuries, friends say, he received in a fight.

Three other names were on the list as witnesses to Sam Carter's murder. One was Garrett Kirkland, Fred Kirkland's uncle. He died in 1952, according to the report, at age seventy-eight. Another was Jason McElveen, who was also present at the Carrier House shootout three nights later. McElveen died in 1983, at age eighty-eight. The third was Orrie Kirkland, Fred Kirkland's father. He was fifty-two the night Sam Carter was killed, but no one, not even his son, can recall the year he died. The FDLE could find no official record of Orrie

Kirkland's death. The best they got was the word of one Levy County old-timer who said old man Kirkland died "many years ago."

Four more names on the suspect list are men who were wounded the night of the shootout at the Carrier House, according to newspaper accounts from the time of the attack and according to witnesses interviewed by the FDLE. Two of those men—Cephus Studstill and Henry Odom—were seen in Sumner late that Thursday night, bloody and bandaged, by Ernest Parham. Studstill, who was twenty-three at the time, died fourteen years later, on the last day of December. Odom is more of a mystery. The FDLE found a 1971 death certificate for a Henry A. Odom in Jacksonville, but they are not sure it's the same man. It is possible, the report concluded, that Odom is alive today. If so, he would be at least ninety-seven years old.

The other two men listed as wounded that Thursday night were Fred Kirkland's brothers, Bryan and Warner. Again, the FDLE could find no record of either man's death, so it is assumed they could possibly still be alive. If so, Bryan Kirkland would be ninety-nine. His brother Warner would be at least ninety-seven.

The last name that appears on the Rosewood suspect list is Red Raulerson. He was a witness to the Carrier house shootout, according to Fred Kirkland. Kirkland says Raulerson is dead now, but he can't recall when he passed away.

The remaining six people on the list are identified by numbers, not names, "due to the weakness of the allegations against them," according to the FDLE. Two were "possibly involved" in the shooting death of Mingo ("Lord God") Williams, and one was "possibly involved" in the killing of Lexie Gordon. Five of these suspects are now dead. The sixth, were he still alive today, according to the report, would be at least ninety-seven.

That was the gist of it. "The Rosewood investigation has now been completed," wrote FDLE Commissioner James Moore in a cover letter to the report, delivered to the state's Attorney General in January of 1995. "All investigative efforts," the report stated, "have been pursued to their logical conclusion."

That included the hunt for bodies possibly buried out in those woods. The FDLE team spent two days pushing through the swampland behind Doyal Scoggins's house and came away with nothing but scratches and insect bites. The last paragraph of the thirteen-page report sums up that search: "The mass grave issue may never be resolved."

And strangers may never stop knocking on the door of Wesley Thompson's trailer to ask about it. No one has heard more about this mass grave than Thompson. It's his property on which the grave supposedly sits. It's his land Arnett Doctor walked around that spring afternoon in 1982, when he stumbled on the headstones of his ancestors. It was Wesley Thompson who offered Arnett a beer that afternoon.

The headstones are still there, still covered with tangles of vines and poison ivy, deep in these woods back behind Doyal Scoggins's house. There are still gators back there, too. And snakes. And green turtle and black catfish, hogs and wild turkeys, possum and rabbits and otter and deer—all the meat a man would need if meat were what he was after. And that is what a group of men huddled here on a recent, wet autumn afternoon were after—meat.

Their bows were strung taut, their steel-tipped arrows glinting in the glow cast from the porch light of the hut behind them. Around the hut perched a half dozen trailers, bent, rusted, empty. A battered pickup truck leaned by a split-rail fence, its windshield shattered, its wheels swallowed by weeds. Beside it, beached like a lost fish, sat an airboat, its caged propeller looming above its stern, the steel wires sharp and shining in the midday mist.

The men were clad in camo fatigues, four of them, each clutching a cold can of beer. They laughed and cursed, paying no mind to the soft sheets of rain sweeping down from the gray sky above, to the sound of their hounds baying in a distant pen, to the chickens and children rooting in the mud by the porch.

There were women inside the hut, tending a pot of beans picked fresh that morning, lima beans. A television was tuned to the Florida–Ole Miss football game, which was just about finished, the Gators ahead by three scores, and so the men had moved outside, where the smallest of them, a wiry fifty-year-old, his chin speckled with stubble, his damp gray hair dangling from beneath a sweat-stained ball cap, was holding court.

Wesley Thompson.

The shack, the trailers, this land, it's all his, his and his family's, he said. "Unless," he added, draining a last swallow from his can and flinging it toward the fence, "the niggers take it away from us."

His companions grinned. One had a compass pinned to the crown of his cap. The small clear bulb bobbed like a Christmas ornament, its tiny arrow quivering as the man laughed.

Thompson pointed toward a stand of cabbage palms, their gnarled trunks smeared with splashes of orange paint. "It was the state government people did that," he said. "They come in poking around, measuring this and that, checking their maps, trying to figure out where such and such was, where the *town* used to be."

A woman—big, brunette, clad in shorts and a T-shirt, with flip-flops on her feet—stepped out from the hut, waving a spoon. Her name is Christy Thompson, Wesley's wife.

"What the shit were they measuring for *anyway?*" she said. "What's to *measure?*"

Her husband nodded, then continued.

"It's been aggravatin'," he said. "People drivin' up in my yard night and day. White people. Black people. Tellin' me they want me to take 'em down to where the train trestle used to be, or over to the cemetery, or what have you. All these news people, all these reporters. I'm *sick* of it. That that happened was in 1932 or 1923 or whenever it was. That is *history.*"

He popped open another can.

"Shit, what has happened is this thing has gotten blowed way out of proportion. Every person in the state of *Florida* is paying for this, and that just don't get it. That's our *tax* money."

His wife took a seat on a wet plank of pine.

"What are *we* getting out of this?" she asked. "We're right in the middle of it, and we ain't got a damn *thing* out of this except people comin' in here and nosing around.

"What I want to know," she said, "is with all this talk about the coloreds and what they're owed, there hasn't been nothin' said about the *white* people. I mean, from what I've heard, the first persons *shot* in this thing were white people."

Her husband nodded.

"Nigger shot a white man," he said. "That's what started it all. Naturally they all come down and started killin' after that."

The dogs had stopped howling. The TV was turned off. The only sounds were the children splashing in the mud and the rain swishing through the trees. A puppy crawled out from under the porch and curled by the woman's feet, beneath her makeshift bench.

"I don't think it was right what they done," she offered, "I mean, these coloreds were human just like we are. But I don't think these ones out there *now* ought to be reapin' all this profit off it either, not when there's other families that suffered from this, too, *white* families, and nobody's said *diddley*squat about them, and they're not speaking for themselves because they just want to let the past *die*."

Her husband stood and stretched his thin, ropy arms.

"That's the way it's always been, up till now," he said. "Nobody ever said much about this, 'specially those that were actually there. You never heard a word from them, not a *word*.

"I bought this place in 'seventy-two," he said. "From the timber company, *that's* where my deed came from. These niggers talking all about how this land was theirs and they're owed something for it? Are you *kiddin'* me? Those people didn't own this land. Shit, *they* were owned, basically. That's what they were, owned by the lumber company."

The others chuckled again. The rain was falling harder now, beads of water hanging from the brims of their caps.

"Those '60 Minutes' people," he said, "I never will forget that. I come home from work over at the power plant, and here's a TV crew set up out there by the gate, and there's two old niggers sitting there in chairs, and here's this other nigger I recognized from the television, that Bradley man, and he's leaning on the fence, talking to the camera and interviewing these other two niggers, and all I could think was what the *hell* is goin' on here?"

He took another draw from his beer.

"I mean, most of the time a black man comes up in this yard, I turn the *dogs* loose on him. We got to feed our dogs every now and then."

His companions snickered. His wife waved them quiet.

"Blacks have *never* been welcomed around here," she said.

"You got *that* right," said her husband. "When I was growing up over in Cedar Key, we didn't know what a nigger *was*. There used to be a few livin' up on what they called Nigger Hill, but there ain't none there now, not 'less they import 'em in and they leave before dark."

More snickers.

"You see them come in once in a while to visit the island," said the woman. "Just like the other tourists. I saw a couple of 'em not long ago, a black man and woman riding bicycles down by the pier, but I guarantee they didn't spend the night. They've *all* been told there's only one way in and one way out and you better be out before dark."

"That's just the way it is," said the man. "This is not just history. I was working with a company out of Gainesville, buildin' a water plant over at Suwannee, down at the mouth of the river, and a bunch of them old-timers was sittin' around there. We had some black men working with us, and one of these colored guys walks over to these old crackers and says, 'Where do the *black* people hang out around here?'

"And this one old fella, he looked at him a little while, not sayin' a word, then he pointed up at a branch on this big oak tree and said, 'Well, the last black that hung out around here hung right up there.'

"Needless to say, them blacks went back up to Cross City for the night, where there's some of their kind, and that's where they stayed."

The others were picking up their weapons now, moving toward the woods. The woman was back in the hut, tending the stove. Wesley Thompson collected some crushed beer cans and dropped them in a pail.

"I don't like any of this," he said, shaking his head and grabbing his bow. "I don't like it worth a *shit*.

"And I'll tell you where it started," he said, lifting his cap and wiping his brow. "It started that Saturday, I think it was, when that colored man come up here poking around."

He pulled his cap back on and shook his head.

"Yep," he said, spitting on the ground by his feet, "that's what it was."

He rubbed the spit into the mud with the toe of his boot.

"Colored man with a cane."

ACKNOWLEDGMENTS

First, I must thank the survivors, who had the courage, kindness and grace to open their lives and share their stories with a stranger: Minnie Lee Langley; A. T. Goins; Wilson Hall; Willie Evans; Dorothy Goins Hosey; Mary Hall Daniels; Margie Hall Johnson; Robie Mortin; and, through his wife Lugenia, Lonnie Carroll.

My gratitude also to the relatives of Rosewood's survivors and deceased alike, who took me into their trust to help me understand: Arnett Doctor; Yvonne Doctor; Eva Jenkins; Vera Goins Hamilton; Mae McDonald; Annie Bell Lee; Altamese Wrispus; Janie Bradley Black; Anna Maude Goins; Dorothy Smith; Gregery Mortin; Albert Edwards; Sylvia Juanita Richardson; Gwendolyn Johnson; and Katherine Hall.

Special thanks go to Ernest Parham, Doyal and Fuji Scoggins, Martha Pillsbury Thompson, and Walter and Carolyn Pillsbury for sharing their own stories and those of their forebears. Also thanks to George Sandora, Leonard Reynolds, Wesley and Christy Thompson, Herb Wilkerson, Eleanor Travers, Kellie Meyhoff, Don Hatcher, Kenny Collins, Lloyd Collins, Liza Collins, Randolph J. Hodges, and scores of others who asked not to be mentioned by name, for helping me see and understand Levy County, both present and past.

In terms of general historical direction, I must first thank the professionals themselves, the members of the state's Rosewood investigative research team: Maxine Jones, Tom Dye, Bill Rogers, David Colburn and Larry Rivers. The staff at Florida State University's Robert Manning Strozier Library, particularly Gay Dixon and Grace Brock, helped steer me into some of the more arcane corners of the state's history. I am also indebted to the staff of Florida A&M University's Black Archives Research Center and Museum. Others who helped with various local history were Midge Laughlin, archivist with the St. Petersburg Museum of History; Liz Ehrbar, director of the Cedar Key Historical Society Museum; the staff at the Cedar Key State Museum; the staff at Dade City's Hugh Embry Public Library; and Jan H. Johannes, Sr., whose history of Nassau County included useful background on the town of Hilliard.

For their guidance through the legal and legislative layers of this story, I thank Steve Hanlon, Martha Barnett, Jim Peters, Richard Hixson, Greg Galloway, Al Lawson, and Miguel De Grandy. I would also like to thank Bo Johnson, Elaine Gordon, Richard Trammell, Pete Antonacci, Manny Dobrinsky, John Long, Bill Posey, Robert Wexler, Daryl Jones and Charlie Williams for sharing their own roles in the Rosewood bill's legislative journey. I am deeply indebted as well to the staff of the Florida Legislative Library Services Division in Tallahassee, especially archivist Delbra McGriff, and to the Florida State Archives, where David Coles and James Helms shared their expert advice.

I offer my gratitude to Greg Durden, Guy David Robinson and Frank Beisler of the Florida Attorney General's Office of Civil Rights for their assistance above and beyond the call of duty.

The library staffs of several Florida newspapers were immensely generous in opening their files to me. Those newspapers, and the particular people who helped me, include: the *Tampa Tribune* (Alyce Diamandis and Buddy Jaudon); the *Tallahassee Democrat* (Deborah Galloway); the *St. Petersburg Times* (Caroline Ziadie); the *Orlando Sentinel* (Cate Nolan); the *Palm Beach Post* (Sammy Alzofon); and the *Nassau County News-Leader* (Mary Hurst).

Journalist Gary Moore, whose 1982 investigation of Rosewood was a catalyst for many of the events that followed, was very generous in sharing his insights and overviews. Also helpful were reporters Peter Gallagher and Charles Flowers of the *Seminole Tribune* and Eric Harrison of the *Los Angeles Times,* producer Joel Bernstein of CBS News, Brad Wasson of the University of Florida's office of news and public affairs, and Judy Sedgeman, former editor of *The Floridian,* the *St. Petersburg Times*'s Sunday magazine. I would like to thank as well Joe Capozzi of the *Palm Beach Post.*

For the photographs that so enrich these pages, I must first thank the families who trusted me with truly priceless personal snapshots and portraits, particularly Arnett and Yvonne Doctor, Martha Pillsbury Thompson, and Walter and Carolyn Pillsbury. I would also like to thank Joan Morris with the Florida State Archives, Kelly Cooley with Florida State University, Lissette Nabut with the *Miami Herald,* Ron Kolwak and Michelle Dwaskin with the *Tampa Tribune,* Hugh Scoggins, Wendy Ledis with the *Palm Beach Post,* and Terry Witt. Beth Bergman of the *Virginian-Pilot* deserves a special nod for her sensitive eye and magical touch.

On the home front, for their support, encouragement, advice, and—in several cases—sheer sweat, I want to thank Millie Johnson, Joan Ange Shepard, Fred Kirsch, Erika Reif, Cole Campbell, Marvin Lake, Wil Haygood, Randy Jessee, Dave Potvin, Carol Taylor, Cass Fullerton, Susan Raihofer, and Kate Murphy.

Finally, for her wisdom, patience and unending enthusiasm, I will always be grateful to my editor Jane Isay. And, yet again, for his faith and guidance I thank my agent David Black.

NOTES AND SOURCES

PROLOGUE

This account of the January, 1923, attack on Rosewood is based on a synthesis of sources. As Florida State University history professor Maxine Jones told me after she and her colleagues on the state's academic study team had finished investigating this event, "It would be impossible to recreate exactly what happened."

My primary sources were the nine living survivors, each of whom I visited at their homes in Florida during the summer and fall of 1994 and the spring of 1995. Two other primary sources—Ernest Parham, whom I interviewed at his home in Orlando in the fall of 1994, and his sister-in-law Martha Pillsbury Thompson, whom I interviewed several times by telephone at her home in Jacksonville—were witnesses to that week's events and helped provide the perspective of the white community in Sumner. All of these men and women—except for survivor Lonnie Carroll, who is too ill to speak—shared with me the experience as seen through their own young eyes. Several spouses and direct descendants of Rosewood survivors shared with me as well the stories their parents had told them about the town and the attack.

Besides my own interviews, I was able to refer to transcripts of sworn statements made by each of the survivors to attorneys from the law firm of Holland and Knight in 1992 and '93. The state's academic study team members interviewed each of the survivors as well in the fall of 1993. The transcripts of those interviews were helpful, as were the transcripts of all testimonies given at the Florida House of Representatives Special Master Hearing conducted in Tallahassee during February and March of 1994.

I was also able to review all affidavits filed with the Florida Attorney General's Office of Civil Rights by Rosewood survivor claimants; many of those affidavits contained useful details about the town and the attack. Also helpful were transcripts of interviews with survivor claimants conducted in the fall of 1994 by Investigator Frank Beisler of the Attorney General's Office of Civil Rights.

The dozens of state and national newspaper accounts published the week of the attack in January, 1923—though conflicting in many cases—were helpful in providing some details of events. Also helpful were several modern-day newspaper and magazine articles written about Rosewood, most notably two lengthy pieces written by journalist Gary Moore—the first published in the *St. Petersburg Times* in July, 1982, and the second published in *The Miami Herald* in March, 1993. An unpublished paper on the Rosewood attack titled "Rosewood, Florida: The Destruction of an African-American Community," written by historian Tom Dye, who was a member of the study team commissioned by the state to investigate Rosewood, provided useful information as well. The state's study team's report, *A Documented History of the Incident Which Occurred at Rosewood, Florida, in January 1923*, along with a detailed review of that report, included a multitude of facts which were crucial in piecing together what transpired that week.

Finally, of course, it was necessary to personally visit the site itself, which I did numerous times during the spring, summer and fall of 1994, walking the acreage behind the old John Wright house, as well as exploring the ground around Sumner where the old sawmill town had once stood.

CHAPTER ONE: OLD NEWS

I first met Arnett Doctor in the law offices of Holland and Knight in downtown Tampa in April of 1994. It had been only twelve days since the Florida Senate had voted in favor of the Rosewood claims bill. Governor Lawton Chiles had yet to sign the bill into law.

Doctor was wearing an Orlando Magic sweatsuit, a ball cap, a pair of high-topped Reebok tennis shoes—and a witheringly skeptical expression. We sat in a conference room with a commanding view of the city's skyline. His leather briefcase, spilling over with papers, file folders and lists of addresses and phone numbers, sat open on the table. During the course of this first conversation, Doctor was coy, careful, suspicious. We were interrupted several times by telephone calls buzzed in by the firm's receptionist. One, Doctor whispered, was from a movie producer. Another, he told me, conspiratorially, was from an *Esquire* magazine reporter. This was apparently a busy man, and he wanted me to know it.

During the ensuing fall, as we spent days together in Doctor's home in east Tampa, he was constantly interrupted by a ringing telephone. The process of verifying and paying Rosewood bill claimants was ongoing by then, and Doctor considered it his duty to hound the Attorney General's office. If he wasn't dialing attorneys or newspaper reporters, prodding the state, he was answering calls from family members anxious to know about the status of the government payments, as well as about any information Doctor could give them concerning the movies and books and magazine articles all rumored to be in the works. So much was in the works in the wake of the families' legislative victory that spring.

As we spent more time together, Arnett began to relax, to open up, to share personal details he had been reluctant to divulge in the beginning, details about both himself and his relatives. Much of the first half of this book revolves around those details, around the shadow Rosewood threw over scores of these families through the better part of this century, and around the struggles and squabbling they faced among themselves during the decade it took for them to finally come together and take action against the state.

This first chapter is based primarily on Arnett's recollections of his boyhood in St. Petersburg. I visited the places Arnett described: Jordan Park, 22nd Street, the Manhattan Casino, South Mole Beach, the Million-Dollar Pier. I also interviewed Arnett's uncle, Arnett Turner ("A. T.") Goins, in August, 1994, at his home in St. Petersburg, where he corroborated, corrected and fleshed out many of Arnett's memories. Arnett's sister, Yvonne, was also helpful during numerous telephone conversations we had in the spring and summer of 1995. Midge Laughlin, archivist of the St. Petersburg Museum of History, shared her personal knowledge and recollections of the city—including her own memories of the Manhattan Casino—as well as providing other details about St. Petersburg's history. An excellent source on the history of St. Petersburg is Raymond Arsenault's *St. Petersburg and the Florida Dream* (Norfolk: The Donning Company, 1988).

I interviewed John Taylor, owner of Lundy's Liquor Store, by telephone in the spring of 1995. Taylor confirmed Arnett's account of the Friday afternoon in 1982 when Arnett first met Gary Moore, although Taylor did not know about Arnett's pistol. "I didn't know he carried a gun on the job," Taylor told me. "I kept a pistol in the store myself, but I didn't *carry* it."

Gary Moore verified the account of his first encounter with Arnett Doctor during a June, 1995, telephone interview from his home in Tupelo, Mississippi.

Arnett could not provide a specific date, or even year, for the death of Wallace Jordan in Lacoochee, nor could any of his Lacoochee relatives, although they all recalled it. In May of 1995, I obtained a copy of Wallace Jordan's death certificate from the Florida Office of Vital Statistics in Jacksonville. The date on the certificate, which did not include the cause of death, was March 7, 1957. That would mean Arnett was fourteen when Jordan died, not ten, as Arnett remembers. But Arnett insisted he was ten, even after I told him about the certificate. "There is no way that happened in 1957," he said. "I was still living in the quarters in Lacoochee when Wallace Jordan was killed. We lived three doors down from the Jordans there. By 1957 we had moved over to Mosstown. There's no *way* that happened in '57."

I then called the Pasco County Sheriff's Department, where Denise Mills, the records clerk, spent two days searching for the record of Wallace Jordan's death. She found nothing. "It's odd," she told me. "There *was* a death, so we should be able to show something. Of course," she added, "way back then there's no telling how they handled things."

As for the account of Arnett's prison experience, it is based on interviews with him and on a copy of his prison record, which I obtained in January, 1995, from the Florida Department of Corrections in Tallahassee. The file described Arnett as "an above average inmate," who "spends his spare time reading."

CHAPTER TWO: A WALL OF DARKNESS

This chapter is based primarily on interviews with Arnett and Yvonne Doctor. A. T. Goins also shared his memories of his sister Philomena's emotional pain about Rosewood. When I visited Vera Goins Hamilton in August, 1994, at her home in Lacoochee, she talked about her older sister, Philomena, and what life in Lacoochee had been like for them all in the 1940s and '50s.

Historical information on the Cummer and Sons Company was found in many newspaper stories and columns on file in the library of the *Tampa Tribune* newspaper. Most notable was a September 15, 1979, article by Dale Wilson titled "Lacoochee Just Couldn't Keep Lumbering Along." Biographical background on the Cummer family and their business interests both in Michigan and in Florida is included in *Florida: Historic—Dramatic—Contemporary: Family and Personal History* (New York: Lewis Historical Publishing Company, 1952).

CHAPTER THREE: "IF THAT AIN'T COUNTRY"

The description of the drive down Route 19 from Tallahassee to Levy County came from my notes taken while making that trip several times during the spring, summer and fall of 1994. The descriptions of modern-day Cedar Key came from several visits made during that same time period.

I interviewed approximately two dozen Cedar Key residents during this time, many of whom asked not to be identified. Among those who did not mind giving their names and who were most hospitable as well as helpful were Eleanor Travers ("Miss El"), owner of the Cedar

Inn motel; Kellie Meyhoff, who tends bar at the L&M; Don Hatcher, a local clam farmer; and the Collins family—Kenny, who runs a small machine shop on the island, his brother Lloyd, who guides tourists on fishing excursions into the Gulf, and their mother Liza, who has spent all seventy-seven years of her life on Cedar Key.

George Sandora, executive director of the Levy County Development Authority in Bronson, spent an October, 1994, afternoon gathering and helping me understand the current demographic and economic statistics of Cedar Key and its surrounding inland area, including Rosewood.

The Cedar Key Historical Society Museum was a source for some of the history of this region. Another source was the Cedar Key State Museum, located at the north end of the island. It was there that I found a copy of *A Thousand-Mile Walk to the Gulf,* by John Muir, edited by William Frederic Bade (Boston: Houghton-Mifflin, 1944), which includes Muir's account of his visit to Florida and Cedar Key, from which the quotations in this chapter were taken.

Search for Yesterday: A History of Levy County, Florida (Bronson, Fla.: Levy County Archives Committee), a series of interviews, oral histories, records and photographs collected by Levy County historians during the late 1970s and early 1980s, contains a wealth of detailed information about day-to-day life in early twentieth-century Levy County. A short, but fascinating section on that same period of time in this region is included in *Florida: A Guide to the Southernmost State,* compiled and written by the Federal Writer's Project of the Work Projects Administration for the State of Florida (New York: Oxford University Press, 1939). An invaluable source as well for the area's history is Tom Dye's master's thesis, titled "Race, Ethnicity and the Politics of Economic Development: A Case Study of Cedar Key, Florida," submitted to the Florida State History Department in the fall of 1992.

Cedar Key's violent heritage is vividly recounted in a July 25, 1959, *Tampa Sunday Tribune* story titled "Cedar Key Old Timers Recall Wild Gun Fights," by Sam Mase. The story, with photographs of barefooted fishermen and graphic accounts of gun battles and knife fights, called turn-of-the-century Cedar Key "probably the toughest town in the South."

Gary Moore described his discovery of the Rosewood story during our June, 1995, telephone interview. The account he shared with me was the same as the author's note that appeared with his March 7, 1993, *Miami Herald Tropic* magazine story titled "The Rosewood Massacre." "I would take weekend trips, looking for color stories," he wrote. "The more obscure, the better." He described coming to Cedar Key seeking a "travel story," but once he was there, he "felt something much deeper." That feeling led him to the discovery of Rosewood. In a synopsis of his research, included among the documents stored at the Florida State Archives, Moore wrote, "Like the public at large, I personally had never heard of Rosewood."

The tales of Rosewood victims' body parts in Levy County abound. Gary Moore described several in his 1982 newspaper account. Twelve years later, an October 16, 1994, *Los Angeles Times Magazine* story on Rosewood by the *Times's* Atlanta bureau chief, Eric Harrison, quoted former *Cedar Key Beacon* editor Robin Raftis as saying she had seen "penises, testicles, fingers, even toes. You name it," she said, "they jarred it." I had tried calling Robin Raftis myself six months earlier, at the *Beacon* office in Cedar Key. Her husband, Mike "Salty" Raftis, answered the phone and told me Robin had left the newspaper and was no longer in town. When I asked how to contact her, he told me they were both working on their own book about Rosewood and neither she nor he would be able to talk to me. This was something I discovered early in my reporting on this story—that a lot of people seemed to be working on a lot of books and movies about Rosewood.

I heard several Rosewood body parts stories myself during my visits to Levy County. The most vivid came from a man I interviewed at his home in Chiefland on the last Friday night of September, 1994. The man—a former administrator with the Levy County Public School system—had written an unpublished, fictionalized account of the Rosewood attack, which was referred to in a December 28, 1992, *Miami Herald* story by a reporter named Lori Rosza. The man told me Rosza had promised she would not use his name in the story, but then did. I left several phone messages on Rosza's answering machine at her *Herald* office over the course of several months, to ask about this and other matters concerning Rosewood, but I did not hear back from her.

The Chiefland educator was reluctant at first to meet with me. Ultimately he invited me to his home, where he and his wife prepared a meal of fried catfish and grouper, caught fresh that day, he pointed out. He exacted the same promise of anonymity from me that he had from Rosza, then he proceeded to talk for several hours about the tales he had heard over the years from old-timers about Rosewood. He too had heard about body parts, but he never believed the stories, he said, until he stopped for gas several years ago at a Pure Oil filling station in Bronson. He was inside chatting with the owner when "a man" walked into the office: "He had something in a bottle and was showing it off. I didn't say a word, not till he left. Then I asked Len what was that in that jar? He said that was that black man's thumb that they cut off in Rosewood. They cut off the man's ears too, he told me. He said some say they cut off his *dick*. That was the first time I ever saw anything like that."

The only threatening encounter I had during my time in Levy County was with a man named Jesse Taylor. People around Cedar Key call him "'Ol Cuz,'" and I was told he was the brother of James Taylor, Fannie Taylor's husband.

It was a rainy Sunday morning when I knocked on the screen door of Taylor's tin-roofed home at the end of a dead-end lane in the center of the island. A large, bald man in stocking feet, slacks and a light sportshirt answered the door. He wore eyeglasses. A slight pot belly sagged over the belt of his trousers. Behind him, a formica table was covered with neat rows of playing cards. I had interrupted a game of solitaire.

I told him I was a writer working on a book, that I was interested in some of the history of Cedar Key, and that I'd heard he was a man who knew more about this town than just about anyone on the island—all of which was true. I did not mention Rosewood.

He remained behind the locked screen door, his eyes squinting as I spoke. "You're not a *reporter* now, are you?" he asked. "Now don't you *lie* to me."

I said again that I was writing a book, not a newspaper article. Again, I did not mention Rosewood—not yet. He stared hard, then let me in, told me to take a seat and settled himself in a large lounge chair. I began to ask a few questions, just chatting—Did he live here alone? Was he retired? What did he used to do for a living?—and he immediately cut me off.

"I thought you wanted to know about Cedar *Key*," he said, narrowing his eyes again and leaning forward. "You *sure* you're not a goddamn reporter?"

So we talked about Cedar Key. In the course of the conversation, he shared a few things about himself. He was about to turn eighty-five, he said. He was a bachelor, never married. He'd done some time as a merchant seaman during his middle years, but most of his working life had been spent right here, on the decks of those fishing boats down by the Cedar Key waterfront.

"Now if you want *bullshit,*" he said, "go on down to those docks. I've heard so many goddamn stories about this and that that was supposed to have happened around here from people who weren't even *born* then. None of 'em knows what the hell they're talking about. Those bastards *love* gossip, and that's what they do. Gossip. Pure bullshit."

The house we sat in was at the island's highest point. I asked him if we were anywhere near the place they called "Nigger Hill."

"This *is* Nigger Hill," he said. "There was niggers lived in this house right here. Almost three hundred of them lived up around here at one time. But ain't none of 'em here any more. Not one. They just left. Left and died out."

We went on chatting for another half hour, talking about hurricanes, about the big cocaine bust they had in town a few years back—"Operation Fishhook," the DEA agents called it—and we talked about the island's art festival, how large it had grown. Then I mentioned this story I'd been reading so much about during the past year, the story of this place they called Rosewood.

He bolted from his chair, sprang to his feet and thrust a thick, quivering finger toward my face.

"*Goddamnit!*" he yelled. "I *knew* it! Rosewood! That's why you came to my house. *Shit!* I *knew* it."

That was the end of the interview. Later that afternoon, with rain still falling in sheets, I drove past the end of that lane. As I went by, I could see four pickup trucks parked in front of Taylor's house. A group of five men, younger than Taylor, a couple cuffing cigarettes, were standing on his front porch, out of the rain. I didn't know if the gathering had anything to do with me, but I wasn't about to stop and find out.

CHAPTER FOUR: GROUND ZERO

The details of Philomena Doctor's life came from interviews with Arnett Doctor in Tampa and with Yvonne Doctor in St. Petersburg, as well as with Philomena's sister Vera Hamilton in Lacoochee. I also spoke by telephone in March, 1995, with Janie Bradley Black in Miami. Black was Lee Ruth Bradley's niece and was very involved in the Lacoochee branches of the various Rosewood families. Her memories of Philomena Goins's matriarchal power within those families concurred with the accounts of virtually all the survivors and descendants whom I interviewed.

Arnett's mother may indeed have shared a stage with Ella Fitzgerald, but Fitzgerald's spokespeople say she did not. When I called Salle Productions, Fitzgerald's production company in Beverly Hills, in October, 1994, Margaret Nutt, who said she has worked with Fitzgerald for thirty years, told me it was "highly unlikely" that Philomena Goins ever sang with Ella Fitzgerald during the 1930s. "As far as we know," said Nutt, "Ella never sang with anyone. They didn't have any 'backup' singers, no chorus. Ella sat with the band back then, as a member of the band. There were no 'warmup' acts either. There was never any other woman but Ella, no woman, period."

The account of Arnett's Saturday visit to Rosewood with Gary Moore comes from interviews with Arnett, with Wesley and Christy Thompson, who own the property on which the small Rosewood cemetery is located, and with Moore. When I visited the Thompsons at their home in Rosewood in October, 1994, Thompson and his wife took me through the woods behind their trailer to the cemetery, where the gravestones still lay, including Martine Goins's, which had been knocked over since Arnett first discovered it. "See," said Christy Thompson, pointing at the stone, "what's the big deal?"

CHAPTER FIVE: THE DEATH OF A DOG

The January, 1923, Florida and national newspaper reports of the events in Rosewood were found in both the microfilm periodicals collection and the special collections department at Florida State University's Robert Manning Strozier Library.

A proliferation of books and articles exists on the "lynching era" in America. Those which provided source material for this chapter, both general and specific, include: *A Festival of Violence: An Analysis of Southern Lynchings, 1882–1930,* by Stewart E. Tolnay and E.M. Beck (Urbana: University of Illinois Press, 1995); *Lynching in the New South,* by W. Fitzhugh Brundage (Urbana: University of Illinois Press, 1993); *The NAACP Crusade Against Lynching, 1909–1950,* by Robert L. Zangrando (Philadelphia: Temple University Press, 1980); *The Anti-Lynching Movement: 1883–1932,* by Donald L. Grant (San Francisco: R and E Research Associates, 1975); *Race Riot: Chicago in the Red Summer of 1919,* by William M. Tuttle, Jr. (New York: Atheneum, 1970); *Racial Violence in the United States,* edited by Allen D. Grimshaw (Chicago: Aldine Publishing Co., 1969); *Urban Racial Violence in the Twentieth Century,* by Joseph Boskin (Beverly Hills: Glencoe Press, 1969); *A History of the South, Volume X: "The Emergence of the New South, 1913–1945,"* by George Brown Tindall (Baton Rouge: Louisiana State University Press, 1967); *Race Riot at East St. Louis, July 2, 1917,* by Elliott M. Rudwick (Carbondale: Southern Illinois University Press, 1964); *Mark Twain on the Damned Human Race,* edited by Janet Smith (New York: Hill and Wang, 1962); *Mark Twain: Social Critic,* by Philip S. Foner (New York: International Publishers, 1958); and *Rope and Faggot,* by Walter White (New York: Alfred A. Knopf, 1929). Of all these books, and dozens more written on the subject of lynching in the South, the only one that mentions Rosewood is Tindall's—and the single sentence it gives the subject short-counts the damage and the deaths: ". . . the race riots petered out in 1923," wrote Tindall, on page 154 of his text. "The last serious affair was at Rosewood, Florida, where a white mob in search of an alleged Negro rapist ran amuck through the Negro community, burned six houses and a church, and left five Negroes and two whites dead."

Details of several of the specific lynchings described in this chapter come from the NAACP lynching records stored at the Tuskegee Institute and included in the appendix to *A Documented History of the Incident which Occurred at Rosewood, Florida, in January 1923,* by Maxine D. Jones, Larry E. Rivers, David R. Colburn, R. Tom Dye and William R. Rogers. This report was the result of the 1993 study commissioned by the Florida legislature to investigate the attack on Rosewood.

An excellent source for the etymology of the term "cracker" is an article titled "Cracker: The History of a Southeastern Ethnic, Economic, and Racial Epithet," by John Solomon Otto in the March, 1987, issue of *NAMES, the Journal of the American Name Society.*

CHAPTER SIX: SWEET POTATOES

This chapter is based primarily on my interview in September, 1994, with Minnie Lee Langley at her home in Jacksonville and several subsequent telephone interviews with her. Supplemental information came from a copy of Minnie Lee's sworn statement recorded by attorneys from Holland and Knight in June, 1992; from a transcript of her September, 1993, interview with Tom Dye of the academic investigative team; from a transcript of her testimony before the Florida House of Representatives Special Master in February, 1994; and from a copy of Florida Attorney General's Office of Civil Rights Investigator Frank Beisler's notes from his interview with Langley in September, 1994.

CHAPTER SEVEN: HARD DIRT

This chapter is based primarily on an interview I had with Arnett T. ("A. T.") Goins at his home in St. Petersburg in August, 1994. Additional information came from Goins's sworn statement given to Holland and Knight attorneys in February, 1993; from a transcript of Goins's September, 1993, interview with Dr. Larry E. Rivers of the state's academic investigative team; from a transcript of Goins's testimony before Florida's House Special Master in February, 1994; and from Investigator Frank Beisler's notes from his interview with Goins in September, 1994.

Information on Goins's life also came from interviews with his wife Anna Maude and with his nephew and niece, Arnett and Yvonne Doctor. When I tried to interview Goins's daughter, Annette Goins Shakir, by telephone in May, 1995, she refused, saying she would call me back after she spoke to her attorney. I did not hear from her again.

The CBS News "60 Minutes" segment on "The Rosewood Massacre" aired December 11, 1983. A videotape of that broadcast provided some of the visual details A. T. Goins referred to during our interview.

The description of "harvesting" logs in the early part of this century came from viewing a videotape I discovered while visiting Lacoochee in August, 1994. I had stopped at the town's only medical facility—a rural health clinic housed in a trailer near the old "quarters" section of town where Arnett Doctor had once lived—to gather what information I might find there about modern-day Lacoochee. As I chatted with Paula Knight, the clinic manager, she mentioned a tape they had in the back room on the history of the old Cummer and Sons Company logging operation. She fetched it for me to watch on the waiting room's television. The tape, narrated by an unidentified former manager of the Cummer operation, included film footage of loggers in the 1940s wading into the swamp to cut timber. "The same way," noted the narrator, "they been doing it since the 1920s." As the huge cypresses fell on film, the narrator lamented, "Almost makes you want to cry when you see them great big old trees taking their final dive." He lamented, too, in his own way, the harsh working conditions endured by the loggers. "It was a hard way to make a living," he said, "but regular work was hard to find in those days, and this was regular work."

The old days of logging in Lacoochee were also detailed in a May 19, 1985, *Tampa Tribune* story by Sara Nichols titled "Loggers Remember When Timber Business Was King."

Several of the Rosewood survivors I interviewed, as well as Ernest Parham, recalled how central the weekend baseball games were to the social culture of Rosewood. The same was true, said many of the old-timers I talked to, of most rural communities—white or black—in this section of the state. Even Martha Pillsbury Thompson, Ernest Parham's sister-in-law, who was fourteen at the time of the attack on Rosewood, recalled how popular the game of baseball was with the men and boys in both Sumner and Rosewood. Her explanation was simple. "There wasn't much to do back then for entertainment," she said. "You found your fun where you could. The men and boys found it in baseball."

The game of "fireball" was described in great detail by Wilson Hall during my interview with him at his home in Hilliard in September, 1994. A. T. Goins concurred with Hall's description of this game.

A definitive source for the history of black professional baseball leagues, teams and players, many of whom were recalled by A. T. Goins, is *The Biographical Encyclopedia of the Negro Baseball Leagues,* by James A. Riley (New York: Carroll & Graf, 1994).

CHAPTER EIGHT: NO EAR ON EARTH

This chapter is based on interviews with Arnett Doctor and his sister, Yvonne, as well as on interviews with various survivors and descendants who shared many of the same rumors about Rosewood, ranging from Sylvester Carrier's escape to the suggestion that Fannie Taylor is still alive. Some—perhaps all—of these stories may be true, but I was unable to verify any of them.

Ed Bradley of "60 Minutes" responded by letter in early March of 1995 to my inquiry if he was indeed related to the Bradleys of Rosewood. "I am satisfied," he wrote, "that there are no family connections."

Joel Bernstein, producer of that "60 Minutes" piece, was the man who, accompanied by Gary Moore, visited Philomena Doctor's home in the fall of 1993 to ask her to appear on the program. He recalled the meeting when I asked him about it during a telephone interview in June, 1995. "She was very persistent, very stubborn," said Bernstein, "and she made it clear in no uncertain terms that she was not interested. But there was nothing confrontational about it. She didn't throw us off her property. It wasn't like that at all. We just said, Okay, and left."

The notion of interracial Masonic brotherhood as an explanation of why a white fugitive would have fled to the black community of Rosewood is embraced by many of the Rosewood families today. But the history of Freemasonry in the South indicates otherwise. In his book *Middle-Class Blacks in a White Society* (Berkeley: University of California Press, 1975), William Muraskin traces the history of black Masonry in the United States from its beginning in Boston in 1775. A "primary attraction of the Order," writes Muraskin, was the vision of this secret society as a future bridge between blacks and whites in America. "The original hope that Masonry offered black men," writes Muraskin, "was the integration of the races in a common brotherhood."

The reality, however, was that black Masons were rejected by their white counterparts from the beginning, especially in the South, especially after the Civil War. "The South did not like the idea of blacks meeting together without supervision," writes Muraskin, "and an organization such as Masonry appeared especially dangerous to them."

By the turn of the century, the climate among white and black Masons in the South reflected the climate among white and black southerners in general. "Scorpio Africanus is simply a brute, with no revenge or resentments, and no regard for the truth or the purity of women," wrote the Grand Secretary of Mississippi's white Masons in 1909. "Whiskey and co-caine and miscegenation are his bane and until some remedy is found for these great evils, the poor fellow will continue to go down lower and lower in the social scale."

According to Loretta J. Williams, author of *Black Freemasonry and Middle-Class Realities* (Columbia: University of Missouri Press, 1980), even Albert Pike, a nineteenth-century Mason regarded as the leading scholar of his time on the history of the sect, stated more than once that he would leave the Order before he would recognize a black Mason as a brother and risk being "contaminated by the leprosy of Negro association."

While history seems to refute the notion that Rosewood burned because of interracial Masonic loyalty, the fact that there was a Masonic lodge in Rosewood and that many of the men among that community were high-ranking members of that Order bolsters the claim that this was more than a mere collection of shanties in the swamp, that Rosewood was a vi-able middle-class community. Masonry, writes Muraskin, has always been "one of the bul-warks of the black middle class. It has worked to separate its members, both socially and psychologically, from the black masses." It has done so, writes Muraskin, by emphasizing, "the values of work, thrift, charity, property ownership, and business efficiency"—precisely the qualities so many Rosewood descendants point to with pride when they recall the black com-munity their parents and grandparents built.

CHAPTER NINE: SMOKE AND FOG

The account of Arnett Doctor's visit to the Levy County Courthouse comes from my in-terviews with him. Physical descriptions of the drive to Bronson and of the town itself come from those interviews and from my own visit to Bronson in October, 1994.

Much of the census and property records information cited in this chapter comes from Arnett's personal files. Some comes from records included in the appendix to the state's in-vestigative study team's report. And some comes from microfilm copies of the 1900, 1910 and 1920 federal census reports for Levy County, which I examined at the Florida State Archives in Tallahassee during my visits there in the fall of 1994.

Details of Ed Goins's business and property holdings in Rosewood can be found in the state's study team report. Statistics indicating the area's economic decline by the early 1920s are also included in that report, as well as in Tom Dye's study of the history of Cedar Key, cited earlier.

CHAPTER TEN: SOUL FOOD

The account of the beginnings of the Rosewood Family Reunions and the conflicts and confrontations that occurred during the ensuing years are based on interviews with Arnett Doctor, Yvonne Doctor, Vera Goins Hamilton, Annie Bell Lee, Altamese Wrispus, Eva Jenk-ins, Janie Bradley Black, A. T. Goins, Willie Evans and Dorothy Hosey.

I found several accounts of the history of the Mosstown section of Lacoochee—including various references to the Depression-era gathering and selling of moss—in the files of the *Tampa Tribune*. The most detailed account of moss gathering was a *Tribune* column by Carol Jeffares published in December, 1984.

Vera Goins Hamilton shared her recollections of Rosewood and of her life after the attack when I visited her home in Lacoochee in August, 1994.

Dade City's Hugh Embry Public Library was a source of several newspaper stories and locally produced pamphlets describing the history of the city's citrus packing industry—particularly that of the Pasco Packing Association, which is known today as the Lykes Pasco Packing Company. A May, 1986, *Tampa Tribune* story written by Leland Hawes, marking the fiftieth anniversary of the Lykes Pasco operation, provided several details included in this chapter.

The Rosewood family members' 1987 visit to the old Wright house was recalled in interviews with Vera Hamilton, Eva Jenkins and Willie Evans, as well as with Doyal and Fuji Scoggins, whom I visited at their home in October, 1994.

The accounts of the interfamily disputes in Rosewood are based on interviews with Arnett Doctor and other family members. The record of Sylvester and Hayward Carrier's 1918 arrest is included in the *State of Florida Prison Record Book, 1900–1920,* which I examined in the Florida State Archives in Tallahassee in October, 1994.

The account of Philomena Doctor's death is based on interviews with Arnett and Yvonne Doctor.

CHAPTER ELEVEN: THE FIRE THIS TIME

I interviewed Michael O'McCarthy several times over the telephone at his home in South Carolina, beginning with two extensive conversations in January, 1995. By then I had already spoken with scores of Rosewood survivors, descendants and attorneys. Whenever Michael O'McCarthy's name was mentioned by any of them, it was with a raised eyebrow and a tone of skepticism, if not outright disdain.

The man I spoke with on the telephone seemed straightforward, if a bit aggressive. He was candid about the details of his past struggles with alcohol and drugs, of his incarceration both in reform school and in prison, and of the variety of motivations that drove him as a political activist, as a radical journalist, and finally as the film producer he is today. As he detailed the twisting arc of the lifelong journey that led him to Rosewood, I found the story both improbable and preposterous, too incredible to believe. Then I checked out what facts I could, and they were all true. His account of the Florida reform school was there, on page 122 of *Growing up Southern* (New York: Pantheon Books, 1981). His behind-bars relationship with George Jackson was there, on page 31 of *Soledad Brother* (New York: Coward-McCann, 1970). He and the counterculture co-authors he claimed were out to expose the entire police state in America were there, lined up in a photograph on the title page of *The Glass House Tapes* (New York: Avon Books, 1973). And there was his photo again, eight years later, in the July 23, 1981, issue of *Rolling Stone* magazine, this time posed alongside some of his Vietnam veteran buddies.

Gary Moore recounted his initial contact with O'McCarthy during our June, 1995, telephone interview. Again, Moore's memory concurred with an account he had already written, this one in a letter dated August 10, 1993, sent to the state's academic investigating team as they were launching their study. "In the summer of 1991," wrote Moore, "McCarthy called me because of my research and expressed eagerness to make a movie about Rosewood, which he said would be built around a presentday [sic] hook: testimony in a courtroom-style setting by aged survivors decades after the destruction. I demurred [sic], saying no such public testimony had ever occurred in real life. McCarthy then stopped calling me. I heard no more from him for more than a year."

O'McCarthy's account of his first meeting with Lee Ruth Davis was corroborated by Davis's niece, Janie Bradley Black. The racial strife and rioting during the 1980s in both the Liberty City and Overtown sections of Miami are well documented in national newspapers and magazines. I drove to Liberty City in March, 1995, retracing O'McCarthy's route through the neighborhood where Lee Ruth Davis lived in 1992. This chapter's physical description of that community comes both from O'McCarthy's memories and from my own notes.

The quotation from the NAACP letter to O'McCarthy comes from a copy of that letter, dated October 29, 1991, mailed from the organization's national headquarters in Baltimore and signed by then-NAACP Deputy Executive Director George E. Carter.

An account of O'McCarthy's pursuit and discovery of Lee Ruth Davis and Minnie Lee Langley is included in the October 16, 1994, *Los Angeles Times Magazine* story by Eric Harrison, titled "A Massacre, The Movies, and the Obligations of Memory."

CHAPTER TWELVE: EAT WHAT YOU KILL

I first met Steve Hanlon at his law office in Tallahassee in April, 1994. In September of that year, I returned for two days of interviews there, followed by numerous telephone interviews during the ensuing months. This chapter is based on those interviews, as well as on interviews with Michael O'McCarthy which confirmed the details of O'McCarthy's initial contact with Hanlon concerning Rosewood.

The descriptions of previous cases handled by Hanlon's Community Services Team came from Holland and Knight records shared by Hanlon and from newspaper accounts. Hanlon's legal services work in Tampa was the focus of a March 13, 1991, *Tampa Tribune* story by Suzie Siegel titled "In Defense of the Poor."

The pro bono division of Holland and Knight was the subject of a *Wall Street Journal* article by Eric Morgenthaler titled "For the Public Good," published April 8, 1994.

Profiles of Chesterfield Smith—each highlighting his housecleaning attitude as president of the American Bar Association and his controversial condemnation of Richard Nixon—appeared in the February 18, 1974, issue of *Time* magazine and in the April 15, 1974, issue of *Newsweek*.

CHAPTER THIRTEEN: TINY ISLAND

This chapter is based on interviews with Arnett Doctor at his home in Tampa, where he shared his files of correspondence from 1991 and '92, when he was trying without success to find legal representation for the families' case.

"Grunting gators" was a common practice among some of Lacoochee's white population as well as its blacks, according to one of the town's white old-timers, a man named Horace Morgan, who described the practice in an August 23, 1987, *Tampa Tribune* story titled "He Recalls Days of Fish and Gators," by Carol Jeffares.

Arnett's account of the monkey on the island was confirmed by Steve Shepard, manager of the John B. Sargent Sr. County Park, where the fishing spot Arnett described is located. "A lot of people have seen this 'monkey,' including some of our staff," Shepard told me when I called him in May, 1995. But the animal, said Shepard, is actually not a monkey at all. "We suspect it's probably a *coatimundi,*" he said, "a member of the raccoon family. It's not an animal usually found in this area, but some people like to keep them as pets, and this may be one that got away, or that someone wanted to get rid of. It's got a long tail, it likes to climb trees and forage along the riverbank, and it's bigger than a raccoon. If you're at a distance, it can sure *look* like a monkey."

Albert Edwards confirmed the account of the claims bill discussion he had with Arnett in a June, 1995, telephone interview from Edwards's home in Deland.

CHAPTER FOURTEEN: ORIGINAL SIN

This chapter is based on interviews with Steve Hanlon, Michael O'McCarthy, Minnie Lee Langley and Janie Bradley Black.

CHAPTER FIFTEEN: A DELICATE DANCE

I interviewed Al Lawson at his insurance office in Tallahassee in October, 1994. A month after that, I interviewed Miguel De Grandy by telephone at his law office in Miami. Subsequent telephone interviews with both men, as well as with Steve Hanlon, confirmed and fleshed out the facts contained in this chapter.

Also helpful were several newspaper profiles of both men. Two *Tallahassee Democrat* accounts of Al Lawson's 1982 and 1986 campaigns were especially useful in understanding his approach to politics. The first, written by Ann M. Doyle and titled "House 9 a Race of Quiet Dignity, Rags-to-Riches," detailed Lawson's 1982 campaign against Bette Wimbish. The second, by Jan Goodwin, described Lawson's 1986 re-election campaign, focusing on his "curious" constituency, including the "Rednecks for Lawson."

In De Grandy's case, the *Miami Herald*'s annual rankings of state legislators were revealing. Each year's ranking provides thumbnail sketches of the leading lawmakers, and De Grandy was ranked among the leaders during his entire time in office, primarily because of his efforts on behalf of his largely Hispanic constituency. After the crucial redistricting process that occurred during the 1992 legislative session, the *Herald* called De Grandy that year's "unquestioned star" and predicted that "when a slew of new minority legislators are swept into office this fall, he can rightly claim a leading role." That prediction would prove prescient when it came time to decide who would sponsor the Rosewood bill.

CHAPTER SIXTEEN: ROAD KILL

Arnett's account of the family uproar that Tuesday in December of 1992, after the news of Minnie Lee Langley's and Lee Ruth Davis's lawsuit was published in the *Miami Herald* and went out on the Associated Press wires to newspapers across the country, was corroborated by several family members, including those named in this chapter. Steve Hanlon verified this chain of events, as did Manny Dobrinsky. Hanlon also verified details of his first phone conversation with Arnett Doctor.

The January 1, 1993, kidnapping and torching of Christopher Wilson was national news, documented in newspapers and magazines across the country, as well as throughout Florida.

Details of Steve Hanlon's drive to Lacoochee came from his memory and from my own trip taken along that same route in August, 1994.

The Lacoochee murder story, titled "Presumed Guilty," written by David Finkel, was published in the March, 1989, issue of *Esquire* magazine.

Some details of Lacoochee's history were found in the Dade City Public Library's file of locally written pamphlets and brochures—collections of local remembrances such as *East Pasco's Heritage,* edited by Eleanor Dunson (First Baptist Church of Dade City, 1976). Much of the Cummer and Sons information came from the sources cited in the notes for Chapter Two.

The descriptions of modern-day Lacoochee were based on my visit there in August, 1994. Background information on the town's economic and racial problems came primarily from newspaper pieces in the *Tampa Tribune,* which routinely covers this west-central section of the state. The recent beatings, shootings and cross-burning were all reported in *Tribune* stories. The community's current poverty and decay were extensively reported in a 1989 series of *Tribune* stories titled "Lacoochee: Forgotten Town," written by Lisa Demer.

The newspaper series on the Ku Klux Klan in Florida, by Fred Smith of the *Tampa Tribune,* was published in April, 1965.

The account of the church meeting in Lacoochee came from interviews with Hanlon and Doctor, as well as with various family members.

CHAPTER SEVENTEEN: THREE MORE NAMES

Michael O'McCarthy shared both his memories and his January, 1993, correspondence with the producers of the "Maury Povich" show to help recount the sequence of events that led to that broadcast. Minnie Lee Langley also shared her memories of that experience during my interview with her. The description of the broadcast itself came from a videotape of that January 18 program.

I interviewed Wilson Hall at his home in Hilliard in September, 1994. We spent half a day at his club, then walked up the road to his sister Margie's home, where I talked with her on her front porch for about an hour. Margie was not doing well; she had just been released from the hospital the day before. A yellow plastic identification bracelet was still on her left wrist.

The 1993 arrest and conviction of former Nassau County Sheriff Laurie Ellis on charges of selling cocaine and marijuana were reported in the *Nassau County News-Leader* in a series of stories written by reporter Sarah Bottoms.

The account of the Hall family's life in Rosewood is based on interviews with Wilson and Margie, as well as an interview I had with their sister, Mary Hall Daniels, in September, 1994, at her apartment in Jacksonville. More information came from subsequent telephone interviews with both Wilson and Mary.

The murder of Emmett Till is probably the most well-documented lynching in American history. A detailed account of his killing is included in Stephen J. Whitfield's *A Death in the Delta: The Story of Emmett Till* (Baltimore: The Johns Hopkins University Press, 1991).

Wilson Hall's account of his brother Sam's whereabouts during the attack on Rosewood differs from that of Sam Hall's granddaughter, Katherine Hall, whom I interviewed by telephone in June, 1995, at her home in Jacksonville. "What I was told by my grandfather," she said, "is he was *there* in Rosewood at the time of the attack. He was working in Sumner, but he was still living in Rosewood. He said he went out in the woods with the rest of them, hiding in the swamp so they wouldn't get killed. I don't know what anyone else says, but that's what he told *me.*"

CHAPTER EIGHTEEN: "ATTENTION WHITE PEOPLE"

The account of the September, 1993, gathering at Florida A&M University is based on interviews with Al Lawson, Steve Hanlon and Arnett Doctor, as well as with the survivors who attended the conference that week and the members of the state's study team who interviewed them there.

I visited the campus of Florida A&M several times during September and October of 1994, primarily to visit the university's Black Archives Research Center and Museum.

Dozens of newspaper stories have been written about Bo Johnson and his political family. Probably the most definitive was a February 14, 1993, *Tallahassee Democrat* examination of Johnson's controversial career titled "Johnson Built His Career on Determination," by Judy Doyle and Dana Peck. A companion piece to that story, titled "Connections With Bond Company Were Secret," examined questions about ties between Johnson's political position and his personal finances. The description of Johnson's personal background is based primarily on those stories and on a June, 1995, telephone interview with Johnson.

The testy relationship between Al Lawson and Bo Johnson was confirmed in interviews with both men.

The problems with the 1993 Rosewood bill and the subsequent funding of an academic investigative team were detailed in newspaper stories and recounted in interviews I had with Steve Hanlon, Martha Barnett, Al Lawson, Miguel De Grandy and Bo Johnson.

The families' anger in the wake of Minnie Lee Langley's and Lee Ruth Davis's original claims bill was typified by a letter written by Yvonne Doctor to Davis following that January's "Maury Povich" broadcast:

"Everyone is upset about the lies that were told," wrote Doctor. "We would appreciate it very much if you would stop now. Because this thing could become very, very ugly in the long run. . . . You know, Lee Ruth, we all have to be careful, because you never know to whom you're speaking and in fact, to whom they are acquainted. There is still alot [sic] of hate crimes being committed today . . . We are not going to stand by and let this continue to open old, old wounds. . . ."

Arnett's hyperbole with reporters during the summer of 1993 was typified by a set of articles published that May in the *Tampa Tribune*. Titled "Razed by Racism," written by *Tribune* reporter Suzie Siegel, the stories contained Arnett's references to Rosewood as a "Black Mecca," etc. Arnett says today that his reference to Atlanta was taken out of context. "I consistently compared Rosewood to Atlanta from the perspective of black unity, black business, and strong civic pride," he says. "The comparison was not intended to suggest that Rosewood was on the same scale, or of the same size, as Atlanta. That would have been ludicrous."

Doyal Scoggins recounted the visit to his home by the Ku Klux Klan during our interview there in October, 1994.

A copy of the "ATTENTION WHITE PEOPLE" flier was included among boxes of records, tapes, transcripts and other material related to the Rosewood bill stored at the Florida Legislative Library in Tallahassee, which I visited in April, 1994. That material has since been transferred to the Florida State Archives.

I called John Baumgardner at his home in McIntosh, Florida, March 27, 1995. We had an extensive telephone interview that evening, and he subsequently mailed me his Ku Klux Klan business card and several recent copies of his monthly *Florida Interklan Report,* featuring articles with titles such as "Who Is White?," a column ridiculing a photograph of Bill Clinton in a yarmulke and calling the President "a closet Christ-hater, a little Jewish want-to-be," and several columns on the subject of Rosewood, which was referred to as "Lawton's Folly."

CHAPTER NINETEEN: DOC WILLIE'S LITTLE GIRL

I interviewed Martha Barnett at her law office in Tallahassee in September and October, 1994, followed by several telephone interviews during the subsequent months. This chapter is based on those conversations, as well as interviews with Steve Hanlon and Arnett Doctor.

CHAPTER TWENTY: SATISFACTION

I visited Maxine Jones at her office on the campus of Florida State University in September, 1994. We had several telephone conversations following that meeting, to confirm, correct, and add to information from that interview.

A week after I met with Jones, I interviewed Tom Dye on the FSU campus as well. I also interviewed William Rogers, David Colburn and Larry Rivers by telephone in June, 1995.

The study team's report and appendix, as well as transcripts of the team members' testimony before the Florida House Special Master in March, 1994, were helpful in reconstructing their experience.

In the course of my own research, I came across many of the same documents the investigative team had studied and so was able to describe some in detail. An example was the Florida State Prison Record ledger book, which a staff member at the Florida State Archives pulled from a back storage room when I asked if they had anything beyond the typed, Xeroxed, second-hand compilations of prison records available in the front room.

The *Washington Post* story which included quotations from Tom Dye appeared May 30, 1993. Titled "Rosewood: The Town That Burned in Shame," it was written by William Booth.

Jason McElveen's account of the attack on Rosewood came from pages 69–72 of Tom Dye's master's thesis on Cedar Key, cited earlier in these notes.

CHAPTER TWENTY-ONE: BACKWOODS FOLKS

I visited Ernest Parham at his home in Orlando in September, 1994. I had come across a photograph of him earlier that fall in the Cedar Key Historical Society Museum, a gangly big-eared boy lined up with his Cedar Key High School classmates on the last day of November, 1922—less than two months before the attack on Rosewood. I could still see some of that boy in the elderly man who answered his door that September afternoon. This chapter is based on that interview with Ernest Parham, as well as on several follow-up telephone conversations we had in the ensuing months.

The account of John Wright's later years came from conversations with several Levy County residents, most notably former Florida state senator Randolph J. Hodges, who recalled his father telling him of the pistols placed throughout John Wright's home, and Doyal Scoggins, who took me to John Wright's grave in the Shiloh Cemetery.

I interviewed Ernest Parham's sister-in-law Martha Pillsbury Thompson by telephone at her home in Jacksonville in May, 1995. Martha is the only living child of Walter Harlan Pillsbury, who was superintendent of the Sumner sawmill at the time of the attack on Rosewood. Her father was indeed part Indian, she said, but like Parham, Martha, who was born in 1908, has no idea of her father's exact ancestry. She did say, however, that her daughter-in-law Carolyn had recently been researching the family's history and might know. So I called Carolyn Pillsbury at her home not far from Martha's.

"We've been trying to track it down for years," said Carolyn, the forty-two-year-old wife of Walter Pillsbury, W. H. Pillsbury's grandson. "What we *do* know," she told me, "is that the Pillsbury family were highbrow people up in Michigan. Very wealthy, very uppity. When one of their sons, Edward, married an Indian woman, they completely ostracized him, paid him his share of the family's business and told him to leave. 'See ya. Take *off.*' Just like that."

By the turn of the century, she continued, "nobody in the family wanted to recognize their background at all. The attitude was, 'No, no, no. No Indians in *this* family.' So now here we are. My children are fifth generation Pillsburys, and they want to know where they came from. *I* want to know."

What Martha Thompson knows is that her father was Edward Pillsbury's oldest son, that he was born in 1875 and that he grew up playing with the sons of a man named Jacob Cummer in the Clam Lake (now Cadillac) area of Michigan. Jacob Cummer was a logging magnate up in Michigan, and by the turn of the century he had moved his business and his family to Jacksonville. According to Martha, her father was a young man playing on a traveling semi-professional baseball team when he bumped into the Cummer boys while passing through Jacksonville, and they convinced him to stay and join the family's business.

"Papa was a sawyer at first," said Martha, "pulling logs out of the St. Johns River right here, where the Cummers had a sawmill. Later they sent him down to the Bahama Islands to build a mill for the company there. It was when he came back from the Bahamas that they asked him to go on over to Sumner."

That was in 1913, just after the Cummers had opened a new sawmill on the Gulf Coast and begun harvesting the abundant cypress there. Ten years later, those woods were almost completely logged out, the company was already opening another mill further south, in Lacoochee, and the Sumner operation was slowing down. That was in 1923, the year the attack on Rosewood occurred.

Martha was fourteen at the time of the attack. She didn't go near Rosewood that week—"I never did go closer to Rosewood than Mr. Wright's house, where we'd go to pick grapes." But she remembers how busy her father was that week, beginning with the first day, the day Aaron Carrier was tortured and Sam Carter was lynched. It was Martha's older brother, Edward, she said, who drove Aaron Carrier to safety that day.

"Edward was four years older than me," she said, "and his friend Burt Phillips had come down to visit from Jacksonville, to go hunting over Christmas season. When this trouble started, my father put this black man in the back of a car, covered him with a quilt, and told Edward to drive him to Bronson, to put him in the jail there for safety. Burt went with him, and I remember, as soon as they got back, *that day,* my father put Burt Phillips on the train home to Jacksonville."

The next two days were frightening, recalled Martha. "There were people just driving up and down the streets with shotguns sticking out of their cars."

The day after the shootout at the Carrier house, Martha said Sumner was filled with refugees from Rosewood. Several of her families' neighbors took in black women and children and hid them from the mobs, she said. Her own family hid "between ten and twenty" women and children in a small building behind their home, said Martha, where they stayed for two nights. "My mother would wait till dark," she said, "and then she'd cook a big old pot of grits and greens, you know, *cracker* food, and she'd carry it out to them."

The blacks weren't the only people terrified of those mobs, said Martha. "Some of the *white* people in Sumner came and stayed in our house," she said, "'cause they were scared to stay in their own. We were *all* afraid. All these cars riding up and down the road with all those guns. We didn't know when somebody was gonna try to shoot *us*. . . . It was just an exciting time," said Martha, "a scary week."

Finally, she said, it ended when the Bryce brothers' train arrived that weekend to pick up the blacks hiding in Sumner and carry them to safety in Gainesville. "I thought it was mighty nice of them to make arrangements to do that," said Martha.

Martha's father left for Lacoochee the next year, but unlike Ernest Parham, Martha does not remember W. H. Pillsbury having any particular problems with the workers there. "In fact," she said, "the Cummers sent Papa a letter commending him for saving all those lives. They said anything they could ever do for him, they would."

And they did, said Martha. Her father left Lacoochee and the company in 1925, retired from the logging business and moved his family back to Jacksonville. A year after that, on a hot June evening, he was driving home from Fernandina Beach when his car developed engine trouble. He pulled off the road, climbed under the gas tank, found a leak, plugged it, stood back up and—"Like an idiot," his grandson Walter told me—lit his pipe.

"He burst into flames," said Martha. "They couldn't do anything for him. He died that night."

CHAPTER TWENTY-TWO: SPECIAL MASTER

I interviewed Richard Hixson at his office at the state capitol building in Tallahassee in October, 1994. This chapter is based on that interview, along with two subsequent telephone conversations.

CHAPTER TWENTY-THREE: THE ELEVENTH HOUR

Interviews with Steve Hanlon, Arnett Doctor, Martha Barnett, Al Lawson and Miguel De Grandy formed the basis of this chapter.

Biographical information on former Florida Governor and U.S. Senator Spessard Holland is abundant. The titles alone of the many newspaper and magazine articles about Holland indicate the man's political complexity: "Sen. Spessard Holland 'Brings Home the Bacon'" (*Tallahassee Democrat,* Oct. 3, 1965); "Holland: 'They Call Me Hopelessly Reactionary'" (*St. Petersburg Times,* Oct. 10, 1965); "Spessard Holland Was a Man of Many Labels" (*Polk Country Democrat,* Nov. 8, 1971). The two instances in which Holland personally confronted lynch mobs were detailed in a *Polk County Democrat* story written on the occasion of his death in 1971.

CHAPTER TWENTY-FOUR: ONE LAST MATTER

Steve Hanlon, Martha Barnett, Richard Hixson, Bo Johnson, Pete Antonacci and Robert Trammell shared with me details of the discussion and decision to have the state defend itself at the House Special Master's Hearing.

I interviewed Jim Peters at his office in Tallahassee in October, 1994, and interviewed him again by telephone in April, 1995, to confirm and add to the information he had already shared with me.

Earnest Lee Miller and William Riley Jent were the subjects of the *Esquire* magazine article cited in the notes to Chapter Eighteen.

Steve Hanlon's comments about Peters came from our interviews at Hanlon's office in Tallahassee.

CHAPTER TWENTY-FIVE: LIKE AN ANT

I visited both the old and the new Florida State Capitol buildings many times during the spring and fall of 1994. The staffs at both buildings—particularly Pete Cowdrey at the Old Capitol—were very helpful in providing historical background on the structures.

Florida State University Professor William Rogers, who was a member of the investigative team that wrote the report on Rosewood, has also written extensively on the history of Tallahassee. The center of the city's slave business, said Rogers, was not far from the capitol, at the city's largest outdoor market. But he has never been able to confirm the popular rumor that slaves were actually sold off the steps of the Old Capitol. "If they did buy and sell slaves there," he said, "it was clearly an exception. Although," he added, " I wouldn't rule anything out, the South being what it was."

Although the Florida Department of Law Enforcement offices in Tallahassee and Tampa could find no official record of patrols provided in response to threats received by Arnett Doctor when I called them in June, 1995, the FDLE office in Tampa acknowledged that they may have provided "unofficial drive-bys" of Doctor's house at the time he received the threats.

The account of the House Special Master's Hearing's opening day—as well as the twenty-four hours preceding it—came from interviews with Richard Hixson, Steve Hanlon, Martha Barnett, Arnett Doctor, Jim Peters, the four Rosewood survivors who testified that day—Minnie Lee Langley, A. T. Goins, Willie Evans and Wilson Hall—Miguel De Grandy, and Al Lawson.

The physical description of the hearing room came from notes made during my visits to the Capitol building.

The dialogue in this chapter was taken directly from transcripts provided by the state Legislative Library in Tallahassee.

That first day's testimony had a particularly strong impact on Bo Johnson, who told me he watched a videotape of the day's proceedings that evening in his office. While he was watching the testimony, said Johnson, two of the Capitol's cleaning staff—both African-American women—peeked in to take a look. Johnson turned and asked them what they thought. "It looks," said one of the women, "like the hometown folks are whippin' up on the big boys."

CHAPTER TWENTY-SIX: AMBUSH

This chapter is based on interviews with Jim Peters, Steve Hanlon, Richard Hixson, Maxine Jones, Tom Dye, William Rogers and Arnett Doctor.

Stan Smith's economic calculations came from a copy of his report submitted to the Special Master, now part of the Rosewood file stored at the Florida State Archives.

Again, the Hearing dialogue came from taped transcripts provided by the Legislative Library.

CHAPTER TWENTY-SEVEN: "HE DIDN'T HAVE A HOLSTER"

Jim Peters shared with me the details of his excursion to Levy County during our interview at his office. I spoke with Herb Wilkerson several times by telephone in April, 1995, to confirm and add to Peters's account of his interview with Wilkerson and Wilkerson's father, James. The description of that videotaped testimony came from viewing a copy of the tape at the state's Legislative Library.

CHAPTER TWENTY-EIGHT: HANDS UNKNOWN

Next to the opening day testimony of the Rosewood survivors, the testimony of Ernest Parham was the most climactic of the hearing's three weeks.

The heart of this chapter comes from transcripts of Parham's testimony that day. Interviews with Parham himself, as well as with Richard Hixson, Steve Hanlon, Martha Barnett, Bo Johnson, Arnett Doctor, Al Lawson, Maxine Jones, David Colburn and Martha Pillsbury Thompson provided context for that testimony as well as for the Rosewood team's behind-the-scenes strategy that preceded it.

Numerous newspaper accounts provided the public statements quoted in this chapter.

A copy of the March 17, 1994, letter from Florida NAACP President T. H. Poole to state Attorney General Robert Butterworth regarding Jim Peters's tactics was sent to me by Guy Robinson of the Attorney General's Office of Civil Rights.

Ernest Parham's interview with David Colburn of the academic investigative team is found in the appendix to the team's report, as cited in this chapter.

The Florida Department of Law Enforcement interviews to which Ernest Parham referred in his testimony were ordered by the Attorney General's office just prior to the start of the House hearing in late February, 1994, according to FDLE agent Arthur Erickson, whom I interviewed by telephone in June, 1995. Erickson said Parham was first interviewed by agents from the FDLE's Orlando office at his home on February 25, the same day the House hearing began in Tallahassee. Erickson himself interviewed Parham at his home in May, after the bill had become law and the FDLE's official investigation had begun.

A thorough account of the Byron De La Beckwith case is Maryanne Vollers's book, *Ghosts of Mississippi* (New York: Little, Brown and Company, 1995).

CHAPTER TWENTY-NINE: A MORAL OBLIGATION

Richard Hixson was very open in sharing and clarifying the reasoning and research that went into the decision he wrote after the Rosewood hearing concluded. That reasoning forms the heart of this chapter.

The copy of the coroner's verdict on Sam Carter's death was provided by Tom Dye.

Robert Trammell and Bo Johnson both confirmed the discussion of Hixson's decision on the amount of compensation to be included in the recommendation.

A copy of Hixson's report is included in the records on Rosewood now filed at the Florida State Archives. I obtained my copy from the state's Legislative Library, where the records were stored at the time I was in Tallahassee.

The account of Arnett Doctor's volatile reaction to the report came from interviews with Doctor, Steve Hanlon and Martha Barnett.

Again, public statements about Hixson's decision came from numerous newspapers' accounts of his report's release.

CHAPTER THIRTY: GOOD FRIDAY

This chapter is based on interviews with Richard Hixson, Martha Barnett, Arnett Doctor, Al Lawson, Miguel De Grandy, Bo Johnson, Robert Trammell, and John Long.

Legislators' public statements included throughout the chapter came from numerous newspaper accounts of the Rosewood bill's journey through the House committees, as did the excerpts from various editorials and letters-to-the-editor.

Official House Committee records were provided by the state Legislative Library Services Division.

The luncheon showdown between Governor Chiles and the black caucus was gleefully covered by the press, which provided many of the details—such as the meal served that afternoon—which are included here.

CHAPTER THIRTY-ONE: AMEN

The heart of this chapter—the House floor debate on the Rosewood bill—came from a tape recording of that debate provided by the state Legislative Library. The physical descriptions of the House and Senate chambers came from notes made during my visits to the Capitol.

The Journals of the Florida House of Representatives provided a detailed account of all bills voted on by the House the day it debated the Rosewood bill.

Interviews with Miguel De Grandy, Al Lawson and Elaine Gordon, as well as observations from Steve Hanlon, Martha Barnett and Arnett Doctor, helped provide background details to what was on the official record.

When I called Bill Posey in May, 1995, to ask how exactly he was related to Samuel Mudd, he couldn't tell me. "I don't really know directly," he said. "My dad told me we were related by marriage somewhere back through there."

Posey's reference during the Rosewood debate to Samuel Mudd's imprisonment in Key West was actually incorrect. Mudd was jailed at Fort Jefferson, a federal prison located sixty-eight miles west of the Keys, among the cluster of islands known as the Dry Tortugas. Several accounts of Mudd's life have been written, the most thorough being *The Riddle of Dr. Mudd* (New York: G. P. Putnam's Sons, 1974), by a historian whose name echoes the dead of Rosewood: Samuel Carter III.

The Senate section of this chapter is based on the Journals of the Florida Senate, as well as on interviews with Barnett, Robert Wexler, Daryl Jones, and Charlie Williams.

CHAPTER THIRTY-TWO: NOTHING BUT SCARS

I visited the Attorney General's Office of Civil Rights in Hollywood in March, 1995, where I spent the day with Guy Robinson and Frank Beisler, who, along with Greg Durden, had spent the previous ten months enforcing the law prescribed by the Rosewood claims bill. During that day's interview and in numerous subsequent telephone interviews, they shared both their personal experiences as well as the official records of their research.

The description of the governor's bill-signing came from newspaper accounts and from interviews with various Rosewood family members.

CHAPTER THIRTY-THREE: WILDFLOWER

I visited Robie Mortin at her home in Riviera Beach the day after I met with the Attorney General's staff. This chapter is based on our interview that day and on several subsequent telephone conversations. I also was able to refer to Mortin's survivor affidavit filed in August, 1994, with the Attorney General's office, and to Frank Beisler's notes made a month after that during his interview with Mortin at her home.

Several newspaper stories were written about Mortin in the *Palm Beach Post* after she surfaced as a Rosewood survivor, and she was featured in the January 16, 1995, issue of *People* magazine. These articles provided additional background for this chapter.

CHAPTER THIRTY-FOUR: FAMILY

In May of 1995, as I neared the conclusion of writing this book, I set out to call all of the Rosewood survivors for final interviews, to catch up with each of their lives at that point. The first section of this chapter is based on those interviews—the ones I was able to obtain as well as the ones I was not.

The chapter's second section focuses on the Rosewood property claimants and is based on interviews with Guy Robinson, Frank Beisler and Greg Durden of the Attorney General's office, as well as on interviews with various Rosewood family members, including Arnett and Yvonne Doctor.

CHAPTER THIRTY-FIVE: SYLVESTER'S SHADOW

This chapter is based on interviews and records shared by Robinson, Beisler and Durden as well as interviews with Arnett Doctor, Michael O'McCarthy, Gary Moore, Steve Hanlon, Martha Barnett, Bo Johnson, Miguel De Grandy, Al Lawson, and Charlie Williams.

Epilogue

A copy of the Florida Department of Law Enforcement's final report on its Rosewood investigation, dated January 18, 1995, was provided by Greg Durden's staff at the Attorney General's office in Hollywood, Florida.

My visit with Wesley and Christy Thompson at their home in Rosewood took place in October, 1994.

The Survivors

Minnie Lee Langley: Nine at the time of the attack, she lived in Rosewood with her grandparents, James and Emma Carrier. She now lives in Jacksonville, Florida.

Arnett T. (A. T.) Goins: He was eight, staying with his grandmother, Sarah Carrier, when the attack occurred. His parents, George and Willie Retha Goins, were away at a logging camp that week. He now lives in St. Petersburg, Florida.

Willie Evans: Born in Sanford, near Orlando, his mother died when he was four and he moved to Rosewood to live with his grandparents, Ransome and Julie Edwards. He turned sixteen a week before the attack. He now lives in Sanford, Florida.

Lonnie Carroll: The son of James and Emma Carrier, he was twelve when Rosewood was attacked. He later changed his name to Carroll. He now lives in New Smyrna Beach, Florida.

Wilson Hall: One of Charles Bacchus Hall's nine children, he was seven the week of the attack. He now lives in Hilliard, Florida.

Margie Hall Johnson: Wilson Hall's sister, she had just turned fourteen at the time of the attack. She now lives in Hilliard, Florida.

Mary Hall Daniels: The youngest of the Hall children, she was three when Rosewood was attacked. She now lives in Jacksonville, Florida.

Dorothy Goins Hosey: The daughter of Perry and Hattie Goins, she turned four the first day of the attack. She now lives in Tampa, Florida.

Robie Allenetta Robinson Mortin: Born in 1915, she was living with her uncle, Sam Carter, and her grandmother, Polly Carter, at the time of the attack. She now lives in Riviera Beach, Florida.

Lee Ruth ("Mossy") Bradley Davis: One of the original two Rosewood bill claimants, along with Minnie Lee Langley, she was seven at the time of the attack. She died in 1993, as the second claims bill was taking shape.

Vera Massadeas Goins Hamilton: A. T. Goins's baby sister, she was with her parents at a logging camp the week Rosewood was attacked and so did not qualify for state compensation as a survivor. She now lives in Lacoochee, Florida.

Eva Jenkins: Born and raised in Rosewood, she was thirteen and staying in Gainesville with an aunt at the time of the attack. She too was disqualified as a survivor. She now lives in Orlando, Florida.

Berthina Edwards Fagin: Born and raised in Rosewood, she was nine when she and her parents moved to the town of Steinhatchee three weeks before Rosewood was attacked.

Her parents owned a home and land in Rosewood, which they lost. She too was disqualified as a survivor. She now lives in Deland, Florida.

Thelma Hawkins: Nineteen at the time of the attack, she had been raised in Rosewood by her uncle and aunt, Ed and Eliza Bradley, who lost their home and five acres of land during the attack. She had moved to Jacksonville before the attack occurred and so was not considered a survivor. She now lives in Dade City, Florida.

Lillie Washington: Born in Rosewood in 1910, she and her family were living in a small village called Lenin, six miles from Rosewood, at the time of the attack. They left soon after, because of the attack, but she was not considered a survivor. She now lives in Gainesville, Florida.

THE ANCESTORS

Sam Carter: A forty-seven-year-old blacksmith, he became the first victim of the attack on Rosewood when he was lynched Monday night, January 1, 1923.

Sarah Carrier: She was the week's second victim, shot to death in her home Thursday night, January 4.

Sylvester Carrier: The thirty-year-old son of Sarah Carrier, he died during the January 4 gun battle at his mother's house.

Lexie Gordon: A fifty-five-year-old widow, she was shot to death fleeing from her burning house on Friday morning, January 5.

Mingo ("Lord God") Williams: A fifty-year-old turpentine worker, he was shot to death Friday afternoon, January 5, while working in the woods outside Rosewood.

James Carrier: Sarah Carrier's brother-in-law, he emerged Saturday morning, January 6, from hiding in the swamps around Rosewood and was murdered execution-style beside the grave of his sister-in-law Sarah and his nephew Sylvester.

Hayward Carrier: Sarah Carrier's husband and James Carrier's brother, he was away on a hunting trip the week of the attack.

Annie ("Sweetie") Carrier: Sylvester Carrier's sister.

Lelland ("Beauty") Carrier: Sylvester Carrier's sister.

Bernadina ("Honey") Carrier: Sylvester Carrier's sister.

Willie Retha Carrier: Sylvester Carrier's sister.

Emma Carrier: James Carrier's wife.

Aaron Carrier: The son of James and Emma Carrier, he was tortured, then escaped the first day of the attack.

Beulah ("Scrappie") Carrier: Emma Carrier's daughter, she helped care for some of the smaller Carrier children in the woods after the attack on Sarah Carrier's house.

Elias Carrier: A Carrier cousin, he was gunned down by Charlie Goins during a church Christmas pageant in Rosewood several years before the town was destroyed.

Lee Carrier: A Carrier cousin, he survived into the 1980s and was a strong voice at family reunions.

Martine Goins: Born a slave in North Carolina, he established the M. Goins & Brothers' turpentine distilling company in Rosewood in the mid-1880s. He died in 1905.

Ed Goins: Martine's younger brother, also born a slave, he ran the family's turpentine business until 1916, when he moved to Gainesville.

Charlie Goins: One of Ed Goins's ten children, he was the man who murdered Elias Carrier.

George Goins: Another of Ed Goins's sons, he married Willie Retha Carrier and had five children, including Philomena, A. T. and Vera.

Philomena ("Sissy") Goins Doctor: A daughter of George and Willie Retha Goins, she was eleven at the time of the attack and was in her grandmother Sarah Carrier's house the night of the January 4 shootout. The mother of Arnett and Yvonne Doctor, she died in St. Petersburg in 1991.

Daisy Mitchell: A daughter of James and Emma Carrier, she was Minnie Lee Langley's mother. She died giving birth to Minnie Lee in 1915.

Theodore Mitchell: Daisy's husband, he left his children with his wife's parents after her death and went to work along the Gulf Coast as a sponge diver.

Ruben Mitchell: Minnie Lee's brother, he lost an eye the night of the shootout at the Carrier house.

Charles Bacchus Hall: He owned a small store, farmed and ran a sugar-cane grinding business, all on his property in Rosewood.

Mary Davis Hall: Charles Hall's wife.

Sam Hall: One of Charles and Mary Hall's nine children, he was fifteen at the time of the attack. He died in Brunswick, Georgia, in 1984.

Dosha Hall: Second-oldest of the Hall children, she was married and moved from Rosewood by the time of the attack. She later settled in Hilliard, Florida, with her sister Margie, where they both eventually reunited with their brother Wilson.

Polly Carter: Sam Carter's mother, she raised survivor Robie Allenetta Robinson Mortin in Rosewood, after Robie's parents divorced when Robie was a baby.

THE WHITES

Fannie Taylor: The twenty-three-year-old wife of a Sumner sawmill worker, she was assaulted in her home New Year's morning, 1923. That assault precipitated the attack on Rosewood.

James Taylor: Fannie Taylor's husband, he was an employee at the Cummer and Sons sawmill in Sumner.

Robert Walker: He was Levy County's sheriff at the time of the Rosewood attack.

Clarence Williams: He was the Levy County deputy sheriff in Sumner at the time of the attack.

Walter Harlan (W. H.) Pillsbury: General superintendent of the sawmill in Sumner at the time of the attack, he is credited with saving the lives of blacks both in Rosewood and in Sumner.

Bryant Hudson: Twenty-five at the time, he was the man who shot and killed Sam Carter the night of January 1, 1923.

Fred Kirkland: A witness to the lynching of Sam Carter, he is still alive today.

Garrett Kirkland: Fred Kirkland's uncle, he was among the mob that witnessed Sam Carter's lynching.

Orrie Kirkland: Fred Kirkland's father, he was also present at the lynching of Sam Carter.

Jason McElveen: A logger and fisherman from Cedar Key, he was present at both the Monday night lynching of Sam Carter and the Thursday night attack on the Carrier house.

C. P. "Poly" Wilkerson: A storekeeper and former quarters boss from Sumner, he was shot and killed by Sylvester Carrier the night of the attack on the Carrier house.

Henry Andrews: A logging foreman from Otter Creek, he was also shot and killed by Carrier the night of the attack.

Bryan Kirkland: He was wounded during the attack on the Carrier house.

Warner Kirkland: He was wounded during the attack on the Carrier house.

Cephus Studstill: He was wounded during the attack on the Carrier house.

Henry Odom: He was wounded during the attack on the Carrier house.

Manny Hudson: He was wounded during the attack on the Carrier house.

Red Raulerson: He was among the group that attacked the Carrier house, but did not take part in the attack.

John Wright: A storekeeper in Rosewood and the town's only white resident, he hid a number of black women and children in his home during the week of the attack.

John and William Bryce: Two railroad conductors from Cedar Key, they brought a train through Rosewood at the end of that week and carried carloads of women and children to safety in Gainesville.

The Descendants

Arnett Doctor: The son of Philomena Doctor, he spearheaded the families' pursuit of a legal claim against the state of Florida.

Yvonne Doctor: The daughter of Philomena Doctor.

Annie Bell Lee: The daughter of Rosewood resident Josephine Evans, she, along with her sister, Altamese Wrispus, organized the first Rosewood Family Reunion in 1985.

Annette Goins Shakir: The daughter of Rosewood survivor A. T. Goins.

Janie Bradley Black: The niece of Rosewood survivor Lee Ruth Davis.

Geffery Mortin: The son of Rosewood survivor Robie Mortin.

Dorothy Smith: The daughter of Rosewood survivor Minnie Lee Langley.

Albert Edwards: The son of deceased Rosewood resident Earl Edwards and a cousin of Arnett Doctor, he was with Doctor when the idea of filing a claim against the state was first discussed.

Spouses

Lugenia Carroll: Lonnie Carroll's wife

Anna Maude Goins: A. T. Goins's wife.

Walter Doctor: Philomena Doctor's husband.

PHOTO CREDITS

INDEX

Page entries in **boldface** indicate illustrations in the text.

N

O

P